"Deborah Jowitt's book on Jerome Robbins is [...] objective study of an extraordinary man who [...] twentieth-century musical theater. It captures the essence of this haunted perfectionist whose choices in life were as fraught with self-doubt as those made in the rehearsal room. Paralleling the fruits of his creative brilliance with the fallout of personal decisions, Jowitt gives us a three-dimensional look at a charismatic and complex character. I thought I knew Jerome Robbins well—I was wrong."   —Mikhail Baryshnikov

"Deborah Jowitt's . . . *Jerome Robbins* is a superb critical biography that vibrantly captures both his conflicted personal life and his remarkable creative productivity. Principal dance critic of *The Village Voice* since 1967, Jowitt had unrestricted access to Robbins's huge archives of papers, diaries, letters, photographs, and tapes, and it shows in the richness and depth with which she delves into his life. . . . This is a vivid flesh-and-blood portrait. Jowitt has written an indispensable guide to understanding and appreciating the man generally considered America's finest native-born choreographer."   —*The Christian Science Monitor*

"The great, endlessly intriguing glory of Jowitt's exhaustively researched and beautifully written new biography is its clarity in describing and critiquing Robbins' long and remarkably varied career. . . . Gossip is cheap, and scandal always readily available. Jowitt focuses instead on three main personal themes that wind through her narrative and intersect like choreographic patterns. . . . What she does do is interweave his insecurities, Jewish identity quest and informant guilt in a broad psychological tapestry that provides an expressive background to his life and artistic choices."   —*San Francisco Chronicle*

"Herself a dancer and choreographer, Jowitt puts the reader fifth-row center to see how Robbins's work evolved and then sailed across the stage. . . . For buffs, scholars, actors, dancers, choreographers, and directors: a vital picture of ballet and Broadway in a golden age."   —*Kirkus Reviews* (starred)

"Given unrestricted access to Robbins's personal and professional papers, Jowitt adds a new [...] . . . Both critically sophisticate[...] [...]t for theater and dance devote[...] [...]*kly* (starred)

ALSO BY DEBORAH JOWITT

Meredith Monk: An Anthology
(edited)

Time and the Dancing Image

The Dance in Mind:
Profiles and Reviews 1976–1983

Dance Beat:
Selected Views and Reviews 1967–1976

Jerome

Jesse Gerstein

Robbins

His Life,
His Theater,
His Dance

Deborah Jowitt

Simon & Schuster Paperbacks

New York   London   Toronto   Sydney

SIMON & SCHUSTER PAPERBACKS
Rockefeller Center
1230 Avenue of the Americas
New York, NY 10020

First Simon & Schuster paperback edition 2005

SIMON & SCHUSTER PAPERBACKS and colophon are registered trademarks
of Simon & Schuster, Inc.

For information about special discounts for bulk purchases,
please contact Simon & Schuster Special Sales at
1-800-456-6798 or business@simonandschuster.com.

Book design by Ellen R. Sasahara

Manufactured in the United States of America

1   3   5   7   9   10   8   6   4   2

The Library of Congress has cataloged the hardcover edition as follows:
Jowitt, Deborah.
Jerome Robbins : his life, his theater, his dance / Deborah Jowitt.
p.   cm.
Includes bibliographical references and index.
1. Robbins, Jerome.   2. Choreographers—United States—Biography.
I. Title.
GV1785.R52J69   2004   792.8'2'092—dc22   [B]   2004045440

ISBN-13: 978-0-684-86985-8
ISBN-10:   0-684-86985-3
ISBN-13: 978-0-684-86986-5 (Pbk)
ISBN-10:   0-684-86986-1 (Pbk)

Grateful acknowledgment is made for permission to quote from the following material:

"I Feel Like I'm Not Out of Bed Yet," by Leonard Bernstein, Betty Comden and
Adolph Green. © 1944 Leonard Bernstein Music Publishing Co. LLC. Administered by
Universal-Polygram International Publishing Inc./Warner Chappell Music, Inc.
All rights reserved. Used by permission.

"New York, New York," by Leonard Bernstein, Betty Comden and Adolph Green.
© 1945 Leonard Bernstein Music Publishing Co. LLC. Administered by Universal-
Polygram International Publishing Inc./Warner Chappell Music, Inc.
All rights reserved. Used by permission.

(continued on page 591)

Acknowledgments

O*ne of the hallmarks* of Jerome Robbins's work was the illusion of community he built onstage. During the five years it took to produce this book, I was given generous and valuable support by several very real "communities" of individuals.

The Jerome Robbins Foundation and the Robbins Rights Trust not only proposed that I undertake this project, but gave me unrestricted access to Robbins's huge archive of papers, both personal and professional, as well as to audiotapes, videotapes, and photographs. I am grateful for the confidence and support of those involved with the foundation and the trust: Floria V. Lasky, Robbins's lawyer; Allen Greenberg, his financial advisor; and his literary executors, Daniel Stern and William Earle. I am especially grateful to Christopher Pennington, administrator of the foundation and the trust, whose knowledge and assistance went far beyond the call of duty, enlivening and enlightening months of riffling through papers—first in Robbins's house, later in the foundation office.

My gratitude extends to members of Robbins's family—to his sister, Sonia Robbins Cullinen, and her husband, George Cullinen; to his cousins Viola Balish, Jack Davenport, Jean Handy, Jackye Lee Madura, and Robert Silverman—and to his friends Mica Ertegun, Michael Koessel, Allen Midgette, Milan Stitt, and Robert Temko. Especially warm thanks to Christine Conrad, Brian Meehan, and Aidan Mooney, who were always available to answer questions, and to Mooney and William Earle for their superb hospitality in Spoleto.

A simple thank you hardly covers the enormous support I received from Madeleine Nichols, curator of the Jerome Robbins Dance Division of the New York Public Library of the Performing Arts Dorothy and

Lewis B. Cullman Center, and her entire staff. That many of the materials bequeathed by Robbins to the library were not yet catalogued, or were in the process of being catalogued, created difficulties that they surmounted with grace and without complaint. I go down on bended knee to manuscripts librarian Charles Perrier for his unwavering support and countless services. My particular thanks go also to Monica Moseley, Francis Dougherty, Philip Karg, Else Peck, Patricia Rader, Grace Owen, Myron Switzer, Danielle Rogers, and the cataloguers of the Robbins archive, Rick Hunter and Sisnur Araujo. Thanks to George Boziwick of the library's Music Division, to Thomas Lisanti of its photographic services and permissions department, and to audio engineer Adrian Cosentini; to Mark Horowitz, music specialist of the Library of Congress; to Charles Markey in the New Jersey Room of the Jersey City Public Library and James Fruscione, assistant director of the New Jersey Division of Revenue; to Nicholas Jenkins, literary executor of the Kirstein Papers and Copyrights, Lincoln Kirstein Estate; to Marie Carter of the Leonard Bernstein Office; to the Lincoln Center press office; and to the press office of the New York City Ballet.

The experience of writing this book would have been impossible without the participation of performers, choreographers, directors, and others professionally associated with Robbins who shared their memories of rehearsals, productions, and more: Anita Alvarez, Margaret Banks, Mikhail Baryshnikov, Jamie Bauer, Sammy Bayes, David and Jeanie Bean, Eric Bentley, Edward Bigelow, Peter Boal, Todd Bolender, Ruthanna Boris, Conrad Bromberg and Nancy Franklin, Isabel Brown, Cora Cahan, Maria Calegari, Victor Castelli, George Chakiris, Betty Comden and Adolph Green, Emily Coates, Bart Cook, William Crawford, Grover Dale, Danny Daniels, Richard D'Arcy, Gemze de Lappe, Shirley Eckl, Eliot Feld, Kristina Fernandez, Horton Foote, Maria Irene Fornés, Gerald Freedman, Jean-Pierre Frohlich, Larry Fuller, Helen Gallagher, Miriam Golden, Virginia Gibson, Robert Gottlieb, Rhoda Grauer, the late Martin Green, John Guare, Peter Hanson, Joel Honig, Barbara Horgan, Mary Hunter, Ann Hutchinson Guest, Louis Johnson, Suzanne Johnston, Neel Keller, Florence Klotz, Arthur Kopit, Hortense Koulouris, Karen Kristin, Ina Kurland, Robert La Fosse, Arthur Laurents, Carol Lawrence, Sondra Lee, Julia Levien, Don Liberto, Annabelle Lyon, Patricia McBride, Allyn McLerie, Dorothy McNichols, Mara, Erin Martin, Peter Martins, Joanna Merlin, Benjamin Millepied, James Mitchell, James Moore, Gregory Mosher, Yvonne Mounsey, Jay Norman, Sono Osato,

Arthur Partington, Austin Pendleton, Delia Peters, Barry Primus, Magnus Ragnarrson, Tommy Rall, Christine Redpath, Janet Reed, Ned Rorem, Herbert Ross, Donald Saddler, Stephanie Saland, Anna Sokolow, Stephen Sondheim, Ellen Sorrin, Thomas Stone, Maria Tallchief, Twyla Tharp, Jennifer Tipton, Beryl Towbin, Gina Trikonis, Kirsten Valbor, Violette Verdy, Edward Verso, Edward Villella, William Weslow, Barbara Whipple, Robert Wilson, Robert Wise, Kate Friedlich Witkin, Elaine Wright, and Yuriko (Kikuchi).

I am indebted to those who allowed me to quote from unpublished correspondence—their own or those they hold the rights to—and other unpublished sources: Louis Begley, Eric Bentley, Edward Burke (for Robert Lewis), Betty Comden, Robert Cornfield (for Edwin Denby), Robert Craft (for Igor Stravinsky), Michael K. Crawford (for Cheryl Crawford), Michael Cristofer, Richard D'Arcy (for Oliver Smith), Brooke Hayward Duchin (for Leland Hayward), David and Robin Fitelson (for William Fitelson), Sarah Harding (for Isobel Lennart), Kitty Carlisle Hart (for Moss Hart), Arthur Laurents, Norma Pane (for Tanaquil Le Clercq), Bentley Roton (for Francisco Moncion), Robert Sealy, the late Ray Stark, and Margaret Styne (for Jule Styne). Thanks to Marinel Abreu, Rosemarie Gawelko, David A. Mintz, Wendy Stillman, and Martin Zelner for facilitating permissions requests.

Martha Swope provided many of the superb photographs that light up the book. I am also grateful to photographers Paul Kolnik and Jack Mitchell; to George Platt Lynes II, Steve Bello (for Philippe Halsman), Gabriel and Avivah Pinski (for Fred Fehl), Virginia Teslik (for Eileen Darby), and Rona Tuccillo of Getty Images for permitting and facilitating reproduction. Ruthanna Boris, Sonia Robbins Cullinen, Gemze de Lappe, Ina Kurland, Jackye Lee Madura, Aidan Mooney, and Donald Saddler lent me photos from their own collections.

My friends and colleagues in the fields of dance, theater, and writing answered questions, passed on valuable materials and information, and helped in many different ways: Jack Anderson and George Dorris of *Dance Chronicle,* Erik Aschengreen, Claire Brook, Carolyn Brown, Ze'eva Cohen, Michael Feingold, Jack Gelber, Beth Genné, Leslie Getz, Joyce Greenberg, Joanna Harris, Judith Brin Ingber, Naomi Isaacson, Ellen Jacobs, Robert Johnson, James Klosty, Leslie Hansen Kopp, Ellen Levene, Alexander Meinertz, John Mueller, Barbara Palfy, Ermanno Romanelli, Janice Ross, Marcia B. Siegel, Ted Striggles, Eric Taub, Tobi

Tobias, Alexandra Tomalonis, Amanda Vaill, Jean-Claude Van Itallie, and Susan Willerman. Robert Greskovic not only served as a constant and gracious hotline for information; he steered me toward videos I might otherwise have missed. Kenneth Geist passed on to me tapes of interviews he conducted in 1983–84, and Nancy Reynolds gave me access to interviews she recorded in connection with her invaluable 1977 book, *Repertory in Review.* Thanks, too, to Bob Lamm and Douglas Lackey for sharing archival material with me. Joan Acocella, Clive Barnes, Arlene Croce, David Denby, Nancy Goldner, Martin Gottfried, Joyce Greenberg and the University of Pittsburgh Press (for Dorothy Bird), Sheldon Harnick, Christopher D. Kerr (for Walter Kerr), Michael Smith, and Stephen Sondheim generously allowed me to quote from their published writing.

Some of the material in passages dealing with *Afternoon of a Faun* and *Antique Epigraphs* are drawn from an essay of mine ("Subverting the Dream-of-Elusive-Women Scenario: Vaslav Nijinsky's *L'Après-midi d'un Faune;* Jerome Robbins's *Afternoon of a Faun* and *Antique Epigraphs*") that I contributed to *Of Another World: Dancing Between Dream and Reality,* a Festschrifft for the Danish critic and scholar Erik Ashchengreen. The experience helped jump-start my writing about Robbins, and I thank the book's editor Monna Dithmer and Museum Tusculanum Press for giving me the opportunity. I have also often drawn on my reviews in *The Village Voice,* which has given me a forum for over thirty-five years. Elizabeth Zimmer, my editor at the paper, provided sage editorial comments as this book developed, as did my esteemed agent Robert Cornfield—himself knowledgeable about dance and theater. Faye Greenbaum and Meital Waibsnaider provided some crucial research assistance. There are two people I couldn't have managed without: Kate Mattingly, whose research skills tracked down many elusive items, and Shields Remine, who not only transcribed hours of tape, but provided always illuminating comments on them.

As every author knows, writing a book is only part of the work. My longtime friend Hannah Pakula helped introduce me to her publisher, Simon & Schuster, where many expert hands spanked and groomed my book into its final form. My profound gratitude to publisher David Rosenthal; to vice president and editorial director Alice Mayhew, who believed in the project, who encouraged me through the writing when I wavered, and whose expert comments helped polish the book; to associate editor Emily Salkin Takoudes, whose invaluable editorial labors, knowledge of dance, and patience with my innumerable questions and panicky moments made the process of publication easier. Others who provided crucial services were Ellen Sasahara, who designed the interior of the book; cover designer Michael Accordino; copy supervisor Leslie Ellen; copy editor Lynn Anderson; proofreaders Jim Stoller and George Wen; Victoria Meyers and Elizabeth Hayes of the publicity department; and Veronica Jordan and the entire legal department of Simon & Schuster.

I could not have managed to complete the research and writing had I not received a Fellowship in 2002 from the John Simon Guggenheim Memorial Foundation, which enabled me to focus my energies more intensely on the book project.

Finally, I thank my family: my son, Tobias Ralph; my daughter-in-law, Regina Ralph; and especially my husband, Murray Ralph, who endured with patience, humor, and remarkable serenity my intense involvement with another man—one whom I struggled to understand and to whose spirit I raise a glass: Jerome Robbins.

Contents

Jerome Robbins

The Rabinowitz Family: Harry, Lena, Sonia, and Jerry.
Jerome Robbins Dance Division,
New York Public Library for the Performing Arts
(NYPL).

1

A Boy of Many Talents

I stand before a mirror. Ahead, two dark eyes are looking back at me beneath a shock of black hair. The face is thin, the eyebrows so bushy as to draw the attention toward them as a diamond on velvet.

Slowly the mask begins to rise, revealing another face. The features of this one are the same but they are distorted into a mask of malignant capability. This also rises leaving me looking at a mask of complete tranquility—peace, quiet, and love, but this rises and another one is shown and still another. . . . Faster and faster they come, spreading over the mirror, the walls, the rooms, the earth. They all look at me with blank vacant eyes where, if they were over my face, my eyes would show through. They are all me, every one. They are all my selves!

Sixteen-year-old Jerome Wilson Rabinowitz penned "My Selves" for his senior English class at Woodrow Wilson High in Weehawken, New Jersey. His teacher gave it an A+.

The essay, which includes selections from his 1934–1935 diary, was prescient in many ways. It hinted at the volatile character of the boy who was to become Jerome Robbins and exposed his ebullient theatricality. Reading it, you cannot imagine this teenager bound for a career in business, medicine, the law, or any other profession toward which his Russian Jewish immigrant parents might logically have pressed him.

The "artistic self" had already assumed pride of place:

By saying Art I do not mean just drawing. I mean music, drama, literature, dancing, handcrafts, and painting. I believe I have some talent in
all of these. I compose and play music for the piano and violin, I have received awards at camps for dramatic ability and handcraft ability. I have
written poetry and prose, and have taken a shot at plays. I have had several scholarships in dancing . . . modern and fundamental, and have
done much painting and other drawing skills outside of school.

   However, I think all these Arts can be expressed in marionettes, their
plays, their stage, the design for the stage, and costumes, the writing of
music and a play for it, and the designing and making of the marionettes
themselves. I get the same physical satisfaction out of doing any of these
Arts as a man does out of being well fed. I can sit gazing on a line of
beauty for hours, memorizing each curve and each arc. That is my artistic self.

Looking in the mirror, Jerry Rabinowitz would also have seen a boy
small for his age, late in maturing, with teeth that seemed outsized in his
thin face. (Later in life, he couldn't be sure whether a portrait taken for a
school yearbook commemorated his graduation from high school or from
junior high.) Compared to some of the bruisers in his senior class picture,
he looks scrawny.

   The Rabinowitzes fostered their children's talents but in 1935 didn't
contemplate their only son's becoming a dancer any more than he did.
Jerry and his sister, Sonia, studied violin and piano, like the offspring of
many immigrant families that honored culture and saw access to it as part
of the American dream. Harry and Lena did count on their son being successful and bringing home the bacon. Of his father, Robbins once wrote, "I
do think he'd stop breathing if he thought air cost money." Sonia, older
than her brother by six and a half years, later said sadly of her parents,
"They didn't really know how to cherish or love. [It was] Make! Produce!"

   In about 1904, Harry Rabinowitz, age fifteen, had left the Russian shtetl
of Rozhanka, 182 kilometers northwest of Pinsk, (a city near the border
between Belarus and the Ukraine), walked across Europe to Amsterdam,
and caught a ship to join his older brothers, Theodore and Julius, in New
York. For a Jew, being conscripted into the Russian army meant a short career as cannon fodder; Harry's parents had to buy him a grave and a death

certificate to avoid punishment for his disappearance, and he traveled by night in company with a Russian deserter—being especially wary at borders, where guards raked the ground so that footprints could be tracked. So innocent was he that looking around the pier, he saw no boat; when someone pointed out the massive shape he had taken to be a wall, he wept at its hugeness and the idea of being inside it.

Lena Rips Rabinowitz (born 1889) had arrived, probably from Minsk, around 1893, together with her parents, Aaron and Ida Rips, her brother Jacob, and her sisters Anna and Mary (three more, Jean, Gertrude, and Frances, were born in America). Her father's seven siblings also emigrated—one by one, in the traditional manner. Pogroms in the "Pale," that much-disputed area between Russia and Poland where Jews were pushed to settle, could erupt without warning. The year after Robbins was born in a New York City hospital on October 11, 1918, there were Passover riots against Jews in Lida, near the Lithuanian border, and thirty-five Jews were summarily executed in Pinsk.

Robbins's parents' work ethic was understandably fierce. Harry Rabinowitz began his career in the United States laboring for $5 a month at a Manhattan delicatessen (where he slept on a shelf behind the counter); later he owned a delicatessen himself, employing his younger brother Samuel and his sister Ruth. By the time his son was ready for kindergarten, the family had moved from Madison Avenue at Ninety-seventh Street, then a largely Jewish neighborhood, to Boerum Avenue in Jersey City, a short block away from a park where kids could ice-skate in winter. Robbins mostly grew up, however, farther north in Weehawken. And during most of his youth, his father ran a modest manufactory, Comfort Corset Company (for "stylish stouts"), in Union City, where Lena also worked after the stock market crash of 1929. The couple took over the factory—originally owned by Lena's sister Mary and her husband, Ben Goldenberg—and its subsidiary, Worthmore Garment Company in Jersey City, around 1934. Before the Depression, they could afford a Packard, bought their son an electric train for Christmas (they were not strictly observant Jews), and sent him to kindergarten and first grade at a private school, the Hudson City Academy, where the pupils learned rudimentary German (Jersey City boasted a sizable German population). But in the early thirties, they were grateful for donations of hot dogs from Harry's brother Julius Rabinowitz, who worked for Hygrade Frankfurters.

On June 23, 1923, at Hudson City Academy's end-of-the-year recital, Jerome Rabinowitz, not yet five, gave what may have been his first public performance. According to the program, he favored the audience with a piano solo and a recitation of "Mauschen" (looking, one suspects, like a "dear little mouse" himself). He also must have appeared in the final "American Negro Slumber Song," because he later recalled being dressed as a mammy, singing a lullaby, and rocking a doll.

At six, he received his first rave review, from a Jersey City paper:

> A special feature of the evening [a recital by the piano pupils of Miss Clara Linda Wright], which had not been previously announced, was the playing of little Jerry Rabinowitz, son of Mr. and Mrs. Harry Rabinowitz of Weehawken, who is a pupil of E. E. Perfield, under whom Miss Wright also studied, and from whom she learned her system of teaching. Little Jerry is only 6, and since the age of 3, has been composing and playing. Last evening, he played two of his own compositions, an 'Indian Dance' and a 'Russian Song.' Both the compositions were typical of the music of the people for whom they were named, and showed a comprehension of music far beyond that of even most adults.

Was he fulfilling a parental fantasy? Some of Harry's favorite radio programs were those, such as the Eddie Cantor show, that featured musical prodigies or encouraged young amateurs hoping for stardom. Jerry was raised on stories about Jewish boys who played the violin for tsars or presidents and grew up to be famous. He felt inadequate. The tales did, however, arouse fantasies of performing before crowned heads in a velvet suit, and "they listened as the whole court did enrapt, spellbound, tears flowing down their cheeks, as I played my heart out for them, & they rewarded me with golden coins worth a fortune, & then I save my dear parents from a life of drudgery, etc." (When Robbins jotted this memory down later in life, he noted that it had come true in a way. His ballets had been performed for heads of state, he had been amply rewarded, and he had financed his parents' early retirement.)

Effa Ellis Perfield taught piano on West Thirty-sixth Street in Manhattan. Lena Rabinowitz thought nothing of ferrying her children across the Hudson, if that was where the best teachers were to be found. Perfield's unconventional style of instruction encouraged three-year-old Jerry in his compositional urges. As a prodigy in training, Robbins had some catching up to do; the household already boasted a star.

Sonia was the dancer in the family. Her brother was still in the womb when she performed on June 1, 1918, at a "reception for Brother Edward C. Havens" in the Grand Lodge Room of the Masonic Club of the City of New York. Amid recitations, solo songs, and musical selections played by the U.S. Naval Band from Pelham, "Little Sonia—The Youngest Child Dancer in the World . . . 4 years old" rendered "Classic Dance." (Shrewd Lena! Sonia was a month shy of her sixth birthday.)

Not every little boy had a sister who danced a "Spring Song" at the Metropolitan Opera House and the Hudson Theater and performed in free concerts organized by Charles D. Isaacson, later a critic for *The Dance Magazine,* at such sites as an insane asylum and Sing Sing prison. "A tiny fleck of loveliness," Harold G. Broland called her in an effusive poem linking her with the marvels of nature. In April 1928, the year Robbins turned ten, sixteen-year-old Sonia performed in Havana with the troupe of girls led by Irma Duncan. Irma was one of Isadora Duncan's first six pupils, the slender barefoot maidens in Greek draperies who had adopted their teacher's name and who toured America just after 1918, fondly referred to by the press as the "Isadorables." Isadora's "Russian Songs" were an important part of Irma's repertory; Sonia was chosen as much for her strong singing voice as for her grace.

Robbins's first exposure to dance was watching his sister practice and sitting on the floor during her lessons—most particularly classes with Alys Bentley in Studio 601 at Carnegie Hall. Bentley was lauded primarily as a teacher of "various aspects of rhythmics," as an instrumental force in shaping music teaching in New York City's public schools, and as a consultant to opera diva Geraldine Farrar. Bentley's ideas about movement were considered liberating, especially the exercises that began on the floor—a radical notion at the time. Sonia spent most of her girlhood summers near the Canadian border, assisting Bentley at her adult camp on Chateaugay Lake in Merrill, New York. Robbins remembered the classes he saw and occasionally participated in when he was in elementary school as Duncanesque—wafting scarves and balloons and letting great music invade the soul. "We did things like 'folding' (slowly collapsing in an embryonic heap on the floor), prancing (a deerlike lifting of the feet from the floor)." He was entranced by the freedom of making up his own dances. His sister, Sonia Robbins Cullinen, thinks it was here that he first came to love the Chopin mazurkas and waltzes that so affected the onstage "listeners" in his 1956 comic gem *The Concert* and on which he built his great 1969 ballet *Dances at a Gathering*.

Sonia may have been paid for some of the appearances she made, although she has no recollection of money changing hands. Perhaps pride in her accomplishments justified all the shlepping (much of it undertaken by aunts), the dancing shoes, the fabric to be run up into silky tunics and beruffled dresses. Certainly her mother took the performances seriously. Sonia remembers a day in the Madison Avenue apartment when, already dressed to perform at school, she spilled boiling milk on her chest. Her father ripped off the frock; her mother repaired it, put a plaster on the quite severe burn, and bundled her off to dance. Only afterward did they visit a doctor. However, Lena Rabinowitz was not really kin to that monstrous showbiz parent, Mama Rose of *Gypsy,* her son's directorial triumph of 1959, and fortunately, she allowed Bentley to guide Sonia into "artistic" directions. Had Lena wanted a career in vaudeville for her daughter, she probably could have engineered one. The family's single theatrical connection, Dan Davenport, the husband of Lena's sister Jean, was reared in the business and had managed troupes and theaters; his British father and uncle, Lew and Vic Cohn, toured on the Heurtigan-Seaman vaudeville circuit as the Davenport Brothers: "World Renowned Acrobats and Premier Artists in their Acts of Posturing, Ground and Lofty Tumbling, Acrobatic Display, etc., and concluding with their Exciting Assault-at-Arms, Friendly Sparring Contest Interspersed with Laughable Situations."

Apart from harboring dreams of high-earning children, Lena encouraged her children's imaginations. She played creative games with them. They'd swipe a wet rag haphazardly over a blackboard and then rush to outline the shapes in chalk before the surface dried. They'd watch the sunset from the porch of a summer cottage on the shore and point out images in the cloud formations. It may have been at Camp Kittatinny that the grown-ups sewed leaves on Jerry's bathing suit and that of his good friend (and second cousin) Viola Zousmer and cast them as Adam and Eve in an act that consisted of their sitting in "an upright box papered with leaves and [throwing] baby green apples at passersby."

Kittatinny was a three-hundred-acre farm near Dingman's Ferry, Pennsylvania. The property, jointly owned at first by the extended family and some of their friends, began as a vacation place for the young couples before the babies started coming. A place where they could relax and cut up. They called themselves the R.F.s—the Regular Fellows. Bungalows were added as the families grew, and eventually—after a deal left Harry and Lena Rabinowitz with the corset factory and Ben and Mary Goldenberg in possession of Kittatinny—the property became a paying children's camp. Jerry—first as a camper, then as a junior counselor—indulged his theatrical bent. He and Viola and pals acted out favorite scenes from silent flicks: tearjerkers such as *Stella Dallas* (1925) with Belle Bennett and Ronald Colman; World War I sagas (*The Big Parade,* 1925); swashbuckling adventures (*The Black Pirate* with Douglas Fairbanks, 1926); epic dramas (*Ben-Hur,* 1926); chillers (*The Cat and the Canary,* 1927). Jerry loved Lon Chaney, and the 1923 *Hunchback of Notre Dame* was a favorite. A photo taken of a group of the kids shows him dressed as the hunchback in Oscar Wilde's *The Birthday of the Infanta;* he's hovering over the others, spreading a black cape probably made by Aunt Gert, who was skilled at ad hoc costume design. Gilbert and Sullivan productions were a staple. Viola Zousmer Balash remembers herself and Jerry as the father and mother in the thriller *The Monkey's Paw* and the day when he riskily flew "like a bird" around the edge of a roof, urging her to join him. From what she says, he obviously learned early how to keep dancers in line: "He did all kinds of performances as a kid—twelve, ten, eleven—he'd get us all together, like the Rockettes: 'SWING your legs! SWING your legs! SWING your arms! SWING your arms!' "

In the family's succession of houses and apartments in Weehawken, New Jersey—a narrow little town about thirty blocks long by six or seven wide, draped along the Palisades across from midtown Manhattan—he entertained his cousins with puppet shows. A basement window made a dandy miniature proscenium stage. He learned early, too, his power as a dancer—thrilled that when he performed his "Oriental" number (dressed as a girl) at a large Kittatinny party, he brought tears to people's eyes (it is not clear whether he had touched their hearts or displayed a budding gift for comedy).

⌒

Robbins accumulated the usual recollections of boyhood—the games and scuffles with cousins and neighborhood boys. The long hill known as "The Volley" (later an exit ramp for cars emerging from the Lincoln Tunnel) made a splendid long sled run. Jerry and Sonia could whiz down it and have their obliging dog Blitz haul the sled back up. But the Rabinowitz home seems also to have been a site for family scenes that rivaled the theatricals he dreamed up, an emotional tinderbox, setting off the domestic melodramas familiar to other offspring of Eastern European Ashkenazi stock. (His sister, it must be noted, remembers few of the incidents that marked him, only unhappiness and dancing.) Included among the leading players—Harry, Lena, Sonia, Jerry—was tiny, sweet grandmother Ida Rips, who moved in with the family after her husband died in 1931, kept kosher, and founded the Ladies Auxiliary of the Sherman Avenue Talmud Torah, and whose English never caught up to her Yiddish.

"I guess my family were 'theatrical' in their behavior," Robbins wrote in the 1970s, when he was contemplating an autobiography. "There were always 'scenes.' Fierce arguments, threats of death, suicide, abandonment, murder & the opposite: laughter, singing, dancing, being crazy, singing fake operas & dancing to records."

Hungry dancer buddies whom he took home for Sunday dinner during the forties recall raucous dinner table talk, two or three Rips aunts (most likely Gert and Jean, who lived nearby then) laughing and cracking jokes with standup verve. "They were funny ladies," says choreographer and onetime Ballet Theatre dancer Donald Saddler, "[they had] that Bette Midler style of delivery." Sonia remembers that Mary was a wonderful social dancer too, and in the days before Gert was badly scarred in a fire, she, Mary, and Jean used to dance at family gatherings—Jean "doing splits off the piano."

Harry—a wag, a tease, and a *tuchis*-pincher" in company—was taciturn at home, tired from his day at Comfort Corset, buried in his Yiddish newspaper. Not fully there for his son (his conception a draft excuse, Harry let him know, even though he'd given Jerry a middle name honoring the nation's wartime president). Harry, Jerry later wrote, scarcely touched his son once he learned to walk. Robbins couldn't remember his father ever smoothing down a lock of hair or straightening a tie for him, let alone playing ball with him. Harry's elaborate jokes could strike a sensitive son as more wounding than funny. The Christmas of the electric train, Harry had dressed up as Santa Claus to reveal the marvelous gift. Later, at a family gathering, when Jerry refused to heed requests to put the train away, "Santa" suddenly appeared with his sack and started loading the toy into it. While the child howled, Harry ripped off the beard and red hat and roared with laughter. Robbins never forgot, or fully forgave, this "double betrayal": Harry compounding the anguish he'd inflicted by laughing with the other adults over how he had fooled his son.

Harry could also be flamboyant when aroused. "It'd start in the kitchen," Robbins remembered, "Sonia and Mother. Pots would be slammed, voices rise; I'll make it myself—my way, your way—aggravation—that killer disease caused by children of martyred parents—smell of onions, eggs, & lox frying—challah toasted—a constant going & coming to the table for plates, salt, butter—the meal being eaten piecemeal—the fight going on . . . and on—and on—until finally hysteria would be reached—my sister goading my mother, my mother weak-kneed, wobbling, crying to God for help to relieve her agony—tears pouring out—down—Sonia obstinate, biting, resistant to Mother act . . ." At the boiling point, Harry wades in, making "cutlass swipes" with his paper, and "like Jove, hurls his Yiddish thunderbolts." Once, teenaged Sonia grabs a brass candlestick and yells that she'll hit him if he whacks her again. Usually, the family scuttles out of his way, and the storm blows over.

When Sonia was left in charge of Jerry, they might have a "Chinese dinner"—working backward from dessert (tea with a gingersnap floating in it) on the assumption that China was on the other side of the globe and therefore upside down. Sibling rivalry between the family's admired dancing daughter and its much younger only son also fueled ferocious tussles. And equally fierce need. When Jerry met Sonia carrying a small bag and heading toward the Jersey cliffs and the 258 steps that led down to the ferry to Manhattan, bent on leaving home after some fight with her mother, he feared she might be planning to hurl herself off the cliff and cried and begged until she turned back.

Lena had attended secretarial college—the only one of the Rips sisters to go beyond high school. She was a power in the Comfort Corset Company and a mover and shaker in civic organizations such as the local branch of the Eastern Star (Harry became a mason in 1925) and the Talmud Torah. Lena was also a leader in the extended family—Viola Zousmer Balash remembers her as "brilliant. . . . She could speak. She was unbelievable. . . . An Eleanor Roosevelt type."

She exercised her power at home. " 'Mother Knows Best,' " wrote Robbins, "was tattooed on my soul." And "[She] set me up for extraordinary standards. As I felt she was perfect (& she wanted me to feel that) how could I ever achieve her love, I who was so imperfect."

A son who doubted or criticized or resisted Lena was in for a scene. In his preteen years, if he got her angry enough, she might pick up the phone and pretend to dial. "Hello, is this the orphanage? Come and get my boy," she'd say, "I don't want him anymore." He'd cry and plead. (Did this happen several times, or was once enough to burn the episode into his memory?) When all threats failed, *she'd* weep and call on the Lord and wish she were dead; he'd hug her—"No, no! I'll be good. I'm sorry"—and they'd sob together.

Among the memorabilia of her son's precocity that Lena saved is an acrostic penciled on rough sketchpad paper:

> Dear Mommy
>   Im very SORRY
>   and so
> S is for sacrifice that you do for me
> O is for oweing which I owe to thee
> R is for rude which Im sometimes to you
> R is for apology Im trying to do
> Y is for you dear, this poem's at its end
>   your my sweatheart my lover
>   and your my best friend.
>   Jerry

Someone—Lena, one presumes—went over this heartbreaking missive with an editor's stern eye and penciled in more appropriate word usage.

⁓

Robbins's first vision of what Judaism could be arrived in a rush of color and singing and flickering light. But not in New Jersey, even though he witnessed some of the rites and absorbed the folklore. His grandmother attended shul, but the rest of the family confined its practice of Judaism mostly to seders and various big holiday meals.

In 1924, with a surprising disregard for potential danger, Lena set off for Rozhanka (ceded to Poland after World War I and by then known as Rejanke) with her children, her cousin "Honey" Zousmer, and Honey's son Jesse. Harry's father needed to see his grandchildren. Little Jerome (Gershin) had been named after him. To six-year-old Jerry, the shtetl was an Eden. In his memory it acquired the kind of golden glow in which Dylan Thomas wrapped his Welsh childhood: "All the sun long it was running, it was lovely." No matter that the village with its one road had no plumbing or electricity, or that some of the houses had packed-dirt floors. "They told me I spoke Yiddish there & that I played with the children of the shtetl all day long in the fields, in the yards. . . . I do not remember one unhappy moment there." He watched with awe while the white-bearded paternal grandfather, "who I loved a lot and who I knew loved me," stopped "a drunk from carousing through the town atop a large farm wagon, lashing his two horses." This grandfather sang Jewish songs at night, and little Jerry, nestled on his lap, sang with him. Reminiscing into a tape recorder more than fifty years later, Robbins's voice breaks when he says, "And it was my home; it was what I belonged to." Ironically, in a 1924 shtetl, surrounded by potentially hostile Christians, he felt no fear, while in America, he came to be afraid of being a Jew.

In Rejanke, the beauty and drama of the Jewish religion took wing for him. And not again for many years. One day, as he sat at the dining room table in Weehawken, memorizing the required parts of the Torah for his bar mitzvah with an old graybeard whom he disliked and who explained nothing, the neighborhood boys he'd just been playing with after school appeared at the room's three windows, "making faces and jeering and imitating" his teacher. To Robbins's shame and rage, the rabbi ignored them and went on with the lesson, even when the kids opened the windows and climbed into the first-floor room. It was Robbins who stood up and yelled at them to go home or he'd call their parents. Perhaps this episode and the frightening fact that, after the age of thirteen, all the sins of this under-sized, "mother-cuddled" boy would be on his own head shadowed his bar mitzvah. And when his throat tightened up and he croaked out words that called for the ringing tones of a boy at the edge of manhood, he wept and cried out for his dead grandfather.

He says he refused to attend services after this. For many years, anyhow. And only later could he acknowledge the influence of his culture:

My being a Jew is not because I was Bar Mitzvahed. It is within the deepest part of my soul which was nourished by the countless unidenti-fied cultural love stories . . . The superstitions, the temperaments, the fears & the glorious good times, the celebrations, food, inflexions, songs; in the fights and the jokes . . . the yiddish jokes I could not understand, but could join in the communal laughter. . . . I knew God must be just within reach. . . . subtly, subtly my heritage was laid open for me and more gently than I ever realized. . . . And from all of that I closed myself off—forgot it & threw [it] out (I was sure).

⌒

Robbins's sister always believed he could have made a career in any of the arts. As "My Selves" reveals, when he was a boy he loved all of them too much to focus exclusively on, for instance, developing his talent for the piano (maybe, too, the Depression ruled out further study). His early literary efforts were rewarded when his teacher, Miss Cora E. Fiske, sent this rather lugubrious poem by eight-year-old Jerry to the local paper:

> Sometimes I dream of funny things,
> Sometimes I dream I'm dead,
> Sometimes I dream that I'm so mean
> I have to go to bed.

At a slightly more advanced age, he adopted a world-weary stance, struggling mightily with issues of rhyme:

> Youth is a thing I can never retain.
> Once I have used it, now tis mislain.
>   . . .
> Old as I am I have still watched the young
> Still watching boys that can skip and can run.
>   . . .
> Oh! If only I could have it once more.
> You can't even buy it with money in store.
>   . . .
> Still dreams of youth I will keep in my head,
> Till my heart stops beating & until I am dead.

It is difficult to figure out exactly when Robbins decided to become a dancer and with whom, besides Alys Bentley, he took the early classes mentioned in his high school essay. Certainly he made it clear to his parents that he was not suited to be boss-in-training for Comfort Corset. He'd loved playing there as a child, he and his cousin Jack Davenport snapping the metal corset stays at each other. It pleased him, too, to see his father in a position of authority, urging on the Italian women in his employ (Jerry loved them all) as they sat at their sewing machines: "Come on girls, no talking no talking—work work that's what I pay you for." It was fascinating to watch Harry's skill at folding pink material into stacks six to eight inches thick, stenciling a pattern on the piles, and "most terrifying, cutting them out with a rotary blade knife cutter which let out a shrill whine when it hit the cloth." Jerry had enjoyed the factory less when he had to sweep threads caught in the splintery floorboards in order to earn his allowance. And at sixteen or seventeen, he didn't last long at "learning the business" of getting longline brassieres out to buxom women. His family managed to send him to New York University for one year, but clearly his mind wasn't on his studies; his highest grades were Cs, and in the spring of 1936, he flunked his second semester of college algebra and trigonometry. In chemistry, which he'd loved as a kid playing with a magic set, he drew a C and then a D. He loathed college.

Every morning, as he walked the short distance through Weehawken's comfortable, largely gentile, middle-class streets to the Palisades and down those 258 steps to the ferry bound for Forty-second Street, he must have seen the Manhattan skyline as more than a splendid vista. It was a place where he could discover for himself who Mr. and Mrs. Rabinowitz's talented little son and Sonia Rabinowitz's skinny kid brother really was.

2

First Steps

Jerry in his "Lazy Boy" at Tamiment, 1941.
Seymour E. Fischer. Courtesy of the Jerome Robbins Foundation.

*L**ater in life,* Robbins regretted his lack of a college degree. Despite years of expanding his mind and a few honorary doctorates (including one from NYU), he still felt somehow at a disadvantage around the highly educated. But at seventeen, his goals were to settle on his life's work and to become financially independent of his family as soon as possible. His decision to concentrate on dancing, as he tells it, seems almost fortuitous. He thought he'd like a career in journalism but couldn't get a foot in the door. His first love being puppetry, he wanted to apprentice himself to Tony Sarg, whose book on the subject he'd admired,* but he was literally rebuffed on the doorstep.

Sonia to the rescue—no longer Sonia Rabinowitz but Sonya Robyns. While supporting herself in New York with a variety of jobs, she'd performed with the Dance Center group (touted in a 1932 program as "America's Only Ballet Company"), run by Gluck Sandor and his partner-wife, Felicia Sorel. Jerry had seen his sister in Sandor's *Tempo (Dance Marathon)* that year at the Barbizon Plaza Concert Hall. Inspired by Sandor's version of *Petrouchka*—the famous ballet Mikhail Fokine had choreographed in 1911 for Serge Diaghilev's Ballets Russes—he constructed his favorite puppet, "The Magician," and planned a tiny basement production of his own.

Sonia thought her brother had a gift for dancing and fought fiercely with her father to let him give it a try. Accordingly, Jerry, eighteen but small and boyish (at sixteen he'd still been able to get into movies as a twelve-and-under), presented himself before Sandor in bathing trunks and a T-shirt. His audition must have taken place sometime in the fall of 1936, around the time that Dance Center was moving into its new home—a loft theater at 118 West Fifty-fourth Street above one of the many livery garages on the block. Possibly he didn't realize how unorthodox an audition it was. After asking to see some elementary moves—running, jumping, turning, and some rhythmical sequences—Sandor had the boy write the numbers 0 through 9 on the air with his arms, then with different body parts, then in various dramatic contexts, ending with instructions to do the sequence as Shiva. *"Who?"* Never mind; Robbins apparently impressed Sandor with his imaginative responses, and Sandor certainly impressed Robbins.

Here is Robbins's description of the man he referred to as his master: "I think he must have been strongly impressed by German Expressionism. In a blink of an eye he could transform his face & body into anything he desired—a bird, a monster, a beauty, a clown, a fat whore, a thin dowager, etc. He was not a mimic & although keenly observant, his own images of

---

* Possibly *The Tony Sarg Marionette Book* (1921), illustrated by Sarg, text by F. J. McIsaac, with two plays for homemade marionettes by Anne Stoddard.

the worlds inside were incredibly abundant & useful." To José Limón—
who appeared in Dance Center productions of the 1930s—Sandor was a
"dynamo":

> He took good dancers, with well-established reputations, unknown but
> talented younger dancers, and aspiring beginners, and by the pure force
> of his indomitable will, molded them into stunning productions.
> Sammy was a martinet, a tyrant, impatient, tempestuous, and explosive.
> He was also lovable, warm, and human, with an irresistible sense of
> humor. But above all else, he was an artist. When the curtain went up,
> there was magic.

Sandor, aka Sammy Gluck, aka Samuel Gluck, aka Senia Gluckoff,
aka M. Senia Gluck aka Senia Gluck-Sandor, is difficult to define in relation to the fermenting dance scene of a New York gradually crawling out
of the Depression. But then, he had always been a chameleon. He had
studied with Mikhail Fokine and performed in his *The Thunderbird* in a
revue at New York's Hippodrome in 1921. During the 1920–1921 season
he'd danced at the Metropolitan Opera in Nikolai Rimsky-Korsakov's *Le
Coq d'Or,* with Fokine's choreography staged by former Diaghilev dancer
Adolf Bolm, and he garnered excellent reviews touring with Bolm's Ballet
Intime. Between 1927 and 1931, he had, with Felicia Sorel, devised and
performed prologues before movies at the Paramount in Manhattan and
elsewhere. In 1931, the same year he founded Dance Center, he choreographed for the ninth edition of *Earl Carroll's Vanities* the ballet *Hands and
Masks,* which had, wrote Robert Benchley in *The New Yorker,* "a beauty
quite out of keeping with the rest of the exhibition." The numbers he
staged for Minsky's Burlesque at the Apollo Theatre on 125th Street were
also viewed as class acts (" 'Madame Butterfly' conceived and directed
by M. Senia Gluck was a real revelation in the way of artistic character
presentation"). The *New York Times* dance critic John Martin appraised
Dance Center's first year of operation in 1931–1932 with considerable
enthusiasm.

> The surprise of the season lay not in the enterprise's shortcom-
> ings, which were few, but in its excellences which were many. In Mr.
> Gluck, it revealed an outstandingly gifted director. Never "arty" always
> theatrical; sometimes a little obscure; remarkably inventive, at times
> straining for originality;... dynamic enough to excuse occasional

crudity: . . . frequently poetical; once in a while given to sentimentality; often embarrassingly daring; always large and vital in intention—such is the catalogue of his choreography. It is in many ways a paradoxical one, but it marks him as an unfailingly interesting artist.

Given such a critical response (including that intriguing "embarrassingly"), one wonders why Gluck Sandor's name is not more well known; he may be remembered by theatergoers primarily as the rabbi in the original 1964 Broadway production of *Fiddler on the Roof*—a role for which the respectful and grateful Robbins sought him out. Eclecticism was crucial to financial stability during the 1930s; it also somewhat befogged Sandor's reputation. His 1932 boast of Dance Center's being America's only ballet company wouldn't have been far off the mark (the Chicago Opera Ballet had been operating since 1925), except that Dance Center wasn't really a ballet company. Sandor and Sorel had also studied briefly with Mary Wigman, the great German exponent of contemporary *Ausdruckstanz* (or Expression Dance) during a 1930 trip to Europe, and possibly also during workshops she taught in New York when touring the United States; 1931 ads for classes at the Dance Center list instruction in "German Technique and Dance." Certainly, photographs of Sandor's work show angular poses molded by emotional intensity; clustered people all gesturing differently, similar to group designs favored by Wigman; and no classical lines. His idea of having different parts of the body "write" different numbers simultaneously seems to have been an original idea—one he deployed in choreographing both concert works and revues.

Dance Center functioned within the emerging modern dance scene. During Robbins's apprenticeship, José Limón, then affiliated with the company of Doris Humphrey and Charles Weidman, not only played Sorel's young suitor (Sandor was her "Spectre Lover") in *El Amor Brujo*, to Manuel de Falla's music, but also Arlecchino in the less praised Commedia dell'Arte piece *Isabella Andreini*. In the spring of 1938, the Dance Center Company appeared on a concert series at Washington Irving High School that featured, among others, the Humphrey-Weidman Company. Weidman premiered *The Happy Hypocrite* at the Dance Center, and African-American concert dancer Edna Guy presented her group there.

During a period of heightened social conscience, when dancers walked on picket lines and the "moderns"—ardent leftists all—donated dances to concerts held to raise money for the Abraham Lincoln Brigade fighting fascism in Spain or the International Labor Defense Fund, Sandor, too, alluded in his work to headline causes such as the Spanish Civil War *(Spanish Dances of War [after Goya])* and investigated African-American culture *(Negro Blues Poem*—a series of solos that Sorel and Gluck performed to Langston Hughes poems set to music by Herbert Kingsley). However, in the 1930s, Sandor, unlike the contentious group of "modern" choreographers then in the limelight—Weidman, Humphrey, Martha Graham, Helen Tamiris, Hanya Holm—didn't seem intent on forging a new and stripped-down vocabulary, and some of his most lauded productions were new versions of scenarios made famous on the ballet stage by Diaghilev's Ballets Russes: *The Prodigal Son, Salome,* and *Petrouchka.* A Dance Center press release advertises *El Amor Brujo* as being "from the repertory of the late Argentina," although Adolf Bolm had also presented a ballet using Manuel de Falla's music and based on its scenario of supernatural possession.

Robbins drank in the atmosphere and devoured the lessons. And took note. Sorel he saw as a cool, intense foil to Sandor's wildness. "Her lids never seemed to raise to make a visual connection with her partners, but connected she was. She used her hands in an archaic way, fingers together, thumbs separated and crooked back toward the hand at the last joint." Robbins began to think about hands. He saw also how Sandor gained power by "[using] space as if it were a thick volume" and took the strategy to heart. Most crucial in terms of forming Robbins's taste and influencing his later way of working, Sandor drummed into his pupils the importance of theatrical credibility. Affiliated with the Group Theatre as an occasional teacher and choreographer, he pushed dancers to think about their characters' backgrounds and perform truthfully in the Stanislavskian sense. His company had acting lessons (Robbins thought perhaps with Sanford Meisner), and Group Theatre actors were sometimes recruited for Dance Center Productions; in 1938, two young men later to make their names in directing were scheduled to appear in a revival of Sandor's *Salome* that never materialized—Elia Kazan taking over the role of Herod from Sandor and Robert ("Bobby") Lewis playing a page.

After Robbins's first season with Dance Center, when he spent the summer of 1937 at Kittatinny as a junior counselor, charged with teaching daily dance classes and staging Saturday-night shows, he consulted with Sandor about his own roles. Koko in *The Mikado,* Sandor told him, had once been a tailor, so Jerry carried scissors and a tape measure and, carried away, gave a snip or two to the Mikado's beard, startling the actor. When Robbins was able to assemble enough cash to see Colonel de Basil's Ballet Russe perform Fokine's *Petrouchka* he found it unconvincing and inferior to the Dance Center's modest version, done to Igor Stravinsky's four-handed arrangement of the score—a production Charles D. Isaacson had praised for its realism in *The Dance Magazine*. It allowed the audience, he said, to "look into the hearts of the puppets."

For performers at the Dance Center's studio theater, concentration was vital. The closest spectators were less than five feet away. Stagecraft was make-do but imaginative, and some talented artists, in addition to Sandor himself, provided decor: Reginald Marsh for *Tempo (Dance Marathon)*, Hollywood-director-to-be Vincente Minnelli (then designing for Radio City Music Hall) for *Salome*. "Everything was a source of invention," Robbins remembered, "from the limitations of money, technique, and his dancers to the water and heating pipes that haphazardly pierced the studio theater stage space." New York dance aficionado Martin Green, who regularly attended Dance Center performances and knew Sandor and Sorel well, remembers a kind of trapdoor in the ceiling leading to the pair's living space, where the performers dressed and made up; through this they could descend to great effect in works like *Salome*, and "there was always a prop coming down through the ceiling. It was fabulous!"

Programs, memories, and critical appraisals offer glimpses of the theatrical ingenuity and boldness that young Robbins sucked up. Sandor's *Petrouchka*, daringly for those days, cast an African-American dancer (Raymond Sawyer) as the Moor, necessitating an amorous duet between a black man and a white woman. His choreographic designs sound vivid; an anonymous critic noted admiringly how in *Salome* (four acts and five scenes), "The men and women of Herod's court sitting on the ground throw one leg over the leg of their partner's in a linked chain." Total depravity did not reign in this *Salome*, and there were no seven veils. At the end, Sorel ("an infinitely subtle blend of prurience and innocence," according to Limón) settled herself over the corpse of John the Baptist—his body covered in black to make him appear decapitated—at which point he sat up and raised his arms above her "as if to plead for her redemption."

During Robbins's apprenticeship, Sandor was in the midst of preparing a major work under the auspices of the short-lived, contention-plagued Federal Dance Project: a radical revision of his earlier *Prodigal Son*, entitled *The Eternal Prodigal* and set to new music by Herbert Kingsley. It played at the Ritz Theatre for a week beginning November 29, 1936. Although Robbins was not in it, he undoubtedly saw it both during rehearsals and onstage. Sandor brought the biblical tale into the twentieth century and staged most of its prologue and six scenes as a dream (the rebellious youth leaves home and falls asleep in a field); it contained elements of *Faust* (Sandor as the "evil genius" luring the musician-hero to destruction) and the Romantic theme of a woman (Sorel) pursued and repeatedly lost—once in a "subway stampede"—and "ideals shattered in the confusion of modern existence." In place of the standard family-reunion ending, the hero is ordered to wander "always searching, fighting for what he knows to be true until the world changes." Heady stuff for an aspiring young dancer-choreographer-dreamer like Jerome W. Rabinowitz.

By the spring of 1937, he had made his debut at Dance Center, but not under that name. A Jewish name might be all right for a producer or a stellar violinist; it didn't, in those days, suit a dancer. Some years earlier, Sulamith Ish-Kishor had remarked in *The Jewish Times* that "few stage artists of recent times have admitted Jewish ancestry." Robbins later said that one of his reasons for joining the theater had been that there was no anti-Semitism there; even so, he had been brought up to believe that to be a Jew meant being in constant danger—whether from outright persecution or ostracism and condescension. After the Anschluss of 1938, in which Germany annexed Austria and Czechoslovakia, terrifying stories of fascist actions against Jews began to leak out of Europe. The guilt-drenched shame common to bright children of immigrant parents also affected him. During those years, he recalled, "I didn't want to be a Jew. I didn't want to be like my father, the Jew—or any of his friends those Jews. I twisted on the two prongs: my own anti-Semitism & the terror of others. I wanted to be <u>safe</u>, protected, assimilated, hidden in among the Goys, the majority."

Following Sandor's example, he tried out a number of names before settling on Jerome Robbins. In that 1937 spring season, "Robin Gerald" (Sandor's suggestion) played one of six companions in *El Amor Brujo* and, in *Isabella Andreini,* one of three jugglers who indulged in "high jinks and impromptu business." By April 1938, he was trying out "Gerald Robins" and had graduated to playing the Lover's friend in *El Amor Brujo.*

His metamorphosis into a dancer was hard won. His parents had offered him $5 a week for a year and no longer; and he was hell-bent to prove himself and become self-supporting by its end. He lived in the family home on Highwood Terrace in Weehawken, trudged up and down the steps to the ferry to save bus fare, ate at the Horn & Hardart Automat on Fifty-seventh Street. In high school, he'd earned money delivering eggs, selling magazines, painting screens for a New York photographer, selling tax bills (whatever this meant, it garnered a high school senior 75¢). As a determined young dance student, he scrubbed studio floors and windows in exchange for lessons, stuck up posters for concerts, and delivered publicity materials to the post office. Sandor got him a job designing and making medallions for the Works Progress Administration production of Kurt Weill and Paul Green's *Johnny Johnson,* which Sandor was choreographing (Jerry fashioned them of too flimsy materials, and they fell apart).

Harry Rabinowitz may not have been pleased at his son's decision to try dancing as a career, but, good with hammer and nails, he helped build seating platforms for Dance Center's new theater. At one performance—possibly the one in which his son was given a chance at a solo in *El Amor Brujo*—he marched up to John Martin and asked whether the kid had talent. Martin said yes, he did. Martin was the authority; what he said went. And after that, apparently, Harry didn't doubt his son could make a living in dance. Even this early, Robbins seems to have developed a powerful ambition, uncommon (or perhaps unrealistic) among dancers, not just to become an artist to reckon with but to become a financial success.

He might have had difficulty fixing on a name, but he was fixed in his goals and eager to develop his dance technique. In later life, Robbins wasn't specific about names and dates connected with his early training, but at some point he took classes in Greenwich Village with a dancer who taught Martha Graham's technique through the WPA; he found the floor exercises tough on his tight hips, even though high extensions and superior flexibility weren't expected of male dancers then. He mentions Charles Weidman as a teacher, and various unnamed others associated with the New Dance Group. He went to Helene Veola for classes in Spanish dance, and to Yeichi Nimura for a demanding combination of modern dance and ballet that also featured detailed Asian-influenced work for the hands. It was Sandor who persuaded Robbins to study ballet, which he disdained until he saw Alexandra Danilova perform the second act of *Swan Lake* with Colonel de Basil's Ballets Russes during the company's April 1937 season at the Metropolitan Opera House and was overcome by the beauty and expressiveness of it all. Perhaps, too, a WPA teacher he first studied ballet with presented it uninterestingly, because once his sister sent him to Ella Daganova, Robbins worked devotedly—sometimes taking two classes a day plus another barre, and writing down every exercise in a notebook. Daganova, an American, had Russianized her name, possibly when she toured with Anna Pavlova; judging by Robbins's daily notes on his studies, she taught three classes a day in her Fifty-sixth Street studio—the strict approach to classical technique devised by Enrico Cecchetti in the later nineteenth century spiked with Dr. Bess Mensendieck's theories about muscle function and body alignment. Daganova's usual classroom attire was a pleated skirt and sweater, and Robbins thought she lacked only a sunshade and the right shoes to look like a professional golfer. For Daganova, he cleaned blinds; male dancers being scarce, such work scholarships weren't hard to come by. George Balanchine's School of American Ballet over on Madison Avenue and Fifty-ninth Street was the only one that turned him down; he couldn't get past the front desk.

He must have demonstrated stage presence before he acquired technical mastery. Lisa Parnova, who often performed with the Dance Center Company, enlisted him as a partner in a program at that haven for choreographers planning to present a single concert, the Ninety-second Street YMHA, on November 20, 1937. Parnova, once a ballerina of the Cologne opera, had been praised for her abilities in modern dance, ballet, and character vignettes in the manner of the acclaimed solo mime artist Angna Enters. Necessity must have dictated Parnova's choice of such a novice as a partner. Perhaps Igor Miladeroff, with whom she toured extensively between 1937 and 1939, was injured or busy elsewhere, because the YMHA concert was twice postponed. Anatole Chujoy, reviewing this fateful event in *The Dance Magazine,* thought that Parnova succeeded best when satirizing ballet conventions. He was less pleased with her serious numbers, "and Gerald Robbins' partnering hinders rather than helps."

At that point Robbins had had only four beginning-level ballet classes. And he was slight. Parnova, dark and beautiful to his eyes, had told him that all he had to do was to put his hands on either side of her waist to keep her on balance and just to think of her as a tall pole. In a duet to Claude Debussy's "The Snow Is Falling," he discovered that the pole she most resembled was a heavy telephone pole and that keeping her straight while she revolved was a chore: "I never could get her back on center once she started off." As for steps, he offered her his two favorites: sissonnes and tour jetés. It was easier to waltz Parnova about to Strauss in their flirtatious other duet: "skinny me in my rented starched clothes—and Lisa in a big hooped skirt."

However, the young dancer was confident enough to throw in his lot with his sister that fall, and offer to teach what little he knew to others. According to a nicely printed pamphlet, "Sonya and Jerry Robyns" (a new name variation that deferred to Sonia's already established stage name) "announce the fall opening of their Dance Studio." The classes, to be held at Dance Center on Saturdays, offered everything the pair knew, and more. They were prepared to teach Rhythms, Modern, and Advanced (four one-hour lessons per month and a practice session for $5; private lessons, $2). Those wishing to learn the waltz, fox-trot, slow fox-trot, tango, and rhumba could make an appointment for half-hour lessons (12 for $10). Sonia cannot remember whether they attracted any pupils.

Early on, Robbins was interested in choreography and enrolled—the only boy to do so—in a composition class that Bessie Schönberg was teaching near Union Square. (Schönberg, a former member of Martha Graham's company, was already known for her classes at the Bennington School and Festival in Vermont, where the modern dance luminaries gathered every summer.) Robbins brought a touch of drama to what sounds like an early version of basic assignments that Schönberg was still giving forty years later to her students at Sarah Lawrence College; she seems to have asked her young pupils to choreograph a study using bending movement, axial movement, swinging, and jumping. Robbins decided he was a hibernating bear awakening in the spring.

> It started with "bending" movement & then went to "circular movement" (sitting on floor I circled my legs about & under me), gradually got up to swinging movement (as I got to my feet & felt the life of spring coming back to me) & ended with "jumping" movement, as my happiness at complete liberation carried me away.

At a 1995 ceremony honoring her, Schönberg claimed to remember this junior effort and said she thought it was fine.

Greenwich Village buzzed with modern dance activity—Martha Graham had a studio on East Ninth Street. However, during the two-year period Robbins worked for Sandor, many of the studios were, like Dance Center, concentrated in the area around Carnegie Hall; hurrying from one to another, perhaps with a stop at the Automat, was no problem. When days ran late, Robbins could spend the night on Sandor and Sorel's couch. It was on that couch one afternoon that he had his first homosexual adventure—or rather, almost had it. In the midst of an embrace, the man, an older dancer on whom he had a crush, cupped a hand over his genitals. Jerry hadn't expected this to happen; he had indulged in mutual masturbation with school friends and campmates but had never before connected sex with the tenderness he felt for his colleague. The man, realizing that this boy was not only young but inexperienced, pulled back. And for the first time, Robbins understood, unhappily, "that I loved a man, that I was queer." A few years later, on tour with Ballet Theatre, curious, perhaps, about what he had missed, he visited the dancer in Boston, slept with him, and never saw him again.

In the fall of 1937, Sandor was able to offer steady jobs to both Jerry and Sonia. He'd been asked to choreograph the dance sequences for a production of I. J. Singer's novel *The Brothers Ashkenazi,* adapted into a play by Maurice Schwartz for his Yiddish Art Theatre. Nine times a week, "Jerome Robbins" danced in two scenes, sang the "International" along with an insurgent crowd, and walked the curtain in for several episodes. Being small, he was tapped to play the father of the eponymous twin brothers as a child (Julius Adler portrayed the character as an adult); his two words, "Yes, Papa" in Yiddish, earned him a mention among those named in the *Daily Mirror* as outstanding (although one of his many aunts told him that someone had coughed and she had missed his line completely). His family, however proud to see him getting steady professional work, was not anxious to see him embark on a career in Yiddish theater; they, too, wanted him to become part of the mainstream (read *goyische*) American culture.

Writing on Yiddish theater in America, David S. Lifson suggests that the initial impulse had risen out of nostalgia for a Europe where Jews had lived in enclaves within the larger society; the gathering place once provided by the shtetl synagogue was replaced by the theater. The old-style, out-of-Russia Yiddish theater involved actors flamboyantly improvising stock characters, with a prompter to keep them on track. As a producer-director-star, Schwartz had loftier goals. As early as 1918, critics had hailed one of his productions as initiating an art movement in Yiddish theater. His company performed plays by Oscar Wilde, August Strindberg, and Henrik Ibsen, as well as those by Singer, Sholem Aleichem, and other Jewish writers. Schwartz's emphasis on naturalism and ensemble playing was as strong as that of the Moscow Art Theater, which had impressed New York on its visit in the early 1920s.

The Brothers Ashkenazi, conveniently for Robbins, was not housed at the theater on Second Avenue at Twelfth Street where Schwartz usually staged productions. By putting on the play at the Jolson at Seventh Avenue and Fifty-ninth Street, Schwartz made it accessible to an uptown Jewish bourgeoisie. The production was opulent. The program lists more than fifty roles; a few of the performers played more than one character and also swelled the ensemble of thirty "men, women, Germans, Chassidim, waiters, weavers, dancers, officers, servants, wedding guests, red army soldiers, Polish soldiers" in an epic that began in the early nineteenth century and ended during World War I. The superb makeup, a tradition in Yiddish theater (and usually created by the set designer), enabled the actors to play a variety of characters; at the first dress rehearsal, Robbins failed to recognize anyone. The saga of the two brothers—the saintly Yacob and the greed-driven Simcha, aka Max (Schwartz)—took in the rise of the textile industry in Lodz, business chicanery, family quarrels, incest, war, the rise of the revolutionary spirit, and anti-Semitism. In the climactic scene, the brothers—reunited through the one's forgiving generosity and the other's remorse—are commanded by Polish soldiers to dance before a jeering mob. Max does this "dance of shame" to save his life; Yacob refuses and is shot.

Robbins didn't particularly enjoy doing the show—perhaps in part because it stalled his flight from his Jewish heritage. Also, Schwartz was an autocrat and a tightwad. The dancers struck for a raise from $10 a week to $15 and got it, but two weeks later he fired some of them. Actors' Equity didn't cover foreign-language productions. Robbins apparently didn't endear himself to the men in the dressing room by holding on to the washbasin to run through his Daganova barre work prior to performances (only later did it occur to him that he might have been in their way). But since he was young and full of himself, the cast members took pleasure in the good-natured game of seeing how many of them could pat his face or pinch his cheek during a crowd scene. His appearances onstage were so far apart that he could mosey around the neighborhood between them.

He must have learned something about the daily grind of professional theater, but when the New York run ended and Schwartz took the com-

pany on the road, he went back to the Dance Center for its April performances—as Gerald Robin. Those were his last appearances with Sandor
and Sorel. He wanted to be dancing more often, and for good pay. The
Dance Center company seemed plagued with difficulties. John Martin
had often remarked on postponements of seasons and cancellations of premieres and suggested that there was friction among the personnel.

Robert Lewis gives an interesting glimpse into Sandor's erratic side in a
somewhat tongue-in-cheek letter to Robbins, written in 1989 after he
heard that Robbins was possibly planning to direct Richard Strauss's opera
Salome:

> Gluck Sandor said, "Bobby, I want you to stand stage center, both
> arms extended out in front. When the curtain rises, each character of the
> Ballet will cross the stage, taking off the black coverings they have on
> over their costumes and dropping them on your arms. You then walk
> off and the Ballet begins." (This device was used by Vachtangov as the
> opening of *Turandot,* too. I don't know who came first.) "Also," Sammy
> continued, "I want you to do it like an eleventh century priest." I com-
> plied immediately. Anything was possible for a young Group Theatre
> actor in those days. Next rehearsal we repeated this opening passage.
> Gluck Sandor stopped me.
> "What are you doing, Bobby?"
> "I am doing what I did yesterday."
> "But I thought I told you to do it like Harry Richman [the comedian
> and singer]."
> Kazan, who was also in the Ballet, and I looked at each other and we
> knew it was time to get back to the quiet normalcy of Lee Strasberg.

Whatever the reasons for Dance Center's closing, it was announced in
The New York Times on November 13, 1938, that from now on Sandor
would put on one-man theater with masks and life-sized puppets in his
new studio at 138 Fifth Avenue—noting that he felt he couldn't afford to
pay live performers adequately. More tellingly (and interesting in relation
to Robbins's own early aspirations): "Gluck-Sandor now feels he would
rather work with dolls who do as they are told and whose personalities do
not interfere with his ideas."

⁓

By the end of May 1938, now Jerry Robyns again, Robbins was gain-
fully employed as a performer in the evening entertainments at Camp

Tamiment in the Poconos. Tamiment had been established in the 1920s by the socialist Rand Institute; during its early years, the adult campers—typically single, young, and Jewish—tended to be affiliated with Rand or profess socialist leanings. By the time Robbins arrived, Tamiment, according to historian Martha Lo Monaco, had a more diverse bunch of paying guests; as dancer-choreographer Ruthanna Boris puts it, the girls were looking for husbands, "and the guys were looking for a fast lay." All was not boating, swimming, or golfing, however; ten lectures by visiting scholars were offered during the summer of 1938 on such topics as "Some Social Influences in Modern Music," "Fascism and War in Current Drama," and "Inside News from Europe." There is no record of whether Robbins attended any of them. He was probably too busy rehearsing.

In 1933, Max Liebman had taken over Tamiment's entertainment component and started raising it to a higher level. At nearby Camp Log Cabin, where he'd worked for the nine previous summers, he'd had to hire waiters who could "wield a wicked tennis racket, shake a nimble hoof on the dance floor, possess a rumbling larynx for poetry reading in a canoe. . . . If he could sing, tap-dance, play a ukelele or paint scenery, he had an edge." At Tamiment, he could employ professionals, among them as many as twelve dancers. Liebman staged a revue every Saturday night in the social hall that jutted two feet out over the lake and boasted a stage sixteen by twenty-four feet. In addition, there were other nights during the week where anybody on the payroll could do just about anything that came to mind: a ballet dancer might attempt a song, a baritone essay a first-ever tap routine, a musician plunge into stand-up comedy, or a dancer with choreographic ambitions test the waters. Their fiercest critics and partisans were the old settlers and families who lived in the bungalow colony, Sandyville, on the premises. Boris: "If Sandyville liked what you did in the floor show on Friday night or the musical comedy night or in the dance concert on Wednesday or Thursday, they let you know, and if they didn't like it, you heard about it right after the performance. They were vocal, they were powerful, and they were mostly all socialists."

Among those who worked at Tamiment in the late thirties and early forties were the comedians Imogene Coca, her husband Robert Burton, Jules Munshin, and Danny Kaye; the pianist, composer, and comedy lyricist par excellence Sylvia Fine (later Mrs. Danny Kaye); playwright-to-be William Archibald (then a dancer). Dorothy Bird and Anita Alvarez came from Martha Graham's group, Archibald, William Bales, Lee Sherman, and Kenneth Bostock from the Humphrey-Weidman Company. Over Robbins's four summers at Tamiment, they mingled compatibly with ballet dancers such as Herbert Ross, Albia Kavan, Miriam Golden, Ruthanna Boris, and David Nillo.

Robbins had actually made his Tamiment debut at the very end of the 1937 summer. While finishing up his chores as a Kittatinny counselor, he'd thought it might not be a bad idea to contact Max Liebman and see if he could try out for the shows he'd heard about. Come and audition, responded Liebman, needing an extra boy for the Labor Day weekend. Robbins got a friend to drive him the fifteen miles from Kittatinny to Tamiment, jumped plausibly, and, when asked for pirouettes, prudently identified himself as a modern dancer who had just started ballet. Ten dollars plus room and board for the week! The ensemble dance he learned, possibly to "Begin the Beguine," embedded itself in Robbins's memory. Almost forty years later, he wrote, "You came in on half toe a step to each every 2 counts with your arms held like you were dancing with someone, & then after 4 steps—whamoo—you flicked your hands to face out instead of in. I thought it was gorgeous." He asked Liebman if he could return the following summer. Yes.

Tamiment was decidedly rustic. Coca, arriving for the first time with her husband, took one look at the communal bathrooms and considered turning around and heading back to New York. At least one performer was supposed to eat at every guest table. Apparently Robbins finally got tired of being asked what he did in the winter: "Wear a coat," he said. Judging from the pictures taken by camp photographer Lewis "Snappy" Goren, the performers had a *little* leisure time; although in one snapshot of Robbins and Albia Kavan lying facedown on a jetty, apparently slumbering, a portable phonograph sits beside them, as if a rehearsal were in the offing or had just ended. Robbins believed himself in love with Kavan, although their relationship was stormy. After the summer, he wrote in a diary what a pleasure it was to "feel her lips and body & see her eyes so full." His crush, however, didn't preclude other sexual adventures and friendships that were useful in a variety of ways. Composer-accompanist Glen Bacon helped him cultivate an appetite for reading, and the exotic-satiric dance team of Mata and Hari exposed him to another developmental experience: they "seduced" him simultaneously. "It felt funny."

On Sundays, Liebman held conferences to thrash out ideas for the revue two weeks off, as well as to make final decisions about the coming weekend's show. This main event was rehearsed Monday through Thursday and had its first run-through with orchestra on Friday morning; its technical and dress rehearsals took up all day Saturday, and the show went on at nine o'clock that night. According to Lo Monaco, Tamiment guests were entertained six evenings a week. Ruthanna Boris remembers one night's being devoted to the resident Madison String Quartet and one to whatever dances the kids could come up with. According to Robbins, there were nightclub floor shows on Thursday as well as Friday, plus a Monday vaudeville he called "schloch night" and "a porridge of leftovers," most of them culled from the Saturday-night revues.

The impetus to try new skills seems to have been strong. Boris recollects that Danny Kaye once got it into his head that he wanted to sing the "Kol Nidre" in true cantorial style; he, the string quartet's cellist Maurice Bialkin, Boris, and Robbins (the two Jewish dancers in the bunch) trucked over to nearby Unity House to get advice on ceremonial gestures (this rival camp, run by the International Ladies' Garment Workers' Union, had a rabbi in residence). Here were two aspiring choreographers—one of them, Boris, a snob about her superior ballet training with Rosina Galli at the Metropolitan Opera—performing movements drawn from Yom Kippur ritual costumed as two Jewish boys (Ruthanna with her breasts strapped down). Kaye and Munshin had a hankering to do a Russian dance and enlisted Boris to help them and to play a flirtatious maiden with handkerchief and red boots. Their undertrained thighs were clearly not up to the stress of *prisadkas;* a brilliant idea struck them. They scavenged empty institution-sized tomato juice cans from the kitchen, strapped them on to their behinds, and, instead of squatting, sat to kick their legs about. "Danny," said Boris, "was born to have the middle of the stage, and when he didn't have the middle of the stage, he became acutely sick. He was voracious. So was Jerry Robbins, only in a different way (in my experience). Jerry had to have it his way, or no way. Danny got into everybody's act in one way or another."

In her memoir *Bird's Eye View,* Dorothy Bird gives an ebullient picture of Robbins dancing in a floor show:

In the cabaret environment he was a spellbinding performer. He was mysteriously confident and outwardly carefree, even casual, about every aspect of his solo work. Jerry was completely prepared for any eventuality that might occur. He choreographed startling, dazzling entrances for himself, certain to capture everyone's attention. He moved improvisationally from table to table, reaching out to people, before suddenly spinning, leaping, and sliding across the floor to another table. He laughed along with the audience, communicating his extraordinary sense of élan, sensitivity to the music, and joy in dancing. As he heard the climactic music, he readied himself to execute the most theatrical exit imaginable. He disappeared to thunderous applause, then laughingly returned to bow, always at ease but in total control.

If Robbins hadn't known before how to pick up material quickly, throw together a routine, adapt to a variety of styles, make a point succinctly, and understand the importance of timing, he learned it now. Much of what he later deployed in original ways in the Broadway musicals he choreographed and/or directed he must have absorbed—either through his pores or his very sharp eyes—during the four summers he spent at Tamiment. The training may have been harum-scarum, picked up on the run, but it was definitely professional.

Many of the Tamiment dance numbers were satires—most often on politics or the theater itself. In the summer of 1938, Coca did a hilarious takeoff on the "Water Nymph Ballet" that George Balanchine had choreographed for a recently premiered movie, Samuel Goldwyn's *The Goldwyn Follies,* featuring Vera Zorina (whom Balanchine was courting at the time). Coca titled her version "Goldwyn's Folly." Robbins made his first appearance of the summer in "No More Waltz in Vienna," choreographed by Lil Liandre. The politically aware audience would have caught every nuance of the irreverent goings-on in a number by Sylvia Fine, "ILGWU Finishing School" (a dig at Unity House, perhaps?), in which Robbins was one of eleven performers (none of the others was a dancer), or "Militant Moe," a sketch by Liebman for Munshin and "Group Dancers." Pacifism got its comeuppance in "Ferdinand," with Coca as the flower-loving bull and Robbins as one of five frustrated matadors.

The roles Robbins played in that first summer's revues attest to his versatility: a devil in "Casey Jones"; a slave in the cotton fields in "Negro Dance Saga: Jungle to Harlem" (choreographed by Jerome Andrews); a newsboy among the city types in "Triangle Murder" by Fine; a beggar in "Zlotopol: In a Jewish Village"; a Garment Center graduate; and other ensemble roles as well.

Tamiment was, as Anita Alvarez said, a "jumping joint." Often several dancers with a lust to choreograph collaborated on a number. For the August 27 revue, *What's New,* Alvarez, Jennifer Chatfield, and Robbins put together a hornpipe trio called "At the Anchor." They all contributed steps, but Robbins masterminded it. (This and the 1939 "Ahoy," with Alvarez, Robbins, and Dorothy Bird—possibly a remake of "At the Anchor"—indicates that his interest in sailors as subject matter came well before his first great choreographic success, the ballet *Fancy Free.*)

Robbins and Kavan may have been an item, but it was Alvarez he wanted to perform and choreograph with. She was, he later wrote, "a ferocious contained tigress of a dancer. . . . She used the floor as easily as one walks over it & her descents and rises from it were one continuous movement through space." The two made dramatic use of a ladder in the very successful "He Done Her Wrong," with Glen Bacon singing the ballad of Frankie and Johnny. Although Robbins and Alvarez concocted what must have been a satirical duet, "Whirling Persians," in 1940, their most notable success was their "Strange Fruit" (1939), to the song made famous by Billie Holiday. Robbins, recalls Alvarez, "was the degenerate Southern gentleman and I was a girl in a sackcloth that he made passes at. . . . What eventually happened was that he grabbed me and we did a lift that went around his back and I slid all the way down in front and landed in a heap. And at the end of the song I rose up with an outstretched palm." She doesn't remember if she was supposed to be black, only that she was being abused. They repeated the duet in New York at the Ninety-second Street YMHA's Kaufman Auditorium on August 31; the program, to benefit the left-wing TAC (Theatre Arts Committee), included numbers by Ruthanna Boris, Agnes de Mille, the comedic mime Lotte Goslar, and the Lindy Hoppers. A *Billboard* writer thought that Robbins and Alvarez's number "revealed them as superlative dancers, and they show-stopped easily. Spotted properly, they should click handily into a revue." (The two did audition for a few shows as a couple, but their partnership evaporated when Robbins joined Ballet Theatre in 1940.)

Quite a few of Robbins's Tamiment ideas seem to have been serious dance-dramas: the timely "Death of a Loyalist" (1939), in which he starred as a prisoner in the Spanish Civil War remembering his past, and "Harlem Incident" (1940), which he described to a reporter in 1944 as "a party of white slummers [actually only two, Ballet Theatre dancers Miriam Golden and David Nillo] invade a Harlem dive, make it surly and self-conscious and almost create a riot." He conceded that he might have compressed the scene a bit too much; seven minutes wasn't a lot of time in which to develop an important social statement. He had thought a bluesy song, "Where's the Boy I Saved for a Rainy Day?," which he staged in 1941 for a big-eyed neophyte named Carol Channing, would have the audience in tears and was taken aback when they roared with laughter. But his "Lazy Boy" was a satirical version of the fence-painting scene in *Tom Sawyer* (with himself as Tom and Alvarez as his overenthusiastic, paint-happy sidekick), and "À la Russe," starring Coca, spoofed some of the *ballets bouffes* endemic to the repertoires of Colonel de Basil's Ballet Russe and the Ballet Russe de Monte Carlo. In that 1944 interview, he called the number "a typical French farce situation—old husband, young wife, about seventeen doors and millions of exits and entrances. Nobody would just leave the stage—they'd have to do entrechats, double tours-en-air, fouet-tés—that's ballet talk for spins, pirouettes, and a lot of fancy business."

Performing with gifted comedians was an educational experience. During Danny Kaye's first Tamiment summer (1939), Robbins partici-pated in "The Richtige Mikado" (Broadway had seen several variants of the Gilbert and Sullivan operetta; *The Hot Mikado, The Swing Mikado,* why not a Yiddish Mikado?), in which Kaye, as Nanki-Poo, wrapped his nimble tongue around Yiddish with a speed that might well have alarmed W. S. Gilbert. And Robbins adored that damaged elf Imogene Coca. "I was as attentive a fan as if I were her understudy. I was thrilled to watch the simpleness and clarity of her mind. Her acting was connected and per-sonal, her taste and sensitivity were almost painfully touching. I believe I learned more from her about timing and humor than [from] anyone else." One of his most treasured memories of those early years was of the August 31, 1940, revue, when he got to join Coca and Burton as one of the three ri-valrous infants in "Triplets" (at Tamiment titled "Three Alike"), taken from the 1931 show *The Band Wagon*. From Robbins's first appearance at Tamiment through his last, the camp proved an income-generating haven when shows he was in closed unexpectedly and during his first two seasons (1940 and 1941) as a member of Ballet Theatre, when bookings were slim.

In 1939, galvanized by Sylvia Fine, Liebman and a nucleus of Tami-ment performers stayed on after Labor Day and worked some of the best numbers from recent seasons into a show to which they could invite agents and producers. Harry Kaufman "discovered" Tamiment and, with the Shubert brothers, brought it to Broadway on September 29 in the form of *The Straw Hat Revue,* conceived and directed by Liebman. The Shuberts nixed serious numbers and pointed political satire. Somber war news from Europe and the possible consequences for America demanded escapism. Tamiment regulars, headed by Coca, Kaye, and Burton, were augmented by new performers, most notably, at the insistence of the Shuberts, baritone Alfred Drake. Jerome Robbins, with a salary of $50 a week, appeared in five numbers. One of these was "Piano and Lute," a sort of competition between ballet and modern dancers. According to Dorothy Bird, it ended with the three supposed modern dancers circling the six spinning ballet dancers—Robbins sliding on his stomach, Bird doing backbends, and Bill Bales kiting about more erect—in a design that spiraled upward toward Ruthanna Boris, sitting on someone's shoulders.

When *The Straw Hat Revue* opened September 29, John Martin, reviewing the show's dance numbers, was especially taken with "Piano and Lute," thinking that Andrews had "attacked the problem of mixing the ballet and the modern dance in quite the best manner that has yet been attempted. Without trying to put them together in any sort of spurious unity, he has kept them quite distinct and contrasted their technical styles most . . . ingeniously." Burns Mantle, theater critic and editor of the annual volumes *The Best Plays of . . . ,* noted that the show "brought in a touch of novelty and lasted until the competition shut it out with seventy-five performances" (it closed December 2). Balanchine and Zorina attended a performance; he enjoyed it, including the spoof of his *Goldwyn Follies* ballet; she was baffled.

While appearing in the show, Robbins struggled to balance serious ambition and youthful high spirits. One night Sonia was waiting to scold him when he came out of the theater. Sylvia Fine had let on that some cast members were worried because he and Richard Reed had been kidding around and camping a bit too much. Upset, Robbins noted firmly in his diary that he could get by without acting up. He worried that he was getting into a rut at the show (Coca cheered him by saying it happened to her too).

Brooding at ten minutes to midnight on the eve of his twenty-first birthday, he wrote:

21 gone and how much have I accomplished. Have still to formulate my ideas on what I want and how to get it. Each day brings more and more resolutions and affirmations. I must declare myself. On this earth, in the dance, with people I meet, with my family. I must be known as positive

sure and firm on what is right. I must deal with people better. With friends, relatives, and all I should be able to meet and yet save what I want for my work and my "self" what I feel is above and almost holy to my deep sincerity of faith in what I'm doing. I must control myself in all ways better. This is a resolution I made at least five years ago—the best ever and the best to be kept.

A few weeks later, in the tiny New York apartment he'd just rented at the imposing 873 Sixth Avenue—6A, with its own bath (he gleefully sketched himself swallowed up in the short, very deep tub)—he was able, at 4:00 A.M., to formulate a fervent mission statement: "My rising eating loving loving sleeping shall all be affected by my faith, I shall be firm and straight and even cruel to be faithful. I SHALL DANCE. . . . My classes shall be my daily worship and workshop."

3

From Broadway to Ballet

Robbins, Lucia Chase, and Yura Lazovsky in Fokine's
Bluebeard, 1941. Sent to company members by Chase as
a Christmas card.   *Courtesy of Annabelle Lyon.*

A*young American dancer* in the late 1930s couldn't afford to
specialize or be too choosy about what kind of work he would or
wouldn't do. Getting into a ballet company was almost out of the
question. For much of the decade, there weren't any established companies. Between 1935 and 1938, the American Ballet Company, under

George Balanchine's direction, was uncomfortably ensconced as the resident company of the Metropolitan Opera, where operas were many and all-ballet evenings exceedingly rare. Even before the relationship was dissolved and the company as such vanished, Balanchine began siphoning off dancers to the Broadway shows and movies he'd begun to tackle with apparent ease, competence, and good manners unusual enough to cause comment. Others joined Lincoln Kirstein's Ballet Caravan, a small, short-lived company (1936–1939) that presented Americana ballets by Americans, such as Lew Christensen's *Filling Station* and Eugene Loring's *Billy the Kid*. The two companies that toured regularly as of 1937—Colonel W. de Basil's Ballets Russes and the Ballet Russe de Monte Carlo—were descended from Serge Diaghilev's landmark Ballets Russes (1909–1929) and maintained a "Russian" profile in terms of both repertory and personnel. In his chronicle of ballet in the United States, George Amberg commented on the slowness of the "natural process of American infiltration [into these companies] by way of the *corps de ballet* and minor positions. . . ."

Like Robbins's appearance in Lisa Parnova's concert, his first experiences on the ballet stage were short-term. He and his friend Harry Day managed to get taken on as extras for the Fokine Ballet's performance of Mikhail Fokine's sexy 1910 orientalist one-act *Schéhérazade* at Jones Beach on July 4, 1937. Fokine's son, Vitale, staged the work. Day and Robbins played two faithful servants of the Shah who return from the royal hunt to discover a forbidden orgy and rush off to break the news of the harem's faithlessness to the trusting ruler and his cynical brother. Robbins, schooled by Sandor, found Patricia Bowman as Zobeide and Harold Hoskins in Nijinsky's role of the Favorite Slave unconvincing as actors: "Everything was done on a huge, over-histrionic base. Their attention seemed more out front than to each other. It seemed eyes didn't see & emotions appeared 'showed' rather than felt." (One wonders if, in applying Group Theatre standards, he took into account the fact that the immense outdoor theater, seating ten thousand and stuffed to capacity, didn't encourage subtlety.) At the critical moment when Zobeide demands to be allowed to kill herself rather than be slain like the hoi polloi of the harem by brawny guards with scimitars, she was supposed to seize a dagger from a handy servant. Robbins, pleased to be given this role, was shocked that Bowman, not immediately seeing the knife stuck in his belt, said, possibly in some irritation, "Where's the dagger?" At Dance Center you never came out of character; a meaningful glance at his waist was the extent to which he would sacrifice his principles to help her out.

He and Day had more dancing to do in Alexander Yakovleff's production of the "Polovtsian Dances" from *Prince Igor* on a special outdoor program to dedicate the 1939 World's Fair. Robbins doesn't seem to have had much respect for Yakovleff, whom he and his buddies dubbed "Yake-flopf," but he was enthusiastic about being one of a band of Tartars "celebrating their wild & ferocious way of life with a stomping leaping almost bacchanalian fervor." One of three soloists, he got to follow the leading dancer in a "whip-like turning entrance" brandishing a bow. There were perks too. Over and over, lines of warriors skipped victoriously toward the footlights—pirouetting, falling to one knee, and loosing a shower of imaginary arrows over the audience's heads. The English folk dancers who preceded the ballet on the program had, in springing about, dislodged coins from their pockets. In between shooting his arrow and rushing back to shoot again, Robbins managed to stow away 45¢ to augment his $2 pay. Another useful side effect: he met Muriel Bentley, with whom he was to perform, on whom he was to set roles, and who was a frequent scapegoat for his temper fits for over twenty years.

Robbins had met Day at Daganova's studio. He wrote "it was good to have a friend," as if he hadn't really had a close one in New York up to then. Both of them slender and on the small side (Robbins had still not reached his full height of five feet, 7½ inches), the two swapped practice clothes for auditions and street clothes for appointments. They spent weekends at each other's family homes. They giggled together; colleagues called them the "Bobbsey Twins." But when Robbins began getting steady work in Broadway shows and Day didn't, they drifted apart.

⌒

The Straw Hat Revue was not Robbins's first musical. Probably around 1937, he had begun to audition regularly, without much luck. For an article he drafted in 1986, he relived his early anxieties, beginning with the morning warm-up at home, the business of choosing just the right clothes, and the wait in the alley outside the theater—ears cocked for helpful tips that might be passed down the long line of hopefuls.

Will you be asked to sing (rare in those days), as there were usually 16 dancers, and the same number of singers, show girls. Is it a big show, period show. And most of all <u>please</u> God, am I good enough, is my technique good enough, will I appear attractive enough, tall enough, talented enough. And as the day grows nearer, the more the fantasies and expectations mount. A job—a job—a job as a <u>dancer</u>—a job in a Bwy show—oh dream beyond believability. How the stakes would rise—a breadwinner—able to get free from the ominous nervous economic fear & strictures. Imagine being free—to be perhaps able to rent a furnished room, buy your own clothes, pay for classes instead of being a janitor for them, or not having to watch so closely how much is spent for each mouthful you ate, to be able to take a streetcar or bus instead of having to walk up the palisades or from the river to 5th Avenue & back. . . .

Auditioning made him feel like an immigrant, an outsider glimpsing a society he yearned to enter; so many of those around him in line were in the know, had already danced in shows. Every rejection widened the gap between him and that enthralling world.

The required time step was always a problem. Seeking help from a tap-dancing Broadway gypsy, he was told that all he had to do was remember a little rhyme and he'd nail the rhythm. Robbins duly muttered:

> Oh my God what a titty,
> Oh my God what a titty,
> Oh my God what a titty
> On the girl last night.

He'd always get a stutter in the steps.

Eventually his improving technique, coupled with a new attitude, paid off. He simply decided to audition as if he knew he already had the job. It worked, and when *Great Lady* opened at the Majestic Theatre on December 1, 1938, Jerome Robbins was in the cast.

Theater critics had been gloomy for some years over the crippling effect of both the Depression and the increasing drain of talent and audiences to Hollywood movies. The 1938–1939 New York season bucked new and irresistible competition in the form of the World's Fair, whose Trylon and Perisphere beckoned the crowds out to Flushing Meadows to stroll or ride through Utopian visions of what technology could accomplish. In 1926–1927, a boom season before the stock market crashed, as many as 260 entertainments had opened in New York (many of them, of course, closing in a few days). In 1938–1939, the total was less than half that.

Burns Mantle, looking back on the season, felt that "it missed the note of experimentation that added so much to the previous season." Still, there was much of quality. Robert Sherwood's *Abe Lincoln in Illinois* and Lillian Hellman's *The Little Foxes* were the most substantial new plays. Helen Hayes starred in *Victoria Regina* and Maurice Evans in *Hamlet.* The list of shows selected for inclusion in Mantle's *Best Plays of 1938–1939* was heavy on romantic comedies, the liveliest being Philip Barry's *The Philadelphia Story* (with Katharine Hepburn and Joseph Cotten), S. N. Behrman's *No Time for Comedy* (with Katharine Cornell and Laurence Olivier), and Clare Boothe's satirical *Kiss the Boys Goodbye.*

An ambitious dancer like Robbins could have auditioned for seven musicals due to open in the fall-winter months of 1938.* Luckily—in terms of his future career—he was among those chosen for the chorus of *Great Lady.* William Dollar, who had worked in both the American Ballet Company and Ballet Caravan, received the credit for choreographing the musical, "for contractual reasons," and possibly did stage a number or two, but Balanchine created the dances. Many of the dancers were his protégés (notable exceptions: Albia Kavan, Nora Kaye, and the Cuban husband and wife Fernando and Alicia Alonso); Robbins had to hone his still rough-edged technique in the company of André Eglevsky (taking a break from the Ballet Russe de Monte Carlo), Annabelle Lyon, Leda Anchutina, Holly Howard, Hortense Kahrklyn, and Olga Suarez.

Great Lady was not a hit. Billed as a "biography with music," it followed the career of Eliza Bowen, a nineteenth-century adventuress with relaxed morals, who lures into marriage a wealthy French merchant visiting her native Providence, Rhode Island. She returns from Paris to Manhattan as Mme. Jumel but is snubbed by elite society no matter how lavishly she entertains. When the show opened at the Majestic on December 1, *The New York Times*'s acerbic drama critic Brooks Atkinson noted that many spectators "wore themselves out with laughing," but he was not amused: "Earle Crooker and Lowell Brentano have written the book with some of the crude delight of sophomores who have just learned about the frailties of

---

* Cole Porter's *You Never Know;* the vaudeville revue *Hellzapoppin; Sing Out the News,* a revue by Harold Rome and Charles Friedman; a musical play about Gilbert and Sullivan called *Knights of Song* that lasted for sixteen performances; the Maxwell Anderson–Kurt Weill *Knickerbocker Holiday,* set in old New Amsterdam; *Leave It to Me!,* by Sam and Bella Spewack, with music and lyrics by Cole Porter; and Rodgers and Hart's *The Boys from Syracuse,* choreographed by George Balanchine.

the sex and hope to devote a lifetime to studying them." They have, he went on, "only one thing in mind. They write of it with the subtlety and capriciousness of a battleship. . . . Ribaldry, like every other topic, needs talent and imagination."

Balanchine was already a showbiz master. He'd choreographed the very successful Rodgers and Hart musicals *On Your Toes* (1936), *Babes in Arms, The Boys from Syracuse,* and *I Married an Angel,* as well as the film *The Goldwyn Follies,* with music by George Gershwin and Vernon Duke. Critics of *Great Lady* complained that his accomplished cadre of dancers had too little to do. And John Anderson of the *Journal American,* enjoying the sight of Anchutina, Eglevsky, and Lyon performing to "swooning waltz music [by Frederick Loewe, later to write the scores for *Brigadoon* and *My Fair Lady*] on a stage bathed in ardent twilight," remarked that "The dancers seemed to be kicking their nimble heels against the stolidity of the plot." And, as Lyon remembers, that pas de trois, and the waltz and pas de sept that preceded it, had no connection to the story whatsoever— not uncommon in musicals of the day.

Balanchine evidently noticed Robbins—giving him "little things" to do—but the show lasted for only twenty performances, and Robbins went very quickly into his next show; on February 9, 1939, not quite two months after *Great Lady* closed, *Stars in Your Eyes* replaced it at the Majestic, with Robbins on the payroll at $40 a week. This was a more savory venture, with lyrics by Dorothy Fields and music by Arthur Schwartz, and starring Jimmy Durante and Ethel Merman. (Twenty years later, one of the chorus boys would direct her in her greatest triumph, *Gypsy.*) Schwartz's original idea for the musical, to be titled *Swing to the Left,* was to have involved the making of a movie by people from New York's left-wing theater (social significance dukes it out with conventions of glamour). Director Joshua Logan ditched this aspect, thinking that political themes and an airy romantic plot didn't go together. Still, the story was rife with opportunities for satire (the movie being shot boasted six assistant directors, of whom Dan Dailey, Jr., was one) and amorous shenanigans. Tamara Toumanova (one of the so-called baby ballerinas discovered seven years previously by Balanchine in Olga Preobrajenska's Paris studio, when she was a startlingly voluptuous twelve-year-old) played the love interest of the leading man that Merman, the star, is pursuing. Carl Randall provided the choreography for a ballet company of twenty-seven that included, in addition to Robbins, the Alonsos, Nora Kaye, and Maria

Karniloff (later Karnilova).* Brooks Atkinson thought that Merman and Durante gave "the gustiest performances of their careers," and that writer, lyricist, and composer "have conjured just the sort of roaring material that makes rare comics out of this pair of inspired groundlings."

Stars in Your Eyes had a respectable run of 127 performances, closing in May, and Robbins had Tamiment to look forward to. In the fall, when many of his buddies joined the brand-new American company, Ballet Theatre (due to make its debut in January 1940), he was tied up with *The Straw Hat Revue*. Did he audition for Ballet Theatre and get turned down? Probably not. He may still have felt insecure about his classical technique and mistrustful of the nature and future prospects of the new enterprise. After all, he had begun as a modern dancer, scorning ballet, and now had a prospering career as a Broadway "gypsy."

Not long after *The Straw Hat Revue* closed on December 2, 1939, Robbins was chosen by Balanchine for the chorus of a revue, *Keep Off the Grass.* When the show opened in New York on May 23, the critics from the city's six daily newspapers agreed that it constituted good-natured summer fare—and, noted Richard Lockridge of the *New York Sun,* "there is always something happening to keep the mind off the war."

The show's cast, notably Jimmy Durante and Ray Bolger, received high praise. Burns Mantle wrote of Durante in the *New York Daily News:* "Age cannot wither the infinite variety of his grunts, groans, expostulations and explosions. He works with the singers, he works with the dancers, he works with a flock of monkeys and he does a lot more for the sketch writers than they do for him." The parade of satires coupled the current hit *Life with Father* and the presidential family in "Life with the Roosevelts" and took aim at the disappointing *Romeo and Juliet* featuring Laurence Olivier and Vivien Leigh as well as at the recently released film spectacle *Gone With the Wind* (with Durante as Rhett Butler, Bolger as Ashley Wilkes, and wasp-tongued Ilka Chase as Scarlett O'Hara). The monkeys played the learned panel in a jab at the popular radio show *Information Please* with Durante as Clifton Fadiman.

Robbins had moved up in Balanchine's eyes. He was assigned to understudy featured dancer José Limón (in Act I's "This Is Spring," Limón,

*Alicia Alonso says that Balanchine choreographed Toumanova's numbers and that Robbins got a chance to contribute some choreography. Robbins never mentioned this himself, and Randall, who had played many juvenile leads on Broadway in the 1920s, was an experienced choreographer of revues and musicals.

Daphne Vane, and Marjorie Moore mixed with "The Dancing Young Ladies as Ponies," and in Act II's "Look Out for My Heart," he and Betty Bruce wielded rapiers before the same dancing ladies—now as a chorus of fencers). In another number, Limón played an amorous faun with Moore and Vane. Being cast as understudy startled Robbins in view of Limón's magnificent brawn and his own wiry physique. Balanchine as Broadway man seems to have adapted to whomever and whatever he was given. At one rehearsal, Limón, noting that Balanchine had choreographed the steps and patterns for the corps that was to surround his solo, asked what Balanchine had in mind for him. "You go in center and do Modern Dance," replied the master.

Tamiment fed Robbins's itch to choreograph by giving him opportunities to cook up numbers. And while pursuing his Broadway career, he made dances whenever he could. *Melodies and Moods,* put on at the Labor Stage on March 25, 1939, by the Bundle Brigade (select members of the Undergarment and Negligee Workers Union, Local 62, of the International Ladies' Garment Workers' Union), lists "Dances and Choreography by Jerry Robbins."

Keep Off the Grass did not last the summer; it closed in June after twenty-eight performances, and on June 25, before going off to Tamiment, Robbins made his debut as a member of the corps of Ballet Theatre for performances at Robin Hood Dell in Fairmount Park, Philadelphia, accompanied by members of the Philadelphia Orchestra. The Alonsos, Muriel Bentley, and John Kriza also joined the company for the scattered summer performances at Robin Hood Dell and Lewisohn Stadium in New York. There he was, amid old and new friends, as a huntsman in *Swan Lake,* a "choreographic poem in one act" (restaged by Anton Dolin after Lev Ivanov's original second act), and one of eight Cavaliers in Mikhail Mordkin's *Voices of Spring,* a "comedy of flirtations" laid in Vienna's Belvedere Gardens.

This easy-on-audiences summer program at Robin Hood Dell (including Adolf Bolm's *Peter and the Wolf* and a solo *Bolero* by Dolin) didn't exhibit the range of repertory that represented Ballet Theatre's loftier aims. The company had emerged from a smaller group founded in 1937 by the Moscow-trained Mikhail Mordkin, who had partnered Anna Pavlova during her 1910 and 1911 American tours. Richard Pleasant, the general manager Mordkin hired in 1938, had more ambitious ideas; he envisaged a sort of museum of dance that would house "the best that is traditional, the best that is contemporary, and, inevitably, the best that is controversial." Lucia Chase, one of Mordkin's principal dancers, was moneyed, and had been contributing to his company. Pleasant persuaded her to play godmother to this new enterprise. This took generosity of spirit on her part. In the Mordkin Ballet, she had danced Giselle; when that company was folded into Ballet Theatre, she would be assigned to small, if telling roles. (Mordkin was to find his own choreography represented skimpily, and eventually not at all.)

When the company opened a three-week season at Radio City's Center Theatre on January 11, 1940, it boasted a lineup of ninety-three dancers, including a "Negro Unit" of sixteen and a "Spanish Unit" of seven. Among the eighteen works presented, audiences could see ballets premiered by Diaghilev's company early in the century—staged by their choreographer, Mikhail Fokine; ballets brought across the ocean by a brilliant young Englishman whose name, Antony Tudor, few Americans knew; a decided departure from tradition, *The Great American Goof,* "A Balletplay" with a scenario by William Saroyan and choreography by Eugene Loring, whose *Billy the Kid* had been one of Ballet Caravan's hottest items. Agnes de Mille used the African-American dancers in *Black Ritual (Obeah),* and José Fernandez created *Goyescas* for the Spanish dancers. The classical repertory was represented by freshened-up productions of *Swan Lake,* Act II; *Giselle* (former Diaghilev star Dolin not only staged them but played the heroes in both); and *La Fille Mal Gardée* (staged by Bronislava Nijinska). Although some of the names on the roster were Russian, the first Giselle was Annabelle Lyon; the Odette, Patricia Bowman; and Karen Conrad danced the pas de deux in *Les Sylphides* with William Dollar. The corps de ballet was resoundingly American. Nora Kaye, who started the season as Nora Koreff (her real name), soon took a stage name that sounded more in keeping with a homegrown company that had heralded its commitment to show "the ballet stepping out from the red plush, gilt and palm, and making its bow in a new dress" and was immediately touted as "a new page in the history of ballet in America."

Robbins fit in excellently. He had performed with many Ballet Theatre members at Tamiment or in shows; others he knew from auditions and classes. The dance world was comparatively small. He had by then a decent technique and was a striking performer. Onetime colleagues Janet

Reed, Miriam Golden, and Annabelle Lyon agree that he didn't conform to the *danseur noble* image in either appearance or style, and he later explained without regret to his parents in a letter, "I am not a classical dancer really you see." Sono Osato, who joined Ballet Theatre in 1941, commended his partnering "because there was real contact with him. It wasn't the body who was just lifting you. You felt that he was *there,* that he was interested; he was doing his thing." He could hold his own in a male quintet for fishermen (Dolin with Fred Danieli, Charles Dickson, Richard Reed, and Robbins) in *Capriccioso,* Dolin's vivacious, elaborately costumed "Italian" ballet to the music of Cimarosa, but he wasn't happy in tights, tunics, and feathered berets. Ballet Theatre colleague Donald Saddler says Robbins loathed being a cavalier in *Princess Aurora,* the last act divertissement of Marius Petipa's *The Sleeping Beauty,* as staged by Dolin. He must have enjoyed the ballet more when he was promoted to vault in as one of the Three Ivans. Later, he partnered Margaret Banks and Barbara Fallis in a pas de trois. But it was as a character dancer that he excelled, and as an actor-dancer he was taken notice of and advanced within the company.

Although Robbins's face briefly cuts across the screen in one of the several valuable silent films of Ballet Theatre excerpts shot in performance and rehearsals by Chicago critic Ann Barzel, it's difficult to locate him as a performer amid the turmoil. However, a home movie, filmed on the rooftop of the Weehawken apartment building where his parents lived during the early 1940s, gives an idea of Jerry the young dancer. First, he demonstrates a balletic front attitude to his mother, then an arabesque. Hanging on to him, Lena copies the moves. He promenades her in arabesque, grinning at the camera, and gives her congratulatory kisses. Then it's Dad's turn; Harry squats down and jumps about (looking as much like a frog as a Cossack) while his son stamps and claps for him. Finally, Jerry takes off in a bravura phrase—quick steps into a canted leap, some spins; he bows in mock elegance, then thinks up more steps, finishing with hopped turns with one leg (foot nicely pointed) out to the side à la seconde. He looks fluent and boisterous, with a kind of witty precision—easy and intense at the same time.

Barzel's films of Ballet Theatre's charismatic stars—Dolin, Laing, Baronova, Conrad, Nana Gollner, Alicia Markova, and others—show that, in any case, their approach to classical technique was less line-oriented than that of later twentieth-century dancers. Nor were the lines as extreme as they later became under Balanchine's influence; no Ballet

Theatre member routinely hit high noon with an arabesque penchée or grand battement. Today's ballet dancer tries to show straight knees and pointed toes as much of the time as the choreography permits—that is, on descending from a jump, the toes stay pointed until the last second; the standing leg is arrow-straight in pirouettes. Ballet Theatre dancers of the 1940s cared less about these issues. On film, they're strong; they attack with verve and expressiveness, and the shape of a phrase seems to matter more than the pictorial beauty of each individual moment.

As a young dancer, Robbins felt his colleagues' power. While he was taking some time out in the Bahamas during the 1950s, ballet music he heard over a café's loudspeaker brought back the ineffable experience of watching the great dancers of the thirties and forties. These stars illumined ballets like Léonide Massine's *Gaîté Parisienne* (1938) and David Lichine's *Graduation Ball* (1940)—ballets that he acknowledged, more than ten years and a world war later, to be banal in subject and so degraded as to be barely watchable. But how entrancing they had been and how those performers carried away their public, especially an ambitious junior dancer with a finely tuned kinesthetic sense:

> I remember the first performance of *Gaité Parisienne* [1938] and how I had waltzed with [Frederic] Franklin and [Alexandra] Danilova, quarreled with [?], marched with Marc Scott* and flicked around with Massine. My hand never did get into the glove he was trying on, while making eyes at D. And I never had a gondola ride as lovely as the one in *Gaité*. But oh when Danilova and Franklin waltzed. . . . Off we glided with them and lifted and turned with them and again that fantastic feeling of this-is-how-it-had-to-end, has-to-live came back to me. . . . No one has ever danced a waltz like Freddie and Shura or were more in love, or lived a more idyllic life than at the moment they came on from the wings, her arm across his shoulder behind his head and started keeping time to Offenbach, the most lovely of waltzes. . . . I was struck by . . . how beautiful it was then and how very much it made me <u>want</u> to dance (and I don't think I'm wrong in suggesting that this terrific impact was felt by all of my generation from Kaye, Alonzo, Kriza, etc. right down). It was dancing, the last that we saw of its kind . . . pure, heartfelt by all on stage and heart accepted by all sitting in the house being warmed and held and given deep happiness. . . .

* Robbins may have been thinking of Marc Platoff, aka Marc Platt.

Because Ballet Theatre made its debut cold in New York, it had few advance bookings. Critics may have applauded, but houses were only half filled that first season. Belief and free classes with Tudor helped hold the company together. Robbins's first contract covered only the June 1940 week of rehearsals, at $20, and the Robin Hood Dell performance week, at $45 (competitive with Broadway and about twice what Ballet Russe de Monte Carlo ensemble dancers reportedly made). He signed another contract for the July dates. After the summer performances, the company was, luckily, invited to the Chicago Opera Company for a six-week residency, beginning November 3. The arrangement worked out better than Balanchine's stint with the Met in that the company danced its own programs twice a week (although it danced them to half-full houses). Assignments for ten operas were parceled out among its dancer-choreographers, Edward Caton, Eugene Loring, Dimitri Romanoff, and Tudor. Tudor applied himself to *Aida.* The mind reels at the thought of the creator of *Jardin aux Lilas,* the genius of reticence and stifled passion—coping with triumphal marches and dancing slaves. In Act III of *Il Trovatore,* Loring cast Robbins and Alicia Alonso as soloists. Robert Pollack commented approvingly in a review that Loring made the dancing a part of the action instead of simply "a gypsy recital divertissement."

Touring with the company around the United States and in Canada, Robbins performed the usual corps de ballet duties, a peasant in *Giselle* and so on, but he began to attract notice in small roles, the Pony Express rider in Loring's *Billy the Kid,* one of the frightened hunters in Adolf Bolm's *Peter and the Wolf.* He and Saddler escorted two *majas,* Alonso and Kaye, in Tudor's *Goya Pastoral* (soon renamed *Goyescas*). Reviewing *Peter* and other ballets for *The Musical Courier* in January 1941, Alexis Dolinoff singled out "Jerome Robbins, whose style is agreeable but who does very little." Before the year was out, Robbins, promoted to soloist status, was playing the role of Peter in Bolm's work. By late 1942, he was playing Billy the Kid's adversary, Alias ("essentially the best performer yet to be seen in the role"), and during a 1941 fall engagement in Mexico, he and Muriel Bentley (who, like him, had studied Spanish dance with Helen Veola) danced the leads in *Goyescas.* Mexicans, he recalled later, did not care for the ballet, and "We must have been something—two Jewish kids (whose mothers had wanted high culture for them) clicking away, banging our heels, hair pomaded, spit curls galore, trying to look Spanish classical."

Agnes de Mille gave him his first big break during the 1941 New York winter season at the Majestic, casting him as one of five performers in her tongue-in-cheek morality play *Three Virgins and a Devil.* The previous spring, he and a few other Ballet Theatre colleagues had been recruited by de Mille for two Sunday performances at Doris Humphrey and Charles Weidman's Sixteenth Street studio theater. The show was *American Legend,* an Americana potpourri of one-act plays, songs, speeches, and dance directed by de Mille's old friend Mary Hunter for her American Actors Company (de Mille choreographed, and Hugh Laing designed the costumes along with Katherine Dunham's husband, John Pratt). Maybe de Mille liked Jerry's gusto in such dances as a "running set," which, like the square dance in her later *Rodeo,* was performed only to calls and clapping. It has also been said that when de Mille was casting *Three Virgins,* Laing recommended Jerry to her as having an excellent rhythmic sense.

The role was that of an inadvertent assistant to the Devil (Loring) in his attempts to snare a priggish virgin (de Mille), a greedy one (Chase), and a lustful one (Lyon) as they strut virtuously to church. Robbins, wearing a wig and a high-crowned medieval hat, was Lyon's nemesis. Practically all he had to do was walk across the stage with a flower. But what a walk! As Sono Osato remembers it, "He came sort of tripping across, and the tripping was very funny because it was real. . . . He kind of bopped and tripped along. He didn't trip over his feet, but he had a kind of little jerky thing . . . he paused and he looked out front in a kind of quizzical way, and then he took the flower out of his mouth and twirled it around a finger. I don't know if he raised his hat. Then he walked off." He ignored Lyon, who was panting for him, but on his return, she jumped onto his back and rode him into the mouth of the Devil's cave.

All the New York papers praised him. John Martin, summing up the season for *The New York Times,* said, "Jerome Robbins in a marvelously devised comedy bit in *Three Virgins and a Devil* could scarcely have been better." Critic-turned-photographer Carl van Vechten took a series of soft-focus portraits of him in costume, toying dreamily with his carnation.

Ballet Theatre was mired in financial difficulties, and Chase was balking at the frequency with which she was asked to write large checks. In the spring of 1941, following this second New York season, the company negotiated a contract with impresario Sol Hurok that would begin in the fall, while Pleasant, unable to secure the funds to continue at the ambitious level he had set, resigned. (During the summer hiatus, some of the dancers went with Tudor to Ted Shawn's Jacob's Pillow in Lee, Massachusetts, and Robbins returned to Tamiment for the last time.)

With the advent of Hurok appointee Gerald Sevastianov as managing director and Vania Psota as regisseur general, a not-so-subtle process of Russianization began. The new productions for the 1941–1942 season were *Princess Aurora, The Beloved* (a ballet Bronislava Nijinska had created in 1928 for Ida Rubenstein's company), Psota's *Slavonika* (starring the adorable Irina Baronova, Sevastianov's wife), revivals of Fokine's *Spectre de la Rose* and a truncated version of Nijinsky's *Afternoon of a Faun,* plus two new Fokine ballets: *Bluebeard* and *Russian Soldier.* However, Ballet Theatre still fostered a kind of democracy. As Saddler said, "One night you might be a soloist; the next night, you were back in the corps." Before Hurok, dancer Dwight Godwin had told Walter Terry, dance critic of the *New York Herald Tribune,* "Why, even the ballerinas take stiff direction without a murmur, and we know that when new productions are cast we of the ensemble have as good an opportunity of landing roles as do the company's already established soloists." That continued to be true. However, beginning in 1943, the company was touted by Hurok as presenting "Russian Ballet," and the dancers called his takeover "the Russian invasion." Robbins later said that for two years, he rarely appeared onstage without sporting bloomers, boots, and a wig.

A *far more devastating event* than a change in management affected not just American ballet but American life. On December 7, 1941, the Japanese bombed Pearl Harbor, escalating Hitler's war in Europe into World War II and ensuring the United States' involvement. Ballet Theatre's touring, never elegant, was fraught with difficulties. The amount of time spent in travel was considerable, given that the company usually performed two to three nights in a given city and one-night stands were common. The railroad cars they traveled in were often attached to troop trains and sometimes unhitched and left on the sidings when more carloads of soldiers were taken on or a route was altered. Dancers have vivid memories of such scenes as the queen of onstage fragility, ballerina Alicia Markova, curled up on her suitcase, dozing, on a Midwest station platform. They might arrive at a performance two hours late, to find the audience still waiting for them; corps dancers were often expected to pitch in and help set up. The trains' dining cars frequently ran out of food, and sleeping cars were scarce. When boarding late after a performance, company members became adept at unscrewing the seat backs and propping them up on suitcases: "five minutes after we left, the train was flat, and we were all sleeping." The buses were worse. An enigmatic entry in the diaries Robbins kept intermittently during these tours, "returned to train . . . made bed & slept with Nora," was possibly unrelated to the affair he and Kaye later had. According to Charles Payne, the management's one-seat-per-dancer rule was augmented by another: two to a berth on the infrequent Pullman cars. Robbins and Kaye may have been doubling up out of necessity—although, as Miriam Golden points out, tired as they all were, they were also young: "The hormones were racing."

The dancers were used to hardship in any case. Even with contracts approved by the American Guild of Musical Artists, they often went for long periods without days off. The management didn't reserve hotel rooms; the dancers had to disembark and start scrambling. Rooms often being scarce, the "Army game"—usually played for the sake of thrift—reached improbable proportions. Two dancers would register for a room with twin beds. As many as six more might sneak up. Putting the mattresses on the floor, they would sleep doubled up, four on the mattresses, four on the box springs.

Members of the company occasionally performed for the troops. And of course, some of the male dancers were drafted. Soon after war was declared, Robbins began to worry that he and the young playwright Horton Foote—with whom he lived for a time at 44 West Fifty-fourth Street, where other members of the American Actors Company were housed—might be called up. Foote was rejected toward the end of April 1942, and around the same time, Robbins was too. Summoned to appear before a draft board, he answered yes to the question "Have you ever had a homosexual experience?" When an examiner asked him if he could specify the date of his last such encounter, he replied, "Last night." He was swiftly classified 4F. The interestingly euphemistic "Report of Induction of Selective Service Man" disqualifies him for the following "defects": "Constitutional psychopathic inferiority" and "Asthma, bronchial." He later hinted that the draft board experience had been extremely stressful. Within the company, Robbins seemed perfectly at ease with his bisexuality, but one diary entry dated January 13, 1942, after a performance at Baltimore's Lyric Theatre contains the curious prayer "Please save me from being 'gay' and dirty."

His remarks to his diary are brief, usually written late at night. He jots down the city, what was performed, and a few observations. One wonders if he noted well the advice printed on the front page of his 1942 "yearbook" under "Rules for Business Men": "Be wary of dealing with unsuccessful men." (Maybe those rules prompted a short story he began on tour and never finished, in which his leading character was a traveling salesman.) His first winter entries indicate that, war or no war, the dancers had plenty of fun together. He records ice-skating, snowball fights (this last after a New York dinner at "Markie's" [Markova] and a movie [*Dumbo*]). Returning to the city after a Princeton performance and a long wait for a train, he wrote, "Sang songs all the way home with Johnnie [Kriza], Muriel [Bentley] & Dick [Reed]." In Quebec, some of them went skating as soon as they'd checked in and tobogganed down a slide that took them directly to the hotel door. In Montreal, he missed a photo call to take a sleigh ride.

But for the most part, Robbins's entries deal with his own dancing— how well or badly he's doing (he accidentally throws his guitar into the audience in *Bluebeard,* he loses his false nose in *Peter*), what he thinks of the ballets and how they're danced, and his ambitions to choreograph. He couldn't sleep for nervousness the night before he made his debut (January 17, 1942) in the major role of the Devil in *Three Virgins* in New Rochelle, but on retiring the next night, he wrote that "Kids thought I'd do it well, but I knew I didn't have enough rehearsals to be relaxed. I did a barre with Ian [Gibson] again & made up . . . in the style of Loring [the role of the Devil had been made on Eugene Loring]—but most people liked it. The performance went by in a flash & how I got thru I don't know except for 2 things. One—I closed in & did 4 pirouettes, + 2. I wasn't at all satisfied by the performance. Would like to do another real soon. [Critic Walter] Terry liked it." Afterward, he and Nora went to the House of Chan for a Chinese meal—"her birthday so I treated." Later, the critic from Vancouver's *Daily Province* would laud his "fantastically agile, apelike devil."

⌒

Ballet Theatre colleagues remember the young Jerry Robbins as a good friend, as someone who was fun to be with, but when writing in his diaries or honing his literary skills in sketches for short stories, he often dramatized his own insecurities. In early December 1942, while Ballet Theatre was maintaining its grueling itinerary of mostly one-night stands, he wrote that he was torn between wanting to go out with the other dancers after the performance and wanting to be alone—"cringing inwardly that he would become the butt, suddenly, of their cattiness." When sketching out autobiographical tales in his notebooks (written in the third person), the convivial Jerry who goes out snowballing with friends becomes a young man convinced he's unattractive and unlikable.

> When the boys decided to go to a nightclub he would refuse to go, saying to himself—I don't want to go out & mess around & pick up people & be gay & chippy—but under it all he wanted was to be that very much—but he wanted to be the most attractive—the most gay & chippy—the center & the happiest. He was afraid of drinking of getting drunk & becoming unhappy. And he was afraid of the casual jibe, the cutting joke. And so he went alone—ate alone—& slept alone—wanting comradeship & joyous company—not knowing if he were superior or inferior because of not getting on with them all.

Certainly, he did spend enough time alone to observe people and places and store away impressions:

> [T]here were things he knew immediately & forever about a city or room or place. In Bridgeport it was a long hill covered with golden autumn leaves, and a house with long windows reaching to the front porch. In Hartford, it was a tea room on a rainy afternoon—a warm wooden room & rich stained table—a pot of tea & cheese and crackers—and a few tables away some drunken middle aged well off woman drinking cocktails & gibbering empty talk & feeling better each moment. In Raleigh it was a long street lined with stores he had walked looking for a place to eat on a warm muggish afternoon. In Washington it was a dark night club with a rumba he went to with a girl he picked up.

Quite a few of the stories he sketched out featured a young man—often as not lonely in a room above city streets—anxious to escape the everyday and hungry for something ineffable. In the paired stories "Lullabye & Reveille," the coming-of-age theme turns autobiographical. His hero (thinly disguised as a teenage movie theater usher) arrives home late at night to his parents' house, and, as he sits typing in his room, he imagines himself confronting his mother: "I've got to take care of myself now Mom. . . . I mean I want to help myself now instead of having you do things for me, you've got to see that." Robbins then explores the sleepless mother's thoughts. Had her son seen the birthday cake she'd left for him in the kitchen? She imagines him coming into her room, "and he would understand and thank her and everything would be cleared up again and he'd talk to her and kiss her and she'd know him again and and . . ."

One curious unfinished tale poured out almost as a stream of consciousness. Robbins's Jewish protagonist is at first termed a "boy," but a few sentences later, he has acquired a potbelly and a big nose. He invites the black elevator operator to his hotel room. What he wants, it turns out, is for the young man to sit with him in the dark and tell him about being black. (The elevator operator keeps asking nervously, "Can I get you something?") Eventually the protagonist explodes into a rage of self-loathing: "But you can laugh—you can laugh—I've heard you—that big gushing cleansing laugh—& have you heard me laugh—have you ever heard the sardonic snigger—sneerish laugh—the tight high frighten [sic] giggle—no—haven't you ever heard me laugh my little laugh—"

Critical attention notwithstanding, Robbins experienced periods of doubt about his dancing too. In a third-person account dated December 5, 1942, he wrote dramatically that when young he had "lived in large sure brushstrokes of life, confident of his talent," but that the fire and conviction he'd once had had vanished "that one year of the tour." He had "performed a bad role [possibly the kid-hero of *Peter and the Wolf*—Annabelle Lyon had urged him to get out of it], asked for the wrong things to do—made a bad decision, compromised with jobs & money. He lost a friend—he had scenes—he was told off as being too aggressive, too swell-headed, too ambitious for his own good." Self-doubt made him both slack off and act with a vengeance like the brat that some thought him.

Finally, he noted, he had pulled himself together. Just as well. Fame and success were already dogging him like that tail he switched about with such aplomb as *Three Virgins'* devil.

4

Learning from the Masters

Robbins in Leonide Massine's role in Massine's *Capriccio Espagnol,* 1943.
New York Public Library.

Antony Tudor was the choreographer almost every Ballet Theatre dancer wanted to work with. Tudor was the one with the
new ideas, the eagle eye for human behavior, and the knowledge
of Freud. Robbins later said that it was *Dark Elegies,* Tudor's heartbreaking study in pent-up grief, set to Gustav Mahler's *Kindertotenlieder,* that

had drawn him away from Broadway and into Ballet Theatre. During Robbins's years with the company, Tudor, then in his early thirties, was a force. Along with his lover, Hugh Laing, he performed in the ballets he'd premiered at Marie Rambert's Mercury Theatre in London—*Elegies,* the ravishing *Jardin aux Lilas,* and the satires *Judgment of Paris* and *Gala Performance*—and in works he created for Ballet Theatre: *Pillar of Fire, Romeo and Juliet,* and *Dim Lustre.* He also played character roles in ballets by others and taught company class. He may not have been a technically accomplished dancer himself, but he knew what was what and how to achieve it. Robbins remembered how "One could see him mold Nora Kaye into an amazing technician. Each day we watched as she could duplicate a series of pirouettes—going from 1 to 6 or 7 in immaculate succession & with perfect control." Tudor also dispensed advice. "*Peter* went better," wrote Robbins in his diary. "Mr. T. said I shouldn't try so hard in it & maybe it'd go easier."

Tudor had something in common with Gluck Sandor. His dancers didn't simply learn steps; they had to know who they were in a ballet and where they came from. Tudor went farther than Sandor in search of dramatic verisimilitude; he pressed the dancers for minute details of a character's life. It was, perhaps, not only a way of getting the performance he wanted but of stimulating his own, often painfully slow, creative process. Those who, like Sono Osato, endured with him the long rehearsal period for his great and moving 1942 *Pillar of Fire* had to know "the time of day, the day of the week, where we had been each time we appeared, and where we were going next." She was sure that Nora Kaye, who played the repressed heroine, Hagar; Lucia Chase as her old-maidish elder sister; and Annabelle Lyon as the flirtatious younger sister knew "the color of the wallpaper in their living room, the hours at which they ate dinner, the furnishings of the rooms in which they each slept." Such fastidiousness about character background resonates in Robbins's own later approach to dramatic ballets. He learned well Tudor's Stanislavskian tactics for getting dramatically rich performances out of dancers.

Tudor would also, as Ballet Theatre principal dancer Miriam Golden said, "get right to the inner you." He accomplished this by detailed direction, by prodding, by bullying, and by picking at a dancer's ego as if it were a scab that had to come off. "When you choreograph, there are two of you creating a dance," Tudor told critic John Gruen years later, in relation to his protégée Nora Kaye. "You've got to get the dancer to climb into the skin of the dance with you. For a while, there are two of you in the same skin. Then, happily, *you* get out of it, and leave the skin to the dancer—and she has to stay with it. If she goes back to herself, the performance won't be any good." He used to speak with admiration of how Kaye rented a studio just to work on the rather bizarre entrance walk of the Russian Ballerina in his wicked ballet satire *Gala Performance.*

As well as showing off his pass-for-Spanish looks and stance in *Goyescas,* Robbins danced an "attendant cavalier" in *Gala Performance,* one of the lesser of the six roles in *Dark Elegies,* and the "boy in black" in *Jardin aux Lilas.* He also had the opportunity to create roles in *Pillar of Fire* and *Romeo and Juliet* (1943). In *Pillar,* he was cast as one of the sleazily voluptuous Lovers in Experience, who apparently inhabit an ongoing party across the road from the heroine's, in the house belonging to the handsome stud (Laing), who both attracts and brutalizes Hagar. Three couples erupt from the house as if Tudor meant it to appear a Pandora's box releasing sexuality into Hagar's guarded world of feeling. Donald Saddler remembers Osato "oozing" out the door and Robbins following hotly.

In Tudor's spare and delicate one-act *Romeo and Juliet* of 1943, to music by Frederick Delius—a medieval painting come to life—Robbins played Benvolio, wenching and fighting alongside Romeo and Mercutio. The choreographer was not one to hand out praise, but in 1945, after Robbins was no longer closely affiliated with Ballet Theatre, a mutual friend wrote him that Tudor admitted that in losing Jerry, the ballet had lost "a vital characterization" and had no strong Benvolio, and that Laing (the ballet's Romeo) had added that "when he played with you, you 'sparked' him and made the motivation clearer and that he missed you frightfully."

Robbins believed that Tudor understood him as potentially something other than a gifted performer. "I was always trying out steps and lifts. . . . Rehearsing *Pillar of Fire* one day, he said, 'I'm stuck. Who has a lift? Jerry?' " Jerry had one, grabbed Muriel, showed it. Tudor pronounced it "perfect," and asked if he could use it. Speaking at a memorial for Tudor in June 1987, Robbins said he had felt he'd been given a metaphoric pat on the back, that [Tudor] was saying, "Go ahead, I believe in you"—although at the time the beleaguered choreographer's own uppermost thought was more likely to have been "Thank God, one more problem solved!"

Robbins also absorbed from Tudor the impression that choreography was an immense struggle. He remembered in *Romeo and Juliet* "a little one-minute dance for a group of about eight people and I think he was there for about a week on it. I mean a *real* week!" *Romeo and Juliet* had to premiere unfinished, with the lovers still alive. Tudor apologized to the audience. Looking back on those years, Robbins could see that Tudor often "got in his own way," getting more and more stiff and stuck in his search for excellence. He admitted offhandedly that this could happen to him too but never completely acknowledged the demonic aspects of his own perfectionism.

Mikhail Fokine had also built his reputation on a kind of believability, but believability within fantasy. Nobody ravished by his *Schéhérazade* when Diaghilev presented it in Paris in 1909, or when the Ballet Russe de Monte Carlo toured it around America in the 1930s, would have believed the ballet presented an accurate view of harem life. However, his concubines wore neither pointe shoes nor tutus, a radical departure from tradition at the time of its premiere. *Les Sylphides,* one of the glories of Ballet Theatre's first New York performance, honored not only Marie Taglioni and other gossamer heroines of Romantic ballet but also—although Fokine never fully acknowledged this—Isadora Duncan. Not only did he use "her" music, Chopin waltzes, nocturnes, and mazurkas, but his freer and highly influential use of the torso, and even some floating arm movements, recalled her.

The ballets Fokine had made since establishing himself in New York in the 1920s were not up to the level of his earlier work, but in *Bluebeard,* he gave Ballet Theatre a crowd-pleaser—a staple of what the company viewed as its "ham-and-eggs" program. Although the ballet consisted of two prologues, four acts, and three scenes, it was short enough to be programmed with two other ballets. Based on the libretto of Offenbach's *Barbe-Bleue* and set to orchestrated selections from that opéra bouffe, the ballet made light of the eponymous hero (played with panache by Dolin), his inquisitive bride (Baronova), and his wife-murdering proclivities; the court alchemist's potions merely put the women to sleep. Interwoven scenarios concerned a princess (Markova) set adrift as an infant and reared as a shepherdess, plus a much-courted queen (Chase).

When the ballet premiered in Mexico City on October 27, 1941, Robbins played one of the queen's lovers, along with Annabelle Lyon (cast as an adoring page), Dimitri Romanoff, Yura Lazovsky, and Saddler. After the ballet's New York debut in November, Walter Terry singled him out as "delightful," and Margaret Lloyd, reviewing *Bluebeard* in *The Christian Science Monitor,* called him brilliant. Robbins and Lazovsky were meant to be Spanish. And Robbins pretended to serenade the queen. The performance in which he accidentally threw his guitar into the audience attests to the wealth of Latin temperament he was putting out. *American Dancer* called his scene and duel with Laing (replacing Lazovsky) "one of the high spots in a ballet that is practically all high spots." Lyon remembers from rehearsals that "Whenever [Jerry] did it, Fokine would just sit back and grin. He really liked him doing it."

Fokine's next effort, *Russian Soldier,* was far less popular. Almost sixty years after its premiere in January 1942, former Ballet Theatre dancers still roll their eyes at the mention of it. The ballet, set to Prokofiev's *Lieutenant Kije Suite,* obviously had immense resonance for Fokine; his native Russia was at the moment struggling against the German invasion. Margaret Lloyd shrewdly characterized the work as a "pièce d'occasion and not a pièce de résistance . . . acceptable in the name of Russia's strength and courage, sweetly nostalgic to those who know and love the land, sad and touching in spite of its sentimentalities." In it, a soldier of the early 1800s (Lazovsky), dying on the battlefield, remembers his past—an idyllic Russian peasant life. Robbins played the officer in command, had a lively bit as the hero's brother during a wedding feast, and, along with other reluctant members of the ensemble, was cast as "wheat," whose reaping by peasants bore a premonitory connection to death's harvest.

The dancers, ambitious and hardworking but at the same time young and full of fun, were not terribly enthusiastic in the studio, and Fokine took umbrage. Sono Osato remembers him demanding, "Who is against this enterprise? You must leave rehearsal!" Writing about the ballet in 1976, Robbins remembered the alarming dress rehearsal with the whole company drilling as soldiers—men and women alike in white tights, black boots, and red coats.

> We quickly found out it was very difficult to know who to line up behind or with now that we were out of practice clothes . . . and men & women looked alike. Bedlam broke loose. You'd be tapped from behind to turn around and be identified. When you turned, your rifle over your shoulder usually knocked off the hat & wig of the person next to you & there was more crotch staring than ever seen anywhere in order to see the sex of the person next to you. You must remember that the backstage was dark, & the ballet as a whole dimly lit so that the memory scene could be mysteriously faded in & out. There were also complete blackouts between scenes. And these really caused havoc. For each of us had many

roles to play & one had to change costumes in the dark. . . . In the dark we would search for our piles of clothing & might be half dressed sometimes . . . before discovering it wasn't one's costume. The solution was to find a secret place or corner backstage where you hoped no one else would choose to hide his clothes & make his change. It got to be more fun making the changes—like a kids' game. As a matter of fact, I'm afraid we didn't take the ballet too seriously except where we were called to do some serious dancing. As a stack of wheat we wore sort of a long full hay overcoat & a tall hay top hat. We stood in rows and moved sequentially as if a wind was blowing over us, and then some girls with scythes would move thru us with cutting movements. 'I'm reaping you' they'd whisper as we'd fall to the floor in a heap & say 'I'm relaxed & enjoying it.' Then one dancer as Death [Saddler] walked thru us & we rolled off the platform behind & ran for our next change of clothes. Some of the girls played nuns. I don't remember how they figured in the story—but I do remember the hilarious & vulgar things (gestures & pantomimes) they would do off stage to try to break us up before they came on.

Saddler, stalking through with his scythe, was lucky to be covered by a dark cloak; heading for Jerry, he couldn't be sure what cutting-up mightn't provoke him to unseemly laughter. Robbins noted in his diary the day before the Boston opening that he didn't perform in *Giselle* or *Aurora's Wedding* that night but had to rehearse in costume "that awful 'Kije'—Ugh!—!!" The next afternoon Fokine was still "making mad changes." However, Robbins got through what he characterized as "a hard variation" and could give himself a pat on the back: "I did very well indeed according to Mr. Fokine's reaction."

Dancing his first Fokine ballet at Ballet Theatre, *Carnival,* Robbins felt that the choreographer disliked him because he couldn't muster—or believe in—the elegance needed for a Romantic waltz, but obviously Fokine took an interest in him early on and prodded him. His solo in *Russian Soldier*'s wedding scene was full of pirouettes and exuberant Russian double turns in the air with the knees drawn up underneath, often landing on the knees. Fokine would exhort, "Good, good . . . but I want 90 percent," holding up a rolled-up newspaper and telling him, "Your feet must go this high." As Robbins remembered Fokine's methods later, "It was never a put down—a trainer & dog relationship—he'd be full of excitement & joy to get me to do more. And I did."

It was during the summer of 1942, in Mexico, that Robbins realized a dream: to play the title role in Fokine's *Petrouchka*.

⌒

That 1942 Mexican sojourn was a dream for everyone connected with Ballet Theatre, and in many ways. During the previous fall, the organization had been invited by the Mexican government to perform at Mexico City's Palacio de Bellas Artes for two weeks. The following summer, the company, strapped by a wartime economy, moved to Mexico for slightly more than four months, ending with almost a month of performances at Bellas Artes in August and September. It was cheaper to live and rehearse in Mexico City, cheaper to have scenery built there, and they performed in other towns as well.

On April 30, Robbins, armed with his draft release, set off for Mexico by car with John Kriza; backtracked from Athens, Texas, to take in New Orleans (which he loved); dropped in on Horton Foote's parents in Wharton, Texas; and in Laredo hooked up with the company (the other dancers had been on a railway coach for sixteen hours). By May 8, he was ensconced in a hotel not far from the Villa Internationale headquarters, where many of his friends were staying, and where he could get meals "$11 a week with room and bath and food pas mal." On May 9, he was playing the piano for company class, a job he occasionally took on.

Over the summer, he made trips to Taxco, Cuernavaca, and Acapulco with friends. He and his former girlfriend Albia Kavan borrowed a car from company manager Charles Payne and drove to Teotihuacán. He read Faulkner's *Light in August*. He wrote stories and sent one to Foote, who liked it. He survived a temporary rupture in his friendship with Foote, getting hysterical but refusing Payne's invitation to go out and get drunk: "I have control, & that is what is important to me—that is what I've found out. And I'm glad to have it. I don't want to drink—& I don't want to sleep around."

He loved Mexico, got a kick out of hanging half out of crowded buses, and watched the inhabitants with the sensitive, acquisitive eye he was also beginning to apply to art. He wrote to Foote of seeing a play in a little caravan theater in Taxco. "And there is an Indian mother with a baby on her back in a shawl. . . . Do you think it will smother. . . . And the mother watches the whole show, the tragedy and the comedy, and her smooth brown cheeks never move and she never laughs or reacts, but watches everything very intently."

In a letter to his young cousin Jean Handy, however, he emphasized, maybe exaggerated, the toughness of the schedule—perhaps because Jean, already studying with Daganova, had notified her mother, Gert, that she was serious about becoming a dancer and the family wanted her to know how much hard work and sacrifice were required. Cousin Jerry wrote:

> I have class at nine every morning. This is followed by a three-hour rehearsal . . . [ellipses were his current punctuation of choice] And these hours we work full out. This brings it to one o'clock. Just time to get back to the hotel for a meal . . . a half hour rest . . . And back to re-hearsal. This time we work till either 6 or 7:30. That is the end of the day as far as the company is concerned . . . But my working day goes on. In the evening I teach a ballet class and take a Spannish [sic] dancing class. This brings me to ten. Then I crawl home and get into bed after a light snack. So for the next eight weeks life is going to be awfully confined to the rehearsal hall and home. We do have Sundays off, but they are mostly spent in bed getting better from the last week and getting ready for the next.*

He revealed to Jean what must have been his own state of mind: "Don't be fooled by thinking that 'dancing' means always having a good time and always performing. It doesn't. I am very very unhappy at it a good deal of the time because I either realize my restrictions, and I have them . . . Or else I am so utterly weary from working so hard . . . Or else I am discon-tented with what kind of ballets we are doing." And he warned her lov-ingly, "If you can't be the best . . . If you haven't made up your mind to be the best . . . You are going to suffer . . ."

Jerry was in the process of making up his own mind to be the best. But rehearsing and performing could not command his complete attention. Ballet Theatre dancers performed in two Mexican films made that sum-mer. One, called *Yolande,* involved Ballet Theatre's production of *La Fille Mal Gardée*. Irina Baronova performed, as did the Mexican comedian Cantinflas, whom the Ballet Theatre gang found to be an entertaining companion. The second, *Yo Baile con Don Porfirio,* featured two dances—

---

* Donald Saddler remembers the schedule being somewhat less grueling. Because of the after-noon heat, the dancers had a break from about 2:00 to 6:00 P.M. This sticks in his mind because Massine used to corral him during siesta to work out ideas for *Aleko*.

a cancan and a polka—choreographed by Jerome Robbins. Jerry proudly referred to it as "my film," and on July 23, because of the money he expected to get from the project, he invited his parents down for a month, "now that things in the factory are slack." He didn't think he could pay for their transportation, but he could manage their room and board, "and here is my chance to [do] something toward repaying you for bringing me up, such as I am. Please, please." However much they might have cramped his style, they could have seen their son being successful and apparently well liked—appreciated for his sense of fun, his friendliness, and his diligence. They didn't come. And their communications distressed him: "I only wish you could write less of a business letter to me once in a while. They all seem so formal. Come on and relax and let me know what's cooking with you all."

Robbins also worked under Léonide Massine that summer and seemed to enjoy it, although he later said he had never considered Massine much of an influence on him. Massine, a protégé of Diaghilev and his principal choreographer during the teens and twenties, had been affiliated with the Ballet Russe de Monte Carlo. He arrived in Mexico City to compose a new ballet, *Aleko,* a tragic drama about a young man (George Skibine) who becomes enamored of a Gypsy (Markova) and ends up killing both her and her Gypsy lover (Laing). Tudor played the pirate chief and Robbins a Gypsy. The music was by Tchaikovsky, and Marc Chagall arrived to supervise the making of the decor and even lend a hand with the painting.

"Started work with Massine," wrote Robbins on July 7. "Like it very much. At least we <u>really</u> dance. Like the way he works with people." Saddler, who understudied Skibine in the title role and on whom Massine worked out a lot of the movement, gives a clue to what Robbins may have appreciated about Massine: "He was the kind that would say, 'Now you have to go here, downstage, in twelve counts. You know what it is. You do it.' And you could stay in character but do something to get there in those twelve counts. So it was wonderful training [for a would-be choreographer]; you thought that you were contributing something." Robbins believed that Markova and Dolin looked "especially wonderful" at the premiere and that the ballet's costumes and scenery were splendid. "It does have a kind of atmosphere about it."

Massine also cooked up a less durable venture—an extravaganza called *Don Domingo de Don Blas* for Mexican Independence Day. With music by Revueltas, decor after Juan Ruiz de Alarcon, a seventeenth-century scenario, and a host of fairly authentic Mexican dances, the ballet made one critic feel as if he'd "had an overly rich fruit cake stuffed down [his] throat." Robbins, in an immense sun disk of a headdress, was one of four "tricksters." It may have been during rehearsals for this short-lived ballet that Robbins slacked off. Charles Payne had to give him a talking-to: How would *he* like it if he were a choreographer and a dancer acted the way he was acting? Robbins retorted that if he ever made a ballet this bad, he'd deserve whatever he got.

Fokine, meanwhile, struggled over the summer with his burlesque ballet *Helen of Troy* (unfinished at its Mexican premiere two nights after *Aleko*). Robbins played Hymen. At the time, he emphasized only that the role was classical and difficult. In later years, he made it sound too pretty for his taste. He had to wear a tunic and a wig he compared to a Brillo pad, topped by a crown of flowers. Holding a wreath in one hand and a torch in the other, "I had to do a rather Duncanesque lot of skipping & turning in attitudes, & swooping happily & gayly about; and I was miserable. . . . I felt very out of my capabilities—noble, clear, 'nice', & aryan!" (This was written in the 1970s, when Robbins was probing his feelings about being Jewish.) Following the first run-through, he wrote his parents that "after working on the classical variation like hell, and getting all worried and upset because I couldn't do it properly, and after almost giving the damn thing up, I did it well enough for Fokine to say that I did it 'very well, very well' and I hope that with a good costume I will be able to get off with the dance." In fact, he had been so self-conscious in the part that, after thanking Fokine for the honor of being cast, he had asked to be taken out of it because he felt he was dancing badly. Fokine refused, telling him that he couldn't just dance one way, that he had to "force [himself] to know and do all kinds of dancing," concluding, "You do it. You keep trying."

⌒

Throughout August, Robbins worked on *Petrouchka,* his obsession. He'd had a dream in high school that he equated with the sad but dauntless puppet—something about being trapped in a rubbish-strewn lot behind a tall schoolyard fence—and had lusted after the role for six years.

It is not hard to see what drew Robbins to this enigmatic ballet, premiered in 1911 by Diaghilev's Ballets Russes and featuring the great Vaslav Nijinsky. Fokine's opening scene and Igor Stravinsky's music depict the hubbub of a Shrovetide Fair in old Russia. No matter how big the stage that houses it, the "street" always seems thronged with revelers: coachmen already drunk, nursemaids, Cossacks, street dancers, masqueraders, a dancing bear and his trainer. They fall silent when the sinister showman draws the curtains of his booth to reveal three life-sized puppets, their arms draped over the stands that hold them up, their legs dancing in place at his command.

Compared with this scene, pulsing with life, the ones that take place "backstage" are sadder. The puppets live in solitary confinement, albeit in gorgeous cells designed by Alexandre Benois. The greedy Moor, the stiff-limbed girl dancer, and the rag doll Petrouchka see one another only when on display or when the showman is observing what happens if he puts them together. While the Moor, in his room, makes clumsy overtures to the shallow Ballerina, whom he regards with pleased curiosity as something only slightly better than a piece of exotic fruit, Petrouchka, who loves her, rattles frantically around his cell. Feet turned in, mittened hands limp, he bangs his head against the wall that separates the two cells. All that he craves—life and love and freedom—exists outside these walls.

The audience doesn't see a behind-the-scenes confrontation between the Moor and Petrouchka, but when the action returns to the bustle of the street, the crowd is astonished to see the puppets running free, the Moor chasing Petrouchka and brandishing a knife, the Dancer running helplessly after them. The excited bystanders obscure the battle, gesturing to the Showman that a man is being killed. The crowd parts before his scorn, and, in a striking *coup de théâtre,* he picks up in one careless hand a limp stuffed doll.

The ending is cryptic. The stage has emptied. The Showman, dragging Petrouchka's body behind him, is startled by a high-pitched, mocking laugh in Stravinsky's music. The spirit of Petrouchka—crowing, undaunted—pokes out of the tent's roof, waving his arms furiously. But suddenly he falls forward, his torso flopping over the edge of the tent. So he dies twice, but for a moment—in a reprieve between the death of powerlessness and the death of nonexistence—he asserts man's lust to triumph.

⌒

For a young man who often thought of himself as a loner, an outsider, a not very attractive person, Petrouchka was an icon. Robbins's usual role in the ballet was as one of the vigorous little coach boys, although he played other roles as well. He hadn't been chosen to understudy Petrouchka, not even, he remarked, "to understudy the understudy." But, asking Fokine if he could just learn the role, he got in line behind Dolin, Lazovsky, and Ian Gibson. In Mexico, Dolin dropped out, feeling the role unsuitable and moving Robbins nearer his goal. At some point, Fokine started giving him corrections. In August, Robbins sent for phonograph records of the music. A debut was scheduled for September 9.

True to his training with Sandor, his work with Tudor, and his own inclinations, Robbins gave hours of thought to the character. He told the critic Clive Barnes years later that he had decided that Petrouchka was "badly painted, so probably couldn't see well or hear well and had a hard time focusing." He devised an impressive crooked-mouthed makeup. The night before his debut, he wrote that he had found a "wonderful analogy & line to work on. The different & 'strange' person—mentally & morally—against the 'proper' [twice underlined] society conventions. Ballerina must be one you love intensely. Magician & walls are the standards, conventions, & hard uncaring egotism of the proper society."

On the day itself, he rehearsed *Helen* and performed as the Chinese automaton in *Coppélia,* feeling quite relaxed; however, waiting in his little fairground booth for the magician to open the curtain and show the three life-sized puppets to the crowd, he came close to passing out from excitement. He evidently made an impressive debut in the role; Tudor told him his second performance a few days later was better than the first, and Sevastianov pronounced him excellent. "Oh god," he wrote in his diary, "I'm so happy that Petrouchka is working out. It means so much to me. I want to be the very best Petrouchka there is. I am & want to be humble & workmanlike before the part. It has to be good. It is me in so many ways. Please let me be healthy about it—And sincere."

On October 25, two weeks after his twenty-fourth birthday, Robbins danced the role in New York (after having almost quit the company—or almost been fired—the week before in the course of a fight with Sevastianov). He got "a short slap" from Martin in the *Times,* but Robert Lawrence of the *Herald Tribune* raved, "His approach was that supreme combination of mechanical and tragic that embody the argument of *Petrushka.* The drooping limbs, frustrated mask, the lightning motility that alternated with his shambling gait made this an overwhelming portrayal." At another performance in November, Lawrence went further, calling Robbins's characterization one that "for dramatic power and sheer emotional appeal surpassed any Petrouchka that this writer has seen."

David Lichine told Robbins that he still needed to work but "that it was the first time in many years he had been touched by the ballet." Dolin thought he ranked among the best Petrouchkas. Family and friends were thrilled.

One important person was not there to give an opinion of Robbins's debut in the role. Fokine had left Mexico City for New York in mid-August. Robbins had been onstage rehearsing *Petrouchka* the very day, August 22, that news came from New York that Mikhail Fokine had died.

There was a loss in Robbins's offstage family as well. His cousin Lewis had been fighting overseas. Robbins's laconic entry for September 25, after the halcyon days in Mexico, reads, "Arrived home. So did Lewis—dead." The next month, in a happier diary note, he recorded an addition to the Rips-Rabinowitz clan. In 1941, Jerry had served as best man when his sister married George Cullinen of the merchant marine; notified of the birth of their daughter on October 13, he wrote simply, "an uncle!"

<hr />

Robbins continued to better his roles. He shocked Massine by asking him if he could understudy him in the farruca in *Three-Cornered Hat*—a ballet created for Diaghilev's company in 1919—but Claudia Cassidy of the *Chicago Tribune* praised him in Massine's 1943 *Capriccio Espagnol* as having "captured precisely the Massine quality of movement," and Massine did allow the ambitious young dancer, a principal in the company as of 1943, to step into his own part for a few performances. He took on various roles in *The Fantastic Toy Shop,* another Massine revival from 1919, and received the following rather revealing review from the *Chicago Tribune:* "The indefatigable Jerome Robbins, in an Ed Wynn, Jr. makeup—managed by a deft trick of timing to steal the stage from the misbehaving poodle" (Karen Conrad and John Kriza played dogs in this ballet bouffe). Except for Alias in *Billy,* Benvolio in *Romeo and Juliet,* and the occasional performance as Petrouchka, most of the roles for which he garnered attention either exploited his flair for Spaniards and Gypsies or allowed room for him to let his comedic talents run rampant, such as Agnes de Mille's Devil or another devil, "Red Coat," in David Lichine's *Fair in Sorochinsk.* The part had been created by Dolin, who capered malevolently through it on pointe in his boots (a feat he was known for and that Robbins did not attempt).

He certainly went to town in the new version of *Helen of Troy,* finished and revised by Lichine a few months after Fokine's death. Balanchine too had a hand in the choreography, at the point when his beautiful wife, Vera Zorina, came in as a guest artist to play the title role. Gone was the classical solo Robbins had sweated over. Now he was Hermes in winged sandals, and, according to him, he pretty much worked out his own characterization. If in the confusion Lichine or Balanchine asked him, puzzled, "Did *I* give you that?" he would look innocent and say, "Yes."

Critics compared him to other Broadway Hermes (or Mercuries)— Richard Whorf in *Amphytrion* with the Lunts and Ray Bolger in *By Jupiter.* John Martin named him "perhaps the single justification for *Helen of Troy,* for he managed to carry its collegiate humor into real comedy." His Ballet Theatre peers were not so approving. Judging from the reviews, he seems to have had no shame. In terms of scene-stealing, "He chewed gum and an apple with equal nonchalance, he broke into a short 'jive' routine and, when he was not the center of interest in the stage proceedings, managed to focus attention by flirting with the audience or filling in for Helen in the arms of her sleeping husband Menelaus." The summers at Tamiment with Imogene Coca and Danny Kaye had served him well.

Surprisingly, the finest of all dance critics, Edwin Denby, loved him in *Helen.* Denby had taken over the dance desk at the *Herald Tribune* when Robert Lawrence was drafted (Lawrence had gotten the job when Walter Terry was drafted). His critical words in 1943 about Robbins's Petrouchka—although leavened by praise—must have been both wounding and thought-provoking: "Robbins sometimes seems to like to jump about for the sake of jumping; and he forgets then not the meaning of his gesture but the illusion on the stage—that is, the reality of a character and of a story. I thought he was too anxious to get across to the audience, too eager to please; he would be more effective with more reserve." But Denby's review of *Helen* presciently brings out how out of place Robbins felt in most of the "Russian" repertoire; the Americanness he was about to salute in his own ballet *Fancy Free* was bursting to get out.

Jerome Robbins, as Mercury, has of course the most original part and he does it beautifully. It is a part in straight American—real Third Avenue, in fact. One of the most interesting things about it is that, where everyone else dances with a particular vivacity, he moves with an American deliberateness. The difference is as striking as it used to be in peacetime abroad, when a stray American youth appeared in a bustling French street, and the slow rhythm of his walk gave the effect of a sovereign unconcern. So Robbins on the stage, by being very natural, looks different enough to be a god; and that a god should be just like someone you see any day on the street is a nice joke.

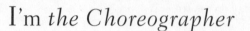

5

I'm *the Choreographer*

Harold Lang, John Kriza, and Jerome Robbins ogle Shirley Eckl in *Fancy Free*.
Fred Fehl/NYPL.

R *uthanna Boris* remembers boarding the bus that would take her to her first summer at Tamiment (1938). Max Liebman had assured her she'd have a chance to choreograph (he evidently told this to all ambitious young dancers but took care not to promise exclusivity). When the friendly man in the seat in front of her turned to introduce himself, she announced, "I'm Ruthanna Boris, and I'm the choreographer." At that, a second head in front of her turned and she found a pair of black eyes regarding her balefully. "I'm Jerome Robbins, and *I'm* the choreographer."

They both must have discovered rather quickly that Jerome Andrews and/or Leon Barto choreographed most of the big numbers and that, while no one was designated "the" choreographer, any talented young person could indeed become "a" choreographer during the season. Early on, Robbins had decided that choreography was one of his missions; within four years, it had become his primary goal. He not only concocted numbers he thought might work for Tamiment, he bombarded Lucia Chase with ideas he hoped she'd allow him to choreograph for Ballet Theatre.

The scenarios confirm Robbins's interest in American subject matter and reveal a spry choreographic imagination at work. He could envision how an idea might be structured in movement and the shape of its dramatic rhythm.

Certainly his distaste for Ballet Theatre's infatuation with Slavic tales fueled his interest in American themes, and he was acquainted with Lincoln Kirstein's short-lived Ballet Caravan (1936–1939) and its repertory of Americana (such as Eugene Loring's *Billy the Kid*). But he was also influenced by the work of the American Actors Company, beginning in the spring of 1941, when he rehearsed and performed de Mille's *American Legend*.

The AAC, headed by Mary Hunter (later Mary Hunter Wolf), was a consortium of actors—among them Joseph Anthony, Mildred Dunnock, and Horton Foote—who had met in Tamara Daykarhanova's acting classes and, in 1937, formed a kind of collective, influenced by Russian models. Their disastrous first production of *The Trojan Women* led them to reconsider their mission. As Foote remembers it, "Mary said, 'Well, you know, I think we're on the wrong track. We're from all over America, and we're Americans, and that's our heritage. I think we should do American plays.'" Improvisations set up by the actors to acquaint one another with their respective backgrounds led, for instance, to a one-act by Foote and then to his first full-length play, *Texas Town,* set in a drugstore in a small town like the one where he had grown up. The play received five off-Broadway performances in April 1941, when Robbins would have been rehearsing *American Legend* with de Mille—and meeting Foote and Hunter.

Around this time, Robbins envisioned a "New York Ballet" for Tamiment that depicted the denizens of *his* "hometown." A cop, lovers, prostitutes, sailors, truck drivers, "city sharpies," a shoeshine boy, and others populated a New York street scene. They walked the imaginary avenues, stopping whenever the cop blew his whistle and freezing while each took a turn to express his or her nature in a brief dance theme. Robbins imagined this opening set to music "like a stirring jazz fanfare for the city." It's as if he already heard in his head the music Leonard Bernstein would write for *Fancy Free.*

He made notes for a ballet, "War Babies," inspired by an article that appeared in the April–May 1941 issue of *Direction.* The author, Hyde Parnow, had interviewed East Side kids "born during the last war and now headed for another." Robbins labeled some of the accompanying photos "use for ballet": a couple dancing outside a billiard parlor, four men in overcoats and hats having a heated debate outside a candy store. Another striking image of a couple dancing moonily might have found its way into *Fancy Free;* his acquisitive eye was always busy storing up impressions. For his scenario, Robbins developed a leading character who would also serve as a narrator (based, like the restless hero of Foote's *Texas Town,* on its author):

> Lennie is tough . . . on the outside. . . . His whole walk is but an outward show of stance in self-assurance which he hasn't, indifference which he isn't [*sic*], and smugness which he is far from. His theme is the callousness which he hates but uses for self protection. He wants love badly. He wants escape badly. Warped into a little sneering person and hating it because of his acute sensitiveness, Lennie is afraid . . . Of the crushing world he lives in.

Members of the American Actors Company were interested in folklore. At some point, Robbins came up with a Wild West idea for a ballet, into which he seems to have planned to incorporate the Frankie and Johnny duet that he and Anita Alvarez had created at Tamiment. His rhythmic ideas are smart. The habitués of a gold-rush bar race to the window, stare out, and return to whatever they've been doing, but as they wait for the door to open and the hero to enter, they slow their activity down "until it's completely suspended."

Foote remembers the AAC members' fondness for a folk song that tells of the exploits of Stack O'Lee, a larger-than-life rascal drawn from Southern folklore—a Tyl Eulenspiegel minus Tyl's redeeming propensity for mocking pomposity and corruption. Robbins drafted a ballet scenario (and perhaps envisioned himself in the leading role). He had high hopes that the powers in Ballet Theatre would go for his colorful rumpus, divided into four scenes and an epilogue. On January 15, 1942, he wrote in his diary that if he doesn't "get anything done," he's going to try nightclub work. He hates the idea but thinks he can earn more money that way.* Three days later, when the company swung briefly into New York, he went to his Aunt Jean's house and the two of them typed out *Stack*. His sister read it and approved. The next day, he gave it to the office (shrewdly sending a copy to himself c/o Comfort Corset in order to copyright it). After performing in Boston on January 21, he reported that "Dorati [Antal Dorati, Ballet Theatre's conductor] likes the ballet!!! Oh god please—I'll be good—I'll work hard—but please let me do what's right & get to do what I want to do."

Stack is born full-sized, with a set of teeth and a lust for women. The Devil, a rather ratty little fellow, thinks it'll be a cinch to harvest this soul for Hell, but Stack keeps outwitting him. It was Robbins's plan to have the performer playing the Devil act as narrator to bridge the scenes, and his script credits Foote with the narration—either as a writer or a potential speaker, or as both. (The idea of an onstage narrator was not as radical as it might seem, since Martha Graham had used an "interlocutor" in her 1938 *American Document* and Eugene Loring had incorporated spoken text into his Saroyan piece for Ballet Theatre, *The Great American Goof*.)

The script for *Stack* is full of bright ideas. In one scene, the audience sees what looks like a heap of colorful skirts; one woman after another pulls away to reveal Stack, seated on a stool with a woman on each knee and a whiskey bottle in his hand. In the ensuing rowdy party, Stack plays the piano and the girls "pick up the rhythms on the chairs and floor"; he joins their increasingly wild dancing, and the scene ends with all the ladies on his lap.

For Scene 3, Robbins planned a chase that would build like the chil-

---

* It was probably after the summer of 1942 that he created a number for Imogene Coca to perform at the Copacabana with four showgirls. However, in devising a parody of *Hiawatha,* he hadn't realized that as Coca doggedly rowed backward on the floor, most of the club's patrons couldn't see her, and when the showgirls bent forward, their gigantic feather headdresses completely hid her. The number was dumped after one performance.

dren's story "The Gingerbread Man." All the people Stack enrages—his huge wife, whose two diamond teeth he's stolen, three bumbling deputies, the Devil—gradually swell the procession that keeps pursuing him off the stage and back onto it. In the end, Stack, hanged for murder, makes nice to Mrs. Devil and her kids and boots Satan out of Hell.

The scenario certainly exhibits wit and theatrical savvy. It may have been rejected because Robbins, at twenty-three, was too much an unknown as a choreographer to be entrusted with such a large-scale venture. His only further reference to *Stack O'Lee* in his journal is a remark that the play *All That Money Can Buy* ("wonderful") was "very close to *Stack*."

Robbins apparently wasn't easily daunted. Even as he was sending *Stack O'Lee* off to be appraised, he was outlining to Sonya his scheme for another, more serious ballet, *Clan Ritual*. For this work, he studied his own family, writing character sketches of his parents, grandmother, aunts, uncles, and cousins. His attempts to loosen his ties to Lena dominated one possible scene he sketched out. He planned to begin with a birth image— a woman sitting on a box in wide second position, or perhaps standing, with the main character, her son, between her feet. When the boy is finally helped to stand on his own and let go of her hand in "the first breaking away of his life, the music cuts off short." Robbins roughed out a promising second scene, a circling dance in rondo form, in which mother and son gradually exchange the roles of leader and follower, but went no further into the details of his four-part rite-of-passage epic.

In his book on the history of American Ballet Theatre, Charles Payne remembered Robbins also having submitted an idea for a Cain and Abel ballet. No plotted-out dance description exists, but an impassioned written narrative drawn from Genesis—beginning with Eve's temptation and developing Cain, the unloved and enraged misfit, into his protagonist—is full of movement images: "And then out of the bushes rippled a snake, and slithered its way to the apple and sensuously wound its coils round and round the apple till its length encircled it. It lifted its head and gazed in the direction of the woman, and then slowly swung and pointed the way of the man. Then slowly it relaxed and laid its head over the bright skin of the apple and slept."

These projected works were, as a matter of course, dramatic; short-story ballets formed the bulk of Ballet Theatre's repertory. There's no record of how many of his ideas Robbins sent to the company's management. In later years, laughing over his youthful chutzpah, Robbins mentioned that most of his scenarios called for fairly elaborate productions, although he prudently opened his outline of *Clan Ritual* by remarking, "This ballet is so essential that it may be done on a bare stage in practice clothes and without curtain scenery."

Eventually some wise person—Robbins thought it might have been the critic Anatole Chujoy—suggested that he might have better luck persuading Ballet Theatre to let him choreograph if he came up with a shorter and more concise plot, and one that involved a small number of dancers and a single set. Judging from a letter written by his friend Charles Payne, he was having trouble finding a workable idea. As early as January 1942, Payne, now Ballet Theatre's executive manager, was covertly advising him on strategies, even coming up with a Horatio Alger scenario set in a Coney Island café, in which a poor dancing newsboy (Robbins?), looked down on by upper-class snobs and falsely accused of a crime, would save the rich girl from drowning and become a hero. It might, thought Payne, turn out to be "an American Beau Danube, which could be worse." Jerry wasn't tempted to undertake this pseudo-Massine ballet and decided to reconsider the Tom Sawyer work he had done at Tamiment. Payne replied with a four-page single-spaced typewritten letter, full of warnings and recipes for success that say much about ballet of the day. He understood how the young choreographer wanted his first work "to be different, unique, and distinctly Robbins." However, he warned, "no matter how intrinsically worthwhile your first ballet is, unless it appeals to the public generally, you will never get a chance to do another." Jerry's idea of introducing each character with a personality-defining solo would never fly: "An opening ballet (which you intend Twain to be) usually starts off with a gay chorus number." And although Payne didn't know *why* this was so, he offered examples to support his theory.

By May 1943, Payne, now in Washington, D.C., and writing on U.S. Naval Reserve stationery, elaborated on an idea he had broached earlier. Getting Lucia Chase interested was key. And how better to get her interested than telling her his ballet would offer her a starring role that made use of her acting ability and was unlike the others she currently played? "Can you make Aunt Polly moderately young, amusing and a real character? Can you, in talking about the character, make it sound very unlike the older sister in Pillar, the nurse in Romeo, the servant in Don Domingo, the society lady in Aleko, etc." Payne analyzed the competition (Agnes de Mille had proposed two ballets), and he outlined exactly what words might convince Lucia to champion Robbins's idea to Gerald Sevastianov.

Luckily, Mary Hunter fed Robbins a timely idea. (This woman, who became a friend for life, was one of those he credited, along with Foote and Tamiment accompanist Glen Bacon, with turning him into a reader; when he was in his seventies and she in her eighties, she was still sending him books and recommending others.) She suggested he take a look at Paul Cadmus's painting *The Fleet's In.*

This 1934 work had caused a furor by offending the secretary of the Navy, to whom it represented "a most disgraceful, sordid, disreputable, drunken brawl, wherein apparently a number of enlisted men are consorting with a party of streetwalkers and denizens of the red-light district. This is an unwarranted insult . . . and evidently originated in the depraved imagination of someone who has no conception of actual conditions in our service." Robbins looked hard at the painting and at Cadmus's *Shore Leave* (also the name of a novel by Frederic Wakeman and a working title for *Fancy Free*), and probably at his *Sailors and Floosies* as well. Cadmus's images were a bit too raunchy for his purposes and if captured in a ballet during wartime would undoubtedly have angered audiences. Still, in Cadmus's satirical realism, there is a refreshing lustiness and a naturalness of gesture and groupings that Robbins would have found intriguing: the girls mockingly accosted, the woman shoving away the guy who gets fresh, the dreamy embraces, the "Come here, honey" tugging, and the sailors' physical ease with one another.

Later, the servicemen-on-leave motif provided Hollywood with plots that captured the lighter side of World War II at a time when military subjects were proliferating. (In 1943, when Robbins dreamed up *Fancy Free,* almost 30 percent of Hollywood features were war-related.) *Seven Days Leave,* an army musical starring Victor Mature and Lucille Ball, came out in 1942, and Gene Kelly's *Anchors Aweigh* (another shore-leave scenario) in 1945.*

Robbins had no real need to study Cadmus's paintings to get ideas. Sailors were everywhere in New York. Passing through Times Square on his way to and from rehearsals and performances at the Metropolitan

---

* *Anchors Aweigh* was released after the premiere of *Fancy Free* and was possibly influenced by it, although according to what Gene Kelly's wife, Betsy Blair, told dance historian Beth Genné, Kelly may have begun mapping out his movie in the winter of 1943.

Opera House, he noticed that they often sauntered along in threes, full of bravado, grasping at pleasure before being shipped out to possible death. He wrote a simple scenario detailing what happens when three buddies on leave, out on the town, end up with only two girls for an evening's fun. By this time, Managing Director Gerald Sevastianov had been drafted, and his successor, J. Alden Talbot, had in the past, according to Payne, been charmed by Robbins's sly off-the-cuff imitations of Fokine and Massine, and was perhaps more sympathetic to non-Russian choreographers than Sevastianov. As Robbins recalled later in an interview with Clive Barnes, not only did the project find favor, but a slot fortuitously opened in Ballet Theatre's 1944 spring season at the Met—possibly because de Mille choreographed only one ballet; her *Tally-Ho,* the other non-Russian hit of the season, premiered two months before *Fancy Free.* He also remembered that Ballet Theatre's powers had been pleased with the dances he had devised for the Mexican film, especially the cancan, which Payne had praised to him for being "distinctly American in mood." Back when the project was approved, however, Jerry didn't spend much time wondering what prompted the decision; he got to work.

The sailor-as-dancer was already something of a tradition. Soldiers march; sailors do hornpipes. One of America's first recorded native-born dancers, John Durang, made his reputation by performing numerous versions of the Sailor's Hornpipe during the years after the Revolution—apparently mixing ballet steps like sissonnes and entrechats with pigeon wings, double shuffles, and such vigorous-sounding moves as "jockey crotch down." (Robbins, it must be remembered, had done *his* hornpipe number at Tamiment in 1939.) In the 1936 movie *Follow the Fleet,* Fred Astaire had shown that a U.S. Navy uniform, with its hip-hugging bell-bottom pants, made an outstanding dance costume. A soldier's bulky belted trousers and tucked-in shirt are far less trim. As Gene Kelly (who played a sailor in four of his films) explained, a gob's snugly fitting clothes don't break the line of the body.

For a choreographer, there was something particularly alluring about the topic of sailors on leave. Their joking camaraderie, their rolling gait, their tight uniforms and rakish caps all fostered an image of cockiness, of sexuality ready to bust out. *Fancy Free* had precedents on the ballet stage, although none achieved the longevity of Robbins's first work or received the reported twenty-plus curtain calls on opening night. In 1925, Léonide Massine had choreographed *Les Matelots* for Diaghilev's Ballets Russes. Its plot, like that of *Fancy Free,* focused on three sailors and two girls. And, as in Robbins's work, each sailor (an American, a Spaniard, and a Frenchman) danced a solo. However, Massine's slight plot devolved on a sailor's wish to test the fidelity of his fiancée (aided by her so-called friend, he and his buddies return from sea disguised by beards and attempt to lure her to a bar). It would be interesting to know if Robbins had seen *Les Matelots* as a high school kid; revived in 1934 for the de Basil Ballets Russes's New York season, it apparently did not go over well and was soon discarded.

On November 14, 1943, a few days after Robbins began rehearsals for *Fancy Free,* a group called the American Concert Ballet made its debut at the Ninety-second Street YMHA. The previous spring, Robbins had been listed as one of the choreographers affiliated with the group, along with such Balanchine dancers as William Dollar, Todd Bolender, Mary Jane Shea, and John Taras, but presumably the chance to choreograph for Ballet Theatre superseded all other plans. Coincidentally, on that Y program, Shea presented her *Sailor Bar,* in which a lonely Navy man (Francisco Moncion) and the girl he has picked up (Jane Ward) are contrasted with less rough and less realistically drawn alter egos billed as their "ideal sel[ves]" (Bolender and Georgia Hiden). One critic praised as "touching and exciting" the "good brawl, the crude heartbreak," and Todd Bolender remembers the ballet being liked when the little company toured. He also remembers Shea being disgruntled when the success of *Fancy Free* overshadowed her ballet but points out that the two works had little in common but sailors and that, given the ubiquity of servicemen on the streets and on movie screens, they were bound to debut on the contemporary ballet stage sooner or later.

Robbins drafted and revised several scenarios for *Fancy Free.* It is surprising how closely the one he presumably submitted to Ballet Theatre's management sometime during May of 1943 resembles the finished ballet. Reading the scenario brings it instantly to life. When the first woman walks on, the three sailors "spruce themselves up. They pick up her walk and rhythms and try to insinuate themselves with her. . . . They snatch her bag and toss it from one to the other. She pretends to be angry with them, and annoyed, but both she and they know she isn't." It's all there, even to the sort of musical moods Robbins prescribed in the margins. The buddies' unison downing of three beers, their paper-scissors-rock game to see who pays, the gum-chewing, the shifts in mood—he evidently planned them all before rehearsals began. He even had a cast in mind; the first girl is called the Brunette, the second, the Redhead. Although brunettes were common enough in the company, redheads weren't; it's safe to assume he envisioned Muriel Bentley and Janet Reed in the roles from the start. The most obvious difference between the scenario and the ballet is that he first envisioned the sailors wearing navy blue uniforms instead of the summer whites in which they eventually rocketed onto the Metropolitan Opera stage on April 18, 1944.

By June 1943, Robbins was casting about for a composer. At some point, he approached Morton Gould, but Gould, Robbins later said, was too busy. Gould himself remembered being reluctant to throw in his lot with a newcomer who was working on spec and had no budget for orchestration or the copying of parts. In late June, Robbins traveled to Philadelphia to meet with another possible composer, Vincent Persichetti, and on August 3, still without a collaborator, he mailed Persichetti a politely desperate handwritten letter from San Francisco, one of the stops on Ballet Theatre's packed summer tour.

Dear Mr. Persichetti,

If you'll remember, I came down to Philadelphia late in June with a scenario for a ballet, and you played for me, but you thought that it wasn't your type of score I wanted. And at that time you suggested Leonard Bernstein. I spent one full day trying to get in touch with him, finally ending up by visiting a non-existent address in New York. As yet, I found no one to do the score for me, & as I am returning to New York later this month, thought I'd try to get on the trail of Mr. Bernstein again. I wonder if you have any further information of his whereabouts. I would appreciate it very much if you would let me know. . . . Or if you know anyone who would know. I could not contact Lukas Foss—, & Marian Bauer. If you can supply me with any means of finding him, please send it to me, in care of Ballet Theatre, 25 W. 45th . . . I hope this finds both you and your wife very well.

Sincerely,

Jerry Robbins

Luckily, Robbins ran into a friend, stage designer Oliver Smith, who would create the set for the ballet. Smith took him to Bernstein's Carnegie

Hall studio. Robbins was twenty-four years old; Bernstein was probably just twenty-five (depending on the date they met—his birthday was August 25) and about to take up his post as assistant conductor to Artur Rodzinski at the New York Philharmonic.

Robbins showed Bernstein his scenario, and Bernstein responded with something he'd written on a napkin at the Russian Tea Room at lunch that day—a tune that had popped into his head. When he sang the melody, "Jerry went through the ceiling. He said, 'That's it, that's what I had in mind!' We went crazy. I began developing the theme right there in his presence." It was perhaps at those first meetings that Robbins developed the habit—later described by Bernstein in a discussion of *West Side Story*—of standing behind his colleague as he played the piano, hands on the composer's shoulders, sending and receiving dynamic signals through touch.

On November 14, three days after Robbins began composing his ballet, Bernstein became the music world's rising star. Bruno Walter, the guest conductor for that afternoon's Philharmonic concert, had taken sick; Rodzinski was in Stockbridge, Massachusetts, immobilized by a snowstorm. At 9:00 A.M., Bernstein was told he'd be going on. Bernstein's biographer Humphrey Burton reports that the *Times* headline reporting his ensuing triumph was printed in the same-size type as "JAPANESE PLANE TRANSPORT SUNK." Offers to conduct swelled his mailbox, and before *Fancy Free*'s April premiere, his *Jeremiah* symphony had been played in three cities.

Robbins's fame would be deferred until spring, but he may have had some inkling of success. On Bernstein's birthday, he scribbled a note to himself in his diary: "Jerry—If you get to [be] a big shot—<u>don't be small.</u>"

His entry for November 11 in Philadelphia says, "Tomorrow start on my ballet. Just movement. . . . Whee." The following day, he worked for an hour and a half with his buddies John Kriza and Harold Lang, with Michael Kidd standing in for himself, and that same day, in addition to performing, managed a trip with a friend to the Navy Yard for a bit of research: "Very very exciting place—went aboard U.S. Wisconsin—cables [w]elders . . . riveters—noise, business, etc.—all so very exciting."

Beginning in January 1944, Robbins logged his progress in his little appointment calendar, a "Dailyaide" ("The Silent Secretary"), along with the ballets performed as the company looped from Tennessee and Texas through Midwest cities to California, Vancouver, and the Pacific Northwest, then back down to the South via Minneapolis, Columbus, and

Cincinnati. He and his cast—Lang, Kriza, himself, Bentley, Reed, and Shirley Eckl, who played the small but crucial role of the gently seductive third girl the sailors catch sight of just before the curtain falls—rehearsed wherever and whenever they could, sometimes for little more than a half hour. *Fancy Free* was hammered out coast to coast on stages, in rehearsal studios, in hotel lobbies, in nightclubs during daytime hours, and on trains. "A lot of counting went on down the aisle," says Eckl. Reed remembered even the city streets as a site for choreography: "[W]e were in Bloomington, Indiana, walking down the street on the way to the theater, and Jerry said, 'I wonder what would happen if—' and he described the girl running and suddenly jumping and the boy catching her. He just talked his image of it as we were walking. I let him walk on ahead a little ways and I said, 'You mean like this?' and I ran down the street and jumped at him. And he had to drop his bag to catch me. That's in the pas de deux we did together."

In addition to plundering his recollections of sailors parading their jaunty personas (more often a bluff) through Times Square and studying the popular dances of the day, Robbins also kept his eyes primed for the telling gesture, the interesting pattern. "If we were on a train and we looked out a window and saw planes flying in formation, Jerry used it in the ballet," said Reed. "Everything he saw that he could use, he did."

The cast members were all his friends, and he built not only on their particular dancerly strengths but on how he saw them as people. "I guess he saw me as a show-off," Lang told writer Tobi Tobias in 1980. "He put in all the things I liked to do: pirouettes, air turns—a lot of high movements, extensions, and jumps." In the forties, few male ballet dancers could execute a double air turn and land in a split, as Lang did in his variation. Kriza was the sweet one. Bentley thought that "Jerry really caught Johnny in that role—the sailor who always paid the check. . . . Johnny was the good one. The one who just loved to dance, loved going to parties, loved to drive his car out on tour, loved people." As for her own part, "That role is me— the first girl. That is a character by the name of Muriel Bentley. She was sharp, she was knowing, she was not a whore, she was bright, she was smart." Robbins had defined Bentley's character, the woman in the tight black jacket and swishing yellow skirt, as being "like patent leather, shiny and bright and crisp." Reed he saw as softer and more innocent, and she, too, said she "never really thought of that girl as anyone but myself." A description of Robbins by Agnes de Mille could easily be applied to the persona he displayed in his own variation: he was, she wrote, "small, dark and lithe, taut as a coiled spring, with crackling feet and fingers, the leer of a satyr, the insinuation of a cat."

Reed had only happy memories of rehearsals, but Bentley did not. When Robbins was unhappy with her performing, he let her know it in words that stung. His first ballet may have marked his debut in the unpleasant practice of scapegoating. Except that Bentley, unlike some of the dancers on whom he vented his frustration in later productions, couldn't be considered a slacker, a slow learner, an apple polisher, or someone he felt was resisting him. She'd been his friend for six years and, according to her, "his first fuck" (among women, that is); out of the studio they remained fond of each other.

Robbins himself recalled that choreographing *Fancy Free* had been easy and pleasant: "I don't remember hitting a snag where I didn't know how to get out of it. Or hitting a block at all." However, his diary records in equal measure elation, frustration, and a fatigue that's not surprising considering the almost daily performing that he was logging in. Around Christmas 1943, he made what would turn out to be a fateful decision: he joined the Communist Party, understanding, he later said, that opposition to anti-Semitism was part of the Party's credo. In early 1944, he took some space in his little book to ponder his insecurities, to write of the beauties of Colorado Springs or Red Rock, to mention the Alaskan Indian fishhook he bought for $5 in Denver ("Must save now, but good!"), to note that he'd finished reading *Lost Weekend* and that he'd been picked up by an oil king in Oklahoma City. Every entry logs his slow progress on the ballet (except for some mysteriously blank pages in February), and by late March, his jottings deal almost exclusively with *Fancy Free*.

[1/20] Kansas City. Got 3 pages done!—It's good too. [He had received parts of the score from Bernstein and figured out how to read them.]

• • •

[1/21] Colorado Springs. Got in around 1 P.M. Ate & then worked a while with Kriza and Rex [Cooper, who played the stationary bartender]. Juney [June Morris?] watched & then I worked alone. . . . Worked on two lifts with Janet & John at theater.

• • •

[1/24] Salt Lake City. Arrived early A.M. Trudged around most of the day looking for room. Finally took Dolin's in the Utah. Rehearsed, got about 7 more bars done. Ate & to theater. Learned how to play *Escalera.* [later] *Capriccio,* phooey, must rehearse if I'm to do it more [he had started dancing Massine's own part].

. . .

[3/4] Seattle, did good *Billy.* Started scene with Janet—may go well.

. . .

[3/6] Victoria, ½ hr. with girls—set entrance. 1 hour with Harold. Set var[iation]. Danced devil in *Fair.* Foo!

. . .

[3/7] Vancouver. 5 hours! Finished 1—& ½ way thru 2. Set pas de deux up to bar. Whew!

. . .

[3/8] Vancouver. Finished 1 & 2. Don't like end of 2 yet—not right musically. Puts accent on 1 instead of 2—movement should be slow & rolling—So far it runs 5 minutes. Felt very depressed after rehearsal. Devil in *Fair* better. & *Helen* v.g.

. . .

[3/17] Minneapolis (*Billy, Romeo, Aurora*). Must have <u>at least</u> 40 hours to complete ballet—now must keep <u>calm.</u> Finished no. 3.

. . .

[3/19] 2 hrs. cleaned 1 & worked with Muriel—got her to react better. Up to pas de deux. Started entrance of V [5]. . . .

. . .

[3/23] Columbus (*Sylphides, Lilac, Helen*) 3 hours—not much done—very hard—set meeting of 5 . . . girls giggles—takes time—Will try & have opening postponed to the 22nd.

. . .

[3/25] Cincinnati. (*Romantic, Peter, BB, Syl, Fair, Helen*) [This was a Saturday with matinee and evening performances.] Have finished 11 minutes of ballet. Got introduction scene straightened out. Must go into boogie woogie scene before variations. First dance needs most work. Leaving on 4:20 train for NY [Sunday]. Maybe by 18th?

Robbins was leaving the tour a few days early, along with Reed and possibly Kriza, to finish the duet and his solo and to consult with Oliver Smith and costume designer Kermit Love. The fact that he'd been on the road had made planning difficult. A model of the set that Smith sent to Vancouver arrived after the company had left, and Jerry felt let down. Nor was he there to do battle when J. Alden Talbot told Smith the set would have to be painted on a single backdrop (Smith handled the matter very wisely, arguing with the union to get the freestanding set built for $250). It was even more crucial that Robbins and Bernstein sit down together.

Ballet Theatre hadn't commissioned a score since 1940, and in spite of Bernstein's sudden fame, he was obviously excited about the project and willing to work extremely closely with Robbins on the ballet. He not only sent Jerry the score as it emerged and revised on demand, he and composer Aaron Copland (with whom he had a close relationship at the time) recorded a two-piano version of the first sections of music on 78-rpm disks and mailed them to Robbins (they didn't actually rehearse with the records, according to Janet Reed, although the first Ballet Theatre accompanist with whom the choreographer worked was unacquainted with jazz and drove him crazy). The very fast and vibrant piano playing on these records is preceded by a little speech by Bernstein, sounding both very young and endearingly pompous:

Dear Jerry,

This is an impromptu apology for these records. They're not so very bad but they're not so very good. I hope they're useful at any rate. I'm looking through the score now, exhausted, and, uh, I think the first one came out pretty well. Number 2 begins on the second side and I made a transition for you with the F sharp and A third. Everything's OK up to [Number] 3 but when all the counterpoint comes in on the two pianos, I'm afraid it's sort of messy.

At any rate check with the music—I mean the printed music—and you'll be able to probably figure out what *should* be happening. It's very hard to do on the piano, but in the orchestra it'll be very clear.

There was some mess in 3 also about turning pages but I think with the music in front of you you can make sense out of it.

The pas de deux is all okay except that on page three, with those three repeated measures, the rhythm was left out on the third measure. You'll have to put it in yourself, mentally. Also some other errors in turning pages. But on the whole good. The variation is about as it should be. Except the ensemble between the two pianos isn't clear. But I think *also* you'll be able to figure it out.

Pardon all the mistakes. [At this point, a voice in the background calls out cheerfully, "All my fault!"] And it was all Aaron Copland's fault because there he sits now. [Laughter]

My love and give my love to everybody in the, uh, thing. And I hope you like it. Good luck Jerry.

Many of Robbins's datebook entries reflect his need to get Bernstein to underline what he was trying to emphasize in the action. The hot young composer-conductor was fulfilling engagements himself, and the dancers remember him occasionally traveling with them. Otherwise, the two fired off letters. In an undated missive, responding to Jerry's queries, Lenny was extremely accommodating: "About the two extra bars on page 6: if you need them, OK; but it makes awful music (Maybe we can straighten it out in N.Y. at the last minute)" and "About the ending of #2: Throw it out. It's not necessary, and I see your point. It's very easily fixed; and I used it at the beginning of #5, where it works much better. Do you want the revised ending immediately?" And, with a touching lack of arrogance: "(There's a phrase most Aaron-like in II—I hope you don't mind. It's so pretty I can't remove it.)"

As spring advanced, the message on the stationery of the Philharmonic Society of New York was more often "For God's sake, get home! I need you!" By March 30, Robbins was optimistically telling his diary, "Got music settled." On April 3, his own variation was finished (or the music for it, at any rate) after a session at Bernstein's that ended at 5:00 A.M. with Robbins sleeping over and included some earnest talk about their respective families and about psychoanalysis. On April 4, Robbins, Copland, and Bernstein dined together; then the two composers watched a rehearsal "and raved." On April 9, Ballet Theatre's season at the Met began, a marathon that required of the dancers two shows on both Saturdays and Sundays and only one day off until performances ended almost a month later (May 7). On April 15, Robbins wrote, "Leonard said he was proud to have done music for my choreography . . . a noble work cause it makes you like all the people in it."

The correspondences between action and music in the ballet's dramatic passages reflect the intensity of the Robbins-Bernstein collaboration. Pauses that increase the drama are built into the score. The alternation of orchestral passages with those for piano alone shape the changing moods and events. When the three sailors open their chewing gum and, one by one, toss the wadded-up wrappers to see how far they'll go, Bernstein provides single notes to accompany each throw. As the men first enter Oliver Smith's ingenious barroom, Bernstein slips in a four-note fragment (related to the third sailor's variation); then, when they thrust their beer mugs high, one after another, to toast the evening's adventure, he lets us hear the triumphant little melody in full (they finally got the drinks they were thinking about as they walked in); after their swaggering, the sweetness of the tune attests to their affection for one another and hints at the golden ephemerality of this day's leave. In the moments when the guys pace, circling, ready to fight over the women, the music's short, repeating rhythms express the rising tension but with a jauntiness that belies serious menace. As they explode into their final knockdown fight, partially obscured by the bar, a drum underscores the punches. When the two women discover they know each other, the piano mimics their high, excited chatter. Anyone who's seen the ballet a few times can hear the score with closed eyes and see the action.

On opening night—April 18, 1944, as scheduled—*Fancy Free* was programmed directly after *Swan Lake,* Act II, and must have seemed novel from the moment its brief overture sounded. As the conductor, Bernstein, raised his baton, a song, "Big Stuff," came from *behind* the curtain, apparently from the bartender's radio,* which was revealed when the curtain rose on Oliver Smith's flexible set—now all street, now all bar, now half and half, depending on the action.

Robbins built the sailors' close bond from the moment Bernstein's irrepressible first bars rang out. The first man to be seen through the bar's side window flips out of a cartwheel to jump straight up and beckon to his buddies over the heads of an imaginary crowd, and they, in turn, cartwheel to join him. A few gestures reveal their mood and their relationship. The third sailor (Robbins) shapes a female form with his hands, the joyful second one (Kriza) springs up and clicks his heels together in the air and shortly—always the patsy—gets good-naturedly tripped but is caught before he can hit the ground. The men's dancing gives us a deeper look at them: their easy unison, the bounce in their walk, the way they take a wide stance and slowly raise their arms and their gaze, leaning back as if trying to take in the enormousness of the skyline.

The first woman to come along (Bentley), with her high-heeled strut, a

---

* The radio was actually a phonograph belonging to Betty Comden; she and her partner in comedy, Adolph Green, great friends of Bernstein's, had raced in a cab to her apartment to grab hers when it turned out that Ballet Theatre had none on hand. Bernstein had written the song with Billie Holiday in mind. The singer on the record, who sounded so much like her, was his sister, Shirley.

snappy red patent leather pocketbook slung over one shoulder, becomes fair game for their high spirits. Their teasing, the third sailor's imitation of her walk, the way they toss the purse back and forth or hold it out of her reach stop just short of real heckling, but Robbins and Bernstein let us feel that potential until the moment she signals "Enough!" and her swains back off like the decent guys they are. There's no real tenderness until the third sailor manages to be alone in the bar with the second woman (Reed).* After a pantomime in silence, in which he shows her how many enemy planes he personally shot down, they adventure into some slinky music, but she too is a "good girl," just being nice to one of our boys in uniform, and when he advances on her she holds up warning hands that say "Take it easy, mister." They may touch each other in the big, soaring lifts that express their mounting attraction to each other, but he decides against even putting his arm around her as they stroll back to the bar.

The choreography delves into all the awkwardness that arises from the three-guys-two-girls scenario. There aren't enough chairs. While couples dance to honky-tonk music, the odd man is always jittering around to cut in. The three men's competitive solos salve matters only temporarily. These solos are the dance heart of the ballet. Bernstein opens his "tempo di galop" with a drumroll as the first sailor spins in the air and drops into a split. And Robbins, after giving the virtuosic Lang every jump and turn he could think of—allowing him a breather to down a shot of whiskey—had him end, riskily, on one leg, the other stuck up to the side and his hands clasped overhead like a champion. The second sailor begins with a "Gosh, me dance?" air, shy, lyrical leg swings, and softly frisky skips, but before long, he's vaulting over bar stools and jumping over his own legs.

The solo Robbins made for himself is perhaps the most unusual in terms of its angularity and changing dynamics, and the most rhythmically sophisticated. Bernstein wrote a *danzón,* a Latin form not unlike the rhumba in terms of rhythm. A newspaper item asserted that it stemmed from a song "The Riobamba," which Bernstein wrote for Jane Froman to sing at the eponymous club, and which Frank Sinatra also sang. (The composer Ned Rorem speaks of Bernstein buying the tune from two Cuban musicians for a thousand dollars.) Especially as danced by Robbins in a

* Robbins originally did the duet. However, in Ballet Theatre, when Michael Kidd (Robbins's understudy from the beginning) took over the role, the duet was performed by John Kriza. Over the years, the duet has sometimes been performed by the second, sometimes the third, sailor, depending on casting.

silent black-and-white film of the original cast's performance, the sailor's swinging hips, his intense looks at an imaginary partner, his raising eyebrows and frequent "How'm I doing?" glances at the ladies suggest a braggart with an inferiority complex.

Bernstein saves his sweetest music for after the sailors' big scuffle. It's a fine contrast to the manly, dust-yourself-off, flick-his-tie assertions that friendship runs deeper than a night's squabble over women. But of course, that third, silky woman and her torchy tune are hard to resist, and as the guys exit, waving "Hey!," they're going so fast that they skid around corners that aren't even there.

The audience loved it. Hitherto most of the "American" works by ballet choreographers—with the possible exception of de Mille's believable and bumptious *Rodeo* (1942), Loring's *The Great American Goof,* and Kidd's *On Stage*—had presented fictionalized historical landscapes peopled by colorful characters, and those in modern dance had tended to conjure up an imagined frontier of open spaces and blazing individualism. Robbins offered a ballet that looked like what you'd see when you walked out of the theater into the 1944 streets. Antony Tudor had sent him a little opening-night card: "I have a nervous presentiment that the choreographic genius of our age may be discovered tonight. I'm trying so hard to be bitter but am really happy because we certainly need a genius around." He was, it seems, prescient, although there were critics who carped. Arthur V. Berger of the *New York Sun* wrote, "The whole production shouts like a billboard poster." B. H. Haggin, writing in *The Nation,* faulted the "aggressive self-intrusiveness of Leonard Bernstein's music."

But John Martin praised the ballet highly in the *Times,* and in the *Herald Tribune,* Edwin Denby confirmed it as a "smash hit," explaining its success in terms of the context in which it was being viewed. "It is a direct, manly piece: there isn't any of that coy showing off of 'folk' material that dancers are doing so much nowadays. The whole number is as sound as a superb vaudeville turn; in ballet terminology it is perfect American character ballet."

Denby mentioned the dancers looking dazed by their many curtain calls, and they remembered being thunderstruck. They read the reviews in the early hours at the party Nora Kaye threw for them in her apartment. Robbins ought to have been basking in approval. He'd made everyone happy and his family proud. However, some colleagues remember that as the party grew euphoric, he became gloomier and gloomier. Others—

Comden and Green, for instance—thought he manifested a kind of fierce, almost baleful triumph: "I showed them!" To be sure, Martin's second sentence had thrown out an unsettling idea: "This is young Robbins' first go at choreography, and the only thing he has to worry about in that direction is how in the world he is going to make his second one any better."

6

Choreographer on the Town

On the Town collaborators Leonard Bernstein and Adolph Green
(rear) and Betty Comden and Robbins (front) toil for the camera.
NYPL.

The success of *Fancy Free* changed Robbins's life in ways both gratifying and disturbing to him. Ballet Theatre immediately scheduled extra performances of the runaway hit, and, while the mingy ten-dollar royalty payments didn't add much to his soloist's wages, producers started nosing around, trying to figure out whether this bright new choreographer might be able to deliver on Broadway. The day after the premiere, he wrote to his cousin Bob Silverman, wounded overseas and recuperating in a British hospital, "Yesterday I was a schnook from Weehawken, and if I went to a producer's office, I couldn't get by the secretary; and this morning twelve producers called me and asked me to do their next show." Had he been any less talented, he wondered, a week ago? He signed with Century Artists to represent and advise him. He moved to a bigger apartment at 34 West Eleventh Street, around the corner from Oliver Smith. He was confident enough of his potential earning power to embark on psychoanalysis with Dr. Frances Arkin in order to free himself of the imps that beset him, whining in his ear: Not good enough! Not handsome enough! Not desirable enough! Not successful enough! And not heterosexual enough.

Sought out by a reporter for the short-lived *NY PM* not long after the premiere of his ballet, Robbins spoke with the unguarded enthusiasm of the inexperienced interviewee: "I've got a dozen ballets I'd like to do, as soon as I get a little time. . . . I'd like to do several plays as ballets. *Street Scene* is one; Clemence Dane's *Coming of Age* is another. I'd like to do a life of Mark Twain, a ballet of Americana it would be. And I'd like to do a ballet I did at Camp Tamiment ["À la Russe"], which was kind of a burlesque on classic ballet."

By May 1, 1944, however, the day after the interview appeared, he had completed a draft (originally designed for submission to the Theatre Guild) of what he conceived of as a "ballet dance play in one scene, combining the forms of dance, music, & spoken word into one theater form." This, in embryo, was a form he would wrestle with on and off almost to the end of his life. He may indeed have cooked up *Bye-Bye Jackie* practically overnight; however, it reads like a dramatic prelude to *Fancy Free,* and a letter from Robbins to Bernstein indicates that a trilogy was discussed. Seventeen-year-old Jackie is itching to get out of his safe Brooklyn neighborhood; he's surprised to find that the girlfriend he's known all his life is also restless, also yearning for something—she doesn't know what. Amid the rhythmic neighborhood games and chatter Robbins maps out, there's admiring talk of an older boy who's just returned from naval duty in the Aleutians. Jackie enlists. In Scene 4, he's in Navy attire, back sitting on his stoop: ". . . [T]he whole scene is based on his adjustment to the uniform . . . changing the way he walks, the way he leans against the post, the way he sits . . . he adjusts the hat till it gives him a cocksure look . . . he tries different ways of saying hello . . . of lighting a cigarette, of changing the whole moody adolescent boy to the exterior of a sure as hell of himself sailor . . . of looking secure and safe."

The successfully cocksure sailor, however, was destined to find a home in a sturdier package: *On the Town.*

It was Oliver Smith's idea to take *Fancy Free*'s basic situation—three sailors on shore leave in New York—and expand it into a musical comedy. He would serve as set designer and, with Paul Feigay, as coproducer. Robbins would choreograph, Bernstein write the score. Both men, according to Smith, at first resisted the idea. Bernstein was ambitious to be known as a composer of symphonic works, and his mentor, Serge Koussevitzky, kept reminding him of his destiny as a conductor. Robbins was intent on developing his reputation as a ballet choreographer. Once Smith had persuaded the two of them, the question became, who'd do the book and lyrics? Bernstein took Smith to the Blue Angel to see one of the regular performances of Betty Comden and Adolph Green; the two at the time constituted, in their words, "the desperate remains of our old nightclub group, 'The Revuers'* . . . hanging on by our still God-given teeth as a duo." Bernstein was not only a friend, he was a fan; they claimed he knew the words to all their songs better than they did. Robbins originally favored Arthur Laurents for the book and John Latouche for the lyrics but was easily persuaded to collaborate with these ardent fans of *Fancy Free.*

Comden and Green had never written a straight song, but blessed with the hubris of youth, they needed no persuading to work on the new musical comedy project as lyricists and bookwriters. The collaborative process that began in late June was probably Robbins's happiest. Four smart young people—all thirty or under—innocent of how painful getting a Broadway show onto the stage could be. Bernstein and Robbins had considerable input into the plot, and the collaborators met frequently, even though Bernstein had conducting commitments and Robbins, now a soloist with Ballet Theatre, was still going on the road. In August, while Jerry danced in Los Angeles and Lenny conducted *Fancy Free,* as well as a Hollywood Bowl concert on his twenty-sixth birthday, Smith sent Betty and Adolph out to California, and for several weeks the four continued to conjure up New York from a Spanish villa in the Hollywood hills. Sprawled on his

---

* The original team, which had gotten its start at Max Gordon's Village Vanguard a few years earlier, had included Judy Holliday, Alvin Hammer, and John Frank.

bed, slightly drunk on a hot night in New York, Smith wrote Robbins a euphoric letter about the project so far and about his own preliminary sketches: "My Coney Island scene is a dream, very funny, and yet very beautiful, and slightly lascivious at the same time. You will love it . . . It will leave almost the entire stage free for dancing."

Initially, all were wary of the idea of three sailors as musical comedy heroes. Recalled Green, "I think we were all secretly afraid that once we presented, articulated, and moved around these three musical comedy sailors we might have what would turn out to be a grade-B movie." The 1943 *Oklahoma!* notwithstanding, Broadway musicals tended toward fluff like *Mexican Hayride,* with Bobby Clark, and *Follow the Girls. On the Town* was witty and occasionally zany, and all three sailors miraculously found girls they hoped to spend the rest of their lives with, but the level of craft and sophistication elevated it. As Bernstein said, "the subject matter was light, but the show was serious." For one thing, its pressured pace and bittersweet edge derived from the fact that these sailors have only twenty-four hours to see New York and possibly find love before they ship out. When the three couples said their good-byes at the dock and sang "Some Other Time," a line about time being "precious stuff" for folks in love would have struck 1944 spectators as especially poignant; the three, like so many other sons, lovers, fathers, and husbands, might never return home. Work had begun on the script only weeks after Allied troops had landed in Normandy and thousands had died. Comden's husband was serving overseas.

In light of all the songs Bernstein wrote and all the dances Robbins planned, it was fortunate that the script managed to attract the veteran director George Abbott—never one to quail at pruning a show into shape. Abbott had cowritten and staged *On Your Toes, The Boys from Syracuse,* and *Pal Joey,* among other hits; his name attracted hitherto reluctant investors to *On the Town.* Asked why he had signed on, he said, "I like the kids connected with the show." "Kids" is the operative word, and the collaborators, for the most part, accepted without protest Abbott's decisions as to what would work and what wouldn't. Who were they to argue with a Broadway pro? When Comden and Green went to him to plead for their original opening and ending, which would have made the entire action of the show a flashback, he said they could have their prologue or him. They didn't take long to make the choice.

On the strength of the script, a friend of Louis B. Mayer's convinced him to buy the movie rights to *On the Town* for MGM before the show opened on Broadway. The preproduction deal brought in money that helped cover expenses, but Robbins had no hand in the 1949 movie starring Gene Kelly, Frank Sinatra, and Jules Munshin. Only four pieces from Bernstein's score were retained, and Comden and Green wrote new lyrics for far blander tunes by Roger Edens. The opening New York montage, with the sailors careering all over town, is terrific, but the choreographic inventiveness doesn't match Robbins's.

On the Town broke some long-standing Broadway traditions. The three women Gabey, Chip, and Ozzie meet aren't dewy ingenues or their stereotypical smart-mouthed, sourpuss girlfriends. They're independent in the way American women had learned to be in wartime. Tough, heart-of-gold Hildy (a part tailor-made for Nancy Walker) drives a cab and is uncompromising about refusing fares she doesn't like the look of and forthright about dragooning a guy she fancies (Chip). Claire de Loon, the intellectual of the trio, is an anthropologist with a runaway libido. Ivy Smith, the Miss Turnstiles whose poster Gabey falls in love with, supports her ballet and singing lessons by doing a cooch number at Coney Island. The casting wasn't entirely conventional either. Early on, the role of Ivy was given to Sono Osato, whom Robbins knew from Ballet Theatre. She had just won one of the first annual Donaldson Awards for best female dancer in a musical, *One Touch of Venus*. Reviewing the show, choreographed by Agnes de Mille and starring Mary Martin, Wolcott Gibbs had referred to Osato as "a marvelously limber girl of cryptic nationality, who led the dancers and alarmed and fascinated me almost unbearably." Perhaps it's fortunate that her nationality *was* "cryptic"; this gorgeous dancer cast as an all-American girl was half Japanese, and her father was currently interned in Chicago (the irony was not lost on Osato). In addition, the team wanted a cast that reflected the diversity of New York, so they hired four black singers and four black dancers and mixed them in with the rest of the cast, unheard of on Broadway at that time. Dorothy McNichols and Flash Reilly did an eye-catching jitterbug in the "Times Square Ballet" that ended Act I, but both McNichols and her friend Jean Handy (the little cousin Robbins had advised about a career in dance was in the chorus) say *On the Town* was the first integrated show on Broadway without the stereotypes and without a separation of black and white dancers.

The three buddies' search for Gabey's elusive Miss Turnstiles sends them running all over town, and in a sense, the city is the star of the show: its subways, its skyline, its nightclubs, Times Square, Coney Island, the Brooklyn Navy Yard, the Museum of Natural History, Carnegie Hall (all revealed through Smith's vivid drops and flats that skimmed in and out). Smith called *On the Town* "a valentine to New York." Even its history gets into the act; Chip (Cris Alexander) reels off from his antiquated guide-book the names of long-gone desirable places such as the Aquarium and the Hippodrome while Hildy jerks her cut-out taxi around, insisting, "Come to *my* place!"

Bernstein's score captured the stress and relentless speed of New York, its changing rhythms, its ongoing traffic and lit-up nights. Like *Oklahoma!,* the show begins on a quiet note. No singing-dancing chorus. Just one sleepy Navy Yard watchman with a formidable bass voice, stretching as he sings, "I feel like I'm not out of bed yet. *(yawns)* A-a-a-a-a-a-h." But when he finishes his brief song and a whistle blows, a flood of sailors cata-pults onstage, and by the time the three heroes have finished their song, the men of the dancing chorus are vaulting across the stage, one hand reaching up to grab the skyline.

> New York, New York, a helluva town,
> The Bronx is up and the Battery's down.
> The people ride in a hole in the groun'.
> New York, New York, it's a helluva town!!

It's as if the shipboard pressure has been building up until, released, the men explode into life, avid to seize not just the day but the whole city.

Robbins, Bernstein, Comden, and Green, with Smith's input, managed to make the musical reflect everything that mattered to them. It was "sym-phonic" in its fusion of elements. Comden and Green, who'd been audi-tioning unsuccessfully for shows as performers, wrote for themselves the fat parts of Ozzie and Claire de Loon. Green's rumpled looks became fod-der for the witty scene in which the anthropologist mistakes the sailor for a museum specimen of *Pithecanthropus erectus* and starts taking his mea-surements. Robbins's dances were a vital part of the action, justified by Times Square's madhouse of human traffic, slow drags in nightclubs, and Coney Island orientalism, and culminating in a dream ballet. Bernstein put almost everything he knew and loved about American popular music into the score: jazz licks, swing, blues, Gershwin, the big baritone aria that makes you think of *Show Boat,* a fox-trot rhythm here, a hint of square dance there. But the vivid musical gestures, surprising textures, complex harmonies, and unexpected rhythmic shifts come from Bernstein, the twentieth-century classical composer. What other Broadway music man of the day would have exploded his opening chorus into raucous counter-point? Abbott teased him about "that Prokofieff stuff" in portions of the score but didn't cut a bar of it.

During a 1981 symposium on *On the Town* that brought the collabora-tors together, Bernstein made it clear just how cooperative the process of putting the show together had been:

> [Jerry] would say, "As a practical matter, I've got to have four more bars here or I can't get my dancers from left to right and offstage," and I would say, "I can't do four more bars, that would just drag it out," and I would do four more bars, then it would usually turn out to be a better piece with the extra material, because Jerry's instincts are incredible, musically.

When the composer loathed what he'd written for "I Get Carried Away" ("this little polka-like cowboy tune. It wasn't like me"), it was Comden and Green who suggested he try it in the minor key: "Suddenly we had this operatic feeling which dictated the whole form of the number, the whole duet quality of those two quasi-operatic voices that brought down the house."

Robbins had never choreographed for so many dancers before, and Abbott's busy schedule allowed only two weeks for out-of-town tryouts (in the end, they had ten days). He brought in his old Tamiment colleague Anita Alvarez to assist him and invited Mary Hunter to lead the dancers in some rather Stanislavskian preliminary improvisations (in one, they had to explore animal behavior) to get them suitably down to earth. How-ever, he seems to have worked confidently and adroitly most of the time. His choreography for the Miss Turnstiles number cleverly pointed up the ephemerality of her sudden celebrity. A line of women sidesteps on, backs to the audience, bent forward, butts wiggling, while an announcer talks up the contest and a spotlight roams over the line. It finally stops, and Ivy Smith straightens up and turns in ecstatic surprise. After a dance of light-ning changes reflecting all the inconsistencies in her effusive contest-entry description ("She's a home-loving type who likes to go out nightclubbing"), the line of next month's hopefuls sidles in and absorbs her back into anonymity.

For the action-packed "Times Square Ballet" that ended Act I, all the ensemble men are in uniform, throwing balls to win stuffed bears when they aren't dancing. Robbins created orderly but combustible traffic patterns for ensemble and principals and played with variants of social dancing as he had in *Fancy Free*—the sailor who slow-drags with his head on his partner's bosom, the girl who decorously keeps her hips pulled back as far as possible. Having composed a satiric "oriental" dance for himself and Anita Alvarez back at Tamiment, Robbins must have had fun concocting the cheap "Turkish" trio at Rajah Bimmy's where Ivy is employed picking up a handkerchief with her talented teeth. When lust and the displays at the Museum of Natural History not only carry Ozzie and Claire away but carry them back to a comic dream of 6,000,000 B.C., three skimpily clad female pterodactyls and three cavemen draw the pair into an improbable prehistoric social dance. Critic Edwin Denby found the most striking number of all to be Robbins's staging of "the monkeyshines of the principals" in the terrific "You Got Me," when Chip, Ozzie, Hildy, and Claire attempt to cheer up the despondent Gabey (he's been stood up by Ivy, who has to work) with a song and dance about all *they* have to give him. (Chip: "You got my whole family in Peoria, for you to see! And it's free, Gabey, it's all free.")

Robbins also had a chance to experiment with less light-hearted dances. One, a pas de deux, expressed the darker side of shore-leave pickups. After Gabey (John Battles) has sung Bernstein's lovely ballad "Lonely Town" and slumped onto a bench, a passing girl (Nelle Fisher), one of a group of teenagers, bumps—or gets pushed—into a sailor (Richard D'Arcy). This sailor wears a dark winter uniform instead of the summer whites of the "Times Square Ballet," and though he begins gently—sitting with her on a bench, measuring her hand against his, her foot against his—it's clear what he has in mind. In Robbins's notes, this guy knows "very well how to manage her, when to show affection, and when he can really come out with his hot lust when it is too late for her to back off." Their duet ends with a clinch, "his hands caressing her body." She pulls away, ashamed and embarrassed, and the sailor, according to D'Arcy, thinks, "What am I doing with this nothing?" When a more knowing blonde slinks by, he follows her without a backward glance. As the innocent backs up, she bumps into Gabey, and though he only means to offer sympathy, "she thinks, 'Oh no, not another one,' and runs off the stage."

The idea of a dream ballet that advanced the plot of a musical was a fairly recent invention, although dream sequences and visions figured in ballets, straight plays, and operettas at least as far back as Victor Herbert's *Little Nemo* (1904) based on the surreal comic strip. *Lady in the Dark* had dream sequences; Balanchine choreographed one, "Peter's Dream," for *Babes in Arms*. De Mille's masterful "Laurey's Dream" in *Oklahoma!* (1943) set a precedent with its somber Freudian undertones; it not only alerted the heroine to the true menace of Judd Fry, it revealed the sexual tension that accompanied her distaste for him. De Mille had also choreographed for *One Touch of Venus* a dream in which the goddess imagined herself a suburban housewife. The ballet in *On the Town* exists to show the doubts that creep into the exhausted Gabey's mind as he sleeps on the subway bound for Coney Island and to reveal how misguided are his visions of Ivy as famous and his seedy destination as a playground for the rich and famous. Cleverly, Robbins turned the rhythmic swaying of the passengers into a somnambulistic dance. "Then from the end of the subway," wrote Robbins in his plans, "Ivy appears, resplendent in a long flowing gown. She drifts toward the dreaming Gabey who looks up. Then she leads him invitingly to the center of the car which splits in half and rolls offstage leaving Gabey and Ivy in a black limitless void."

Actually, Oliver Smith's sparkling dream Coney Island materializes in blue as a "wonderful, suspended, fluid and dreamy sophisticated place for rich people." While the glamorous and coolly impersonal denizens of this space dance, Gabey fantasizes himself as "the Great Lover," and a dream double (Ray Harrison) enters to execute what's described in the script as a "jazzy, slick, ingratiating, torchy, sexy dance." "It was a long, hard dance," remembers Allyn McLerie, who performed in the ensemble and later played Ivy, "and he ended up on people's shoulders, but there was no applause." (Robbins became known for downplaying a climax or undercutting it in order to avoid breaking the flow he'd built.)

A prize ring of white ropes and poles is set up on a diagonal, and in it Ivy and this self-assured Gabey spar. Apparently Robbins, busy with the ensemble, left this "fight" until a few days before the traditional Boston tryouts that preceded a Broadway opening. According to Osato, he finally arrived at rehearsal, grinning and carrying a length of red jersey. He handed one end to her and the other to Harrison.

Next, with a slight shove, he set me turning into its length until I was wound in Ray's arms. It worked. Then we spent hours experimenting, winding the jersey around my waist, chest, and neck until it finally ended up as a turban round my head. Enormously pleased with his invention, Jerry said, "Now Ray will pull on one end and your hair will tumble down."

This fantasy-Ivy lassoes Gabey with her turban and wraps him up like a spider putting a fly into cold storage. She is declared the victor in the bout, which the real Gabey watches in horror.

Considering the complexity of the show and the short tryout period, it's not surprising that in Boston, Robbins apparently succumbed to nerves and disappeared for forty-eight hours. A few dances were still unpolished. A solo for Osato "in one"* wasn't working, despite the promising idea of having her dance in a Carnegie Hall corridor to whatever music she hears coming from the studios: "[H]e had done a dismal little solo for me, really—listening at the doors of Carnegie Hall. I felt like an idiot. Just trip, trip, trip, listen at the door, trip, trip, trip, listen at the door. And I remember I danced it once and I think one person applauded one clap. And I remember thinking to myself, 'Oh-oh, it's got to be better than this.'"

According to Richard D'Arcy, the efficient and impatient Mr. Abbott called in Alice Dudley (an old Tamiment colleague of Robbins's) to finish the choreography, but before she could do anything, Robbins reappeared and created a simpler and more effective little solo—remarking years later how helpful and encouraging Osato had been. As Osato observed, "You know, most people don't come to rehearsal and say, 'This project is too immense for me.' They look as though they can handle it. But looking back, I think it just overwhelmed him and he got to the point where he had to go away and just sort of catch his breath."

As of December 15, while Jerome Robbins was polishing his *On the Town* choreography, the troublesome Jerome Wilson Rabinowitz ceased to exist—on paper anyway. Sometime in the fall of 1944, he decided to legalize his professional name. What is more remarkable is that he applied for the name change together with his mother and father. It was as Harry

---

* "In one" is theater lingo for the strip of stage closest to the audience. With a curtain closed behind it, the action "in one" can cover a scene change that otherwise might slow down the pacing of the show.

and Lena Robbins that they would hereafter attend his openings, proud to be acknowledged as his parents.

When *On the Town* sailed into New York on December 28, 1944, spruce and smart and ready to lure the holiday crowd, one critic, John Chapman of the *Daily News,* found it "dullish" and sighed, "Cripes, what I would give to see a good old hoofing chorus again!" Writers at the other New York papers, however, were far more enthusiastic about the show's originality. Jack O'Brien of the Associated Press relished the "opportunity to heave his hat into the stratosphere and in general start the sort of journalistic drooling over a musical comedy that puts an end to all adequate usage of superlatives." The most constructive criticism for Robbins came from Denby: "Just now, his ideas do not develop in space easily, but he doesn't try to cover up by complicated patterns or ornamental gestures; he concentrates instead on clarity of impulse and variety of pacing." Louis Biancolli, writing perceptively in the *New York World-Telegram* more than a month after the opening, thought he detected a revolutionary change in the world of musical comedy: "We're used to actors bursting into song in a musical. Now they burst into dance . . . and we accept it." He felt that the entire production

> had been planned, worked out, and delivered in a ballet key. By that I mean the sense of kinetic action is felt, even where ballet isn't the featured factor. Ballet and song often appear geared to a dynamic pattern, as if any moment things will blaze again into dance. I sensed that repeatedly in the Bernstein music.

The collaborators were dazed to find lines at the box office. After the opening, Robbins and Nancy Walker hied themselves to one of those studios where anyone could record something on a tiny 78-rpm record. You can hear the euphoria crackling through as they try giddily to sing "New York, New York"; Walker manages to belt out a line or two, but Robbins keeps dissolving in giggles, and eventually they both crack up.

On the Town racked up 463 performances on Broadway (plus a national tour) and might have run longer had the end of the war not taken some of the edge off its subject matter. A February 1945 program contained a jingle by playwright George S. Kaufman urging the audience to buy war bonds ("The bonds that you purchase today, tra la / Go only for winning the war. / But each little dollar you pay, tra la, / Will bring you that dollar and more"); by May, Germany had surrendered, and, by August 14, Japan. No longer were sailors going off to a war from which they might never return.

⌒

Robbins's name appeared in the show's advertisements and programs not just as the choreographer; *On the Town* was "based on an idea by Jerome Robbins." If the success of *Fancy Free* had changed his life and his status in the dance community, *On the Town* pushed him a step higher on the fame ladder, bringing in offers and necessitating decisions. In a *Cue* interview published in March 1945, he mentioned that he was working on Aaron Copland's opera *The Tender Land* (a project that would not come to the stage until nine years later) and had been offered two productions of Gilbert and Sullivan's *Pinafore* (one with an all-black cast). Jerry, who'd acquired a reputation for pushiness among his Ballet Theatre colleagues and for being something of a user, told John Kriza that he could no longer be sure who really liked him and who simply wanted something from him.

He began his career as a dog lover by getting a squash-faced Belgian griffon that many of his friends thought horrid. He hired a clipping service to help him fill the scrapbooks his sister had started for him and, deciding he needed help handling phone calls and correspondence, enlisted an aunt—probably his Aunt Jean—to help him. Many years later, he told a young assistant, Rhoda Grauer, a charming story—undoubtedly dramatized for the occasion—about this "professional" relationship. When the phone rang and someone asked for him, his aunt would say, "Just a minute, please," call him, and hand him the receiver. He explained to her that the reason he needed someone to answer the phone was that he didn't wish to talk to everybody; she should please take down name, number, and message and tell the caller he wasn't in. Aunt Jean: "Jerry! I can't *lie!*" After some thought, her nephew worked out a solution: "All right, I tell you what. You say, 'Just a minute, I'll see if he's in,' and then you look for me, and if you don't see me, go back to the phone and say, 'I don't see him!' " Thereafter, every time the phone rang, he would hide in a closet.

At some point after *On the Town* proved to be a hit, Robbins assumed the mantle of the good and successful son and offered to finance his parents' retirement. Comfort Corset as a corporation had been legally dissolved in 1943; an outside company sent the factory the garments already cut, and Comfort's employees stitched them up. Harry and Lena could now move freely between their Weehawken apartment at 17 Fifty-first Street (for years Robbins's own legal address) and a cottage in Bradley Beach on the New Jersey shore and spend more time visiting with their grandchild, Cydney Cullinen (to be joined in 1946 by a brother, Robbin). Robbins felt munificent, but with leisure time to fill, says their daughter, Sonia, "they complained all the time."

Robbins kept no datebooks or calendars for 1945 (at least none seems to have survived), nor did he save—as was his later habit—every letter that dropped into his mailbox. Perhaps he was too busy juggling offers and plans, still somewhat unsure of what direction he should take or how much work he could reasonably manage. We don't know how he felt about a film deal with Samuel Goldwyn, the first of his edgy encounters with Hollywood. Articles in three different newspapers from February 1945 indicate that he had signed with Goldwyn to create the numbers for a film (possibly *Wonder Man*) starring his old Tamiment colleague Danny Kaye; one writer has Robbins and Kaye heading for Hollywood on May 1. Robbins told an interviewer for *Cue* that he had plans to involve the camera in the dancing. However, on April 2, Leonard Lyons reported in his syndicated column "The Lyons Den" that Robbins had told Goldwyn he no longer wanted to go to Hollywood. The columnist prodded Robbins: Was this a personal matter? Was he in love? Yes, Robbins told him. And she doesn't want to go to Hollywood? No. "OK, you can tear up the contract," concluded Lyons. Whether the "personal matter" and being in love had a connection was moot, and Jerry cleverly allowed Lyons to assume that the amour was a woman. His analyst, Frances Arkin, believed that homosexuality was "curable" and, with Robbins's cooperation, worked with him to that end. Gossip queen Dorothy Kilgallen's March 14 column mentions that Robbins and actress Lois Wheeler, then performing in *Trio* on Broadway, seemed to be "a Sardi romance," and in 1999 Wheeler told writer Greg Lawrence that a marriage between them had been mentioned. The real issue may simply have been a disagreement with Goldwyn.

Robbins still had one foot in the ballet world. In March, he wrote an article for *The New York Times Magazine* called "Ballet Puts on Dungarees," talking about the new informal, "American" tone in classical ballet—a tone that might help make ballet less of an elitist institution. A week before Lyons reported that the Hollywood deal was off, Robbins signed a new principal's contract with Ballet Theatre for the company's Metropolitan Opera season. It's clear that he dictated the terms to the new directors, Lucia Chase and Oliver Smith: He would dance only in *Petrouchka, Fancy Free,* and *Helen of Troy* for $150 per performance. He would do *Petrouchka* only on weekend evenings, except during any extension of the season. A substitute (probably Michael Kidd) would dance *Fancy Free* on the four Saturday matinees, and, during the possible extension, Saturday matinees and one evening each week. He would not rehearse these ballets. For the rest of 1945, he would be paid $50 per performance. With the advice of his agent, he was on his way to building his reputation as a shrewd businessman. Chase and Smith were undoubtedly eager to have him. The season's ad featured *Fancy Free,* and R.B. of the *New York World-Telegram* reported that on the first anniversary of the ballet, Sol Hurok presented Robbins with a gold watch onstage.

During Ballet Theatre's season, if Lyons is accurate, Robbins also found time to create an eight-minute song-and-dance routine with Edward Chodorov and Colonel Jay C. Flippen, "the veteran vaudevillian," for Chodorov's play about a touring USO troupe in Italy, *Common Ground.*

It was incumbent upon Jerry to choreograph a second ballet, and in the spring of 1945, he drew up a list of nearly twenty ideas. Some were rehashes of his Tamiment hits such as "Frankie and Johnny" ("might be very exciting done with colored cast"). One, working the Americana vein, was about "country life"—barn dance and all. One, hard to imagine as a ballet, was a psychologically charged glimpse into an ultimately tragic friendship between two men—one "wealthy, crude, yet sensitive," the younger, "bitter, slightly talented and vicious" (perhaps a painter and a critic, he thought). In keeping with his Communist Party connections and social conscience, he mentioned a scenario, not fully formed in his mind, that would deal with the rise of fascism and plotted a "Negro Ballet" that would contrast the South during slavery with a Harlem scene. He thought about approaches to *Cinderella* (using Eric Coates's music) and to the *Pagliacci* story. He jotted down in his list Copland's *Quiet City* (he finally got around to it in 1986). And he began to think about a ballet based on S. Ansky's play *The Dybbuk* (which materialized in 1974).

He also outlined in some detail an ambitious *Cook Book Ballet,* which was to be a compendium of the elements of theater: slapstick, production numbers, tragic scenes; he had myriad ideas for little acts. Never choreographed, the outline nevertheless generated ideas he would use later in shows and ballets; for instance, a tall-man-short-woman gag found its way into *Look Ma, I'm Dancin'!,* others into the hilarious "Comedy Tonight" opening of *A Funny Thing Happened on the Way to the Forum.* The dancers for *Cook Book* would be onstage warming up as the audience entered, and, knowing the financial state of ballet companies, he would have them clad in practice clothes, "& use only those props you might find in the theater, a ladder—chairs—pail—horses—etc." (He took a similar approach to props and scenery in his 1946 ballet *Summer Day* and his 1976 *Ma Mère l'Oye.*) The above words were to be part of an opening speech delivered by Robbins, during which he planned to acknowledge to the audience the influence of Thornton Wilder's *Our Town,* with its Stage Manager narrator. In his patter, he would introduce members of the troupe by name and remark, "By the way, I'm Jerry Robbins—I dance in this now and then too. This is all very unorthodox, I know, but so is Saroyan—& *I* respect him."

He was apparently still reluctant to drop *Bye-Bye Jackie.* According to Bernstein's biographer Humphrey Burton, Robbins approached Bernstein about writing music for it and Lenny turned him down. Robbins's list of future projects noted that *Jackie* was to have a score by Paul Bowles. In his memoirs, Bowles, at the time a neighbor of Robbins's in Greenwich Village, recalled the choreographer talking to him that spring about composing music for the ballet that turned out to be *Interplay.* Bowles wrote of their conversations, "He worked in a very different way from the choreographers with whom I had previously collaborated. To me everything he said had the air of being supremely subjective, almost to the point of being hermetic. For Jerry it was somehow connected with the psychoanalysis he was undergoing at the time. We never managed to get anything decided during our discussions, and finally we gave up the project. Later Morton Gould wrote the score." Bowles was wrong about that last. Gould was not commissioned to write the score; his *American Concertette* for piano and orchestra predated the ballet. Robbins's list of possibilities included a work to the Gould piece: "This would be a bright dancey ballet to the Morton Gould suite which is in four movements and includes a polka and blues. The whole suite is based on [a] jazz flavor. Runs about fifteen minutes."

Bowles's words about Robbins's psychological approach seem more applicable to the story of *Bye-Bye Jackie* and its restless young hero than to *Interplay,* Robbins's frisky second ballet. Although later in his career, Robbins spoke as if he had always planned to follow *Fancy Free* with a plotless work, since "*Fancy Free* . . . was so specifically a story," one can speculate that *Bye-Bye Jackie* somehow became *Interplay*. Both were conceived for eight dancers. Robbins could have taken the Brooklyn neighborhood kids and the games they were to have played and abstracted them for his new ballet.

Interplay was not choreographed for Ballet Theatre, although it entered the company's repertory in October 1945. Robbins got an offer he was not about to refuse: Billy Rose signed him to find dancers and create a ballet for a new revue, *Billy Rose's Concert Varieties,* opening at the Ziegfeld Theatre in June of that year. For his $1,000 a week, with a guarantee of four weeks, he was also required to perform in his own work.

This was a show with ambitions. Louis Kronenberger, in a review titled "Culture Larded with Comedy," said it fell "halfway between art and entertainment." Music critic Deems Taylor served as master of ceremonies for a potpourri that included Spanish dancers Rosario and Antonio, Katherine Dunham's troupe, the Salici puppets, Mexican tenor Nestor Chayres, and boogie-woogie pianists Albert Ammons and Pete Johnson with Sidney Catlett on drums. Imogene Coca did several numbers, including the Tamiment "PM of a Faun" with William Archibald. The other comedians were Eddie Mayehoff and Zero Mostel (the latter imitating a politician, an opera singer, and a coffee percolator). Robbins remembered it as "a wonderful show." The critics were skeptical. Like most, George Jean Nathan thought that art and vaudeville were uneasy partners: "If you are going to mix culture and corn, it's better to serve the corn cob and not go for half measures."

Some of the highest praise went to Robbins, and when Ballet Theatre premiered *Interplay* on October 17, John Martin noted that "Jerome Robbins' *Interplay* set out quite deliberately to prove that not all American dance theatre works had to be storytelling, genre or period pieces, but that a purely formal approach could be made to composition in a strictly native vein and still be good. Mr. Robbins certainly made his point."

Irene Sharaff's costumes aided the ballet's bright, clear image. In the *Concert Varieties* version, Robbins had worn a yellow velvet shirt with green stripes and Janet Reed a yellow tunic with green stripes over a long-sleeved green shirt (she loathed it). A backdrop showing swings and slides added to the kids-at-play look. Sharaff dressed all the men in black tights with different-colored long-sleeved T-shirts with modified turtlenecks and the women in black tights and long-sleeved black leotards topped with short colored tunics, open on the sides. The tights are footless and the ankles are bare, giving the illusion of bobby socks. Robbins cast *Fancy Free* buddies Harold Lang, John Kriza, Janet Reed, Muriel Bentley, plus Tommy Rall, Melissa Hayden, and Roszika Sabo; Michael Kidd was listed in the program, but Fernando Alonso danced instead. By then busy with a new musical, *Billion Dollar Baby,* Robbins only occasionally performed in the ballet. (In the *Concert Varieties,* he'd danced the leading role in every section of *Interplay* every night, plus Saturday and Sunday matinees, and nearly killed himself.)

In *Interplay,* Robbins took a lighthearted view of American teenagers, or rather of American dancers *as* teenagers; the games they play have both vernacular and balletic elements. The darker images of youth that he dealt with later in *New York Export: Opus Jazz* and *West Side Story* never found their way into this ballet. The swinging ponytails, leapfrogging boys, and considerate bumptiousness suited the war years' optimistic vision of American culture—an apple pie cooling on every windowsill.

A program note explained the title: "There is interplay among the dancers themselves. There is interplay of classical ballet steps and the contemporary spirit in which they are danced. There is the interplay of the dancers and the orchestra, interplay of piano and other instruments and an interplay between classical and jazz elements."

Robbins might well have taken to heart Edwin Denby's words about his choreographic ideas for *On the Town* not developing in space, and indeed, in reviewing *Interplay,* Denby praised Robbins's grasp of how time, generated by the "musical architecture" of the jazz-infused score, was made to interact with the architecture of the stage space. "Free Play," the ballet's first section, skedaddles all over the stage, its re-forming, developing patterns keeping the spatial picture building. One guy dances, a second enters, they travel stage right together to pick up a third, then dance down left to capture a fourth. Arms around one another's shoulders, backs to the audience, they step side to side. After one of them breaks into a brief, explosive, in-place solo in one corner, they absorb him into a line stretching from front to the rear of the stage, play a little canonic game about leaning sideways, and then take off as a squad. After the women enter, Robbins weaves all manner of patterns—playing vertical lines against diagonal ones and a snaking farandole against a grand right-and-left in a circle against two country-dance ranks—boys facing girls. At one point, all eight dancers come forward, peer into the pit, and boogie for a few seconds, as if each, carried away by the music, were improvising a wild response to Gould's hot licks.

Throughout the ballet, Robbins uses steps that allude to popular dance and games or stunts: leapfrog, hopscotch, cartwheels. The leader of the second section, "Horseplay," ends his solo balancing on one leg, the other stuck out to the side, hands clasped overhead in a victory gesture—the way Lang ended his *Fancy Free* number; also reminiscent of the earlier ballet is a competitive bit when two of the guys step wide over each other's feet, each trying to get ahead. The dancers whip off a variety of classical steps: many, many turns of different sorts, pas de chats, chassés, grands jetés. But the choreography emphasizes a more grounded preparation, so it looks as if they are bursting into spunky motion. Robbins also played around with ballet's courtly behavior: little bows and greetings (especially noticeable in the second section, which Gould titled "Gavotte," and in a pas de deux, "Byplay," which Reed performed with Kriza in the Ballet Theatre version).* The duet featured conventional partnering techniques as well as some unusual lifts; in one of these, the woman is lifted high, then slides down and around the man's body as he turns, ending on the floor. The effect is both easygoing and sensual, as if both kids were enjoying the prolonged and variegated contact.

The tone of the ballet is breezy—even, at times, a bit cute—and for once it seems appropriate to call the performers "girls" and "boys" (as many ballet and Broadway choreographers traditionally do, even though some of these perpetual adolescents may be in their late thirties). The dancers seem to have an irrepressible energy and to change their minds every few seconds without pausing for thought. As critic Marcia B. Siegel has pointed out, the duet is "romantic out of all proportion to the casualness of the encounter." Often the two do the same steps side by side, like pals. The more sensual partnering suggests that these young people from a more innocent age find themselves trying on intimacy the way they'd investigate a new game, without committing themselves to it. They end sitting cozily close on the ground, but their pose is without erotic overtones.

In *Interplay*—relaxed, rough-edged, unpretentious, but fastidiously structured—Robbins established an aesthetic that was to remain crucial to

---

* Many of the impressions of *Interplay* are drawn from a 1945 silent film of the Ballet Theatre cast that featured Harold Lang, Janet Reed, and John Kriza.

his work. He built an image of community. The dancers may face the audience quite a lot of the time, but they seem to be dancing for each other and *with* each other. Inaugurating a device that heightened this impression—a device he would use many times—Robbins made them spectators too. The men lounge on the floor and watch the women as they weave nonchalantly around the area. One man, winded, sits in a downstage corner during the second section. As the third section begins, Reed tries to get him on his feet to dance with her, but he waves her away; it's almost accidental that she and Kriza begin to move together. During the duet, other dancers pick up the music's dreaminess and stand at the back or down in front, silhouetted, slowly shifting their hips from side to side. The last section, "Team Play," which presents balletic virtuosity as a competitive sport, uses "behavior" in a more obvious way. After a face-off in which two guys want to outturn each other, leaders choose teams, and each dancer gets a chance to shine for a few seconds. Out of the huddles, handshakes, and excited jiggling in place, every step becomes fodder for the competition; fouetté turns, tours en l'air, girls dragged in splits. A canon looks less like a compositional device than a bout of follow the leader. It was fortuitous that *Interplay* was made for only eight dancers; Robbins could teach himself the fundamentals of choreographing for a ballet ensemble before he had to deal with a full corps.

Interplay may be easygoing, but it's far from easy. Rehearsal footage from the 1990s that shows Robbins rehearsing members of the New York City Ballet reveals how critical timing, focus, and impetus were to him from the very beginning, as well as illusory spontaneity. He loved to have dancers look as if they were doing a step for the first time, no matter how many hundreds of times they'd practiced it. That air of discovery became one of the hallmarks of his style and, ironically, something to be labored over in rehearsals.

⌐⌐

Robbins moved into a better apartment in mid-August 1945. For $165 a month, he leased the entire fifth floor and roof terrace at 24 West Tenth Street. It was furnished and included a piano, which "the landlord may remove if at any time he may desire to do so." Jane and Paul Bowles lived at 26, Oliver Smith (he and Bowles were distant cousins) at 28, Bernstein at 32. They used to visit one another by crossing the roofs. Years later, a young friend of Robbins's expressed awe at these giants of the theater behaving like kids. Jerry: "We didn't know who we were then."

In the 1970s, when he was jotting down memories for a never-completed autobiography, Robbins wrote nostalgically of his time on Tenth Street and the unplanned gatherings at Jane Bowles's late at night (the Bowleses, an unconventional couple, had separate flats). "Somehow we'd all be lying on Jane's huge bed, like at a picnic or on the beach. And we'd talk. I don't even remember about what. Someone would tell a story or play some music. Those evenings I felt as if Jane's bed became some special raft on which we all floated off, lolling, resting, talking, being silent but so easily comfortable in each other's presence." He loved Jane Bowles's writing and yearned to direct her play *In the Summer House;* "Oliver, producing it, chose someone else (wisely)."

Jerry's cousin Robert Silverman recalls the heady game playing that went on in those apartments—not only charades and word games, such as Twenty Questions, but a sort of musical quiz with dollar stakes. They'd sit in a circle on the floor and put one player in the center, along with a hat for the money, and he or she would try to identify musical excerpts sung by the others in turn. Silverman, himself a musician then training at Juilliard and much later the publisher of *Piano Quarterly,* was awed by the brilliance of the company. On one evening, the players were "Jerry, Adolph, Lenny, [composer] Marc Blitzstein, myself, and maybe a couple of other musicians, and we'd throw out things like the second theme from the Borodin String Quartet, second movement." Adolph Green could beat everyone at this game. Jerry must have held his own. In one testament to his musicality, which Silverman calls "tremendous," the two of them sang in the car all the way from New York to Providence, playing around with Bach's two-part inventions. "I'd give him the theme; he'd start, and I'd come in. We also made up rounds; we harmonized."

Robbins later wrote that in the Tenth Street days, he had affairs with men and women and went to meetings of his Communist Party cell: "Both seemed to be conducted under water."* During this year stretching from

---

* Robbins stopped going to meetings in the spring of 1947. In 1980, he wrote in his notes, "My leaving the party was not because I thought they were a threat to the U.S. in any way. The party seemed too feeble, chaotic, unbalanced, in at least the area I was exposed to, to seem anything more than noise making rowdyism—If there were any stronger strains, strings or strengths around it, I never saw it."

summer 1945 to summer 1946, he enjoyed the company of duo pianists Robert Fizdale and Arthur Gold (who at some point rented the apartment of the inveterate traveler Paul Bowles), Edwin Denby, and the dancers Francisco Moncion, Todd Bolender, and Tanaquil Le Clercq (shortly to become founding members of George Balanchine and Lincoln Kirstein's new Ballet Society), as well as the up-and-coming actor Montgomery Clift, with whom he was beginning a sustained and well-camouflaged affair.

A pattern was developing in Robbins's professional life. From 1944 to 1955, he choreographed a musical comedy a year and one or two ballets almost every year. The alternation seemed to suit him. Broadway shows inevitably involved compromises; in the ballet world, he had near autonomy. And the two mediums yielded different sorts of satisfaction—one significant difference between them being the amount of money each brought him. The two also fed each other artistically; devices, even movements, from a ballet might find their way into a musical and vice versa. However, none of the musicals he worked on between *On the Town* and *West Side Story* twelve years later was constructed on a dance impetus. Finding ways to brighten an existing plot with clever numbers had its attractions but wasn't ultimately as satisfying.

He discovered that he loved doing research. Three of the 1940s musicals he choreographed after *On the Town* were set in the American past: *Billion Dollar Baby* (1945) in the late 1920s, *High Button Shoes* (1947) in 1913, and *Miss Liberty* (1949) in the 1880s. He immersed himself in each period, discovering the popular dance forms on which he might build, as he did with the Charleston for *Billion Dollar Baby.* He explained to an interviewer that he had studied magazine cartoons of the twenties for this show and gone to the Museum of Modern Art to look at silent movies of the period. Four of his successful ventures were directed by George Abbott, which meant that they were lean and fast-moving despite their intricacies of plot—true musical comedies, rather than romantic plays with singing like Rodgers and Hammerstein's *South Pacific.*

Robbins was in the middle of choreographing *Interplay* when he began work on a second project involving Gould's music. Among the offers Bernstein turned down in April 1945 was Oliver Smith's new Broadway venture, which Smith had hoped would unite the *On the Town* team. Koussevitsky had given Bernstein holy hell after *On the Town.* "His attitude was unequivocal: a potential great conductor must not dissipate his talents." That summer, Gould joined Comden and Green—who were still performing in *On the Town*—in turning out the book and music for *Billion Dollar Baby,* a cautionary tale about the late 1920s, and in October rehearsals began. Robbins signed a six-week contract to serve as choreographer at $750 per week plus 1 percent of the gross. Abbott directed, and Smith designed the decor, as well as producing the show.

Billion Dollar Baby appears to have puzzled the public. Gould's music was bright and sophisticated but not of the caliber of *Interplay*'s *American Concertette.* Twenties nostalgia had not yet burgeoned; Helen Gallagher, who danced in the show, thinks even the costumes and hairstyles may have jarred 1940s audiences. More importantly, as Comden and Green point out, *Billion Dollar Baby* viewed the 1920s from an unusual perspective. Their book was no Jeeves and Wooster romp or as giddy as the 1949 *Gentlemen Prefer Blondes* or the much later retro hit *The Boy Friend.* "We tackled the end of the twenties when the crash came. The whole show built up to the 1929 stock market crash. . . . It was a very sardonic show and was not totally merry because it has this very tough ending." And a comedy that related Prohibition not just to wild parties, bobbed hair, and short skirts but to mob killings had a dark side. The critics, perhaps inevitably, compared it with *Pal Joey* because of its intermittently comedic gangster population (one song, "Speaking of Pals," referred to the many former cronies it had been necessary to bump off). John Chapman of the *Daily News* liked it better than *On the Town,* and Howard Barnes of the *Tribune* called it a "honey," but most reviewers, such as Ward Morehouse of the *New York Sun,* equivocated, saying that the show displayed not much humor but had "considerable life." Louis Kronenberger's thoughtful review in *NY PM* was titled "A Fine Try Just Misses," and amid the praise and respect that he doled out for the venture, he zeroed in on what he saw as a major flaw: "For one thing, it can never quite make up its mind whether to burlesque an era or to catch its real quality of melodrama." He also disparaged a "hammer and tongs quality that never lets up, that begins as exhilarating but winds up as wearing." Toward the end of his life, Abbott ungenerously and rather inaccurately blamed a part of the play's less-than-dazzling success (it managed 220 performances) on its leading lady, Joan McCracken: "She had fat legs and you can't have a great beauty queen have fat legs and have it convincing. She had what we called ballet legs in those days."

This heroine was not the good girl audiences root for. Maribelle Jones is pretty and charming, apparently innocent, and absolutely without scruples. It's not that she loves money, she says, it's that she loves the things you can buy with it. Having missed out in the finals of the Miss America contest, she abandons her nice boyfriend, who works on the Staten Island Ferry and enters marathon dance contests, and works her way dubiously upward—seducing a bootlegger's shill; his gangster boss (played with comic ferocity by David Burns), who runs a speakeasy; the boss's bodyguard; and finally a billionaire. As a result of her machinations, men are killed and romances wrecked. By way of a moral message, things end well for the nice guys, and news of the Crash comes at Maribelle's wedding to her billionaire. Pandemonium invades the ceremony as half the people, unaware of what's happened, celebrate and the rest panic. As the bride is tossing an expensive bracelet to the crowd, the groom is scrabbling to pick it up.

The show gave Robbins fine choreographic opportunities, the most memorable of which was "Charleston." Adolph Green thought it was one of Jerry's best show numbers. It happened downstage, outside the speakeasy. One of its impressive aspects was the way Robbins individualized the chorus dancers (he and Agnes de Mille were among the few Broadway choreographers who took pains to do this). Each person has a distinctive, if stereotypical, character and attacks the Charleston in his or her own way. Besides the policeman, who begins the number by walking perkily into view on his toes, flipping a foot out in a hint of a Charleston and swinging his club, Robbins delineated a Park Avenue couple (long cigarette holder), a collegiate couple wearing raccoon coats and swigging from a flask, another young couple, an old couple, a red-hot mama, three identical flappers, gangsters delivering boxes of booze (the cop turning a blind eye). They don't arrive onstage all at once but come and go, infected by the dance and emitting little cries of "Whoopee!" or "Hotcha!" by way of punctuation. A shy girl, shocked by the drinking of the college pair, gets dragged into the speakeasy by a "good-time Charlie" hoping to wash away her primness with bathtub gin. Ann Hutchinson Guest, who played the part, recalls what happened: "A bit later, the door opened, the gangsters rolled out backward, and then I came out, just pushing them away, and then went into this terrific shimmy (which was why the costume had to have a lot of fringe). And then the music went silent while I suddenly looked down and saw [my] hips going and [*shocked scream*] stopped them." In the end, Robbins brought everyone onstage to exhaust themselves with a knee-twisting, foot-flinging dance that lands them flat on their backs, weakly lifting a leg or an arm now and then and half sitting up to sigh a

"Whoopee!" or two before gathering their strength to rise, jump, enter the speakeasy, and dash out again for an applause-grabbing group pose.

The plot included two dream sequences. In one, Robbins satirized silent-movie clichés, at the same time hinting at Maribelle's voraciousness. She imagines herself as a succession of film queens driving men mad. First, she's a little darling like Lillian Gish, whose bashful country-boy suitor (supposedly based on Hollywood star Richard Barthelmess) holds out a bunch of flowers. She's so overcome he has to chase her around the couch with it. Their lips move exaggeratedly. "For *me?*" she mouths as he proffers a ring, and then she whacks him with the bouquet in her delight. Next, a slinky Maribelle is swept off her feet by a whip-wielding Rudolph Valentino type who trades her rose for his cigarette and pulls her into a tango. Finally she's a Theda Bara–style Cleopatra, seducing a slave (Robbins was thinking of Ramon Novarro) who's fanning her. He kisses her foot; she points to her knee; he kisses that. Then, at her command, he drinks poison and dies at considerable length. In the end the men all fight over her, and, in a comic melee, as all three struggle for a knife, she gets stabbed. The startled suitors drop kisses on her as they leave.

In the other, darker dream, Maribelle, contemplating a future with Rocky, the bodyguard, imagines a dank scene in a nightclub, where a couple of hookers in singlets and tight short pants flirt and indulge in rather acrobatic shenanigans with thuggish customers. McCracken performed a steamy pas de deux with James Mitchell (as Rocky's dance double). The dream ends when he grabs her by neck and ankle and flips her upside down, evidently making it clear to her that any future life with him will involve danger on every level.

Telling a reporter of his many ideas for "ballet plays," Robbins mentioned that he had used these ideas a bit in *Billion Dollar Baby*'s "final psychological ballet." He created the duet before the show ever went into rehearsal. Like McCracken, Mitchell was dancing in *Bloomer Girl,* a show celebrated for Agnes de Mille's choreography, when Jerry invited him to be in *Billion Dollar Baby.** Mitchell accepted. Then Robbins said he'd have

---

* De Mille tolerated the loss of Mitchell; she wouldn't stand in the way of what was obviously a good career move for him, but, in a letter to Jerry dated October 24, 1945, she was not so sanguine over the loss of some of her ensemble: "I don't think it is quite ethical to tease the chorus boys away at a time when they are so dreadfully difficult to replace. . . . I cannot bear to think of you and me playing at this cut-throat game, and caring not a damn what hurt we do to one another's works and reputations. Out of friendship and respect, I think we should not raid one another's shows unless we can better the lot of the individual dancer."

to audition. As Mitchell remembers it, the "audition" turned out to be two weeks of rehearsing for several hours a day: "He choreographed the entire pas de deux that I did with Joan McCracken. The entire thing. Lifts, everything. He was small enough that I could lift him." The union, Actors' Equity, was not as strong then as it later became, and Robbins was without shame; he finally said that he guessed Mitchell could do the part.

Dancers remember with delight the funeral procession for Dapper that was added during tryouts in New Haven. The gangster's henchmen and girlfriends cross the stage "in one," holding up signs betokening revenge on Rocky, as well as such sentiments as "I was Dapper's best girl." Each "lady's" bouquet of calla lilies is larger than the one before. As Arthur Partington (the cop in the Charleston) remembers it, "Dapper's girls were all in black and white with big hats and veils and doing Black-Bottom-dirty bumps and grinds. . . . The guys would stop and do a buck-and-wing for about sixteen counts and then continue on." Several critics singled out a number that satirized the Ziegfeld showgirls, with lavishly befeathered singers, who doggedly continue to flute, "A lovely girl is like a lovely bird," even as Rocky is shooting his boss, Dapper Dan.

A couple of numbers Robbins did not choreograph occurred during a dance marathon. Danny Daniels, the tap dancer extraordinaire who played Champ, Maribelle's original boyfriend, had auditioned for the show with a solo he'd choreographed while in the Army. The creative team liked the dance a lot. As Daniels tells it, when Champ and his partner, Esme, are declared victors in the marathon, "They [Robbins, Abbott, and Gould] arranged for the winner to go kind of berserk and grab the drumsticks from the announcer." Then Champ launches into the virtuosic solo. Daniels also choreographed the dance steps that accompanied a song he had to deliver, "I've Got a One-Track Mind," while Jerry labored over the Charleston and the second-act ballet. Daniels received neither program credit nor extra pay: "I never even thought of it, to be honest with you; I just wanted to do a good number."

Robbins won his first Donaldson Award (a precursor of today's Tony) for *Billion Dollar Baby*'s choreography. Doubts the critics and the public had about the musical did not apply to him. He was, wrote Lewis Nichols in *The New York Times,* "generally accepted as the hero of the new show." *Billion Dollar Baby* closed in the fall of 1946, but Robbins wasn't finished with it. Sometime during the next summer, he began to map out in detail a potential film version. Penciled inside a script are the words "screen version—I did or wrote dance sequences & discussed whole picture with J. [Jerome] Chodorov."

In the projected movie Maribelle is nicer—a gullible Staten Island kid, pushed by an ambitious mother. Robbins thought of her as adapting to the driven ways of the people she meets, her conscience dizzied by the mad whirl of late-twenties gaiety. In the end she returns to her home and good old Pa and looks pleased when her original modest-income boyfriend comes calling.

Robbins's notes reveal his fascination with cinema, the acuteness of his visual sense, and the way dance rhythm underlies some of his most ambitious ideas. The beauty contest was to have a "jazzy distortion. . . . It is the contest as seen through the eyes of nerve-wracked Maribelle [Miss New York] and from our looking back at the disjointed twenties. It should look somewhat like a more humorous version of the fair grounds of *The Cabinet of Dr. Caligari*." He wanted the camera to tilt down, cut diagonally across, and peer up at people to give the feeling that everything was going too fast and edging out of control. The floats on which each contestant entered were to be "exaggerated symbols," and he saw Maribelle perched on a papier-mâché skyscraper, her pose as precarious as her future. He envisioned the judges' inspection of girls and ensuing consultations occurring at lightning speed (he used the technical term "undercranked") with the bevy of girls diminishing accordingly.

Among his elaborate plans were a yacht sequence involving a rolling ship and Maribelle's growing drunkenness as she wheels between Dapper and Rocky. He suggested that three girls being pursued by three gangsters be suspended slightly on piano wires "so they can achieve weird balances in compensation for the boat tilts." Here's how he saw the final wedding-plus-stock-market-crash: "The picture bursts and flies into pieces and becomes confetti-like as it swirls about." Amid the montage are shots of a banker's car being sucked from his garage, his wife's jewels and furs falling from her.

He ended his notes, "In other words treat the whole film as a musical sequence, so that the all over feeling of the picture has a complete style of its own as *Henry V* [he had seen Laurence Olivier's film in June] and *Caligari*." We may never know if it was a version of these ideas that he submitted to Hollywood or what was made of them. Were they found pretentious, too fancy, or out of line coming from someone who'd been consulted primarily as a choreographer? In any case, in August, Robbins was paid

$2,500 for his work on the screenplay, but the picture never materialized. (At the same time, he also made some kind of contribution during the shooting of David O. Selznick's film of *Portrait of Jennie,* starring Jennifer Jones, for which he also received $2,500.)

Hollywood sang him a siren song, but firmer commitments on the West Coast continued to elude him.

7

The Broadway-Ballet Seesaw

John Kriza, Robbins, and Nora Kaye at the climax of Robbins's *Facsimile*.
Jerry Cooke/Getty Images.

Mention *Robbins's name* to just about anyone even vaguely connected with the theater, and you're likely to be told a version of the same story. It's the one anecdote about Jerry Robbins that has been handed down with relish from one generation of Broadway gypsies to the next and passed around ballet companies. Some people are sure that the event it chronicles happened during a rehearsal of *West Side Story*. Others argue that it must have occurred during *High Button Shoes*. No, says a third, "I was in that show, and I never saw it." Another decides, "I don't believe it ever happened." It takes a bit of sleuthing to track down the facts: the episode occurred, several dancers agree, during a rehearsal of *Billion Dollar Baby*.

This is the story: Robbins is onstage, his back to the footlights, giving the dancers notes. As he enumerates their failings and what they damn well better do to improve, he begins backing up. They all watch him, silent, frozen. And they remain silent as he steps off onto air and falls into the orchestra pit. After the fall, says James Mitchell, "Nobody moved. Luckily he didn't fall hard; he fell into the tympani. It was stage right and the drum section was set up, so he had a little cushion. And he might have grabbed onto the apron or whatever. But nobody really moved. Nobody ran forward and said, 'Oh, my God!' It has become the myth that nobody helped him out. Just let him crawl up." Nobody is quite certain whether the dancers were furious enough to let it happen or whether they were simply paralyzed—unable to believe he wouldn't notice what he was doing—or whether they were so used to not interrupting that they couldn't break the pattern. In the 1980s, Robbins countered a query about it by a lover, Brian Meehan, only by saying, "That's not exactly what happened."

Why do showbiz folks cherish this story? For one thing, it presents the foul-tempered choreographer getting his comeuppance from dancers, who by tradition and out of necessity are docile. The nonintervention of *Billion Dollar Baby*'s cast members took passive resistance to new heights. And it must have given Robbins pause. He could be considerate, high-spirited, and fun to be with away from work—going to the beach or Coney Island amusement park, for instance, with dancers he considered friends. His sense of humor could flash out at work, too. He was famous for his giggle. Several of the women he worked with fell in love with him (and undoubtedly some of the men did as well). However, he could turn into a Mr. Hyde during rehearsals—especially rehearsals of shows, when the pressure was more intense. "He was," says James Mitchell, "the most charming, lovable son of a bitch that I have ever known." (Others, such as William Weslow, who danced for him in the 1950 musical *Call Me Madam*, would place "sadistic" prominently among those adjectives and drop the "lovable.")

When Robbins was a chorus boy himself, in *Straw Hat Revue*, he wrote disapprovingly in his diary of choreographer Jerome Andrews's difficult rehearsal manners: "I think Jerome doesn't really want to act the way he does when he directs except that he really can't help it." He saw this, yet took no lesson from it. His temper was a demon that wanted out when the going got rough, and it brooked no interference from his more rational self.

Many choreographers have a reputation for being nasty. The dictatorial ballet master with the little cane is a familiar figure in ballet lore. A dancer familiar with Robbins during his first decades as a choreographer might well have said to another, "You think Robbins is bad? Try Antony Tudor or Jack Cole." Many years later, Robbins wrote this about Cole, whom he very much admired, for *Vanity Fair:* "He had the temper tantrums of a child whenever any little thing didn't go exactly his way. . . . It was as if Cole, finding the world imperfect, was trying to choreograph a super-perfect world of his own, where people—dancers—behaved ideally and exactly as he wanted. And when that didn't happen—watch out." Jerry might have been looking into a mirror. George Balanchine, too, could be cruel; he just never used bad language. The rages, cutting remarks, and occasional spiteful behavior are not excusable, but they are understandable. In none of the other arts does the artist have to create a work from scratch with materials that get injured, have upset stomachs, talk back, or can't learn fast. Every choreographer has experienced times when nothing looks right. Deep down, he or she knows that the problem may lie with the steps, but it's easier to believe that the dancers just aren't doing them right or giving their all. Choreographers whom dancers love, such as Donald Saddler, struggle against assigning blame too readily. Not Jerry. Ann Hutchinson noted that when asking to see a section he had choreographed the day before and finding it unsatisfactory, he would be far more likely to say, "What *are* you doing? I never gave you that" than "Was that what I did yesterday? I don't like it. I want to change it."

With any choreographer, there's a necessary degree of molding that goes on. Like Tudor, Robbins could be ruthless in the ways he goaded dancers into doing more than they thought they could. Helen Gallagher, in the chorus of *On the Town* and a featured player in *High Button Shoes,* brings to mind Tudor's modus operandi when she talks of Robbins: "The way I remember it . . . he would take the skin off your bones and then build you back up. That's how he did it. He destroyed you in order to make you into what he wanted you to be." She acknowledges that the process was risky, "but if you loved him—and we did—and loved the work . . . I mean, we were *crazy* about working with him." That "we," of course, does not include everyone who ever danced for him but those he particularly admired, who showed they liked him, and who weren't afraid, either of him or of the level of commitment he demanded. Nor does it include the dancer in *Billion Dollar Baby* who used to shake when Robbins looked at him hard and to whom, according to Virginia Gibson (then Gorski) of *Billion Dollar Baby,* Jerry said things like "I want this lively, *lively,* and if you don't do it, I'm gonna stick a firecracker up your ___." (Robbins put it more bluntly than Gibson.)

Sondra Lee, a dancer in *High Button Shoes* and Robbins's Tiger Lily in *Peter Pan,* gives an excellent impression of a dark mood coming over Robbins. "He would turn black. His eyes would darken and his lips would swell. And his eyes went out of focus. They were shifty, nervous. They would almost vibrate." When he looked like that, dancers knew better than to speak to him. Says Gallagher:

> If he got blocked, I mean, a black pall would descend. It was just *oppressive,* and we'd all just sit around. . . . Because the way he got over it always was to have a scapegoat. . . . He would end up screaming at somebody, and then the work could come, but it could be as much as three days, and the ones of us who considered ourselves "his" dancers— the ones he'd rehearse things on or go to the beach with—we would sit there and say [to ourselves], "Oh, please, let him even scream at *me,* anything to get over this." Because it was such fun working with him. I would sell my soul to the devil to work with him.

Lighting designer Beverly Emmons, who worked with him much later, put it succinctly. With certain directors, when things weren't turning out the way they wanted, "You had to scrape them off the walls. Jerry looked around for someone to kill."

The victim might be a dancer who didn't seem to be fully invested in the choreography. Or simply someone who got on his nerves in some way. Perhaps it was Jerry's inner Lena (the maternal voice goading him to seek the grail of perfection) that caused him to drive himself and his casts hard and to create version after version of the same passages of choreography. He resented people who didn't give their all over and over. Until his last, slightly mellower years, he seemed to work with blinders on, impervious to performers' fatigue or looming injury. Suzanne Johnston was a dancer he liked both professionally and personally. She tells a curious story. While she was dancing in the road company of *High Button Shoes,* her fiancé, stationed in Panama with the Air Force, was killed on a mission. She thought she'd better perform that night, rather than sit in her room and go out of her mind with grief. Robbins came up to her afterward and rebuked her for looking lackluster, without her usual sparkle. She told him what had happened. He said only, "If it had been anyone but you, that person would have been out of the show." It was as if he simply hadn't been able to process what she'd said, so focused was he on his vision and her dereliction. And yet this is the same man who, in Spoleto in 1973, when his young assistant, Rhoda Grauer, received news of her father's death, sat beside her holding her hand for an entire evening. Grauer, of course, was not a performer putting his work in jeopardy.

Sensitive to the opinions of others in regard to his work, he was quick to interpret a look or a shrug as implicit criticism. Allyn McLerie, who had first adored him as a starry-eyed young dancer in *On the Town* and of whom he was very fond, noticed during rehearsals for *Miss Liberty* (she played the lead) that he was teaching a dance not to her but to her understudy, Maria Karnilova. She called him and asked him what the matter was. "He said, 'I don't know, Allyn Ann. You know, I've changed. You've changed. Somehow you take the starch out of me. I feel that you're criticizing me.' I was *criticizing* him?!" They worked it out.

He particularly disliked performers who flaunted their own egos or curried favor. "When Jerry could smell that," says Sondra Lee, "his eyeteeth got fur."

However, he often backed off when people stood up to him privately: "Don't you *ever* speak to me like that again." And he admired spunk, because, paradoxically, he didn't enjoy being thought a villain. When Lee was cast in *High Button Shoes,* she was very young and *very* naive. She went up to him and said she thought they ought to have a coffee and talk. Why? She wasn't sure—just for them to get to know each other better. He gravely agreed, and if he hadn't loved her before, he did thereafter.

On certain occasions, Robbins could be childishly malevolent—especially with male dancers he craved who were not yielding to his advances. Malevolent because the punishment was not the product of a sudden burst of rage but something that had to be planned. In *Call Me Madam,* William Weslow knew a solo bit of Tommy Rall's that Weslow refers to as the "Wild Man from the Mountains" (part of a Gypsy number that was later dropped). As Weslow recalls it, at the final run-through before an invited audience, just before the company departed for out-of-town tryouts, Robbins called Weslow aside and told him that when Rall came onstage, he wanted Weslow to do the whole routine in back of Rall—"full out, all the screams, all the pirouettes." Weslow argued that he couldn't do that; it would upset Tommy, etc. "Shut up and do it!"

> So Tommy came out—"Yaay yowww!"—and I came out—"Yaay yowww!" We started the à la seconde pirouettes and everything. All of a sudden, Tommy stopped and said, "Wait a minute, Bill, what are you doing?" And I said, "Well, Jerry told me to come out and do it full out in back of you." So he said, "Jerry, did you tell—?" Jerry said, "No, I didn't. That pushy little son of a bitch. He's just trying to get your role, that's all."

According to Weslow (Rall doesn't recall the episode), Robbins, who was unsuccessfully pursuing him, was trying to foment hostility between the two men.

Dancers who wished to work with Robbins put up with the problems in exchange for the rewards of performing choreography that excited them. Agnes de Mille had been a major figure on Broadway since *Oklahoma!,* yet, says dancer Arthur Partington of Robbins, "He was *it.* He was *the* choreographer you wanted to work with. I did a couple of shows with Agnes, then I did several shows with Jerry, and then about five shows with Michael Kidd. Nobody was in his league. And, personality aside, it was fabulous working for him."

Performers were not the only ones to experience the demands of collaborating with Robbins and the eruptions of his seemingly uncontrollable temper. He became notorious for taking scissors to costumes in front of their appalled designers. In 1948, Monty Proser, the coproducer of *High Button Shoes,* clearly spoke from a position of knowledge: "That little squab has a flame in his belly. I wouldn't want to be the sucker who tried to stop him from doing what he wants to do."

Jumping back and forth between Broadway and the ballet world not only nurtured Robbins aesthetically; the former subsidized the latter. Robbins, while chiding Ballet Theatre's management for letting financial considerations derail the pursuit of excellence, never wished to consider "starving" and "artist" as interdependent terms. In 1946, his finances were in good shape. His ballets earned him a pittance, but it was a fairly steady pittance. His $10 per-performance royalties from *Fancy Free* averaged $50 a month between May and August (he continued to fume for years over the ironclad contract he'd signed in his eagerness to get his first ballet produced). His *Interplay* royalties were $20 per performance, and the total for the year came to $153. For *Facsimile,* his 1946 offering to Ballet Theatre, he was paid $1,500 plus per-performance royalties of $25. The musicals earned considerably more. In the spring of 1946, *On the Town* was still running, after which it went on the road. His *On the Town* credits for both choreography and original idea yielded 2.5 percent of the gross. A typical weekly royalty check amounted to $826 (of which he had to pay his agent 10 percent). His royalties from *Billion Dollar Baby* were figured at 1 percent; the show typically grossed $30,000-plus a week. In 1946, a year when his weekly expenses (judging from the sums he typically withdrew from his checking account for that purpose) amounted to $100, these fees added up to a considerable income. And back in 1944, his bank account may have been bolstered for some time to come by a lump sum paid him by MGM for the film rights for *On the Town.* Even before the lease on his Tenth Street apartment expired, he moved to 421 Park Avenue, at Fifty-fifth Street, and started interviewing maids.

With *Billion Dollar Baby* up and running, Robbins turned his attention to Ballet Theatre. In a couple of ways. *The New York Times* had already announced that he had teamed up with playwright Arthur Laurents to write what became, in 1948, *Look Ma, I'm Dancin'!,* a musical based on his own touring experiences with Ballet Theatre and his struggle to succeed as a choreographer. However, on February 15, 1946, Laurents signed a letter saying he couldn't write the book "due to the pressure of other matters" and offering to surrender any ideas or suggestions he had contributed in discussions (he had written a scene-by-scene outline and come up with the title). The "other matters" came down to pressure from Laurents's then-psychoanalyst, Theodore Reik, who seems to have considered "versatility" a dirty word and wanted Laurents to concentrate on his play *Heartsong.* "This man made me crazier than I was. But I *knew* I was crazy, and I desperately wanted help, and anything he told me. . . . So he said don't do it, and I said I couldn't do it, not realizing that wasn't a very decent thing to do. Jerry was furious and got me to sign this paper giving up the whole rights, which I thought was only fair." Robbins, undaunted, continued to turn *Look Ma* over in his mind.

His 1946 datebook, which begins in May, reveals that Robbins saw a lot of Montgomery Clift, with whom he was by now much in love. Also that he attended Horton Foote's new play; Gian Carlo Menotti's operas *The Medium* and *The Telephone,* produced by Lincoln Kirstein's newly founded Ballet Society; and the Old Vic's now-legendary New York season featuring Laurence Olivier and Ralph Richardson. He visited his therapist, Dr. Arkin, Monday mornings, with a few extra appointments when needed. In May, he also took ballet classes with Helene Platova—sparingly, it must be admitted—to get himself in shape for Ballet Theatre's first London season. In addition to appearing in his own ballets, he wanted to dance *Petrouchka* a few more times and had consented to do *Helen of Troy* and *Three Virgins and a Devil* as well.

During the spring of 1946, Robbins was functioning as a member of Ballet Theatre's Artistic Advisory Committee, in charge of making suggestions about repertory, company policy, and more. The other members were Aaron Copland, Henry Clifford, Antony Tudor, Agnes de Mille, and company directors Chase and Smith. Among the planned ballets that failed to come to fruition was an abstract work by Robbins to Vivaldi music. He had specified in his contract that he would require forty-five hours of rehearsal time for it. Getting those hours proved to be impossible. Ballet Theatre's rehearsal schedule didn't begin until mid-May, and the company sailed for London in late June for the opening of its Covent Garden season on the Fourth of July. Twenty-one ballets from the repertory had to be prepared and kept in shape. Robbins worked on the Vivaldi during the London season. However, Frederick Ashton, the Sadler's Wells Ballet's esteemed principal choreographer, was teaching a group of Ballet Theatre dancers his charming 1937 skating ballet, *Les Patineurs* (which was to become a repertory staple), and Tudor, as artistic administrator, was hogging rehearsal hours to polish his *Undertow* (he was evidently nervous before an English public that had considered his move to America in wartime a kind of defection). Robbins, whose demands for inordinate amounts of rehearsal would always be a cause of hair tearing on the part of company directors, abandoned the Vivaldi and, after dancing one final *Petrouchka,* flew home on July 28. Apparently he was not leaving out of pique; the company's run had been extended to the end of August, but he had planned on staying only a month.

He could leave London with the knowledge that *Fancy Free* and *Interplay* were audience favorites and that the company as a whole had made an excellent impression, especially in terms of its "modern" ballets and the theatrical flair of its performers. Ballet Theatre was exactly what the English expected something made in America to be, and after the grimness of the war years, they were ready to celebrate vigor and high spirits. One can detect just the faintest condescension in *The Times* of London's critic's warm appraisal: "Its characteristics are, as one would expect, vitality and gusto, technical accomplishment and a very high polish, and an informing humor with less emphasis on charm and lyrical feeling."

The hiatus gave Robbins time for a Nantucket breather and a visit to Stockbridge to confer with Leonard Bernstein about their collaboration on the other work he had planned for Ballet Theatre's fall season at the Broadway Theatre, *Facsimile*. This season was the company's first since the management had terminated its agreement with Sol Hurok, and it found itself up against a rival, ensconced for a simultaneous season at its own previous stomping ground, the Met. The unquenchable impresario Hurok had decided to present another ballet troupe: The Original Ballet Russe of Colonel de Basil. The Original had spent much of the war years, 1942–1946, touring Latin America and, despite Hurok's recruitment of prestigious stars such as Alicia Markova and André Eglevsky, was in ragtag shape (it was said that the touring schedule had been grueling and classes to keep the dancers in shape rare). Ballet Theatre, at the Broadway, countered this new sort of Russian invasion with an opening-night program that trumpeted its contemporary point of view: *Interplay, Pillar of Fire,* and *Fancy Free.* It had lost one *premier danseur* (Eglevsky) but had gained Igor Youskevitch, discharged from the U.S. Navy and almost as splendid as ever. New York's ballet public was looking forward to Robbins's new ballet, and, in a nod to the rivalrous situation, Edwin Denby titled his *Dance Magazine* account of the season "Ballet Theatre Wins."

Robbins logged approximately 120 hours of rehearsal on *Facsimile.* The premiere had to be postponed seven days—to October 24, 1946. (During the last weeks of rehearsal, he upped his sessions with Dr. Arkin to four times a week.) Originally the cast consisted of A Woman, A Man, Another Man, and Some Integrated People (a chorus of eighteen). As rehearsals progressed, the eighteen became ten, and during the dress rehearsal the ensemble listed in the program disappeared altogether—leaving only the "three insecure people" and baffling both critics and audience.

Robbins built the ballet on Nora Kaye, Hugh Laing, and John Kriza. However, he, not Laing, danced the first man on opening night, and friends and family sensed a connection between the situation depicted and Robbins himself, maybe even a situation involving him and his intimates, Kaye and Kriza. Certainly the work reflected an interest in psychology that choreographer and composer shared—an interest fueled by their own psychoanalysis, as well as by current trends in the arts. In 1944, Martha Graham had made *Herodiade,* her first major work in which the movement was impelled by the heroine's interior dilemma. In 1946, she produced the highly symbolic, almost graphically Jungian *Dark Meadow,* and *Cave of the Heart,* which probed the jealousy of Medea, revealing plot incidents through the perspective of the character's memory. Antony Tudor's 1945 *Undertow* took a Freudian approach to the formation of an agonized young murderer, complete with the traumatic childhood scene in which he sees his father and mother copulating. Too, the optimism that had prevailed during the war years was undermined by anxiety and restlessness as servicemen returned from overseas and tried to fit into new lives or take up former ones, while working wives returned to home and hearth and got pregnant.

In his history of Ballet Theatre, Charles Payne mentions that "*Facsimile* was intended to explore and elaborate an observation" by the medical researcher Santiago Ramon y Cajál: "Small inward treasure does he possess who, to feel alive, needs every hour the tumult of the street, the emotion of the theatre, and the small talk of society." The tone of the ballet couldn't have been more different from the cheeky verve of Robbins's two previous works. In the first place, it was a ballet about adults. *Facsimile* depicted a triangle, but not a conventional one; the men, despite tensions between them, shared the woman. It is pretty clear, however, from a fragmentary black-and-white silent film of Kaye, Laing, and Kriza, that the choreographer was primarily intent on bringing out the superficiality of these people's lives and desires, the idleness that leads them into potentially harmful games. Eroticism provided the key to translating his ideas into a physical language, and Bernstein created a score that began with the voice of a solitary oboe and ended on the same mournful note, as if all the dramatic effervescence and argumentative syncopations of the middle sections had failed to coalesce.

Few performers could have rendered Robbins's ideas with the nuance and drama of his original cast. He had already tested a working relationship with Kaye, whom he valued for her intellect, wit, and the powerful onstage presence she revealed, most particularly in Tudor's ballets. On the occasion of a benefit on May 2, 1946, for the Greater New York Committee for Russian Relief, he staged *Afterthought* (not usually listed with his ballets) for the two of them to Stravinsky's *Five Easy Pieces*. She is the linchpin of *Facsimile*—a highly gestural ballet with little dancing for its own sake. Robbins decided shortly after its opening to call it "a choreographic observation." The three protagonists try out attitudes, stop to see what kind of impression they're making, try something else. They react to one another's least move with amusement, excitement, despair, or suspicion.

The original program note strained for ambiguity. "Scene: A lonely place. Time: The number of minutes the ballet takes, or that many days, weeks, months, or hours." The lighting suggested night, maybe on a beach. Although Irene Sharaff costumed the two men in subtly decorated crewnecked shirts and belted footless tights in hot colors, Kaye wore a vividly striped leotard that resembled a bathing suit, Smith's spare set suggested remnants of a pier, and the piece of fabric Kaye drew between its poles—and behind which her shadow was briefly seen—might have been a bathhouse curtain. One critic's analysis refers to the first man entering with a towel over his shoulder and to a "beach robe" that the woman picks up at the end and runs off with. It is perhaps significant that another film, one that never materialized, was supposed to be shot on Nantucket in 1949.

Kaye is the aggressor. She lures the first man playfully. He's timid, or feigns timidity—dare he touch her?—and makes rather theatrical gestures, like pressing his hands to his heart or dropping to his knees and covering his eyes. As they sit, he kisses her foot, her knee, her lips. She doesn't point out the spots where she wants to be kissed as does Maribelle-as-Theda Bara in *Billion Dollar Baby,* but she might just as well. They lie on the floor side by side as if in postcoital relaxation. When they sit up, he seems surprised to see her there, and after each new kiss or stroke of a cheek, they lean back and size each other up. They dance together briefly.

When Kriza enters cockily, Laing ushers him toward Kaye. She and Laing crouch while the newcomer dances, making gestures of interest and approval. An uneasy threesome forms. They're able to dance side by side, laughing and a bit silly in an affected way. But they're easily bored with everything they start. As John Martin wrote in a perceptive review, "Without inner resources of any sort, they play around dangerously with psychological thrills." Laing appears upset when Kriza carries Kaye in a seated position, kicking gaily; and he's unprepared when Kriza tosses her to him. At another point, Laing runs in a circle embracing Kaye's foot while Kriza holds her in his arms and spins with her. Their closeness breeds unpleasantness. When Kriza and Kaye drop to the floor, Laing staggers wide-legged over them. They tangle. Kaye appears to sob. They tangle again before falling to the floor. The design, as careful as it is violent, looks like a Monkey Puzzle knot. Kaye screams "Stop!" (a bold departure from ballet's mute tradition). She sits for a moment, hand to brow, and then races away distraught, the "beach robe" streaming out behind her. The men withdraw, Laing upset, Kriza more nonchalant.

Denby thought the ballet "a big step forward by an honest, exceptionally gifted craftsman." The opposite viewpoint was expressed in extreme and mocking form by Robert Sylvester in the *New York World-Telegram*'s opening-night review:

In comes John Kriza in red underwear. Everybody gets all mixed up, kissing Nora some more, until at one point Kriza nearly kisses Robbins. Then Robbins kisses Nora's foot while Kriza kisses her on the kisser and runs her around Robbins like he was a maypole.

The facetiousness and vicious put-down may have rankled, but the reputations of neither Ballet Theatre nor Robbins were hurt by the fact that a few kisses had to be excised in Boston and that *Life* magazine devoted an elegant photo spread by Jerry Cooke to *Facsimile*'s more erotic moments.

Kaye received much praise for her stunning performance, although James Mitchell, who took over Laing's role when the piece was revived for Ballet Theatre's European tour in 1950, doesn't think she cared much for the ballet. Mitchell also tells a curious story about *Facsimile*'s choreographer. Robbins, in Europe to check up on details for the ballet's Paris opening, cornered Mitchell onstage shortly before the curtain was to go up. "Do a pirouette," he said. Mitchell whipped one off. "Do two pirouettes." Taken aback, Mitchell complied. "Do three." That was stretching it; Mitchell hadn't had a great deal of classical training, but terror galvanized him, and he did three turns. Robbins said, "*That's* the way I want your hair," turned on his heel, and drew a stool into the downstage wing, the better to keep his eagle eye on the performance. Was this a slightly crude directorial strategy to make Mitchell look and feel confused and excited, in keeping with his character? Or was Robbins subscribing to a common—and risky—belief that getting a performer nervous gives him an edge onstage?

In the spring of 1947, Robbins countered his steamy trio with a witty send-up of the standard classical pas de trois for Ballet Theatre's rival, the Original Ballet Russe, spending a week on the road with the company in order to prepare the work (one wonders how Lucia Chase and Oliver Smith reacted). *Pas de Trois,* set to the minuet of the will-o'-the-wisps and the waltz of the sylphs from Berlioz's *The Damnation of Faust,* featured Alicia Markova (at the premiere Rosella Hightower replaced Markova, who was downed by illness), Anton Dolin, and André Eglevsky. (During these early years of American ballet, leading dancers such as Markova, Toumanova, and Massine jockeyed bewilderingly back and forth among Ballet Theatre, the Ballet Russe de Monte Carlo, and the Original Ballet Russe.) *Pas de Trois,* Robbins's fourth ballet, appeared on the Original's last four programs in March, and although audiences enjoyed it, it made a minor impression, despite opportunities for virtuosic dancing and some good jokes. To Lillian Moore of *The Dancing Times,* it was "an irreverent and diverting bit of nonsense, a not too subtle but uproariously funny satire on classical ballet and the affected stage manners of ballerinas and premier danseurs," and John Martin cited with relish Eglevsky's elaborate and portentous preparation for a single, negligible pirouette and described a moment that foreshadows Robbins's hilarious "Mistake Waltz" in his 1956 *The Concert:* "[T]hey sneak glances at each other's fifth positions and resentfully shift the other foot forward to conform. . . ." After *Facsimile,* *Pas de Trois* may have given the choreographer valuable practice in devising nonthreatening ways to tangle two men and a woman together.

In 1947, Robbins also contributed a ballet to a May 12 program by the American-Soviet Musical Society that featured music for theater written by Russian and American composers. Serge Koussevitzky, the president of the society, knew Robbins's work through the choreographer's association with Bernstein, and composer Marc Blitzstein, who provided production support, may also have been instrumental in persuading Robbins to make a work for the event. Robbins again cast a satiric eye on ballet, but in a gentle way. Sergei Prokofiev's *Children's Suite* returned him to a world of innocence: a duet, *Summer Day,* for himself and former Ballet Theatre colleague Annabelle Lyon. The program note explained the premise: "Children while playing together make a comment on adults' behavior. In the same way, the child dancer whose imagination is stimulated by stage props improvises his impression of a professional." Lyon remembers that they started out in practice clothes. "I think he wore tights and a knit shirt. I was in *Carousel* at the time, and we used underclothes from that costume: a pair of short little panties, with ruffles around the legs. . . . Somebody added a peplum layer to make it look something like a little skirt." As photos show, tambourines elicited a tarantella, a hair bow rendered Lyon doll-like—a Coppelia—wings turned her into a sylph and so on. This slight piece gave Robbins a chance to explore further his interest in behavior that looked spontaneous and in dancers pretending to be people pretending to be dancers. Or in creating the image of people who just happened to be dancers. Walter Terry's review indicated that Robbins was right on the money:

> Quite naturally, the youngsters find much that is worthy of spoofing and they comment actively upon the dreariness (although their manner suggests that they recognize it as essential) of balletic exercises, of the false elegance that occasionally infects ballet and of the movement idiosyncrasies of well known individuals or types in the ballet world. Mr. Robbins has woven these dance cultures together with seemingly natural but carefully choreographed movement, such as a walk, a yawn, a passing gesture, a glance, and the result is a ballet, or a theatre piece, which presents a refreshing brand of satire.

It should be noted that *Afterthought* and *Summer Day* were Robbins's first "piano ballets." For the latter, accompanist Ray Lev, a woman with whom he had worked in Ballet Theatre rehearsals, was placed onstage. The little piece entered Ballet Theatre's repertory on December 2, and Robbins, after performing on opening night with Ruth Ann Koesun, handed over his part to John Kriza.

Pas de Trois and *Summer Day* hint that Robbins was gearing up for *Look Ma, I'm Dancin'!,* with its satiric view of the ballet world. At a cocktail party, he had met radio writers Jerome Lawrence and Robert E. Lee, whom he shortly recruited to produce the book, and was expecting the semiautobiographical musical he had dreamed up to be produced in 1947. While aboard the *Queen Mary,* bound for England for Ballet Theatre's season in the summer of 1946, he had penned a letter to "Dear Boys" (Lawrence and Lee), complimenting them on a scene they'd drafted and indicating that he was mitigating the discomforts of the tour by considering the experience as research that "will come in handy later on when direction and staging is necessary." His Ballet Theatre pals held a party in someone's bunk, and a steward, appointed to tell them to be quieter, got sucked in. "It wasn't long before Muriel-Lily [he was obviously observing Muriel Bentley for character traits that might suit his good-hearted heroine] was sitting next to him, sharing her paper cup of booze and lukewarm water . . . asking him all about decks and watches." The dancers gleefully dredged up incidents that stock every touring company's oral history of onstage goofs, "like the time Charlie Dixon's pants slowly dropped down and he couldn't pick them up because he had a girl sitting on his shoulder. . . . That was an exit!"

In September 1946, Robbins met with Hugh Martin, who was to compose the music and lyrics. A little over two weeks after *Facsimile* opened, he was involved with auditions and readings to do with *Look Ma*. His diary records that on December 30, 1946, he went roller-skating with Nancy Walker, who became the show's star, and during the spring of 1947, he conferred with George Abbott, who, in the end, would both produce and codirect the show with Robbins. However, *Look Ma* was delayed (Oliver Smith had considered producing it but did not), and on August 11, Robbins began rehearsing *High Button Shoes,* also involving Smith as set designer and Abbott as director.* For this show, Jule Styne wrote the music and Sammy Cahn the lyrics. The book was adapted from Stephen Longstreet's novel *The Sisters Liked Them Handsome,* with Abbott and the show's star, comedian Phil Silvers, jiggling Longstreet's script into the desired shape over the author's protests.

Silvers played the made-to-order role of Harrison Floy, a small-time con man adept at charming the ladies and coaxing money out of folks' pockets. Patent medicines, fake jewels, cars he doesn't own—he'll sell anything. He's also good at gambling swindles. Perpetually on the lam, he and his sidekick, Pontdue (comic Joey Faye), decide to try their fortunes in Floy's hometown. There his shenanigans focus on the Longstreet family but eventually involve practically the whole town. Before he's done, he has

---

* Actually, Robbins's friend Mary Hunter was slated to direct the show but was fired by the producers for incompetence. When she fought the issue (she and Robbins shared the same lawyer, William Fitelson), Robbins and others testified as to her abilities. She won a settlement and continued to receive royalties of .75 percent. *The Respectful Prostitute,* which she did direct, opened during the arbitration.

flirted with Mama Longstreet (Nanette Fabray, cast despite her youth) enough to make Papa (Jack McCauley) jealous; managed to become engaged to the daffy Longstreet daughter, Fran; unsuccessfully attempted to fix the important college football game by injuring and demoralizing the team (including Fran's boyfriend); and passed the family a Model T for $100, "practically free," which they later find out they have to buy from Ford. His final triumph is to sell swamp land belonging to Papa for $500 down payments per lot and make off to Atlantic City with the money (and Fran) before the angry buyers discover that they sink in mud up to their knees when they step on their new property. The Longstreets and the town bask in a happy ending, and Floy and Pontdue are once again on the run. Even as the crowd is singing "He Tried to Make a Dollar," the scoundrel is hopefully spieling about a powder made from the glands of female tigers.

Audiences that had felt little affection for a musical like *Billion Dollar Baby,* set in the year the stock market crash ushered in the Great Depression, could watch *High Button Shoes* and feel a twinge of nostalgia for the halcyon days before World War I, when automobiles and silent movies were a novelty, when the tango was shocking enough to be forbidden at the Yale junior prom, when ladies' bird-watching clubs met in front parlors, and when girls went bathing in the sea wearing several layers of clothing. *Meet Me in St. Louis,* for example, had succeeded as a novel and a film musical (1944). Besides, *High Button Shoes* was a sly, bright show that made people laugh at the ongoing waltz between gullibility and enterprising rascality.

Robbins told a reporter, "First I had to get the style and then I had to distort it. If I had done it exactly as it had been done, then it might look tame, might even be boring. It's like furniture. You don't furnish your home exactly as the Victorians did, for instance. You combine it with modern stuff to spike it up and give it emphasis." He read up on Vernon and Irene Castle's instructions for the Castle Walk, a polka, and a new "denatured" tango in which partners never touched (she kept her hands on her hips, he kept his in his pockets). He used the first in a postgame celebration in the Longstreets' garden and both it and the polka to accompany Fabray's flirtatious song "Papa Won't You Dance With Me" at the picnic held to promote the land sale. The tango (definitely not "denatured") made its appearance in a scene between the idle Longstreet son, Willie (Paul Godkin), and the family's maid, Nancy (Helen Gallagher).

For some reason, Robbins was reluctant to start on the tango. Gallagher says that he sent her and Godkin down to the theater basement to work on it with his former mentor Gluck Sandor, who was acting as his assistant. There was also a certain tension between the former Ballet Theatre colleagues Robbins and Godkin because Robbins had outdistanced him (Godkin gave his notice opening night to accept a choreography job, and Donald Saddler replaced him). Up through the last run-through before the company left town for tryouts, Abbott was asking, "Is that number finished, Jerry?" and Jerry, focused on other numbers, would claim he hadn't had time. This would not be the last occasion when distaste for something or someone led him dangerously close to cutting his own throat.

During tryouts in Philadelphia, when the scene arrived, Saddler would pull down the shades and try to inveigle Gallagher into joining him in the tango he was trying to learn from a book he'd ordered; after a few steps they'd run out of choreography and have to quit. "In would walk Nan Fabray, and the whole audience went 'Awwww!' [in disappointment]. You could hear it." Finally, says Gallagher, Abbott threatened to finish the tango himself, and for a more practical reason: Fabray needed more time to change her costume. "At six o'clock [Jerry] broke the dancers, and he stayed with us for twenty minutes and finished the number. In twenty minutes! And he said, 'Well, that's it! I've got to get back to teach a class' [to warm up the dancers for the performance]. He didn't want anything to do with that number, and we stopped the show cold that night. But the reason we stopped the show cold was because it was all about two people who didn't know what they were doing. And literally, we did *not* know what we were doing." The duet was successful enough to call for a brief, comic encore after the next scene. In a scratchy movie of Saddler and Gallagher filmed from the wings, you can see how hilariously botched the tango moves are. She bangs her knee on the ground; their legs fly out every which way and get tangled. He chases her about, grabs her, and they prowl sultrily, pressed together spoon fashion. In the encore, the hitherto shy maid grabs a shawl, bends Willie back over the table, and kisses him hotly.

One of Robbins's favorite numbers in *High Button Shoes* (he liked it enough to include it in his 1989 anthology of high spots from his musical comedy career, *Jerome Robbins' Broadway*) was a gentle, almost minimal soft-shoe number for Papa and Mama to accompany the song "I Still Get Jealous When I Look at You." The steps, which emerged from a stroll back and forth, are simplified versions of those that might have been done on any vaudeville stage by a couple of guys with canes and straw boaters, but Robbins shaded them with a touching combination of sedateness and roguish delight; the dance recalls this long-married couple's youth and makes them feel just a bit reckless.

A quiet little triangle that Robbins dreamed up and Abbott accepted appeared as an interlude in the procession of people crossing the stage "in one" to go to the picnic. Tiny Sondra Lee, playing a girl just edging into adolescence, entered with an older boy (Arthur Partington). Lee remembers the staging as very sensitive. "The little kid wanted to play youthful things and jump on his back and sort of imitate him, do the kind of sweet things that kids do when they can't express themselves." Partington tripped and fell at the feet of the beautiful Jackie Dodge (one of Robbins's most adored dancers); teasing him about his embarrassment, she drew him into a flirtatious duet, which ended when her boyfriend arrived to take her along to the picnic. "And then," says Partington, "Sondra comes on and wants to get back in the game and start playing around, and I push her and knock her down." What Lee remembers is that "the little girl saw him do this sort of awkward movement that the older girl taught him and she begins to cry and he holds her nose and tells her to blow it in his handkerchief and placates her in a very gentle, more worldly way than he would have if he had just played with her as a little girl." Then, as the curtain rose behind them, they joined the dancers going to the picnic.

Robbins was very adroit at depicting childhood, willing at times to come close to cuteness and sentimentality and yet not falling into that trap. And "I think," says Lee, "that he understood the outsider at every stage of life." More intimate dances, like this one and the little duet for Nelle Fisher and Richard D'Arcy in *On the Town,* gave him a chance to show how "serious" ballet ideas could balance the big production numbers that gave a show its wallop.

The jewel of *High Button Shoes,* however, is the hilarious Act II opener, "Chase Ballet—à la Movies of 1913." It starts innocuously in Atlantic City, with a singing chorus of girls in bathing attire delivering "On a Sunday by the Sea," diving into a succession of cardboard waves, and flirting with a lifeguard. A pair of twin girls meet up with twin boys to dance while Floy and Pontdue sneak around, and Willie, missing his chance to recover the bag of money from the land scam, ogles the ladies. But the number escalates into a hilarious chase, replete with double takes and missed connections; the beach frolics get mixed up with the Longstreets' attempts to get their daughter and the money back from Floy. A squad of bumblingly acrobatic Keystone Kops straight from a Mack Sennett silent movie mixes in. In the midst of struggling with the difficult number, Robbins hit on the idea of adding a Charles Addams-ish family of crooks—Father, Mother, and Baby—who are trying to steal the loot themselves. From then on, "his mind raced, and we were off and going," says Partington. Lee remembers Robbins taking her out on the sidewalk and rolling her in the dirt, both of them laughing like crazy, because Baby Crook needed to look grubby.

Before long, everyone in the ballet is tiptoeing in and out of Smith's row of bathhouse doors, emerging in odder and odder combinations, one of which includes a stray gorilla. In what *Time* magazine called "a masterpiece of controlled pandemonium," the police appear disguised as cossacks and dance accordingly. The crooks acquire tambourines and turn Italian. Suddenly there seem to be two bags of money. One gets filched right in the middle of a group tug-of-war. At the end, a bag is kicked and thrown, but as the entire ensemble strikes a pose, it drops into Floy's lap as neatly as does the gift Robbins has just tossed the audience.

As Arthur Laurents has remarked, "That kind of stuff in Jerry's hands was not musical comedy in my opinion; it was really—I don't know whether you want to call it farce—but it was a notch higher." The ballet showed how deeply Robbins was able to grasp the style of a source—the speed and exaggerated clarity of silent-movie comedy—and translate it into a number for the stage.

The whole thing is as intricately constructed as watchworks. There's not a single misstep in it. It was Robbins's ingenious sense of timing and contrast and build—so deliciously displayed here—that began to make him sought after to doctor shows that were in trouble. However uncertain he sometimes was in rehearsal—trying now this version, now that one— he knew when something worked or didn't work, and usually knew why. *High Button Shoes* received mixed reviews when it opened in New York on October 9, 1947, but it ran for 727 performances and garnered Robbins a Tony and a Donaldson.

From his experiences working in both musicals and ballets, Robbins was aware of the differences between choreographing for dancers and directing actors. Perhaps partially in preparation for *Look Ma, I'm Dancin'!,* he began studying how to foster the kind of performances he wanted and to gauge the impact of directorial suggestion. In October, he joined the brand new Actors Studio, headed by Bobby Lewis and Elia Kazan—two men he'd known since his days with Gluck Sandor and Felicia Sorel. Feeling a nostalgia for the old Group Theatre era (1931–1941), Kazan and Lewis had decided to start an organization that would give theater professionals similar opportunities to experiment and expand their craft. Contentions over how Konstantin Stanislavski's system was to be interpreted were still boiling and, according to Lewis, he and Kazan wanted to incorporate into the teaching of actors some of the changes of emphasis that Stella Adler had brought back from her conversations with Stanislavski in Moscow.

Among the members of Lewis's advanced group at its inception (Kazan took the younger performers) were Marlon Brando, Montgomery Clift, Maureen Stapleton, Eli Wallach, Anne Jackson, Herbert Berghof, Sidney Lumet, and Jerome Robbins. The class met three days a week, at first in a vacant church on West Forty-eighth Street. "My group," wrote Lewis in his autobiography, "would rehearse scenes in all styles, with particular emphasis on the process of 'inner action' or 'intention' (subtext), plus a healthy discouragement of working for emotion for the actors' own sake rather than for its relevance to the character and play." Without dispensing with the emotional truth so central to Stanislavski's teachings, Lewis was moving actors away from a slouch-and-mumble style and toward a sense of how era, social status, and even clothing affected behavior. It should be remembered that Brando, who had made his name as the loutish Stanley Kowalski in Tennessee Williams's *A Streetcar Named Desire* in 1947, had made his stage debut as the languishing young Marchbanks in Katharine Cornell's 1946 production of George Bernard Shaw's *Candida* and in 1953 received an Academy Award nomination for his Mark Antony in the film of Shakespeare's *Julius Caesar* and won the British Academy Award for Best Foreign Actor.

It's possible that Clift influenced Robbins's decision to join the Studio. Whether or not that's the case, Jerry participated fully in classwork. Lewis cast him in a scene from Clifford Odets's *Waiting for Lefty* as a victim of anti-Semitism—a young Jewish hospital intern—and remembered the look on Jerry's face when Lewis commended his emotional quality but remarked that "his physical movement was a bit awkward." Although Lewis resigned from the Studio over disagreements with Kazan in the spring of 1948, Robbins, judging from his 1949 calendar, continued to attend sessions with the various guest teachers Kazan brought in. The careful investigations of character in relation to situation expanded on the ideas Robbins had already absorbed from Sandor and Antony Tudor and reinforced his insistence on believable behavior even in plotless ballets.

Fetching offstage images abide from these years in the recollections of those in Robbins's circle, such as the twenty-three-year-old Brando kidnapping the twenty-eight-year-old Clift from a party at Robbins's Park Avenue apartment and the two zooming off on Brando's motorcycle together—in retrospect, seriously endangering the future of American theater and film. Apparently, few associates were aware of how intimate and emotionally charged the relationship between Clift and Robbins was. Clift had been behaving according to an unspoken Hollywood rule: he concealed his homosexuality by dating attractive women. As did Robbins— although Robbins was seriously interested in romancing the opposite sex, half hoping, with Dr. Arkin's help, to become a committed heterosexual. At approximately the same time he was involved with Clift, Robbins was considering marriage with the attractive blonde Rose Tobias (then an aspiring actress, later a casting director).

Rehearsals for *Look Ma, I'm Dancin'!* finally began late in 1947. Perhaps as a demonstration of his faith in its eventual success, Robbins asked for his $6,000 fee as "dance director" all at once so he could invest it in the show (he was also to receive 1.5 percent of the gross). The plot is relatively simple. While the Russo-American Ballet Company is slogging back and forth across the United States, two new arrivals shake things up. One is Eddie Winkler, who's done his apprenticeship on the borscht circuit and is hell-bent on becoming a serious choreographer before he's twenty-five, no matter how many toes he steps on. The other is good-natured Lily Malloy, who has also weathered a stint or two in the Catskills and wants to become a great ballet dancer; her family has amassed a fortune from its Texas brewery, and she is prepared either to subsidize the company or buy it outright. There are romantic tussles and fallings-out among Eddie, leading dancer Ann Bruce, and Larry, who's smitten with Ann. There's a bit of courtship foolery between the two juvenile leads. But the heart of the show is the life and financial perils of the company, and Eddie's progress as a human being and a choreographer.

The shipboard letter Robbins had written more than a year before made it quite clear just how much of himself went into the character of Eddie:

I think the essence of the story, and central conflict is the struggle of Eddie and his ambition driven actions (which are in part hostile gestures) in a friendly society. I am sure that Eddie is aware of these gestures, and of their hostility, to some degree . . . so that there is always some conflict and guilt when he goes chasing after the white horse of success rather than being a decent human being. . . . That conflict makes him a deeper character, and helps the audience understand him and warm to him. And as a character, it gives Eddie a hectic and stumbling quality . . . trying to plunge ahead, trying to understand what exactly feels wrong when he makes a mistake and senses censorship . . . trying to rationalize his way out of all guilt and responsibility on the grounds that the kids should understand that he really likes them, but he must get ahead. It is this "must" which is the sick thing in him. He feels that when successful everyone will like him . . . all the world will be his. All this stems from a great insecurity of feeling not accepted by anyone. I guess this really stems from his childhood life as a kid in a go-getter aggressive family. I think this was solidified in adolescence when the awareness of the huge world around him, plus the insecure feelings of being an adult (in a city) drove him desperately to plunge for recognition and attention by climbing the success ladder. Never-the-less, Eddie is a sensitive boy, not so far gone that he can't see outside of himself enough to see his mistakes (maybe dimly). . . . But in any moment of stress or anxiety the MUST and drive feelings carry away the insecure feelings.

The credits for the show read "Conceived by Jerome Robbins" and "Direction and Choreography by George Abbott and Jerome Robbins," which is to say that Abbott's directorial hand may have extended to certain choreographic decisions and that Robbins had a say about how "his" characters functioned. He had modeled them on individuals or types familiar to him. The producer, F. Plancek, stands for Sol Hurok. The choreographer, Vladimir Luboff, is modeled vaguely on Léonide Massine; he's prone to describing his future works in rhapsodic terms: in his Beethoven ballet, "spirits of darkness" reside in the piano. He announces at various towns where the company performs, "I must create a ballet about your beeootiful city" (possibly a reference to the Russian Massine's attempts to make "American" ballets such as *Saratoga* and *Union Pacific*). The company boasts a typically tempestuous Russian diva, her put-upon partner, and a wise-cracking dancer who travels with a pet bird named Pavlova.

The character of Lily Malloy owes a great deal to Lucia Chase, but in the interests of comedy and with Nancy Walker playing the role, all the two have in common is that they bankrolled ballet and were driven to dance. Lily is coarser, far less talented as a dancer, and perhaps more immediately chummy and lovable than Chase. As Arthur Laurents said of his original plans with Robbins, "Lucia had aspirations and she had taste, and as I recall it, that song about 'the third girl in the fourth row' would never have been in the show we talked about. It wasn't that kind of show." However, Walker, flat-footed and looking as if a tutu were an alien object that had landed around her, made the audience laugh with her balletic ineptitude (perhaps the source of Robbins's later, brilliant "Mistake Waltz" in *The Concert*). And the echt musical comedy number by Hugh Martin that Laurents was referring to got off some catchy in-jokes:

> I'm the first girl
> In the second row
> Of the third scene
> Of the fourth number
> In fifth position
> At ten o'clock on the nose.
> I'm the first blond in "Scheherazade,"
> The first swan in "Swan Lake,"
> Then I play the thorn in "The Specter of the Rose."
> In "Igrouchka," I'm a fairy,
> In "Petrouchka" I'm a bear,
> And in "Sylphides," I am something
> That will really curl your hair.

Robbins was able to cast many of the performers he'd worked with before, and others that he'd admired. From *On the Town* came Walker and Alice Pearce, who'd played Walker's eccentric roommate in that show (and had been the only cast member to make it into the film). Harold Lang was cast as Eddie and Janet Reed as Ann. Katherine Sergava, formerly of Ballet Theatre (and Agnes de Mille's "Dream Laurey" in *Oklahoma!*), stormed through the part of ballerina Tanya Drinskaya. Virginia Gorski (later Gibson) of *Billion Dollar Baby* played the juvenile lead Snow White opposite Don Liberto's Wotan. Tommy Rall of Ballet Theatre had a speaking role. Other favorites from Ballet Theatre and various musicals filled the ranks of the Russo-American Ballet Company, among them

Margaret Banks, Richard D'Arcy, Charles Dickson, June Graham, Eric Kristen, and Ina Kurland.

The script made the most of sly allusions to the rival Ballet Russe companies and their similar repertories. Here the Russo-American Ballet and its competitor follow each other around the country, one boasting *The Cossacks on Parade,* the other *Parade of the Cossacks.* References to the "army game" crop up, with Lily gamely hiding various freeloaders in her hotel room, and Robbins created one of his sensational in-and-out mix-ups, "Pajama Dance," in which he went to town on the hidden and not-so-hidden lusts of ballet dancers on tour. In Smith's Pullman car set, dancers pretending to sleepwalk pop in and out of berths and disingenuously pursue one another. Those emerging from curtained upper berths land smoothly on others' shoulders, creating a double-decker sleepwalker, four hands out groping the air. Double takes spawn switches of direction as someone more appetizing than the current object of pursuit walks by. Richard D'Arcy remembers that he caught June Graham up in a leap as he hurried along and then switched her to face the other direction, creating the illusion of a take in midair. Robbins made the small-girl-tall-man joke with Herbert Ross and Ina Kurland into a running gag.

He also reworked his Tamiment "À la Russe" as "Mademoiselle Marie," with music by Trude Rittman, the arranger, accompanist, and dance music composer par excellence. This is supposed to be Eddie Winkler's creation; he has browbeaten the dancers through rehearsals and told them that it would be their fault if the ballet failed. However, it seemed to Ross more like a satire on Massine's ballet bouffe *Mademoiselle Angot* than a fresh and innovative work. In this pseudo–French farce, Walker played a nymphomaniacal honeymooning bride through whose hotel room and vast armoire passed not only her doddering bridegroom (Ross) but a sexy bellboy (Rall), the innkeeper, maids, servants, aspiring lovers, an unexplained cadre of Russian serfs, and eventually the entire company as gypsies, sylphides, fauns, and other ballet escapees. A portion of Robbins's preliminary notes gives an idea of the rapid-fire entrances and exits and interrupted amours he planned:

> husband—lech theme
> interrupted chambermaid 2
> husband leaves
> waiter come in—polka

interrupted chase by bellboy with bandages
grande passion again
interrupted by husband—suspicion
exits john
entrance of lover—flowers
mad mazurka exit to bed
husband reenters—suspicion
to lech—
interrupted
by hot chambermaid with message
exit husband exasperated
bell[boy] reenters—bandaged completely
grand passion
interrupted by cop and robber
then by house dick & finally husband
& furious chase . . .
fast chase—fugue music

Herbert Ross remembered it as having been "full of Jerryisms. You know, Boy Scouts running in and out and saluting on their knees." Robbins asked Ross to do rapid hopped pirouettes à la seconde while removing his trousers (*not* easily managed) and liked the effect so much that he had other men pull off the same stunt and got Ross another pair of pants to layer over the first so he could keep the joke going. "I wound up doing something like sixty-four turns in second," said Ross. "Jerry thought that was hilariously funny; I never got the joke at all, but he would sit there whooping with laughter." In the course of popping into and out of beds, doors, and the armoire, some people flee into others' clothes. Tommy Rall ended up dressed as an aproned maid.

A shocked Plancek strides onstage and stops the ballet, but of course it's a hit, and Hollywood wires Eddie offers. One of the problems with the show's believability, however, was that "Mademoiselle Marie" was no *Fancy Free* to ignite a career. In one song, the juvenile lead Wotan (Don Liberto) and Lily ask, "Why don't we do a jazz ballet about jazz?" but one never materializes. Eddie, nicer now and somewhat humbled by success, enthusiastically pitches a ballet that will be "new and American" with talking and singing in it: "We figured we've been dancing Water Lilies and Louis the Fifteenth's bad dreams about long enough. We've decided we'd just be ourselves, Mr. Plancek . . . our own generation." That's never shown either. Robbins-Eddie did create a more serious modern ballet, but it had to be excised, leaving only photographs and dancers' memories of heavy velvet outfits by John Pratt.

Aside from the sleepwalking number, Robbins's most interesting contribution was a duet near the end between Ann and Eddie. She's practicing in a Des Moines theater basement, while *Swan Lake* is being performed on the stage overhead. She begins to dance to music of the Act II pas de deux, and Eddie steps in to partner and encourage her: He: "Three turns?" She: "Just two." He: "Try three." She does, and he praises her. She's surprised he knows *Swan Lake.* He retorts, "I'm that clever Winkler boy." They continue to dance and talk, becoming more involved in the ballet's love story, freezing when anyone walks through. By the last ten bars, they're about to kiss when he drops her; he's just had a great idea for a ballet. It'll feature talking and dancing!

The show opened on January 29, 1948, and the critics were not overjoyed. Some pointed out tolerantly that this was Lee and Lawrence's first Broadway script, and showed it. (Interviewed in Philadelphia during tryouts, Lee said, "One thing we've learned on the road is that the book of a musical isn't written; it's re-written. The cutting gives it life." And Lawrence estimated "gloomily" that about three thousand words had been cut along with two ballets and three new sets.) Although Brooks Atkinson of the *Times* rated *Look Ma* a "top-drawer Broadway show" and Robert Coleman of the *Mirror* chalked it up as "another hit for George Abbott," others were less pleased. Louis Kronenberger called it "one of the brightest children I've ever flunked," and Ward Morehouse opened his review with "A good idea . . . goes wrong." Walter Terry made the most interesting point: "[F]or whatever reason, *Look Ma* emerged as a comedy about dancing, rather than a dancing comedy."

Everyone adored Walker. "She dives into an indifferent book and score and flings handfuls of it across the footlights," wrote one reviewer. Terry found her a wonderful dancer "in the sense that she does everything wrong so perfectly . . . she persecutes a pirouette unmercifully, she mangles entrechats, her leg in jeté behaves as if it were a pile-driver and her balletic line is beyond description."

By the end of March, the show had a net loss of almost $120,000, but it began to make a profit in the first days of April. A capital contribution of $195,000 later in the month erased the remainder of the debt, at which time $75,000 was distributed. Robbins can't have received much for his efforts. The show closed in less than six months. Richard D'Arcy thinks that Walker was beginning to slough off and that her terrific performance had slipped a notch (perhaps for personal reasons; she had become romantically obsessed with Harold Lang).

Given his personal investment—both financial and emotional—in the show, Robbins must have been disheartened. His commitment to *Look Ma* was given a boost a year later, however, when Paramount saw potential in it. On December 20, 1949, *The New York Times* reported that the studio had acquired the film rights for between $60,000 and $75,000. The following year, Robbins's notes show him struggling valiantly to adapt his plot into a vehicle for Betty Hutton and Fred Astaire. While retaining most of the ideas and numbers, he had to drop the character of Eddie and create a new one for Astaire. This hero was to be a successful Broadway tapper from a hoofing family who's come to Hammerlocker Falls, where his younger brother is touring with a ballet company. His aim is either to help his brother make it big in ballet or to get him out of the company and onto Broadway. Hutton was to play Lily (now called Molly and a good dancer—just not a ballet type), and she and Astaire end up returning to Broadway together.

As might have been expected, Robbins became enthralled by what film could reveal. His notes show what an astute grasp he had of the movie-musical aesthetic. He devised a daydream for Molly. Sitting in the audience watching a ballet, she projects herself into it:

> As she waltzes and sways from side to side, the audience's heads tilt from side to side in sympathy. She begins a variation; she starts to perform incredible feats. CUT TO Corps de Ballet and audience's reaction to the fantastic amount of pirouettes she performs, she herself a picture of nonchalance, sucking teeth. She leaps and as she takes off, CUT TO audience, all heads tilting up higher and higher as if watching a pop fly to outfield. She performs some entrechats, going up, feet beating madly as she polishes her nails. She has visions of the orchestra having to hold notes forever while she does her tricks; her swiftness and her agility making gusts of wind, rattling sheet music and programs and making skirts fly.

Finally she is shot by the villain's arrow (moving both audience and conductor by her death scene). She kisses her prince's hand in farewell and finds herself back in her seat kissing the hand of the man next to her.

The idea of a film based on the musical fluttered around for a while. *Dance Magazine* reported in February 1952 that Robbins was waiting to see a film script of the musical written by Preston Sturges before signing a contract. But no movie materialized. According to Sturges's biographer Donald Spoto, the film was canceled when Hutton pulled out in a huff; the studio wouldn't hire her husband, choreographer Charles O'Curran, as director. Astaire and Hutton did make a picture together in 1950: *Let's Dance.* It bore absolutely no resemblance to *Look Ma, I'm Dancin'!*

8

Balanchine's Right-hand Man

Tanaquil Le Clercq and Robbins in George Balanchine's
Bourrée Fantasque.   *George Platt Lynes/NYPL.*

*I*n *late 1948,* Robbins was riding high. An article in *Esquire* reported that since he had, with distinction, choreographed four shows and five ballets in four years, Roseland had given him a plaque naming him "Tops in Terpischore" [*sic*]. Offers abounded. However, in October, he saw a performance of George Balanchine and Lincoln Kirstein's

Ballet Society in its first season as the New York City Ballet—a season that, coincidentally, began on his thirtieth birthday. Although he had worked for Balanchine in two shows and, very briefly, in Ballet Theatre, and had followed his career, he was utterly bowled over by a "rapturously" danced *Symphony in C,* especially by the second movement and the nineteen-year-old Tanaquil Le Clercq. She fell backward into Francisco Moncion's arms like an enchanted princess finally surrendering to desire, and Jerry fell in love—with that image, that choreography, that dancer. "So I wrote George or Lincoln or someone there, and said, 'Do you need someone . . . Is there any way you need me?' And they called and asked if I wanted to do a ballet, and also if I wanted to dance." Before the end of the year, Robbins was a member of the company and already composing a new work.

Robbins's early journals profess no particular reverence for Balanchine, but colleagues from those days had noticed his adulation: "From the very beginning, Balanchine was what he wanted to be," recalled former Ballet Theatre dancer Isabel Brown (Mirrow). When Balanchine remounted his 1933 *Errante* as *The Wanderer* for Ballet Theatre in 1943, choreographed *Waltz Academy* for the company the following year, and created *Theme and Variations* in 1947, Robbins asked to observe rehearsals and to understudy Hugh Laing in *Errante.* In several later interviews, he also referred to an important conversation with Balanchine that occurred one summer, probably 1945, when the two chanced to take the same ferry from Nantucket.

> And in those days, what with my modern training and my guru [Sandor] having been completely affected by Stanislavsky because he worked with the Group Theatre, my approach toward ballet was very dramatic, theatrical, concentrated, and I felt that anything at all could be told by dance. And he said, "Well, it doesn't have to be so theatrical." He said, "There's a stage; it's empty. Four girls come on and dance with one boy. They go off and leave him alone. It's theatrical." He said, "Then six girls come on and dance on the other side. That's theatrical. And then two people do a solo, and it's just two people who are dancing and then they go off. And that's already theatre and entertainment."

For a choreographer who began in modern dance, believing that great art emerged struggling from the deep recesses of the soul, "It was just like the light had been turned on about what choreography was really *about.*"

Balanchine was fourteen years older than Robbins and steeped in the imperial Russian ballet traditions. Jerry may also have been struck not only by the older man's choreographic brilliance but by the ease with which he put ballets together, especially in comparison to Tudor. And to himself (he could devise movement speedily; it was the agonizing selecting and polishing that ate up time). Robbins needed more than a hundred hours to compose the nineteen-minute *Facsimile*. The following year, Balanchine managed to turn out the thirty-two-minute, four-movement *Theme and Variations* in only thirty-nine rehearsal hours.

Robbins's decision to approach Kirstein and Balanchine in October 1948 may have been prompted by considerations beyond admiration for their work. For one thing, he'd just weathered his first major flop, the musical comedy *That's the Ticket!* (originally titled *Alfred the Average*)—a failure that had also marked his debut as a director. He wrote later that Joe Kipness, the ebullient coproducer of *High Button Shoes,* had offered it to him, and that Robbins had thought he wasn't ready. "[Joe] tore up a telephone book in front of me, looked me in the eye & said I won't take no for an answer, and didn't."

The show must have been designed to capitalize on election-year antics. Harry Truman was battling New York's governor, Thomas E. Dewey, for a second term, while the Progressive Party nominated Henry Wallace. The story, by Julius J. and Philip G. Epstein, with a score by Harold Rome, involves a third, ultra-right-wing political party—sort of a moneyed-old-boys club—that needs to find a replacement for its ninety-year-old presidential candidate (he has just expired in the arms of a lascivious actress). Their man should look good but not be too bright. The party boss's daughter solves their problem. Wandering tipsily in Central Park, she meets a frog. The old kiss-me-I'm-an-enchanted-prince idea. The prince who wakes up beside her the next morning is a medieval knight in full armor (Leif Erickson), who can neither read nor write—in short, and with a bit of coaching, the perfect presidential candidate. The Democrats and Republicans go out looking for frogs.

The script gets dubious comic mileage out of juxtaposing daffy contemporary conservatism with Alfred's ancient variety (uppity servants should be slaughtered, the party boss should wash the feet of his high-ranking guest, and why not invoke *droit de seigneur* when a serving maid gets married?). The heroine and the gradually acclimatizing knight fall in love, but the actress, somehow an incarnation of the witch who enchanted Alfred, invades their wedding and tangles the plot into farcical knots.

Jerry thought the idea amusing and liked Rome's score, but it didn't take long for the novice director to realize he was in over his head. He didn't really know how to guide actors. Dancers wait to be shown what to do and then absorb it as quickly and efficiently as they can. "One of the reasons we dancers loved him," said Allyn McLerie, "was that he was a delight to watch. . . . A dancer copies the choreographer and tries to be him. You really try to do the movement exactly as he's doing it. And that was fun because he was wonderful, so you felt yourself doing something nice. You couldn't wait to try to get that movement exactly as he did it." Most actors tend to form their own ideas about character, to dislike being given line readings, but they also need the director to clarify his intent. Robbins later wrote, "I made mistakes about the style of the show, the sets [by Oliver Smith], some poor casting, and worse performances that I couldn't straighten, and to boot, assigned the choreography elsewhere [to Paul Godkin] (as I knew I couldn't do both in 4 weeks rehearsal) & it didn't score. Added to that, the two leading ladies [Edna Skinner and Kaye Ballard, then a novice in the theater] seemed to have some bond going, for if I [made a] cut in their lines or scenes, both would become recalcitrant. The whole venture was a mistake & it closed out of town in Philly in 6 days. I was numb and relieved both."

Isabel Brown (Mirrow), then a seventeen-year-old dancer in the show, felt Robbins was "hamstrung by the script," and did what he could to salvage a dismal book. No matter how many patchwork rewrites he asked for from the Epstein brothers (who'd done far better work on the screenplay of *Casablanca*) or how much tinkering he did with Godkin's choreography (one dubious highlight had the dancers tottering around in armor), *That's the Ticket!* never worked. It may have been Robbins's decision not to bring the show into New York. He had asked for, and gotten, his name in type one point larger than anyone else's. Wisely, he didn't want his first directorial credit to be attached to a flop.

Around the time Robbins joined the New York City Ballet, he was also contending with a broken love affair. Montgomery Clift felt his skyrocketing career increasingly endangered by the relationship. He had captured the public's attention with his first two films, *Red River* and *The Search*. He was a different sort of movie hero: sensitive, vulnerable, yet fearless, he looked like a man with complex hidden anguish twisting his vitals. Both films were released in 1948. When *Red River* opened, Clift was already working on the film version of *The Heiress,* playing the caddish Morris Townsend opposite Olivia de Havilland. By the end of the year, *Variety* had declared that his was "one of the most unusual rises to stardom in all of Hollywood history. . . . With only two films released, *Red River* and *The Search,* and with no studio backing, he has suddenly become one of the two or three most in demand male players in Hollywood and can pretty much have his choice of parts at any studio." Clift signed a three-picture contract with Paramount; he also broke off the liaison. Jerry was devastated.

Robbins felt perhaps less of a dichotomy between Broadway work and concert work than did Leonard Bernstein, but ballet was certainly a less stressful form to work in: there was no cadre of collaborators haggling in hotel rooms. It's interesting, however, that after the frustrating and chastening experience of *That's the Ticket!,* he hadn't simply returned to Ballet Theatre, although he made sure that door stayed opened. (Lucia Chase continued over the next few years to try to coax him back to choreograph, and he evidently made proposals of his own.)* Too, he occasionally had to skirmish with Ballet Theatre over renegotiations of his *Interplay* and *Facsimile* contract. (The *Fancy Free* agreement, with its $10 royalties, proved almost impossible to break; he wasn't able to wrest it from Ballet Theatre's exclusive control until 1980.)

If Robbins had weighed the New York City Ballet and Ballet Theatre solely in terms of their respective stability and prospects, he'd have been faced with a six-of-one-half-a-dozen-of-the-other decision. During Ballet Theatre's spring season at the Met, the house was half full much of the time, and he must have been aware that the company's finances were in a parlous state. Necessary organizational changes in 1947 had absorbed it into Ballet Theatre Foundation, Inc., an educational corporation, and complications resulting from the altered tax status made it impossible for Lucia Chase to continue donating 30 percent of her income. As yet, Ballet Theatre had not seriously courted other investors. By the end of July 1948, the dancers were laid off, with assurances that the company would surely be able to resume operations by the following January. Ballet Theatre did

* For instance, on March 3, 1949, he wrote to his good friend Robert Fizdale, of the piano duo Gold and Fizdale, that he might appear with Ballet Theatre in April, and sometime in 1950, he told Fizdale that he was still waiting for Lucia to "make up her mind about the Bowles piece."

in fact not revive until March 1949. The New York City Ballet was scarcely a solid financial organization, but it stood at a threshold marked by a change in status and name.

Robbins had apparently not considered joining the company when it debuted as Ballet Society in 1946, shortly after Kirstein finished his three-year military duty. Bristling with elegant taste, venturesomeness, and a degree of snobbery, Ballet Society functioned as a subscription organization. Its members (800 at most) got tickets to presentations of new operas and ballets, as well as copies of *Dance Index,* an ongoing series of erudite and wide-ranging monographs on dance. Seasons were short (sometimes a single performance) and often held in the same bleak venues the modern dance audience was accustomed to, such as the Central High School of Needle Trades auditorium or Hunter College Playhouse. Kirstein's private fortune, like Chase's, couldn't bankroll his enterprise indefinitely— indeed, at one point, he suggested they merge their companies.

In the spring of 1948, however, Morton Baum, the chairman of the finance committee of the City Center, saw and was enthralled by one of the company's first nonsubscription performances during Ballet Society's brief rental season (five shows in all) there on West Fifty-fifth Street. Baum was in charge of policy and operations at the Shriners' former Mecca Temple, which had been seized by the city for back taxes and turned into a cultural center offering low-priced tickets. He offered the company a fall season of two nights a week (the low-attendance Mondays and Tuesdays) during the New York City Opera's season, with the understanding that Balanchine and the dancers would participate in the operas as well. It wasn't an ideal arrangement, but Kirstein accepted it. Fortunately, Baum was ready to go further and convinced his board to back him. In 1949, City Center assumed the new company's operating costs and placed the ballet company on an equal footing with its constituent opera and drama groups, guaranteeing it two seasons a year.

In casting his lot with the company, Robbins certainly did not expect monetary gain or even a decent living wage, despite the company's improved status; the dancers still subsisted part of the year on unemployment insurance and the odd freelance dance job, although they may no longer have had to pose for figure-drawing classes at the Art Students League or seek other kinds of temporary work. Robbins perhaps sensed a pattern of development that could put the company on a more solid footing. And, of course, he could always pay a visit to Broadway during slack times at

NYCB. It must have been understood that he would disappear between seasons to choreograph musicals. Balanchine himself maintained an eclectic schedule. Beginning October 14, 1948, three days after New York City Ballet's fall season started, New York City Opera premiered four productions with his choreography. A highly successful musical he'd tossed off, *Where's Charley?*, opened in New York on October 11, 1948, the same day NYCB's season began (and the day Robbins turned thirty).

The New York City Ballet had good reason to be interested in Robbins. For many years after the enterprising, brilliant, and moneyed Lincoln Kirstein brought George Balanchine to America in 1933 to establish a school and company (originally the American Ballet Company), the choreographer didn't always receive the critical acclaim that later came to him. John Martin, a champion of modern dance, had initially put him down. How could a Russian choreographer, formed in Saint Petersburg and Paris, contribute to the development of American ballet? Unlike Robbins, Martin was not entranced by *Symphony in C:* "Mr. Balanchine has once again given us that ballet, this time for some inscrutable reason to the Bizet Symphony . . . [using] all of his familiar tricks, some of them charming, some of them forced, some of them slightly foolish." Although Balanchine was certainly the linchpin of New York City Ballet, Kirstein had presented works by other choreographers during the brief lifetime of his Americana company Ballet Caravan, and he continued the practice in Ballet Society and New York City Ballet. Todd Bolender, John Taras, William Dollar, Lew Christensen, Fred Danieli, even the young modern dancer Merce Cunningham contributed works to the repertory.

Ballet Caravan had produced at least two important works in the American vein, Eugene Loring's *Billy the Kid* and Lew Christensen's *Filling Station.* Kirstein obviously believed that Robbins could enrich this aspect of the repertory and provide contrast to the master's largely plotless ballets via dramatic works with a contemporary slant. It was clear to everyone that Robbins was being brought in as a resident choreographer, a kind of "sidekick" to Balanchine. In letters Kirstein wrote to Robbins over the ensuing years, he placated the choreographer when necessary, shamelessly flattered him, spoke for Balanchine (who wasn't a letter writer), proposed ideas for ballets and nixed others, as well as regaling Jerry with hilariously scurrilous gossip and opinions that acknowledged their fraternity in New York's gay world. For the most part—certainly during the early years of their relationship—Jerry seems to have valued Lincoln's erudition and taken in stride the eccentricities here described by Maria Tallchief in her memoirs:

> [Y]ou never could tell when you greeted him if he would be friendly or curt, or even what he was thinking. Conversations with him could be disconcerting. In the middle of a sentence he'd suddenly turn around and walk away. A military buff, he sometimes dressed in khaki shorts and matching shirt as if he were a colonel in the British raj. Other times he'd wear white shoes that clashed with the black suit he invariably had on.

Bolender remembers that when Robbins arrived, the dancers all thought, "Well, what's he coming for? And in such a position: coming in as a choreographer. Everybody was a little bit nervous. But then we all knew Jerry and we knew he was talented." And they knew that he took some adjusting to: "He could be absolutely lovable. And just such an angelic person. And then shift. I remember this from the early years. How wonderful he would be, what a nice person he could be, and how much you wanted to be with him. And then suddenly he would do something just ghastly, which made you immediately wonder, Have I misread this character?"

The Guests, Robbins's first ballet for the company, premiered on January 20, 1949. In later years, he denied that it was based on Shakespeare's *Romeo and Juliet* or had any bearing on *West Side Story,* but its basic armature—a boy and a girl from two rigidly divided social groups fall in love—resonates with both. His collaborator, Marc Blitzstein, like Robbins, had a strong social conscience and what Lincoln Kirstein referred to as "Leftist attachments." At this point in his career, when Robbins was choreographing essentially lighthearted period musicals, he brought to his ballets the kind of serious ideas that could be found in contemporary plays of the 1940s and 1950s, such as Arthur Miller's *Death of a Salesman* and Tennessee Williams's *A Streetcar Named Desire. The Guests* was planned as a critique of intolerance and the treatment of minorities. Blitzstein built his original scenario around a labor-appeasing competition sponsored by a large department store among its employees; the winners—one male and one female—would be chosen to model a clothing line. Management's strategically friendly gesture came to naught when it was discovered that one winner was black and the other white. Robbins, perhaps mindful of working in a Balanchinian world and remembering the fateful conversation on the Nantucket ferry, stripped the plot of details. Speaking in the 1950s to Selma Jeanne Cohen about his choreography, Robbins explained that "*The Guests* portrayed a social problem in terms of classic dance. Here, the drama was achieved through the use of space design involving large groups. I wanted to get at the essence of the conflict rather than depicting a specific situation, so the drive was not to look individual, the gestures were not to be personal."

He also mentioned to Cohen a fact that had shaped, and would continue to shape, the way he made ballets: "Having started as a modern dancer, I am somewhat influenced by its approach to dancing though I work within the ballet idiom." He was referring to the practice of allowing subject matter to determine form and movement choices. In the case of *The Guests,* his basic plot—the brave individual(s) pitted against a conformist society—actually linked it with modern dance works of earlier decades, such as Martha Graham's *Heretic* (1929) and Doris Humphrey's *With My Red Fires* (1936). More important, as Walter Terry pointed out in a 1966 article entitled "Dance Me a Dance with Social Significance," the kind of abstraction Robbins dealt with in *The Guests* was "a distinctively American choreographic concept. This has to do with distilling, with procuring the essence. Modern dance had known this for a long time (there were no cowboys or Indians in Martha Graham's monumental classic *Frontier*). Robbins did not give us the geographical location, the time, the names of the antagonists in *The Guests.* He gave us the core of conflict and the characteristics, the individual and the mob, with which it was met."

It was Terry, too, in his review of the ballet's premiere, who praised Robbins's use of the "drama of space" and likened his charged architecture to that of German-born choreographer Hanya Holm, one of the pioneers of modern dance in America.

Despite the abstract aspects of *The Guests,* it carried forward Robbins's interest in creating enclosed worlds onstage. A program note identified *The Guests* as "A ballet in one scene concerning the patterns of adjustment and conflict between two groups, one larger than the other." The group Robbins called in his notes "the included" consisted of eleven dancers, the "excluded" of seven. Judging from the memories of observers and performers and from Robbins's early notes, the two groups have come to a gathering that features a competition for the larger group only. He himself played a character he originally thought of as the "Discriminator," but later labeled the Host.

The ballet used not only the classical vocabulary but its good manners. The Host subtly shepherds the separate groups, but the opening dance makes it clear that this is largely unnecessary; everyone accepts the status quo, with the "excluded" ghettoized in space, deferential, though always treated courteously. Early on, Robbins, like the Montague boys crashing that fateful Capulet party, hit on the idea of masks. The alpha group dons these to parade before the host cum contest judge. "[The masks] are the market-place," Robbins wrote in his notes, "the supposed anonymity and equality of all comers (applicants for jobs, university entrance, immigration, etc.)." What the host has not noticed is that two of the "included" decline to compete and their masks are donned by others—one a girl from the nonelite group. In the showing off of individual brilliance, the young man performs a solo that Robbins referred to in his notes as "chipper, assured" and the young woman a gentler one "with lyrical arm movements." They are selected, and this development leads to one of those pas de deux in which two relative strangers, or even antagonists (think of Fred Astaire and Ginger Rogers) gradually fall in love as they fall into step. Maria Tallchief, the strong young half–American Indian dancer whom Balanchine had married and was refining into a prima ballerina of consequence, danced the duet with Nicholas Magallanes; she remembered that it was lovely and full of lifts. (Critics, many of whom thought the ballet a minor effort, praised this passage.)

The preordained unmasking takes place, and, not surprisingly, there is consternation among the guests. The host separates the lovers, and, despite their efforts to be accepted by one group or the other, both societies reject them. While working on the ballet, Robbins reminded himself that "This work shouldn't be negative; there is plenty of evidence of surge and resistance to discrimination; this work is actual proof; things look up; maybe the pattern of bias and prejudice isn't fully broken down in this piece—but at least there is a clear attempt made, with tiny slow gains." However, he opted for an ambiguous conclusion, with the young man bearing his chosen partner away, leaving an angry host and a baffled, discomfited assembly.

Balanchine watched the growth of the work with interest, dropping by rehearsals almost every day, "a supportive gesture" that Robbins valued. Knowing masks were needed, the boss went out and bought some for his new colleague. Robbins told Balanchine's biographer Bernard Taper how amazing he had found this: "Here I was, just a young choreographer, and there was the great master of our age bringing in props to help me, as if he were some fourth assistant to the stage manager."

The reviews were mixed—encouraging, but not raves. Doris Hering of *Dance Magazine* likened the ballet to a "newborn child" in terms of potential: "small and perfectly formed, but as yet not quite coordinated." Robbins acknowledged to Robert Fizdale that the variety of interpretations "floored" him. He himself thought that "the whole latter half is exactly right. . . . The first half holds mostly by hindsight." He was clearheaded enough to understand that something needed fixing: "The final feeling of the ballet is one of simpleness so that the audience has had the tragedy happen without fuss or ornamentation. This is its best asset but it also leads to the ballet being called naive or overstated."

By the end of the year, John Martin, who'd initially been disappointed, noted the results of Robbins's revisions and declared that "what emerges now is a taut and brilliant theatre work with a style all its own." When the NYCB visited London in 1950, the press was enthusiastic. Robbins must have been gratified by James Monahan's insights in *The Manchester Guardian*:

> [Robbins] has done something which looks simple but is not. He has, with small modifications, married an entirely classical technique to a tiny sketch of a story—a story which is all mood and atmosphere and which never tries to say anything which could be better said in any other medium. Because of his delicate sense of the dramatic, his sense of music, and above all, his respect for the limitations of the classical dance, he has turned his forbidding little scenario into a work rich in imaginative suggestions.

Despite Robbins's later denial of connections between *The Guests* and *West Side Story*, it seems more than coincidental that, according to Bernstein, Robbins found time in early January 1949, even as he was sweating through preparations for *The Guests*, to meet with him and with Arthur Laurents to discuss an idea he was fired up about for a musical theater work. Bernstein wrote in a "log" he concocted for publication after *West Side Story* saw the light of day eight years later: "Jerry R. called today [January 6, 1949] with a noble idea: a modern version of *Romeo and Juliet* set in the slums at the coincidence of Easter-Passover celebrations. Feelings run high between Jews and Catholics. Former: Capulets; latter, Montagues. Juliet is Jewish. Friar Laurence is a neighborhood druggist. Street brawls, double death—it all fits."

Small wonder that Robbins saw Dr. Arkin as many as four times a week in early January. In addition to cramming in as many rehearsals as possible before *The Guests* premiered on January 20 and brainstorming ideas for the project the collaborators thought of as *East Side Story* (it was, at that point, set on Manhattan's Lower East Side), he was also making plans to choreograph a far more frivolous musical, *Miss Liberty,* with music by a composer he greatly admired: Irving Berlin.

By March he was deep in preparations for *Miss Liberty,* as well as taking ballet classes at the School of American Ballet (in those days, there were no special company classes for NYCB dancers), going to the Actors Studio, and educating himself in the history of art by attending the Metropolitan Museum's twice-monthly Monday-night lectures. By March, he had also made his debut as a New York City Ballet dancer in Bolender's *Mother Goose Suite,* taking over the choreographer's own role, Hop o' My Thumb. Despite the name, this was not an antic part. In Bolender's take on Maurice Ravel's *Ma Mère l'Oye,* a woman dreams her youthful adventures, and in these fantasies, the fairy-tale figures assume transformed significance. Hop o' My Thumb is pursued by a girl representing the bird who eats the crumbs he has dropped as a trail to guide him home again. "The bird-girl drapes her long blond hair over the boy's head, ensnaring him. The boy is undisturbed." He dances with the dreaming girl too, but clouds waft him away from her to the one he truly loves. Robbins wrote to Fizdale that "Dancing in Todd's ballet was finally lots of fun. I say finally, because I went through much anxiety beforehand, not having performed in over a year, dancing a classical variation which I never have done, and having a pulled tendon in one leg, but came time of performance and I relaxed, enjoyed myself and heard that I danced very well." He began to take an interest in the company as a whole. Watching from the wings, he was able to tell Fizdale (a great admirer of Balanchine) that "Todd's new ballet *Image of the Heart* was very interesting. It is romantic, mysterious and morbid all at the same time. [Beatrice] Tomkins [*sic*], Moncion and LeClerque [*sic*] very good, Tanny dancing with more truth and subtlety than I have ever seen before."

If one can discern a governing principle in Robbins's working life at this point, it seems to be that he wanted it all. He never, as far as we know, expressed the idea that there was such a thing as being too busy or too sought after, or that he was keeping too many balls in the air. He thrived on hatching plans for ambitious ballets while garnering kudos and money from musicals and pursuing film possibilities. During his first stint at the New York City Ballet, Robbins outdid Balanchine in jobbing around. Between 1949 and 1956, when he began to withdraw from the NYCB, Balanchine's right-hand man would work on seven musical comedies, doctor at least four more, provide dances for an opera (Aaron Copland's *Tender Land*), and teach *Interplay* in Israel—in addition to creating nine ballets for NYCB, collaborating with Balanchine on two, restaging one (*Interplay*), and performing in most of his own ballets plus four by Balanchine and one by Bolender.

For a while, none of his Broadway activities conflicted with his duties at New York City Ballet, where, as of 1949, he was billed as "Associate Artistic Director." From the end of its City Center season in February 1949 until rehearsals began the following October, members of the NYCB performed in only two productions that Balanchine choreographed for the New York City Opera in April and a ballet of *Cinderella* for CBS's "Through the Crystal." In between these, they jobbed around or collected unemployment insurance and went to class.

~

Robbins had read of the plans for *Miss Liberty* while managing to take a break in Europe. The show emitted signals of being a hit. Irving Berlin would write the music and lyrics. Moss Hart, half of the celebrated comedy-writing team of Kaufman and Hart, and a successful director, would take charge of his first musical. Robert Sherwood, the author of such impressive dramas as *There Shall Be No Night, Abe Lincoln in Illinois,* and *The Petrified Forest,* was to make his debut as a musical comedy writer. Robbins bit and, knowing no more about the venture than these sterling names, "Zing like an arrow I went to the phone and called my agent and said try to get me that show." The contract he signed at the end of February guaranteed him $750 a week for rehearsals plus .75 percent of the gross receipts for the first 25 weeks of New York performances or until the original production costs had been recouped, at which time his take would be upped to 1 percent.

At a 1990 Memorial for Irving Berlin, Robbins claimed he'd had a "ball" working on *Miss Liberty:* "I was asked to do dances for almost all of the musical numbers. My inventions and imagination were very very hot those years and nothing daunted me. I'd plunge in, come up with something, and show it to Moss and Irving and into the show it went." He loved the era and locales in which the plot unfolded: "Wonderful period, 1890s, New York, Paris, Cancans, Policemen's balls—the unveiling of the Statue of Liberty." Oliver Smith was on hand, along with costume designer Motley, to provide a handsome surround.

Robbins was a little less sunny about working on *Miss Liberty* in a letter he wrote to Mary Martin and her husband, Richard Halliday, in 1955, explaining the kind of oblique dealings he didn't care for. The *Miss Liberty* team had asked to see what he'd accomplished in only five days; he had complied, even though he felt the request was premature since he usually threw out everything he'd done in the first rehearsals. They raved. Then Hart asked him to lunch:

> We spent the first hour and a half talking about how he had used his shows therapeutically to help him over problems, and the benefits that he was able to derive from applying his analysis to his shows and vice-versa. I sat in complete bewilderment. In the next half-hour, he pussy-footed around some more concerning how difficult it was for him to find an approach to collaborate with me as we had never collaborated before. The last half-hour he finally got around to telling me that they didn't like what I had done so far. In the last five minutes, I set him straight and told him that the best way to work with me was to let me work, and when I had finished to show them what I had done, and then I would accept any criticism, and as for collaborating with me, the only way I could work with him was if they were completely direct with me and straight-forward about anything they had to tell me.

The trouble was that Berlin, Sherwood, and Hart believed the advance publicity. They produced the show themselves, putting up, it was said, $175,000. Allyn McLerie, who played the title role, noted that "They were always worshiping at one another's shrines. 'You are the best this, you are the best that.' 'No, no, you are the best.' Here were all these geniuses."

In the smash hit *Annie Get Your Gun,* Berlin had worked to integrate his songs with the characters and atmosphere of Buffalo Bill's Wild West Show, coming up with a raucous cross between 1890s pop and Tin Pan Alley that suited *Annie*'s lusty-voiced star, Ethel Merman. This time he made it clear that "These songs will be hits all by themselves." Many of them were written before Sherwood had finished the book. "I Love You" made the hit parade prior to the show's opening, and Robert Coleman's opening-night review in the *Daily Mirror* mentioned that some songs had already aired on the radio. However, during the show's very long hot-summer tryouts in Philadelphia, the cast remembers him as insecure: "Irving was always around with little candies in his pocket, and he'd hand them out to anybody, and he would ask people how the show was doing." But he stoically wrote new songs as numbers were cut. Sherwood was charming but rarely sober. At conferences, Hart might say that something wasn't working, to which Sherwood would blurrily respond, "*I* like it." That was that. McLerie learned later from Hart that at some point during the Philadelphia run, he had simply given up; furthermore, his struggles with Sherwood had taken so much time and effort that his shaping of the show had been largely limited to directing traffic. He'd get to polishing the actors later, he told both himself and them.

The plot hinges on a fictional case of mistaken identity, embedded in an historic event. It's 1886, and the Statue of Liberty is about to be erected in New York. In the midst of a newspaper war between Joseph Pulitzer of the *New York World* and James Gordon Bennett of the *Herald,* the *World* has raised $100,000 to complete the pedestal. Maisie Dell, a feisty writer for the *Police Gazette,* persuades Horace Miller, a young photographer at the *Herald* whom she fancies, to go to Paris, locate the girl who modeled for the statue, and bring her to New York. What a scoop for Bennett's paper and a boost for Horace, Maisie suggests, and she manages to persuade Bennett to put up the money for the voyage.

Frédéric Bartholdi's mother actually posed for Liberty, but when Horace enters the sculptor's studio, he sees a beautiful young girl standing there torch in hand. How should he know that Monique Dupont is an impoverished flower seller seeking work as a model and that Bartholdi has gotten her to strike the familiar pose for fun? The plot goes from uproar to uproar. Comic disguises, evasions, and disappearances ensue. Eventually, with Bartholdi's intervention the drama is resolved happily, and in a somewhat treacly finale, Monique leads the chorus in singing Berlin's setting of Emma Lazarus's poem "The New Colossus" ("Give me your tired, your poor").

One problem with the scenario was that the character of Monique lacked spice ("a pallid part," Brooks Atkinson of the *Times* called it).

Maisie (played by Mary McCarty) was far more interesting. McLerie, who had scored a big hit in *Where's Charley?* and left that show to do this one, was too inexperienced to shape the part on her own. She remembers asking the beleaguered Hart if she could smile sometimes, and he gratefully urging her to go ahead. Ethel Griffies, in the role of Monique's grandmother, had played an array of character parts in Hollywood and for many years before had kicked up her heels in the London music halls. She could still kick—and high, too—and she knew just what to do with any number she graced. "Probably the authors didn't intend Griffies to be the star," remarked Atkinson, "but that is how it worked out." In a review titled "*Miss Liberty* and Miss Griffies," Robert Sylvester said thankfully that "[she] ought to be arrested just for the way she leers at the audience."

Berlin's "Let's Take an Old-Fashioned Walk" was just about everyone's favorite song, and Robbins devised a charming stroll for McLerie and Eddie Albert as Horace, with the lighting creating the effect of sudden rain and the chorus singers and dancers (including Robbins's Ballet Theatre friends Maria Karnilova and Tommy Rall) joining in. Of all the collaborators, the choreographer came off best. "It is Robbins and his nimble dancers who contribute the chief sparkle to a sputtering show," wrote Howard Barnes in the *Herald Tribune.* John Martin thought that "Of Robbins' five Broadway shows thus far it is easily his best; it finds him inventive, charmingly evocative of period and atmosphere, witty with his own quiet kind of comment, as well as full of raucous rumpus when occasion demands." In a tricky little routine that Martin found delightful, three chuffing male dancers became a train to transport Miss Liberty around to adoring reception committees. Robbins also brought on corps members as sharks to follow Horace's "Little Fish in a Big Pond" and staged a "tumultuous Paris masquerade" in Act I with clowns, circus dancers, and strongmen; McLerie danced with Rall (playing a Lamplighter) in the sweet "Paris Wakes Up and Smiles." A ballet near the Brooklyn Bridge celebrates Miss Liberty's arrival at the opening of Act II, and a couple of numbers later, the dancers go to town in the "Policeman's Ball" (the fleeing Monique has taken cover at this rowdy celebration and ends up taking part in it, with Rall as a nimble dandy). A "Follow-the-Leader Jig" at the ball turns into a competition battle. During the dark days in Philadelphia, when New York friends took the train down and made it clear they thought the show was in trouble, Hart penned a heartfelt note from the Ritz-Carlton hotel:

Dear Jerry—

It is my fond hope that this is my last musical, but if ever again I should be idiotic enough to do one I would refuse to do it without you.

This is a rather involved way of explaining my admiration and gratitude for your job but admiration and gratitude it is.

Moss

During the hectic tryout period, Robbins lost the number he was most attached to, "Mr. Monotony." A chanteuse delivers a torchy song about a woman drawn to a jazz trombonist, whom she later kicks out (literally) in favor of a clarinetist. The trombonist's insistent bass has palled, and the more lively clarinetist prevails. McLerie danced it with Rall and Bill Bradley, who mimed their instruments while tossing off virtuosic dance riffs and dueling hot licks. "Mr. Monotony" stopped the show. Rall remembers that someone dared Berlin to drop it, even though, flimsily offered as an entertainment in a dance hall beer parlor, it suggested an improbably sexy side of the demure French girl who had refused to undress for a sculptor in Act I. Rodgers and Hammerstein, among the many who traveled to Philadelphia for a look-see, told the collaborators that "Mr. Monotony" had to go. In subsequent years, Robbins kept trying to get this number to Broadway; it was dropped from both *Call Me Madam* and *Two's Company*. Unable to remember it by the time he was putting together *Jerome Robbins' Broadway* in 1988, he choreographed it anew. Before too long, the jinxed dance had disappeared from the show; a singer delivered the tale alone onstage.

Miss Liberty couldn't compete with deeper musicals like *South Pacific* and *Lost in the Stars,* nor did it have the vivacity and wit of *Kiss Me, Kate.* Reviews from the eight New York dailies were mixed, and the show ran for 308 performances.

⁓

Robbins dived back into the New York City Ballet. By mid-October, he was in rehearsals but still found time for weekend pleasure and romance. In the next-to-last entry in his datebook before he got too busy to keep track, the writing sprawls across the pages for October 21 and 22, warning: "Go Away!! You Fool. if you dare—& Stay!!"

Balanchine made every effort to integrate Robbins into the company and to capitalize on his talent. He paired him with Tanaquil Le Clercq in the first movement of *Bourrée Fantasque,* making shrewd use of Jerry's impish proclivities and sense of timing and the sophisticated wit that gave Tanny's glamour its enchanting edge. Taking advantage of Robbins's dramatic skills, Balanchine revived his great *Prodigal Son,* choreographed in 1929 for Les Ballets Russes not long before the death of the company's founder, Serge Diaghilev.

Choreographed to several festive pieces by the French composer Emmanuel Chabrier, *Bourrée Fantasque* set out to be a stylishly insouciant romp, a charmer. Doris Hering thought it looked like a "French Christmas tree." Walter Terry noted shrewdly that *Bourrée* "takes a fleeting jab at the choreographer's own tendency to wind dancers into daisy chains and it tosses in activities that border on the acrobatic, yet its vocabulary, both balletic and gestural, is primarily academic and its choreographic form is as flawless as that to be found in any one of Balanchine's puredance masterpieces." Balanchine chose his cast wisely. Tallchief and Nicholas Magallanes danced the romantic second movement ("Prelude"), and tiny, saucy Janet Reed led the "Fête Polonaise" with Herbert Bliss.

In the first movement, the choreographer cracked gentle jokes around the fact that on pointe Le Clercq—wearing Karinska's short, off-the-shoulder black tutu with a black-trimmed gold bodice and a lacy little chapeau and wielding a fan—was taller than Robbins in his black beret. Le Clercq had a lot of fun dancing with Robbins and once told an interviewer that "Jerry always said, 'You are the French maid walking her poodle,'" adding, "I do not think Mr. B. saw it like that." Tallchief thought the whole ballet elegant and remembered that the company was surprised at all the opening-night laughter during the first movement. Yet Terry, who was something of a sucker for good comedy, called Robbins "agile as a leprechaun and twice as mischievous" and thought he "created a character which must be classed with his immortal Hermes [in *Helen of Troy*]." *Bourrée Fantasque,* however, required more of Robbins than his comedic flair. Balanchine tossed entrechats and échappés into the ensemble finale like popcorn.

Watching a video of *Bourrée* as revived for the 1993 Balanchine celebration, one can only guess what Le Clercq and Robbins made of the ballet. Although the music begins with a circusy flourish as four men and four women enter, it becomes quieter, rather like a protracted cadenza, during part of the first-movement duet. The steps are quick and bantering, as if the two were enjoying being slightly at odds. As they enter together arm in arm, she leans forward when he leans back; this motif is repeated. He lunges to grab her, and she fans herself in vigorous disapproval: a gentleman *asks* for a lady's hand. Much of the time, he is more smitten than she—attempting to land kisses on her, crawling after her like a seal. He kneels and offers his thigh for a chair; they have a little conversation—he nodding insistently, she shaking her head: "Oh, no!" In one bit of virtuoso slapstick, while he's concentrating on supporting her in a front attitude, his hands at her waist, she leans forward, whips her lifted leg around behind him and whaps him on the back of the neck. He looks over his shoulder in puzzlement but sees no one. So involved with her is he that she manages this feat twice without his ever catching on. Amid the hornpipe steps and high kicks, their prancing forays with the corps, and an argument that tangles their arms together, they remain fond of each other. When he drops to one knee and puts his hand dramatically over his heart, she touches her heart too.

Had Balanchine been a fortune-teller, he couldn't have expressed more clearly the relationship that would shortly develop between Robbins and Le Clercq. Despite the age difference (he was thirty-one, she twenty), they were in many ways two of a kind—not unlike a pair of talented, ambitious, and very smart siblings. They wrote bantering letters when apart. They shared a sharp wit and a zest for games (especially charades and all manner of word games; she considered herself a champion at Botticelli). He loved her deeply—rather more than she loved him—and was puzzled when she occasionally turned a cold shoulder for no reason that he could discern.

Prodigal Son, with its Prokofiev score and decor by Georges Rouault, was an essay in modernism. Boris Kochno's scenario stripped away details of the biblical narrative so that dancing and structural devices (like the tower that becomes a table, a wall, a treacherous ramp, a boat) could convey the tale. There is no virtuous brother jealous of the father's love for his errant son, only two daughters, docile to the point of invisibility, and a pair of disloyal servants. The riotous living in which the Prodigal wastes his substance is encapsulated in a scene of debauchery, seduction, and torment amid a spooky throng of bald thugs masterminded by a bandit queen—a variant of the familiar predatory female who thrilled audiences in such Diaghilev productions as Fokine's *Cléopâtre* and *Thamar.*

The ballet presented Robbins with an enormous challenge. Later New

York City Ballet aficionados, accustomed to virtuosos such as Edward Villella and Mikhail Baryshnikov (or Peter Boal, who was coached in the role
by Robbins in 1986), may wonder how Robbins managed that iconic high
leap with which the biblical miscreant expresses his longing to be quit of his
father's house. Reading the reviews, it seems as if Robbins's leaps and turns
never stood out as such, although he told Nancy Reynolds in 1974 that he
remembered some steps Balanchine had given him to perform with the
male ensemble that Villella wasn't currently doing. His costume was less
the Roman warrior's outfit it usually is today and more a modest version of
what Serge Lifar had worn in the original 1929 production: knee-length
tights and a gathered shirt with a white turban whose hanging ends mingle
with a short white cape. In photos, with his dark skin and white teeth, Robbins looks very Middle Eastern and very much the rebellious, skinny boy.
Certainly, given his modern dance background, he felt at home with the
often clumsy steps Balanchine used in this ballet and understood perfectly
the son's emotional journey from pride to humiliation at the hands of the
venal Siren and her squad of goons, followed by the humble, agonizing
crawl homeward and final poignant climb up into his waiting father's
arms. The difficult part, Robbins recalled, was avoiding self-pity.

The original Siren, Felia Dubrovska, by then teaching at the company's
affiliate, the School of American Ballet, was on hand to help Balanchine
recall the choreography. Although Dubrovska was tall, Balanchine assigned the plum role of the siren to Tallchief, who was shorter than Robbins, thus depriving spectators of a towering Siren enfolding the small boy
with her spidery arms and legs (a feature of both the original and subsequent productions). Tallchief herself felt miscast, and the critics were not
enthusiastic, but they raved over Robbins. His performance was, recalled
playwright Robert Sealy, "like the best kind of silent movie acting. . . . It
was distant, mysterious, thrilling, like reading an illustrated Bible story by
flashlight in the dark." A year after the ballet was performed on the
company's first trip to Europe that summer, a friend in Paris wrote Robbins, saying that his performance in *Prodigal* was one of the most moving
things he had ever seen. Struggling to find the right word for the quality
he so much admired, the correspondent settled on *pudeur*. "Discretion is
not the word, because discretion could have a weaker meaning, weaken
the expression. Pudeur doesn't. It goes with the greatest strength too. It
has something to do with the fact of not showing off, of not dancing to use
the dance and the part to one's own profit, but of dancing for the part and

for the dance. It's almost a moral attitude." This captures exactly what Robbins hoped for from dancers in his own works. He shared *Dance Magazine*'s award for "outstanding performing dancers" of the 1949–1950 season with Martha Graham.

~

While Robbins was rehearsing *Prodigal Son,* he was preparing his own ballet, his most ambitious to date. *Age of Anxiety,* inspired by W. H. Auden's poem, premiered on February 28, only three days after the Balanchine revival.

Auden had begun writing his epic odyssey in 1944, during World War II, but it was first published in the United States in 1947 and spoke also to the restlessness and uneasiness of the postwar years. Auden, who had emigrated to America, was much lionized in Manhattan—especially within the intellectual gay community, but in all artistic circles. (Invited to dinner by Balanchine in 1948, Igor Stravinsky and his wife asked if they might bring Auden along.) Lincoln Kirstein, a close friend, was certainly familiar with *Age of Anxiety,* and so was Bernstein. In fact, the scenario Robbins devised for his ballet was determined less by the poem than by Bernstein's musical setting of it in "The Age of Anxiety," Symphony No. 2 for Piano and Orchestra (1948).

As Bernstein biographer Humphrey Burton has pointed out, the work is, in places, more like a concerto than a symphony, but the composer wrote that, rather than use the piano as a virtuoso voice, he had conceived it as "an almost autobiographical protagonist," involved, like the four protagonists of Auden's poem, in a search for faith—for something to hold to in troubled times.

Bernstein's belief in the creative agility of his unconscious mind and his continuing interest in psychology may explain in part his attraction to the poem. As John Fuller, author of *W. H. Auden: A Commentary,* has convincingly suggested in his analysis of the poem, the four lonely people who meet in a bar are not only real characters, each symbolizes one of "the four faculties indicated by [Carl] Jung's *t'ai chi t'u,* a diagrammatic representation of the processes of the psyche." Thus Rosetta, a Jewish department store buyer, represents Feeling; Malin, an officer in the Canadian Air Force, stands for Thinking; Quant, an Irish clerk, is associated with Intuition; and Emble, a young naval recruit, with Sensation. They embark on a journey—what Bernstein called a "dream odyssey"—without actually moving any farther than the distance from their bar stools to a booth. They seem to achieve some success, some self-knowledge, but fulfillment is denied them, "For the world from which their journey has been one long flight rises up before them now as if the whole time it had been hiding in ambush, only waiting for the worst moment to reappear to its fugitives in all the majesty of its perpetual fury." In a cab, on the way to Rosetta's apartment for a nightcap, the four intone a "Dirge" for the loss of "our lost dad, / Our colossal father"—possibly mourning, Auden hints, the death of Franklin Roosevelt but, more profoundly, the absence of heroes to whom they can turn.

Here is how the composer described his penultimate musical resolution of Auden's "Epilogue":

> What is left, it turns out, is faith. The trumpet intrudes a statement of "something pure" upon the dying pianino: the strings answer in a melancholy reminiscent of the "Prologue": again and again the winds reiterate "something pure" against the mounting tension of the strings' loneliness. All at once the strings accept the situation, in a sudden radiant pianissimo, and begin to build, with the rest of the orchestra, to a positive statement of the newly-recognized faith.

A less daring choreographer would not have tackled Auden's complexities, even in an abstract way. Bernstein's music must have given Robbins courage; it has that American sound, occasionally Coplandesque, often redolent of jazz rhythms and full of artful syncopations. The overall contrast between minimal passages and great stacks of chords give the symphony an enormous sense of drama as well as conveying the tension between quiet thought and restless action.

Robbins, of course, steered clear of complicated narrative details. Praising the ballet, Doris Hering stressed that "[Robbins] makes no attempt to lean upon the literary framework. It speaks instead with the infinite eloquence of the kinetic language. In other words, Robbins has penetrated into that fluid realm where only movement speaks."

It is instructive to leaf through Robbins's copy of the poem and see what he underlined, what he jotted down in the margins. His choreographer's eye tends to pick out verbs, allusions to emotional states that can be physicalized, and images that suggest spatial configurations, as well as phrases he considers key to the poem's meaning. So as "The Seven Ages" section begins, he writes: "watching, observing—fear of action—defiance/plunge—the smile, cough." He underlines Malin's words: ". . . his inner life/Is a zig-zag, a bizarre dance of / Feelings through facts . . ." and plucks sexuality as an approach to the Third Age from the words, ". . . however violent / Their wish to be one, that wild promise / Cannot be kept . . ." He extracts from Emble's speech on the Fifth Age "To be young means/To be all on edge, to be held waiting . . ."; and, from Rosetta's, "Unattached as tumble-weed. . . ."

From Auden's characters' occasional glances into the mirror over the bar, Robbins conceived some of the ballet's most striking images. In "The Seven Stages," the four characters (originally played by Tanaquil Le Clercq, Todd Bolender, Francisco Moncion, and Robbins) acquire dou-bles, who imitate their gestures. An ensemble of sixteen women in sleeve-less red leotards and faceless in fencing masks, in Moncion's words, "become obstructions, they become hurdles, they become alleys." There was also a passage, he remembered, "where they were like turnstiles and we had to break through them; they lined up in various directions and we had to find our way out of the maze; they shifted directions, which caught us against the wall." In black-and-white fragments, filmed from back-stage, Nora Kaye (who replaced Le Clercq when the latter injured her ankle) confronts her double through a line of women, who turn to face now one protagonist, now her image, and block any merging.

The film scraps, mystifying though they are out of context, are stun-ning. We can see the simple beginning after the four have entered, when they walk into a close circle and gaze at one another. In a 2000 interview, Bolender tried to describe and demonstrate that opening:

> And then we reached out and touched each other this way [formally and reticently, yet inquisitively]. And then we did a grand plié, all four of us, with knees straight forward. And then we rose up and we dropped our arms and then we would look—I would look at you and you would look away from me. And [that pattern passed] right through the line and then back again until finally it ended back at this person and then we would look at each other across [the circle], like that. Then we started to back away from each other and then one person would start off in one direction and another and another and another. And then suddenly a sweep of dancers would come through and they would pick up one of the people.

This led into the variations representing the seven ages of man—a man struggling out of infancy, a woman dancing with the impetuousness of youth, lovers, and so on. The film captures a solo performed by Kaye (possibly that second variation) that is startling in its vitality. The steps are balletic: front attitude on pointe drawing in to passé, for instance, but Kaye uses her torso in such a full and free way that the movement looks unusually bold and three-dimensional. The film also shows parts of several striking duets; one performed by Kaye and Moncion suggests the impossibility of truly merging; held, she stretches away from him, yet leans against him when he pulls her in. At one point, he catches her in midair and she hangs, curled in fetal position, over his arm.

A restless energy informs the group; in one phrase, they leap and hop, thrusting their legs now front, now back, now side; they dash past the camera. You can understand what Bolender meant when he said that "[Jerry] seemed to focus the very word *anxiety* in his movement—jagged, almost unrelated things, like tics sometimes, throughout the body." He might have been describing the "Masque," where the four characters and the ensemble begin by twitching, as if Bernstein's jazzy scherzo for piano and percussion were jolting through them like some kind of forced laughter. They throw their legs front and back in a desperately jolly Charleston—both separately and in a linked line; because some people face forward in the line, others the reverse, the steps look dislocated. Men and women engage in dissolute ballroom dances, the women hanging on their partners, legs dragging in weariness or intoxication.

What the film doesn't reveal is any glimpse of the "Dirge," with its homage to Auden's "colossal father" (nor does it show Oliver Smith's spare but realistic set of city buildings). Robbins put his own slant on the "Dirge" (which may have contributed to Auden's reputed dislike of the ballet). He conceived a black-hooded, puppetlike figure, tottering on platform shoes. Edward Bigelow, who played the role, himself contrived what he describes as "high wedgies" on which he could "lumber around—a walking prop." The principals and ensemble fall on their knees before him, but he, an unstable and imperfect "god," created from their own need, collapses and falls. Nor did Robbins, who was somewhat skeptical of religion, imply faith in God as a solution to anxiety. His four reiterate their opening circle, bow to one another, and go off in separate directions, somehow strengthened by the fellowship they have discovered and the new awareness it has roused in them.

Given the scope of the ballet, you might guess that the process of hammering it out was harrowing, but apparently, beyond the occasional flare of Robbins's redoubtable temper, it was not. Bolender remembers "wonderful rehearsals":

> Jerry would call us in to rehearsal at maybe noon and then we would work until about six o'clock. And he'd say, "Let's have some food." We'd go out and have dinner for an hour or something, come back, and we'd work until midnight. Just the four of us. . . . We had a great time. He started giving us different names. He called us Pussyfoot and Piston and I've forgotten what—each one had a different name. Oh, and Puce. It always had a "P." . . . And then, of course, he would think up a new name, and we'd all fall down on the floor laughing. We were so exhausted by that time we would laugh at anything. But the thing between the four of us was that we worked together marvelously. It was really a unit. And I loved the ballet. He gave me things that expanded me, I felt, and sometimes he'd fight with me about getting things. He'd say, "Do it bigger, don't be so lazy. Get into the air." And so I did. It was very exciting.

Observers, too, found *Age of Anxiety* exciting but not easy. John Martin prepared his readers by writing that the ballet was "quite as obscure as Auden's poem and just as unavoidably unresolved. But if you are interested in seeing one of the most sensitive and deeply creative talents in the choreographic field tackling his most profound and provocative assignment with uncompromising vision, you will find the piece completely fascinating. [Robbins's] intuition is uncannily penetrating, his emotional integrity is unassailable, and his choreographic idiom is lean and strong and dramatically functional."

Age of Anxiety, like all Robbins's early ballets, asserts an absorption with communities and human interaction that would also, in different ways, shape his later ballets and, eventually, his musical comedies. He didn't often focus closely on the inner feelings of a persona, as did Martha Graham, or dissect characters with the Freudian precision of Antony Tudor. The sailors of *Fancy Free* seek to reveal their individuality through showing off, but it is their comradeship that we remember. The kids of *Interplay,* the bored trio of *Facsimile,* the lovers of *The Guests,* and the four searchers of *Age of Anxiety* define themselves through how they behave within a group—through how that society makes them dance.

Dance Magazine accorded Robbins another accolade for the 1949–1950 season, to go along with the award for his performance in *The Prodigal Son*. This one went to *Age of Anxiety* as an outstanding achievement in choreography in the ballet category. Robbins shared the honors with Herbert Ross (for *Caprichos*) and, more important as far as he was concerned, with George Balanchine and his new *Firebird*.

9

Walking a Tightrope

Nicholas Magallanes and Nora Kaye in Robbins's *The Cage*.
Walter Owen/ NYPL.

Balanchine *often worked correctively,* giving a female dancer steps that might expand her range or pressing a male dancer into a different sort of role. Casting a shrewd eye on Robbins, he decided that the younger choreographer needed prodding; he agonized too much over his ballets. Balanchine's idea was that you made a lot of ballets, and even if a few of them were bad, you learned something, and eventually you became more fluent; if you were lucky, one of those works would be great. For the New York City Ballet's 1950 spring season at City Center, he corralled Robbins into a joint project. To loosen him up about choreography, he decided that they'd make *Jones Beach* together. The music was contemporary: the first of the very young Dutch composer Jurriaan Andriessen's *Berkshire Symphonies,* and Jantzen, the bathing suit company, donated appropriate beachwear in return for the publicity. The project sounds like something Lincoln Kirstein could have concocted; giving the public an occasional novelty made good business sense.

The ballet was mapped out in four sections: "Sunday," "Rescue from Drowning," "War with Mosquitoes," and "Hot Dogs." Perhaps it was as a sardonic allusion to Jantzen's largesse that Balanchine remarked, "I hate mosquitoes. I think if I give them free advertising, they may be kind to me later."

Here's how Robbins described the collaborative process to Ellen Sorrin:

I was rehearsing in one room and he was rehearsing in another. And after about an hour and a half, two hours, he came out and said, "Okay, come on. Come with me." So I went into the other room and he showed me how much he had choreographed . . . and said, "Okay, you go on." I said, "What do you mean?" He said, "You pick up where I finished and you go on for the next part," and he walked out. I just dove in, picked up where he stopped and went on choreographing. I had no idea what it was about. And I went on for another hour and a half, and I said, "Okay, your turn," and back he went. I think he did the second and third movements himself, except that he turned one of them over to me after he'd finished and said, "You play with it. If you want to change anything, change." And then the last movement he choreographed on me.

Even from still photographs of the ballet, notably George Platt Lynes's exquisite compositions, you can tell that the high point of *Jones Beach* was Balanchine's second movement, a duet for Le Clercq and Nicholas Magallanes, in which Le Clercq is bewitchingly limp (the positions Balanchine—and Magallanes—managed to get her into are extraordinary) and her rescuer is making love to her even as he engages in artificial respiration. Robbins did quite a lot of work, apparently, on the mosquito section, in which, according to *Dance Magazine* critic Doris Hering, "seven pretty little female mosquitoes pricked their way around three robust reclining

males. A mighty battle ensued and ended with the men standing in triumph like big-game hunters over the inert form of—one mosquito." (A
year later, Robbins turned the tables in his far darker insect ballet, *The
Cage.*) Robbins and Tallchief led the last section, which brought back the
full company. Lynes's photos show the two in attractive, sweetly amorous
duet poses against a soft-focus beach, but Le Clercq told Rick Whitaker of
Ballet Review, "They came tearing on upstage left, made a diagonal, and
performed a fast and jazzy number. Then they came way down to the orchestra pit and pretended to roast hot dogs."

John Martin called *Jones Beach* "a piece of vivacious nonsense." However, two days later, he devoted a Sunday article to Robbins, commenting
that in *Age of Anxiety,* he had reached "artistic maturity," and that his joining New York City Ballet was a fine thing for the organization.

Robbins seemed committed to the company. Although he went to Hollywood in April to confer about the planned movie of *Look Ma, I'm
Dancin'!,* it was also reported in the *Chicago Tribune* that month that he
had backed out of an agreement to choreograph *Pal Joey* on Broadway because he wanted to travel to London with the New York City Ballet. However, the contract he signed with the company in June suggests that he
might not have planned to be there for the entire Covent Garden season
(July 10 through August 19) or for the engagements in provincial English
cities that followed. This may have been because he had signed another
contract later in June, agreeing to choreograph a new musical that was
scheduled to begin its New Haven tryouts on September 11. *Call Me
Madam* had a book by Howard Lindsay and Russell Crouse, the successful
creators of *Life with Father,* and music by Irving Berlin. George Abbott
would direct. Robbins wrote succinctly to Robert Fizdale: "nice fee and
percentage. Will do it." With that in the offing, he could well afford to
dance in Britain with NYCB for $84 (or "not less than $72") a week.

Ironically, England didn't get to see much of Robbins the dancer.
His performances in *Age of Anxiety* and *Bourrée Fantasque* were admired,
but he injured an ankle, and Francisco Moncion danced his role in *Prodigal Son.*

Since, with some notable exceptions, British ballet inclined toward narrative classics and dramatic modern ballets, attempts had been made to
prime Londoners for the New York City Ballet's cool style and Balanchine's plotless works. Richard Buckle's magazine *Ballet* had printed a
typically erudite two-part article by Lincoln Kirstein, avowing that

There is, in the best examples of classic American style, a leanness, visual asceticism, a candour, even an awkwardness which is in itself elegant, shared also by some of our finest Colonial silver, the thin carving on New England grave slabs and in the quicksilver of Emily Dickinson's unrhythmed quatrains. And sometimes there is a galvanizing, acetylene brilliance, a deep potential of incalculable human strength which, particularly between our wars, is a novel and hopeful guarantee.

Londoners did not fully buy this. *Orpheus* won "passionate admiration," as did *Prodigal Son* (although critics didn't care much for Balanchine's *Firebird,* finding it neither sufficiently like Fokine's original nor a radical departure). They weren't bowled over by New York City Ballet's new *Illuminations* by their own Frederick Ashton, with music by a British composer—Benjamin Britten's settings of some of Arthur Rimbaud's poems—and costumes by a British designer, Cecil Beaton. They admired Balanchine's *Serenade,* which exuded Romantic feeling (just as they could warm to *Ballet Imperial,* which he had recently staged for the Sadler's Wells, in part because it had tutus and grand manners—a Petipa ballet without a plot). However, the no-frills classicism of *Concerto Barocco* and *Symphonie Concertante,* along with the company's cool performing style, came under fire, striking many critics—with the notable exceptions of Clive Barnes and Richard Buckle—as somehow meager. (Buckle went so far as to mock his colleagues for their addiction to "psycho-sexo-dramas" and traditional story ballets in a wicked satirical playlet titled "Critics' Sabbath.")

It's not surprising, then, that *The Guests* and *Age of Anxiety* received good marks for Robbins's assured handling of serious dramatic subject matter. And when Ballet Theatre (temporarily billed as American National Ballet Theatre) played London hard on the heels of New York City Ballet (August 27 to September 19), offering *Fancy Free, Interplay,* and *Facsimile,* he came in for additional critical attention. Although *Facsimile* was, on the whole, considered interesting and not too likable—if wonderfully performed—the two earlier works, according to critic Mary Clarke, were already "firm favorites in London," remembered from when Ballet Theatre played there in 1946.

∼

Like all the musicals Robbins had choreographed since *On the Town, Call Me Madam* didn't offer him opportunities to mold the script's ideas through dance or even, as he later said, "opportunities for me to cut loose," although he did his damnedest to create them. During the rehearsal period, he wrote to Fizdale that he hadn't so far gone through "great turmoil and anxiety with the show . . . but on the other hand I don't feel I've turned up with anything special either. . . . This has really been a whore's job: doing it for money."

A vehicle for Ethel Merman, the story had been inspired by President Truman's appointment of wealthy Washington hostess Perle Mesta as ambassador to Luxembourg (even though the program prudently, if waggishly, noted "Neither the character of Mrs. Sally Adams, nor Miss Ethel Merman, resembles any other person, living or dead"). In her ability to dominate a stage, Merman resembled few other living performers either. The story was slight but sufficient. Mrs. Sally Adams, possessed of an enormous oil fortune, is good at heart but a bit uncouth, apt to put her foot in her mouth, and used to solving problems by tossing money around. Appointed to the tiny, poor, but proud principality of Lichtenburg, she learns a few lessons, as do the Lichtenburgers, starting with the distinguished premier, Cosmo Constantine (played by Paul Lukas) with whom she falls in love. Irving Berlin's bright and tune-rich score played American brashness against the little country's music-box quaintness.

Call Me Madam was a perfect Cold War musical, reflecting in a lighthearted and satirical way European stereotypes of the "ugly American" and attempting to correct them. The "Washington Square Dance" presents Mrs. Adams's ball, tongue very much in cheek, as a great equalizer, a sort of microcosm of America where people of all persuasions and backgrounds dance together. Squarely. Berlin, like Robbins the son of Russian-Jewish immigrants, was a patriot, and a fragment of his "God Bless America" wells up in the score. Sally gives a topical slant to her calls: "Dive for the oyster, dig for the clam" is followed by an exhortation to do the digging "for Uncle Sam," and "one for the money, two for the show, three to get ready" points to the looming danger of "Uncle Joe."

The United States' shift toward conservatism was noted and approved in one number. Although the national election was two years away and the candidates undeclared, the marching song "They Like Ike" gave Dwight Eisenhower's eventual campaign a boost and a slogan. The song was purportedly a wacky argument between Democratic and Republican senators and congressmen, but Berlin's lyrics portray President Harry Truman only as an incumbent with squatter's rights.

There's a dichotomy in Robbins's musical comedy work. On the one hand, he could demonstrate an extraordinary grasp of the whole, whatever he divined that to be, and how every part should reinforce the main theme. Notes he wrote in the margins of scripts in progress often took the tack "What is this scene really about?" Or "How does this relate to the key idea?" His sense of how to determine this idea and shape material around it made him invaluable as a "show doctor." On the other hand, he naturally approached each new musical with an eye to getting as much interesting dance into it as possible. This second Robbins, the creative wildfire, often had to cut numbers he had slaved over—bowing to the decisions of collaborators that the first Robbins knew deep down were inevitable.

He optimistically planned a ballet for *Madam*. The Lichtenburg leader was to show Sally Adams some native dances. It was for this festive occasion that Robbins concocted the solo for Rall that William Weslow referred to as the "Wild Man from the Mountain," embedded in some unbridled Gypsy dancing for the ensemble.

Kirsten Valbor, who danced in the show, attests to the slimness of the pretext: "They talked about the wild people that lived up in the mountains. It was the most awkward introduction . . . 'Oh, here they come now!' and then 'Oh, look, they're starting to dance.' Then we started to dance. How convenient!"

But she thought the number itself was "a phenomenal piece of choreography. . . . It was a *killer*. The tempo kept building up, and, God, we all had floor burns and bruises. We'd get off the stage and just fall over; you couldn't breathe anymore. But it was wonderful." There were spectacular lifts: "We were spun around in some strange way on the floor and swept up over [our partners' heads] and I don't know what." At the end, the Gypsies clustered around Rall, who began to whirl an enormous artificial bird at the end of a rope. It made a clicking sound ("k-ta-k-ta-k-ta-k-ta"), and as its circle enlarged and became more rapid, so did the dance. Weslow remembers the kaleidoscopic effect that the costumes gave, "those beautiful reds and purples and greens and oranges and yellows and blacks. We just dazzled as we went around the stage."

Jerry's beloved friend Slim—formerly the wife of film director Howard Hawks, then married to *Madam*'s producer, Leland Hayward, later the wife of British banker Sir Kenneth Keith—had less charitable memories of the number. In her memoir, she said that the whirling bird "looked like an out-of-work bat with a glandular problem." (She should know; she salvaged the creature, had it decked in flowers, and sent it to Jerry as an opening-night gift. The two of them kept exchanging it until they got sick of the game.)

As might have been expected, the wild orgy of dancing was cut. All that remained in the way of Lichtenburg culture was the tinkly, catchy song-and-dance "Ocarina," with two musicians billed as "Potato Bugs" soloing on the flutey sweet-potato-shaped instruments.

Jerry had to weather another disappointment. Berlin had brought along the discarded "Mr. Monotony," and Robbins set it on Muriel Bentley, Rall, and Arthur Partington. It was jammed into the script as a cultural artifact that Sally Adams was importing to introduce Lichtenburg to American jazz. Donald Saddler, who had come up to Boston to assist Robbins (and staged "It's a Lovely Day Today"), remembers watching the show beside him one night. "Mr. Monotony" began. "It went like gangbusters. Merman introduced it [i.e., sang the song] and exited, and when she came back she couldn't go on because they were applauding so much. Jerry said, 'Watch, Don, it's going to go out.' " It did.

Robbins did persuade Berlin that, with "Mr. Monotony" gone, the beginning of Act II needed more dancing. Like what, for instance? " 'Look, just give me something to dance about and I'll do it.' Stop—freeze—a look on Irving's face. 'Not bad,' he said, 'Damned good title.' " In a few days, Berlin came up with "Something to Dance About"; it gave the dancers—Bentley and Rall were featured—a chance to zip from fox-trot to tango to waltz to rhumba while Merman belted out the song. (Robbins's retrospective verdict was "OK. No great shakes.")

The cuts and substitutions didn't help Robbins's disposition. Although on breaks in Boston during tryouts he and some of the male dancers would sit in the park and make up bawdy limericks about other dancers in the show, especially the women (Valbor remembers being miffed because their first effort to immortalize her was so polite), rehearsals were less agreeable. Robbins would take out his frustrations on Weslow or his old friend Bentley. If Rall dropped her in a lift, it was her fault. The others averted their faces. He also attempted, in the name of realism, to savage the gorgeous heavy costumes that Madame Karinska had hand-embroidered to designer Raoul Pène du Bois's specifications—slashing them ragged, ripping out sleeves (Karinska screaming in horror) before he was stopped.

Despite his own dissatisfaction, Robbins had predicted early on that the show would be a hit. With a top ticket price of $7.20, *Call Me Madam* opened in New York on October 12 with a stunning advance sale of $1,000,000 and ran for eighteen months. "Let's not pretend that the book is immortal," wrote Brooks Atkinson in the *Times,* but, like his confrères, he hailed Merman ("still lighting up like an inspired pinball machine") and thought Berlin had produced "one of his most enchanting scores." Robbins was scarcely mentioned in the reviews. John Chapman of the *Daily News* called his dances "smart, bright," Howard Barnes of the *Herald Tribune* thought them "gay," and William Hawkins of the *New York World-Telegram* trotted out "fresh, young dances."

Six years later, Robbins wrote Slim Hayward from Copenhagen that he'd been invited to attend the premiere, in Odense, of a "light opera." Sure, he had said. What was it? A translation of an American light opera entitled *Call Me Madam.* Had he ever heard of it? Robbins finished this account with "(sound of a falling body, mutterings [?] of 'that goddam bird will never let go etc.')."

⌒

After Call Me Madam opened, Robbins left for Europe. If the show was sanguine about the future, many in America were not, he among them. Nuclear war seemed a strong possibility. Schoolchildren were being taught to crouch under their desks should a bombing materialize. He wrote Fizdale that he was "horrified (yet amused in some way). . . . They are completely preparing us to accept the idea of New York and other cities being destroyed."

He had another reason to be uneasy. His two years in the Communist Party were coming back to haunt him, and his behavior and career decisions for the next three years would be to some degree influenced by fear.

Robbins had gotten an inkling of what he was up against back in February. He was scheduled to appear on Ed Sullivan's Easter telecast when his agent, Howard Hoyt, learned that the show's sponsor, Ford Motors, had ordered Sullivan to clear all potential performers with the watchdog magazine *Counterattack.* Sullivan checked and found that Robbins had a record of Party membership and support for alleged front organizations. It was suggested that the choreographer bow out with a telegram about not being able to clear the music rights "or some such excuse."

Justifiable postwar fears about Soviet expansion, fueled by the 1948 Communist coup in Czechoslovakia, and the threat of Soviet espionage and possible sabotage within the United States were breeding hysteria. The ranting of Senator Joseph McCarthy of Wisconsin and the vigilantism of the congressmen making up the House Committee on Un-American Activities had turned the search for Soviet agents into a horrid carnival of confession, blackmail, and accusation. As Arthur Schlesinger, Jr., remarked of HUAC's highly publicized investigations of communism in Hollywood in his review of Victor Navasky's important book *Naming Names,* "The Committee's inquisitorial zeal had no justification in the protection of national security, nor in the need for legislation, nor in the oversight of government, nor even in the discovery of known facts, since it had independent access to Communist Party membership." Even many staunch anti-Stalinists and those who, like Robbins, had years before turned away from the Party and its agenda were appalled by how easy it was to ruin a career on the flimsiest of evidence.

Robbins seems to have panicked after a meeting with Sullivan. Hoping to clear his name, he and Hoyt met with Theodore Kirkpatrick, the ex–FBI agent who published *Counterattack.* He decided against writing, as he was urged to do, a confession of his former Communist affiliations for the magazine, even though Kirkpatrick told him "that it was to his definite advantage that he straighten himself out as soon as possible for if an Atom Bomb were to be dropped the FBI would no doubt pick [him] up among the first of those rounded up." In April, Robbins and Hoyt went to the FBI, apparently expecting naively that if Jerry admitted he'd joined the Party in late 1943, left it in disillusionment three years later, and lent his name to several supposed "Communist front" organizations he had mistaken for good causes, he could avoid public testimony.

The FBI agent who wrote the report doubted Robbins's veracity (although he probably wouldn't have picked up one whopper Jerry let fall: he said he'd attended the Cultural Council for World Peace in 1949 at the Waldorf-Astoria because he had always wanted to meet Aaron Copland). The agent thought that Robbins had no interest in telling the FBI anything it didn't already know but rather wanted to interject the agency into a "squeeze play" between Sullivan and *Counterattack.* An undated "Letter to the Director" notes that Robbins had been "unable" to remember names, dates, or places.

It must have been these events that Robbins was referring to in an enigmatic and emotional meditation written in Paris on Monday, November 13. He speaks of his own talent—to him, a frail and incomprehensible gift, something that could be withdrawn at any time—wondering why "it" still comes out of him. And "Will it still come out of me after that confession and giving up is over with?"

At the Hôtel Quai Voltaire, recently turned thirty-two, he meditated somberly on Faust, "Not as an aged man who dotes and pines—but as a man 35–40 who already knows his youth had passed." He waxed poetic in regret for an unnamed lost love: "And now is the time when pain will come and nicely touch the falling heart. A drop [edited from "spot"; was he considering publication some day, or was he a perfectionist even in the privacy of his mind?], the first to fall when the lover sees another love, deceived. . . . I have never regretted a tie gone by before. . . . Why now?"

Feeling fragile, perhaps because he'd completed, not altogether to his satisfaction, his six-year analysis with Dr. Arkin, he concluded, "When will I find myself & what I believe in again. When can the 'I' join the 'me' and be whole to work together again."

Nevertheless, he didn't spend his time in Paris being glum. With the French dancer-choreographer Jean Babilée and his dancer wife, Nathalie Philippart (then guest artists with Ballet Theatre), he went to see some Balinese dancers and sketched one in his journal. He hooked up with old Ballet Theatre pals during the company's Paris appearances (November 17 to December 6). Two days after his dark period, his mood was beginning to lift:

Nora [Kaye] is staying with me. I like it. I like the companionship & like the sex. I guess yes it's like we have been married for 10 years & some of the excitement of a younger & more passionate kind of love (& not just sexually passionate) is missing. Nor do I feel a be-all-and-end-all feeling about it. Nor do I at all think it a negative thing to say we get on well. It's more than that, but that is plenty. Nor am I putting myself on any test basis. What is, is, & what will be, will be & I no longer expect perfection or disaster from myself. I'll indulge I guess sometime elsewhere & otherwise sexually, I think—but now this with Nora feels like home.

A few lines later, he returned more optimistically to his theme of two days before: "Maybe the splits & seams in me are coming together again—maybe it's all coming together & I'll not be afraid to look at people & feel [a] fraud. Where does the talent come from I wonder, when I have felt such a hoax."

This last was, sadly, a theme that he would repeat over the years, even as he accumulated wealth, awards, and successes, and his reputation as a great American choreographer became established.

On November 15, the very day Jerry was writing his heart out in a Paris hotel, the New York City Ballet was opening a monthlong season at City Center. Why wasn't he performing? The ankle he had injured in July should surely have healed. Why had he not been there to choreograph a piece for the company he so admired? His relationship with Balanchine was not turning into a close personal friendship as he had hoped, yet he had written to Fizdale around the time of the London season, "I have gotten to be closer to George & love him very much." His fear of being hauled up before the HUAC and his inner turmoil over his career seems to have had a paralyzing effect.

However, Robbins came out of his funk and fairly bubbled to Fizdale in a December letter from Paris. He did mention that with the "war news looking so bad," perhaps they'd like him to ship Fizdale and Gold's car, "George"—named in honor of Balanchine—home to the United States. (Robbins had been using George in Europe while the pianists used his car in New York.) But everything else was written on a high. Ballet Theatre was having a tremendous success in Paris; as in London, *Fancy Free* and *Interplay* were favorites with the public. He had three new ballets "under the skull." He was off to Berlin, then back to Paris, then to New York for three months "to do one ballet for *Anna and the King of Siam* for Rodgers and Hammerstein. It is just a lovely work—and is all I have to do in the show." Then he planned to return to Paris to work with "a new French company in Monte Carlo." That would eat up April, May, and June. In July, he'd make a new ballet in Venice. In addition, he had "many other commitments & wonderful plans to return and work."

Strange that the New York City Ballet doesn't seem to figure in this busy schedule, especially since Nora Kaye had left Ballet Theatre to join Balanchine's company—in part to work with Tudor, who, along with Hugh Laing and Diana Adams, had also severed his connection with Lucia Chase and Oliver Smith's company and was to set several works on the Kirstein-Balanchine enterprise. While Kaye was making her NYCB debut in February, somewhat miscast in Balanchine's classical *Pas de Trois,* and the master, his marriage to Tallchief dissolving, was premiering his haunting masterpiece *La Valse,* starring his new love, Le Clercq, Robbins was busy with *The King and I.*

However, a newspaper article dated February 14, 1951, indicated that Robbins would be free to dance his roles in *Age of Anxiety, Bourrée Fantasque,* and *Mother Goose,* and, for whatever reasons, he did not, after his triumph with *The King and I,* spread his talents over Monte Carlo and Venice. Instead, in June, he presented the New York City Ballet with one of his best works and Kaye with one of her most stunning roles—that of the Novice in *The Cage.*

∽

It's easy to understand why Robbins found *The King and I* a tempting project. Richard Rodgers and Oscar Hammerstein II were the current kings of musical theater, and Jerry had yet to work with them. De Mille had choreographed their two biggest hits, *Oklahoma!* and *Carousel,* as well as choreographing and directing their prestigious and innovative flop *Allegro* (*South Pacific* had no choreography to speak of). The show—starring the marvelously versatile English actress Gertrude Lawrence in what would be her last role and the less well known and furiously charismatic Yul Brynner—offered Robbins one of his favorite pastimes: to research and reinvent another era—and, in this case, another culture.

A successful movie, *Anna and the King of Siam,* starring Irene Dunne and Rex Harrison, had already been made from Margaret Landon's novel based on the diaries of Anna Leonowens, a widowed Englishwoman who, in the 1860s, went to what is now Thailand to tutor the crown prince. The tale cried out for musical treatment. The clashes and deeply buried love between a proper lady raised in a Western republic and a feudal monarch equipped with a multitude of wives could not only yield both tragedy and comedy, they could generate cross-cultural lessons in song, and sermons that danced.

Little had been written specifically about the dances of Siam. Robbins found useful material on neighboring Cambodia and Laos in such books as Raymond Cogniat's *Danses d'Indochine,* which includes photos of masked demons and "Khmer Dancing Girls" as Apsaras (or celestial dancers) in their high-tiered golden headdresses. He probably also saw articles in the September and October issues of *Dance Magazine* written by the dancer-choreographer Mara von Sellheim, who performed simply as Mara. Before the war, this woman, born in Manchuria of Russian-French parentage, had become proficient in several Asian forms, studying Cambodian dance at the court at Phnom Penh. At the time that Robbins met her, she was running a small company in New York. He was very taken with her. She assisted him in the initial mapping out of "The Small House of Uncle Thomas," a dance-theater piece that "Mrs. Anna" and the king's wives create based on a book she has introduced them to: Harriet Beecher Stowe's Civil War–era novel, *Uncle Tom's Cabin*. (Mara's scribbles in the margins of an early script, for instance, warn him against having trained poodles play the roles of the bloodhounds pursuing Eliza: "No!!! Jerry— this is Catskills kitchy. Out.") In a long session in early January 1951, she taught Robbins and a small group of dancers a considerable amount of the vocabulary and conventions of Cambodian court dance and demonstrated appropriate styles for the characters. Of course, being scrupulously "authentic" was never an issue for a choreographer on Broadway; Rodgers's music was hardly that. Robbins learned that in Cambodia only demons hopped but he could have Eliza hop steadily in her flight like a little cardboard puppet in a groove, being slowly pulled across.

Mara was paid and offered credit as "dance advisor" in a box after the cast list. A novice on Broadway and given bad advice, she didn't realize this was a generous offer and declined, thinking a box meant being hidden away. Additional misunderstandings resulted in her not being further involved with the musical* (much later, she wondered if Robbins had not simply gotten all he needed from her). Michiko, the Japanese dancer who played the "Angel from Buddha," became Robbins's "Consultant on Oriental Dancing" (she, like the show's leading dancer, Yuriko, had studied with Teiko Ito, who taught a potpourri of Asian styles). It was Michiko who taught the dancers the skills that Robbins needed.

"The Small House of Uncle Thomas" does honor the Cambodian court-dance custom of an all-female cast in terms of the principal dancers, as well as making use of some of its flexible hand gestures, hyperextended elbows, crawls, and the "celestial walk" (standing on one bent leg, the dancer raises the other bent leg behind her, flexed foot flat to the sky) or a similar pose kneeling. And designer Jo Mielziner provided gorgeous and more or less accurate costumes, masks, and headdresses.

The choreographer employed his usual Stanislavskian strategies to

* Robbins was accustomed to soliciting and/or accepting uncredited contributions from Broadway performers such as Danny Daniels. Mara went on to choreograph (and direct) many productions of *The King and I* in summer stock. "For Whom the Bells Tinkle," an article by her in *Dance Observer,* April 1953, contains the enigmatic tribute "Jerome Robbins took—with my compliments—the Cambodian Apsara—to Broadway."

bring the performers up to snuff dramatically. When Gemze de Lappe, one of Agnes de Mille's favorite dancers, was auditioning, Robbins demonstrated some movements, then told her to do them growling like a lion. "Dancers never made any noise in those days. I could feel the entire group just go 'gulp.' I wanted to fall through the floor. I started growling and roaring. After I'd been doing it for fifteen or twenty seconds, I stopped being inhibited about it. I could see what he was after. . . . A wonderful lesson for me." She brought that ferocity to the masked role of the ballet's villain, Simon of Legree.

The tactic worked rather less efficiently when Robbins asked Yuriko, who was playing Eliza, to rush about the studio shrieking, "Help! Help!" while jumping and executing little upthrust Eastern gestures of fright. After she'd exhausted herself, he said, "Now keep everything except the voice." At the next rehearsal, she did what she thought he wanted. "What's the matter with you?" he demanded. "You have no Asian quality in your dancing." Yuriko, used to Martha Graham's foibles, found a way to accommodate both style and terror.

However the idea came about for "The Small House of Uncle Thomas," it made the ballet integral to the plot. The harem would entertain a visiting British embassy the king was anxious to impress, not simply with a display of exotic loveliness but with a musical playlet that caught the show's important subtext: the plight of the king's newest wife, Tuptim (played by Doretta Morrow); like Eliza, she is enslaved and separated from the man she loves. The ballet's subversive message of freedom only gradually dawns on the king, and the performance gives Tuptim, its writer and narrator, the courage to flee the court.

Robbins seems to have had a good deal to do with the ballet's overall form. Handwritten drafts of the scenario exist among his papers. It is his penciled notations in a typed script that altered Tuptim's line "I beg to introduce King of Kentucky, Simon of Legree" to "I regret to put before you King Simon of Legree" and he who added the term "scientific dogs" for the bloodhounds who pursue Eliza. Trude Rittman, who had composed the dance music for many shows, devised a delicate, rhythmically clever percussion score that simulated a gamelan and accented the sudden concluding poses and rising excitement in a stylistically appropriate way. It was also vital that the music and the words of the text reinforce each other. Yuriko confirms the importance of the Robbins-Rittman collaboration to the final version of the ballet: "He would say some phrase and ask, 'What do you think of this?' And she would say, 'Oh, that's great!' And then she would start composing and ask, 'What do you think of this, Jerry? This just came into my mind.' "

Robbins made astute use of a number of Asian conventions, several of them from Japanese Kabuki theater: black-clad stage assistants and symbolic props like handheld ribbon whips for rain, a length of fabric to represent water. Eliza, Uncle Tom, Topsy, and Little Eva, ceremoniously introduced, enter singly like characters in a Noh drama. But he added savvy touches that would charm a Broadway audience. As the masked dogs crawl along in pursuit of Eliza and bend to sniff the ground, each shivers one leg in the air like an excited wagging tail. When Eliza emerges from a rainstorm, she gently shakes water off the little doll she carries to represent her baby; the music underscores the shakes with light tinkles of percussion. In a sweet, typically Robbins moment, the Angel, leading Eliza across the river that Buddha has conveniently frozen for her, gives her a little lesson in ice-skating—slithering sideways on one foot, the other daintily raised in celestial walk position. Forgetting for a few seconds that a pack of hounds and the evil master Simon, carried along in an aggressive pose by soldiers, are hot on their heels, they take childlike pleasure in the slippery surface.

Robbins also set Lawrence and Brynner (once a circus acrobat) polka-ing in "Shall We Dance?" A fan dance for Michiko became central to the little cultural exchange between Anna and the king's wives, "Getting to Know You." The cleverest idea in this number was having four wives scurry to form a living hoopskirt around Michiko so she could better imitate the movements of "Mrs. Anna." The Act I "March of the Royal Children," which charmed Anna—newly arrived and already deciding to leave this barbaric place—into staying at court, shows Robbins's canny ability to orchestrate an event.

You can read in his notations in one script (using the child performers' names) exactly how shrewdly he planned the scene to delight both Anna and the audience. It became a game for the spectator to guess just which of the thirteen children would enter next and what minute character variations would be wrung from a walk, a bow to the king, a greeting to Anna, and a retreat to one of the waiting mothers. Some carry out their duties in exemplary fashion, which highlights the "different" ones, and the tiniest provide a high degree of adorableness and some concern that they'll screw up. One daughter starts to examine Anna's dress when a finger-snap from

Daddy sends her in retreat. The Crown Prince Chululungkorn strides in with a brusque precision and arrogance that shows he's his father's son. The family's main charmer is a little girl who enters in a rush, smiling, and runs up to hug her father. He snaps his fingers; she bows, crestfallen, but is grinning again by the time she's back in place (he makes it clear she's a favorite). On the last beat of the music, they all bow together, and in the ensuing applause, Anna removes her bonnet. She'll stay.

On March 29, 1951, when *The King and I* opened on Broadway, few people would have been bothered by the plot's implication that Western ways were superior. Given the tastefulness of the scenario and production and Yul Brynner's charm, the Siamese court and its tyrant—caught between tradition and inevitable "progress"—came across as winning.

Among the sheaf of telegrams Robbins received was one saying "BEST WISHES FOR A BRILLIANT SUCCESS FROM LINCOLN GEORGE AND THE WHOLE COMPANY."

The critics from New York's five daily papers weren't so sure it was brilliant, although all found it enchanting. Most mentioned that, of course, it wasn't *South Pacific*. That Rodgers and Hammerstein show had edged the Broadway musical a notch further into mature drama. But Brooks Atkinson of the *Times* felt that "Strictly on its own terms, *The King and I* is an original and beautiful excursion into the rich splendors of the Far East, done with impeccable taste by two artists and brought to life with a warm, romantic score, idiomatic lyrics and some exquisite songs." He thought that Robbins had "put together a stunning ballet that seasons the liquid formalism of Eastern dancing with some American humor." The show ran for a record 1,246 performances.

The later (1956) Twentieth Century–Fox film of *The King and I,* for which Robbins restaged his choreography, embellished some of the production details of "Small House": a gamelan played Rittman's music. Simon's evil fingernails were three times as long and the handheld tree branches fancier. The rain was a sudden dramatic spray of rice-paper streamers—an effect used in Kabuki theater to symbolize a spiderweb; it had to be imported from Tokyo. The film, directed by Walter Lang and shot in CinemaScope 55 by Oscar-winning cinematographer Leon Shamroy, was said to have cost $6,500,000. Press releases hyped the construction of three hundred fountains.

Robbins and some of the original dancers—Yuriko, Michiko, Gemze de Lappe, and Dusty Worrall among them—went out to Hollywood in the fall of 1955, and, true to form, he came down hard on his cast, fretted over camera angles, and did his best to control every aspect of his numbers. This excerpt from a long memo to conductor Alfred Newman is telling:

> After Bar 55 (the introduction of the slave, Eliza) we have opened the sound track and Eliza needs a little something to bring her on before the gong on Bar 55-A. I would suggest perhaps a repeat of the bell rattles we use in the opening sequence, very soft, just to lead her in, or else absolutely nothing, which is kind of mysterious and beautiful. (By the way, let's be sure that all the answer gongs are heard as in Bar 61, third beat, and Bar 18, 1st beat) . . .

With this exhaustive attention to detail, it's small wonder that he wrote to Arthur Laurents,

> Needless to say, the first day was like being tossed in the washing machine, and I never spent a more miserable night [than] after it, but since then they found out I don't withdraw and sulk in a corner but keep fighting back and that a great number of my ideas are good and that all in all I'm a fairly creative guy. I saw the first two days "rushes" and was so pleased with them. They seem to have caught the delicacy, humor and poignancy all at once.

Robbins wanted and was given considerable control. The score was recorded in six-track, high-fidelity stereophonic sound. One innovation was the use of three-way closed-circuit television to enable simultaneous recording on three separate studio soundstages. For the ballet, Newman was on one stage with the musicians, Tuptim (Rita Moreno) on another with Robbins and the dancers, and the singing chorus on a third. The dancers marked their parts quietly while Robbins mouthed the words for Moreno to follow and, in effect, conducted the conductor and everybody else.

By the time the shooting was over, he could report that he was pleased with most of the ballet and that "the scars and bullet holes are scarcely visible." When the picture was released, the movie's producer, Charles Brackett (also the Academy Award–winning writer of *Lost Weekend*), wrote Robbins that he found "the reviews and the clink of coins at the box office just delightful—and I'm infinitely pleased that your wonderful contribution is appreciated so universally" and signed his letter, "My love and thanks to you."

⌒

The New York City Ballet's 1950 performances in England had given the company cachet on home turf, and the experience—its most sustained period of work so far—had undoubtedly helped weld the dancers into a stronger ensemble. During the first of two seasons that Robbins missed— four weeks at City Center from November 15 through December 14— John Martin finally and fully embraced the Balanchinian aesthetic. The company, he felt, was "at the top of its form."

> And what a company it is! Without any stars in the narrow sense of the term . . . it has a brilliant set of leading artists. . . . Here, too, is an en- semble of note; there was not one of them last night who did not dance as if she were herself a prima ballerina, yet with a feeling for the unity of the group and the framework of the composition. What more one can ask of any company it would be difficult to say.

Although Morton Baum was not in a position to guarantee the NYCB seasons far in advance, the company managed not only its February 1951 performances at City Center but another series in June, plus early-fall ap- pearances before the November season. In April, in Chicago, it gave its first U.S. performances outside New York. Still, it is indicative of the shakiness of the company's position that it seems to have been assumed that Balanchine would earn his living choreographing musicals, judging from a proposed agenda that Lincoln Kirstein attached to a letter to Betty Cage (then his secretary, soon thereafter the company's general manager) dated August 25, 1950. Among the points that Kirstein intended to pre- sent at a meeting with Baum was one concerning pay for Balanchine. He noted that the choreographer had been receiving about $300 a week from *Where's Charley?* but the show was closing, a national tour was still hang- ing fire, and his royalties were bound to be reduced.

> It is a waste to force him into trying to find a musical-show, and besides his well-known contempt for Broadway does not make it any more likely that commercial producers will want him. Does the City Centre of Music And Drama consider Balanchine an item for which it is con-

ceivable there may be some budgetary considerations, similar to Halasz [Laszlo Halasz, the director of City Center's opera company]. The difference is in this: Balanchine is the equivalent of Verdi, Puccini, Mozart and Wagner in his own right; he is both creator and interpreter of a classic repertory and is recognized as the greatest living choreographer, the equal of a Picasso in painting, Gide or Eliot in literature; a Strawinsky, Schoenberg or Hindemith in music. Is he owed anything by the City Centre?

In March, Balanchine duly made a foray to Broadway to choreograph the musical *Courtin' Time,* while Robbins, even before *The King and I* opened in New York, took for the first time a job spiffing up someone else's musical: *A Tree Grows in Brooklyn,* George Abbott's adaptation, with Betty Smith, of Smith's best-selling novel; Abbott directed the musical, and Herbert Ross choreographed it.

Jerry then took steps to rededicate himself to the New York City Ballet. On April 19, 1951, while he was in Hollywood conferring about the resurrected idea of a *Look Ma, I'm Dancin'!* film, Claudia Cassidy announced in the *Chicago Tribune* that he would be coming to that city with the company "after all" to dance *Bourrée Fantasque, Mother Goose,* and at least one performance of *Age of Anxiety.* It was also noted by newspaper columnists that Robbins and Nora Kaye had set an April date for a wedding. Instead of either dancing in Chicago or marrying Kaye, Robbins had his appendix out and choreographed *The Cage.*

Theater gossip has occasionally bruited about the notion that creating this deadly little masterpiece about a man-killing bunch of spidery females and casting Kaye as its protagonist was Robbins's revenge on her for breaking their engagement.* In fact, he and Kaye remained on excellent terms, and the ballet can more easily be considered a gift from him to her. Since joining the company, she had not had any major roles created for her that made use of her gift for drama. Tudor had built his *Lady of the Camelias* around Laing and Laing's new love, Diana Adams.

One startling thing about *The Cage* is how swift and brutal it is. The curtain goes up, Stravinsky's 1946 Concerto in D for String Orchestra rises

---

* Arthur Laurents, who also had an affair with Kaye, doubts that the marriage plans were serious. Kaye, who did marry four times, was both adventurous and easygoing about sex and was attracted to many gay colleagues. "She was going to marry us all."

from the pit, and spectators confront a spiderweb of ropes being pulled toward the ceiling.* The ritual is already under way. A scantily clad, wild-haired bunch of women—the company's taller dancers—slash their limbs against the air and use their pointe shoes like ice picks. Company dancer Ruth Sobotka's costumes made the creatures appear transparent, with curling black lines like intestinal tracts on their nude-colored leotards. Not since Doris Humphrey's 1929 *Life of the Bee,* thought Walter Terry, had a choreographer so successfully evoked a nonhuman community. Robbins told critic Robert Sabin in 1955, "I did not have to confine myself to human beings moving in a way that we know is human. In the way their fingers worked, in the crouch of a body or the thrust of an arm, I could let myself see what I wanted to imagine. Sometimes the arms, hands, and fingers became pincers, antennae, feelers."

The dancers' splayed fingers and hyperextended elbows had migrated from *The King and I,* and Kirstein noted the possible influence of Apollo's just-born solo in Balanchine's eponymous ballet and the dance of the Bacchantes who tear his hero apart in *Orpheus.* However, *The Cage* as a whole alluded more potently to *Giselle.* Robbins transformed Act II of the Romantic 1841 classic, with its betrayed, man-hating Wilis and their deadly queen, into a primal ceremony. The killing of two male invaders of this female domain becomes a required rite of passage for the "Novice."

This adolescent creature enters with her head covered by a white veil, as in *Giselle,* but when that is whipped off, she still wears for a few minutes what looks like the remains of an insect's chrysalis. The movements Robbins designed for Kaye are extraordinary. At first, she stands on pointe, knock-kneed and wobbling. Her movements are preternaturally limber, yet tentative, as if she hasn't yet fully learned how to use her body. She opens her mouth in silent howls. Her short, slicked-down hair (Robbins had been struck by how Kaye looked coming out of the shower) has the wet look of the newborn and adds to her vulnerability. As she gains in strength, her coiffure begins to look more like a carapace. She has no problem dispatching the first male intruder by stomping on (actually close to) his supine, twitching body and then getting his head between her legs and twisting. She arches her spine and rubs the outsides of her arms down the

* The highly effective raising of the ropes came about by accident. After a stage rehearsal, lighting and set designer Jean Rosenthal was lowering what was to have been a tight overhead web to check the ropes when Robbins noticed the loosened web and mandated that initial and effectively symbolic image.

insides of her thighs—grooming herself after the kill. Her strutting dance of triumph, mouth now opening in a silent victory yell, wins her the approval of the group. As they leap forward on a diagonal, their force appears to roll the inert male's body in the opposite direction and offstage (a clever reference to the way *Giselle*'s Wilis pass the hapless Hilarion down the line and into the lake).

But the second movement of Stravinsky's concerto sweetens, and Robbins harkened to what he heard as an expression of "love and tenderness, of individual human emotion." This is the crux of the ballet; something stirs in the Novice at the sight of the second male intruder—*Giselle*'s Albrecht, if you will (Nicholas Magallanes was the original victim). John Martin worried that this episode "almost went into pas de deux territory." However, by mixing pas de deux behavior—the man turning the woman, supporting her in balances, she casting herself on him—albeit with insect-like deformations of the classical vocabulary, Robbins made an interesting point. His original idea had been "to 'project' what occurs when a human goes against the norms of society; then the individual is either destroyed or has to revert to the inherent pulls of the tribe—the blood instinct of a cult, or race, or clan rides strongest above everything else." But the nature of the duet lends the violent sixteen-minute story the aura of tragedy. In the third movement, the Novice, like Giselle, attempts—if ineffectively and briefly—to protect her mate, but instinct reasserts itself, and she allows herself to be carried by the tribe to the fallen male and suspended over him to begin the kill. We feel horror at the inevitability of it all, but also a small spasm of pity for the killer.

According to Arthur Laurents, on opening night Kaye added a sudden contraction of the body after she had killed her mate. Jerry was furious, but the gesture stayed in—a human reaction of revulsion.* Still, the Novice's remorse (if that's what it was) is short-lived. The fierce but efficiently organized kingdom clears away the second body and welcomes her into its celebratory dance. Doubtless many people, like John Martin, felt the ballet to be an angry piece, "decadent in its concern with misogyny and its contempt for procreation." But many also agreed with him that *The Cage* was "a tremendous little work, with the mark of genius upon it." Walter Terry spoke admiringly of its "remorseless beauty."

* Nothing quite like this stands out in current performances. If Laurents is referring to the slight convulsion of the Novice when she is lying collapsed facedown on top of the Intruder's body, the impact of the gesture is ambiguous and not pointed up.

Kaye received raves for her performance. Bernstein wrote her that "I loved you for your beautiful way of conveying horror. God what an artist." Terry aptly called her "frighteningly inhuman, provocative, and glitteringly feral." Writing of her performance in later years, Robbins agreed:

> She didn't ever play human or have human responses. She was much more terrifying & unearthly. She performed the role quietly. With a beetle's eyes & no expression. As one cannot read into [the] eyes or thinking [of] an insect she remained appalling in her surrenders, instincts, and actions—an extraordinary creature—not a ballerina doing ketchy movements.

At the time, however, Robbins seems to have pondered the charges of misogyny. He must have enjoyed a letter from a ten-year-old fan, Karen Kissin, daughter of the Robbins family doctor. He had invited her and her parents to the premiere of *The Cage*. She reported that her mother thought "you don't like women very much, but I told her you just don't like nasty women." He apparently worried that he and Kaye had made the Novice too inhuman. During the summer, when Robbins was in Europe, Tanaquil Le Clercq wrote him, obviously in response to some doubts he had communicated to her, "I don't see <u>love</u> in *The Cage* at all—It isn't there, so why do you expect it? It seems to me she just 'uses' Nicky then kills him—like the bees? If she <u>loved</u> him which insects <u>don't</u> wouldn't she protect him? You don't kill when you are in love only kill <u>with</u> love—I think it's fine the way it is."

The Cage was a long time developing. Previously, Stravinsky had been Balanchine's exclusive territory at the New York City Ballet. Robbins had discovered the music about two years before he choreographed the ballet; it was on the other side of a recording he had purchased of Stravinsky's *Apollon Musagète,* the score for Balanchine's *Apollo* (perhaps the idea of a newborn discovering how to move—a scene in *Apollo* that Balanchine omitted in later years—seeped through the vinyl). He thought the concerto dramatic and filed it away as a possible future project. He actually had Amazons in mind when he started rehearsing and had the dancers "clattering around the studio with shields and swords." Interestingly, Robbins later said he had thought of Le Clercq long before he choreographed the role of the Novice on Kaye—her long, thin legs, her coltishness, her youth.

Subletting his apartment for two and a half months, Robbins left—or fled—New York for Europe immediately after the premiere of *The Cage*. He did not return to participate in the NYCB's early fall season and practically had to be dragged back for the later one. He had reasons to leave the country that were stronger than his love of Europe's art treasures and scenic villages: on March 21, HUAC had turned its attention to Hollywood for a second time, and its first witness, actor Larry Parks, star of *The Jolson Story,* caved in. His agonized performance as a cooperative witness spurred Ed Sullivan to attempt to end Robbins's evasiveness. His front-page article in *The Philadelphia Inquirer* bore the headline "TIP TO RED PROBERS: SUPENA JEROME ROBBINS." The misspelling, repeated in the article, is not Sullivan's only error. He wrote that Robbins "figured importantly in Hollywood" and claimed that Robbins had said that joining the Communist Party had enhanced his career as a dancer. "Their [the Communists'] directors moved me from the second row to the first row; their newspaper and magazine sympathizers started giving me all sorts of publicity. Overnight I became a celebrity in my field." Sullivan's article urged HUAC to put the squeeze on the choreographer, who might be more cooperative now that Parks had shown the way.

Robbins, alarmed, put himself in the hands of R. Lawrence Siegel, of Pepper and Siegel, whom Victor Navasky describes in *Naming Names* as a "preeminent attorney, special counsel to the ACLU." An FBI report dated April 20, 1951, says that Siegel appeared at the New York office on Robbins's behalf and "stated that the subject had told him things and wanted to be reinterviewed by the FBI to furnish information about his Communist Party activities that he had not mentioned on 4/25/50." Robbins was scheduled to appear at the office the following day. There is no record of what he said or whether he even showed up, but all through the summer and fall, the committee examined witness after witness from Broadway and Hollywood, and, judging by Robbins's behavior once he was in Europe and out of reach, he had no reason to believe he would *not* be summoned before HUAC.

However, ensconced again at the Hôtel Quai Voltaire in Paris, he was able to forget that terrifying prospect for a while. And he found a new lover, with whom he was to embark on a five-year affair. He and Buzz Miller locked eyes at the Lido; Miller had just finished performing with a show Kay Thompson had brought over. Jerry must have seen him before without realizing it. The dancer, twenty-one or twenty-two when they met, had come from Los Angeles to New York in 1948 with *Magdalena,* an admired but short-lived show choreographed by Jack Cole; Robbins, a fan of both Cole and the show, saw it several times. Robbins invited Miller to go to Chartres for a special mass where the crippled were blessed; he and Swen Swenson (then dancing at the Lido) picked him up at 5:30 A.M. Horsing around amid the gargoyles on the cathedral roof, both were aware, Miller said, of the chemistry happening between them. Swenson took the train back to Paris and the Lido, and, in an unseasonably cold July, Robbins and Miller spent the night in a small village near Chartres and continued on through Brittany together. Forty-seven years later, Miller, talking to Brian Meehan, remembered that night as "if not perfect, the nearest thing that I have known to perfection." Perhaps it was for Jerry too. He found Miller on the beach the next morning. "The first words he spoke," said Buzz, "were, 'I suppose you know I'm engaged to Nora Kaye.' And I said, 'OK.' What could I say? I'd never heard of Nora Kaye, and if he was engaged to her, that was fine by me. It was never brought up again. He didn't indicate I was to leave, so we went off to Finistère and had a wonderful time." Robbins's words may have been as much to protect himself from his own strong feelings as to warn Miller that this might be just a fling.

On July 15, Robbins wrote a happy letter to Robert Fizdale. The trip had been "wonderful . . . so many unexpected loveliness and laughs." He talked of picturesque little fishing villages, "fantastic calvaries—I want to do a ballet on them," ruins at Carnac, forests, religious processions, swamps, and Buzz.

> The initial, impossibly rapturous bloom has finally dispelled—& now there is a very sweet, intelligent shy boy who seems to be quite a wonderful companion in many ways. . . . I guess now I have the defenses up & the realistic world around me. However all has been a marvelous experience & it looks like we'll continue through Europe after Israel.

In this letter, Robbins also noted gleefully that he was managing the European sightseeing courtesy of the American Fund for Israel Institutions—flying to and from Israel on a round-trip ticket via Europe, with another stopover in Greece. The fund had begun its cultural mission by sponsoring (with the participation of Sol Hurok) visits to America in 1947 by the Palestine Symphony Orchestra (soon to become the Israel Philharmonic) and in 1948 by the venerable theater company Habimah; it was now considering doing the same with a dance company. Robbins was to make a survey of dance in Israel: modern dance, ballet, and folk dance. As he announced at a July 20 press conference upon his arrival, "We would like to explore whether it would be feasible to bring a group to the United States for a good-will, non-profitable tour."

Judith Gottlieb, head of the fund's Tel Aviv office, set up a busy schedule for his visit, and, as might be expected, choreographers beseeched him to look at their work. He met individually with Gertrud Kraus, the noted Viennese dancer-choreographer (a resident since 1935), who had just organized the Israel Theatre Ballet, and his fellow American Talley Beatty, who was acting as guest teacher and choreographer to Kraus's group. He met the prominent ballet teacher Mia Arbatova and Sara Levi-Tanai, the director of Inbal. He taught a class at Arbatova's studio and then talked with a group of twenty-six dancers and choreographers. He saw the Habimah Theater do Bertolt Brecht's *Mother Courage* and traveled to Ein Harod for a performance. He visited Jerusalem and was scheduled to visit other cities: Haifa, Aco, Safad, Tiberias.

He was excited by Israel and by the spirit of the people he met. The experience gave his perceptions of Jewishness a new dimension. He had also invited his mother and father to Israel, at his expense ("Can't you just imagine the tons of guilt I'm shedding with this gesture!" he wrote Fizdale). They were satisfyingly overcome. "Dearest Sweetest Jerry," wrote Lena, "It is needless to say how we feel. Emotions swept us away & we are still dazed."

Robbins now had an assistant who could arrange such matters as a parental voyage and, in fact, handle his correspondence, field calls, advise callers, and perform a multitude of services. He could stay away from New York for protracted periods of time, knowing that the roof would not fall in. He relied on Edith Weissman, as did many others who did business with him. She usually knew which way the wind was blowing. When she died more than thirty years later, in 1982, he was holding her hand, and friends knew enough to send heartfelt messages of consolation.

After his return to Europe, Robbins wrote to Judith Gottlieb that he had "found in Israel a strong desire to feel the connection with the past and to create an Israeli culture. . . . However, there is no knowledge of how to do this through dance." He cared enough to return to Israel the following year and forge closer ties with its dance community. In the meantime, the company that most impressed him was Inbal. Inbal performed neither ballet nor modern dance nor the created folk dances that sprang up after the country became independent of Britain. Sara Levi-Tanai drew from the traditions of the Yemenites, a group often looked down upon by Israelis of European extraction. Ululating voices, hand gestures, and the fierce pride of a desert people allied them with Middle Eastern and North African cultures. To Robbins, Inbal had a kind of authenticity that other groups were still struggling to find.

While he carried out his mission and resumed traveling about Europe with Buzz Miller, his agent and lawyer plied him with news and advice that might influence his decisions about the future of his career. Howard Hoyt revealed a juicy offer from Paramount in a letter to Paris dated July 12: "They would like to make a deal for you to be a producer, director, writer and choreographer, however, as far as choreography is concerned, you would have the right to reject any picture we felt was wrong for you. They would like to build you into one of their top men." Paramount was offering a five-year contract with a starting salary of $1,500 a week for fifty-two weeks a year. Hoyt mentioned several properties, including *Look Ma, I'm Dancin'!* (the script Jerry had been working on in April). By August, a letter from Siegel, Robbins's lawyer, to his client in Athens indicated that Paramount was upping the ante: a starting salary of $1,750 a week, an eight-month year, and a six-year contract, although he recommended a one-picture deal or a three-films-in-two-years one. Twentieth Century–Fox was also sending a script for Jerry's consideration.

Hoyt's letter of August 24 found Robbins in Venice, and it's clear that Jerry was worried that if he accepted a Hollywood contract, he would be more visible and hence more vulnerable to HUAC's bloodhounds. Hoyt attempted, cryptically, to reassure him:

> If anything did happen and you were with Paramount . . . they would certainly seek to protect that investment. . . . Paramount—Segal [*sic*] makes this point—is about the only studio that would be in a position to do that for you, in view of the fact that their higher-ups have nothing to worry about. This is one reason why some of the most important people in pictures still have not been touched.

What is interesting in all this correspondence is the way Siegel couched his advice to Robbins. Meant to be reassuring, his letters could have been almost calculated to induce fear. Many years later, in 1991, Robbins sought to determine whether the man advising him might not have been an undercover FBI agent. In an August letter, after saying that the situation looked "not dark but bright," Siegel mentioned the Donaldson Award Robbins had received for *The King and I:* "I feared for a while that the resulting publicity might be a green light for your enemies to open fire. Fortunately, nothing of the sort occurred; of course, there is no guarantee that the thing may not be picked up by *Counter-Attack* or somebody else in the future, to your embarrassment and injury."

He comforted Robbins with the news that HUAC had announced that the session beginning September 17 would be its final one. But he went on, "Meanwhile the Senate Committee under McCarran is conducting its own hearings. To date, there has been a great deal of gossip that this Committee is going to invade the New York entertainment field but thus far the rumors are unsupported entirely by official announcement or action."

The oddest communication was one in which Siegel indicated that he'd heard from Howard Hoyt that "[Oliver] Smith has threatened to 'expose' you unless you agreed to his demands. Several times before Hoyt had telephoned me to give me similar messages; in the past, however, Lucia Chase was also mentioned by Hoyt as a person who was going to hurt you." Siegel suggested that Jerry ignore these "threats." No correspondence exists that reveals Robbins's reaction to this news or explains why Ballet Theatre's directors, one an old friend and frequent collaborator, would resort to blackmail. Years later, when Robbins was going through this material in his archives, he sent a copy of the letter to Oliver Smith with a penciled query, "What's this all about?"

Robbins eventually decided not to tie himself down to the lucrative film contract. Meanwhile, New York City Ballet was tugging at him, tactfully implying that for an associate artistic director, he was certainly not very visible. By the end of August, Hoyt informed him that Kirstein wanted him back in New York as soon as possible. Balanchine and Kirstein were planning a ballet based on Richard Strauss's tone poem *Till Eulenspiegel,* to star Robbins. It was likely that Balanchine would then be going to Hollywood to choreograph *Hans Christian Andersen* for Danny Kaye. Hoyt reported that Kirstein was "looking for you to supervise the company in

Balanchine's absence" and said he'd told Kirstein that Robbins would be heading home by ship on October 8.

Kirstein wrote Robbins letters full of Balanchine's plans for *Tyl,* and kept him up to date with company news and plans. Nora wasn't dancing enough and needed a new ballet. So did Maria. He regaled Jerry with descriptions of Todd Bolender's *Miraculous Mandarin,* a usefully sexy ballet that neither he nor Balanchine greatly admired. "Melissa [Hayden] is in her seventh heaven; she is the Bette Davis of the dance and there is a bucket of guts for her to put her points in." The company founder proved a master at behind-the-scenes gossip, describing a "terrible series of hysterical incidents" at a *Mandarin* performance:

Hugh [Laing] tore off his clothes and LEFT. Todd [Bolender] wept and shrieked. Milly [Hayden] went crazy. BUT, they danced like angels, and the boys, including Jacques (sex box) d'Amboise, exuded blood and gism from every pore; it was really coherent and afterwards Oliver Smith said it was better than the Turkish Baths. I do not, however, think that this means it is a repertory favorite.

Francisco Moncion, too, sent vignettes of company life. Laing was being difficult, and Lincoln had to step in. "On two occasions now [in *Cage*], Nora has practically kayoed Michael [Maule, the first intruder] by kicking him in the chin. Last time so hard that the opposite eardrum rang like a fire alarm and he had to have it looked at."

Moncion also unburdened himself of some worries about the New York City Ballet's future, including an oblique plea for Robbins's return:

The company is growing well, if a mite too fast. As long as the emphasis does not change, we as a group will be safe. However, if the trend shifts to theatrical artificiality in place of sheer sincerity of approach, we will be in trouble. An audience or public will sense that soon enough. Syntheticism cannot be disguised for too long, and as associate artistic director, I hope you can help guide the path of the company. I'm not moralizing, but after the terrific effort we've made, and the love of work and ideals poured into those early "Ballet Society" days when we practically worked for nothing, it would be tragic to see all that go for naught and the path take new unwholesome twists. We did a great deal of spade-work to get this thing going, and it's all worth preserving. Don't you think?

It may be that Moncion was referring to the version of *Swan Lake* that Baum was more or less compelling Balanchine—"much against his will"—to choreograph on the grounds that the "classics" drew audiences. Kirstein, too, worried that Baum might be "forcing us more and more toward corn," even as Baum was trimming the New York City Opera seasons to make room for more ballet.

Le Clercq, who was out with an injured ankle that summer, wrote Robbins charming letters that ought to have made him homesick for the New York City Ballet. Included in one was a clipping about Thomas Mann's novel *The Holy Sinner;* she explained that the story centered on a man whose parents were brother and sister and who later married his mother: "Here is a plot right up your alley. No?"

She responded firmly to what must have been a rather impassioned why-not-me letter on Robbins's part in regard to her affair with Balanchine: "I just love you, to talk to, go around with, play games, laugh like hell, etc. However I'm in love with George—Maybe it's a case of he got here first—Maybe not—I don't know—anyway I'm staying with him. Can't we be friends? Like they say in the movies—"

In September, Lincoln stepped up his campaign to get Jerry home in early October, since Balanchine was expected to depart for Hollywood on October 24 (by October 10, however, a rescheduling of the shooting forced his withdrawal from the project, and Roland Petit choreographed *Hans Christian Andersen*). Esteban Francés's decor for *Tyl,* wrote Kirstein temptingly, suggested a dark combination of Zurbarán and Bosch, and the ballet was to be "a great spectacle involving the liberation of the provinces of Belgium from Philip II, and has wild inquisition scenes, ball—tortures, and liberation." If Jerry wasn't interested, he added slyly, Balanchine would give the title role to Hugh Laing. He dismissed the version of *Tyl* that Jean Babilée was choreographing for Ballet Theatre: "he's a cuties-pie [*sic*] and Balanchine's version is furiously cruel; there is no classic dancing in it; a lot of mime and expressive nonsense. Please do it."

In letters to Betty Cage that Kirstein wrote from London while laying the groundwork for the 1950 British tour, he stresses the value of Lew Christensen to the company. Christensen, the first American Apollo, was a talented choreographer and served as Balanchine's valuable, hardworking assistant in preparing for the overseas tour (had he been significantly younger than Balanchine, Kirstein might have pushed him as a future heir to the company). When Robbins was mentioned, it was slightingly; re that tour, "I would give ANYTHING if Robbins never came at all" and re the fall plans, "If Robbins has to do something it can be next to nothing." Yet, over and over in Kirstein's letters to Jerry that autumn, Lincoln larded his advice on present needs and future plans with compliments. *Age of Anxiety* badly needs Jerry's attention (with Le Clercq nursing her damaged ankle, Kaye had taken over her part). Nora wants him to revive and revise *Facsimile*. No to a new version of Nijinsky's *Jeux* that Robbins had proposed but a fervent "yes" to a scenario about an animal trainer (Lincoln, his considerable creativity underused, bubbled with suggestions about title, casting, music, setting, and costumes). And Jerry must do something to "an important American score": Thomson, Copland, Sessions, Barber, "but PULLEEEASE not Paul Bowles" (Bowles's work, Kirstein allowed, "simply musically has charm, but can't we have more?").

In short, Kirstein knew the company needed Robbins. Why shouldn't he, Kirstein said, "fit in films, shows AND ballets? Balanchine always has." And "we will be able to pay you from now on on something more than an honorary basis." And "Balanchine wants to give you more authority if you can be counted on to want to take it." And urgently:

> I believe you are the only choreographer alive who can take George's place; historically speaking you are not as fortunate as he; he was a classic dancer, trained under the Empire and the early USSR, and he had Diaghilev, and you alas, have only me; but what is more important; you are an American with an amazing gift for gesture; no one else has it.

Kirstein was aware of the political high wire Robbins was walking and his fear of falling. Le Clercq was not. And she wrote a perplexed letter, quoting back to him something he had written about "being stranded in Paris not knowing if I'd ever be able to return." She's glad he's all right now, but, what, she asks, is the problem? What "news" came? Has somebody died? Has a lover left him? She quotes him again: "Doesn't anyone know what's happening to me?" No, what?

Jerry continued to delay. Buzz Miller had gone back to New York in August, overwhelmed and confused by the strong emotions the relationship with Robbins had engendered. And Robbins embarked on a three-week fling with composer Ned Rorem, meeting interesting new people in Paris and considering collaborating with Rorem on a ballet. He wrote

Kirstein that he couldn't return. He hoped Lincoln knew by now—could tell from his previous letters—"how much I enjoy the company and the people connected with it and what real pleasure and gain it has been for me to work with it." He had been looking forward to home and *Tyl.* "So you should know that it isn't just a mad whim or sudden shift of affection or attention or caprice that has made me not return and stay here. You remember that awful business I went thru . . ." Here the draft breaks off.

Tanny lost her twenty-two-year-old temper and penned a note on a tiny sheet of onionskin paper:

Hy—

Just heard the news.

I think you stink. If you are sick why don't you come back? Better doctors food etc—

If you can't dance you could at least come back and help—my god you have your name on the program as doing something, having some interest in the company—As far as I can see all you do is put in a few (three ballets) then rush off to Europe, or to make money—If it were me I'd say "it's been swell, good bye"—You are a wonderful dancer, and you never dance—The best young choreographer and never choreograph—What the hell goes on?

I'm sorry if this makes you so mad you won't write to me, I wish you would just explain—I'm understanding but to a point —Love, Tan

Then there's another sheet with no salutation and no signoff:

Can't you think of anything besides yourself—What about Til— George wanted it for you—I'm sure if it had not been for you he would [never] have touched it—But still he has to go through with it, do it for someone else—And really you might have decided a little earlier—Your last postcard sounded chatty enough.

I really don't understand you—I think you are an S.O.B. I mean it.

Suppose George does have to go to Hollywood—Don't you care that *Age* is ghastly,—You are marvelous and we have a magnificent *Cage,* a shaking *Age,* and no *Guests*—And BT does *Fancy Free, Inter-*

play and *Facsimilie*? [*sic*] Doesn't seem to be an overabundance of Robbins choreography does there—What are your reasons? What <u>can</u> they be?

This missive is postmarked October 19. Ten days later, Robbins flew back to the United States.*

<hr>

* The dates and the reasons for Robbins's change of heart are not entirely clear. In a letter of October 13, 1951, Siegel wrote Robbins that Hoyt had told *him* that the choreographer would be returning November 1. If this were so, Hoyt would surely also have notified Kirstein and Balanchine, rendering Le Clercq's letter unnecessary. In a preface introducing three letters from Robbins to Ned Rorem published in *Dance Chronicle,* Rorem gave an October 23 date (Rorem's birthday) for Robbins's departure from Paris. However, a letter Robbins wrote from New York to Rorem in Paris on Sunday, November 5, says he has been home a week, and one dated November 14 indicates that he has been home for two weeks. It would be tempting to credit Tanny with influencing Jerry's decision to return.

10

Ballet Haven

Tanaquil Le Clercq and Francisco Moncion in
Robbins's *Afternoon of a Faun.*
Frederick Melton/NYPL.

Variety announced Robbins's return to the New York City Ballet
with the headline "TOP B'WAY CHOREOGRAPHER ROBBINS DANCES
WITH TERP TROUPE FOR BARE MINIMUM," noting that he'd be making $85 to $100 a week with the company, while receiving about $700 a
week in royalties from *The King and I* and *Call Me Madam.*

The discrepancy that surprised the trade paper didn't bother Robbins. Working at the New York City Ballet gave him something more than autonomy as a choreographer. A Broadway show creates a temporary world; people spend all of their working hours and many of their after-work hours together. When the show closes and they go their separate ways, there's always a little wrench. A ballet company, despite changes in membership, is a more stable community. The New York City Ballet was always there for Jerry—an artistic home to return to.

However, despite Robbins's affection for the company, returning after such a long absence was not easy. Just back in New York and having a dinner break between rehearsals, Robbins wrote morosely to Ned Rorem from his apartment: "rain stained ceilings, peeling walls and torn carpets, like it's all crumbling from every direction at once." Two weeks later, he was still not happy: "I feel absolutely choked here . . . theres no air thers [sic] no light theres no beauty theres certainly no Life here. I miss Paris even more than I did when I first got back, and every time I walk on the street I think of how very beautiful it must be there." In addition, his schedule was imprisoning: "From ten in the morning til eleven at night Im dancing, rehearsing or choreographing . . . and all I see is the inside of the studio and my apartment." Yet for all his griping, he plunged into the work, aware of how valuable he was to the company as both performer and choreographer.

The critic Edwin Denby, returning to New York in 1952 after four years abroad, wrote a long and remarkable essay on the New York City Ballet's style. "American ballet," he said, "is like a straight and narrow path compared to the pretty primrose fields the French tumble in so happily. The NYC style is the most particularized and the clearest defined of all the American ones; the most Puritan in its uprightness." He found the dancing "limpid, easy, large, open, bounding; calm in temper and steady in pulse, virtuoso in precision, in stamina, in rapidity. . . . Never was there so little mannerism in a company, or extravagance."

Denby preferred those very ballets the British had found dry in 1950: Balanchine's *Symphony in C* and *Concerto Barocco,* along with *Four Temperaments* and the new *Caracole.* The company as a whole, he thought, looked finest in such "dance ballets," while the corps and some of the leading dancers were fairly hopeless at anything that required miming or acting. He praised both Robbins and Kaye, who had both "long ago learned to do without the insistent projection that so often spoils ballet acting," and thought he discerned their beneficial influence on some of the other NYCB principals.

At this point in the company's development, Kirstein, and probably Balanchine too, knew that audiences used to the story ballets of Ballet Theatre and the Ballet Russe companies were not ready to accept a repertory consisting entirely of plotless works. Consequently, dramatic ballets requiring more than just dancing were a necessity. During the 1951–1952 season, Balanchine presented his one-act *Swan Lake,* Frederick Ashton choreographed *Picnic at Tintagel,* and Antony Tudor restaged his *Lilac Garden* (featuring the Ballet Theatre cast of himself, Nora Kaye, and Hugh Laing, plus Tanaquil Le Clercq) and created *La Gloire,* in which Kaye played a great tragedienne in decline (Sarah Bernhardt was the inspiration). Other ballets, such as Balanchine's *Prodigal Son,* Bolender's *Miraculous Mandarin,* Robbins's *The Cage,* and Ruthanna Boris's comic delight, *Cakewalk,* also needed strong, unmannered acting.

And Balanchine recognized that skill in Robbins. Le Clercq's hunch that he would never have choreographed *Tyl Ulenspiegel* had he not been able to build it on a dancer like Jerry was surely correct. The role fit his assistant choreographer's talents perfectly. Playing the legendary rascal immortalized in Richard Strauss's 1895 tone poem, *Till Eulenspiegel's Merry Pranks,* op. 28, Robbins could be impish, crude, malevolent, and heroic in rapid succession. Balanchine had gone beyond the original character's exploits to make sport of the aristocracy and clergy, and, drawing on an 1867 novel by the Belgian writer Charles de Coster, given the tale a socially aware edge that was not out of keeping with Robbins's own three previous works for the company. This Tyl was a rapscallion Flemish patriot harassing the Spaniards who were occupying sixteenth-century Flanders. A prelude made the situation clear. Two children—one representing Philip II of Spain as a boy, the other, in rags, the young Tyl—play bastard chess on a huge slanted table; the little peasant forces back the prince's armada with a loaf of bread.

Robbins later recalled the excitement of working with Balanchine, who could demonstrate to inimitable perfection the stances and deeds of his hero. However, the ballet itself proved to be a nonstop obstacle course, in which Jerry spent as much time rushing offstage and changing costumes and masks as performing. Todd Bolender, who later took over the role, loved the "sense of conspiracy, because you would appear from someplace and sneak back and go around and come out as something else." Most critics agreed with Anatole Chujoy, who wrote in *Dance News* that Balanchine had been hampered by the shortness of the score (twelve to fifteen minutes, depending on the tempi): "Tyl just did not have a chance. No sooner had he begun a scene, or a prank if you will, than the music drove him right out of it."

Tyl's mischief centered on King Philip (Brooks Jackson) and his retinue of courtiers, soldiers, and clergy, especially a duke and duchess (Frank Hobi and Beatrice Tompkins). Along the way, he rescues a victim of the Inquisition. A set of contact prints by photographer Walter Owen gives a good idea of the shenanigans Balanchine devised and how brilliantly Robbins pulled them off. Here he is disguised as a monk; the duchess has been sufficiently deceived by his mock saintliness to kiss his hand. Here, in beggar's rags, he cavorts lasciviously with the duchess and her two beruffed ladies, falling to the floor with her in a tangle. Here, disguised with buckteeth and a scraggly beard, he pretends to be an artist and gets the court to pose for him for what must have been a very long time. He masquerades as a buffoon. The king threatens him with an arrow, and he counters with a net. At the climax, Spanish soldiers attack him. Kirstein's description of the splendors of Jean Rosenthal's lighting and Esteban Francés's set brings to life the story's dark side: ". . . the backdrop suddenly evanesces into a sheet of fire, in which the owl, like the heart in a human body, stands silhouetted as a steadfast symbol of Tyl's courage." Bolender, however, remembers the bravura of fencing with the men and flipping the swords out of their hands, and, judging from *Dance Magazine* critic Doris Hering's account, lusty comedy was seldom far away: Tyl takes on three swordsmen—riding one while he fights another, thrusting between his legs to attack a man behind him, and tricking them into fighting one another while he plays an imaginary fiddle. At some point Tyl upends a Spaniard in a barrel, his legs kicking upward—a sly Hieronymous Bosch image. Playwright Robert Sealy, recollecting his impression thirty years later, conjured up an arresting picture of Robbins: "In a fright wig and with a mad bow-legged crouch, he ran through the legs of the world, kicking, goosing, leering at the prissy and highborn, knocking over the tabletop kingdoms of the world. His eyes were like naughty coals, the glowing center of the work." Even at his hanging, Tyl tricks the world—and death. His spirit, like that of Robbins's beloved Petrouchka, is unquenchable. By some connivance, King Philip replaces him on the bier, Tyl goes home with his wife, and the Flemish flag is raised in triumph.

Tyl was, as Chujoy put it, "a detailed, complicated pantomime, rather than a ballet in the accepted sense." Just as well. Robbins had not spent his time in Europe taking daily ballet classes; a friend writing from Paris to compliment him on his reviews reminded him how he'd used her dining table for a barre, "grunting and groaning . . . agonizing over the short rehearsal period and how long you haven't been dancing." Walter Terry noted in the *New York Herald Tribune* that "because [Tyl's] antagonists tend to be cardboard, the magnitude of his conflicts is somewhat lost." But he was unstinting in his praise of Robbins:

[A]s striking as the decor is and as pictorially arresting as the Balanchine ensemble designs are, it is Mr. Robbins's performance which captures and revitalizes the spirit and the purpose, the wit and the warmth of a great legend. . . . Mr. Robbins permitted us to see [the] contradictory elements of Tyl's nature. He made us love him and laugh at him, disapprove of him and weep for him as he capered disrespectfully and irresistibly throughout his fantastic adventures. He made myth into a human being, an unlikely one perhaps, but human nonetheless.

Ironically, Balanchine, the master of what he once termed "storyless" ballets, had created a rowdy and subtly political drama that involved more gesturing than dancing. *The Pied Piper, Ballade, Fanfare, Afternoon of a Faun, Quartet,* and *The Concert*—the ballets that Robbins made for the New York City Ballet between the end of 1951 and 1956, when his connection with the company loosened for a while—may have had narrative elements, but they focused on dancing and music and the world of the artist.

While he had been in Europe, facing an unpleasant political reality, he had begun to eschew fictionalized societal realities. He had fiddled with the idea of a highly escapist fantasy, but never developed it: a ballroom being readied for a party is invaded by a pair of elves (invisible to humans)—"two moonbeams who play and caprice." While gallivanting with Ned Rorem, in addition to planning a collaboration with him, he also conceived *Madame Auric's Lover,* inspired by the ménage à trois maintained by composer Georges Auric, his wife, Nora, and her lover, Guy de Lesseps. Kirstein was taken by the possibilities: "Lincoln had the marvelous idea of the woman first appearing in sidesaddle riding clothes boots whip etc, heavy black skirt pulled up on one side. Then she would remove the riding outfit and [c]ome down in her underskirt." (It's not clear whether this or the Rorem work was the "animal trainer" ballet Kirstein referred to in the letter mentioned earlier.) These ballets, too, never materialized. Robbins found Rorem's score, jokingly titled *Ballet for Jerry* after Aaron Copland's working title for *Appalachian Spring—Ballet for Martha*—not to his taste.*

Instead, for the New York City Ballet's satisfyingly long season (February 12 through March 16), Robbins began work on *The Pied Piper.* He had originally planned to set it to Paul Bowles's double piano concerto (with Fizdale and Gold at the pianos), but the City Center pit couldn't accommodate two pianos and an orchestra, and, Robbins wrote Rorem, "they couldn't afford to put the rest of the orchestra on stage." He turned to his other choice (and one Kirstein approved), Aaron Copland's Concerto for Clarinet and String Orchestra, with Harp and Piano, composed in 1948 for Benny Goodman.

For *Pied Piper,* Robbins returned to a premise he loved and had explored earlier in *Summer Day.* The stage is bare, except for a ladder and some boxes to sit on. The dancers are "themselves," wearing their chosen practice clothes and gradually wandering onto the stage, where they're drawn into motion—not by props or costumes this time, but by the music. The eponymous piper is the onstage clarinet soloist, who, in the ballet's wild and most memorable last section, induces a kinetic frenzy—sucking the dancers toward him by the seductiveness of his playing, then shooting them back across the stage or propelling them into a wild Charleston. When they collapse exhausted, like the revelers in the *Billion Dollar Baby* Charleston, the music moves their quaking limbs as if the notes were marionette strings. Walter Terry put it well in an ecstatic review: "[T]hey lie on the floor in a vast vibrating mass, they freeze into contorted immobilities, they pretend to resist or they yield crazily to a screaming command of the clarinet, to an irresistible rhythmic pattern, to a musical jolt, to the lash of a cadenza, to the tickle of a single-pointed note."

Copland's music, however, begins quietly and moodily, and Robbins segued into it by having the clarinetist (Edward Wall) stroll onto a dimly lit stage, sit, turn on a light, check his score, and try a few notes before the orchestra takes up the first section. Diana Adams and Nicholas Magallanes appear in a lit doorway, as if from backstage, to begin a gentle pas de

---

* Some of Robbins's ideas for that ballet went into his *Ballade,* and Rorem orchestrated the music for a project by the great French actor Jean Marais.

deux with the same tentativeness, while a spotlight throws their shadows on the back wall. Jillana and Roy Tobias, Janet Reed and Todd Bolender, Melissa Hayden and Herbert Bliss, Tanaquil Le Clercq and Robbins were the other principal couples, along with an ensemble of twenty-three. Reed is a little hellion, an instigator of jazzy movements when the tempo heats up. She leads one guy in a chase around a huddle of dancers. When he catches up with her, she slaps him. He manhandles her into a lift. When another fellow turns from the clump and socks her aggressor, she draws out index-finger guns and shoots them both. Unfortunately, the scraps of film shot by Ann Barzel don't show Robbins and Le Clercq.

Pied Piper, like *Interplay,* mingled classical steps and jazz, but the feel was a little looser and more relaxed—dancers letting off steam rather than well-behaved kids at play. Later, Le Clercq summed it up: "It was more like his shows. Happy go lucky. Very clever. It was a good ballet." Although it had a solid structure, Reed thought of *Pied Piper* as close to improvisation: "It seemed to me it was thrown together. We just got in the studio one day and the music played and I started to do a lot of crazy stuff and it just—that was it." Not surprisingly, when the company went to Europe in the summer of 1952, the European press found the ballet typically "American" in its informality, humor, and rhythmic pep. If Robbins had wanted to affirm his "Americanness" to a doubting Senate committee, he couldn't have done it more brightly.

Kirstein, delighted with *Piper*'s success, sent a review of it to Frederick Ashton, who was due to come shortly from London to begin work on *Picnic at Tintagel.* Ashton wrote Robbins a charming note: "You are a bright boy. You seem to go from strength to strength & I am delighted you are not deteriorating like the rest of us. I always have had the greatest admiration (as you know) for your gifts & consider you the best of the young & the only one with real mastery. Won't be long before we all have to cede to you." Ashton had heard that Jerry was rehearsing his *Illuminations* and was very pleased: "I love your generous spirit." Robbins did at times take his title of associate artistic director seriously.

From Aaron Copland and a spunky jazz ballet, Robbins turned to Claude Debussy's *Six Épigraphes Antiques,* a piano piece for four hands written in 1914, and *Syrinx* (1912) for unaccompanied flute. His friends Fizdale and Gold brought the music to his attention. (Ned Rorem believes that the erudite duo pianists were responsible for at least 75 percent of Robbins's musical choices.) The music for *Ballade* carried Robbins back to

Picasso's blue period with its elongated circus acrobats and mournful clowns. Boris Aronson, who had been a mainstay of Maurice Schwartz's Yiddish Art Theatre, designed the set and costumes.

Ballade seems to have mystified many people when it premiered in the company's February–March 1952 season. John Martin found it "cute, cloying, and self-conscious" and unoriginal, linking it to Lew Christensen's *Jinx*, Antony Tudor's *Undertow*, and Frederick Ashton's *Illuminations*. Walter Terry, however, found its enigmatic poeticism "enchanting, so much so that I wished that I could see it through three times (perhaps more) in a row."

Edwin Denby liked *Ballade* because it "didn't get started in that fascinatingly literal gesture of [Robbins's] that is wonderfully contemporary but so resistant to development, to the spontaneous kind of development." The remark was in tune with Denby's criticism of Jerry at this point in the choreographer's career:

> Robbins's dramatic line, the dramatic power of a piece, is developed not from the central impulses to dance—in ballet characters normal as breathing—but it is developed by applying an obsessive rhythm to what for the characters is incidental gesture. It is like seeing someone punished very heavily for a small fault, and the main drama never coming to light. It is as if the characters were not free agents—they act under compulsion.

Denby might have been describing the difference in approach between a choreographer bred in the ballet tradition, who thinks in terms of "steps," and a master of modern dance such as Martha Graham, for whom emotion molded the whole body into a heightened gesture. Despite Robbins's mastery of the ballet vocabulary, he still, to some extent (as he told Selma Jeanne Cohen in a 1954 interview), thought like a modern dancer.

Denby's remark about Robbins's characters usually not appearing to be free agents is ironic in the context of his critique of *Ballade*. When the curtain rises on the ballet, snow is falling, and seven characters are slumbering on chairs in a state of hibernation. To the wisp of a solo flute air, a balloon vendor enters and places one in each inert hand. The balloons pull them up into life; they bow to their mysterious master, and he leaves. Robbins likened the limp figures to the roles that dancers must fill:

There's that Petrouchka costume laying on a rack somewhere—there's the role in limbo. . . . It's only when someone gets into that role that the role comes to life—exists again—and then when that person stops, the role collapses. The roles are endowed by whatever artist it is that happens to dance them.

The dancers were dressed in costumes suggesting Commedia dell'Arte characters. Three males tumbled about in what dance writer Francis Mason remembered as a "rushing, circusy number." (One of them, interestingly, was the black dancer Louis Johnson, who took class at the School of American Ballet and who appeared as a guest artist.) Nora Kaye, dressed as a Harlequin, performed a vigorous, somewhat acrobatic solo. Roy Tobias wooed a doll-like Columbine (Janet Reed), who offered him a heart that leaked sawdust. Tanaquil Le Clercq, dressed as Pierrot, rebelled at the realization that she lived only through the power of the balloon and let hers go. When the man retrieved his balloons, only she remained awake, unable to stir her comrades—facing an independent but lonely future.

Casting Le Clercq as the rebel says something about how Robbins saw her. Unable to be contained by any one kind of role, Tanny—shared as muse between Robbins and her now husband, Balanchine—could be heartbreakingly innocent, Death's chosen partner in Balanchine's *La Valse;* an elegant and spicy *femme du monde* in *Bourrée Fantasque;* or the gawky, leggy, gum-chewing girl in *Pied Piper.*

Balanchine gave Robbins suggestions for improving *Ballade,* and while touring Europe with the company that summer, Jerry gave it some thought: "No sets—just those chairs—& a few metal tables, a little like a lost cafe. Costumes are skirts, pants, overalls, sweaters—sort of St. Germaine [sic] after a siege. And more relationships between the people & less Commedia dell'Arte. Not exactly clear on it yet." He remained fond of the ballet and considered reviving it several times, but it vanished. The same Debussy pieces inspired his very different 1984 ballet *Antique Epigraphs.*

Ballade premiered at City Center on February 14, 1952, and on February 1, Robbins appeared as one of three cavaliers in Balanchine's new *Caracole,* a theme and variations set to Mozart's Divertimento no. 15 (related to, but not exactly like, the later ballet titled after the music). Balanchine had decided that Robbins would understand the classical vocabulary and the

NYCB's company style on a deeper level if he danced in a formal, tutus-and-chandeliers ballet like this one. There he was, a thirty-three-year-old choreographer of consequence, in tights and tunic, wearing a hat with a curling plume, he and Nicholas Magallanes flanking the European-trained *danseur noble* André Eglevsky.

Edwin Denby found the ballet "heavenly. . . . If you watch the steps, in the variations for instance, a single step or brief combination will flash out sharply visible, so astonishing is the contrast to the step before it. The shape of the step appears unexpected as lightning and, lightning-like, vanishes—or like the pulsating brilliance of a butterfly on the ground, as its wings open and shut." Jerry, apparently, held his own in all this intricate beauty (including heavy duty as a partner), but the headgear distressed him. In 1957, after seeing *Divertimento No. 15,* he wrote to Le Clercq (he was disappointed; he had thought it was going to be a "<u>new</u> ballet"), con-fessing himself "haunted by the terrible image of myself in pink tights, black velvet vest with lace at the collar and a huge tam with a white feather. Do you think George was being mean putting me in that?" Jerry's mother may have initiated the hat's status as a sore point. According to Maria Tallchief, Lena came backstage and said "sugarhead," then shook her own head: "Oh, Jerry!" He began to think about retiring from per-forming. But for the time being, he danced some of his old roles in the sea-son, and his ballets figured prominently: four performances of *Ballade,* eight of *Pied Piper,* four of *Age of Anxiety,* and four of *The Cage.* The com-pany honored him with its first all-Robbins evening.

Jerry also agreed to tour Europe with the NYCB in the summer of 1952.

The FBI had not believed that Robbins was telling the truth about severing his connection with the Communist Party, and he was, rightly, still uneasy. Shortly after his reluctant return from Europe to do *Tyl,* he had invited Buzz Miller to live with him at Fifty-fifth Street and Park Av-enue. Brian Meehan, who often spoke with Miller during his last years, said Miller told him that on one of his first nights in the apartment, "Jerry woke up screaming out of his sleep and he was saying, 'They're outside, they're outside, they're looking in the window, they're taking our picture. Go outside, go look at the fire escape.' " Apparently this happened often. "He even would forbid Buzz to spend the entire night in his bedroom be-cause, he said, 'We're going to fall asleep and somebody's going to sneak into the apartment.' He would have these paranoia attacks in the middle of the night." When he began to choreograph the musical *Two's Company,* he cast Buzz as one of the dancers but apparently asked him to move into a hotel during part of the New York rehearsal period so they could arrive separately and be seen heading for different destinations at the end of the day; Buzz, surprised and hurt, obliged.

Their five-year relationship was very loving. The apartment in the five-story building with its Spanish stucco roof had been the home of the photographer George Platt Lynes. Some of his furniture—driftwood tables and the like—remained, and, best of all, there was a darkroom, where the two men expanded their mutual interest in photography. They had more in common than that. Although Miller had grown up on a farm in Arizona and won poultry contests and Robbins was a city kid, they had both taken piano lessons early, shown talent, and preferred improvising and writing their own pieces to learning the standard repertory. One of the highlights of Miller's youth had been playing the cello in a string quartet three nights a week in the high school auditorium. His easy acceptance of his homosexuality may have helped Jerry to worry a little less about his own. It is a measure of how some gay men of the day conducted themselves that Robbins was dumbfounded when Miller, after one of their first nights together, got out of bed and walked across the room naked, without grabbing a robe, a towel, or a pair of shorts first. Apparently, no lover of Jerry's had ever been so at ease with his body and his desires. When Robbins was in Europe with the New York City Ballet in the spring of 1952, they reminisced in letters about the previous summer in Venice, when they had picked up a couple of young male prostitutes ("brownies" was their code name) on a bridge in Naples and taken them off to Capri for a highly pleasurable time.

The New York City Ballet's five-month tour began in Barcelona on Tuesday of Easter week and opened in Paris on May 8. Robbins, who had been in Israel, flew to France just in time to get ready for the first performance there. He wrote Buzz the next day from his regular hotel, the Quai Voltaire. His bag had been misplaced, and he had had to go on with Tanny in *Bourrée Fantasque* in borrowed shoes, costume, and makeup. The evening, he noted, was a triumph. "Nora did a fabulous Cage—roars from half the house, silence from the other."

The trip to Israel had been an invigorating change of pace. Like Leonard Bernstein—who had gone to Palestine in 1947 to work with what was then the Palestine Symphony Orchestra—Robbins continued to be enthralled by the spirit of the country, its sense of new beginnings, new possibilities. He even met some cousins, possibly ones who had fled Rejanke during the war.

This time, the American Fund for Israel Institutions sent him not only to meet with members of the Israel dance world and further assess the state of the art but to conduct a workshop. He taught *Interplay* to four ballet dancers from Mia Arbatova's studio and four modern dancers. Photos show him, immaculate in white shorts, T-shirt, socks, and only slightly dingier ballet slippers, demonstrating to a rough-and-ready bunch, and in one shot he's surrounded by a group from the studio, with a happy grin on his face. There is some evidence that he seriously discussed with Gertrud Kraus the possibility of his settling in Israel and codirecting her struggling Israel Theatre Ballet. Kraus got the impression that he was frightened about returning to America. However, Jerry often made impulsive gestures to people he liked who were in need, only to draw back later. He flew to Paris, and the Israel Theatre Ballet disbanded.

But his feelings toward the dance community in Israel were warm, almost paternal. A six-page letter he wrote in July to Judith Gottlieb in the fund's Tel Aviv office was meant to be shared with teachers and dancers, many of whom had written him their ambitions and complaints. He praises them for what they have accomplished in a short time and tells them that "Of course, there are problems" and dissatisfactions, but voicing them is healthy, provided they are then handled cooperatively. He divined both a prejudice against imported techniques and an undue impatience to see results from them.

> There is no such thing as a foreign technique to a dancer. There are no dances (to a true dancer) which is alien. Everything you are being taught, and particularly the modern and ballet technique, whether they come from Europe or Zululand, is a result of years and years experimentation and development. You must learn these techniques to have mastered them, and only after can you be in a position to continue experimentation, growth, and development, making these various techniques into your own, so they are no longer alien, no longer strange, no longer foreign. . . . I found in Israel, that there was too much desire to feel the link [with Israeli culture], and to feel an Israeli culture, and absolutely no technique as to how to go about feeling it. . . . Don't be over

nationalistic. Dance is an international art and the Israeli dance will emerge not so much because you consciously <u>force</u> it as it will emerge from the influence of the country and the way in which you wonderful people will dance it.

He realized that professionalism was a new concept for many of the Israeli dancers, and he hoped they "had gotten over the need to be entertained and kept amused. . . . I so want to come back and find you all more developed, more versatile, more professional, more disciplined and happy with each other and with what you have been doing: and it needs day to day constant work and effort." When he returned, he warned, he wouldn't want to work with anyone who had not been laboring "diligently and cooperatively with the group" (it is not clear whether this was meant for Inbal or for the dancers he'd worked with in Arbatova's studio). But he ended his scolding on a soft note: "Here I go finding myself criticizing again, but believe me, the above remarks only rest on my love and devotion to all of you. I miss you and found it a terribly difficult adjustment when I returned to my company."

⁓

He wasn't exaggerating the adjustment—a "shock," he called it in a letter to Robert Fizdale. However much pleasure he derived from being one of the gang, he got a larger dose of it than he needed touring with the New York City Ballet. He was getting too old for cramped dressing rooms and backstage games:

> Suddenly I felt like I was back in Ballet Theater struggling for recognition & attention. I hated being a member of a travelling company again—resented the whole thing & felt it completely degrading to stand in line for money, pick up & return shoe bags & costumes, get assigned a dressing room that was poor, etc. etc. As a matter of fact I've so hated dancing that I've spoken to George & I'm coming out of Bourrée and Piper & will only dance Tyl as there is no replacement for me—& Anxiety.

In this sour state, he felt himself in competition with Balanchine for attention ("his name plastered all over the affiches and no one else's") and for Le Clercq ("I don't see much of her as George dictates everything—even that she should not learn Nora's role in Cage"). It was still the first month of the tour when he wrote Buzz Miller that he thought he might leave and come home in mid-June, and then again from London in July, "I'm coming home, shh don't tell anyone."

Despite Robbins's sense that he and Balanchine were in competition, Balanchine went out of his way to be helpful. When the French clarinetist hired to play for *Pied Piper* in Paris was horrified at the prospect of being onstage and would play only from the pit, Balanchine offered to mime the role. He enjoyed himself to the hilt, embellishing his part each night. Robbins was moderately grateful: "As Tanny said turning pale while watching him, 'what a ham.' It may make a difference in their relationship."

The Robbins ballets were a great success in Europe. *The Pied Piper* happily reinforced the European public's vision of Americans as young, spirited, and a little brash. "The rage of the first season in Paris," Robbins wrote Fizdale, "was *Piper* with *Cage* a close second. The papers carried headlines about them & long articles were written." Perhaps Balanchine suffered mild attacks of jealousy too. Writing home to Robbins from a later European tour, Le Clercq announced, "I think George was a bit irritated as he said to me, 'You don't have to take any classes [to dance *Pied Piper*], no developpés, no turn-out, personal triumph, etc.' " And she added, "You struggle through things like *Caracole* (I struggle) then go out & have a ball." *Age of Anxiety* was the hit of the Florence engagement. For the return dates in Paris, Robbins's name would be "right under George's." *The Cage* received some inadvertent publicity when the burgomaster of the Hague decided, based on the reports of Dutch critics who had traveled to Florence and found the ballet pornographic, that it should not be performed. Robbins threatened to withdraw all his works if this were acceded to, and Kaye indicated that she would refuse to appear in *any* ballets. Kirstein gloated over the resultant sold-out houses.

For Robbins, almost better than rave reviews was the fact that "Igor now calls me Jerry!!" Stravinsky had come up to him at a reception, "put his hands on my waist & rocked me gently saying 'Jerry, come to my rehearsal tomorrow yes, & rest well for tomorrow's performance. You have great success here, I am so happy.' I felt like Christ had looked over the crowd, picked me out & blessed me."

The New York City Ballet went on to London without him. Composer Samuel Barber had invited him to Corsica. Together with Frederick Ashton and the great Sadler's Wells ballerina Margot Fonteyn, the American choreographer Ruth Page had rented the celebrated Villa Cimbrone in

Ravello for the summer and asked Jerry to drop by ("Can't you see the bodies being tossed over the cliffs now").

It's interesting to note how differently Robbins delivered information to Fizdale and to Miller (he was an adept chameleon in his correspondence). From Paris, he elaborated to Buzz about the celebrities he'd met dining at Maxim's—not only had the Duchess of Windsor been seated on his left and Aly Khan on his right, but "Scattered around were other odd counts dukes ambassadors and stinkingly wealthy folk. The luncheons at Versailles, and the cocktail parties in fabulous homes have piled up." Then he played it down: "[B]ut you know what? I've had it. All the time the same faces wherever you go. It's like being with a different kind of ballet company on tour." As for the proposed Ravello visit, he simply rated it as sounding "too marvelous. Want to come?"

It was, however, to Fizdale, not Miller, that he expressed his darkest feelings. Hedonism brought guilt, and in the same letter about his social whirl, he unburdened himself:

> O Christ I feel helpless and scared when I think of how I have the gift to coreograph [sic] and how time is passing and Im [sic] not working and seem to be carousing and drinking and whoring. "Live it up" seems to be my motto for a while, while the other Jerry stands aghast and white being raped, destroyed, defiled and maligned. And like a merrygo-round out of control, the days pass one two, one two day night day till the result is just a blur.

However, by late July, back home, the "other Jerry" had already doctored one show and was about to start choreographing a new one. He assumed he'd be ready to rejoin Balanchine for the company's November season.

Wish You Were Here had already opened in New York when some salvage work was deemed necessary. Josh Logan had not only cowritten the script (based on *Having a Wonderful Time,* Arthur Kober's play about the goings-on at Kamp Karefree, a Jewish summer camp in the Catskills), he had coproduced it with Leland Hayward and was credited with "direction and dances." A *New Yorker* profile of Logan by E. J. Kahn, Jr., notes that he had been trying to fix the show all along; after the critics lambasted it for not having the tenderness of Kober's original play, he altered the entire plot after the New York opening and, according to the article, called Jerry in to stage a new number, "and Robbins injected fresh spirit into the weary dancers, who, by special dispensation from Chorus Equity, were putting in a good deal more rehearsal time than the union ordinarily permits after the show has opened." Donald Saddler also had a hand in rejuvenating the numbers that Logan had created with a couple of assistants. According to Nancy Franklin, who was in the show, Robbins was called in because no one had been able to stage to Logan's satisfaction a campfire scene that turned into an orgy, and Logan "blew his stack: 'No! This is not what I want! I want this to look like one *gigantic* ratfuck.' " Jerry obliged—at least as far as Broadway raunch could go in the conservative 1950s.

⌒

In his lengthy July letter to Judith Gottlieb and the dancers in Tel Aviv, Robbins had told them that the show he was about to embark on was a revue, to star Bette Davis, and he had no idea whether she could sing or dance. However, he was excited that Nora Kaye would be in the show and he could "do some ballets for her." Maria Karnilova was also featured.

Davis could sing a little, but, as a Detroit critic put it at the show's out-of-town opening, she was "not the world's greatest singer by about twelve city blocks." Nor could she really dance, despite having studied years earlier with Martha Graham at the Anderson-Milton School and with the Ruth St. Denis–style orientalist Roshanara. In fact, she had a distinctive gait; as playwright Arthur Laurents put it, she walked "like a bear," swinging her right arm forward when she stepped on her right foot. Robbins told Miller that he'd never seen anything like it. Wisely, in her numbers, he made the dancers move as much as possible the way she did.

The movie diva was excited about returning to the theater and about gracing a revue; certainly the job would be a change of pace from her most recently released pictures, *Phone Call from a Stranger,* in which she played the brave invalid widow of a no-good husband, and *The Star,* which cast her as an actress with a downward-sliding career reexamining her life and not-so-nice deeds. A successful performance in *Two's Company* might give her a new image. She could show off her skills in such numbers as "Roll Along, Sadie," a takeoff on Somerset Maugham's *Rain;* a parody of Noël Coward's *Private Lives;* "Purple Rose," in which, two teeth blacked out and scraping a washboard, she played the lead singer in a hillbilly band; and "Jealousy," described by *The New Yorker* as a "moderately painful scene based on passion and jealousy in a tenement and having, I guess, something to do with the works of Arthur Miller." (Davis appeared as a complete frump, and the target was more likely *A Streetcar Named Desire*.)

But Davis was nervous from the beginning. In Detroit, she fell onstage during her opening number, "Good Little Girls," and had to be carried off. She told the newspapers that, having not slept in twenty-four hours, she had passed out. The dancers told Arthur Laurents she hadn't fainted, she had fallen because she'd forgotten the lyrics and was looking for a way out of her dilemma. However, she endeared herself to the public by reappearing shortly and announcing, "You can't say I didn't fall for you." The song was replaced by the more appropriate "Turn Me Loose on Broadway," in which Robbins had her whirled around by four male dancers.

The number of the star's costume changes was almost exceeded by the number of contributors who were brought in as the show limped from rehearsal to tryouts in Detroit, Pittsburgh, and Boston, en route to Broadway. Charles Sherman was responsible, with Peter de Vries's help, for most of the sketches, but new writers were continually solicited for new material. Ogden Nash supplied lyrics for most of Vernon Duke's songs, but Sammy Cahn and later Sheldon Harnick also made contributions. Josh Logan was invited to Detroit to give advice. The revue, a dying form at this point, lends itself to patchwork tinkering.

Arthur Laurents wrote a sketch he thought Davis liked, in which she was to parody herself: "My feeling was she had to kid herself right away, and then she'd have the audience, including the critics." Davis got cold feet and instead settled on an imitation of Tallulah Bankhead carrying on at the premiere of a Bette Davis film, while Kay Medford did Davis. Based on what he'd seen in Detroit, Laurents wrote Robbins an affectionate nine-point advice sheet. The first piece of wisdom—"I strongly suggest (again) that you take your name off the 'Entire Production' credit line. No use taking the rap for Sherman"—turned out to be unnecessary. Davis brought in her old mentor John Murray Anderson to spruce up the show, and *he* got the "Production Supervised by" billing.

Robbins went to town on dance numbers. In "Esther," a Latin spoof sung by the six "Teen Aces," Karnilova, as a "sex loving Caribbean babe," exhausted one partner (comedian David Burns) but had better luck with Buzz Miller as a "Native." Three other numbers featured Kaye. One, "Baby Doesn't Dance," was meant to show her talents as a comedian—"a Fanny Brice routine," says Arthur Laurents. "She came out in oversized shoes and stepped out of them in ballet slippers." This heroine couldn't get a man because she couldn't dance—presumably ballroom style; the vision of Kaye clowning in ballet class apparently didn't quite work. In planning the meatier "Haunted Hot Spot," sung by Ann Hathaway, Robbins wrote a detailed scenario (with bits of dialogue by Horton Foote) for this tale about Flame, a seductive nightclub dancer (Kaye), who gradually switches her affections from her pianist to her drummer (Bill Callahan and Miller played the musicians) and is shot by the former. Her ghost haunts the place. In Robbins's preliminary scenario, it sounds like a dark-toned version of "Mr. Monotony," with symbolic lighting: "[O]ver the course of [Flame's] dance the pianist's shadow diminishes and the drummer's gets larger and larger until his huge shadow is dominating her and the dance and she is completely abandoned to his rhythm and dynamics."

For the Nash-Duke "Roundabout," with some of Duke's best music and a few spoken words, Robbins adapted the basic theme of Arthur Schnitzler's play *La Ronde* to a cycle of cynical, sometimes cruel children's games played by well-dressed men and women. Kaye, ensnared by the rules in some sort of wheel of love, is spun from one man to another and into frustration, fear, and disillusionment.

To Brooks Atkinson of the *Times*, Robbins and the dancers, "putting their heads together and keeping their feet pretty consistently off the ground . . . account[ed] for most of the freshness, spirit, grace and intelligence of the production." Nancy Walker, loving "Haunted Hot Spot" and "Roundabout" (in that order), sent Jerry a note: "Jesus, Baby, you're the end!" Davis was not blind to the fact that Robbins was giving Kaye star turns.* Laurents remembers one dark night in Detroit:

> The producers were going to tell Bette Davis off. So everybody stood outside her dressing room. (I remember somebody said, "Don't flush the toilet! Can't you *see* we're eavesdropping?") Anyway, instead of them telling her off, you heard Bette's voice say, "This whole show is routined so *Miss* Nora Kaye can change her costumes!"

But Davis was game. She had actorly skills, charisma, and fervent fans, and, as one critic wrote, "You like her exceedingly and you keep, as you

---

* At one point before the Detroit tryouts, Davis refused to continue working with him and threatened to quit. Robbins signed a letter drafted by Michael Ellis, the show's producer, saying that the only reason he, Robbins, had agreed to take on the show was to work with her and assuring her that she would be great in it.

might say, 'pulling' for her, in all the curious adventures which befall the star of a big, lengthy revue." Walter Kerr wrote with edged affection in the *Herald Tribune* that "Indeed, Miss Davis unbends so much that there's some doubt whether she'll ever be able to straighten up again."

The show wasn't doing great business, and when Davis developed osteomyelitis of the jaw, there was no point in continuing without her. The New York run ended after ninety days. Davis and Robbins had had their differences, but when she was honored by the Kennedy Center in 1987, he sent her his congratulations, and she replied, "Dear Jerome Robbins, Time does heal <u>all</u>."

⌒

During the Two's Company tryouts, Robbins managed to stage *Interplay* for the New York City Ballet (it premiered eight days after the revue did, on December 23), and although Kaye was on leave from the company, once the show opened in New York, she performed with NYCB some Sunday nights when Broadway theaters were dark. Robbins, too, occasionally returned to do his old roles, including the pas de deux in *Interplay.*

It's ironic that in taking on *Two's Company,* which—given all the necessary tinkering—involved more time and energy than he had hoped to expend, Robbins didn't choreograph the show that ought to have suited him perfectly: *Wonderful Town.* It's laid in New York's Greenwich Village during the 1930s, and the production involved some very good friends. Five weeks before rehearsals for this show were to begin on December 15, the composer and lyricist at work on the adaptation of Joseph Fields and Jerome Chodorov's play *My Sister Eileen* quit because of disagreements with the original authors. George Abbott, the musical's coproducer and director, called in Betty Comden, Adolph Green, and Leonard Bernstein. The three worked with uncanny speed to meet the time constraints of the show's star, Rosalind Russell, but the *On the Town* team turned out the transformed hit without its fourth member, Jerome Robbins. Donald Saddler did the choreography.

Jerry, however, did end up participating in the tale of two sisters who come to New York to seek their fortunes. This was Saddler's first Broadway job, and it was a strain to work with the speed required. He was so nervous that he had lost his voice. For one thing, Saddler says, at a dangerously late date, while the show was in Boston, they didn't have a strong opener. Dr. Robbins was sent for. He suggested that it would be a good idea to introduce the denizens of the arty Greenwich Village neighborhood to the two starry-eyed new residents, Eileen and Ruth. Comden, Green, and Bernstein came up with a song, "Christopher Street," and Jerry quickly put together a number celebrating the diversity of types roaming this Depression-era "Bohemian" enclave, handing it over to Saddler to polish. Saddler remembers his friend making a number of astute suggestions. "He would say, 'Don, why don't you have them come in with a whirl instead of walking?' " "Everything was very good," says Betty Comden, "it was just taken several notches above where it had been and made really great."

Robbins was evidently as savvy about Russell's limitations as a dancer as he had been about Davis's. As Comden remembers,

When they got to the "Wrong-Note Rag," . . . he said to Rosalind, "Well, what would *you* do with this song if you heard it? What would you do if you had to get up and cut up?" So she got up and did a few steps, you know, her own. And he taught those to the whole company. Very smart.

A story that Humphrey Burton repeated in his biography of Bernstein has Robbins being called in because the dancers dropped Rosalind Russell in the "Conga"; it seems to be unfounded. Saddler says that Robbins didn't touch the number in which Russell, as Ruth, roisters with a bunch of naval officers. In fact, Russell was a good sport about the manhandling. According to him, she said, "Don, don't spare me. I'll crawl on my hands and knees; I'll do anything if it gets a laugh" and told the men to throw her around just the way they did Albia Kavan (Saddler worked out the lifts for Russell on his assistant, Robbins's old sweetheart), including straight-arming her high for a final pose. William Weslow, who danced in the show (and whom Robbins, as was his wont, treated viciously), tells a story that might explain how the rumor started. Russell was supposed to be dropped and caught. On opening night in Boston, at the moment when she was sitting on Weslow's back amid a clump of guys, her Mainbocher dress started to slip and plummet her downward too soon. To save her from falling, he thrust an arm between her legs. (Abbott loved it. But Weslow remembers Russell saying something like, "Oh, George, please, no. I can hardly pee for two days with this, I'm so sore. If we did that every night I don't think I could stand it.")

Wonderful Town was indeed wonderful—and a tremendous success. Olin Downes of *The New York Times* thought of it in terms of opera and waxed effusive over Bernstein's score:

> In days to come it may well be looked upon in some museum exhibit as the archetype of a kind of piece which existed peculiarly in America of the neon lights and the whir and zip of the mid-twentieth century. . . . [W]e are coming to believe that when the American opera created by a composer of the stature of the Wagners and Verdis of yore does materialize, it will owe much more to the robust spirit and raciness of accent of our popular theater than to the efforts of our emulators, in the upper aesthetic brackets, of the tonal art of Bartok, Hindemith, and Stravinsky.

Saddler received a Tony (the show won a total of eight). Robbins took no credit for what he contributed, which seems to have been slightly more than his contract, dated January 26, 1953, called for. This document merely states that he was to assist Donald Saddler during the next two weeks and that "It is understood that you shall not be required to provide [Robbins pencils in "or execute"] any new ballets [Robbins: "or dances"] of your own." For his services, he received $1,000 plus .5 percent of the gross "from each and every company giving performances of the Show in the United States and Canada under our auspices."

<hr>

While it may seem as though Robbins drifted in and out of the New York City Ballet when it suited him, his words to Nancy Reynolds in 1974 affirm that it was indeed a haven for him and that working there was a necessary tonic:

> That whole period was a very, very creative one for me. The big thing in my head was that George made me feel so clearly that what was important was dance. Nothing else. And that place was a workshop where we were all working on some marvelous laboratory experiment called "Dance." It didn't matter who contributed what and how it worked out, but to work on it was the important thing. It was quite different from the atmosphere at Ballet Theatre where . . . there was this choreographer and that choreographer, and you did your work, and they were doing theirs, and you had to fight for time, and the sense of it was competitive. With George it wasn't that at all. It didn't matter if it was his

work or my work. What was interesting was the art of dancing, something that was there for all of us to work with.

For the New York City Ballet's 1953 spring season, Robbins prepared two works simultaneously. It's likely that one, *Fanfare,* was suggested by Balanchine and Kirstein. Princess Elizabeth was to be crowned Queen of England on June 2, and Balanchine, something of an Anglophile since his days there in the early 1930s staging numbers for Charles Cochran's Revue, wanted a new piece for that evening's celebratory program. The music for *Fanfare* was *The Young Person's Guide to the Orchestra,* op. 34, by British composer Benjamin Britten. Its mix of pomp, whimsy, and sweetness suited both the occasion and Robbins's gifts. The other new ballet was much more personal: a new version of *Afternoon of a Faun,* using the Debussy music that had inspired Nijinsky to choreograph his *L'Après-midi d'un Faune* in 1912. Robbins's nymph of choice was, naturally, Tanaquil Le Clercq, with Francisco Moncion as the "faun." He had wanted Buzz Miller to play the role, as a guest artist, but some miscommunication between Miller and Balanchine scotched that. (Miller later told Brian Meehan, "That is me. I am that boy.") Jerry also considered Louis Johnson, the gifted black dancer who had appeared in *Ballade.* A chance glimpse of Johnson had been crucial to his vision of the work: "I walked into a rehearsal studio and Louis Johnson was practicing a *Swan Lake* adagio with a student girl. They were watching themselves in a mirror. I was struck by the way they were watching that couple over there doing a love dance, and totally unaware of the proximity and possible sexuality of their physical encounters." Johnson had one rehearsal with Robbins and Le Clercq and heard no more; perhaps the New York City Ballet was not yet ready for a racially mixed pas de deux.

In April, Jerry wrote to Buzz, who was working out of town, with news of the house he planned to build in Fire Island Pines (he'd owned a lot there since the late 1940s, and Miller owned an adjoining one), the doings of their oversized puppy, Otis, whom he referred to as "our son," and the progress of his two ballets. About the Britten piece: "Yvonne Mounsey, the queen in 'The Cage,' is slightly marvelous as the harp. And the drum section looks like it will be very funny . . . a huge camp for Todd (only I do it better)." He had reworked the beginning of *Faun* for the ninth time "(actually!) and yesterday I seemed to break some of the ice around it. God I hope so. I had to address and be asked questions by the N.Y. Ballet Club on Sunday and boy were they curious about Faune. So is everyone. So am I." This season was an ambitious one, with new ballets by Bolender and Lew Christensen, as well as by Balanchine. Robbins noted that there were some financial worries about the season—he wasn't sure how serious—but was "going to put the bite on" about twenty-five people and ask for money.

In this letter, he returned yet again to his fatalist view of the ephemerality of talent and was delighted that his hadn't dried up yet.

> You know talent is really a gift from nowhere, alighting on some poor slob in spite of himself; and anyone who thinks that he has something to do with it himself is nuts. Sure, if you've got it doesn't mean it will come out and be clear. That takes work, and effort and technique (and on my part hell of a lot of agony). But the nice thing with me is that the older I grow the more I appreciate what I manage to do and that gives me great happiness in this world.

Romola Nijinsky said that her husband had never read the poem by Stéphane Mallarmé that had inspired Claude Debussy's music (although Nijinsky's lover and mentor Serge Diaghilev knew it). It is certain that Robbins studied it in translation. And he had probably seen some rather distorted versions of Nijinsky's ballet that the Ballet Russe companies toured. In 1912, Nijinsky had embraced ideas that came to define early modernism in dance: economy of means, angularity, clarity of design. His nymphs in their handsome Greek draperies arrived to bathe in flat, two-dimensional processions, like those crossing a wall in friezes or running eternally around an archaic vase. Compressed into the same narrow, horizontal corridors of space, the faun roused himself from sensuous reverie and pursued them in a path that snaked across the stage. The ballet's stylized vocabulary stymied Parisians, used to seeing the world's greatest jumper show his skills, and many were shocked by the ending with its fairly obvious depiction of the onanism that's only hinted at in the poem. When the Chief Nymph fled the Faun's attentions, she dropped her scarf; he carried it back to his rock, arranged it in the semblance of a supine woman, lowered himself deliberately onto it, and arched upward in a silent orgasmic outcry.

Robbins deleted the attendant nymphs and recast the principals as young contemporary dancers meeting in a studio. His hero, bare-chested and wearing tights, is asleep on the floor when a young female dancer enters to practice some steps. Jean Rosenthal's set and lighting create an idyllic studio: white floor, transparent white fabric "walls," and beside the stage-right barre, a filmy curtain that stirs slightly in an unseen breeze. The scrim that initially veils the scene casts the audience as voyeurs, but as it rises and the man wakes and stretches to the music's opening notes, the audience understands the stage's "fourth wall" to be the studio mirror. (So mysteriously potent is this illusion that it's surprising to discover that Robbins originally considered placing the imagined mirror on one side of the "room.") While his choreography is fully three-dimensional, the dancers, continually appraising their movements in the mirror, stress the almost two-dimensional legibility that is crucial to ballet's presentation on a proscenium stage.

Robbins's vision was contemporary and natural. He had remembered the way one day in class a teenager (Edward Villella), standing next to him at the barre, "suddenly began to stretch his body in a very odd way, almost like he was trying to get something out of it. And I thought how animalistic it was . . . that sort of stuck in my head." After the woman has walked lightly on tiptoe behind the transparent wall to its doorway, she presses the points of her slippers into a resin box, adjusts the belt of her pale blue tunic, enters, and studies her pose in the "mirror" without seeing the sleeping man. Robbins imagined her, he said, having just washed her hair, and it hangs free. The two young people gradually begin to dance together, and, although the fact that their eyes remain fixed on the mirror has suggested narcissism to some viewers, their gaze doesn't really express self-love. They look into the glass to see what they *might* be, at how they transform themselves through the rituals of ballet. *We* see through the mirror into their desires.

Their pairing seems to happen naturally, from the moment he goes behind her where she is doing her quiet exercises at the barre, places his hands on her waist, and lifts her. Against the mood of sensual reverie that seeps from Debussy's music, they act no roles; they simply explore the steps as if discovering them—almost "marking" them the way dancers sometimes do in rehearsal (a look Robbins loved). Unlike Nijinsky, Robbins felt no need to invent a vocabulary. The ballerina's sudden spin, stopped by her partner's arm, her introspective attention on how a lift feels, build narrative onto classical steps and strategies. His dancers too occupy a drowsy sunlit space that is suddenly infused with a reticent but unmistakable sexual tension, but it is a place of safety for them, a room where their daily work occurs.

All the gestures but one allude to their lives as dancers. At the climax, as they kneel on the floor, the man leans gently forward and kisses the woman's cheek. She watches this in the mirror, turns to look at him, and then—gazing back at their reflections—touches the spot with her hand. It is a moment fraught with irony. So intent are these young people on their reflected otherness that even an intimate gesture must be studied for its effect. When the two are feeling out their pas de deux, he often grasps her body and presses it to him; yet at the moment "real life" enters the studio, the suddenly electric point of contact is very small—the size of two lightly pursed lips.

Robbins took only the basic structure from Nijinsky's scenario. His "faun" wakens to the presence of the solitary nymph, encounters her, and, after she has left, goes back to his place on the floor and stretches out. Perhaps he has only dreamed her. Some years after the ballet's premiere on May 14, Robbins added a gesture. Just before curling up, the man arches up from the floor, a chaste allusion to Nijinsky's climactic moment. Robbins did draw on imagery from Mallarmé's poem (as well, perhaps, as some ideas from Mikhail Fokine's *Narcisse,* a vehicle for Nijinsky based on the myth of a man doomed to fall in love with his own reflection in a pool). Moncion has spoken of gestures like "pushing through the reeds on a hot, humid afternoon." The lonely faun of the poem dwells beside a lake. At one moment, Robbins's nymph is seated on her partner's shoulder; as he gazes up at her and she down at him, very lightly paddling her feet in the air, they might be seeing each other as reflections of the ambition they share. Later, standing behind her, he frames her head almost awkwardly within his angled arms and, in the next instant, lowers and tilts that frame to catch her stretched body as she dives through it.

It is one of Robbins's greatest works.

There have been many fine interpretations of this small masterpiece, but the original cast can be said to embody most fully the choreographer's idea (a silent black-and-white film, shot slightly from the side, is the only record of Moncion's and Le Clercq's performance). Moncion conveys a restrained yet intense sensual interest in Le Clercq from the moment he awakens at the sound of her footsteps to the moment when she backs out of the room and he, kneeling, raises his head slightly, as if scenting the trail of her perfume. She can seem innocent, hastening away from him, but a minute before, she has slowly turned one bent leg in and out, watching him in the mirror watching her, very aware of her seductiveness. Interestingly, in another early film, made by the Canadian Broadcasting Corporation, Le Clercq danced with Jacques d'Amboise, who played the man as a young tough. He brought out the hoyden in her.

Mallarmé's faun dreamed of two nymphs—one chaste, one more knowing.

> Reflect . . .
>   whether these women you ponder
> might embody your fabulous senses' desire!
> Faun, illusion escapes the eyes of the first,
> Blue and cold as a weeping spring.
> But the other, all sighs, would you say she is different,
> Like a hot day's wind in your fleece!

It is possible to interpret these nymphs as two aspects of the eternal feminine. Whether or not Robbins and Le Clercq consciously followed this reading, they reembodied it as the play of conflicting feelings within one young woman. Le Clercq's father, a professor at Queens College and a Mallarmé expert, wrote Robbins, "What you have understood so well is that the two nymphs of the original are one and the same. The very text, obscure as it is, proves it. . . . You have reached the core of the meaning that poor sterile Mallarmé was unable to convey and that all his commentators have missed."

Fanfare, still regularly performed by the New York City Ballet and other companies, has never been considered a great ballet, but it's bright and full of fun and offers many juicy little roles. It may have been one of Balanchine's devices for further educating Robbins. Jerry had never made a ballet that employed a large ensemble—all thirty-four of whom would have to be onstage for the statement of Britten's weighty theme (drawn from Henry Purcell's incidental music for *Abdelazar, or the Moor's Revenge*) and for its restatement in fugal form at the end. In shows, of course, he often had to manipulate crowds—and did it brilliantly—but in a grand ballet of this sort, the ambiance is more formal, less character-based, with some dancers as moderately anonymous contrapuntal background to fore-grounded soloists.

Still, he knew what he didn't want to happen. Once, when he had had to miss a rehearsal at the last minute and asked Balanchine to take over, he'd found that his colleague had pushed forward with the restatement of Robbins's theme. Jerry didn't like the unison (he had counterpoint in mind), so he revised what George had done. Balanchine never let him forget it: "I fixed it, but you changed."

Robbins followed the composer's educational scenario. A Major Domo, dressed as a Beefeater guard, although in slightly more muted colors, announces each section—first, the introduction of each family of instruments, then lengthier variations for each instrument. Irene Sharaff costumed the groups in different colors—short tutus for the women, monochromatic tights and leotards for the men. The ballet announces itself as regal—everyone wears a crown of sorts—and the entrances, with the various groups bowing to one another, cast these embodiments of the orchestra as courtiers. Through this device, Robbins was able, to some degree, to pursue his interest in depicting a community. "Instruments" acknowledge one another, vie for prominence, and fall in love.

The theme-and-variations form in ballet functions on the interplay of familiarity and surprise. A spectator may not pick up a step in all the transformations wrought by changes in order, rhythm, speed, design, but may recognize some as already seen. The movement theme in parallel ranks that Robbins devised for the processional opening isn't quite meaty enough to provide material for all the ensuing variations, and he doesn't follow the process scrupulously. He uses in different ways his theme's formal bows, reiterates its arabesques, and finds ways to alter a bent-kneed step and send it into the air, but also adds new material.

Courtly manners translate into both exaggerated politesse and pomposity, with fine comic results. In fact, the jokes, at which Robbins excelled, tend to be what one remembers from the ballet. The hot-tempered trumpets duel, and one accidentally runs the other through and lugs him offstage, miming, "I didn't mean to" to the audience. The three trombones are soldiers, with the mustachioed tuba as drill sergeant taking bows for their every accomplishment. The double-bass soloist so excites two cellos and two violins with his escalating jumps and somersaults that they cluster around him and applaud. The four French horns menace the string group, most of whom depart in haste, leaving the violins clustered around the harp, fluttering their hands like the swans in *Swan Lake* cowering before the huntsmen.*

Robbins had a field day with the three men depicting the full array of percussion instruments. They enter smartly right after the trombones and tuba drill, drop into at-ease positions, and stare at the audience. When they unwisely clap their hands overhead, the noise of their cymbal hats makes them wince. After every slow retreat, skipping ponderously with bent knees to muffled drumbeats, they turn and advance to embody other struck instruments—scampering and quivering their hands to the triangle, smacking each other in the face to the whip. When the castanets sound, the ringleader (the part made for Todd Bolender) bursts into an eccentric and thoroughly astonishing Spanish dance.

Women impersonate the lighter instruments: there's a pretty little trio for two flutes and a piccolo, with a wandering oboe entering for a legato solo, a dance for six perky violins, and one for a trio of cellos. The harp is queen and has a fine solo as befits her status. One highlight is an extremely pretty duet with lifts for the violas.

Walter Terry, one of the critics who very much admired *Fanfare,* found that the "plan has provided Robbins with magnificent opportunities for the creating of mass action and of delicate detail, and he has functioned in both areas with wit and brilliance." But others were less enthusiastic. The ballet does feel slightly enslaved by its structure, bright little package that it is.

⌒

The New York City Ballet's season opened on May 5, with Robbins's two ballets still to premiere. That same day, the House Committee on Un-American Activities finally closed in on him. During the Eighty-third Congress, hearings reached epidemic proportions. HUAC collected testimony from more than 650 witnesses in 178 days. More because of its high visibility than of the number of genuine subversives involved, the New York theater world was one of the targets. Robbins was called to testify on the first day of the hearings. The account of his testimony makes interest-

* Both this and the double bass's variation were changed in 1975; the bass was originally more incompetent, and the horns were originally women. There weren't a lot of men in New York City Ballet in 1953. When Robbins set *Fanfare* for the male-rich Royal Danish Ballet in 1955, the horn section assumed the casting it has today.

ing reading—an unpleasant drama, with the unctuous, self-satisfied inquisitors nailing their squirming witness.

Robbins was last to testify that day, accompanied by his lawyer, Robert Siegel. He followed playwright Arnaud d'Usseau, who gave the committee members something of a hard time with remarks such as "there have always been people who are in the minority, who have dissented. I think any writer who is worth his salt is critical of our society. I believe, with Shelley, that poets are the unacknowledged legislators of the world." Poetry? Representative Harold H. Velde (ex-FBI) opined that d'Usseau was "getting into the field that is entirely foreign to our hearing today, and our purposes."

The committee obliged Robbins by turning the lights off (thus thwarting film and television cameras) and prodded him into a testimony that was both frank and disingenuous. He gave them his background. He tried to explain, in response to the questions of the committee's counsel Frank Tavenner, what a choreographer was and how he did what he did. Yes, he had, in December 1943, applied to join what was at that time known as the Communist Political Association—becoming a member of what he identified as the "theatrical transient group"—and had left the Party in the spring of 1947. Yes, he had participated in so-called front organizations that seemed to stand for things he believed in, not knowing they were controlled by Communists. At the time, he had thought the Russian Communists were against fascism and anti-Semitism and in favor of artistic freedom. When asked why he had defected, he focused on Soviet policy toward art and artists; he couldn't comprehend how art [implying of high quality] could be labeled "fascistic, bourgeois, decadent, degenerate" if it didn't conform and art of dubious quality praised on the basis of its message. He related that he was annoyed to have been asked by a member of his cell if dialectical materialism had influenced *Fancy Free*.

A member of the committee proposed adjourning for the day, but Siegel urged that they continue the hearing since Tavenner had only three or four more questions. At that point it became clear that Robbins wanted this to be over, that he had come prepared to name names; he spilled them out with almost no prompting. Lettie Stever (who worked in the office of Jerry's agent Dick Dorso) had recruited him. Among those who had attended meetings over his three-plus years as a Communist, he said, were the actors Lloyd Gough, Madeleine Lee, and Elliot Sullivan; playwrights Jerome and Edward Chodorov; left-wing critic Edna Ocko; and Lionel

Berman (party functionary and contributor to *The New Masses*). Ocko had organized the TAC cabarets that had given Robbins's youthful choreography one of its first New York showings. Madeleine Lee had been a friend; he'd met her at a party, where she had clued him in on the latest social dances he needed to know for *Fancy Free*. He had worked with Edward Chodorov and even more with Jerome (and had perhaps been in contact with him quite recently: *Wonderful Town* was based on the play J. Chodorov had written with Joseph Fields).

Representative Bernard Kearney thanked him for his frankness and commented on the unusual forthrightness of his testimony. Representative Gordon Scherer revealed that he himself was going to see *The King and I* that very night and would now appreciate it all the more. Representative Clyde Doyle put Robbins through a couple more hoops. He wanted to know why the choreographer had been so cooperative, knowing he would be branded a stool pigeon by some. Doyle extracted a "yes, sir" to the query "In other words, you feel you are doing the right thing as an American?" He then applied an oblique pressure similar to what had driven Robbins away from communism:

> Now, let me say this too: You are in a wonderful place, through your art, your music, your talent which God blessed you with, to perhaps be very vigorous and positive in promoting Americanism in contrast to communism. Let me suggest that you use that great talent which God has blessed you with to put into ballets in some way, that interpretation.

Robbins replied that his work had been acclaimed in particular for its "American quality." Doyle urged him to "even put more of that in where you can appropriately."

It was over.

Except that it wasn't, of course. Colleagues were outraged and appalled, as were his sister Sonia and her husband, George. Some friends became former friends. Others—Mary Hunter and George Abbott, for example—expressed sympathy for Jerry's ordeal without either condoning or condemning him. The FBI continued to keep a file on him and paid periodic visits, sure that he had more to tell, but he refused to be squeezed any further.

Robbins never fully understood why he had named names. In 1989, preparing an autobiographical theater piece, he sought (perhaps to assuage his conscience) to find out if the names he had given had already been named by others. According to the report he commissioned, no one else had mentioned Stever, Ocko, or Lee. Many years later he told a young intimate, Michael Koessel, that he knew he had done the wrong thing.

Why had he done it? As a patriotic duty? Because he thought his career would be ruined? Because he was afraid of being outed publicly as a homosexual? His terror may have been far deeper seated and more irrational.

Years later, trying finally to come to terms with being Jewish and to embrace it, he wrote in a notebook:

It was my homosexuality I was afraid would be exposed I thought. It was my once having been a Communist that I was afraid would be exposed. None of these. I was & have been—& still have terrible pangs of terror when I feel that my career, work, veneer of accomplishments would be taken away (by HUAC, or by critics) that I panicked & crumbled & returned to that primitive state of terror—the facade of Jerry Robbins would be cracked open, and behind everyone would finally see Jerome Wilson Rabinowitz.

11

Taking Charge

Robbins and Mary Martin practice flying
for the camera on the *Peter Pan* set.
NYPL.

*A*rthur Laurents believes that Robbins cooperated with the
House Committee on Un-American Activities because he
wanted to work in motion pictures. The only films he actually
made, however, were those based on musicals he'd had a hand in, *The*

King and I and *West Side Story* (one that he was deeply interested in during the 1960s, a British movie about Nijinsky, fell through). He turned down a number of offers. On June 30, 1953, Hollywood's *Daily Variety* noted that a deal was cooking for him with Harry Cohn at Columbia Pictures; he'd be the studio's dance director. In July he was said to be in Hollywood discussing the plan. By September, New York's monthly *Dance News* was presenting the job as a fait accompli and listing five films he would choreograph, including *Pal Joey* and a new musicalization of *My Sister Eileen*. That was the end of it (*My Sister Eileen* became, in 1955, the first film Bob Fosse choreographed on his own). However, the next project Robbins tackled was in television and sponsored by Ford Motors, the company that backed *The Ed Sullivan Show* and had ordered Sullivan to check proposed guests on the show for possible Communist affiliations before signing them. Had Jerry refused to cooperate with HUAC, it's doubtful that he would have been able to participate in the Ford show. If that had influenced his testimony, he never admitted it, even to himself.

Perhaps he declined the Columbia offer, as he had the Paramount proposal two years earlier, because he couldn't bear the idea of being tied down for a long period of time. His zigzags between Broadway and the ballet world in the 1950s seem to have been predicated on more than making money ("You must explain to me some day why you need so much money," Le Clercq once wrote to him) and his ongoing need for the artistic stability of Balanchine's world; he thrived on variety. Some advice he gave to Buzz Miller, when Miller was having a success with a new act for supper clubs featuring himself and George and Ethel Martin, may also have been advice he kept in mind for himself during these years: if the initial excitement about the act waned, he wrote, "Try if possible to get some immediate engagement right away so that you are in the light even if its not the best one."

In 1953, he was primed to explore both new media and new roles—in particular, that of director.

Broadcast before a large live audience at the vast old Center Theater at Rockefeller Center on June 15, 1953, the "Ford 50th Anniversary Show" (titled "The American Road") was a major event in television history: a two-hour presentation by the Ford Motor Company. There were no commercial breaks, although two of the hosts, the beloved puppets Kukla and Ollie, sang "There's Nothing Like a Model T" against a hilarious old film sequence in which Harold Lloyd went crazy with a car, and footage of Model Ts being assembled at the Ford plant figured in the parade of modern inventions that made life easier for folks.

Jerry's good friend Leland Hayward, who produced the event, had been brainstorming for some time, with the assistance of Robbins's cherished mentor Mary Hunter. The important issue was to show "who we are and how we got that way." Robbins was also involved in the process of figuring that out, judging by nine undated pages of thoughts he addressed to Hayward after a long, busy confab with Hunter over Lewis Allen's script. His concern, as usual, was to locate and stress the central core on which everything else should depend.

"Concurrent with each period & the things we talk about we have to have constant references to the change in growth to the American character. How did the key inventions, incidents, historical events, effect [sic] the American character." They needed, he thought, to show how the relations between men and women, rich and poor, politicians and the public, the United States and the world had changed: "I think that if we don't stress this or at least let this lead us and make it the spine of the show, which after all is the premise of the show, that we are again falling back onto doing a picture book effect of American life." He liked what they had, but it didn't go far enough for him. "Let's take the first World War. If part of the emancipation of women came out of that—let's show it, let's tell it."

Leland and his wife, Slim, called Jerry "Gypsy" in fond moments, and Robbins's long message ends affectionately, "This is all for now. We have been here sweating for hours while you have been boozing it up. I'm tempted to [laugh from Mary in the background] sing a few gypsy songs."

Clark Jones directed the epic, while Robbins provided the choreography and staging for the musical numbers, but he is one of those acknowledged in the credits for his valuable contributions to the whole.

It would have been a miracle if the show had been able to bring out everything the creative team hoped for, but it was immensely entertaining, with news about political change and two world wars entering swiftly if somberly between visions of what people had been wearing, what plays and movies they'd been seeing, and what inventions had changed their lives. Edward R. Murrow, cigarette usually in hand, introduced most of the political segments, Oscar Hammerstein II, the theatrical material. Wally Cox, star of the NBC sitcom *Mr. Peepers,* provided a running gag as the bespectacled nerd, in each scene reading a different self-improvement book that would, he hoped, make him popular (although showing no signs of success in any endeavor). The great African-American contralto Marian Anderson sang, as did a succession of crooners (Rudy Vallee, Bing Crosby, Frank Sinatra, and Eddie Fisher). Howard Lindsay and Dorothy Stickney enacted a witty male-female confrontation at the beginning of the century (a scene from Lindsay and Russell Crouse's *Life with Father*), and Mary Martin spoke Emily's final moving monologue from Thornton Wilder's *Our Town*.

The two hours ended with a short, extremely serious conversation between Murrow and Hammerstein about the future fifty years. They stood before the camera as if on a street corner and talked about the perils of the atomic bomb and the Cold War, about how the United States, with world leadership "thrust upon us" and vying with Russia for the hearts and minds of other nations, must guide the world to peace not by bombs or dollars but by example. And, in a startling, not-so-veiled reference to the ongoing hunt for subversives, Murrow wondered what kind of example the United States would be to other countries "[if] we confuse dissent with disloyalty. If we deny the right to be wrong, to advocate minority, unpopular, unorthodox views," adding, "Nations have lost their freedom while preparing to defend it." (It is impossible, in the twenty-first century, to imagine a major television entertainment serving up the notion that America could "destroy itself from within.") Dorothy Kilgallen, whose syndicated column ran in the conservative Hearst newspapers, seems to have been the only critic who objected to the sequence, titling her review "Sad Spots Flaw in Big TV Show."

Mary Martin and Ethel Merman were the stars of the endeavor, and Robbins staged numbers for each. To illustrate the zest of jazz, Merman sang "Alexander's Ragtime Band" in front of a Dixieland band. In military uniform, she embodied the lighter side of World War I, trouping gamely with four guys while belting "Mademoiselle from Armentieres." Together, she and Martin strutted with hats and canes, lip-syncing an old record of a vaudeville routine. In the show's great climactic number, they sang old favorites seated on stools (Hunter's idea), occasionally moving off them and into affectionate poses with each other. Still dazzling on the kinescope of the show (black-and-white) is the "I" section, in which they trade first lines of songs beginning with "I," ending with a contrapuntal blend of "Tea for Two" (Mary) and "Stormy Weather" (Ethel) before charging into the final "There's No Business Like Show Business."

Robbins lifted choreographic material from his old shows. A display of changing fashions in bathing suits, decade by decade, borrowed the cardboard waves and the structure of his in-and-out-of-bathhouses ruckus from *High Button Shoes*. Pairs of dancers modeled the outfits, while the invisible Kukla and Ollie narrated and spoke occasional lines for them. To illustrate the wild side of the 1920s, the riotous "Charleston" from *Billion Dollar Baby* was transferred intact, with many from its original cast. But thanks to the magic of television, Robbins was able to add a footnote, drawn from his plans for the never-made film of that show: the wealthy couple from the dance buys a paper with news of the 1929 crash, and as a voice solemnly lists the price drop for each stock, garments disappear off the woman's body one by one; she vanishes when she's down to her skivvies, and then the man loses *his* clothes.

A medley of dance crazes from the waltz to the lindy gave Robbins the opportunity to have the camera occasionally tilt and spin with the dizziness of it all. But the most ingenious new number was one he staged for Martin. To illustrate at a hectic pace the changes in women's fashions over fifty years, Irene Sharaff designed a long stretch-jersey sheath for Martin. By hiking it up or pulling it down, unzipping a section to show some leg, adding a belt, a half skirt, and a variety of hats, she could become a hobble-skirted damsel, a flapper, a Joan-Crawford sophisticate, and so on, in seconds. *New Yorker* fashion writer Lois Lane provided the sly voice-over commands and commentary, and Martin, working hard to keep up with the fickleness of fashion, charmed the audience. In the end, to the pronouncement, "Shape marches on!" she walked away from the camera exhausted, getting lower and lower and finally toppling over.

In July, Jamison Classics decided to market Sharaff's design as the "Mary Martin Dress," and Martin offered Jerry a piece of the action: "In view of the fact some of the inspiration for such dress may have been the result of the contribution which you may have made to the performance by me," she would pay him, out of her royalties, ten cents for each dress manufactured and sold. (The "may have"s are interesting, as if he had insisted and she had acquiesced, but certainly Robbins figured importantly in the concept of the number.)

The "Ford 50th Anniversary Show" cost $500,000, and *Newsweek* reported that 47,500,000 people had seen it. Hayward, Jones, Robbins, and Martin all won television's Sylvania Awards—Martin specifically for "outstanding individual variety performance" in the fashion satire. Priced at $3.85, the long-playing record of the show jumped off the shelves.

Abetted by her research for the Ford show (or perhaps it was vice versa), early in 1954, Mary Hunter produced a modest but successful touring production, *Musical Americana,* billed as "A Folk Concert in Song and Dance." Robbins's files for the television production contain lists she compiled, including ones of great old films and an impressive summary of events in American history and culture from the 1850s to the 1930s that may have been as much for her own project as for Leland Hayward's. Among *Musical Americana*'s numbers were a vaudeville built around daunting inventions—automobile, telephone, phonograph, etc.—and an affectionate satire by Hunter on the kind of silent movie that typically starred Mary Pickford. Ray Harrison was the choreographer, with "additional choreography by Jerome Robbins." Harrison contributed the eighteenth- and nineteenth-century material, and Robbins, again plundering his own oeuvre, contributed the twentieth-century dances. Somehow he found the time.

⌒

The scars from the short-lived *That's the Ticket!* in 1948 had healed, and Robbins very much wanted to plunge into directing again. Plunge he did (with the usual detours to make ballets), although the experiences weren't all satisfying. In 1954, he directed Aaron Copland's opera *The Tender Land;* codirected a musical, *The Pajama Game,* with George Abbott; directed *Peter Pan;* and considered directing *The Skin of Our Teeth.*

Over the summer and fall following the Ford show, Robbins may already have begun giving thought to the scenario of *Peter Pan,* going back to James M. Barrie's children's book and play. Edwin Lester was to present the musical on the West Coast the following summer with Mary Martin as its star and Broadway as a possibility. Although the New York News Service put out the word on July 12, 1953, that Robbins was set to choreograph *The Girl in Pink Tights,* Agnes de Mille did that show. He spent time in Europe and by December was off to Israel and Inbal, this time with Anna Sokolow. He didn't have time himself to bring Inbal's vibrant dancers to the peak of discipline needed for their projected European and American appearances. Courtesy of the American Fund for Israel Institutions, he took Sokolow to do the job.

He and she greatly admired and respected each other. Like him, Sokolow was born in New York of Russian Jewish immigrants. Even before she left Martha Graham's company in 1939, she was making powerful, tough-minded works with a strong left-wing political cast. Aaron Copland and Leonard Bernstein, both fans, met for the first time at a concert of hers. She had done splendid work with companies in Mexico. A woman of formidable integrity, she too could be hard on dancers and the actors she taught at the Actors Studio. She understood that Jerry's demands and temper fits didn't spring from egotism. In a 1999 interview, old, sick, heavily medicated, and having trouble speaking, she suddenly said (comparing him to certain other successful choreographers of her acquaintance), "He didn't think the sun shone out his ass."

Anna fell in love, as Jerry had, with Sara Levi-Tanai and her company and returned for three months in the summer to give those dancers, and others, classes in technique and composition. Robbins himself remained committed to the developing dance scene in Israel, and they must both have been gratified by the warm reception that greeted Inbal when the company first performed under Sol Hurok's management in Europe in 1957 and the United States in 1958.

Robbins came home from Israel to more than Christmas with Buzz Miller. The New York City Ballet had returned from a ten-week tour of Europe in mid-November and needed him. For the winter season opening January 5, 1954, Balanchine produced his most elaborate work yet for the company: a remounting of Lev Ivanov's 1892 *Nutcracker;* he had danced in it at Saint Petersburg's Maryinsky Theater when he was a little student in the Imperial Theater School. It was the company's first full-length ballet, and although credit for the first complete American *Nutcracker* belongs to William Christensen and the San Francisco Ballet, most ballet audiences had seen only a truncated suite of dances to excerpts from Tchaikovsky's score. Jerry, in his seldom-invoked role of associate artistic director, chipped in. While Balanchine was busy with the Act I Christmas party and the last-act variations for the various dancing sweetmeats, Robbins handled the battle between the toy soldiers and the marauding mice, a bit of mayhem staged and costumed to be pleasantly scary and not really alarming. The padding in the rodents' gray suits wobbled endearingly as they ran, and although they tucked little ballet-student soldiers under their furry arms in the battle's darkest hour, even the Nutcracker's duel with the dreaded Mouse King had its droll aspects.

Worried about how the public would respond to *The Nutcracker,* the company programmed it in clusters during its ten-week City Center season. The public—paying the theater's popular prices ranging from $3.50 for seats in the orchestra and the front of the first balcony to $1.50 for the back of the second balcony—liked it fine. City Ballet fans of those days remember with delight the Christmas tree that, on City Center's modestly equipped stage, had to sit on the trappings of its own larger self, so that when it grew in little Marie's dream, it creaked and clanked upward as its lower layers dropped, lights and ornaments wobbling precariously. The ballet, of course, became a staple of New York Christmases and, in various versions, a staple all over America. Robbins has never been given program credit for his contribution.

Age of Anxiety, The Cage, The Pied Piper, Afternoon of a Faun, and *Fanfare* were all danced during the season, along with sixteen Balanchine ballets, including the new *Opus 34,* Ruthanna Boris's *Cakewalk,* and Lew Christensen's 1938 *Filling Station.* Only Balanchine's *Serenade* received more performances than *Piper* (nine to seven during the first month).

Keeping his image as a committed ballet choreographer fresh in both his own mind and the public's—as well as nourishing himself with a creative job that involved no argumentative collaborators—Robbins set a work, *Quartet,* to Sergei Prokofiev's String Quartet no. 2, op. 92, written in 1941. He had heard the music in Israel but was offended when some critics, notably John Martin of the *Times* and Rosalind Krokover of the *Musical Courier,* thought they detected an influence of Israeli folk dance—Martin going so far as to call the ballet a "fantasia on Israeli folk themes" as in "pastoral festivals the young dancers used to present for us in the early days of the Israel republic." The issue is moot. Israel, as a new melting-pot society, had created folk dances that showed the population's varied ancestry. In any case, what Krokover called "the lyric oriental flavor" of the music's adagio movement stemmed from a love song of the Caucasus, which Prokofiev had used as material.

According to Robbins, he was shaping *Quartet* as a purely classical work when Balanchine came into rehearsals and told him it had to be Caucasian. "Once he put that into my head, the ballet started to go that way more and more." So the ballet steps and folk steps mingled—apparently somewhat uneasily, although Martin found the piece "charmingly composed" and offered an interesting comment: "[The music] gives an air of remoteness, which, in conjunction with the use of the alien medium of the classic dance, makes those folk measures seem like something remembered from afar." Jerry had intended to have Le Clercq in the ballet, but she had to have her appendix out. Patricia Wilde and Herbert Bliss danced the spirited first movement, Jillana and Jacques d'Amboise the tender second, and Yvonne Mounsey and Todd Bolender the darker, more rushing last movement. Four additional couples backed the principals. As with *Fanfare,* Robbins had (according to Martin) a little trouble manipulating all fourteen dancers in the final ballabile. Karinska's silk costumes were, apparently, gorgeous. Reading the scant information on this seldom-performed ballet, one wonders if some of the feelings in it found deeper, more accomplished form in Robbins's exquisite 1969 *Dances at a Gathering.*

The Nutcracker premiered on February 2 and *Quartet* on February 18. On February 26, Kaye appeared for the first time in the season in *Age of Anxiety* (Robbins danced in it too, as he had done in mid-January). Before the New York City Ballet's season ended, though, Robbins was busy directing Aaron Copland's first and only opera. *The Tender Land,* produced by the New York City Opera, was not a success, despite some fine musical writing. It was set in small-town America, and its plot begged comparisons with *Oklahoma!* and even closer ones with William Inge's play *Picnic,* although it was in the works before *Picnic* premiered. The critic of *The Saturday Review* didn't think *Tender Land* could really be called an opera, and he blamed the "inept book" for its failings, muttering about a heroine "whose biggest deal is her high school graduation."

The inspiration for the opera had been James Agee's *Let Us Now Praise Famous Men,* and more particularly Walker Evans's stark photographs of southern tenant farmers that accompanied it. Copland's lover, Erik Johns, under the pseudonym of Horace Everett, wrote the libretto. Robbins was eager to work with Copland, and the opera offered possibilities for a director-choreographer. Essentially the story is of a girl's coming of age. Her graduation party is also a celebration of the spring harvest. The barn dance affects and is affected by events. On that evening, the heroine, Laurie, falls in love with Martin, one of two itinerant men who've appeared and offered to help with the harvest. Suspicious that the pair are the drifters who have recently molested some other girls in the vicinity (one of them, Top, is coarse-mannered), Laurie's mother calls the sheriff. Even though it turns out that the real miscreants have been caught, Laurie's autocratic grandfather orders the men off the place. The smitten couple plans to elope, but Top persuades Martin to leave without her, proffering two good reasons: (a) Grandpa Moss will sic the law on them, and (b) what sort of life does a tramp have to offer a girl? Laurie decides it's time to leave home anyway; as Grandpa realizes, she's harvested her childhood and must make a new beginning.

Robbins came out of it pretty well. Douglas Watt of *The Daily News* found his staging "mannered," and the *World-Telegram and Sun* critic, Robert Bagar, referred somewhat sourly to the staging's "quota of plastic posturing," but he thought that Robbins's Act II dance party, in which the performers sang as they moved, was one of two high points. Olin Downes wrote in *The New York Times* that "The most deeply emotional and imaginative passage of the score, at least at a first hearing, is the moment when the dance that has been sheer romping and gaiety suddenly is transformed, as the figures of the dancers become shadowy, and the music becomes that of the inner world of tenderness and longing."

Three days before the opera premiered on April 1, Robbins wrote to Arthur Laurents (who, blacklisted in Hollywood, had decamped for Europe) that the experience had been "one of the worst . . . I have ever had in the theatre—somewhat akin to a nightmarish dream of slowly sinking in quicksand while everyone is standing around asking if everything is under control. No wonder the opera looks the way it does." By April 5, he was more sanguine, telling Lincoln Kirstein that he'd had "a good experience in many ways, in spite of the old pancakes that run the company." In Boston working on *The Pajama Game* and deep in plans for *Peter Pan,* he still fired off notes and corrections on *Tender Land* (fifty for Act I, twenty-three for Act II) to his assistant Robert Pageant and lighting designer Jean Rosenthal after the opera's premiere and announced he'd be coming into town and expected to rehearse the cast for three hours.

He liked *The Pajama Game.* The book, adapted by Abbott and Richard Bissell from Bissell's novel *7½ Cents,* played merry, if serious, hell with unionizing attempts in a pajama factory, and Richard Adler and Jerry Ross wrote a raft of memorable songs, including the ballad (perfect for John Raitt's warm baritone) "Hey There." Abbott wanted Robbins to do the choreography, but Robbins must have realized he had enough on his plate (*The Pajama Game* began rehearsals on March 10, *Tender Land* premiered on April 1, and *Peter Pan* was simmering). Buzz Miller urged Jerry to see the movie of *Kiss Me, Kate,* in particular a number Bob Fosse had staged for himself and Carol Haney. Fosse was hired. But coproducer

Harold Prince—himself, along with his partner Robert Griffith, a relative newcomer to producing—was worried whether the relatively unknown Fosse could deliver. In a letter to biographer Greg Lawrence in 1999, Prince recalled that "I, while agreeing to give Bob Fosse the contract, insisted that we have a protective backup—in this case, Jerry Robbins. Abbott agreed; and so did Jerry, who wanted to become a director and divined that if he insisted on co-directing credit, the word would be out in the field."

Fosse did a fine job, creating at least one sensational number for the musical, "Steam Heat." This trio, danced by Carol Haney, Peter Gennaro, and Buzz Miller, offered what were to become Fosse trademarks: the tilted bowler hats, slouched torsos, hyperactive pelvises, and sharply profiled stances. Robbins, queried the following year by David Hocker of the Music Corporation of America about what he himself had actually contributed to *The Pajama Game,* submitted the following tentative list:

1. Helped re-stage the opening
2. Staged about half of "Racing with the Clock" and the fade-out of the first scene
3. Worked with Johnny Raitt on "New Town" ["A New Town Is a Blue Town"]
4. Completely staged "I'm Not at All in Love"
5. Staged reprise of "Her Is"
6. Completely staged "There Once Was a Man"
7. Completely staged "7 ½ Cents"
8. Completely staged the finale after the dance that opens it
9. Staged the bows and curtains
10. Re-staged "Small Talk" and re-staged the reprise of "Hey There" with Janis [Paige].

It would have been unlike Robbins not to do something to earn his directorial credit (and the Donaldson Award he received as codirector). Or, put more bluntly, hard for him to keep his hands off. In a memo he mailed to Abbott after returning to New York following a March 26 run-through in Boston, he offered opinions about the overall shape of the show. There were too many old men in it, he thought, and too many roles that paralleled one another, spreading the material too thin.

We have a gold-mine in Carol [Haney] and the more things we give her to do all through the show, the better show we're going to have. If she, Mabel and Hines, Sid, Babe and Hasler could get clear of Poppas, assistants, stooges, and all that other mess, the story and show would be better. I think it's a very good idea putting "I Love You More" in the picnic scene as a stunt that Sid does for them and pulls Babe into. It helps them enormously and brings that number into a better position.

Stephen Sondheim, who says that Robbins "was the best stager of musical numbers—I think in my lifetime, anyway—in the Broadway theater," mentions Jerry's particular gift for dealing with numbers that did not involve dancers ("although he hated doing them"), offering as an example "There Once Was a Man," from *The Pajama Game,* "in which he had two klutzes on the stage and made them absolutely like Astaire and Rogers."

Fosse, whose first Broadway musical this was, remembered that when he came to "7½ Cents," the first big vocal number, he just let the cast stand and sing (as Abbott had advised when Fosse went to him for help). The result was terrible. Fosse, humiliated though he was when Jerry dropped in to start over, nevertheless stayed to watch.

I think I learned more in a couple of hours watching him stage than I had learned previously in my whole life. . . . He was very sweet about it and as he did the number he would consult with me and ask me what I thought. (I had no opinion at all I was in such awe of the man.) And in two hours he staged this song absolutely brilliantly. And I am so glad. I think it was a turning point in my career as a choreographer. I get the idea now and I see what you can do and what should be done and how to go about it and everything, and it's been something that's been of value to me for the rest of my career.

Fosse remained an ardent Robbins admirer, once making the sad remark "I think Balanchine and Robbins talk to God and when I call he's out to lunch."

⌒

Mary Martin and her husband, producer Richard Halliday, had wanted to put on *Peter Pan,* with Martin playing the title role, for about thirteen years when Edwin Lester, a director of the San Francisco Civic Opera, asked if they would like to come up with a new musical version, to open in San Francisco and then move to Los Angeles for five or six weeks of the Los Angeles Civic Light Opera's season. Two relatively inexperienced young people, Carolyn Leigh and Mark Charlap, were signed to write, respectively, the lyrics and the music (Martin had been charmed by a song of Leigh's, "Young at Heart," which she'd heard on the radio). They were taking something of a chance on Robbins, too, despite the good experience Martin had had working with him on the Ford show. When he received his first *Peter Pan* payment of $2,000 on March 12, 1954, neither *The Tender Land* nor *The Pajama Game* had opened in New York, and his skills as a director were unproven.

The project, however, was perfect for him. As Mary Martin said, "It was destined that Jerry come into our lives at this time. He was the one and only one to choreograph AND direct *Peter*. You see, Jerry IS Peter Pan." She must have been remembering not only his youthfulness but the playfulness of his imagination. He cherished youth onstage (shades of that doleful poem little Jerry had written about his vanished childhood: "Still dreams of youth I will keep in my head, / Till my heart stops beating & until I am dead"), and he had a gift for creating an illusion of innocence. Who better to tackle the tale of a boy who wanted never to grow up? Instead of achieving only that dubious dream, the Peter of the musical that was taking shape signified an unquenchable spirit—crowing "I am Youth, I am Joy, I am Freedom!"

The play has something of the English pantomime about it, with the "principal boy" being played by a woman and elements of slapstick mixing with more sophisticated jokes. Its fantastic elements are eccentric. An upright English family has a large dog as its children's nurse; a boy's shadow can be lost and end up folded in a drawer; children who fall out of their prams end up in Neverland. Barrie's whimsy is often treacly. There was no getting around Peter's plea to the audience "If you believe in fairies, clap your hands!" That spring, Robbins, with Hunter as his associate, worked to combine elements from Barrie's play and children's book and the scripts used for various productions starring Maude Adams, Eva Le Gallienne, and, most recently (1950), Jean Arthur. He was hoping he could "find a way of doing it freshly and less stickily, less cutely, more robustly." The Indians would be portrayed as children, capable of being frightened by their own bravado, like the "wild Indians" of parental rebuke frisking in the night garden. Wendy, her brothers, and the Lost Boys would be played by real children. The pirates would be big lummoxes, fierce but slow-witted and cowardly—easily conquered bogeymen. And, in a rather Freudian touch, the accomplished British actor Cyril Ritchard would play not only their leader, Captain Hook, but the children's obtuse father, Mr. Darling.

There were snafus. Would Oliver Smith be doing the sets? Yes. No. Lemuel Ayres? No. Peter Larkin was signed. And Motley for the costumes. Jean Rosenthal wasn't free to do the lights. Who then? Eventually Peggy Clark. The back-and-forth correspondence between Lester and Robbins is sizable. In mid-March, Jerry was pleased with the way the songs were coming along. He loved "Moose" Charlap's music, although he had some initial worries about Leigh's lyrics:

> The only possible problem that we may face is the tendency of Carolyn's to always write toward the hit record rather than toward the situation of the show. She shies away from using Peter and Wendy's names or specifics that might make the song unusable in general context. However, I keep hitting her on the head and I just hope I'm not hurting my fingers to no avail.

In May, auditioning began in New York, and by the end of the month, Robbins was enlisting casting help from Eugene Loring, who by then had a school in Hollywood. He needed "small, young boys" and "practically midget girls." One of Jerry's favorites, tiny Sondra Lee, was to play Peter's lovelorn Indian ally, Tiger Lily.

One delicate matter concerned Heller Halliday, the daughter of the star and producer. In January, it was announced that she would play the leading female role of Wendy. Robbins and Hunter thought this would be tricky and worked to dissuade Martin and Halliday without offending them. After considering several other possible uses of Heller, they eventually decided that she would play Liza, the child maid, and show up in the dream kingdom to which Peter lures Wendy and her brothers. Robbins worked hard to define her character: "prim, proper and prosaic in a humorous fashion with a very proper little walk and her hair pinned tightly on top of her head. And when she leaves the stage you should feel that she would give Never Land a thorough scrubbing." He was never able to make her appearance in Peter Pan's domain completely convincing, even though Peter's reprise of his cocky Act I song, "I've Gotta Crow," as a lesson in self-confidence for the little slavey, was made all the more charming by the fact that audiences knew this to be a mother-daughter act.

While the musical was taking shape, Robbins had to cope with a personal tragedy. On April 12, Lena Robbins died of breast cancer. Her son must have known it was coming (there are allusions in his autobiographical jottings to a double mastectomy). But the shock was enormous, and he disappeared for long enough to worry the show's producers.

By the time *Peter Pan* opened at San Francisco's Curran Theater on July 19, it was clear that Charlap and Leigh couldn't write all the songs the show needed. At some point in the proceedings, Leonard Bernstein was approached about the music, since he had written songs and incidental music for the 1950 Broadway production, but his songs didn't suit Martin's voice, and he wasn't prepared to write new ones. Betty Comden, Adolph Green, and composer Jule Styne came up from Hollywood, where they were working, and agreed to pitch in. Sondra Lee remembers curious ticking sounds seeping into her hotel room all night, only later realizing that it was Comden and Green, pecking away at their typewriters. Songs were still being put in and taken out during the Los Angeles run.

The collaborators, according to Comden and Green, had a fine time, but a certain amount of desperation inevitably prevailed. Writing to Buzz Miller from Hollywood's Chateau Marmont, Robbins was self-deprecating and not exactly sanguine: "Occasionally someone comes up with an idea for a big production number and everything inside me gets worried and cold because I don't think at this point that I could work up enough steps and ideas to fulfill anything very large." His contribution to a 1990 tribute to Jule Styne catches something of the atmosphere. He, Comden, Green, and Styne had been laboring in the basement nightclub of the Beverly Hills Hotel when an argument erupted.

> It ended with Jule stomping off in an unprecedented huff, leaving the rest of us crestfallen, downcast. . . . We moped about for some terrible minutes—then suddenly we heard a loud "Ta Da!" and from behind a set of drapes on the bandstand, out bounced Jule presenting himself like a big star show-girl, but stripped down to his boxer underwear and looking, as he always does, like some delicious cupid—all rosy and full of laughter, primping down to the nightclub floor singing his own musical accompaniment. The only thing missing was another Jule Styne to play the piano for his show—as he sashayed around—broke us up— and healed any damage that might have been done.

What Comden and Green instantly perceived about *Peter Pan* when they first saw it in San Francisco was, says Comden, that "It wasn't a musical. It was a play with songs." And Green adds, "We wrote songs that turned it into a musical." Comden: "We felt it needed a big theme number that would convey what Barrie was about and what *Peter Pan* was about— the magical aspect of it. So we wrote 'Neverland,' which is the theme song." Liking and respecting the songs that Charlap and Leigh had written for Martin ("I've Gotta Crow," "Flying," and "I Won't Grow Up"), they also felt that a duet between the two stars was needed and concocted "Mysterious Lady." Peter tempts the entranced Hook, singing while "she" flits between trees, keeping out of his sight (but not the audience's). The number showed off Martin's little-known coloratura and gave a new dimension to the entranced but increasingly befuddled Hook—until he catches on and nabs Peter.

The San Francisco critics put Ritchard and Lee above Martin in their praise, and visiting friends urged her to bow out, but she stuck with the show, only refusing to agree to go to New York with it until she felt comfortable with its final shape (this number in, that one out, please). There was nothing wrong with that shape when *Peter Pan* opened for a limited Broadway run on October 20, and the critics clapped their hands for more than Tinker Bell's resuscitation. Robbins's placement of reprises enhanced the tale's cyclical elements, such as the children's return home and Wendy's daughter Jane's years-later flight with Peter. Mary Martin had found a perfect blend of charm, cockiness, and a brusqueness that fooled no one, and Leigh and Charlap's songs for her captured the rhythmic and lyrical perkiness that had characterized her numbers as Ensign Nellie Forbush in Rodgers and Hammerstein's *South Pacific* ("A Wonderful Guy" and "I'm Gonna Wash That Man Right Outta My Hair"). Walter Kerr of the *Herald Tribune* raved, "It's the way *Peter Pan* always should have been and wasn't."

Ford and RCA Victor sponsored a live broadcast of the show (slightly edited) for Producers' Showcase on March 7, 1955, after the show had closed. Robbins's inventiveness comes across clearly even in a blurry copy of a kinescope. Martin doesn't just fly, she swoops above the stage, legs spread as if leaping; the fact that she bends her leading knee with each change of direction gives the impression that she is controlling her motion. In contrast, Wendy, John, and Michael—novice flyers—scrabble their legs in the air and barrel clumsily around the nursery, shrieking in delight.

Ritchard plays Hook as an over-the-top escapee from Restoration comedy, and Robbins has him carried onstage in a sedan chair. Some of his pirates constitute a traveling band, so that they can strike up a tango at his command while he dreams up a poisoned cake for the boys in song and nimble dance; next time he plots, it's a tarantella. When, in Act III, he announces himself pridefully as the "greatest villain of all time," he does it in waltz rhythm, and the pirates (who've been quarreling over stuffed animals stolen from the captured children) dance around him as prettily as they're able.* In the orchestral reprise of "Neverland" that brings Liza to the magic isle, a grove of trees dances around her, as well as the children's three busy guardian animals: a lion, a kangaroo, and an ostrich.

Some of the staging concepts are ingenious. Peter's lost shadow is given a thematic echo in "I've Gotta Crow," when Peter creates a minuscule shadow play with his hands on the nursery wall. In Robbins's notes: "His right hand becomes a bird, the fingers of his left hand a tasty meal. After eating the fingers and thumb, the bird dispatches the stump by pushing it down out of sight. Then the bird looks to the right and turns back and confronts, face-to-face, another bird—both gasp with surprise, one makes affectionate overtures to the other, ending in a pecking fight." Peter has to call Wendy to separate them. When the boys accidentally shoot Wendy out of the sky (a button stops the fatal arrow), they erect a house around her unconscious form, singing lustily. Peter paints a door, and on the last beat of the music, it opens and out she steps, smiling and ready to play mother to the tribe. Robbins's direction gently brings out the irony of these boys who don't want to grow up; amidst all the hot pursuits, they playact the proper family behavior they had left or never known. The little Indians' bent-over walk and "Ugga-wugga" chant may not be politically correct, but they are, after all, children of another age and another country playing at what they think Indians might be like. Sondra Lee's blond pigtail says it all, as well as some of her double takes; she has to think *hard*—as if she's in charge of a game she doesn't know too well. These Indians, even when shushed by Tiger Lily, tend to be scared of their own shadows and shriek easily (their leader included). As the collaborators had hoped, *Peter* worked for both adults and children. Besides exhilarating singing and

---

* Among the pirates can be glimpsed Paul Taylor. The choreographer has said that he was fired by Robbins during the show's run, having begun to finesse a required backflip that had broken his nose (Sondra Lee corroborates this). But there he is, listed in the credits of the telecast and backing Captain Hook with gusto.

dancing, the grown-ups could enjoy the screwy family values, the suave comedy of Hook, and the almost-grown-up love that Wendy, Tiger Lily, and his guardian fairy—that flickering light, Tinker Bell—feel for the uncomprehending Peter. Kids could love the wildness of children free of parents, the flying, the magic, the chases, the animals; the show projected the giddiness of a night when no one tells you to go to bed.

The telecast was so successful that the same production of *Peter Pan* was remounted for television on January 9, 1956, with Martin, Ritchard, and Lee again heading the cast but with Vincent Donehue credited with its direction for television (this is the *Peter Pan* currently available on video). The stage version has been revived many times, more or less with Robbins's concepts but without his choreography and direction.

⌢

Even before Peter Pan opened in New York, Lincoln Kirstein was anxious to pin Robbins down for the New York City Ballet. Somewhat sour about the fact that Balanchine "thinks he has to do *House of Flowers*,"* he mentioned that a revival of *Tyl* was in order, in response to numerous requests, and that Balanchine had in mind to choreograph Stravinsky's *Pulcinella,* to feature Robbins.

Jerry had ideas of his own—principally a ballet based on S. Ansky's play *The Dybbuk,* with Leonard Bernstein as composer. He had listed *Dybbuk* among his possible projects back in the 1940s, and his interest in Israel may have fired him up. Perhaps, too, his brooding over the death of his mother dredged up connections to the Russian Jewish culture that had spawned her.

The negative response of Kirstein (and Balanchine via Kirstein) to his proposal shocked and deeply offended Robbins. Neither of the two, apparently, cared for Bernstein's music, and they evidently imagined that the collaboration would produce a kind of danced folktale in a vernacular style. Robbins's reply to Kirstein reveals not only outrage but his insecurity about his role as a "classical" choreographer in a company molded by Balanchine. "[George's] suggestion that I do it for Inbal is about as valid as my suggestion that he do *Apollo* for the Greek Folk Dancers that were over here or the *Western Symphony* for a group of cowboys." He was discour-

---

* Balanchine did choreograph the musical by Harold Arlen and Truman Capote. However, he decamped in Philadelphia, and Herbert Ross finished the dances.

aged that Balanchine mistrusted his ability to "convert the material into dance terms suitable for our company." Kirstein's soothing response rebuked Robbins for not pitching his project to Balanchine in person (and more directly let him know that Balanchine had been hurt when, in an interview the previous summer, Robbins had credited only Agnes de Mille, Michael Kidd, and himself with generating a new attitude toward ballet in musical comedy).

As often when offended, Jerry yielded to a "So there!" impulse for revenge. Nora Kaye, feeling out of place and underused in New York City Ballet, had returned to Ballet Theatre in 1954. If Bernstein could complete the score for *Dybbuk* over the winter, he wrote Kirstein, he would offer the ballet to Lucia Chase as a vehicle for Nora. (It is indicative of how deeply Balanchine's opinion affected him that after 1974, when he and Bernstein finally created *Dybbuk* for NYCB, Robbins kept pruning narrative elements away, making the story of possession less and less comprehensible, until the ballet ended up as a set of variations for male dancers.)

Robbins created no works for either New York City Ballet or Ballet Theatre in 1955. Not long after *Peter Pan* began its New York run in late October 1954, he was diagnosed with hepatitis and spent most of the rest of the year recovering from it. In January 1955, he was called in to doctor the musical *Silk Stockings,* during what one critic noted as a "long, turbulent tryout tour." He had originally been slated to choreograph and direct it. The previous April, it had been announced that *Silk Stockings* (based on the 1939 film *Ninotchka,* in which Greta Garbo was seduced from her duties as a Soviet agent by Melvyn Douglas as a happy-go-lucky American) had been postponed until December, when Robbins would be free to work on it. Instead, Cy Feuer directed the musical, which starred Hildegard Neff and Don Ameche, and Eugene Loring choreographed it. So Robbins ended up having at least a hand in its considerable success; his estimated income for 1956 includes $3,000 for his contributions to *Silk Stockings.* In April 1955, after the first *Peter Pan* telecast, he went to Boston for another salvage job—one he preferred not to list on his résumé. *Ankles Aweigh* was "a nautical musical," according to the script that his agent Howard Hoyt urged on him. "This is the story of a movie starlet who, just at the critical point in her career, falls in love with a navy flier and of how the conflict of their careers keeps them apart—even to the point of denying them a honeymoon." The book was by Guy Bolton and Eddie Davis, with music by Sammy Fain and lyrics by Dan Shapiro. It starred the sisters Betty and

Jane Kean. Shipboard comedy that involved a spy ring, the heroine posing as a sailor, and a running gag to do with events conspiring to keep her a virgin did not make for a very trenchant show, although the ending—she gives up her career to make her marriage work—would have struck 1950s audiences as happy. Jerry wrote Mary Martin and Richard Halliday that *Ankles* was "something I never would have had anything to do with except as a favor to Howard Hoyt, who is producing it, but I'll be glad when it's all over."

The momentous collaboration that was to result in *West Side Story* had already taken fire again in 1955, but the collaborators all had projects that pulled them away on and off during the two years of preparation. Robbins seems to have been closely involved with Arthur Laurents's play *A Clearing in the Woods,* and there was talk of him directing it—his first attempt to shape a nonmusical work. It's easy to see why he was drawn to it. In this mysterious and haunting drama, a woman, Virginia, enters the shadowed clearing near a cottage where she had used to summer. There she encounters a little girl, a teenager, and a young woman. As their tense scenes with one another and with three men develop, she finally comes to realize that Jigee, Nora, and Ginna are herself at different stages of her life. She doesn't like them, because she doesn't like her present self, and her coming to terms with that dislike is what drives the plot. The blend of the real and the surreal, as well as the heroine's intolerance of imperfection in herself and everyone around her, were right up Robbins's alley.

Laurents in recent years has written and spoken of how his disenchantment with Robbins was triggered by Jerry's testimony before HUAC, but they were apparently still close at this time. In a letter to "Dearest Crow," in reference to *Clearing,* Laurents wrote, "I have never felt such joy and excitement working in anything or with anybody as I have and do on this play with you. It's fun for both of us. As you say, we may and probably will have hassles in the bad periods that always seem to come up, but I think that by then we will have such a solid foundation of us-ness that it won't matter." In the end, and for different reasons, Laurents and Robbins both had reservations about Jerry's directing *A Clearing in the Woods,* which— postponed due to work on *West Side Story*—opened in New York on January 10, 1957, with Kim Stanley in the lead and Joseph Anthony as director. Though garnering considerable praise, the play lasted for only thirty-six performances. *West Side Story* put that "us-ness" to the test.

Before Robbins began to devote himself exclusively to *West Side Story,* he completed four other projects, reenvisioning his contributions to *The King and I* for film, choreographing *The Concert* for the New York City Ballet, setting *Fanfare* on the Royal Danish Ballet, and directing and co-choreographing the musical *Bells Are Ringing*.

The Concert (or, The Perils of Everybody) is generally considered one of the world's few genuinely funny ballets. The work in its present form is not exactly the one the critics praised with not-so-faint cavils at its premiere on March 6, 1956. John Martin titled his review "A Half Riot." Imaginatively hilarious incidents were undercut by corny ones. Subsequent changes Robbins made after the first performance, in 1958, when he staged the work for his Ballets: U.S.A., and in 1971, when *The Concert* returned to the New York City Ballet's repertory, made it the comic gem that continually convulses audiences.

As was usual with his ballet choreography of this period, Robbins began not simply with his chosen music but with a concept *about* the music—the Chopin piano pieces so often used to accompany ballet classes. His idea was fruitful, inspired by the fantasies that we tend to have while listening to music as well as by cravings to interpret that affix a nickname such as "Raindrop" Prelude to a piece written by a composer uninfluenced by the weather. Robbins once said that a drawing by Saul Steinberg may have inspired him (it's likely, too, that he took in those *New Yorker* idylls by William Steig in which a portly mustachioed everyman frisks like a faun at the sight of a plump lady in flowered dress and sun hat).

He had toyed with the idea of music-inspired fantasies as early as October 1953, when he had set down some ideas centered on Christmas shopping entitled "Nineteen Days to Go." In one undeveloped sketch, a woman with hours of buying ahead of her "is somehow inveigled into an hour of musical appreciation." Her concerns about her gift list and her need to get on with her task get mixed into fantasies spawned by what she hears—perhaps, thought Robbins, cherished warhorses such as the William Tell Overture, Schubert's "Marche Militaire," Chopin's "Minute" Waltz, and so on.

When Ballets: U.S.A., the small company Robbins put together in 1958, presented *The Concert,* he acquired the two frontcloths by Saul Steinberg that are still used today (the first a back view of a theater audience, the second a front view), but the ballet is presented on a bare stage equipped with a grand piano. In an inspired touch, Irene Sharaff dressed all the dancers in light blue leotards, distinguishing them only by their accoutrements: a hat here, a collar and tie there, skirts, and, for the Groucho Marx of a henpecked husband, glasses, vest, boots, and garters.

Later audiences don't see the madly dashing "Minute" Waltz solo or a dance for four men (three in pajama tops, one in pajama bottoms), a subway sequence, a scene consisting of blackouts to music, a murder pantomime (a second one still remains), or a serious, meditative solo for Tanaquil Le Clercq. Over time, Robbins altered and added as well as cut.

The opening remains a brilliant introduction. The pianist enters and makes a major event out of dusting off the keys of the onstage instrument, eyeing the audience balefully at the sound of a chuckle. The principal characters enter singly and in pairs, carrying folding chairs, and settle themselves to listen to Chopin's "Berceuse," op. 57, which has already started. Robbins limns them all in a few brushstrokes: the rapt young man, perhaps a music student, who places his chair to define the first row; the two women in hats whom we imagine have just been shopping and who disturb him by chattering and unwrapping candy; the loopy beauty (the role created for Le Clercq), who plants herself close enough to lean adoringly on the piano; the tough, militant young woman; the husband and his domineering wife; and a small, shy, bespectacled young man. A latecomer causes a disturbance; he has no chair, but he has a ticket. An usher dutifully walks around asking to see tickets and moving people out of one place and into another. Eventually, the tough girl, left standing, snatches the chair from under the Le Clercq character, who—completely engrossed in the music, head on the piano—remains sitting on air. It's a wonderful moment, but it's not pumped up as the end of the scene; the changing places goes on, further revealing the characters, until the young man in glasses is glared out of his seat by the wife and ends up having to hunker down on the floor.

One of the sweetest dances has no dance movements in it. To the gentle strains of the Prelude, op. 28, no. 4 (as in many of the scenes, the orchestra joins the pianist so smoothly that the transition is barely noticeable), the performers walk quietly about. Someone senses rain and opens an umbrella; another picks up the idea. This copycatting goes on for a while as dancers accumulate onstage (the cast includes a fourteen-person ensemble). Even as some people are popping their umbrellas open, others are sticking out hands, verifying that the shower's over, and folding theirs. Later, while they stroll, they begin to pair up, two under one umbrella. Then there are four to an umbrella, then eight. By the end all are crowded under one umbrella. There's something curiously poignant about this foolish, unquestioning herding that lies so gently against the music and leaves more and more people unprotected.

The Concert is rich in ballet satire. Robbins kids the hearty Russian character dances he got so sick of during his Ballet Theatre days, as well as the complicated daisy chains and cat's cradles Balanchine often creates with his ensemble. For hilarity, the jewel of *The Concert* is a corps de ballet in disarray. Men race about, carrying women in absurd ways, as if they were lugging department store mannequins against a deadline. After placing them incorrectly many times, they manage to arrange the women in a fetching cluster. On the last chord—presto!—the six dolls become a corps de ballet. The joke is that they're dangerously underrehearsed. The situation wasn't all that far from the truth of life in a ballet company, and Robbins's shrewd timing of mistakes and adjustments blew it into delicious comedy. What keeps the mayhem from being just a string of gags is that the women really *dance* to Chopin's posthumous Waltz in E minor, executing choreography that pokes mild fun at Fokine's *Les Sylphides* (whether arms flap up first or down first becomes a major decision). Sometimes the music has to stop so that one woman can semiunobtrusively nudge an errant colleague back into the lineup, but the corps weathers every possible kind of upset to strike its final triumphant tableau.

Robbins occasionally plays against the music. The delicate Prelude, op. 28, no. 7, accompanies a session in which the daffy romantic tries on hats. And through the ballet run the triangular goings-on among her, the husband (originally played by Todd Bolender), and his wife (Yvonne Mounsey). Even through most of a demanding little solo and the ensuing butterfly mating chase, the husband, though equipped with wings and antenna, retains his cigar.

Balanchine was very fond of *The Concert*. Not only did he often watch it from the wings, but at one performance, he went on for Bolender on rather short notice. Sam Lurie, whom Robbins had hired as a publicist in 1954, sent Jerry a letter on March 9, 1956, enclosing reviews. Todd had contracted the flu, and Lurie had heard about the resultant backstage scurrying around from lighting designer Jean Rosenthal after the performance. Cuts had had to be made and lighting adjusted. It had been "quite a job getting George into the costume," but he had been brilliant in the opening section.

Robbins told Maria Tallchief he had wanted to revive *The Guests* for this season, but his work on *The Concert* had proved too time-consuming. To fill in the gap, Balanchine tossed off *Allegro Brillante,* a ballet that has been seen in companies around the world. *The Concert* premiered on March 6. By April, Robbins was having a first go at setting a work of his on a foreign company. The company was the Royal Danish Ballet, and the work was *Fanfare.* He had been negotiating with the Danes since the beginning of 1955, never able quite to pin himself down to a date until a few months before his arrival at the end of March 1956. It took a number of urgent cables before Irene Sharaff's designs were sent. Through it all, executive director H. A. Brøndsted and Vera Volkova (the Russian teacher-pedagogue and unofficial adviser to Brøndsted and then–artistic director Niels Bjørn Larsen) remained unfailingly polite and patient.

Copenhagen couldn't measure up to the excitement of Rome or Paris as far as Jerry was concerned, and he spent time reading Shakespeare's tragedies, *Island in the Sun, The Blackboard Jungle,* and *Trial* as background for what was to become *West Side Story,* as well as giving some thought to *Bells Are Ringing,* the musical by the *Peter Pan* rescue team of Comden, Green, and Styne, which he was to direct when he returned. Nevertheless, the Danish hospitality disarmed him. Volkova and her husband had him to dinner the night he arrived. The critic Svend Kragh-Jacobsen invited him for a drink and a meal and to meet his mother. The Ballet Club persuaded him to speak on a subject of his choice. He visited museums, including the theater museum in the lovely little eighteenth-century Court Theater. And he was impressed by the opera house system, which each year selected ten little children out of three hundred and trained and educated them into adulthood. He wrote Slim Hayward of visiting the Royal Danish Ballet classrooms and the "beautiful, wonderful atmosphere" there.

> The children themselves look like a roomful of trolls and elves. They all wear the uniform of royal blue wool tights and sweaters, most a little baggy at the knees. They are beautifully behaved and dance already quite well. They do their entrechat sixes already and the girls are bour-réeing on point. The girls always dip into a little curtsey when they enter or leave or pass you, and the boys bow. They are delicious angels all. The next older class goes from ten to about fifteen and this is even more delightful.

In a few years, he expected, there'd be a great group of male dancers:

> They are so amazing. Completely free from any bad mannerisms, musi-
> cally sensitive, technically already near perfection, and what we Ameri-
> cans like to think of as really wholesome and uninhibited. You see,
> because they have started dancing so early, they are completely normal,
> and have not selected la danse as an outlet for their neurotic needs. They
> throw themselves into anything that is given to them, dance or acting.

Fanfare pleased the Danish audience and most of the critics, and, as
Jerry wrote Slim, how could one not be entranced by reviews full of words
like "fart" and "prik" (best translated as "speed" and "exactitude")? "Can
you see the possibilities of fractured Danish?"

Back in the States, he was addressing Volkova as "Dear Verushka" and
telling her how he had loved working with the Danes. Brøndsted wrote
him praising *Fanfare* and "his marvelous cooperation with the company."
Jerry looked forward to seeing them all again when the Royal Danish Ballet came to America in the fall, and the company began negotiating to acquire more Robbins ballets.

However, shortly after arriving in Copenhagen, he had unburdened
himself to Slim. He was nursing an Achilles tendon he'd pulled a couple of
months earlier and having one of his down, self-questioning moments: "I
know I should accept the challenge of doing new things, trying new ballets, extending myself further with each effort, and ever since I've been
sick, I feel like playing it safe, repeating what I've done and not risking the
position I've gained for myself." But even as he writes, he knows he must
push himself: "I suppose behind it all is such doubt about myself as a director which is what I'm moving toward, and equal doubt about contributing
anything further as a choreographer which I'm moving away from and
perhaps won't be able to get back to. (Just think, I'm able to tell you all this,
dear doctor, and it doesn't cost twenty-five an hour either.)"

Toward the end of his April stay in Denmark, he wrote her that upon
his return, he planned to start "getting into a snit about *Bells Are Ringing*. I
might as well start early, I always get into one anyway." He thought he'd
rent a house on Fire Island in which to do that.

⁓

Comden, Green, and Styne had been writing away while Robbins was in Denmark. Betty and Adolph had conceived *Bells Are Ringing* as a gift for Judy Holliday, their beloved friend and former colleague in the nightclub team the Revuers. Holliday was now a Hollywood star, having won one of the rare Academy Awards given to a comedian for her savvy portrayal of a dumb blonde in *Born Yesterday* (1950). She had recently triumphed in *The Solid Gold Cadillac.* But few knew of her sand-in-silk singing voice or her capacity for poignancy.

Bells may not have revolved around the most original idea, but it was smart and charming—the third Comden and Green musical, following *On the Town* and *Wonderful Town,* to take place in a bustling, nicer-than-life New York, where people knew their neighbors well enough to sing on the street together and subway trains were a great place to dance. As Ella, one of three women fielding the telephones at Susanswerphone, Holliday could assume various roles with panache, affecting a Parisian accent when taking messages for a French restaurant, impersonating a stern Santa Claus to help a client make her little boy toe the line, and turning quavery and soothing to deliver news (mostly bad) to a failing playwright (Sydney Chaplin), who's attempting to bolster his insecurity with women and liquor and who calls her "Mom." Visiting (in disguise) a surly Method actor to help him get a job, she wore a leather jacket and out-Brandoed a clutch of Marlon's unsuccessful imitators.

Warmhearted Ella, unlike her boss, Sue (Jean Stapleton), enjoys giving help and advice to her clients and bringing certain ones together for their mutual benefit. By the time the plot tangles have been resolved, Jeff, the playwright, realizes that Mom and the delightful "Melisande Scott" who arrives at his apartment seeming to know a lot about him, who gets him writing again, and with whom he falls in love, are both Ella. The subplot involves a vigilant cop who's bent on proving that Susanswerphone is a call girl operation, and Sandor, a suave bookie with a continental accent (Eddie Lawrence), who pretends to be a record company executive, romances Sue, and sets up a racket in her office. Bets are disguised as orders for platters: "300 albums of Beethoven's Tenth, opus 6, LP" means "Put $300 on number 6 at Belmont, on the nose" (it's when Ella, apprised that Beethoven didn't write a Tenth Symphony, assumes there has been a mistake and changes the order that Sue's problems with the watchful police begin to wind down and Sandor's begin).

While Robbins was in Copenhagen (and contemplating staging a ballet for the Paris Opera), work on the script of *Bells* had been proceeding apace. Debates over whether Peter Larkin could design the show, which Robbins wanted very much, or whether Oliver Smith would, had to take place via letter and cable (Raoul Pène du Bois eventually did the job). Comden and Green fired off cozening letters to get Robbins home in time to cast the show before actors scattered for summer jobs, "So finish with the Danes, grab a vacation and get your international ass back here. . . . With so much at stake we would feel happy & confident if we had your lapels to clutch—and your shell-like ears to pour our venomous script into." Once back in New York, Robbins had the job of pressuring Holliday to arrive before mid-July so Herb Greene could work with her on the songs and Robert Tucker and/or his wife Nenette Charisse could polish up her dancing.

Anxious to pull off with distinction the direction of what had all the earmarks of a hit, Robbins asked that his major credit read "Entire Production Directed by Jerome Robbins," but the bottom of the program's first page would read "Dances and Musical Numbers Staged by Jerome Robbins and Bob Fosse." In addition, Robert Tucker served as an assistant to the choreographers and Gerald Freedman as assistant to the director.

Holliday had worked on a couple of pictures at Columbia with Freedman as dialogue director and was instrumental in getting him to work on *Bells*. She knew and liked Robbins but wasn't sure she trusted him to work with actors. And Freedman (later a director and teacher himself) says that

> [Jerry] didn't tell me then but he told me a little later [that] he was intimidated by Judy Holliday, because she was the intimidating maven in that group, in that very bright group: Leonard Bernstein, her husband [David Oppenheim], and Jerry, Betty, and Adolph. She was clever, she was very knowledgeable, she had read a lot. And of course she had this reputation as being a wonderful, truthful actress. And I think he welcomed the idea of a buffer between him and Judy. Anyway, that was my understanding of it.

Making use of an assistant became a modus operandi for Jerry, and Freedman and others worked with him in this capacity on later shows. On *Bells,* he could help with Robbins's still-unsolved problem of adjusting to the differences between how dancers were used to working and how actors liked to work. As Freedman has said, "You can use imagery with dancers, or metaphor: 'You're like a speeding train,' 'You're like a herd of buffalo.' Dancers are used to taking that idea and kinesthetically appreciating it and doing something with it. Actors don't know what you're talking about. They get the idea, but 'Yes, what has that got to do with the scene?'" And the leading man, Sydney Chaplin, although charismatic and sexy with a pleasant baritone, had limited skills in terms of song and dance. Robbins knew what he wanted but not always how to get there. Freedman did the bulk of the work with the actors on the dialogue scenes.

Bells boasted two songs that became hits: "The Party's Over" and "Just in Time." Comden, Green, and Freedman all speak of Robbins's skillful handling of the latter, a love song. It was the first number he staged in the show, and he managed to make it look as if it were being improvised on the spot. Ella and Jeff meet in Central Park. He plans to take her to a party of theatrical notables; she thought they were going dancing. So he draws her into a simple ballroom dance, as he begins to sing to her. When passersby gather to watch, they get a little more ambitious and work into what the published script describes as "a corny little song and dance routine made up of scraps of old vaudeville and musical comedy numbers." In the end, the fun folds back into tenderness. "He was so extraordinary with those simple numbers," says Freedman. "Here was this dance genius who could strip himself down to the simplest, most effective movements for an Ethel Merman, a Judy Holliday. I learned a great, great, great deal. . . . He never let [the movement] get in the way of lyrics. He never made them look bad. He never gave them too much to occupy their minds. I think he was masterful at that."

Robbins and Fosse divided the musical numbers. Fosse handled some of the vocals and the numbers that burgeoned from song into crowd action, such as Jeff's "I Met a Girl," as well as big dances, such as "Hello, Hello There!"—a convivial subway meet-and-greet prompted by Ella that turns into a wild cancan. But inevitably, Robbins's polishing extended to everything. According to Freedman, Robbins staged most of the numbers involving Holliday. Peter Gennaro contributed to the delirious "Mu-Cha-Cha," in which his character, Carl, gives a quick dance lesson to Ella to prime her for her date with Jeff. Two numbers—Fosse's staging of a glitzy-tacky nightclub act and Robbins's of a jazzy dance at a party in Jeff's apartment—ended up being pared down to a mere suggestion of themselves. A dancing quartet of men who joined Judy in her opening song, "It's a Perfect Relationship," was dispensed with, although in 1959 she persuaded Jerry to let her reinstate and recast the number, subject to his approval.

Fosse did not list *Bells* among his major achievements, and Robbins, although he clearly admired Fosse, allowed himself to become petulant and ungenerous in a letter to Le Clercq: "One terrible part of the show is that Bob Fosse, who did most of the dances, managed to eke out a bad second hand version of dances I have already done, so that it looks like I have just copied myself and repeated badly what I once did well."

The tense week before *Bells* opened in New Haven in October, Jerry also patted himself on the back a bit for Tanny's edification: "You would have been real proud of me, never lost my temper and the company all is in such good happy spirits and I get on well with them much to everyone's and my surprise. However I really prefer dancers to actors, dancers are a much hardier and tougher bunch." To Vera Volkova in Copenhagen, he wrote that although the show seemed to be successful, "I don't care for it too much myself." *Bells Are Ringing* opened in New York on November 29, 1956, and ran for three years, in good part because of Holliday's irresistible charm. Robbins didn't participate when she repeated her role in the 1960 film costarring Dean Martin, and the irreplaceable Holliday died five years later.

~

Robbins was, he regretted, too busy putting in fourteen-hour days to see the Royal Danish Ballet perform in New York. At the same time, the New York City Ballet, touring Europe, was delighting audiences in Copenhagen. Vera Volkova, recuperating from an operation and so not traveling with her company, was deeply impressed by *Afternoon of a Faun* and thought *The Cage* also "an inspired masterwork."

Tanaquil Le Clercq was not to perform either ballet ever again. It was in November, during that Copenhagen season, that she was struck down by the polio that rendered those long, articulate legs speechless for the rest of her life. She was twenty-seven years old. According to Barbara Horgan, because the Salk vaccine was still so new, it was being given only to those under sixteen or pregnant. Ironically, Tanny hadn't minded; she thought it might have had an adverse effect on her dancing. Her husband, Balanchine, was not only anguished but guilt-racked; years before, he had prepared for a March of Dimes benefit a little ballet in which he played the specter of Polio and teenage Tanny his victim, and he was a superstitious man.

At first she could breathe only with the aid of a respirator, but in a little more than a month she could do without it and was gradually regaining the use of her upper body and arms. Jerry wrote every few days; he sent orchids. Le Clercq's mother, "Aunt Edith" to him, replied at Tanny's dictation, adding her own notes ("She is so brave she would break your heart"). Although in a letter scrawled to Jerry with her stronger left hand, Tanny railed against the catastrophe and confessed to weeping "all the time," she never, Edith Le Clercq wrote, let Balanchine see her cry. For her first proud letter written with her more-affected right hand, she held the pencil and her mother moved the paper against it. Endeavoring to sit without the aid of nurses, she feels "like a filet of sole trying to balance on its tail."

Robbins attempted to match her in wit. All that winter, when she was hospitalized in Copenhagen, and during the rest of 1957, which she spent at the famous sanitorium in Warm Springs, Georgia, that attempted to rehabilitate the paralyzed, he regaled her with tales of his doings and the New York City Ballet, and she delved for the humor in hospital life. (He visited her once at Warm Springs, and she began missing him seconds after he left; few Warm Springs patients could match her in cleverness and playfulness the way he could.) During the transitional month of March 1958, when she was at Lenox Hill Hospital in New York, he visited often, laden with food, toys, and books to read to her. In Warm Springs' therapy classes, she proudly wove him place mats. They began an unspoken competition in the x'ed kisses that ended their letters; boomerang x's, migrating x's; these got more and more elaborate until she ended the game by remarking that "someone" coming upon his letters might misunderstand.

One sadly ironic tale: Robbins had asked if he could send her anything at the Copenhagen hospital. Yes—and typically, she disguised her need for comfort with a jest: "I would like an animal to sleep with (lower those eyebrows!)." What she wanted was "a softish, cuddly, something. . . . Also if he could have a nice expression." Jerry, bursting to do his best for her, missed the point and sent her an enormous stuffed dog, "Morgan." She adored him, of course, and all the nurses dropped in to admire, but he was too big to sleep with her; he had to sit on a chair close to her bed.

She wondered if Jerry had had fun picking him out. One hopes her mother never told her that a helpful overseas friend of Robbins's had done the shopping, decked the dog with a nosegay, and had it delivered.

Robbins had offered to take over the New York City Ballet for a while so that Balanchine could stay in Copenhagen with Le Clercq. Accounts of how he fulfilled this task vary. Betty Cage, the company manager, with whom he tangled to the end of his days, has said that when Balanchine actually took him up on his offer, he said via long distance that he was tired from his work on *Bells Are Ringing* and had to take a rest. However, when Jerry made the offer, he was still out of town with *Bells,* and in a letter to Le Clercq dated December 3, four days after the show opened in New York, he says that he had told Kirstein that he expected to go into "the new show" (*West Side Story*) at the end of February, and that although he did have to take a week or two off either before the NYCB season or during *Nutcracker,* he would do everything but choreograph a new ballet: rehearse his works and George's, replace people, and so on. When he got back to town, Cage informed him that Kirstein had said that Robbins would be away for a few months, so Todd Bolender, Francisco Moncion, and Vida Brown had been put in charge. Fine, he doesn't want to take anything away from the three; the responsibility is good for them, he thinks (and was probably relieved), but he's sure Lincoln has told John Martin and Walter Terry, "so again I have done another lovable thing in the eyes of New York. . . . Sometimes I think Lincoln's genius lies in lousing things up better than anyone else."

He had started rehearsing *Age of Anxiety* the evening he wrote of the mix-up, and before long he was trying to put his travails in an amusing light for Tanny in Copenhagen: "all those new little corps de ballet girls' faces look pale, harried and full of counts." And:

All the new kids are flailing away at each other in the Charleston, twitching like crazy and trying to look intense because I tell them to, but I know damn well they have no idea of what the hell is going on or what the music is like, and my dear once they get into those masks and can't recognize each other all hell will break out.

His Achilles tendon was better and, he told her, "Don't laugh. I'm thinking of going to class." A *Herald Tribune* news item dated December 16 mentioned that he *was* supervising the company, along with Bolender and Brown. He watched the progress of Moncion's new ballet, and Bolender's. As usual, NYCB company life was marked by get-by tactics and minor crises. John Mandia hurt his foot the day he was to perform in four ballets programmed for the all-Robbins night. In the scramble to reassign roles, Vida Brown decided that Arthur Mitchell and Robert Barnett could share his role in *Age*. Problem: there was only one costume. "Then they began making plans, something that went like this: 'So after the dirge Bob Barnett rushes offstage and Arthur Mitchell puts on the costume and comes back for the gallop and then he gives the costume back to Bobby for the walks and after the walks Bobby changes into [his own costume for] the images.' " Rehearsing Ann Crowell and Roland Vazquez in the middle section of the pas de deux from *The Pied Piper,* the choreographer asks them what the steps are and how they they fit the music. They show it differently each time, giggle and shrug when this is pointed out to them. Finally he asks, " 'Well, when did you do it last?' (hysterical laughter): 'Last night.' "

Tanny had heard that Lincoln had slapped Gian Carlo Menotti and wanted the full story. Jerry obliged: Kirstein had indeed slapped the composer, whose dance-music-theater work *The Unicorn, the Gorgon, and the Manticore* or, *The Three Sundays of a Poet* had been commissioned by the Elizabeth Sprague Coolidge Foundation and, like all Coolidge commissions, premiered at the Library of Congress. New York City Ballet members danced and mimed the words of a singing chorus. Kirstein had slapped Menotti because Menotti had insisted that John Butler choreograph the work, and Butler had insisted on having Lee Becker, a noncompany dancer, in the cast (in the end, Menotti prevailed, slap or no slap).

Robbins rarely gossiped about the private lives of others, but he could be devastating about their public ones. Le Clercq's painful days and restless nights were undoubtedly cheered by the following word painting about the 1956 *Dance Magazine* awards honoring Agnes de Mille and Martha Graham: "The long table that they were all seated behind made it look a little like the Last Supper and there seemed to be an unconscious competition between Agnes and Martha as to who looked the holiest. Martha won hands down of course with that bony white face and black velvet dress. Agnes only looked like she had been drinking for three days and was trying to look saintly. But for a while it was nip and tuck as to which one was going to rise to heaven first."

In November, Le Clercq's doctors and all who loved her and her inimitably beautiful dancing had hoped she might recover the use of her legs.

She wondered if she might be up and walking by the summer of 1958. Balanchine was to choreograph dances for *A Midsummer Night's Dream* at Stratford, Connecticut, and John Houseman had asked her to play Titania. At Warm Springs, she was given classes in standing several times a week, but at some point she and the staff were forced to realize that she wasn't improving.

In one of his letters, Robbins told her of a comedy-fantasy ballet he was thinking of choreographing, one inspired by the three animals in *Peter Pan*. The lion would be "in a long romantic cape à la Lifar in *Giselle* and the kangaroo in a little tutu doing the Rose Adagio (wouldn't it be fun?)." But he didn't make another work for the New York City Ballet until 1969 and he later said he had lost the impulse to do so when Le Clercq, his muse, could no longer dance. Certainly he may have come to realize that or to believe it, but he did very much behave as if he wanted to continue—on his own terms, of course—as part of that ballet community that he cherished. For the next few years, he and Kirstein engaged in an epistolary pas de deux—Lincoln inviting him to participate, Jerry offering suggestions for ballets and excuses for not making them.

And, in fact, something epochal did intervene: a tale of two communities, *West Side Story*.

12

Tony Loves Maria

Jets to Sharks: "Beat it!" during the filming of
West Side Story's opening scene in Manhattan.
NYPL.

W*hen you mention the name* of Jerome Robbins to people
not deeply attuned to dance or theater, an unspoken question
sometimes hangs in the air. Then you say, *"West Side Story."*
And as soon as they're reminded that Robbins choreographed and directed that show, they understand that he was important, deserving of

fame. Professional companies have performed the 1957 musical in cities all over the world. High school drama teachers regularly put it on. When Robbins returned to the New York City Ballet in 1969, Peter Martins, then a young dancer recently arrived in New York, knew him only as the man who had made *West Side Story:* "That's who he was, to me, growing up in Denmark as a kid . . . he was a giant. I didn't know him as a classical ballet choreographer. . . . And so I don't know whether I was really equipped to truly appreciate him or even understand him as a classical choreographer. He was the man who did this [*snaps fingers*]. And that's what I fell in love with."

Despite some flaws, *West Side Story* is an epochal piece of theater. No previous Broadway musical had ended Act I with two dead bodies onstage and Act II with a third. There had been ambitious dances integral to a show's plot before—such as Agnes de Mille's often-cited "Dream Ballet" from *Oklahoma!*—but none in which dance is a way of defining character from the outset. The restlessness and hostility of the Jets and Sharks emerge primarily through rhythmic motion. And the 1961 film gave that choreography and the tragic tale it powered enduring life. In 2000, when some of the stars of the movie got together for the television cameras to commemorate its fortieth anniversary, Rita Moreno remarked that people often come up to her on the street and tell her, "You are Anita." Not, she marveled, "You *were* Anita. You *are* Anita."

In 1985, the four creators of *West Side Story* came together in a Dramatists Guild symposium: Leonard Bernstein (music), Arthur Laurents (book), Jerome Robbins (director-choreographer), and Stephen Sondheim (lyrics). Thirty-something years later, they were cordial and complimentary to one another. Why dwell on disagreements? They recalled the excitement of the collaborative process, the "aspiration" that Robbins defined as mattering most to him:

> I wanted to find out at that time how far we three, as "long-haired artists," [Sondheim joined them later] could go on bringing our crafts and talents to a musical. Why did we have to do it separately and elsewhere? Why did Lenny have to write an opera, Arthur a play, me a ballet? Why couldn't we, in aspiration, try to bring our deepest talents together to the commercial theater in this work? That was the true *gesture* of the show.

As Laurents had foreseen, the tale of the making of *West Side Story* that emerged at that forum was a kind of *Rashomon*—a story told from four different points of view. The collaborators' memories dated from 1949, when, according to Bernstein's fabricated diary quoted earlier, Robbins got him excited with the notion of an updated *Romeo and Juliet*. Robbins has said that the idea came to him when a friend, who was considering an offer to play Romeo, complained that the character seemed passive and wondered how he could bring it to life. Jerry came up with modern analogies, such as hostility between Jews and Catholics, to explain the enduring feud between Montagues and Capulets.*

Robbins introduced Laurents to Bernstein, who had been brought to tears by Laurents's play *Home of the Brave,* about anti-Semitism faced by a Jewish soldier in World War II. Yet, following some hot discussions, what was originally called *East Side Story* was shelved. One early version pitted Jews against Italian Catholics (news of Juliet's cousin's death was to come during a family seder). Both Laurents and Bernstein came to feel that such a conflict would evoke that long-running sentimental comedy of the 1920s, *Abie's Irish Rose,* and lost interest.

These two agreed at the symposium that the impetus to take up the project again in 1955 occurred when the two met at the Beverly Hills Hotel in August—Bernstein on the coast to conduct and Laurents there working on a movie. Dangling their legs in the hotel pool, they gradually drifted onto the subject of *East Side Story* and current newspaper headlines about violence between juvenile gangs of Chicanos and Anglos. Eureka! Robbins readily agreed that ethnicity rather than religion should be the crux and gangs, rather than families, the antagonists. The Jewish kids became Puerto Rican and the Italian gang a mix of European immigrant stock (Nora Kaye counseled Laurents to make the hero Irish or Anglo-Saxon in order to have a light-skin-dark-skin contrast).

However, Robbins had urged Laurents and Bernstein to reconsider the updated *Romeo and Juliet* earlier in the summer, when a project the two

---

* It has been assumed that the actor was Robbins's then-lover, Montgomery Clift. But this doesn't jibe with a story Clift's biographer Patricia Bosworth had from actor Kevin McCarthy. It was 1947, and McCarthy, playing Romeo for CBS's *Omnibus,* was having trouble with the death scene and asked Clift for help. The two men worked together one whole night (McCarthy's actress wife obligingly dead for them, then replaced by a pillow when she finally went to bed). Clift enacted the whole scene, completely at home in the character and "agonizingly brilliant."

had planned to collaborate on (a musical based on James M. Cain's novel *Serenade*) fell through. Judging by a letter dated July 19 from Laurents to Bernstein, which included a skeleton outline, the plot shift had begun before the legs-in-the-pool moment. The subject of gang warfare was timely and hot, Laurents affirmed. It was filling the newspapers and was beginning to attract the attention of moviemakers. Why not work to get their show on Broadway in the spring of 1956?

Robbins, who, as producer Harold Prince confirms, dreaded the beginning of rehearsals and would do anything to delay the process, worried about a spring opening. Bernstein was working on a major project, his musical play *Candide;* developing several programs for the highbrow television series *Omnibus;* and leading six concerts at Carnegie Hall in December. Laurents was working on getting *Clearing in the Woods* produced. Later, he would take on the screenplay of *Anastasia.* Robbins, although no longer supposed to direct *Clearing,* was on the coast working on the *King and I* film and had no intention of shelving other musical offers and opportunities to choreograph ballets (he created *The Concert,* staged *Fanfare* in Copenhagen, and directed *Bells Are Ringing* before casting and rehearsals began for *West Side Story* in 1957).

Between October 1955 and spring 1957, he also contended with his grief over Tanaquil Le Clercq, his responsibilities at New York City Ballet, and the unraveling of his relationship with Buzz Miller. The break was accentuated by a housing crisis. The building at 422 Park Avenue was being torn down, and Robbins and Miller had to vacate apartment 4 by June 15, 1955. Buzz found a place at 825 Second Avenue. Jerry declined to join him there (although he sent him a Franklin stove for the new place when he learned one was needed). He himself found a duplex apartment in the house at 151 East Seventy-fourth Street owned by the writer Muriel Resnick and her husband. By January, Edith Weissman's daily memos to Robbins reveal that Miller did live for a while in the Seventy-fourth Street apartment. And in March, Robbins became a co-owner of three contiguous parcels of land that Miller had bought in Fire Island Pines in 1954 for $5,200. Oliver Smith ends an April 5 letter to Robbins in Copenhagen with "Please give my best to Buzz." Nonetheless, Laurents says that when Robbins was leaving Copenhagen and coming to Paris, Miller, already in Paris, left for home, indicating that all was not well between him and Jerry. Years after the decisive break occurred, Miller told a friend that he had never really understood why it had happened, and both men suffered for some time thereafter, although they stayed on good terms personally and professionally.

Despite Robbins's worry over a spring deadline, *West Side Story* proceeded at a good pace. Letters that passed back and forth in October and November between Robbins at 1833 Franklin Canyon Road in Beverly Hills and Laurents in Manhattan, or at his house in Quogue, Long Island, reveal the rather complicated maneuverings that brought forth *West Side Story*.

When Bernstein decided he couldn't write all the lyrics, Comden and Green turned out a six-page story plan "that contained a lot of jukebox jitterbug and that ended with a swooning Juliet in a reprise of the balcony scene." But Betty and Adolph were up to their necks in *Bells Are Ringing,* and a movie was in the offing as well. Laurents suggested young Stephen Sondheim. His stuff was "as fresh as theirs but also has a tender quality—which I have never found in their work." Sondheim was more interested in writing both music and lyrics than doing the words alone, but his mentor, Oscar Hammerstein II, advised him that he would profit by working with Bernstein, Laurents, and Robbins.

Laurents, in his letters to Robbins, became spokesman for the New York team—which Robbins in his darker moments feared was a cabal. It has been noted that *West Side Story* has one of the shortest books of any musical on record. Its passions rage primarily through song and dance. The correspondence reveals how much was pruned away, first from Shakespeare's story, then from Laurents's script. Except for the fact that the lovers did not kill themselves, the core of the original plot and the principal characters remained. Juliet's cousin Tybalt became Maria's brother Bernardo, and he acquired a girlfriend, Anita. Romeo's spirited friend Mercutio became Riff. Paris, the man Juliet's parents wished her to marry, was transformed into Chino, an arranged husband for Maria. As in Shakespeare's play, Bernardo stabs Riff unfairly when Tony, out of his new love for Maria, attempts to intervene in the fight; in his rage over Riff's death, Tony stabs Bernardo. All the adults, except for the two cops, Schrank and Krupke; the hapless high school teacher, Glad Hand, who polices the prom; the Bridal Shop owner; and Doc the druggist (the Friar Laurence equivalent), disappeared, including the uncle originally planned for Juliet-Maria and "Francey," the equivalent of Romeo's Rosalind. Maria's parents are represented by a muted offstage voice calling her in from her fire-escape balcony and, in the touching "wedding" at the Bridal

Shop, by dressmakers' dummies. Laurents wanted to base the character the collaborators first referred to as "Tante" (a version of Juliet's nurse and go-between) on a woman he adored, jazz singer Anita Ellis, who he hoped might play the role. She would be a few years older than the gang kids. On October 18, Robbins dictated a nine-point commentary on the outline. Among them was his reaction to Laurents's vision of that character. (Gerald Freedman, Robbins's assistant on the show, thinks Robbins had Muriel Bentley in mind as a prototype, and she did, at some point in *West Side Story*'s long history, play the role.) Wrote Jerry to Arthur:

> You are away off the track with the whole character of Anita. She is the typical downbeat blues torchbearing 2nd character (Julie of *Showboat*, etc.) and falls into a terrible cliché. The audience will know that somewhere a "my man done left me" blues is coming up for her. Furthermore, this puts the girl above the age limit that the gang should have and completely disturbs their adolescent quality. If she's "an-older-girl-kicked-by-love-before-experiencing-the-worst" (and I'm quoting you) she's much too experienced for the gang, or else is sick, sick, sick to be so attached emotionally and sexually to a younger boy of a teen age gang. I can't put the above strongly enough and at the risk of offending you, Arthur, forget Anita and start writing someone who is either older, (like Tante) or younger with the same emotional timber [*sic*] of the rest of the gang.

In the end, all that remained of Anita Ellis was her first name.

In the letters, you can feel those conjuring up *West Side Story* struggling—as Bernstein defined it in his "Excerpts from a *West Side Story* Log"—"to tread the fine line between opera and Broadway, between realism and poetry, ballet and 'just dancing,' abstract and representational. Avoid being 'messagy.' The line is there, but it's very fine, and sometimes it takes a lot of peering around to discern it." Robbins wrote Laurents that his dialogue "relaxes into a legitimate play tempo rather than a lyric drama tempo which is different than life like or straight play tempo. You would sense this immediately were it put upon the stage. The larger-than-life approach, the balletic approach which you have captured at times is exactly right and you must keep it in mind all the time. If you keep each scene down to strict story points, (outside of Romeo and Juliet themselves) you will be writing perfectly for this type of show."

Laurents responded, disagreeing about the inadvisability of "legit play tempo," adding, "True, I have found out that in the legitimate theatre, talk will hold once a tense situation has been established, and I have tried to do that in musical form. But if, as you suggest, the script is pared—except for the love scenes—to story points, then we will have a conventional musical with two-dimensional characters. Furthermore, the gangs will be unsympathetic because there will be no understanding of their characters or feelings." (This turned out to be exactly what some disparaged about *West Side Story*.)

Meanwhile, Bernstein and Sondheim were turning out songs. Laurents found the music "brilliant and exciting" and the song for the balcony scene "beautiful" but wrote Robbins that he craved some "prettier, more melodic songs" to set it off: "What the result of all this careful (and I have been) prodding will be, I don't know. At least, it has made [Bernstein] decide to fool around with the song called 'Maria' and develop, if possible, the really very pretty opening bars to that."

The four had to decide whether Maria would die in the end like Juliet and, if so, how. Would she take poison? Would she rush to the Bridal Shop where she and Tony had plighted their troth and stab herself with a pair of scissors? Instead, she became an impassioned spokesman for an end to the streets as battle zone. One particularly brilliant idea of Laurents's: The message that in Shakespeare's play never reaches Romeo and so causes his despairing suicide was reconceived in a way that brought the racial tension to a boil and made it the direct, as well as the indirect, cause of the tragedy. Enraged by the death of Riff, the Jets have not only taunted and demeaned Anita, the messenger; they've started to molest her. When Doc intervenes, in fear and vindictive anger, she blurts out the lie that Maria is dead.

Laurents had worried about having the gang members too tough to arouse empathy, but he'd also not wanted to make them *too* sympathetic: "[w]e might tend to remove them too far from truth and pretty them up into being Rover boys of 1956. I am <u>not</u> for keeping or making them hoodlums—I found the gang in 'Jungle' [the film *The Blackboard Jungle*] distasteful and overdrawn . . . but I do think we must watch how far we go." A draft of the script opens with a lot of comradely talk by the Jets, using some of Laurents's made-up slang, such as "Clam it! You sockomorphic creepsters!" (In the final book, Laurents's use of this gang-speak was sparing and less elaborate.) In one version, they argue about whether to join the Army. In another, they get carried away by the news of the first rocket landing on the moon and dream of taking off into the blue. The latter was originally a song, set to what eventually became the sensational, almost wordless "Prologue," in which Robbins introduces the Jets through movement and dance alone: their restless finger snapping, their prowling the streets, and their encounters with the Sharks marked by ambushes, attacks, and exaggerated, false politeness.

The collaborators riffed off one another. A "dummy" lyric, written by Laurents to indicate to Bernstein and Sondheim the desired direction for the song Maria would deliver over Tony's dead body, became her climactic speech. A few weeks before the show's Washington, D.C., opening on August 19, Bernstein and Sondheim developed a line from a speech Laurents wrote for Tony—"It's right outside the door, around the corner, but it's comin'!"—into the song "Something's Coming." Bernstein also borrowed from his own work; the music for two songs he'd written for *Candide* became Tony and Maria's "wedding" song, "One Hand, One Heart," and the bouncily sardonic "Gee, Officer Krupke."

While the script was taking shape, the search for producers and investors began. A musical with corpses was a hard sell. Quite a few turned the show down, among them Leland Hayward and Rodgers and Hammerstein. Bernstein, Laurents, and Sondheim sent the first act to George Abbott and followed it up with a visit. "Lenny was very nervous," Laurents wrote to Robbins, "(God! how he talked on and on) played too loud, badly, they both [Bernstein and Sondheim] sang like desperate frogs!" Abbott offered praise and criticism and told them their brainchild "could be a wonderful show," although he found the characters "unsympathetic" on the whole. Perhaps fortunately, Abbott did not get involved, because all his reservations about the script suggested that he would have wanted to sweeten it a little. Finally, Roger Stevens agreed to take on the musical, and Cheryl Crawford of the Theatre Guild joined him in April 1956. The opening was deferred for more than a year because Bernstein's *Candide,* which had been temporarily shelved for lack of the right lyricist, was "on again."

In April it was decided that Oliver Smith would design the scenery and Irene Sharaff the costumes. Smith wrote an exuberant letter to Robbins in Copenhagen on April 5:

Your idea of the abstraction of locales existing in space is very correct; any literal interpretation of the city will get lumpy and terribly oppressive. I see the sets in rich, almost renaissance colors. . . . I think there should be an almost aerial magic, very poetic and dream like. My eyes are peeling the skin of the city and looking everywhere. Each set should be like a serious modern painting. . . . Nothing is more beautiful to me than a row of doors, nailed up to hide a vacant lot, a solitary "El" column, rusted and deep red and blotched with turquoise black, dark red fire escapes, and brick buildings the color of dried blood . . .

He was thrilled to be working on the show, still *East Side Story* but shortly to be known by its interim title, *Gangway*.* Smith did have a reservation about the script: "No where do these people exhibit any charm, or good fellowship. They seem humorless except in a very wry way."

Cheryl Crawford had her doubts almost from the start. The decision to use fresh, young, relatively unknown performers was another liability. Trying to argue down the amount of royalties the collaborators had requested, she noted in a June 1956 letter to Robbins that she and Stevens "both feel that exciting as the show can be, it is no cinch and I think all of you realize that too. It has very few of the customary Broadway values of comedy and splash with three killings and music leaning to opera and it must be cast brilliantly with no names which means the chance of big out of town losses and difficulty in getting benefits and a theatre." By January 1957, when Robbins was already auditioning performers, she had other criticisms. She found the main characters "sketchy," the beginning and ending still unresolved. She noted a lack of wit. "I think most of the segues from speech to music are inexpertly handled, much too primitive for this kind of show . . . the songs just don't come out of the dialogue in that inevitable way that we are used to in our best musicals." After mentioning that Chita Rivera, George Chakiris, and Pat Stanley would be excellent casting possibilities, she returned to her gloomy attack: "Now it might be that if we had types like the performers above and more lightness and fun, it <u>could</u> be a show that summer audiences would go for, but not in its present version."

Lightness and fun. It might have been predicted that Crawford would pull out. Which she did on April 2, 1957. Fortunately, Roger Stevens held firm, and Robert Griffith and Harold Prince, who had already declined to produce the show, reconsidered and came on board. Almost immediately they threatened to pull out again, because Robbins, feeling overwhelmed,

* *Gangway* was the working title until quite late in the game (dancer Gene Gavin remembers seeing that word stenciled on the sets, but *West Side Story* was in place when rehearsals began).

thought he couldn't choreograph the show as well as direct it. The result of the standoff was that Robbins, furious, backed down, but managed to wangle an unprecedented rehearsal period of eight weeks—twice what had been agreed on—an assistant to the director (Freedman), a cochoreographer (Peter Gennaro),* and dance assistants for both Gennaro and himself. Prince and Griffith stuck with *West Side Story*.

Casting, as always for Robbins, was time-consuming. Jets and Sharks and their girlfriends had to look like teenagers. Almost everyone had to be able to dance, sing, and act—not so common among Broadway gypsies of the day, when shows still often distinguished between the singing chorus and the dancers. He jotted down possibilities. Edward Villella (but can he sing?). Jerry Ohrbach (but can he move?). Some performers auditioned over and over. Larry Kert, a friend of Chita Rivera's (the show's Anita), was high on the list to play Bernardo, the leader of the Sharks. Then he was advised to work on Tony. Yet another tryout clinched the leads for him and Carol Lawrence, who had already auditioned more than a dozen times. Robbins told her to hide, and she found a ladder leading to a little overhead platform. When Kert was called in, he was instructed to find "Maria" without calling out and waking her parents. By the time he'd located her, clambered up, and delivered his lines, they were both charged up enough to move everyone watching.

Robbins had been preparing even harder than usual to direct this show, still struggling over how to inspire actors. He enrolled in Stella Adler's scene analysis class, which involved investigating all the ways a scene could be construed and played. Adler was known to be a Tartar. To Tanaquil Le Clercq in Copenhagen, Jerry wrote that she screamed at all the students that they had no talent, and he added virtuously, "The more I see of others' classes and rehearsals, the more of an angel I feel I am." Still,

---

* Robbins drew up his own contract with Gennaro on June 14, 1957, at the start of rehearsals: "I hereby engage you as co-choreographer to create, in conjunction with myself, the choreography for the dramatico-musical production presently entitled 'GANGWAY.' " He undertook to pay Gennaro fees and royalties, as well as first-class transportation for the choreographer and his wife and child. However, he added, "It is hereby agreed between us that there shall belong to me exclusively, and you hereby assign to me, any and all rights in and to any and all choreographic material created or suggested by you in connection with the Play (hereinafter called 'your said choreographic material and conceptions') and I shall have the right freely and without compensation to you to copyright in my name during the initial and renewal terms, use, or corporation that I may in my sole discretion select, your said choreographic material and conceptions created or suggested by you as fully as if your said choreographic material and conceptions had been originally created or suggested by me."

he found Adler's sessions "both crazy and wonderful. She's really madly inspiring or maybe it's just inspired madness, and makes what hair I have stand on end."

He had done his own research, of course. He looked at movies about tough kids and street life: *The Blackboard Jungle, Rebel Without a Cause, Crime in the Streets, On the Bowery.* He went to a high school dance in Puerto Rican Harlem and wrote to Le Clercq about it:

> They do dances that I've never seen before, evolving their own style and approach. In one dance, after starting with your partner for about 2 bars, you leave and separate and never touch or make any contact again for the whole rest of the dance. When you look at the floor each person seems to be having a ball on their own but I'm told that the partners know damn well who they're dancing with.

It's possible that Robbins's reticent and touching "cha-cha" during the dance at the gym had roots in this perception. Tony and Maria, mesmerized by their first sight of each other, stand face-to-face, not touching but moving slowly in instinctive synchrony (*they,* however, are gazing at each other, as if a glance away would break the spell).

Robbins's usual Method tactics came with him into the first rehearsals at the Chester Hale Studio on Fifty-sixth Street. He posted newspaper articles on gangs for the cast to read. Chita Rivera remembers the revelatory moment of seeing on the bulletin board a clipping with a photo showing the victim of a gang killing. Robbins had written above it, "Read this; this is your life."

The actors playing Jets and Sharks were not to fraternize during rehearsals or eat lunch together. Lee Becker, who played Anybodys, the Jets' unwanted tag-along tomboy, ended up being shunned by both groups. Rivera and Jet Tony Mordente (A-Rab) married during the show's run, and Rivera wrote a ruefully teasing letter to Robbins from the dressing room: "Tony is really *in* the show because he hasn't said a word to me yet (I'm a Shark). It's the damndest (wow) show I've ever been in." There were to be no anonymous chorus boys and girls; they all had names. The script's stage directions offered clues to the Jets' characters: A-Rab is "an explosive little ferret who enjoys everything and understands the seriousness of nothing," Action, "a catlike ball of fury." All were advised to figure out who they were, their family background, their day-to-day lives.

During the first weeks of rehearsal, Robbins worked with the dancers and Gerald Freedman with the principal actors. Carol Lawrence remembers Freedman as "the gentle one who drew our own personal truths out. Jerry was very caustic; Freedman was nurturing and loving." Robbins rode his actors hard. They called him "Big Daddy," a name that conjures both a paternal figure you could joke with and a ruthless dictator. Lawrence had appeared for her first audition in heavy makeup and big gold earrings—her idea of Puerto Rican; Robbins told her to wash her face and come back, and it's as if throughout rehearsals, he was still figuratively trying to scrub her clean. He was merciless in trying to dig performances out of Larry Kert and Mickey Calin (Riff). (His temper was probably not sweetened by a note of cavils from Laurents, who praised the staging as "magnificent," then added, "But I do not think, as yet, that it is well directed." He was not happy with Kert's work; Robbins would "make him better or not succeed as a director.")

Robbins pushed everyone past the comfort level, sometimes blind to everything but the task at hand. Carol Lawrence tells a curious story. When the Utopian dream of "There's a Place for Us" erodes into the old savagery, Maria is supposed to be hoisted and hurled, to be caught by others. Robbins was rehearsing the "Maria Lifters." After approving their grips, the angle, and so on, he told them to go ahead and throw Lawrence—not noticing that the "Maria Catchers" had not been primed. Maria landed flat on the floor. After the first horrified moment and a second moment in which it was ascertained that Lawrence wasn't badly hurt, Robbins ordered the move repeated, "this time with the Maria Catchers."

While many feared his wrath, with Chita Rivera, trust seemed to be the guiding force. "I just loved him so much. He's responsible for so much of whatever there is that's professional and good about me in the theater. I used to say that if Big Daddy had told me to jump off a building's fourth story and land on my left foot in plié, I would know it's possible because he could never steer me wrong." Robbins loved her back.

Experienced dancers understood Robbins better than actors and singers did. They coped with learning and remembering countless versions of the same sequence. For a dancer, a negative criticism—unpleasant as it is—can be challenging; it gets the adrenaline flowing, boosts the jump higher. But from Lawrence's point of view, "You can't manipulate an actor into being more poignant. You really denigrate his sense of confidence, and then he will not venture, he will not risk because of the humiliation he feels." Yet both Lawrence and Kert said later that, painful as their experience had been, they'd work for Robbins again in a minute.

And he made astute decisions. Peter Gennaro, who was adept at Latin rhythms, staged "America"—in which Anita quashes nostalgia for old San Juan—choreographing the vibrant dance that grew out of it for Shark men and women. Robbins took the men out of the number, thus giving the show a women's group to balance the dominant warring males and turning "America" into a dazzle of swishing skirts, rapidly flicking feet, and scornful female tongues.

Given the unusual amount of rehearsal time, he could try different strategies. For "Dance at the Gym," he worked in one studio with the Jets, Gennaro in another with the Sharks. Neither group knew what the other was doing, nor had they heard the music in its entirety. The point of this number is that it develops into a dance competition between Sharks and Jets, with each side trying to startle and outdo the other. "We were young," says Rivera. "We didn't know anything about acting. So he made it very real." When the two groups came together in rehearsal for the first time, the excitement was palpable. "We would start our section; then the Jets would pull a stunt and get our attention, and then we were blown away. It was really like a wonderful game; we were just taken by it."

The collaborators tinkered with the show during the rehearsal period, and some important numbers were written and/or staged at the last minute. On August 8, just eleven days before the Washington, D.C., opening, Bernstein reported gleefully to his wife, Felicia Montealegre, that he and Sondheim had written a new song for Tony ("Something's Coming") the day before and "It's really going to save his character—a driving 2/4 in the great tradition (but of course fucked up by me with 3/4s and what-not)—but it gives Tony balls—so that he doesn't emerge as just a euphoric dreamer." According to Sondheim, Robbins staged the clever intricacies of "Gee, Officer Krupke" in no time, three days before the company left for D.C. A song, "Kid Stuff," written in Washington for the youngest Jets—Baby John, A-Rab, and Anybodys—never made it into the show: too musical-comedyish. Sondheim tried to inject some substitute lyrics into Maria's flirtatious 6/8 rhapsody, "I Feel Pretty." He had a point; lines such as "It's alarming how charming I feel" would have been more appropriate in a Noël Coward revue than emerging from a naive Puerto Rican girl newly arrived in America. His colleagues wouldn't let him change a thing.

Early in the show's infancy, Nora Kaye had predicted that Bernstein, Laurents, and Robbins would never be able to work together amicably, and there were times when tensions ran high. Sondheim told Bernstein biographer Meryle Secrest that at the dress rehearsal in Washington, Robbins ran down the aisle and told conductor Max Goberman to make an alteration in the music of "Somewhere." Bernstein, sitting at the back of the theater, got up and left. Sondheim found him in a bar with five scotches lined up in front of him. Robbins defended himself in a 1994 letter to Charles Harmon of the Amberson Group, on receiving a copy of the published score of *West Side Story*. He began by mentioning how closely he and Bernstein had always worked together. They had a long-standing joke: "I would pick up on one of his dance gestures and include it in the choreography and he would pick up on a musical idea of mine and include it in each piece." Then came his version of the event:

> My tactics in jumping in at that dress rehearsal were not the best, I must admit, but I thought Lenny had agreed with me, as he had seen the rehearsals. There was no dancing at that moment but it was an extremely sensitive transition in the show. The song "Somewhere" began, and either the orchestrators or Lenny started it originally with a complete orchestral background (as it appears ten bars later at bar 132). I felt it was too full, too heavy to plunge into immediately, and believed the song should start simply, purely—out of the sky, and then blossom into fullness. When I rushed down the aisle, I never realized that Lenny was present and upset, nor did he ever mention it to me over all the years.
>
> In view of Lenny keeping those suggested changes for the run of the show, for all the cast albums, and for his Symphonic Variations of West Side Story, I take it that he also approved of it. I'm very proud of that final transition that he wrote, particularly when he kept it in even this, his first published score of *West Side Story*.

Bad manners aside, Bernstein had reason to trust Robbins's sense of what was right. Sondheim, too, acknowledged that Jerry was "unequivocally one of the most musical people I've ever met. . . . You either feel music or you don't. And he's one of the people who does. It has nothing to do with being able to read music or tell F-sharp from F-natural."

There was also some contention over billing. After the Washington opening, Bernstein generously ceded his credit as co-lyricist, giving Sondheim the standing he deserved. But Laurents tried and failed to persuade

Robbins to relinquish the "Conceived by" credit he was getting in addition to his name in a box as director and choreographer. It should be noted, however, that despite the many acrimonious remarks that were made by various of the four collaborators over the subsequent years, they continued (in various combinations) to collaborate and often sought advice and help from one another. "Despite everything," said Laurents of Robbins years after *West Side Story,* "we had a special feeling about each other."

West Side Story asserted its break with tradition in its first moments. No rousing overture. No opening song. The first sound after the curtain rises on the Jets hanging out is a finger snap. As the snaps accumulate, the audience understands not just the guys' nothing-to-do, looking-for-trouble mood but their solidarity. Bernstein's rhythmic complexity, Robbins's sense of drama, and their intuitive grasp of each other's vision work brilliantly. The composer uses silence to underscore wariness, waiting, or a break in tension, after which the Sharks may pounce again or a Jet whirl to confront trouble on a burst of music. The few words, such as "Beat it!," are embedded in the musical texture, along with the sound of whistles and squawking horns. Robbins's choreography and direction meet the rhythmic changeability, require it. In this turf war, bravado, stealth, fear, playfulness, and anger meet in combat, revealed in actions that shrug their way into dance and as quickly drop back into everyday behavior. A walk becomes a saunter, acquires a bounce, becomes an easygoing chassé or a soft-edged turn in the air. By the time you notice that the two groups of boys are dancing, you've understood the restless animosity that powers the movement, and it becomes as interesting as the steps. By the time the Jets sing their song of unity, you know the premise as well as you would after Shakespeare's brawling between Montagues and Capulets in Verona's piazza.

Bernstein's compositional foreshadowings and echoings elevate the drama. When Maria and Tony first see each other at the gym during the turf-war-as-dance-contest, you hear a fragment of their later poignant duet, "There's a Place for Us," and, as they meet, a trace of "Maria" before he even knows her name. "Maria" slides into their balcony scene under the stars too, before they sing "Tonight." The brilliant quintet that reprises "Tonight" ironically merges separate starry-eyed lyrics—with Anita zestily imagining how fine sex with Bernardo will be after the rumble, while Riff's and Bernardo's gangs brag about the victory that each is counting on. And, as Bernstein had noted elatedly in the letter to his wife quoted earlier, he constantly played games with cross-rhythms and changing meters, a compositional intricacy that comes across as vitality. When Maria flounces deliriously around the Bridal Shop singing the happy waltz, "I Feel Pretty," her girlfriends chorus in a different rhythm, but still in 3/4 time, giving their comments an affectionately mocking edge. And the reaching-for-Heaven strains of "There's a Place for Us" end the story as a dirge.

The production of *West Side Story* was innovative in terms of its design too. At the 1985 symposium, Sondheim, who appeared less satisfied with *West Side Story* than the other three collaborators, spoke most eloquently of the blend of music, book, lyrics, dance: "More than subject matter its innovation had to do with theatrical style. We were influenced by the movies—there was a fluidity to the staging, which had a cinematic quality. . . . No show had ever been staged—I'm talking about the larger sense, not just Jerry's work—or conceived this way as a fluid piece which called on the poetic imagination of the audience."

Oliver Smith's sets obviated in all but a few cases the convention of staging some scenes "in one" so that a set change could be made behind the first-wing curtain. As Keith Garebian writes in his book *The Making of West Side Story,* "The floating fire escapes suggested a breathless isolation, the shabby tenement walls of a building whirled away, fences and windows disappeared in the doomed lovers' defiant freedom." As Maria whirls exhilaratedly in the white dress Anita has made for her, the apartment where the Puerto Rican girls have gathered slides away and bright ribbons stream down to turn the stage into the gym. She spins off as the Jets and Sharks and their girls, dressed in their best, spin on. Irene Sharaff's costumes are real clothes, but there is a subtle color scheme in effect: blues and mustards for the Jets; shades of red, brown, and purple for the Sharks.

Audiences in Washington were thrilled by *West Side Story.* Justice Felix Frankfurter was observed to have wet eyes after the first act. When the show reached New York on September 26, 1957, the critics had mixed reactions. John Chapman of the *Daily News* loved it. Robert Coleman of the *Daily Mirror* declared it a "sensational hit!" and praised its "tremendous drive. It moves with the speed of a switchblade knife." But Ward Morehouse was put off by the grim subject matter, confessing that "I admired it more than I enjoyed it," and the *Herald Tribune*'s Walter Kerr, although he was enthusiastic, had some cavils. He found the show

> rushingly acted . . . and it is, apart from the spine-tingling velocity of the dances, almost never emotionally affecting. Perhaps the echoes of another Romeo and Juliet are too firm; the people often seem to be behaving as they do because of arbitrary commands from a borrowed plot. Perhaps the near-absence of comedy whittles away the substance of ordinary humanity. Perhaps these teen-age gangsters are too ferocious, too tawdry, too intent upon grinding their teeth to interest us compassionately for two and one-half hours. They terrify us in their drive; they do not touch us in their bewilderment.

On the other hand, the brilliant English theater critic Kenneth Tynan, who came from London to assess the musical in 1958, thought that Robbins had "probably over-stylized a situation too fresh and bloody to respond to such treatment. The boys are too kempt; their clothes are too pretty; they dope not, neither do they drink. This makes them unreal, and gives the show an air of sociological slumming." His final sentence took away the sting: "Yet it compromises only on the brink of greatness; and that, surely, is triumph enough." And his descriptive powers caught the essence of *West Side Story*'s style:

> The score, by Leonard Bernstein, is as smooth and savage as a cobra; it sounds as if Puccini and Stravinsky had gone on a roller coaster ride into the precincts of modern jazz. Jerome Robbins, the director-choreographer, projects the show as a rampaging ballet, with bodies flying from the air as if shot from guns, leaping, shrieking, and somersaulting; yet he finds room for a peaceful dream sequence, full of that hankering for a golden age that runs right through American musicals, in which both gangs imagine a paradise where they can touch hands in love, without fear or loss of face.

In a sense, what some have seen as *West Side Story*'s failing is also one of its strengths. There is no larger society—although a prejudiced one is assumed—and the adults are either barely there (the owner of the Bridal Shop), corrupt and bigoted (Schrank), not very bright (Krupke and Glad

Hand), or a compassionate voice of doom (Doc). The city, unlike Shakespeare's Verona, is not shaken to its basements by the strife. The Jets and Sharks, Maria and her Tony, are alone in the city, almost its only visible inhabitants. Yet their unrealistic isolation heightens another, very real kind of isolation—that of first- or second-generation immigrants from their parents. When Doc gives a weary "When I was your age . . ." Action's not having it; that's what his father tells him, that's what his brother says, and he hits back: "You was never my age—none of you!" Whatever these kids are experiencing growing up in America, their families can't fully understand. The ending, which some spectators find corny and which brings a lump to others' throats, is orchestrated by Maria herself in her new, powerful, grief-altered persona and immediately understood by her peers. After Schrank moves in as if to take charge of Tony's body and she shrieks, *"Don't you touch him!"* the adults simply stand there, while, in response to her unspoken wish, some of his friends lift him. He's heavy, he's about to slip from their grasp, and the Sharks step forward to help. The image isn't rational, of course; it would take more than this to end the hostility between the two groups of angry children, but for the moment it fulfills Tony and Maria's dreams of peace, and ours for them.

West Side Story was a hit with audiences and became a classic, although a miscalculation resulted in its closing perhaps prematurely. In mid-July 1960, the weekly gross dipped temporarily, and the four creators agreed to cuts in their royalties (Bernstein's usual rate was 3 percent, Laurents's and Robbins's 2 percent, and Sondheim's 1 percent). The show had moved from the capacious Winter Garden to the smaller Alvin, and Harold Prince had already announced the December 1960 closing when a lowering of ticket prices (the top weeknight price for orchestra seats had been $5) began to bring new crowds to the theater. The announcement couldn't be withdrawn since another show had already been booked into the Alvin. However, a second company toured *West Side Story* around the United States, and a London production ran for nearly three years. Starting out with an all-American cast and rehearsing at the Alvin Theatre while the original production was still at the Winter Garden, it soon had a part-British cast, with Robbins periodically dropping in and firing off critical notes to his deputy, Kenneth Le Roy (who played Bernardo), or laying down the law about replacement performers to producer Hugh "Binkie" Beaumont. In 1964, the musical won unanimous raves when Gerald Freedman and Tommy Abbott, one of the original dancers, reproduced it faithfully for the New York City Center Opera. Before long, *West Side Story* had been seen in major European cities and in Tokyo.

In the process of birthing the first *West Side Story,* Robbins had enlivened his love life as well as increasing his income and his fame. Gene Gavin noted that during the show's pre-Broadway run in Philadelphia, Lee Becker (the hapless "Anybodys") told Gavin that Robbins had asked her to marry him. Robbins had indeed hoped yet again that he might establish a stable relationship with a woman, but again it didn't work out. In November 1957, he wrote Robert Fizdale from St. John. Buzz Miller had been down twice. "When I see him, I always see why it couldn't work, but when he's not there, I build up a picture of the good times and forget the evil ones." As for his more recent romance:

> What happened with Lee? Turned out <u>she</u> had the problems, not me, and so furiously did they emerge I never had a chance to act up and twist about myself. It's a shame because I really dug her in a big way and felt that perhaps everything was going to fall into place AND HIGH TIME. At any rate she took to spinning like a top, till I grabbed her shook her and tried to get to her. Impossible at this point. She doesn't feel good enough for me!? She says. How about that. Isn't that the switch of all time. Maybe when I get back she'll have calmed down a bit.

Evidently she did not. But Robbins was also involved with Tommy Abbott. Their relationship doesn't seem to have been a romantic love affair but rather an affectionate sexual friendship between a young man and an older one, and a professional association beneficial for both. Abbott was one of those performing and helping out during Robbins's brief, passionate, and frustrating stint on the *West Side Story* movie.

⌒

Jerome Robbins codirected the United Artists film of *West Side Story* with Robert Wise (who also produced the picture), and they both won Academy Awards. Many in the entertainment business also have heard that Robbins was fired by the executive producers, Harold and Walter Mirisch. What is generally not known is that even though Robbins left Hollywood with much of the movie still to be shot, he had a great deal to say about the editing, and Wise was as accommodating as he felt it possible to be.

The plan was to start shooting in late July 1960, and be finished by the end of November. But as early as March, Robbins and Wise were making test shots at locations around New York, using different filters, and trying out parts of the Prologue with a small cadre of performers. Robbins flew to Hollywood for consultations with Wise and Ernest Lehman, who was writing the screenplay. And, as expected, he fired off earnest and driven messages to Wise from an island vacation (also mentioning waterskiing and learning to do a front flip on the trampoline). He worried that they had not yet solved the basic problem of filming *West Side Story*. In an April 4 letter to Wise, he outlined what he felt this problem to be: "Our approach to the original production was to present it with the same time-free, space-free, image-evocative method of a ballet. . . . I am not talking about the 'ballet' or 'dancing' but about the concept and style of the whole work which made it so individual." He didn't feel that any of the approaches discussed so far had generated a correspondingly innovative use of film. "The problem now is to find a new set of conventions, inherently cinematic, which will also convey the essence of a show whose essence is not in any of its separate elements . . . music, movement, sets etc . . . but in their organic unity." Unless they found that new style, he warned, they'd end up with "a very tough, possibly moving, straight story-telling job, but lets all hold our breath when ever anyone sings. The dances I could bring down to a pretty real approach . . . and I think I could justify and involve them easily into the film. But boy, whenever you start to sing you run the risk of falling between a Doris Day musical and Carmen Jones. The dances will come on without a bump, but watch them musical numbers!"

Wise responded soothingly to his codirector's worries. He and his team also felt they hadn't yet found the right approach, but were determined to discover it. "We have to find a photographic and cinematic treatment that will act as a catalyst between the real and the unreal." Casting involved more debates, although Robbins agreed with the Mirisches' decision not to give the role of Maria to Anna Maria Alberghetti, the silver-voiced young soprano whom Hollywood had been trying to turn into a second Deanna Durbin: "Its absolutely true that Annamariaspaghetti's name is death at [the box office]. Mention her name and you think of a symphonic orchestra and a family of pretty dolled up Italians singing from opera in a high Jeanette McDonald [sic] vibrato." Natalie Wood couldn't sing—Marni Nixon dubbed in her limpid voice—but she was a bankable star, and she and Robbins came to adore each other.* She gamely took morning class with the dancers, even though she had to stop before the difficult steps began. Jerry was less enthusiastic about Richard Beymer, who played Tony: he was tall, he could move well, but he couldn't dance or sing (his voice, too, was dubbed), and Wood wasn't wild about him. Robbins gave Russ Tamblyn (Riff) a hard time but was pleased with Rita Moreno (Anita). The cast was studded with veterans of the various stage productions of the show: David Bean, Tommy Abbott, David Winters, Tony Mordente, Jay Norman, Eliot Feld, and George Chakiris (who had been playing Riff in the London production and was released to be the film's Bernardo). By May, Robbins was ensconced at 916 North Foothill Road in Beverly Hills, enjoying a swimming pool and other luxuries (Edith Weissman and Mattie, his cook, came along).

Mistrustful of Hollywood ways, Jerry was fully aware of how much he was rocking the boat. To Bernstein, who had written that he approved of the idea of filming "Cool" in a garage, Jerry replied, "My garage idea is a good one but true to Hollywood standards turns out to be a super garage and I seem to be spending most of my energy in pushing walls closer to each other, washing colors out of the sets, and acting like a sheep dog in trying to keep the script in a nice well-directed herd aimed for the success it was in New York. I run from side to side barking warning noises about strayed lines, changed lyrics and cut choruses. My they're getting tired of me."

It had been agreed that Robbins would rehearse the dances and musical numbers in advance of shooting, while Wise worked on the book scenes. He naturally fiddled with the choreography ("Version 16a or 16b?" the dancers would ask) to adjust it to the cinematic plot and informed Bernstein that some musical adjustments would be needed because on film, the action evolved more gradually. In the Prologue, for instance, "the musical material now is terribly stretched and extended. . . . The 'whole' flow of the prologue is dissipated." His later memo of July 18 shows that he was already well versed in the lingo and demands of film. He explained how, between measures 59 and 62, the last part of the Jets' stroll down the street,

---

* Wood and Robbins remained close. She addressed him as "Mole" in her letters and signed them the same way. Until her accidental death by drowning in 1981, she attended many of his openings and ballet premieres, and a signed photograph of her stood on one of Jerry's bedside tables.

when the walk began to build and hint at dance, and the moment when 85, the "sailing step," moved into 86, the "big strut," "the camera WHIPS and we pick up the Jets in the new location . . . there may be something very exciting in a startling percussive insert for these WHIPS (one or two bars)."

Sondheim, too, had to do some extra work, since some of his lyrics didn't suit Hollywood's idea of what a general public could hear. A verse in "Officer Krupke" offended: "My father is a bastard/My ma's an SOB/My grandpa's always plastered/My grandma pushes tea." Interestingly, Sondheim was asked only to alter the first three lines (perhaps the censors thought the tea in question was part of a small Earl Grey racket), and "My sister wears a mustache/my brother wears a dress" passed muster.

After some soul-searching, Wise, who was producing the film for the Mirisches, had accepted the idea of two directors. Although he knew the musical forms (as an editor or assistant editor he had worked on many Astaire-Rogers musicals), as well as the business of prescoring and working with playbacks, this was his first time working with a choreographer, and, after all, Robbins had conceived the show. The two maintained an easy rapport, as far as the cast could see. Jerry walked around and squinted at the action through a viewfinder, and the two conferred. Wise has said that they'd agreed that Robbins would decide how to film the dances and musical numbers, while he, Wise, would be there to make suggestions and facilitate Jerry's desires. Wise would be in charge of the dialogue scenes, but Jerry would be there to make suggestions. As Wise recalls, "That's the way I went for about sixty percent of the film."

The plan was to begin the "location" shots August 8 in New York: the "Prologue," "Jet Song," "Something's Coming," and "Maria." Most of the buildings around Sixty-fifth Street and Amsterdam Avenue had already been torn down to make way for Lincoln Center, but the contractors had agreed to leave some facades standing as they gutted from the back. The playground on which Wise's spectacular opening helicopter shot descended was at 110th Street and Second Avenue. By August 24, Robbins and the dancers were supposed to wing their way back to the studio to rehearse "America," now revised to include the male Sharks again.

Jets and Sharks (minus the principals), encouraged by Robbins not to fraternize and to think competitively, blew off a very creative amount of steam that hot, moist August. David Bean (a Jet) recollects some of their shenanigans:

We'd write on little tiny strips of paper, "The Jets are the greatest, the Jets are the greatest." Millions of them. We'd sit up nights doing this. We'd have these big tubs, buckets full of these things. And then we got sheets. We bought big sheets. Each sheet had a letter: J E T. And it said "THE JETS ARE THE GREATEST." Do you know how many sheets that was? On all of the buildings, the tenement buildings around this playground, we had "THE JETS ARE THE GREATEST." At a certain given time we threw the sheets over the buildings and on top of the school we had an effigy of a Shark hanging over the side. And then we threw these millions of little leaflet things that said "The Jets are the greatest." This was a huge campaign.

The local landlords, scenting Hollywood money, claimed hefty damages for broken skylights. Although the young dancers denied messing with anything, they were thereafter asked to stay in the bus until needed. And told not to do any more rain dances to relieve the heat and get a respite from shooting.

Old habits are hard to break. Robbins wanted to shoot sequences in different ways, so he could choose which he liked best. He couldn't fathom, or didn't care to, the cost of 70-millimeter color film. And the records show that where the standard was to print one take and keep one in reserve, he was averaging three. One of his assistants, Margaret Banks, says he'd often ask for more than that. Banks had been a dancer with Ballet Theatre when Robbins was in the company, but more recently she had been an assistant to Gene Kelly. So she knew movies and the movie business. One of her jobs was to keep Jerry in check. She had a hard time of it, especially when sitting with him to watch the rushes of a given day's shooting.

I would say to him, "Jerry, we can't print that (it would be sixteen bars of music); we can't because there's a hair on the lens." And he would say, "Well, print it anyway. I want to look at it." Or I'd say, "Jerry, we can't print that; there was a bump on the track." "Print it anyway." "Jerry, it's unusable." "I know, but I want to see what went wrong."

The picture was supposed to cost $4 million. Banks guesses that by the time they left New York, they'd already spent about that, and they were behind schedule. "Maria" and "Something's Coming" appear to have been shot in the studio, and it is George Chakiris's memory that Richard Beymer never got a chance to work with Robbins during the actual filming. Harold Mirisch's note to Wise and Robbins on September 12 expresses admiration for the New York footage but underlines a request to pick up the pace, now that they were back in Hollywood, and to do without alternate versions. On September 15, he had to remind the directors of these words and cites the shooting log to underscore how much time he thought they'd wasted on September 13:

> 9–9:52 rehearse Anita's song
> 10:35–11:06—shot 171, 14 takes
> 1:28–2:10 shot 172—4 takes
> 3:55–4:52—rehearse

Around October 25, he and his brother fired Robbins. Wise has since, tactfully, said that they decided two directors took up more time than one. But it's pretty clear that the Mirisches considered Robbins mostly to blame for the delays and mounting costs. Jerry left in a rage. According to Gina Trikonis, who played Riff's girlfriend, Graziella, he worked the Jets remorselessly through a rehearsal and then told them that just because they'd completed a good portion of the film, they were not to think they couldn't also be replaced. The next day he was gone from the set. His departure didn't solve the schedule problem. His principal assistant (and a boyfriend), Howard Jeffrey, who quit when Robbins was fired, reported in December that he'd talked to Natalie Wood, who was upset about the way things were going, also mentioning that Wise, with the help of Maggie Banks, Tommy Abbott, and Tony Mordente, had been shooting the "Dance at the Gym" for fourteen days and were just up to Tony and Maria's little "cha-cha."

Jerry was missed by many in the cast. Certainly his assistants, including accompanist Betty Walberg, knew *West Side Story* inside out. So did many of the dancers. But it was his show; he knew exactly how all the performers should fit into it and how to help them—pressure them—to do so. George Chakiris remembers that when Robbins would walk in after the dancers' morning class, "the atmosphere absolutely changed. It was like electricity. It was like, okay, we can't play around over here. Now we've got to—it was because he demanded so much of you even though he didn't say that. . . . It wasn't verbalized; you just knew . . . because he demanded a lot of the same of himself, if not more."

Trying to tie up *West Side Story* business with his lawyer William Fitelson, Robbins estimated that he had shot approximately 40 percent of the film and prepared and rehearsed 70 percent (scenes, musical sequences, "rough rehearsals," and talks with the cast about the characters), in addition to previous (unpaid) weeks of preparation and consultations and three weeks of cutting and editing. Because he rehearsed every musical number, memories differ considerably as to exactly which ones he was there for the actual filming of: the "Prologue," for sure, and "Jet Song" and "America." Probably for "I Feel Pretty." Maybe for the "Rumble." Definitely not for "Dance at the Gym" or "Officer Krupke." The dream ballet that in the stage version expands from "There's a Place for Us" was dropped, never even rehearsed, perhaps because dancing in an idyllic film limbo would strain credulity after the "real" streets and tenement rooms.

The "Prologue" reveals how intricately Robbins, with Wise's input, used the camera to emphasize the Jets' and Sharks' hostility, the aimless energy that underlies their tossing a basketball, the run-down city streets that channel and intensify their rage. The cutting and choice of angle keep changing our viewpoint so we become as wary as the kids as to where the next attack will be coming from. After Bernardo whirls out of one shot into a dramatic close-up of him in his red shirt against a red wall, he, Jay Norman, and Edward Verso charge toward us, dancing; a couple of measures later, they're moving away, backs to the camera. Just as quickly, their small figures advance again to burst into their big side kick. In the playground, on the cry, "Go!," the camera is looking down; then, as many hands reach up to catch the ball, we see the action from below. Guys jump up in one location and come down on the beat in another.

Robbins's notes dated December 12, after he'd seen a rough cut of parts of the film with Wise; later notes taken at a session when another cut was run for them on April 2, 1961; and additional notes he sent to Wise and Mirisch on April 12 after going over the film reel by reel with the film's editor, Thomas Stanford, show his fierce determination to get it right. His main concern was that the story and emotions be revealed as strongly and clearly as possible—even, he stressed, at the expense of the choreography.

His early comments extend to small details, such as "There is possibly one too many snaps before the ball hits the fence. It's a question of metric phrase." Or, in regard to "Cool," "Would like to see how the effect of the flare from the headlights photographs. If it is the right effect use it slightly from the beginning and step it up with each section so that by the big chorus it is way out." He was bothered by "the cutting away from Natalie just before she begins singing on 'I Feel Pretty' which is a terribly abrupt, awkward start. Everything should be done to stay with her so that she can be seen to arrive at the song logically, even to throwing Yvonne's lines to her from off camera as she puts the scarf around her shoulders." Wise took this advice, as he did Robbins's desire to insert, during the "Prologue," a close-up of the three Sharks playing cards so the audience would know for sure whom the Jets were scaring.

Later, Jerry's requests for change focused on "Dance at the Gym" and the first meeting of Maria and Tony:

> The most important aspect of the whole Dance Hall is that each gang is desperately _rivalling_ with the other and aggressively _taking_ the dance floor away from each other. In its present cutting this story is lost and it looks like "general dance enthusiasm." Before the Sharks start their own mambo you do not see them (in any shot including both groups) leave the Jets and move to their own conference. The Sharks (in a shot including the Jets) should be seen to withdraw and then take over the dance hall; then the Jets (in a shot including the Sharks) should be seen gathering and taking it back and dispersing the Sharks; then the Sharks reassemble and take it back, and the Jets re-counter. When Riff and Graciela are dancing competitively against Bernardo and Anita, the _total_ picture, including both couples, isn't seen until the very last minute. One doesn't get the impression that this is a highly pitched and desperate gang fight for supremacy. It is of utmost importance because Tony and Maria must meet at the _fiercest_ moment of the gang's crescendoing competitive dancing. This is terribly important to remedy.

Although he found the return to reality after the lovers' meeting "marvelously done" and "an absolutely brilliant moment in the film," he was disappointed by the moments of their meeting, the crucial instant of their sighting each other across the room and being drawn together by some kind of witchery of love.

Wise thought many of his codirector's points well taken but decided against repositioning "America," as Robbins had requested (reminding Wise that he, Jerry, had yielded to Bob in the switching of "Officer Krupke" to the first part of the film and putting "Cool" in its place just before the "Rumble"). In line with Robbins's critique, Wise reported that he had also done some recutting to adjust the competition in the gym. In addition, he had "initiated the additional optical work we discussed in the meeting of Tony and Maria. If I can possibly squeeze the time the day I shoot the process I will also pick up the big head close-ups of Tony and Maria in the meeting. In the meantime I've cut in more of the over-shoulders that we have on the scene."

Finally the Mirisch Company's lawyer, Ray Kurtzman, informed Jay Kanter of MCA that there were apparently no more major disagreements in regard to the cutting and editing of the picture. There followed some wrangling as to exactly what credit Robbins deserved, but certainly he received enough credits—as codirector and choreographer and for conceiving and directing the original stage version. He also received more than $250,000 from United Artists in addition to annual royalty payments. And two Academy Awards.

West Side Story swept the Oscars: for best costume design (Irene Sharaff reconceiving her Broadway clothes), set decoration, art direction, film editing, color cinematography, scoring of a musical picture, and sound. George Chakiris and Rita Moreno beat out Montgomery Clift and Judy Garland in *Judgment at Nuremberg* for the Best Actor and Best Actress in a Supporting Role awards. *West Side Story* was voted the Best Motion Picture of 1961, and Wise and Robbins shared the Best Achievement in Directing. Gene Kelly also presented Jerry with a special award for his choreography.

In those days, Academy Awards acceptance speeches were brief and straitlaced. Robbins, smiling and bowing stiffly, said he was deeply grateful to the academy for the honor (the choreography award) and wanted to thank all who'd been in front of and behind the camera. Accepting kisses and statues from Rosalind Russell for directing, neither he nor Wise mentioned each other. Robbins thanked the producers of the movie and of the original play, naming only Harold Prince and "the late Bobby Griffith," and left the stage.

Bosley Crowther of the *Times* and Stanley Kauffmann of *The New Republic* praised *West Side Story* extravagantly (Kauffmann: "the best film musical ever made"), prompting, perhaps, Pauline Kael's furious *Film Quarterly* review of the picture and, by implication, the stage play that had spawned it, as pretentious ("How can so many critics have fallen for this frenzied hokum . . . ?"), especially as compared with *Singin' in the Rain,* her candidate for all-time best Hollywood musical.

Robbins's own view was more measured. In an October 1961 letter to Richard Buckle, he wrote:

Saw film of *West Side Story*, and it's about the way I figured it to be. Some of it is wonderful and exciting (and I don't mean just everything I did) but some of it gets bogged down in the lack of understanding of what the scenes or the musical numbers were about. And occasionally "Hollywood" rears its ugly head and splatters the screen with the soft lights streaming from Heaven or garish technicolor or STEREOPHONIC SOUND.

And later, to Buckle again, he delivered an opinion on his trophies. The Oscars have "no faces, no fingers, no asses, no balls, no nothing. . . . They're bland like Hollywood, they're gold and glued over." He put his in the basement.

13

Exporting America

Robbins putting members of Ballets: U.S.A. through their paces.
Philippe Halsman © Halsman Estate/NYPL.

B*etween the opening* of *West Side Story* at the Winter Garden in September 1957 and the release of the film in the summer of 1961, Robbins fielded and tossed a multitude of offers. His files bulged with requests for interviews, for money (from the Lena Robbins Foundation—since 1970 the Jerome Robbins Foundation—which he set up in

1957 to give grants to artists), for jobs, for recommendations; with invitations to sit on a panel, serve as an honorary chairman, write an article, come to a party. Would he read this script? Would he consider directing this play? This musical comedy? Could Ballet Company X please do *Interplay*? With the help of the invaluable Edith Weissman, he acknowledged them all. Letters to friends, colleagues, and well-known people he dictated or wrote himself, but Weissman knew how to speak in Robbins's voice. Many responses begin along the lines of "The project sounds interesting, but my schedule is too full for me even to consider it . . ." or "I'm sorry, but I'll be out of the country . . ."

He made time, however, to compile lists of possible funders to facilitate Inbal's American tour, writing a testimonial to accompany the solicitation, and was proudly present when the company made its much-praised New York debut on January 6, 1958. He and Anna Sokolow gave a party in the company's honor at Fizdale and Gold's apartment. And in 1960, the American Israel Cultural Foundation thanked him and Martha Graham for their inspiring talks at a gala that raised $9,500 for Inbal's choreographer-director, Sara Levi-Tanai.

He was good about recommending dancers who had worked with him. Michiko of *The King and I* hoped for Rockefeller Foundation funding to study Balinese and Javanese dance. He wrote a letter on her behalf. The Greater New York Chapter of the National Foundation for Infantile Paralysis solicited a donation. In 1957, with Le Clercq much on his mind, he signed over his royalty fee of $488.50 from the performance of *Afternoon of a Faun* on Canadian television. He was glad to be interviewed by Bernard Taper for Taper's biography of George Balanchine. And he was on hand in 1958 to receive a *Dance Magazine* award from Agnes de Mille. He must have laughed upon reading a letter that began, "The Relaxation Guidance Center is conducting the first of a series of studies on how well-known people relax."

Photography was one way Jerry relaxed, and he was tremendously pleased when David I. Zeitlin, who was planning a book of photographs by famous people and had solicited some from him, praised his pictures highly. He had no trouble clearing the decks to send the requested comments about each photo selected for the book, sounding very knowledgeable. "Clown" he had shot from the ring in Madison Square Garden with a telephoto lens:

The negative is somewhat larger, including a blurred raised arm and some distracting elements in the background. I cropped it to that shape because I was struck by the compositional effect of the strange areas of black and white. By so cropping it, it made the contrast and balances a little eerie, and the impression of mystery of what goes on behind a clown's face was thus heightened. I printed it on #5 Kodbromide paper to heighten the contrast and increase the grain. The eyes of the clown were a bit dodged so they didn't come out as black holes.

His social life was, as usual, full during these years, judging by a long, newsy letter he wrote Richard Buckle about the 1959–1960 holiday season (just after which he'd had to fly to Chicago because the national company of *West Side Story* was "falling apart"). Dickie, or "Bucky," as Robbins sometimes addressed him, was a wit, and Jerry enjoyed rising to his epistolary level, manifesting a certain glee as he told of Balanchine and Le Clercq's Christmas Eve dinner party for ten or twelve. Suzanne, a maid who did Jerry's heavy cleaning, came to help: "She walked into the kitchen and I introduced her to George who was in a terrible old shirt, carving up a turkey, way past his elbows in grease. I said, 'This is Monsieur Balanchine who speaks French also.' She immediately launched into a torrent of tu-toyed French thinking it was one of the help!"

West Side Story had redefined his status in the theater, and he seems to have been veering between exercising the lighter side of his musical comedy bent and investigating more "high art" ventures. On one hand, in October 1957, he tried hard to interest Leland Hayward in an idea he'd had for a musical he envisioned for Mary Martin and Ethel Merman that

> could be a hell of a show for both the girls. Start them out almost dowdy, living together in some mid-west town, school teachers, put them on a real Cook's tour (about which I have many wonderful ideas) take them through Europe and have some marvelous and fantastically funny things happen to them, some sort of romance, and finally a returning back to the U.S. mid-western school, richer, wiser and a little sadder and happier in experience.

He went on to propose possible writers, lyricists, composers. But he also wrote to Rudolf Bing, director of the Metropolitan Opera—who had several times approached him about taking charge of a production—wondering if Bing had selected a director for Alban Berg's *Wozzeck* (he was too late). Leo Kerz, a stage designer turned producer, aroused his interest in directing Bertolt Brecht's *Man Is Man* in 1958 and then in 1960 excited him by proposing that he direct Eugène Ionesco's first full-length play, *Rhinoceros,* which was to star Zero Mostel, but Robbins was unable to make a commitment at the time Kerz needed one. His participation in another project of Kerz's—a new version of the Brecht–Kurt Weill *The Rise and Fall of the City of Mahagonny*—was scotched by the *West Side Story* movie's schedule.

Robbins kept being drawn back to the New York City Ballet, and when Balanchine, in Warm Springs with Tanny, sent word that he hoped Jerry would do Stravinsky's *Capriccio* for the company's winter season of 1957–1958, he did start work on a ballet (though perhaps not that one). However, he wrote Robert Fizdale that he felt that the atmosphere of the company had changed and after two rehearsals "found myself settling for poor stuff." He fled to a favorite spot, Trunk Bay, in a remote part of the Caribbean island of St. John. A year later, in response to a request that he do something for the company's tenth-anniversary season, he offered a plan for *Capriccio* that charmed Lincoln Kirstein—"a horrifying children's fairy tale about birds"—but by then he was too embroiled in another project to take it on.

During the almost four years between *West Side Story*'s Broadway opening and the release of the film, he brought off two major achievements: directing and choreographing the musical *Gypsy* and founding his own company, Ballets: U.S.A.

~

Ballets: U.S.A. came about rather by accident. In 1957, the composer Gian Carlo Menotti approached Robbins about contributing to a three-week festival he was planning to inaugurate in Italy during the summer of 1958—one that would honor the classics of European music and theater and introduce contemporary American composers and artists in all fields to Italian audiences. The lovely Umbrian hill town of Spoleto won out over nearby Todi, because it boasted two theaters: the Caio Melisso, a seventeenth-century jewel box (at that time, run-down and used for showing movies), and a crimson-and-gilt nineteenth-century opera house, the Teatro Nuovo.

For that summer and for many summers thereafter, the attractions were, on the whole, small scale and the Festival of Two Worlds atmosphere intimate. Spoleto was not Edinburgh, with its seven halls and crowds large enough to justify simultaneous performances. Alberto Moravia, in his 1958 program essay, "The Arts in Spoleto," speaks of events such as the Festival dei Due Mondi as being "inspired by what I might call 'nostalgia for the Court' "—for a time when rival dukes vied with one another to see whose dancing master, whose court composer, and whose painter could produce the most exquisite entertainments. The souvenir program attests to the elegant, erudite, and slightly offbeat taste that guided some of the choices. The best-known and most elaborate of the summer's operas was Verdi's *Macbeth*. The young American composer Lee Hoiby premiered a three-character work, *The Scarf*. The other three presentations were examples of the Italian Baroque—comic and entrancingly suitable to the stage of the Caio Melisso—such as *Il Maestro di cappella,* Domenico Cimarosa's witty intermezzo about a conductor who can't control his orchestra.

Conductor Thomas Schippers, not yet thirty, was Menotti's artistic director for music, while José Quintero was in charge of drama, John Butler of dance, and Giovanni Urbino of fine arts. One of the three plays chosen was an Italian comedy; the others were Eugene O'Neill's *A Moon for the Misbegotten,* starring Colleen Dewhurst and Richard Kiley, and Alphonse Daudet's *L'Arlésienne,* with incidental music and choruses by Georges Bizet. The dance offerings were companies assembled by Robbins and Butler. Butler had a long-standing professional relationship with Menotti; he had choreographed the annual productions of the composer's Christmas opera, *Amahl and the Night Visitors,* since 1950, in addition to staging his "madrigal opera," *The Unicorn, the Gorgon, and the Manticore,* with the New York City Ballet in 1957.

When he was invited to participate, Robbins's initial plan—since many fine musicians would be assembled in Spoleto—was to tackle Stravinsky's *Les Noces,* a project he had been pursuing unsuccessfully for some time, and invite Herbert Ross to stage his hair-raising *The Maids,* based on Jean Genet's play, but with the vicious and demented serving women played by men. *Les Noces* fell by the wayside, in part because it was impractical to tour with (it called for four grand pianos, chorus, and percussion), and after the Spoleto Festival, Robbins's group was to perform at the World's Fair in Brussels for a week; he was also hoping for more European engagements. *The Maids* was dropped because it was shocking and, therefore, in terms of Cold War diplomacy, not the best thing to represent American culture at a World's Fair. John Martin, attending a New York run-through in practice clothes of the newly christened Ballets: U.S.A. program, just before the company was to leave for Italy, was pleased to note that "wiser heads have eliminated [it] from the schedule." In a telegram dated April 18, 1958, to the Spoleto Festival office in Rome, Robbins indicated that he had given up *Les Noces* and *The Maids* in order to secure the American National Theatre and Academy's "financial endorsement" (he gained additional support from Philadelphia's Catherwood Foundation).

ANTA had been chosen to administer the President's Emergency Fund for International Affairs, set up by President Dwight D. Eisenhower in 1954 to export American art as a weapon in the Cold War. Since the end of World War II, ANTA had been acting as the State Department's agent in securing services and raising money for companies deemed worthy of traveling abroad. Peer panels in each discipline, like those later set up by the National Endowment for the Arts, sought art that would present America in a favorable light as a cultured nation.

Instead of *Les Noces* and *The Maids,* Robbins would present his comic gem, *The Concert* (now to have decor by Saul Steinberg), *Afternoon of a Faun,* and Todd Bolender's *Games,* set to the Stravinsky-Pergolesi *Pulcinella.* In *Games,* Robbins gained a piquant opener that showed his pickup company at home in classical steps, plus Bolender himself to reprise his comic turn as the henpecked husband in *The Concert.* Robbins was also working on a new jazz ballet with decor by painter Ben Shahn and music by a young composer, Robert Prince. It was this work, *New York Export: Opus Jazz* that he came to consider one of his best and that would knock Europe on its ear.

The company of sixteen dancers was scheduled to perform in the Teatro Nuovo nine times during the festival's three-week June schedule. Butler's smaller ensemble, which included Buzz Miller, Carmen de Lavallade, and Tina Ramirez, would also perform nine times, but in the Caio Melisso, which the festival had restored to its ancient splendors.

Menotti had requested that Robbins find young, relatively unknown dancers, rather than established ballet stars. Auditions began in January. They were more like unpaid rehearsals (common before Actors' Equity ruled against them). Robbins invited dancers he liked to come in and do a little work, and colleagues recommended others. In February they were given morning class and taught excerpts from the repertory, including the material that he was developing for *Opus Jazz*. Carolyn Brown—available because the Merce Cunningham Dance Company, of which she was a vital part, had no work in May and June—learned most of *Afternoon of a Faun*, with Jay Norman as her partner. In the end, of the around twenty picked, only sixteen could go; the others found out by scuttlebutt that the budget had been tightened.

Only a few of those chosen for Ballets: U.S.A.* were primarily classical dancers. Barbara Milberg and Joan Van Orden had been in the New York City Ballet, for example, while Jay Norman came straight from *West Side Story* and Sondra Lee was not notably balletic (she was overheard assuring Robbins at the "auditions"—where she was learning Le Clercq's role in *The Concert*—that since it was only February, she had plenty of time to brush up her pointe technique). Says Lee, "I think we all in some crazy way spoke his language—but in different tongues, because we all came from different places in the dance world—and in our training as well; we were all very well trained." And together they fit the "U.S.A." part of the company's sobriquet, especially as Europeans might perceive it: young, fresh, peppy, up for anything, and coming from a variety of cultural and racial backgrounds.

The company flew to Europe in May to learn the repertory and complete *New York Export: Opus Jazz*. The kids were wild with excitement on the plane, despite snafus that delayed their arrival until late at night, and, says Lee, they faced television crews at the airport in Rome bedraggled and resembling "a shipload of immigrants." It must have been well after 2:00 A.M. when the bus got them to Spoleto and they were taken off to the various private homes where they were to be billeted. Lida Gialoretti, Menotti's assistant in charge of housing, had to reassure one woman, who finally opened her door, took one look at the very beautiful young John Jones, and shut it again, crying out that she was afraid. She had never seen a black man before, and no one had prepared the festival staff for such a possibility. However, the Spoletini quickly fell in love with all the young Americans, especially after the first performance.

The whole Ballets: U.S.A. (BUSA) experience was a new one for many

---

* Wilma Curley, Patricia Dunn, Sondra Lee, Gwen Lewis, Erin Martin, Barbara Milberg, Beryl Towbin, Joan Van Orden, Tom Abbott, Bob Bakanic, Todd Bolender, John Jones, John Mandia, James Moore, Jay Norman, James White. Lee injured herself severely and had to drop out.

of the dancers and for Robbins as well. The first morning, they met in the Piazza del Duomo, near the top of the hill. At one end was the thirteenth-century cathedral, the vault above its altar resplendent with Fra Filippo Lippi's immense fresco of scenes from the life of the Virgin Mary; opposite the cathedral, a stone stairway that Robbins later described as "[draping] like a swag down into the piazza. There is something exhilarating about its sweeping descent, [which] broadens & eases as it arrives at the square." Everything was enthralling: the narrow, ancient streets, the view of the valley and the Apennines, the outdoor cafés within walking distance of the huge rehearsal hall above the elegant opera house, or the gym of a nearby convent, where the dances were hammered into shape. The place seethed with celebrity artists: Samuel Barber (he was on the board of advisers, along with Lincoln Kirstein); Alexander Calder, supervising the mobile he had designed for Butler's *The Glory Folk;* Ben Shahn creating the back-drops for *New York Export: Opus Jazz*. Saul Steinberg designed a witty new frontcloth for *The Concert,* depicting an audience at the Melisso. At the restaurant Pentagramma, where the festival elite regularly lunched, they were served by its owners, one a daughter of Arturo Toscanini, the other the widow of Guido Cantelli. For some company members, this was the first time they'd found boxes full of ballet slippers made to their size wait-ing for them. Romances blossomed, and everyone reveled in working to-gether in a ravishing environment for nearly two months.

⌐

In 1961, two years after Ballets: U.S.A. toured Europe and was visiting England again, the London *Observer* likened *New York Export: Opus Jazz* to a "hurricane . . . sweeping over Europe to leave a holocaust of broken *brisés* and bent arabesques in its wake." Spoleto was the first to feel that force, and the reaction was equally extravagant. In 1958, no one in Europe had seen a ballet with movement that was contemporary in quite this way—respectful of form, obstreperous in content. A triumph of astute theatricality.

The disaffected young people of *New York Export: Opus Jazz* might have migrated from *West Side Story.* The ballet is to the musical as Robbins's *Interplay* is to his *Fancy Free.* In making *Interplay,* Robbins abstracted the behavior of *Fancy Free*'s boisterous sailors and girls into a classical ballet with jazz elements that celebrated youthful verve, friskiness, competition, and budding romance. *New York Export: Opus Jazz,* despite elements of a mean-streets narrative akin to that of *West Side Story,* is, like *Interplay,* a suite of dances, formally constructed to give the impression of spontaneity, even of improvisation. Almost all the movement is rooted in the vernacular, as is Prince's music. The orchestra, under its thirty-two-year-old conductor, Werner Torkanowsky, was augmented by four jazz musicians.

Robbins was not the only choreographer of the 1950s who was dealing with the alienated young people of the day. In the spring of 1958, Juilliard Dance Theatre—then a semiprofessional company directed by modern dance pioneer Doris Humphrey—premiered a work by Anna Sokolow called *Session 58* to a jazz score by Teo Macero. It's possible that Robbins saw it; not only was Sokolow a friend and admired colleague, but Humphrey had been trying to get him to choreograph a work for the company since the group had been formed in 1954. The title of the influential book *The Lonely Crowd,* by David Riesman, Nathan Glazer, and Reuel Denney, might have applied to any number of Sokolow's works, including her 1956 masterwork *Rooms.* Although her dancers flocked together, they often seemed mired in private but explosive misery; potential lovers averted their faces or threw their heads back even as they reached out to each other. *Session 58* began with the dancers at the back of the stage. Suddenly they all raced forward, stopped dead at the edge of the pit, as if some hostile force were emanating from the audience, then backed up slowly, staring.

Robbins used a similar belligerence at the beginning of *Opus Jazz,* and one can also posit an homage to Sokolow in two later works he made for Ballets: U.S.A.: *Moves* (1959) and *Events* (1961). The first of Ben Shahn's five backdrops for *Opus Jazz* suggests wires or television antennas against a pale sky. The dancers saunter onstage, giving the spectators long stares before clustering at the back and swaying from side to side. Like the gang members of *West Side Story,* these kids draw confidence from being together. Their movements, building on the forms and style of social dance, are jazz-infused but joyless. They snap their fingers and crouch over to strut, holding their hands in front of them like paws. Occasionally, they throw both arms straight up or cock a hip. Traditional patterns—couples facing each other in a line, semicircles, chains—unroll via "cool," into-the-floor steps. In the third section, "Improvisations," Robbins creates the illusion of a jam session by having those not dancing hang around watching, clapping to egg on their friends. Three guys do show-off moves—squats, spins on their knees; one does a satiric little "bump" as he leaves.

The elegantly composed last section is just what its title says, "Theme, Variations, and Fugue." One dancer begins with simple, deliberate moves to Prince's ABCs-elementary theme. Reach a foot to the side, return it. Repeat to the other side. Step back, return the foot. Step forward, etc. Speed it up. As the compact variations develop, Prince adds instruments and Robbins accumulates dancers—now a couple performs, then three women, now five men. Three couples break into a Lindy step, eight burst from a Texas Star pattern, and the men turn their partners like rambunctious musicians spinning bass viols. Then, from a clump, they all erupt again, singly or in small groups, into the fugue, until all of them are going at once, following their separate strands, which—true to fugal practice—shorten here and lengthen there until everyone's together again.

The second and fourth sections introduce darker elements. In "Statics," three wary, aggressive men dance to percussion alone, as if they indeed had rockets in their pockets. When a woman (Patricia Dunn) walks in, they hurl themselves randily about on the floor and watch. She's dreamily alluring, aware of their interest. One of them pulls her into a rough sexual duet that turns the others on. When she gets up, they're ready for her— five of them now—but she's still composed, not prepared for what happens. Eventually, they spin her from one man to another and hurl her offstage. Given the stylized New York skyline effect of Shahn's backdrop, it looks as if they're throwing her off the roof, but the dancers don't believe that Robbins intended to give that impression; after gang-raping her, they just toss her roughly away, in BUSA dancer James Moore's words, "like she was a piece of garbage." "Passage for Two" was originally performed by a black man and a white woman (Jones and Wilma Curley), and that casting subtly emphasized the discomforts and tensions that would plague an interracial relationship in the fifties. The two size each other up and edge into a pas de deux in which sensuality and wariness merge. When, kneeling, he slides his face up her body, she arches in response. But they rarely look at each other, and sometimes it seems as if they're trying—and failing—to fit their bodies together. Toward the end, she wraps one leg backward around him and grabs her foot, ensnaring him; the snare alters as he lifts her to his shoulder, but he remains within it until she reclines precariously (no hands) at a slant on his back. They exit in opposite directions.

The New York Times's music critic Howard Taubman's review from Spoleto was titled "Ballet: Rousing Success." Here was a company that truly represented America. Why not export it and show the Russians a thing or two? Within days, Robbins heard from Leland Hayward (or "Haywire," as he occasionally signed his cables to Robbins). The producer wanted to present BUSA on Broadway. And how about a one-hour television special? He'd already met with William Paley, head of CBS.

After performing at the Brussels Fair, at the Maggio Festival in Florence, and in Trieste, BUSA opened at the Alvin Theatre in Manhattan. Works by Robbins were simultaneously on view in four other theaters: New York City Ballet was performing at City Center and Ballet Theatre at the Met; *Bells Are Ringing* and *West Side Story* were running on Broadway. Perhaps in order to have an all-Robbins repertory, Jerry dropped Bolender's ballet and concocted a new curtain raiser, *3 x 3,* to music by Georges Auric. *Variety* called it a "delightful improvisation to the now whimsical, now plaintive accompaniment of a wind trio." It was not just the sound of the music that was whimsical; the bassoonist, oboist, and clarinetist wore very long tail coats with outsized top hats and sat on stepladders. A rehearsal excerpt shown in a film prepared by the United States Information Agency prior to the company's 1959 European engagements reveals little that looks improvisatory. Three women in pointe shoes scamper and skip in close formation, while the choreography plays rhythmic games with six-count measures: 1-2-3-4-5-6 versus 1-2-3-4-5-6. Three men replace them with the same rhythms and similarly perky steps. Robert Sabin of *Musical America* gave *3 x 3* grudging praise by comparing it to a work by the French choreographer Roland Petit (whose company had appeared in New York in April) that he had *really* hated: "[*3 x 3*'s] attempted French chic, brittle cuteness and thinness of texture is a masterpiece compared to Mr. Petit's 'Contre-Pointe.' " John Martin disliked the ballet, and in fact, Robbins wasn't satisfied with it either.

Martin also found fault with the casting of *Afternoon of a Faun* (Jay Norman and Wilma Curley). However, he loved *The Concert* (with Maria Karnilova appearing in Le Clercq's role for the Alvin season) and *New York Export: Opus Jazz.* As did everyone. Opening-night telegrams took BUSA's success for granted. "YOU ARE HEREBY NOTIFIED THAT YOU ARE BEING INVESTIGATED FOR MONOPOLY OF CHOREOGRAPHIC SUCCESS," wired dancer-choreographer Paul Godkin. *West Side Story*'s Chita Rivera and Tony Mordente teased the young cast: "NOW DON'T BE NERVOUS. ITS ONLY THE BIGGEST OPENING OF YOUR CAREER NOTHING TO BE ALARMED ABOUT." Jule Styne sent the following ebullient message as one Jewish male to another:

YOU MURDERED THEM IN SPALETTO [*sic*]

AND IN GOOD OLD BRUSSELS TOO.

THEY WILL BE CHEERING YOU FROM THE GHETTO

BECAUSE YOU ARE THE DANCING JEW.

GOOD LUCK AND LOVE . . .

Lincoln Kirstein was already hungering for *Opus Jazz*. He'd seen it in rehearsal in Spoleto and praised it lavishly: "[N]o one but you has understood Jazz so well in its flexibility and no one has had the gift to make it so interesting." The opening-night wire signed "George and Lincoln" said, "BEST WISHES FOR THE MOST BRILLIANT SUCCESS AND WE ONLY HOPE THAT WE WILL BE THE RESIDUAL FRAME FOR YOUR MASTERPIECES."

Despite the acclaim, the U.S. tour didn't last as long as had been hoped; there hadn't been sufficient time to publicize it. It did, however, recoup the cost of the New York season. In June 1959, Robbins again took BUSA to Spoleto and then shepherded it on a tour of sixteen European countries*—playing international festivals in seven of these. The reviews touting the company as a perfect cultural export had reached the U.S. government. This time, the troupe of twenty dancers,† two conductors, six musicians, and a staff of four was presented by Leland Hayward in association with the International Cultural Program of the United States, administered by ANTA. The program had already had excellent success with the José Limón Company's tour of South America in 1954 and the Martha Graham Company's Asian tour of 1956. The imprimatur, however, didn't mean that the State Department and the President's Emergency Fund paid all the bills. Barbara Horgan (then an assistant to Betty Cage at the New York City Ballet), who had been loaned to Robbins for the summer, mentioned in a letter to Jerry the likelihood that he would get the $50,000 he needed from ANTA (the net cost of the tour turned out to be $248,000). The United States Information Agency, and American embassies in the countries visited, were expected to run interference, play host, and inform the local press—functions they did not always perform

---

* In addition to Spoleto, BUSA performed in the following cities: Paris, Tel Aviv, Istanbul, Salzburg, Belgrade, Dubrovnik, Athens, Edinburgh, London, Copenhagen, Stockholm, West Berlin, Warsaw, Barcelona, Madrid, Lisbon, Monte Carlo, and Reykjavík.
† Tom Abbott, Bob Bakanic, Jamie Bauer, Muriel Bentley, Wilma Curley, Patricia Dunn, Lawrence Gradus, John Jones, Gwen Lewis, Erin Martin, Jane Mason, Michael Maule, Christine Mayer, Barbara Milberg, James Moore, Jay Norman, Bill Reilly, Douglas Spingler, Beryl Towbin, and James White.

Both photographs courtesy of Sonia Robbins Cullinen

Jerry's sister: "Little Sonia," the dancer.

Jerry's grandfather with his daughter Chana Merel, her husband, Motke Stein, and their children, Yosef Yitzhak and Sara Frime. The woman on the left is Alice Rabinowitz, the wife of Jerry's uncle Julius.

Courtesy of Jackye Lee Madura

Jerry's grandmother, Ida Cooper Rips, and her daughters. Left to right, youngest to eldest: Frances, Gertrude, Jean, Mary, Lena, Anna.

Jerry the modern dancer at Camp Kittatinny, ca. 1937.

Jerry holds back the crowd in Gluck Sandor's *El Amor Brujo*. At right: Sandor, Felicia Sorel, and, under duress, José Limón.

Straw Hat Revue (1939). From right to left: Alfred Drake, Albia Kavan, Ruthanna Boris, unidentified, Jerome Robbins, Dorothy Bird, unidentified.

Camp Tamiment, PA. 1939 "Snappy"

Hanging out on the Tamiment dock: left to right: Eddie Gilbert, Richard Reed, Fred Danieli, Anita Alvarez, Jerry, and Albia Kavan.

Robbins (1942) plays the Devil in Agnes de Mille's *Three Virgins and a Devil*.

Ballet Theatre dancers waiting at the train station in Mobile, Alabama, December 16, 1942. Left to right: Albia Kavan, Roszika Sabo, Anton Dolin, Adolf Bolm, Alicia Markova, John Taras, Sono Osato, Annabelle Lyon.

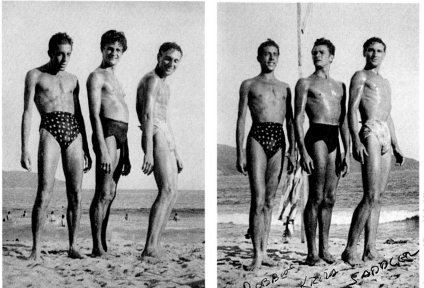

On the beach in Acapulco in 1941, Jerry, John Kriza, and Donald Saddler (sporting bathing suits they made themselves) mock the current "before and after" advertisements. Charles Payne snapped the pictures.

Hermes (Robbins) rebukes Paris (André Eglevsky) in David Lichine's *Helen of Troy* (1942).

Fred Fehl. Courtesy of the Jerome Robbins Foundation

Antony Tudor rehearsing Ballet Theatre dancers.

Sketches of *Fancy Free* sent by Jerry to Donald Saddler, who was stationed at an army base in Alaska.

A Coney Island outing: rear, left to right: Helen Gallagher, Donald Saddler, and Jackie Dodge; front: Arthur Partington, Ina Kurland, and Jerry.

Lisa Larsen, Graphic House/NYPL

Hero pursues sylph: Annabelle Lyon and Robbins in one vignette from his *Summer Day* (1947).

Eileen Darby, Graphic House/NYPL

The bathing beauties of *High Button Shoes* frolic by the sea.

New York Public Library

The choreographer of *Look Ma, I'm Dancin'!* and its star, Nancy Walker, crack up at a photo shoot.

George Balanchine, Tanaquil Le Clercq, and Nicholas Magallanes picnic outside a motel in Indiana during one of the New York City Ballet's tours (early 1950s).

Jerry confers with Leland Hayward and Irving Berlin during rehearsals or auditions for *Call Me Madam*.

The King and I's Eliza (Yuriko) flees Simon of Legree. Scene from the 20th Century Fox film.

Robbins rehearsing his *Interplay* in
Israel with Israeli dancers. From left:
Zohara Gil-Bar, Robbins, Moshe Lazra,
unknown, Yitzhak Mashiach, and Yona
Zilberman.

Buzz Miller in 1951.

Balanchine's Tyl Ulenspiegel
(Robbins) plays yet another
trick on the Duke and
Duchess (Frank Hobi and
Beatrice Tompkins.)

Judy Holliday and Sydney Chaplin making up for *Bells Are Ringing*.

The "Butterfly" Ballet in Robbins's *The Concert*, 1956. Center: Todd Bolender; right: Tanaquil Le Clercq.

Tanny Le Clercq on the roof of the Lenox Hill Hospital, spring 1958.

West Side Story codirectors Robbins and Robert Wise during the filming of the musical.

Ballets: U.S.A. in *New York Export: Opus Jazz* (Gwen Lewis, center).

Robbins's *Les Noces* with Erin Martin as the Bride.

Robert Maiorano and
Sara Leland in *The
Goldberg Variations*.

Watermill's hero (Edward
Villella) ponders his past.

Ringmaster Robbins
marshals his squads of
School of American
ballet students in *Circus
Polka* for the New York
City Ballet's Stravinsky
Festival.

Patricia
McBride and
Helgi Tomasson
in *Dybbuk*.

Aidan Mooney and Jerry at
play in the Tivoli Gardens,
Copenhagen, 1978.

Suzanne Farrell and Peter Martins in the "Fall" section of Robbins's *Four Seasons*.

Jerry and Jesse Gerstein at Water Mill, July 23, 1978.

Suzanne Farrell, lifted by Joseph Duell and Adam Lüders in the apotheosis of *In Memory of . . .*

Jerry looks at a book with Daniel Stern and his children Adrien (standing) and Alice. Taken at Robbins's house in Bridgehampton.

Sonia Robbins Cullinen and her brother at a gallery in Brattleboro, Vermont, that was exhibiting some of her artwork, September 1984.

Jean-Pierre Frohlich (left) and Robbins rehearse Alex Ketley, Seth Belliston, and Kristina Fernandez in *2 & 3 Part Inventions*, 1994.

Coaching a *Fiddler on the Roof* number from *Jerome Robbins' Broadway*. Behind Robbins: Christoph Cabellero. To Robbins's right: Elaine Wright, Joey McKneely (with fiddle), James Rivera, and, slightly behind him, Alexia Hess.

Martha Swope. Courtesy of the Jerome Robbins Foundation

Old colleagues get together to help reconstruct numbers for *Jerome Robbins' Broadway*. Left to right: Cris Alexander, Nancy Walker, Adolph Green, Betty Comden, Jerome Robbins.

with skill or grace. A USIA documentary film was sent around to introduce the company. It showed the choreographer leaving his house, lighting a cigarette, climbing into a taxi, and rehearsing his dancers, after which they performed the last section of *New York Export: Opus Jazz.* Leon Leonidoff agreed to act as impresario, as he did for the New York City Ballet's tours of Europe, despite ANTA strictures that limited his freedom to make bookings.

Those strictures proved to be as galling to Robbins as Broadway's compromises. The toppling of Wisconsin's Red-hunting senator, Joseph McCarthy, in the Army-McCarthy hearings of 1954 had not dispelled the nation's fear of communism as a creeping menace, and the government was determined to win the crucial worldwide popularity contest that the United States was waging with the Soviets. ANTA's Dance Panel in 1959 included many dance notables.* They were obligated to consider what companies and, indeed, what dances, might promote understanding and appreciation of American culture and, in some sense, to grapple with the impossible: How *might* such and such a country respond to such and such a ballet, to what degree might its people misunderstand a choreographer's ideas? Should they have been able, for instance, to predict that some Poles would be disturbed by *The Concert,* fearing that Robbins was making fun of Chopin, their national treasure? During the tour, while being lauded by the foreign press and public, Robbins received worried and admonishing letters from ANTA's general manager, Robert C. Schnitzer, written on the letterhead of the International Cultural Exchange Service of the American National Theatre and Academy. And Schnitzer must have become accustomed to bracing himself for the angry responses.

Most of the difficulties concerned a ballet that was supposed to be set to a commissioned score by Aaron Copland, perhaps the major "American" composer. As *New Yorker* critic David Denby has written of him,

> [H]e established what most people still think of as the very sound of American classical music. This new "American" sound was rangy, big-bodied, and clean-limbed—rarely sensuous. Its lyrical element emerged in the tender gravity of hymnal tunes. There are two inimitable Cop-

---

* Critics Ann Barzel, Margaret Lloyd, Walter Terry, Emily Coleman, John Rosenfeld, and Alfred Frankenstein; teacher-writer George Beiswanger; Hyman Faine, executive secretary of the American Guild of Musical Artists; Martha Hill, noted modern dance educator and the director of Juilliard's Dance Department; Lucia Chase; and Lincoln Kirstein.

land moods. One is a stomping, pounding exuberance in which, say, some threadbare cowboy song gets recharged with dance rhythms as complex and exciting as any that Stravinsky ever came up with; the other is elegiac and beautifully forlorn. His music, both rugged and touching, evokes the gathering strength of a newly powerful country—the open spaces and the metallic hardness of the industrial present—and also the isolation felt by people living on the plains or amid skyscrapers and empty streets.

Is it any wonder that all concerned were delighted to learn that Copland was writing music for Robbins?

The work, tentatively titled *Theatre Waltzes,* was to show off the company in "pure dance terms" using the ballet vocabulary. In a letter to Copland, Robbins hoped the piece would be "a declarative statement—open, positive, inventive, joyous (rather than introspective)." Although Jerry's scrawl to Aaron at the top of his notes asserts that "These are only ideas—and all can be thrown out if anything suggests something else. Feel <u>Free</u> [underlined twice]," he lists twenty-two possible waltzes, such as "Tea Room Waltz," "Ice Skating Waltz," "Cartoon Waltz," "Waltz for an Odd Number of People."

To ANTA's and the panel's dismay, Robbins decided not to proceed with the ballet.* Justifying himself after the fact, he reminded Robert Schnitzer that he hadn't received Copland's full score until the day before leaving for Europe. According to a later explanation of the genesis of *Moves,* Robbins wrote that Copland, in the midst of composing, had warned him that the music wasn't turning out exactly as either of them expected. He'd found the few pieces Copland played for him to be "a beautiful score, quite lyric and much more serious and difficult than I had expected. . . . Subsequently Aaron made me a tape of the music and on lis-

---

* The score, originally called *Music for J.R.* and finally titled *Dance Panels: Ballet in Seven Sections,* did honor Robbins's original waltz idea, although, according to Copland's biographer Howard Pollack, "Copland's highly stylized approach rarely evokes traditional waltzing, in part because syncopations and fermatas often obscure and halt the music's flow." The Bavarian State Opera tried to entice Robbins to choreograph it, but he declined, and the Opera's music director, Heinz Rosen, staged it to premiere on December 3, 1963. John Taras used the music for a narrative work, *Shadowed Ground,* which he choreographed for the New York City Ballet in 1965. It is difficult to understand Robbins's unwillingness to tackle the score. He admired Copland and had, in 1958, also considered doing a formal ballet to the composer's music for the film *The Red Pony.*

tening to it I realized that because of fatigue from my work on *Gypsy* [the musical had premiered on May 21, 1959] and the depth of his score, it would be foolhardy to attempt it if I rushed into rehearsal without assimilating the score. Meanwhile I had started to try some movements with the company (when I was in town for a day) to see if I could begin to grasp any of the mood of the Copland piece." James Moore has a memory of working briefly on steps that were in 3/4 time, and Erin Martin thinks that the company pianist Betty Walberg may even have played some of the music. However, she also recollects that a couple of days later, Jerry said, "Let's try something." She thinks "that it caught fire with him and he forgot about the waltzes." The "something" turned out to be working with no music at all, and he was intrigued with the way the movements looked when performed in silence. The ballet *Moves* was born.

Schnitzer predicted that the State Department would be very unhappy.

The company showed *Moves* at a run-through before leaving for Spoleto. Although Robbins acknowledged that it needed some cutting, it was enthusiastically received—even, apparently, by Copland, who came backstage: "[H]e said he felt *Moves* was exactly the kind of work we should show all over Europe because it's so different and provocative and controversial for a European audience." The panel disagreed and strongly advised that the ballet not be shown in certain countries—notably in Eastern Europe, Scandinavia, Spain, and Greece. Polled, the panel members suggested that *Interplay* be prepared as an alternate, in part because half the program was set to European music. Robbins had suggested this himself but then demurred because he felt *Interplay* was in some ways too similar to *New York Export: Opus Jazz.*

While the company enjoyed new sights and appreciative audiences, the letters and cables that crossed the Atlantic were frequently acrimonious. "Dear Jerry" kept telling "Dear Bob" how much *Moves* was appreciated, how the attaché in Dubrovnik had felt the public had been slighted because it didn't get to see the new work. Having roasted in Tel Aviv's summer with Erin Martin down with something, two dancers injured, and another, Jane Mason, giving notice, and having had to cope with a few more problems, Robbins whined and lashed out, "It is absolutely cruel and unthinking, and practically fascistic, for you to maneuver me into a position where you place the whole responsibility of the whole President's Touring Program onto my shoulders" (this letter he wisely decided not to send). Eventually Schnitzer, perhaps soothed by the glowing reports of the company, gave up and allowed Robbins to program the ballets as he saw fit; cordial relations were reestablished. The disputes show how extremely wary ANTA was on the government's behalf and the amount of second-guessing the panel felt was necessary.

Moves, remounted in 1970 for the Joffrey Ballet and later for the New York City Ballet and other companies, accomplishes for the viewer very much what it did for Robbins. He wrote that this intense scrutiny of dance on its own, without music, costumes, or scenery, "places the dancer's body under a magnifying glass. The relationships on stage are different in silence. Nothing is holding the dance or the emotion but the movements and their relationship to each other." The dancer's entrance is as confrontational as that in *Opus Jazz* but suggests no particular social sphere. They walk onto the stage in a line across the back, then turn, come forward, and look at the audience inscrutably. Their first strident gesture—thrusting their hands forward, palms out—softens as they melt into a slight bow. Without music, their moves—one man sliding a foot out, another relaxing and folding his arms, and so on—seem to come in response to one another. When one ducks and runs, hands seeming to brush something unpleasant from around her head, the others follow suit. The fact that they can't rely on music makes them seem preternaturally aware, listening for the sound of a footfall, sensing a stirring in the air, watching out of the corner of their eyes.

The ballet's striking duet has something of the same feeling as the duet in Balanchine's 1957 *Agon.* The man slowly manipulates the woman into cruelly uncomfortable positions, surveying the results of his molding and pondering the next move. The beginning is almost like a dark modern version of the moment in *Swan Lake,* Act II, when the Swan Queen sits folded over with one foot stretched out in front of her, and Prince Siegfried gently bends, takes her hands, and raises her onto one delicate pointe. Here, the woman is facedown on the floor; she lifts her bracing hands and, arched up in extreme tension, twists to look from side to side. After she has slid one leg around into a split, her partner pulls her into a sitting position and, brusquely but without rancor, folds her arms behind her and bends her head back. Seconds later, he presses down on her lifted palms, testing how far this one, now that one, will lower. Even after she stands, everything looks difficult, uncomfortable. Their rhythms become those of a sparring match, the two watching each other's steps, she hurling herself at him like a projectile; but in the end, he carries her off nestled in his arms like a child.

You can almost hear music during a men's quintet; their bold unison struts and jumps in place, as well as their athletic combats, beat out a rhythm. In contrast to their brisk, macho display, four women dream in a pool of light, sweetly helping one another into arabesques and making soft gestures that suggest they're pulling sounds out of one ear, then another; even when they strike out in space, weave a "London Bridge," or pose like pinup girls—one leg straight, the other coyly bent—they seem docile. The next movement contrasts partners supporting each other in slow, smooth balances (three pairs: man-woman, man-man, woman-woman, plus one extra woman) with various of them leaving one relationship to walk matter-of-factly into another or exit the stage. One person always does the sequence unsupported, while another, far away, partners air.

The last section reminds the audience that this is a community of dancers. It begins like a warm-up with one man stretching up, then bending over and bouncing to relax his muscles. The exercises escalate until what seem like hordes of dancers are bounding across the stage, flying into lifts. But they finish by reprising moments we've seen before, and, in a line again, they repeat their opening gestures, turn, and walk away into blackness.

When the company presented *Moves* in New York in 1961, John Martin said it was the Jets and Sharks gone "arty." But in Copenhagen, the critic of *Politiken* wrote, "It's like having lost one sense and having another sharpened." The work further formalized and, to a degree, balleticized the choreographer's vision of alienated young people.

Today's dance audiences may need to be reminded how innovative Ballets: U.S.A. seemed in its day, especially in Europe. In the end, the company garnered exactly the responses that ANTA and the State Department hoped for and justified its mission as an instrument of cultural diplomacy. Houses were packed. Belgrade added a Sunday matinee to the four performances already planned, and tickets sold out within an hour of the announcement. Julian Holland's review of the company's London opening, titled "The Greatest Thing in Ballet for Twenty Years," noted that "There was Dame Margot Fonteyn clapping her hands ten minutes after curtain fall," and suggested that the Foreign Office cancel the dancers' visas so they'd have to stay indefinitely. *Le Figaro* also mentioned the enthusiastic responses of Parisian theater and dance luminaries. The critic of Berlin's *Der Tagesspiegel* announced that

> None of the illustrious ensembles of the new world has loosened the ties to the classic tradition of Europe like this one and none has more unmistakably turned national mentality into movement. The nonchalance and, when it matters, the terse, unchangeable consciousness. The self-irony and the naturalness of taking possession of space.

The "tour analysis" that reported triumphs and difficulties country by country summed up BUSA's impact in words sure to delight U.S. government circles:

> There have been brilliant successes before and since—symphony orchestras, choral groups, jazz ensembles, other dance companies, and so on. But only "Ballets: USA" was hailed everywhere as something new, fresh, original, and inherently American, growing out of and depicting the vitality of American life and art, and more, acclaim for an American creative genius.

Robbins weathered the four-and-a-half-month tour and its preliminaries with unusual grace, agreeing to interviews and preparing statements about his creative process ("[I]t's like rolling a snowball down hill, not quite sure what kind of a figure you are going to have at the end of it or what kind of patterns you're going to leave behind you as you go along"). He went out on a limb with a program essay to prime audiences ("We in America dress, eat, think, talk and walk differently from any other people. We also dance differently"). As a goodwill gesture, he handed out boxes of tights and ballet slippers in Poland, Yugoslavia, and Israel. He waived his usual fees for the USIA film and agreed to let the Yugoslavian television station broadcast *Opus Jazz* so all those who couldn't get into the theater could see it. He delighted a state department official by arranging, while in Reykjavík, a scholarship at the School of American Ballet for a seventeen-year-old Icelandic dancer, Helgi Tomasson.

As usual, Robbins snarled at certain dancers when under rehearsal stress, while confessing to another, "You know, I have no control over it. . . . When I start working, my focus is so intent on what I want that everything else is an interference. Everything else is a bother, and I push it away. I don't see it. I lash out. I do. It's not good. I can't help it." Yet he fraternized with them as if he were their age instead of twenty years their senior. He invited his favorites to share his Spoleto quarters. While rehearsing in New York, he, Muriel Bentley, James Moore, and designer Bob Mackintosh formed the Alte Kocker Kosher Kasha Kard Klub, a Friday-night group to play poker or hearts that included occasional mystery guests such as Stephen Sondheim and Broadway lyricist Sheldon Harnick and expanded to games of hide-and-seek or Sardines (one of Jerry's favorites). And he was tremendously proud of "his" dancers. He refused to attend a press conference luncheon with just a few of them in Salzburg; all twenty must come, or none. To Leland Hayward, he praised, as well, lighting designer Nananne Porcher, pianist Betty Walberg, and Jeannot Cerrone, the company's manager ("a treasure, a diamond mine, and the Big Father of us all, and a wonderful person all put together. I have never seen anyone work so hard . . . even moving luggage.").

Robbins seems to have enjoyed himself tremendously, despite the hassles. He visited historic sites in Israel. He ran into Bernstein in Salzburg ("The kissing bandit was at his best," he wrote Fizdale). A small diary that he kept off and on has the following entry for Thursday, July 23: "Fabulous day at Speigle's [producer Sam Spiegel] yacht. 11:30 Pat [Dunn, of whom he was becoming enamored], Tom [Abbott], Betty [Walberg], Normans & Stones [Jay Norman and Gwen Lewis were married; so were Erin Martin and production stage manager Tom Stone]—off to Cap Ferrat—swam and waterskied—bravo! ate great meal on boat slept—swam, skied, sunned—off to Menton for dinner there then back around 12. Just beautiful the whole thing. Incredible life can be such a joyous thing with friends."

Fortitude was called for on many occasions. He cracked a rib in Belgrade. At the last minute before the company was to fly from Stockholm to West Berlin, a U.S. Embassy official in the latter city balked at the flight plan: The airplane was scheduled to land in Communist East Berlin; the company would have to pass through the Brandenburg Gate on foot to waiting buses, which seemed to "invite adverse propaganda." In the absence of any other offered plan, BUSA boarded. An embassy official in Copenhagen managed to have the plane land in Hamburg, where the company had to wait for eight hours, arriving in Berlin at 1:30 A.M. Another Cold War snafu developed around the trip to Warsaw.

En route from Athens to the Edinburgh Festival in stormy weather, the small plane carrying BUSA's scenery, costumes, and some of the company members' personal effects went down some fifty yards off the Italian coast, with no loss of life. Everyone rose to the occasion, including friends in the London company of *West Side Story*. ANTA came up with financial support. The dancers and others foraged in Edinburgh department stores for substitute clothes, practice wear, ballet slippers, and sneakers that could, in a pinch, cover the repertory (*Afternoon of a Faun, New York Export: Opus Jazz, Moves,* and *The Concert*). The New York City Ballet sent its *Faun* set.

Robbins, at his charming best, made a curtain speech when the company opened at the Edinburgh Festival, describing what the audience *would* have seen had all the proper costumes, scenery, and props been there. Then he and some of the crew went down to London, the next tour stop. Ben Shahn flew over from New York, and in the week before the company was due to open in Covent Garden, the scene shop there reproduced his drops for *Opus Jazz*.

"The dancers themselves were magnificent," Robbins wrote Bob Schnitzer. "All of them went to work, made hats, painted butterfly wings, sewed snaps, cut costumes, put in elastics, and you would have been very proud of their not only rising to the situation, but, in Edinburgh, [they] actually surpassed themselves dancing like they've never danced before." He couldn't resist emphasizing for the State Department's benefit: "We were all very proud of being Americans, I can assure you." He had lost his luggage in the crash too. In London, Jenny Nicholson Cross, Robert Graves's daughter, who was one of the Spoleto Festival's two press representatives, bought him shoes and socks (and caviar). After BUSA had gone on to Copenhagen, Tony Mordente, in London with *West Side Story*, flew over bearing trousers.

The dancers' resourcefulness certainly did them no harm in the eyes of the press. One Edinburgh critic raved that "Jerome Robbins' Ballets: U.S.A. is tremendous; it lives, it works, it's about them, it's about you, it's about dancing, it's about music, it's one of the three most important ballet companies to visit Britain in thirty years."

Ed Sullivan and Robbins seemed to have established amicable professional relations in the years since Sullivan had exhorted the House Committee on Un-American Activities to summon Robbins to testify. Obviously he approved of Robbins's performance as a friendly witness. The Broadway Jets had performed "Cool" on *The Ed Sullivan Show* in 1958. On November 29, 1959, after BUSA's triumphant tour, Sullivan presented the company in excerpts from *The Concert,* fulsomely inviting Jerry to stand up from his seat amid the studio audience and be applauded.

⌒

Robbins's professional life was marked by the impetuous way in which he would express interest in a project and then pull back. This extended to his private life. He loved to be needed but sometimes regretted offering help. During BUSA's week in Brussels, he composed an extraordinary letter to Robert Fizdale. Fizdale's relationship with the designer Arthur Weinstein had just foundered, and the pianist was desolate. Jerry poured out sympathy and wondered tentatively if he and Fizdale might forge a closer relationship and whether doing so might imperil their friendship, whether the "Arthur G. [Gold] thing"* would work out, and whether Fizdale could stand Jerry's personality over time ("God knows I'm a lot to handle, but I feel you'd bring out the best in me"). "You mustn't worry about me or this letter," he went on, "I mean if you weren't absolutely honest in your heart & reply we wouldn't be as strong friends as we are now. What I mean to say is that I love you very much, that if this does or does not happen will not change my feelings toward you because I don't think I could ever feel rejected by you. I guess I really love you so much with a deep deep friendship that the move to become lovers is a little step—& that if it did not happen would not change the base and strength of my feelings for you."

He worried over the letter the minute he'd composed it and the next day added a note explaining that he had made the gesture because of his love for Bobby and distress at his suffering. But, he said, he hadn't thought out "the consequences or actualities." Was he withdrawing the offer? Did he send either letter?

In 1959, he responded to another friend's need, and this time he didn't go back on a spontaneously generous offer. The marriage of Leland and Slim Hayward—two people he loved very much—was breaking up. He thought of them as "practically my foster parents." Slim was the needier,

---

* Fizdale and Gold shared an apartment and a career, but although they had been lovers beginning in their student days at Juilliard, at this time both had other affairs. The complexity of the relationship Robbins refers to is revealed in a letter he wrote to Tanaquil Le Clercq on October 8, 1956. He had gone up to Snedens Landing to have dinner with "Bobby and the Arthurs. . . . Arthur Weinstein is being very successful, Bobby's skin is more transparent than ever and Arthur Gold is once more alone."

the one being left. Robbins cabled her to come to Spoleto. "I have to work all the time," he told her, ". . . but you can be in the theater, eat every meal with me, and never leave my side. If that's what you want to do." She came. In her autobiography, Slim—by then Nancy, Lady Keith—wrote that

> That was just the beginning of his kindness. Once Jerry had finished his work in Spoleto we rented a car and drove all over northern Italy. We stayed in funny, small hotels, stopped at quaint restaurants, looked at beautiful things. We were on a safari to track down every Piero della Francesca we could find, and we saw quite a few of them. The trip was a great comfort, as if the world had reached out to put its arms around me.

Perhaps it was during this excursion that Robbins's fascination with the Italian Renaissance painter Piero della Francesca began. "He's so cool—so objective—he's like Balanchine," he wrote years later. Like the ideal Balanchine dancer, whom the master likened to angels, the ravishing heavenly celebrants in Piero's nativities do not comment on the message they deliver or the joyous event they praise. It was, in part, the wealth of Quattrocento art that kept drawing Jerry back to Italy.

Robbins's commitment to Ballets: U.S.A. remained strong, despite obstacles. Menotti asked him to be the festival's artistic director for dance for the summer of 1960, although a letter from Robbins to Richard Buckle indicates that Menotti did *not* invite the company. In any case, Robbins, adroit as he was at juggling jobs, couldn't have managed both a Spoleto season and the filming of *West Side Story*. And, while he was busy with the movie, he received news from ANTA's Robert Schnitzer that State Department sponsorship for a 1961 tour was not possible. The powers in government wanted to "balance the program," feeling that orchestras and dance companies had received the "lion's share" of the overseas assignments and that the focus for the next two years should be on dramas and musical comedies.

Enter Rebekah Harkness, the widow of Standard Oil Corporation heir and philanthropist William Hale Harkness, whose death had left her a multimillionaire. At first it seemed as if this ballet-struck Lady Bountiful wanted to corral Robbins to head the "American Ballet Company of Monaco," which she proposed to establish in December 1961. Instead, she was persuaded to sponsor BUSA in its 1961 Spoleto appearances and subsequent European tour. Robbins, while agonizing over the editing of the *West Side Story* film, planned a company of twenty-four, trying to reassemble his dancers and inviting others to audition. A dozen BUSA veterans signed on. Among the newcomers were Glen Tetley (as a guest artist), Scott Douglas, Veronika Mlakar, Richard Gain, Susan Borree and Francia Russell of the New York City Ballet, NYCB apprentice Kay Mazzo, and, fresh from the *West Side Story* movie, Edward Verso.

For what was to be the final season of Ballets: U.S.A., Robbins mounted *Interplay, Afternoon of a Faun* (most often featuring John Jones and the delicate fifteen-year-old Mazzo), and *The Cage* (Mlakar and Martin shared the role of the Novice). The new work was *Events*—another look at an alienated society, with a score by Robert Prince, which, Robbins wrote Nora Kaye, was "just the end . . . more of one piece than the first score and much more weird twelve toneish full of all new kinds of sounds and dynamic theatrical sections."

Some spectators thought they had detected an allusion to the atomic bomb in *New York Export: Opus Jazz,* perhaps at the end of the first section when the clustered dancers all look skyward and then tumble down. The reference was even stronger in *Events*. This is not surprising. Between 1958 and 1961, relations between the Soviet Union and the United States underwent a series of tensions and crises—over the status of Berlin, over Fidel Castro's takeover of Cuba (which came to a head in the Bay of Pigs episode in the spring of 1961), over what appeared to be the Soviets' considerable lead in missile capability.* Concerns about the threat of imminent thermonuclear war were escalating, and Soviet rockets could carry large bombs. In *Events,* which Robbins conceived in eight flowing-together sections, he approached several kinds of fallout. His rough notes for himself speak of a society both numbed by crises and waiting for the next one to strike:

> The fall out (non-radioactive) that we are subjected to seems to be quite subjective and not connected directly or consciously to any nuclear explosions (testings). A deep and pervading radiation seems to be abroad—the subjecting of humans to day to day living crammed full of

---

* The "missile gap," widely believed to be true at this time, later proved an illusion. John F. Kennedy declined to investigate it too carefully when he was running for the presidency against Richard Nixon, since it supported his campaign theme: that the Republicans had allowed the United States to fall behind Soviet Russia in the development of long-range missiles.

an immoral fallout that is subtly . . . and penetratingly changing our views and acceptance of an unstable teetering world.

Four dancers stood out. Something about the relationship of these protagonists to the group evokes memories of the four protagonists of Robbins's 1951 *Age of Anxiety.* They seem to be participants and leaders, as well as wandering observers in a society at risk. The crowd's bouts of fevered gaiety and panic and its brief worshiping of an inappropriate god also recall the earlier ballet. Shahn's backdrop for the first section suggests a stylized array of buildings. In a silent, hard-to-see black-and-white record film of *Events* (with most of the performers in rehearsal attire), Patricia Dunn, Glen Tetley, Edward Verso, and Richard Gain slump on a haphazardly placed group of chairs, from which they erupt in nervous, jagged spurts, then relax again. Everything they do looks edgy, cautious. Verso seems to sense danger from above. Others join them in a version of the Twist that is so somnambulistic as to be barely recognizable. At one point, Dunn stretches and preens in a disaffected way, arms clasped overhead. A man seated at her feet suddenly snaps his legs around hers like pincers. She seems oblivious. As he scrabbles about her, she wipes her cheek, strokes her neck, lifts her arms again.

Two of the episodes tell dark tales. In one, Tetley very explicitly seduces the younger Verso. The boy is restless, clearly an innocent. The man wanders in. At first they communicate in looks and gestures, but then Tetley walks Verso into a series of sexually charged negotiations that also, symbolically perhaps, suggest lessons in flying—pulling one of Verso's arms and one foot up backward, forcing him to arch until his foot almost touches his head; lifting him; tipping him upside down; finally laying him on his belly, taking his hand, and running in a circle to make him spin. When Tetley leaves, Verso makes a gesture that looks angry or disgusted, knocks a couple of chairs over, and sprawls across two others. In his notes, Robbins titled this part "A Walk in the Air." (Erin Martin also learned Verso's part. Perhaps Robbins was uncertain how audiences would respond to a male pas de deux; perhaps he was experimenting with onstage gender roles for his own edification.) The next section he called "An Entertainment," and there's little doubt that he intended a statement about racism by casting John Jones as one separate from the others. The goings-on prefigure the emergence of "radical chic," whose beginning was officially marked by Leonard and Felicia Bernstein's 1970 party in support of the Black Panthers. The crowd admires Jones, mocks him, butters him up, and, finally, forgets him. When he dances, fast and wild and showy, the others, flanking him, stare and imitate. At one point two men grab him and bat him back and forth between them, as if he were some kind of toy. While he dances with a woman, they clap his rhythms, beat on pretend drums. As if playing the savage he thinks they think he is, he pretends to devour his partner. They attack, then stroke him. He scatters them by swinging a chair and letting it go. He's carried off like a champion in a rhythmically clapping procession, but as they exit, he gradually slips off backward and slides to the floor. Only the four notice and stop. He gets up, walks slowly away, and then aims at them a jitter of gestures with an angrily ironic Uncle-Tom edge.

In another scene, a woman (Kay Mazzo) is lifted high; people swing in on crutches, dropping them as if in the hope of a miracle cure by this temporary goddess, then dragging them away, little better than before. At the very end, a curtain billows down and the atmosphere becomes more frantic. People cluster, then break apart, race about, leap, and fall quivering. Some sit on the chairs and twitch, some stand limply. The curtain rises again. Fragments from the earlier sections recur like passing memories. Near the end, a man runs in, slips, falls, and wriggles, and Shahn's large cutout of a torso with a bent arm and fist descends on him from above.

(Shahn was not happy with the "falling man" and offered to redesign it for free but wrote that he was "pleased and profoundly moved by the entire work. I am wholly convinced that you have extended the scope of ballet as an art form, and I am happy to have played some part in that realization.")

Walter Terry noted in the *Herald Tribune* the resemblance between *Events* and *Age of Anxiety* and posited "a quest to find something, bad or good, in a world of uncertainty." But this foursome is not a group brought together by chance embarking on a search for truth; these comrades—if that's what they are—are themselves stalkers and victims in a world dominated by fear. And the choreographer leaves us in no doubt as to what terrifies them. Richard Buckle wrote in London's *Sunday Times* that "The bomb which was threatening in *Opus Jazz* falls at last, and we think, christmas, Robbins has the bomb like some choreographers have gypsies." *Events* was flawed, but no one could deny its flashes of brilliance. When the company opened in New York that fall with two different programs, Terry spoke of "many marvelous and pertinent and even powerful episodes" but thought that "the final impression also includes a realization that things seemed a bit forced and that a jazz dance vocabulary was pushed beyond its inherent assets." Despite his remark about Gypsies, Buckle—who saw the ballet both in Spoleto, before some set pieces were eliminated, and in London—praised it: "The choreography as a whole is so finely wrought, fitting so loosely in the brash and thrilling post-jazz score of Robert Prince, and certain episodes shine out with such poetic intensity, and there is so much drama and invention in it that the ballet is a kind of landmark."

Robbins may have come to think of *Events* as too literally linked to nuclear disaster. Of the three major works he made for Ballets: U.S.A., it has never been revived, and on May 19, 1962, at Madison Square Garden, as part of a birthday salute to John F. Kennedy, Ballets: U.S.A. made its final appearance.

14

Everything's Coming Up Roses?

Gypsy's star and its director:
Ethel Merman and Jerome Robbins.
NYPL.

M ention the original production of *Gypsy* to anyone who saw it, and their eyes light up. "The best damn musical I've seen in years," raved Walter Kerr in the *Herald Tribune*. *The Sound of Music* may have trounced *Gypsy* in the 1960 Tony awards even more drastically than *The Music Man* had triumphed over *West Side Story* two years earlier, but the book of *Gypsy,* by Arthur Laurents, was certainly one of the finest ever written for a musical. The show boasted lyrics by Stephen Sondheim and a score by Jule Styne (orchestrations by Sid Ramin with Robert Ginzler, dance music by John Kander, with additional music by Betty Walberg). In the ads and the program, Robbins's name appeared in a box: "Entire production directed and choreographed by Jerome Robbins."

The lust for credit that prompted his insistence on the box may have been increased by the fact that—because of his preoccupation with Ballets: U.S.A. during the summer and early fall of 1958 and then his labors in England on *West Side Story* prior to the opening of the London production—he didn't participate in the early stages of the show's creation or have as much control over the result as he usually craved. However, he most certainly had a hand in turning *Gypsy* into the beautifully integrated construction it was. Gerald Freedman, assisting him again, compared the musical to "the Queen Mary coming in for docking . . . just this immense, perfect machine." Lighting up its deck: Ethel Merman in the prime role of her career as the monstrous and unstoppable Rose who's bent on making her daughters stars on the vaudeville circuit—blind to their desires and unwilling to believe that vaudeville is dying.

In his autobiography, Laurents lays out the show's genesis smartly, if not with absolute accuracy: *"Gypsy* had two producers: David Merrick and Leland Hayward. . . . [Merrick] owned the rights to Gypsy Rose Lee's imaginative autobiography; Hayward was an agent turned producer who owned the rights to Jerry Robbins. Both he and Merrick wanted Jerry to choreograph but Jerry wouldn't do either unless I wrote the book." And though Laurents had been leery of turning *Gypsy: A Memoir* into a musical, he became more interested when he discovered that domineering mother Rose had been even less like her scented name than he had realized. The mother-daughter lesbian cocktail parties and Rose's possible murder of a recalcitrant chorine never made it into the show but helped flesh out a character that Keith Garebian, author of *The Making of Gypsy*, identifies as "seething with volcano-force anomalies . . . crazy yet funny, pitiable and savage, sinner and sinned-against." Merman hesitated not a moment in accepting the part. It might have been written for her muscular, brassy delivery, her powerful voice and biting diction. Rose was a primal force, a tidal wave; onstage, so was Merman. But the character was not

written as a one-dimensional killer mom, and Merman trusted Robbins to help her bring out what was needed.

In June 1958, Robbins was in Spoleto. Hayward advised him of developments via cable. Sondheim, recommended by Laurents, was again thwarted from writing both music and lyrics:

> ETHEL MERRICK ARTHUR MYSELF AUDITIONED STEVES STUFF
> TODAY WITH HIM SHE IS MAD ABOUT HIS LYRICS BUT WORRIED
> ABOUT MUSIC PARTICULARLY AS YOU KNOW BECAUSE OF HAPPY
> HUNTING EXPERIENCE UNKNOWN COMPOSER* IN MEANTIME
> JULE STYNE BACK HAS ABANDONED COMDEN GREEN SHOW AND
> HAPPY BIRTHDAY HYSTERICAL ABOUT GYPSY HAS NO OTHER
> COMMITTMENTS AND WILLING WORK WITH STEVE MERRICK
> MERMAN ARTHUR MYSELF VERY AGREEABLE THIS IDEA AND AM
> ASKING IF HE IS WILLING CABLE YOUR OPINION AND APPROVAL.

Sondheim's mentor, Oscar Hammerstein II, urged him to take the job, as he had with *West Side Story*—this time because writing for a star like Merman would be a valuable experience.

In one way, Gypsy was a less ambitious show than *West Side Story.* Its writers had no illusions that they were breaking ground in creating a new form of musical theater. On the other hand, they were building on the now-established notion that a musical could have the power of serious drama, that the songs and dances could deepen it rather than decorate it. The showbiz ambiance, a satisfying and familiar one in musicals, could justify as many numbers as needed. Yet in the sleazy hotel rooms, grimy dressing rooms, stage-door alleys, and vaudeville theaters that Jo Mielziner so sensitively designed, a psychologically rich story could develop. Illuminated by Robbins's direction, it developed on the run, in tune with Rose's hectic pursuit of her dream and structured like a vaudeville show, with short scenes punctuated by blackouts and announced by signs

---

* In *Happy Hunting,* which opened in December 1956 and closed shortly thereafter, Lindsay and Crouse had written a role for Merman that fell somewhere between Mrs. Sally Adams of their *Call Me Madam* and *Gypsy*'s Madame Rose: a nouveau-riche Boston matron so enraged by Grace Kelly's failure to invite her to her wedding to Prince Rainier of Monaco that she decides to nab a titled husband for her reluctant daughter. The inexperienced songwriters, Matt Dubey and Harold Karr, failed to provide Merman with strong material.

framed in lightbulbs. When Rose and her daughters hitchhiked across the country—along the way kidnapping likely little boys for the act Rose was concocting—signs with the names of cities were hand carried across the stage to mark their progress. In one brilliant moment, the child performers of "Baby June and Her Newsboys" were replaced on the move by their teenage counterparts in the dimly flickering light of a lobsterscope—all in profile, doing the trudging step known as "trenches"—with one cast magically replacing the other in the same awful Stars-and-Stripes finale before a blackout excised them both.

Robbins, as one might expect, wanted to bring vaudeville and burlesque to life in all their tawdry colors. He searched the memories of an old vaudevillian, Jack Haskell (who later sued, unsuccessfully, for credit and money). However, as the show developed, and especially in its fraught Philadelphia tryouts, during which David Merrick was sure they had a bomb on their hands, several big numbers disappeared, along with a couple of songs. Gone was the prologue meant to convey a panorama of the kinds of acts that toured the circuit. Gone were the jugglers and acrobats rehearsing in hotel corridors. Gone, too, the splashy holiday number to frame Gypsy's climactic strip, "Three Wishes for Christmas"; almost all that remained was a Christmas tree and a gift box for Gypsy to emerge from.* Robbins, nevertheless, succeeded in summing up burlesque in "You Gotta Have a Gimmick," a lesson for Gypsy by three hardened strippers, with Jerry's old friend Maria Karnilova (Tessie Tura) making an impressive debut as a singing, dancing actress. Tessie with her delusions of "artistic" dancing, Mazeppa with her trumpet, and Electra with her lights in strategic places (inspired by a real stripper who'd auditioned), all did the same tired bumps and grinds. And, abetted by Raoul Pène du Bois's costumes and Mielziner's scenery, Robbins made hilariously tacky kiddie numbers in which June—whether backed by newsboys or farmhands—changed costumes and reemerged to do her splits and twirl her batons dressed as Miss Liberty, while three of the boys paraded and did their specialties in uniforms of the armed forces, with her reluctant sister Louise (later Gypsy) costumed as Uncle Sam.

One of the most successful dance numbers was Jerry's tenderest: the unassuming and charming Astaire tribute, "All I Need Is the Girl," in

* When Arthur Laurents directed the London production starring Angela Lansbury, he replaced the Christmas number with "Salute to the Garden of Eden," which appears in the published book. Gypsy came out of an apple.

which Tulsa, one of the boys in Rose's act (now grown up and restless), sings and—describing the choreography as he goes—works out a tap number for himself, gradually drawing a smitten Louise into it.*

The power of *Gypsy*'s script and songs lies partly in the fact that Rose is utterly unaware of what drives her until the last moments of the show: she has been living through her daughters, especially "Baby June"—singing and dancing with her four "newsboys." Years later, June is still doing the same dreadful number, with adjustments, as "Dainty June and her Farmboys," and vaudeville is dying around her high-kicking young legs. When June elopes, Rose shoves Louise—long in her sister's shadow—into the spotlight, fronting a group of underaged bleached blondes in a "Spanish" take on her sister's routine. June had gone from childhood to young womanhood greeting her public with the same awkward spin, kick, and split, the same old "Let me entertain you." It's not until Louise—through a fluke seized on by Rose—embarks on a career in burlesque and becomes Gypsy Rose Lee, the connoisseur's stripper, or "ecdysiast," that her mother, in the show's sensational climax, "Rose's Turn," reveals an inner child greedy for center stage. Singing "Mama's lettin' go" in a bitter, brassy litany, she suddenly falters on her next "Mama" (Merman never quite got that right—she wasn't a falterer) as she realizes what has been happening all these years. Finally, with a bravura and a craving that's as heart-wrenching as it is horrifying, she launches herself into her final rant:

> Well, someone tell me, when is it my turn?
> Don't I get a dream for myself?
> Startin' now it's gonna be my turn!
> Gangway, world,
>   Get off of my runway!

* Robbins, initially unwilling to choreograph *Gypsy* as well as direct it, hoped that Danny Daniels would stage the numbers. Daniels was busy choreographing for television's *The Voice of Firestone,* but during a week or so when the show didn't require him, Daniels says he dropped in on *Gypsy* rehearsals and used his tap expertise (Jerry never did get much beyond the time step) to create material for Baby June's backup boys and "All I Need Is the Girl." "I didn't just do the tap choreography," he says of the latter, "I staged the whole number. The concept, of course, was Jerry's, and it was a great concept." Daniels wasn't paid, but "You know something? I didn't even think about it. I was working with Jerry. I was doing this fabulous show. I was making good dough, a weekly salary [on the television series]. The money didn't mean anything to me; what meant something to me was pleasing Jerry and to do a good piece of choreography." Daniels was indirectly recompensed. Leland Hayward dropped in on a rehearsal, liked what he saw, and invited him to choreograph "The Fabulous Fifties," a 1960 television special conceived as a follow-up to the Ford show, which Robbins had declined to do.

Startin' now I bat a thousand!
This time, boys, I'm takin' the bows and
Everything's coming up Rose—
Everything's coming up roses—
Everything's coming up roses
This time for me!

As Louise/Gypsy comes into her own and her mother's power dwindles, both realize that love is what they never got enough of and if it comes mainly from an audience's hungry gaze and warm applause, so be it.

Robbins had originally thought that "Rose's Turn" might be a nightmare ballet, in which fragments of numbers and images from her past would swirl around her and spark her realization that the need for fame had ruined her life. But he couldn't make it work. In a single session in the grubby rooftop theater of the New Amsterdam, Sondheim and Robbins roughed out the number as a song, with Sondheim doing musically what Robbins had planned to do with movement: collaging fragments of Styne's score. "It was," Sondheim remembered, "one of those things you dream of when you're a kid. You write a song with the star, only it was Jerry Robbins as the star. He started moving, performing a strip, sashaying back and forth on the stage, and I started to ad lib at the piano with the tunes that were already written." In the finished number, previously heard words and musical motifs, altered and distorted, whirl past as visual images had originally been supposed to do, contributing to the sense that Rose is falling apart.

As a director, Robbins worked sensitively and respectfully with Merman. He tried out his ideas with her understudy, Jane Romano, with Freedman standing in for Jack Klugman as Herbie (the mild and obliging man who takes on the management of Rose's kiddie act because he sees the good in her, finds her sexy, and is a born pushover). It is difficult to determine how much of her shattering performance was due to the script, how much to her own persona, and how much to Robbins's direction. Sondheim, while acknowledging that she was thrilling, thought it was the material performing for her: "Ethel's imagination and brain were not great but she was given material that fed into her, both Arthur's stuff and [Jule's and my] stuff; it fed into something she could do, low comedy and anger." Freedman took a different view, recalling to Jerry in 1993 that Merman's "commitment all during the rehearsal and tryout period seemed heroic to

me, and along with your guidance and her willingness to accept it, produced this overwhelming presence and performance."

The difficult decisions, the altercations, the angry confrontations that beset the putting together of *Gypsy* have been exhaustively discussed in Garebian's book about it; Laurents's autobiography, *Original Story;* Craig Zadan's *Sondheim & Co.;* Meryle Secrest's biography of Sondheim; and Greg Lawrence's of Robbins; as well as in a Dramatists Guild Symposium of 1981 (in which Robbins did not participate but parts of which he later refuted). Gypsy Rose Lee had cheerfully admitted that not all the colorful stories in her memoir were strictly true and made no trouble about Laurents's inventions (such as Herbie). The collaborators' principal hurdle was getting a release from June Havoc, the "Baby June" on whom Rose's ambitions had focused. Havoc was by then a successful actress, playing Titania in *A Midsummer Night's Dream* up in Stratford and not on the best terms with her sister. She put them off and insisted on a multitude of minor revisions in the script. Finally the producers and Laurents balked. For tryouts in Philadelphia, they cleverly altered the name from June to Claire. Havoc found being left out altogether more appalling than being misrepresented.

One backstage tale about Robbins is revealing. For whatever reasons, he was not pleased with Lane Bradbury's performance as June. When Bradbury failed repeatedly to handle some business with a teapot that he had made an unpleasant issue of, he went backstage during a performance and removed the batons she had to twirl during her number, forcing her to improvise. His colleagues were outraged, and when the show arrived in New York, Merrick needled him in his opening-night telegram: "DEAR JERRY, THANK YOU FOR A WONDERFUL SHOW. PLEASE LEAVE THE BATONS ON THE PROP TABLE TONIGHT. ALL GOOD LUCK."

One difficulty that plagued *Gypsy* centered on Louise/Gypsy's striptease, a moment the audience had been waiting for since the beginning of the show. For one thing, the producers were aware of the laws governing "obscenity, lewdness and immorality with respect to public performances." For another, although Gypsy had to be sexy, the real-life Gypsy Rose Lee, within the context of burlesque, had been a class act. During the tryouts, Laurents typed Jerry a note about the strip as it stood:

> We are all absolutely convinced that the moment Louise steps out of that dress, she is cheapened and vulgarized. The audience does not want

to see it. They want to see her tease, and love her when she does. But the movement is vulgar, the rolling up in the curtain is vulgar—terribly so—and the moment makes her cheap, common, ordinary—and hurts both Louise and Rose for the rest of the show. If you feel that she must be nude, please restrict to a flash when she is in the white furs. Perhaps if it [is] as though the furs slipped without her knowledge, and then she quickly pulls them back with a smile, it would be acceptable. . . . Please keep her a lady.

The strip ended by not fully satisfying anyone, including the audience, which worried Leland Hayward. Robbins left for Spoleto and Ballets: U.S.A.'s big tour very soon after *Gypsy* opened, and then, happy to be in a creative situation he alone controlled and working very hard, he had no wish to think about the damned strip or hear about Merman and Sandra Church feuding.

Hayward was busy producing Rodgers and Hammerstein's *The Sound of Music,* but his letters and cables followed Robbins around Europe. The show needed its director for a few days, he warned in August, suggesting that Jerry think of his royalties should the show falter. He's happy for the success of BUSA (which is, of course, his success too, as its producer); however, "I know you're so rich, and so popular, and so famous, and your waist is so tired from taking bows, that it's mundane to think about a show like 'Gypsy' that's grossing almost $83,000 a week, but you just simply have to, Jerome my beloved." To get the wallop and the applause Hayward wanted, Robbins advised a new costume and several times suggested with some exasperation that they put Church in pasties and G-string (something Church was unwilling to consider). Eventually, Hayward wondered slyly whether Robbins would mind if he brought in Danny Daniels to fix the strip; he even threatened to do something to it himself, bringing down not only the obvious response, "No other choreographer or director will touch this show," but also a more detailed reaction that reveals both Robbins's sense that *Gypsy* was Laurents's baby and his disappointment over the loss of his number (which, at the time, he'd known was inevitable, given that it added twenty minutes to an already overlong production):

Every time you have to close the curtain on the Christmas tree after opening on it, you have a let-down. Now, here are the things we've already gone through. If we finish on the big strip with the big production, Arthur hits the ceiling that the play's gone out the window. Right?

Because of all these problems something had to suffer and I took the rap. The original Christmas tree number was wonderful but everyone felt that it made the end of the show. Now you tell me what the Hell to do! Will Arthur write a scene so there's no stage-wait, so that we can finish on the number big? The number doesn't have to be longer than it is but just finish big in the set and add the snowballs dropping and the curtain closing in on her and the production number, I'm sure that it will get a hand. The terrible part is that it goes to such a height, opens on a Christmas box, and then she steps out and does nothing and shows nothing. Now this will give you a little to think about and stop making cracks about all the money I'm earning while working my ass off for the State Department (and your name, which is on every poster and bill, as well as mine) O.K.? O.K! . . . We've tried everything but shooting off fireworks, which I'm willing to try providing Arthur has an idea.

The show ran on Broadway for a year and a half. Merman went on the road with it but wasn't even approached about playing Rose in the 1962 film. Producer Frederick Brisson struck a deal with Warner Bros. that entailed his wife, Rosalind Russell, being handed the role, which she played, wrote Sondheim's biographer Meryle Secrest, "as a cross between a hockey mistress and a society matron." Natalie Wood played Louise and Karl Malden, Herbie. Paul Wallace, the original Tulsa, got to reprise his role. Leonard Spiegelgass manipulated Laurents's book into a screenplay, losing something in the process. Given Robbins's Hollywood reputation after *West Side Story,* no one invited him aboard. Mervyn Le Roy directed the film, and the creators of *Gypsy* disliked it intensely. The 1993 television movie starring Bette Midler hews more closely to the original production.

Robbins was at least peripherally aware of the ferment that characterized the art world of the 1960s and as the decade progressed took notice of the irreverent experiments in dance and theater going on in the churches, galleries, museums, nonproscenium stages, and parks of Manhattan. As early as 1957, Allan Kaprow, a graduate of the legendary composition class that John Cage taught at the New School for Social Research between 1956 and 1960, had staged his first gallery event, and in 1959 his *18 Happenings in 6 Parts* had coined the term for a new genre of obstreperous performance. Cage's class attracted writers and visual artists as well as composers, all taken with the idea of breaking down the boundaries between the arts and insisting that any everyday object, sound, or movement could be an element in art making. The Fluxus group of artists carried these liberating ideas into meticulous absurdity, and Judson Dance Theater, with its first showing in 1962, brought similar iconoclastic redefinitions into dance performance. Over the decade, groups such as Julian Beck and Judith Malina's Living Theater, Joseph Chaikin's Open Theater, and Richard Schechner's Performance Group experimented with texts and staging designed to transgress the traditional "fourth wall" between spectators and performers.

The decade was also marked by social agitation, especially to affect the status of African Americans, but also that of women and homosexuals; by the relaxation of censorship laws; and by insistent questioning of conservative institutions—political, social, and educational—by young people in cities around the world. Opposing the war in Vietnam became a rallying point, as did trying to halt the destruction of the environment. The country mourned the assassinations of its president, John F. Kennedy; his brother Robert, the attorney general, who was campaigning for the presidency; and Martin Luther King. And it danced to records of the Beatles, whose wry, ebullient songs altered the course of American pop music with their first appearance on *The Ed Sullivan Show* in 1964; a sizable group of white American males discovered they could shake their hips without compromising their masculinity.

Robbins kept his eyes and ears open. (He also started a beard—the well-trimmed one that he kept for the rest of his life—and began, in his forties, to enjoy the free atmosphere, the scent of marijuana, and the relaxed fashions that were, in some circles, replacing the suit and tie.) Having proven a success in the fields of ballet and musical comedy, he turned his attention to straight plays. Motivated to seek not only success and what he deemed to be higher artistic status but to expose himself to something new and mind-expanding, he didn't seek out comedies or realistic contemporary dramas. None of the three plays he directed during the 1960s was a conventional choice or one guaranteed to attract a large audience and add to his by-now-considerable wealth. And all offered ample scope to his sense of fantasy and his choreographic eye.

The first of these, *Oh Dad, Poor Dad, Mamma's Hung You in the Closet and I'm Feelin' So Sad* (a "Pseudoclassical Tragifarce in a Bastard French Tradition"), had been written while its very young playwright, Arthur Kopit, was on a postgraduate fellowship from his alma mater, Harvard.

Robbins had fallen in love with the script even before *Oh Dad* was performed in London in July 1961 starring Stella Adler and directed by Frank Corsaro. Undaunted by the fact that the British production did not fare well with audiences and critics, he wanted to direct the play in New York and scouted for a producer. Roger Stevens produced the play off-Broadway at the Phoenix on East Seventy-fourth Street, the intrepid theater organization run by Norris Houghton and T. Edward Hambleton. By August 18, Robbins was cabling Stevens to try to get Geraldine Page or Katharine Hepburn (in that order) for the role of Madame Rosepettle, a monster mother of a very different order from *Gypsy*'s Rose. Since *Oh Dad* was short (about an hour and twenty minutes), it was decided that another play by Kopit should precede it, and in September the precocious playwright sent Robbins the half-hour *Sing to Me Through Open Windows*, which he had written between his junior and senior years at Harvard.

Both plays, in diverse ways, presented the preposterous as everyday occurrences and lent themselves to a choreographic staging. Their moments of wistful lyricism, the wit with which Kopit infused horrifying or tragic subject matter, show a subtle influence of French playwrights such as Jean Giraudoux and Jean Anouilh. Some of this was conscious on the part of an ebullient, cocky, and terrifically smart young writer. "The feeding the alley cats to the piranha fish," says Kopit, "came from something Marcel Aymé had written, and I was certainly aware I was influenced by Anouilh's *Waltz of the Toreadors* and even *The Visit*. . . . It never occurred to me that the play had any professional potential or I would have been more cautious." Yet, as Kopit notes, *Oh Dad*'s indefinability and its energy are part of its strength. "It just bubbles along in its strange way."

Robbins noted to himself that the script "for all its horror has fun in it. Its wildness is exciting—its horror is vicariously thrilling—like a roller coaster ride—or a fun house trip. One is scared, knowing it's all rigged to scare—one wants to be scared." Incidental music by his Ballets: U.S.A. composer Robert Prince was commissioned to enhance the sense of fantasy. Designers William and Jean Eckert came up with a trick set and found a way to create a silver piranha and two Venus flytraps that growl and snarl, grow huge, and try to lasso people with their branches (puppets were the solution to the latter—manipulated by sticks from backstage and strings from above). Robbins's fond landlady, Muriel Resnick, thought the plants looked like "cunts with teeth."

Kopit had wanted his heroine to have "a romantic sort of soft name" to contrast to her favorite flesh-eating plants and to reinforce the image that under her apparent amiability, there's something lethal. Her visitors' names—Rosalie and Roseabove—are variations on her own, since to the playwright "it seemed as if they all needed to belong in the same kind of incestuous hermetic hothouse world." Madame Rosepettle (Jo Van Fleet) travels with the corpse of her husband; stuffed, it hangs in the closet of the apartment she's just rented in Havana. She also keeps her seventeen-year-old son, Jonathan (or whatever name she cares to call him), in a hothouse environment. Madame Rose of *Gypsy* paraded her daughters before a sordid world; Madame Rosepettle, who goes out on nighttime missions to kick sand on lovers on the beach, wants to save her son from "a world waiting to devour those who trust in it; those who love. A world vicious under the hypocrisy of kindness, ruthless under the falseness of a smile." Dressed like a ten-year-old, never allowed out, he whiles away the hours with a stamp collection of dubious worth, a coin collection, and a horde of books he treasures.

There was meaty material for a choreographer turned director in the entries of bellboys (never properly tipped) who bring in Madame Rosepettle's possessions; in the nightmarishly spinning waltz into which she draws the entranced (and ensnared) Commodore Roseabove (Sandor Szabo) who thinks to court her; in the scene in which Rosalie, the sensual babysitter from across the way (Barbara Harris), attempts to seduce the increasingly terrified Jonathan (Austin Pendleton) and is smothered. Nancy Franklin, who understudied Harris, says that every single moment of this murder-seduction with the stuffed corpse of Dad falling out of the closet and onto the bed was designed: "You just followed the choreography, and it had to work." As one critic, Harry Altshuler, later pointed out, the whole play was, in a way, a dance.

Jerry planned a compelling movement image to end the play, presumably after Madame Rosepettle has returned to a dazed son, an apartment in disarray, and two human corpses plus those of her fish and her plants and delivered her closing line ("As a mother to a son, I ask you, *What is the meaning of this?*"): "They [mother and son] look at each other. The lights start to grow brighter—become intensely bright—unbearably bright on stage. Rosepetal [*sic*] & Jonathan hold looking at each other—then like sparrows—look around them—concentrating on objects—ceiling—roof—curtains—doors—turning their heads in sudden bird like movements. Suddenly they catch the audience in their look. Hold. Blackout fast & then lights up fast!"

The young playwright hovered over rehearsals, but Robbins made it clear that he didn't care for instant feedback, even during breaks. Kopit wrote Jerry notes on little "Don't Forget" pads, one clump of which he signed "Bernard Shaw." But he was awed by Robbins's "visual brilliance and sense of space. I knew the play required a refined and precise visual imagination, one that had restraint so that it didn't just go crazy all over the place, because it couldn't go out of control. Jerry was very controlled."

Sing to Me Through Open Windows was peopled by a dying magician, Ottoman; a boy, Andrew, who seems to visit him once a year; and a clown, Loveless, who is a sort of servant to the magician. Two rites of passage seem to converge: the boy's coming of age and the magician's death. The clown assists at both. On this visit, the musician's tricks misfire in macabre ways: the rabbit is dead, the magician as ringmaster can't control the clown as panther, the clown has used up all his jokes. At the end, after a mysterious lighting change, the magician dies and the clown puts his body into his trunk of magic tricks. Snow falls. The boy, who has seemed to depart, reappears out of the shadows and watches as the parts of the room slide offstage, taking the clown with them. Only the trunk remains. The boy gazes at it and leaves.

It has been suggested that this inscrutable ending puzzled influential viewers (such as Leland Hayward) who saw rehearsals and/or a preview and that their responses may have contributed to the decision to drop *Sing to Me*. Kopit has said that the complicated set change between plays took almost as long as the opener—too long to expect an audience to wait—and that his enigmatic and melancholy playlet left the audience in no mood to laugh at the absurdist extravagances of *Oh Dad*. Had Van Fleet been able to establish *Oh Dad* as a dark comedy with her first entrance, perhaps the problem wouldn't have arisen, but comedy wasn't her forte. Kopit, Austin Pendleton, Barry Primus, and Gerald Hiken, who played the magician, have said that Robbins staged *Sing to Me Through Open Windows* marvelously, with the sense of fluid motion and fantasy that one would expect. And Robbins was extremely attached to the play.

To establish an ambiance of serious daffiness and prime the audience for *Oh Dad*, Robbins commissioned Fred Mogubgub, the creator of Mr. Magoo, to devise films to function as a prologue and fit between scenes two and three. It was a kind of animation—in Kopit's words "a series of still images that were made to move. It was very stylized. It was wonderful. . . . very funny . . . sort of macabre"; its seminarratives played around with the play's title.

Despite all his work at the Actors Studio and with Stella Adler, Robbins—often inarticulate under pressure—had difficulty finding the words that would spark the kind of performance he wanted, yet not foist his concept on an actor too early. It was for that reason that he hired assistants he trusted (Bill Daniels served in this capacity on *Oh Dad*) to convey what he wanted from a scene and then let preliminary work with the actors be done without him. He would shape the result. He did, however, in some cases show respect for a performer who had ideas of his or her own. Barry Primus, who played one of the bellboys in *Oh Dad,* tells how "on the second or third day of rehearsal he was staging us in different patterns with hatboxes. It was very choreographic. . . . I thought what a great idea it would be if I couldn't see where I was going. So I piled a bunch of boxes in front of me as if I was blind and I came out and disturbed the pattern and just sort of moved around and got bumped, and Jerry said, 'What the fuck are you doing?' from the back of the house. Without thinking, I yelled back, 'I'm *trying* something!' And he yelled back and then he was quiet." Primus found out later from Betty Walberg that Robbins had been intrigued by this young guy who had ambition, ideas, and gumption. Jerry never yelled at him again.

Austin Pendleton thinks that Barbara Harris both unsettled and excited Robbins. Harris had worked with Compass and then with Second City, cutting her teeth with such crack improvisers as Mike Nichols and Elaine May.

> In rehearsal, she never did anything the same way twice. . . . It was terribly challenging to him but he loved it. There were times I think he was frustrated because he would see her do something so extraordinary and the following day she would be doing something completely different. But then he began to be aware that she would either find her way back to what she had done before or she would abandon it in favor of something new that was even better. In her own way she was as much a perfectionist and a striver as he is. He became aware of that quite quickly. . . . And he quickly learned he had to be kind of an editor of her rather than an instigator. . . . He kept an eye on her and when he thought she would go way far afield he would tell her. He would like

hand her a theme and she would do all the variations on it. Then he would edit it. Among his gifts is an incredible eye. . . . He would say, "Now that thing you're working on now, that's good." And, "that thing you're working on now, that's not going to lead you anywhere." There came a point kind of late in the rehearsals, in the previews, when what she was going to do began to emerge and to be formed and he would just begin to add things. He would say, "At this moment I think you should do this, and at this moment I think you should do that." And all the little things he gave her at that point were just inspired because he knew exactly where she was coming from by then.

Robbins was loyal to performers he respected. Pendleton had wanted the part of Jonathan ever since he had read the play while at Yale. After seeing the London production, he wangled an audition, and after five or six more auditions, with Robbins championing and advising him, he won his first Broadway role at twenty-one. A problem developed. Pendleton was a stutterer but had conquered that on the stage. Robbins encouraged him to use the stutter, since Kopit had written it into some of the lines. A few weeks after the opening, Pendleton suddenly found that there were performances when he couldn't control it, distressing himself and his fellow actors and jeopardizing the play. He was ready to give his notice. Robbins, informed of the problem, asked Pendleton to stop by his apartment for a talk and refused to let him quit, quoting people who'd admired his work in the play, and more or less telling the actor that he had an obligation to his own talent to stick with it and to get speech therapy, both of which Pendleton did. If he had been allowed to walk out, he later realized, he might never have acted again.

After *Oh Dad*'s run at the Phoenix ended, the play went on the road, returning to Broadway on August 27, 1963, with British comedienne Hermione Gingold playing Madame Rosepettle. Some of the critics condescended to a play written by one so young, the *Journal American*'s John McClain calling it "Arthur Kopit's little rasher of nonsense." Although Paul Gardner of the *Times* found Gingold's comedic style too broad, the play, he wrote, "remains original and fresh. It makes you wonder what happened to all the people you should have loved."

Jerry was back in analysis, and one might wonder what he, prone anyway to self-examination, made of the fact that he directed three works in close succession that featured "Mom" at her most indomitable, domineering, and castrating. Of these three fierce matriarchs—Rose, Madame Rosepettle, and Brecht's Mother Courage—the last is the most complex. Tough and lusty, she has lost what idealism she had years ago, and, as she lugs her peddler's wagon across battle-torn Europe for the twelve years that the play covers, she focuses only on the strategies and dubious business transactions that will enable her and her three children to survive.

Robbins did not initiate the idea of his directing *Mother Courage and Her Children: A Chronicle of the Thirty Years' War,* although he greatly admired Bertolt Brecht's plays and his ideas about politics and theater. In the summer of 1961, Cheryl Crawford wrote to him in Spoleto, "Jerry dear, For at least twelve years I have been in love with a play which I think is the greatest that has been written in our times." Furthermore, the rights had just been cleared. "Everyone has been after it. But I have it." In two weeks, assured of Robbins's interest, she was mailing off the galleys of Brecht expert Eric Bentley's revised translation to him in London and listing possible leads, including Anna Magnani, Bette Davis, Siobhan McKenna, Simone Signoret, Uta Hagen, Geraldine Page, Lotte Lenya, Anne Bancroft, and "Ethel Merman! Brecht's wife thinks she might be marvelous. Says she is the only indestructible woman she saw over here." (Merman read the play with interest and thanked Jerry for thinking of her, "but I must be honest with you and say that I could not possibly visualize myself in the part. If I ever do a straight play, I would prefer something in a lighter vein.")

Many years later, still rueful over what he felt to have been a flawed job on his part, Robbins admitted that he hadn't been ready for Brecht and confessed to having felt trepidation about the project from the start. As his second job directing a nonmusical, it was a huge challenge. He attacked it optimistically, reading a typed copy of H. R. Trevor-Roper's "Notes on Thirty Years' Wars"; studying Jacques Callot's sketches, *The Miseries and Disasters of War;* gathering photographs of contemporary refugees trudging muddy roads. He slogged through a translation of Hans Jacob Christoffel von Grimmelshausen's seventeenth-century tale *The Adventurous Simplicissimus,* on which Brecht had drawn very lightly. He read Mordecai Gorelik's essay "An Epic Theatre Catechism," which laid out Brecht's ideas. Those ideas stood between him and the play like a wall he felt obligated to scale. Although he perused pictures of the Berliner Ensemble production, when Estelle Parsons offered to send him Brecht's director's notebook for the epic production featuring Brecht's wife, Helene Weigel, he declined, saying he'd had to put his own copy away: "It's been too influential." What he would appreciate, he wrote, was a copy of the letter Brecht had sent to his company when they were opening in London: "It goes very much with my own production ideas."

There has been some debate as to what his own ideas were and why the production didn't live up to expectations. Some felt he had hobbled his own creative gifts in being too respectful of Brecht (even to the extent of trying to duplicate what he could glean of Brecht's own production); others felt that he had not fully understood Brecht and had resorted to strategies that worked in musical comedy. Both sides agreed that there was something unfulfilled about his *Mother Courage*.

Robbins understood that in some sense, Brecht's work "isn't really an anti-war play, it's an anti-'business-as-usual' play, and it's a tremendous anti capitalist play as well"—applicable, he felt, to present-day America. Struggling for her children's survival during the religious wars that ravaged almost all of Europe between 1618 and 1648, Mother Courage is, unluckily, off trying to make a deal, haggling over prices, every time they are in jeopardy. Having tried to keep a recruiting officer from tempting her eldest, Eilif, to join up, a possible sale lures her away, and he's easily dragooned. Later, during a brief peace, when he's brought to say good-bye on his way to be executed for the murder and pillaging that had made him a hero in wartime, she's not there, having hastened away to sell her goods before prices fall. She's not there when her naive and honest son Swiss Cheese makes a misguided decision that costs him his life, nor at the heartbreaking moment when her mute daughter, Kattrin, drums from the rooftop to warn the villagers in the valley below of an impending attack and is shot. Courage is part of a scabrous horde of parasites who live off battles. In the end, she's pulling her cart alone, following yet another regiment while soldiers sing the bitter words she chanted eleven scenes and twelve years ago: "Let all of you who still survive / Get out of bed and look alive!"

At one point it seemed as if Geraldine Page was going to play the title role. Robbins had already started raising money, using her name (as coproducer with Crawford, he was responsible for raising $75,000), when some complicated and vexing maneuvers involving Page, Crawford, and the Actors Studio ended with Page doing Eugene O'Neill's *Strange Interlude* instead. Robbins had no doubts as to Anne Bancroft's talents, but he feared—and so did she—that she was too young (thirty-one) to give the part sufficient weight. Once she was signed, he gave her pictures to look at—images of war, Brueghel's paintings of peasants, and so on. In early December, he took her down to Eaves, the costume house, and tried padding to give her sagging breasts and additional girth, put a skullcap on her head, and blacked out a tooth. Barbara Harris was cast as the camp follower Yvette Pottier, Mike Kellin as the Cook, and Gene Wilder as the Chaplain. Zohra Lampert, Conrad Bromberg, and James Catusi played Mother Courage's children.

Eric Bentley thinks that Robbins never understood fully the emotion and the humor of Brecht's play. The two locked horns early on. After one fraught session, Bentley sent a sharp letter, hoping to clear the air and perhaps set forth some ground rules: "It may be that some people are spurred on to work better by being told that what they have done is amateurish, incomprehensible, boring, impossible etc. I am not one of them." And he reminded Jerry that *"Mother Courage* cannot be put on in America without my approval and collaboration, as I proved in a two-year-long lawsuit. So it is very much to your interest to get what you can out of me, rather than to goad me into becoming hostile to you." He received an apology.

Even as the opening loomed, Robbins asked for cuts, as well as revisions of the text where he felt the translation was awkward. Bentley feared that the cuts might ruin his reputation as a translator and warned Jerry that, while it was fine to try to win the kind of public that might dislike the play, if they made too many alterations to achieve that goal, they might well alienate people who did or would like Brecht, without necessarily gaining a new public either. This was not the kind of problem Robbins usually encountered working on Broadway, where the aim was to achieve a momentum that pulled the audience along on greased wheels.

Robbins understood the requirements of Brecht's Epic Theater in terms of actors. Too, Brecht's theory of alienation might have resonated for him with Balanchine's ideas about reticent performing. "The Epic character," wrote Gorelik, "explains himself fully on stage and by means of his actions; it is not necessary to know his complexes, to guess at his childhood traumas, or even to know his past personal history." Yet, he added, this did not preclude the *actor* learning this. And Jerry, steeped in Stanislavskian ideas, took this last as permission to employ his usual strategies—setting his actors, for example, to play Monopoly that they might experience the lust of buying and selling. Robbins may have begun

his work trying to reconcile two theoretical approaches, as well as keeping in check his musical comedy self and what Stephen Sondheim has called his "ability to button a number."

Eilif, Courage's elder son, has a militant song and dance in Act I. Conrad Bromberg, who played the role, worked on this with Robbins, then by himself according to instructions he'd been given ("I didn't know shit from choreography, but I was doing a whole bunch of sword things—I had the *Gayne* ballet suite going in my head, or something like that"). Jerry polished up the result, and, as Bromberg remembers, "People looked at it and said, 'Gee, Jerry, that's great!' He looked at it and said, 'Naah, it's too Jerry Robbinsish. . . . I want Brecht.' " Out went the syncopations, the lifts of the legs. "What he finally gave me was kind of clunky, as if you were dancing in armor . . . and very blunt . . . it went right with the music."

Bromberg, later a playwright and director, remembers how tidy the production was. At some point Betty Walberg, Robbins's invaluable rehearsal pianist and composer of dance music for some of his shows, brought the actor a message from the director. Were there shields in his costume? Yes. Was he using an antiperspirant? No. Would he please do so? Jerry didn't care to see sweat stains. Bromberg associates this with Robbins's ballet background. "Here you are wanting to do a Brechtian sweat, piss, mud, and blood production but you don't want to have sweat marks under [people's] arms 'cause dancers never show that they sweat. You don't want to show that it's work. You kind of want it to look pristine. As opposed to Brecht, where the more mess you could make the better. It was that kind of thing—where he was at war with himself about it."

Several critics noted, sometimes approvingly, the spareness and lack of mess in the production. The actors carried on the minimal sets (except for the backdrops, which occasionally held projected photographs of war). As in Chinese opera, the commander's tent in an Army encampment consisted of two poles with some rags hanging from them, two chairs, and a table. Although pots and pans hung on Courage's cart, few were used. Eilif had his sword, the cook his soup ladle, Kattrin her drum.

It didn't help Jerry's self-confidence or his temper that he received many notes from Bentley and from his nervous coproducer, Cheryl Crawford, throughout rehearsals on all aspects of the production. "Annie often stops between sentences and has 5 thoughts instead of one" (Crawford). "Isn't the emotion of Courage facing Swiss's death <u>diffused</u> by playing so hard the relationship with Kattrin? The European actresses have made the scene much more moving by concentrating on the reaction to the death of Swiss" (Bentley). In addition, Crawford passed on worrying reactions from others, such as this one attributed to a friend's friend who had seen the Berliner Ensemble: "Mother Courage is a queen—a GIANT—and should not be played like a jewish peddler. She is an <u>executive.</u>" This person also wanted to see red light used in the war scenes and didn't care for having the actors change the scenery.

Robbins was seldom too proud to take advice. Next to Bentley's comment, he penciled "to do," and after the criticism of Tharon Musser's lighting, he jotted "lights 10 up." But he did respond with irritation to a harsh criticism from Bentley around two weeks from opening night; Bentley missed the rage that Brecht felt against the world, and he regretted a lack of pungency in the altered script: "Our text, too, is toned down. Lacks the full Brechtian violence, just as the rest of the production does. . . . This is the Brecht production in which expressions like 'pisser' are replaced by banal adjectives such as 'terrific.' " Robbins responded, "I would like <u>more</u> pungency in text not just prudishly inserted minor 'dirty' words."

Beset and floundering, Robbins unfairly savaged one cast member, changed his mind often, and demanded drastic revisions in Ming Cho Lee's set (Lee may have made as many as six different versions, and the useful turntable, employed in Brecht's production, never made it past the model stage). The originally scheduled opening was postponed, and rehearsals resumed. An article written by Stuart W. Little during the three weeks of previews Robbins had chosen over out-of-town tryouts mentioned how signs held up to announce scenes had been replaced by actors stepping out of character to recite the "chronicles" during scene changes. At one point Robbins tried having all the actors seated onstage all the time, then discarded that as distracting, but had them begin the play by lining up before the audience (no opening curtain) and announcing their own names.

The reviews were mixed but largely respectful, with the exception of Martin Gottfried's in *Women's Wear Daily* (headlined "Brecht's 'Mother Courage' Murdered on Broadway"). John Chapman of the *Daily News* praised the "visually stunning and imaginatively devised production." *The New York Times*'s Howard Taubman wrote that the play "has been staged by Jerome Robbins in a worthy manner that recalls the production by Brecht's own Berliner Ensemble, and at the same time has its own signature." Walter Kerr began his *Herald Tribune* review with some knowledgeable remarks about Brecht's theories, including his belief that the "power of the theater to spellbind through illusion must be broken," and called Robbins's production "austere and honorable."

Bancroft was widely praised for a magnificently convincing portrayal. The New York accent that Taubman found distracting didn't seem to bother most of his colleagues. Many critics singled out Zohra Lampert for her profoundly moving performance as Kattrin. Both Melvin Maddocks of *The Christian Science Monitor* and Richard Watts of the New York *Post* felt that she provided, in her final scene, the single emotionally charged moment in the play. And Michael Smith of *The Village Voice* gave detailed praise to both her and Barbara Harris.

Although Smith's review began with a sharply critical summation—"This is the season in which plays on Broadway are rendered unrecognizable"—and applied words such as "mutilation," "castration," and "disfigurement" to *Mother Courage* (along with productions of *The Cherry Orchard, A Doll's House, Andorra, Strange Interlude,* and others), his view of Robbins's conception aptly engages the issues that Robbins had faced:

> The production has a stark, virile, elegant grandeur of scale that is extremely exciting. Much of the detail is exquisitely crafted. But at some point Robbins seems not to have trusted himself enough or to have become too much in awe of his project. He set himself the task of presenting "Mother Courage" in terms accessible to a Broadway audience, wisely abjuring any attempt to create the famous Berliner Ensemble production, and clearly he worked with devotion. But the production is much too heavy. Everything is insistently deliberate and implacable, and the actors all seem to be aware that they are performing a masterpiece, that this is a Major Event. There is almost never a moment in which they just act, just play the play, just do what they are doing. The production seems continually to be judging itself; and this has the effect of not holding the emotion away from the audience as Brecht said he wanted . . . but of making the emotions ring hollow. A work of art has to come to life before its status as a masterpiece matters at all.

Midway through directing *Mother Courage* Jerry was jolted into pondering the theater business:

> [I]t seems to me that working in the theatre for the creative people, is like being a terrible work horse who slugs his way or plods his way to

get to a certain point. Thrown over him are all the nets and luggage and fight debris and carriages of everyone making money on his effort because when you come right down to it, the only thing that really keeps the theatre going is that work horse. The work isn't me, the director, but the author who decides to write it and then the director and the actors who decide they have to play it. There is also a demand for the spectators to see it and in between the need to create it and the need to see it is a whole vast intricate merciless industry and business. . . . I get depressed because of the enormity of the snake-like business shifts and deals, issues and solutions and cross purposes and snarlings all to personal ends and in a way it really is like MOTHER COURAGE.

One might point out that he, too, thought of everything he undertook from a "business" point of view as well as from a creative one. On his terms, *Mother Courage* succeeded on neither count. The play closed on May 11 after fifty-three performances during which it failed to lure the Broadway audience. Cheryl Crawford wrote Robbins a weary letter. The production had roused great interest in Brecht's play within the theater world, but "I found it interesting to see what happens to a producer of plays like these. Anne made $27,000, you made $14,500 and I made $1350 which didn't do much more than cover my office deficit."

⌒

Many offers came Robbins's way during the early 1960s. He was always on the lookout for the most lucrative deal, or the most challenging project, or the most interesting collaborators, but fear and his perfectionism were also dampers. Many times, he would turn down a likely job because he worried that he wouldn't have adequate time to do it justice. In juggling offers, mulling over a decision too long, or postponing a production, he sometimes lost out.

During the first Ballets: U.S.A. summer, for instance, he had been delighted by the news that Leland Hayward had persuaded William Paley of CBS to save a television slot for the company in the fall. CBS needed positive confirmation from Jerry by a certain date and didn't get it. The bad news that the deal was off reached the choreographer in Brussels: Robbins's reply blended disappointment with excuses and inducements, ending with "WHAT CAN BE DONE URGENT LOVE GYPSY." In 1963, he was approached about directing Paddy Chayefsky's play *Revolt,* which he had

read and loved. When he didn't respond to repeated requests for a decision, his lawyer, William Fitelson, sent this message to him in Spoleto: "Yesterday Paddy Chayefsky called to tell me that his frustration turned to shock, then to fury at your silence and discourtesy. I tried every excuse to calm him down. He was calm when the call ended, but he did say there was no use in considering the matter any further because he would not, under any circumstances, permit you to do the play."

Living such a charged life, it's no wonder that Jerry collapsed from time to time and granted himself a vacation. He made the happy decision in 1962 to rent a house in Snedens Landing, across the George Washington Bridge and north along the Palisades about ten miles. He was already familiar with Snedens and Ding Dong House before he signed the two-year lease on May 24 ($275 a month for the first year, $300 for the second). Fizdale and Gold had rented property in Snedens, and Aaron Copland had lived in Ding Dong House, one of a number of cottages acquired by Mary Lawrence Tonetti (whose father had bought a farm in Snedens in 1870) and leased to artist friends. She, like her husband, François Tonetti, was a sculptor—a pupil and associate of Augustus Saint-Gaudens. It was from Tonetti descendants that Robbins rented the house he continued to use as a retreat until 1975. From the second-floor porch that spanned the long white house or from the top of the sloping lawn, he could gaze down at the Hudson River framed by trees.

It was just as well that he acquired this haven for getaways and periods when he wasn't rehearsing. Between *Oh Dad* and *Mother Courage,* among the projects he failed to fit into his schedule were two musicals that he wanted very much to choreograph and direct and on which he had done preliminary work. Ironically, both shows—*A Funny Thing Happened on the Way to the Forum* and *Funny Girl*—ran into problems and eventually sought his services as a play doctor. Ambitious as he was about "serious" theater, he wasn't ready to kill the Broadway gypsy in himself, especially when the financial rewards were considerable. Too, doctoring a show was easier than being in on one from the beginning. Instead of sweating through creative hassles, he entered in shining armor to save someone else's botched effort.

His involvement with *Forum* had begun in 1958. In February of that year, while auditioning dancers for Ballets: U.S.A., he outlined to Leland Hayward the plot of Larry Gelbart and Burt Shevelove's wacky reassessment of Plautus's *Miles Gloriosus* and sent along a list of the characters and ideas for casting. It was a scenario that appealed to the side of him that had concocted the uproarious Mack Sennett chase scene in *High Button Shoes*. The slave Pseudolus is hell-bent to win his freedom by managing to help his young master wed Philia, the girl he craves. Philia is a recent arrival at the next-door establishment of Marcus Lycus, which teems with pulchritudinous slaves for sale. In thwarting her promised delivery to the ferociously vainglorious captain Miles Gloriosus, Pseudolus sets off a series of misunderstandings that require increasingly complex and preposterous— and often backfiring—ruses on his part, involving men in female disguise, switches of identity, misleading messages, and a mock death.

In the end Harold Prince, not Leland Hayward, produced the show. Stephen Sondheim was finally making his Broadway debut as both lyricist and composer. Jerry, however, was occupied with the *West Side Story* film in the fall of 1960 and couldn't commit himself to a directorial stint in February. By June, nevertheless, he was auditioning and discussing casting with Prince, who was interested in securing Milton Berle or Phil Silvers for the role of Pseudolus and planning to talk with Bert Lahr about playing Senex, Pseudolus's master. Rehearsals were to start in October. In July, busy with Ballets: U.S.A. in London, Jerry pulled out. Sondheim says that a letter he sent his colleagues from Greece arrived torn in several pieces as if to indicate acute distress. Robbins wrote Prince that he knew everyone concerned would

> be pretty teed off at me, and from their point of view, justly so. But the essential thing is that I don't have a firm enough grasp on the show to go into rehearsal. It must be no news to you of my consistent hesitations and reservations over the show, and unless I have a real inner conviction and incentive for <u>any</u> work I'll do a poor job. All other reasons are really incidental. I'm sure that even I could deal with my exhaustion if I had enough security about the show. It's beside the point to reprise all the tardiness of the collective authors' efforts or to point out that their own various commitments over the past few years have delayed the show [,] arriving at a point unacceptable to me.

In the remarkably courteous and understanding letters that preceded and followed this explanation, Prince pointed out that, although he and the writers had been willing to postpone rehearsals and the opening for four or five months, Robbins had not left any leeway in his own schedule:

"Your other commitments loused us up and I was not willing to ask the boys to wait a whole year."

Forum went into rehearsal with George Abbott, by then seventy-five years old, directing and Jack Cole handling the choreography. At tryouts in New Haven, Boston, and Washington, D.C., the show was, says Sondheim, "a disaster." Despite the comic talents of Zero Mostel (Pseudolus), Jack Gilford (Hysterium, Pseudolus's antagonistic fellow slave), and David Burns (Senex), audiences weren't rolling in the aisles and didn't much like the show. Jack Cole, recalled Abbott many years later, "couldn't finish the thing." At Sondheim's suggestion, Robbins was called, and Abbott (according to Jerry, who considered him a "sort of guru of mine") welcomed him "with open arms." Said Abbott later, "[Jerry] could work with Sondheim, which I couldn't. Sondheim didn't trust me at all." Perhaps Abbott had sensed that, despite the courtesy that marked their working relationship, Sondheim was not as impressed with his skills. "I just didn't think he had any talent," Sondheim told Meryle Secrest years later.

Robbins arrived in Washington from the Academy Awards in Hollywood with his twin Oscars on April 10, 1962, and took in a performance of the show with Ballets: U.S.A. stage manager Tom Stone the night before BUSA danced in the White House before the Kennedys, their distinguished guests the shah and empress of Iran, and a glittering assembly. In London, Princess Margaret had attended the stage version of *West Side Story,* and in February, the movie had been chosen for the Royal Command Film Performance. With Iran's empress wearing an impressive tiara while she watched his ballets in D.C., little Jerome Wilson Rabinowitz's I'll-show-them dream of performing before crowned heads had come to pass.

The previous evening had been less pleasant. According to Stone, Robbins left his seat at intermission emanating serious displeasure. That night, he agreed to try to fix the show for .5 percent of the gross, no fee, and no credit, but he must have realized that the experience would be fraught with tensions. Mostel, who'd been blacklisted, had a poor opinion of informers and made no bones about his disdain for Robbins. Jack Gilford was married to Madeleine Lee, one of the seven Jerry had named before HUAC back in 1953.

Nonetheless, although Mostel might make disparaging remarks about Robbins—some intended to be overheard—and may have welcomed him to the job with "Hiya, loose lips" (Jerry reportedly laughed), in a desperate situation professionalism outweighed animosity. And Jerry had only a week in Washington and a few previews in New York to bring off a rescue mission.

His main contribution, everyone agrees, was to get Sondheim to write a new opening number to substitute for the pretty "Love Is in the Air." (Sondheim had jettisoned an idea similar to what Robbins had in mind and written this to satisfy Abbott's criterion that the opener be "hummable.") To Robbins, the issue was basic: "[T]he opening song did not say what the show was about" and so didn't set a tone the audience could respond to for the rest of the evening. Sondheim and Robbins came up with the tuneful and brilliantly witty "Comedy Tonight," in which Prologus introduces the performers as a group of comedians about to present a lusty knockabout play. Robbins had the brainstorm of starting with three men billed as "proteans" who hustle scenery and props about, pop into and out of doors and disguises at lightning speed ("A proud Roman. A patrician Roman. A pretty Roman. A Roman slave. A Roman soldier. A Roman ladder . . ."), and do business with a variety of unlikely props. An extra leg figures importantly and hilariously. The company enters to join the fun, and the audience gets it: love and death and war are going to be rinsed in laughter.

Jerry also staged the climax, involving three vestal virgins, of the final preposterous chase scene, which Sondheim calls the "funniest bit in the show outside of the opening number." In itemizing his contributions— probably for his lawyer in the event of possible future hassles—Robbins wrote that he had also staged "chase" material for Zero and the soldiers and done a version of the entire chase, which "was reworked again by Abbott." In addition, he mentioned restaging the songs "Lovely," "Pretty Little Picture," "That'll Show Him," "I'm Calm," "Impossible," and the finale. Abbott recalled Robbins working on the second-act pantomimes in which people keep mistaking the door that leads to their heart's desire and popping out later, mystified, drained, horrified, or delighted, depending on what they encountered within.

In a flippant letter to Richard Buckle, Robbins remarked that he had put his "magic little finger" to a variety of small details ("beef up trill in orchestra during Act II till stab" reads one of his memos to himself). According to Sondheim, one of Robbins's major suggestions concerned the set. "He said, 'You're being killed by the set. It's too busy. You can't see the actors.' Tony Walton refused to change the set, so what Jerry did was, he went down with Ruth Mitchell, the stage manager, one night when Tony was not around in Washington, and they painted over some of the set and they cut—they literally sawed off—a couple of finials, which were heads, to make the set simpler so the actors could be seen."

Sondheim, however, sent his colleague thanks for more than opening-night flowers. Jerry's inventiveness and wit had helped make the show a success, and its composer was grateful.

Robbins's early involvement with *Funny Girl* ran deeper. He had signed a contract to direct and choreograph the musical on February 21, 1962, five days before *Oh Dad, Poor Dad* opened. Because of his contributions, he would collect royalties as an author. He also negotiated to receive $60,000 for the motion picture rights the day the play opened in New York—threatening to back out of the deal when producer Ray Stark balked.

Based on the career and difficult offstage marriage of Florenz Ziegfeld's star comedienne, Fanny Brice, the scenario offered Robbins a return to the world of vaudeville that had drawn him to *Gypsy,* as well as a chance to bring to life the turn-of-the-century community of emigrant Jews in New York that his own family had been a part of. Jule Styne and Robert Merrill were to write the music and lyrics, and screenwriter Isobel Lennart was developing the script from a story she had written.

Two potential hazards were apparent from the beginning. Stark (who had put money into *Oh Dad,* even while advising Jerry not to undertake the play) was married to the daughter of Fanny Brice and Nicky Arnstein. Although Arnstein had been a reckless gambler by profession and been lured into participating in a scam that had landed him in jail for a while, his daughter wanted his character to emerge as sympathetic. Lennart had been nominated for three Academy Awards (for *Love Me or Leave Me, Lost Angel,* and *The Sundowners*) and written the screenplay for *Anchors Aweigh,* starring Gene Kelly and Frank Sinatra, but she was a novice as far as developing a Broadway musical went.

What made the initial process agreeable—and inevitably more diffi-cult—was that Lennart and Robbins got on like a house afire. He flew out to the coast for a week's work with her in late March and continued to con-fer with her, Styne, and Merrill over the summer, incidentally letting her know in early August that he had just had a long talk with the twenty-year-old singer-actress who'd attracted much notice as the dippy secretary Miss Marmelstein in *I Can Get It for You Wholesale* and that she, Barbra Streisand, would read for him the following Monday. However, at a meeting of all the collaborators in New York on September 20, 1962—the last of several sessions Lennart termed "ghastly"—Robbins resigned. Rehearsals had been scheduled to start that fall, and to that end, he had persuaded Cheryl Crawford to postpone *Mother Courage*. (Ironically, the two of them had consented to the delay because Ray Stark had agreed to invest $125,000 in the Brecht play.) Now, with Robbins feeling strongly that it would take the rest of the year to get the *Funny Girl* script in shape, he was forced to choose between the two plays, and he chose *Mother Courage*. To be sure that his contributions to the script of *Funny Girl* could not be used without his permission and that he would get credit as an author if any *were* used in the production, Robbins detailed, at the request of William Fitelson, every idea he had contributed to the script as it then stood or that had come out of a conference in which he had been a "most active participant."

One of his concerns was that Lennart not think badly of him, and she set his mind at rest: "I've told you that no matter what happened with the show, all you'd ever hear from me was that you'd acted honestly, as I expect a friend to—and with consideration and sensitivity to my feelings. I said that because I believed it. I say it now, to anyone who asks, because I still believe it. And I thought I'd like to say it once more to you."

Funny Girl languished for more than a year and reentered Jerry's life early in 1964, during its tryouts in Philadelphia. The show, starring Streisand and Sydney Chaplin, was in trouble, running far too long. The prominent director Garson Kanin couldn't seem to pull it together. His love of theater history and urge to bring the vaudeville atmosphere to life may have undermined the need to keep the show rolling.

Larry Fuller, who was the show's dance captain, remembers the dancers being onstage rehearsing the latest changes in Philadelphia when Stark appeared in the shadows under the balcony with a figure beside him and addressed the cast. " 'Ladies and gentlemen, I would like to introduce Mr. Jerome Robbins, who will be taking over as director of *Funny Girl*.' And of course everybody exploded in enthusiastic applause and screaming, because we thought, 'Oh, thank God, we may actually make it, and the show may work.' " Jerry rolled up his sleeves and waded in. The production stage manager and stage manager quit in support of Kanin, and he replaced them with his Ballets: U.S.A. colleagues Richard Evans and Tom Stone, who knew intuitively how to give him what he needed in a hurry. Kanin disappeared, and Jerry wrote him a gracious note: "I want you to know that I consider 'Funny Girl' your show. I was hoping to work on it with you, but Ray, in deciding to take advantage of the little time left out of town, felt it could only proceed this way. I'm very sorry indeed, believe me. I just hope I fulfill the very wonderful job you've already left here."

He was not so gracious to Carol Haney, whom he had loved as a performer in *Pajama Game*. He preferred, when doctoring a show, not to rechoreograph it but to work with the choreographer, and he was hard on Haney. Stone and Karen Kristin, a neophyte dancer in the show, thought he was unnecessarily harsh in putting her on the spot in front of the cast at a time when problems Haney was having in her private life made her especially vulnerable. According to Kristin, he "kept saying, 'It's wrong, it's just wrong.' And he wouldn't be specific with [Carol]. . . . And so she kept going back and changing and changing." The Act I number "Cornet Man" had been praised out of town, but Robbins found it too good to be believable as a second-rate vaudeville house's offering. The dance was pared to what the chorus referred to as the "chicken scramble," and the dancers essentially became moving scenery behind Streisand and Buzz Miller.

The Ziegfeld extravaganza "Rat-Tat-Tat-Tat," a World War I number, featured tappers and showgirls and a Ziegfeld staircase, with fancy lighting and changing formations and a precision drill with guns. Said Fuller, "We came marching over the stairs as the set opened up, and we did like a chorus and a half or so of tap dancing with little toy wooden rifles and all dressed as doughboys in the Irene Sharaff tradition. And then we hit a pose at the side of the stage and Streisand came on and sang 'Private Schwartz from Rock-a-way' while we stood in two lines and she walked in and out of us. She finished her section, and then we did a kind of dancey tag." Robbins prodded variant after variant out of Haney, although dancers who suffered through the process couldn't remember for sure how the final version differed from the original one. The neighborhood waltzing in "Henry Street" he had her make less splashy, giving the cast a characteristic note: "Look, you're her neighbors, you're not dancers. When you're waltzing, you have to have fun. This is a block party. This isn't a dance class."

As Robbins scissored and pruned and redirected the show, however, it took fire. Fuller affirms that "his biggest contribution was making the show have a shape and a rhythm and seeing that the absolute most important thing we had was [Streisand]." At the end of the following year, Robbins made it clear how much he admired the young star-to-be in an unpublished essay he titled "Barbra: Some Notes":

> During the rehearsal, in her untidy exploratory meteoric fashion she goes way out, never afraid to let herself go anywhere or try anything. . . . Her performances astound, arouse, fulfill. When she sings she is as honest and frighteningly direct with her feelings as if she was, is, or will be in bed with you. The satisfaction she gives also leaves one with terrible and pleasurable hunger. For what will become of this woman. She is still unfinished. . . . With all her talent and radiance, glamor, uniqueness, passion and wit and spontaneity—she is still forming. There is more to come.

To establish Fanny as a survivor and the bright center of her own narrative, he shifted the emphasis to Streisand's role and, with a deft and wily hand, pared down Sydney Chaplin's role as Nicky Arnstein while still trying to satisfy Frances Stark's wishes that her father come across as a nice guy, even as he did bad things and ruined the marriage. Robbins resisted efforts to have Fanny's last song be about the man she loved and lost (as it is in the movie starring Streisand and Omar Sharif); instead, however lovelorn, she reprises her grand "Don't Rain on My Parade."

While Robbins, Streisand, and all concerned were still laboring in Philadelphia, an exultant Ray Stark wired him on behalf of the producer and cast:

> I HAD TO GO TO A FUNERAL IN NEW YORK BUT WILL BE BACK IN
> THE AFTERNOON STOP YOU HAVE A FREE HAND TO DO ANYTHING
> YOU WANT AND THE KEY TO THE VAULT FOR MY MONEY BELT IS
> UNDER THE RUG IN THE BATHROOM STOP I REALLY AM THRILLED
> WITH EVERYTHING YOU'VE DONE ON THE SHOW AND THE
> INSPIRATION YOU'VE BEEN TO EVERYONE CONNECTED WITH
> IT MANY MANY THANKS

He also proposed that Robbins be credited in the program and the record album with the line "Production supervised by Jerome Robbins."

When the show finally opened in New York at the Winter Garden on March 26, 1964, Robbins's name appeared on the program just above Garson Kanin's and in the same-size type. Buzz Miller sent him an opening-night message: "MUCH LUCK AND MANY THANKS AND YOU KNOW WHAT YOU REALLY ARE GREAT."

15

The Sixties—A Fiddler on His Roof

"If I Were a Rich Man." Zero Mostel in *Fiddler on the Roof.*
Friedman-Abeles/Billy Rose Theatre Collection, NYPL.

D*uring the early 1960s*, Robbins maintained a curious juggling act between surefire commercial work and his desire to
direct unusual plays or choreograph ballets. In the heady atmosphere of Spoleto he could indulge the latter; he was always welcome at the
festival in whatever capacity. In the summer of 1963, the Teatrino delle

Sette, a new little performance space underneath the Caio Melisso, was at his disposal. With a small group of dancers, he produced three "sketches" (and at one showing thrilled the Spoletini by appearing in place of an injured dancer). *Anonymous Figure,* to music by Teiji Ito, featured an immobile Jamie Bauer plus Robert Thompson, Helge Grau, and Arlan Wendland, who, through gestures and stylized movement, commented on or embodied her plight (Bauer thinks the piece might have been inspired by a newspaper account of a drowning). According to one Italian critic, *The Last Night,* set to Charles Mingus's progressive jazz, conveyed an impression of disjointed nightlife, with the dancers (aided by lighting) flickering in their revels like fireflies and moths. *A Little Dance* was performed to Dave Brubeck music by Sondra Lee, Patricia Dunn, Thompson, Bauer, and Grau: a "delicious dessert." These minor works also figured in a one-night-only performance in the Caio Melisso on July 9, along with André Gide's short play *Le Treizième Arbre* in Italian translation, directed by Luchino Visconti.

Robbins also exercised his interest in theatrical fantasy by directing a fourth sketch for that July program. At his invitation, Paul Sand, then working with Second City, had come to Spoleto with a solo playlet he had written, "Luis: From Work." Robbins's interest in the work attests to the allure that offbeat, slightly surreal plays held for him. Luis, a young Puerto Rican immigrant, practices his English by conversing with his potted geranium, recounting his impatience with his coworkers at the office and playing the phonograph for his plant, which grows large and sleek under his attentions (Allen Midgette, a boyfriend of Jerry's, was delegated to crouch under the table, replacing the geranium with ever-more-voluptuous specimens). As Luis grows more fluent in English and confident in his new life, he becomes less nice. In the end, he breaks a flower off the plant, sticks it in his lapel, and goes off to his date with the cashier at work, telling the geranium not to wait up. The Italians loved it.

From that playful summer, Robbins returned to the world of Broadway and the plotting of his next big project: directing and choreographing *Fiddler on the Roof.*

⁓

"*Fiddler on the Roof* . . . is one of the great works of the American musical theatre. It is darling, touching, beautiful, warm, funny and inspiring. It is a work of art." So raved John Chapman in the *Daily News* on September 23, 1964, the morning after the show began its run on Broadway. Yet *Fiddler*—which played for 3,242 performances (nearly eight years) and which before another decade passed had been seen in more than twenty countries, ranging from Japan to Argentina to South Africa to Turkey to Australia—initially frightened away potential producers and backers and gave its creators the jitters while they were writing it and husbanding it through out-of-town tryouts. How could a musical based on the Yiddish tales of Sholem Aleichem appeal to a general audience? Right before the New York opening, after eight weeks of rehearsal and eight weeks on the road, Robbins goaded his cast into extra rehearsals by telling them that they could either work a little more and maybe be part of a hit, or they could cry mercy and play to the congregations of synagogues.

The travails of Tevye the milkman had already been seen onstage in New York. Maurice Schwartz had staged in Yiddish the story of a poor man who drags his rickety cart through a turn-of-the-century Russian shtetl to sell his wares, debating with an apparently attentive but hardly benevolent God about the *tsuris* caused by headstrong daughters who were refusing arranged marriages. Schwartz had also played Tevye in a 1939 film, *Tevye* (with Jacob Adler as the village's Russian Orthodox priest), which focused on the marriage of the third daughter, Chava, out of her faith and presented the Christians as caricatures of boorish nastiness.

It was important to *Fiddler*'s creators to deal with larger issues: oppression of a minority by a powerful majority and the minority's ability to survive with humor and dignity. Book writer Joseph Stein's parents had emigrated from Poland, and, according to Richard Altman (Robbins's assistant on the project and the author, with Mervyn Kaufman, of a book about its gestation), "For Joe, this show was an obvious labor of love, dedicated to the memory of his father." And Robbins, making notes on his heritage for his projected autobiography some years later, wrote, "*Fiddler* was a glory for my father—a celebration of & for him." He had come to know Harry better—and respect him more—while doing research for *Fiddler*. It was also a way of resurrecting the little shtetl he had so loved as a six-year-old. Trying to secure Ruth Mitchell's services as stage manager, he cabled her, "DEAR RUTHIE—I'M GOING TO DO A MUSICAL ON SHOLEM ALEICHEM STORIES WITH HARNICK AND BOCK STOP I'M IN LOVE WITH IT IT'S OUR PEOPLE."

Stein had worked previously with *Fiddler*'s composer, Jerry Bock, and its lyricist, Sheldon Harnick, on *The Body Beautiful* in 1958 and with Bock on *Mr. Wonderful,* starring Sammy Davis, Jr. Bock and Harnick had collaborated on four shows, including the Pulitzer Prize–winning *Fiorello!* (1959). Harold Prince, ready to produce *Fiddler,* advised them to get Robbins to direct and choreograph. They may not have been prepared for the fervor and fury Jerry would bring to the mix. While Stein worked on the book in New York and Bock and Harnick hammered out the music and lyrics as they toiled in London with Prince on the flop-to-be *She Loves Me,* Robbins nagged the songwriters to hurry home and delved into the culture of the shtetl via numerous books and articles.

During rehearsals, Jerry took Altman and his dance assistant Tommy Abbott and various other cast members to Jewish weddings and marveled over what he later described as "the virile ferocity of the dances. Without any constricting elements except a rudimentary rhythm & an avid impulse to express their communal joy—the men stamped, kicked, hit the floor and [illegible]—tossed their arms about, flung their bodies around—each individual taking off as the ecstasy and inspiration moved him." The paintings of Marc Chagall's figures cartwheeling through vivid skies also became an inspiration for him and for the sets by Boris Aronson (Jerry had approached Chagall about doing the sets, and Chagall had politely declined.) The show's opening image of the fiddler spooling out his music while perched on a pointed roof—a symbol of spiritual hardiness and precarious balance—came from a Chagall painting. In Robbins's mind, the fiddler symbolized the dilemma of Tevye: a man perched between a centuries-old way of life and a changing world.

It was Robbins who pressed the collaborators to come up with a strong theme that would both embrace and transcend the tale of daughters who wish to marry for love. Harnick told Altman that Robbins

> was like the world's greatest district attorney, asking us question after question, probing—"What's the show about?"—and not being satisfied with the glib answers we were giving. We kept saying, "Well, it's about a dairy farmer and his daughters and trying to find husbands for them," and he kept saying things like, "Yeah, but that's the Previous Adventures of the Goldberg Family," and he didn't want to do that.

Pauline Kael, in reviewing the film of *Fiddler* (which she called "the most *powerful* movie musical ever created"), remarked that Tevye was a male Mother Courage, not a male Molly Goldberg. That was closer to what Robbins was after.

Once the men figured out that the spine of the musical would be about tradition and its erosion, Robbins insisted on bringing out that theme, most notably in an opening song, "Tradition." Harnick remembered that he "would say again and again, 'Well, if that's what the show is about, why isn't it in *this* scene? Why isn't it in *that* scene? Why don't we see it in *this* character or *that* character?' " If they disagreed, he'd tell them to get another director. His vision, said Harnick, "extended down to the littlest brushstroke in the scenery and the triangle part in the orchestra."

In notes written early in 1964, Jerry defined this core idea in terms of the leading character: "The drama of the play is to watch a man carefully treading his way between his acceptance of his sustaining belief (that way of life that is centuries old, practiced as if it were still in the middle ages, which protects & defends him & makes his life tolerable)—and his wry questioning of it within the confinements of the belief. He always asks why—& He ducks and weaves with the events around him still managing to straddle both sides—his traditions & the questioning of it."

The director's fastidiousness extended to casting, and he took some interesting risks. Who could have imagined that Maria Karnilova, his former Ballet Theatre colleague and the creator of *Gypsy* stripper Tessie Tura, could triumph as Tevye's sharp-tongued, down-to-earth wife, Golde? He wanted Joanna Merlin to play one of the daughters (she had auditioned memorably for *Mother Courage*) and wouldn't give up when Bock and Harnick were less than impressed by her singing voice, necessary for the second daughter, Hodel. He accompanied her to her next voice lesson, discovered to his delight that she had solid chest tones, and convinced his colleagues that she could play Tzeitel, the eldest. She got the part at her eighth audition (before Actors' Equity ordered that performers had to be paid for auditioning more than five times) on November 22, 1963, and she came out of the theater to learn that President Kennedy had been shot.

Robbins and his colleagues may have thought of Zero Mostel for the part of Tevye on the basis of seeing him in Arnold Perl's *The World of Sholom Aleichem* on television (Perl's adaptation of three stories aired on WNTA on December 14, 1959). Mostel played three roles: an Angel in "Bontche Schweig," the Teacher in "A Tale of Chelm," and Uncle Max in "The High School." Having weathered Zero's hostility during *A Funny Thing Happened on the Way to the Forum,* Robbins wrote an imploring letter to "Dear Zee," who had schedule conflicts. "Please," he wrote, "don't make me do this without you. Please." Austin Pendleton from *Oh Dad* became Motel the tailor, and Jerry summoned his onetime mentor Gluck Sandor to play the rabbi. Actors, singers, and dancers begged to audition; some, when they thought they'd done badly, wrote asking for a second chance—and often got one.

It was determined that the musical would begin rehearsing on June 1, 1964, open in Detroit for a four-week run on July 18, play Washington, D.C., for another month, and come into New York's Imperial Theatre on September 22. Over the spring months, Robbins pressed his colleagues hard. He had warned himself to avoid the picturesque and not to romanticize the characters: "They are tough, working, resilient, tenacious; they fiercely live and hang on to their existence; they have the word, everyone else is wrong; we are not to see them thru the misty nostalgia of a time past, but thru the every day hard struggle to keep alive and keep their beliefs." This belief infused his notes to Bock, Stein, and Harnick. After telling the "boys" in March that "Again I feel I have the treasure of the season and I'm grateful to all of you for being able to work on it," and having said in one April missive that he thought the score wonderful, he then zeroed in to criticize it as "one-dimensional":

> There is an insistent repetitiveness of a Russian-Jewish song to such extent that its beauty becomes a whine . . . Missing in the show is the toughness, tenaciousness, robustness, virility and hard core resilience of the people. Nostalgia and sentiment should be made because of the fierceness and passion of a lost time. If every song is sweet, sentimental sad, touching and nostalgic, all will come off as Second Avenue.

("The Boys," in an undated reply, addressed him as "Dear Reb Robbins.")

Length was a problem from the beginning. In a note ominously titled "Book Changes to be Completed by Author in April," he announced that forty pages of script had to be cut: "No arguments on this—this is fact." *Funny Girl,* he explained to Stein, had suffered because the rehearsal script, "which was well written and carefully plotted for character, was not written within the time and tempo schedule of a musical, and when it was ripped to pieces to bring it down to size only a soap opera paste job could be done to make anything recognizable and tell the story." He didn't want to go through that again. At some point, Stein added a P.S. to the discussion of what to cut: "How about cutting out the intermission. Smoking is bad for them anyway."

The surgery continued during rehearsals and tryouts. Aronson's set took up too much space. He fumed and reconfigured it. The reviewer who covered the Detroit opening described the show as "lacklustre" (the direction), "serviceable" (the production elements), and "pedestrian" (the dancing) and mentioned that it was about half an hour too long. Beatrice Arthur, who played Yente the matchmaker, found her part diminishing bit by bit. Songs were dropped. "If I Were a Woman," a song for daughter number two, Hodel (Julia Migenes), and Perchik (Bert Convy), her idealistic young student-agitator sweetheart, was replaced by a brief dance that charmingly reveals the musical's theme: Perchik invites the doubtful Hodel to try a new kind of dancing (a citified ballroom dance in which men and women embrace!); it opposes village tradition, but what could be the harm in something so delightful?

Songs were not the only casualties. Robbins had labored over a dream ballet to follow Chava's announcement that she will marry Fyedka, a Gentile, and Tevye's declaration that, in accordance with tradition, she is henceforth considered dead. Her ghostly image was to follow him while dancers whirled around him. Jerry had cast Tanya Everett as Chava because she was a dancer. The ballet got shorter and shorter until all that remained was Tevye's heartbroken song about the little girl he had loved, while, behind a scrim, the mother and three daughters moved quietly together in a memory of Chava's childhood days.

However, even as everything deemed extraneous was dug out and discarded, Robbins worked in a Detroit hotel room with Tommy Abbott and Betty Walberg to create the brilliant "bottle dance" for four especially nimble male wedding guests with strong thighs and cast-iron knees. "Do You Love Me?" (a song for Tevye and Golde that Robbins had insisted be written in order to give husband and wife a substantial moment together and that remained his favorite moment in the show) was moved to a better spot in Act II.

Whatever the writers, directors, designers, cast, and crew went through, *Fiddler on the Roof* emerged shining. Martin Gottfried wrote in *Women's Wear Daily* that

What Jerome Robbins has done is to create a time, a feeling, a warmth, and an enormous excitement that bristles through between emotions strong enough to put permanent lumps in mass throats. He has done it with time, with swirling color, with rhythms, with rushing sweeps of changing moods. He has done it with movement that for sheer beauty and relevance is paralleled only by his own *West Side Story*. He has also done it with a Jerry Bock score so lovely, so original, so rightly apt as to establish the composer securely in Broadway's first rank.

Several New York critics had quibbles. Bock's music would sound better with better singers (Norman Nadel, *New York World-Telegram and Sun*); the show lacked "something of the compelling dramatic power implicit in its story" (Richard Watts, *New York Post*). But as Howard Taubman noted in *The New York Times*, "criticism of a work of this calibre, it must be remembered, is relative." They all adored Mostel, whose dancing Jerry had likened delightedly to "the shifting of a tub full of jello," and his name figured in almost every headline. "To see him dance," said Gottfried, "is to see an angel in underwear, to listen in on his conversations with God is to be privy to the secret of life." Only Walter Kerr's review in the *New York Herald Tribune* seems to have seriously upset Robbins and everyone involved with the show. "I think it might be a charming musical," he wrote, "if only the people of Anatevka did not pause every now and then to give their regards to Broadway, with remembrances to Herald Square." After reading another half-critical, half-admiring piece by Kerr in the *Tribune*'s Sunday magazine on October 11 (an unpleasant surprise for Robbins's forty-sixth birthday), Jerry drafted a long response, attempting to rebut the critic point by point. The article fueled a feeling that had been smoldering in him throughout the difficult months of preparing the show: in order for *Fiddler* to have the success that pleased and enriched everyone concerned, compromises had had to be made, each one of them painful.

The musical was beautifully orchestrated, from Stein's down-to-earth dialogue to the moments of rapture that seize the group, from the serenity of Tzeitel and Motel's wedding, which, wrote Kerr, seemed "to lift a dozen families into the night air by candlelight," to the sudden shock of cossacks disrupting the revelry following it. Robbins built the first song, "Tradition," on a folk-dance walk, with a slight upward bounce on the accented count that gives it a lilt. As the members of each family group—the papas, the mamas, the sons, the daughters—step forward to sing and gesture their roles in the community, the body language becomes increasingly complex and the younger people cover more ground than their elders, as if tradition can barely contain their spirits. Individuals, including the Russians who stroll through, are introduced by Tevye, while a chaining dance freezes and resumes, freezes and resumes.

The scene in which Tevye agrees to marry Tzeitel to the elderly butcher Lazar Wolf escalates from a puzzled conversation (Tevye thinks Lazar Wolf wants to buy his cow, not marry his daughter) to a drunken revel and brings out the precarious status of these Jews in a village controlled by Russians. Robbins brilliantly used movement styles to convey both the cultural differences between Jews and Gentiles and the potential for harmony. A hush falls when five Russians walk into the tavern, but they order drinks and keep to themselves. The audience can almost forget they're there, until above the villagers' boisterous drinking song "To Life," a single sustained note rings out and everyone falls back. It is one of the Russians, and his golden tenor ushers in his friends' very civil congratulations to the prospective in-laws. Their fierce dancing (including the squat kicks called *prisadka*s) causes the intrigued Jews to back away and then follow after. Suddenly a Russian extends a hand peremptorily to Tevye. "Who, me?" he mimes, but allows himself to be drawn into a slow, stamping Russian walk. As the music speeds up, the Jews, old and young, begin their own kind of dancing in a chain, while the Russians pass squatting under the arches made by their clasped hands. Before long, Jews and Christians have merged in lines that weave and pivot in ingenious ways until, wild with drink and happiness, some of the men spin off to fall in a heap. The precariousness of this fellowship is made clear when the crowd staggers away and the constable enters to warn Tevye with some embarrassment that the authorities have mandated a little dustup—no, not a pogrom, just something to show he and his men are keeping the Jews of Anatevka in their place. At the end of the play, when the village is dismantled and the families stand alone, you remember those circles and chains.

One danger the show's creators had foreseen was that Mostel was unable for long to hold in check his comedic urges and his talents as an improvisor. Robbins had given it two months, and he proved to be right. Indeed, controlling the level of Tevye's shtick and his ad-libbing remained a problem for the stage manager and the collaborators. However much Mostel amused audiences, this show had come to represent a people and a way of life, and the Jewish community wanted it to stay true to their culture. Judah Nadich, rabbi of the Park Avenue Synagogue, had written

Robbins shortly after *Fiddler* opened that he took deep satisfaction in the musical's fidelity to the spirit of Aleichem: "It faithfully reflects both his humor and pathos, the 'tears dipped in honey,' as Heine once described true Jewish humor."

Fiddler triumphed at the 1965 Tony awards, named the best musical. Robbins won for his choreography and direction. Stein, Bock, and Harnick were honored for their contributions, as was Harold Prince for producing the show, Patricia Zipprodt for her costumes, and Zero Mostel and Maria Karnilova for their performances. However, when the Mirisch brothers decided to make a film of *Fiddler* starring Topol, who had played the role to acclaim in London, they were not willing to take on Jerry Robbins. *West Side Story* had convinced them that "he didn't seem able to pick up the tempo and style of picture-making." Amid all the congratulations—telegrams, notes, hugs, words of praise—one stood out: Harry Robbins, né Rabinowitz, came backstage with open arms and tears in his eyes.

Legions of dancers, dance enthusiasts, and dance scholars owe much to *Fiddler on the Roof.* In December 1964, Robbins assigned to the Dance Collection of the New York Public Library one quarter of a percent of his author's royalties from *Fiddler*'s box-office receipts and one quarter of a percent of the royalties from his subsidiary rights as author. The income was to establish what was originally called the Lena Robbins Dance Film Archive, to acquire and preserve archival films, and to film important new dances. Six months later, he assigned it an additional one quarter percent. The income for what's now known as the Jerome Robbins Archive of the Recorded Moving Image has been considerable. For July, August, and September of 1968, for example, Tevye's tribulations earned it $5,570. To this day, with productions of *Fiddler on the Roof* being staged all the time and recordings and videos still being sold, the money keeps coming in.

———

Robbins was never without projects simmering on a back burner. At least as early as 1962, the *On the Town* team—he, Leonard Bernstein, and Betty Comden and Adolph Green—had been discussing collaborating on a musical version of Thornton Wilder's *The Skin of Our Teeth,* and on December 27 of that year they drafted agreements to form a joint venture for the "purpose of producing and operating a dramatico-musical play." Wilder's work is seemingly set in small-town America, but the family pets are a dinosaur and a mammoth, and the Ice Age (read nuclear dev-astation) is coming. Delivering wit and fantasy in down-to-earth tones was something at which all four excelled.

Their schedules kept getting in the way. Finally on January 4, 1965, the show's potential producer, Leland Hayward, issued a statement announc-ing that the project had been canceled but that "The four plan to work to-gether on another project in the future." That, alas, never came about. Robbins, queried in 1993 by Humphrey Burton for Burton's biography of Bernstein, stated a previously unvoiced reason for abandoning *Skin*. Bur-ton had asked whether Bernstein was becoming more difficult as a collab-orator. Robbins penciled in the margin for his secretary to answer: "No—we did not want to think of a world after a nuclear war."

Around the same time, a project that Robbins had dreamed of for many years was about to come to life onstage. Lucia Chase had decided that, as part of American Ballet Theatre's twenty-fifth anniversary season, she would commission a new ballet by Jerome Robbins, set to Igor Stravin-sky's "ballet cantata" *Les Noces,* first staged by Bronislava Nijinska for Di-aghilev's Ballets Russes in 1923. As Jerry had already discovered, this was no small undertaking, given that it involved a chorus, four solo singers, four pianos, and a number of percussion instruments. Fresh from *Fiddler* and the compromises he had had to make in material that he cherished, Robbins could bring to *Les Noces* his deepening interest in ritual as well as the Russian folklore he had studied. The tradition of matchmakers and arranged marriages that had figured in *Fiddler* could be viewed from a dif-ferent perspective, without having to yield to the requirements of a hit musical.

For about ten years prior to Chase's offer, he had been hoping to cho-reograph either *Les Noces* or *Le Sacre du Printemps* (the Ballets Russes premiere with choreography by Vaslav Nijinsky had incited riots in the theater). His plans had always been foiled, either by others or by his own crammed schedule. These were two magisterial Stravinsky scores that he knew Balanchine would never choreograph: both were highly dramatic, with strong scenarios that would be impossible to ignore. Robbins's frus-trating pursuit of these Stravinsky masterworks explains why Lucia Chase's offer was so timely and welcome.

October 1953. La Scala has invited him to stage *Les Noces,* and he writes to Stravinsky, asking the composer to explain his approach and how he as choreographer can best fulfill the musical ideas. Stravinsky is encouraging but taken aback: How can one discuss such things in the mail? Jerry pursues him:

> I notice that sometimes you fit and reshift the words to accommodate them within a set metric pattern and at other times you change the time signature to fit the rhythm of the words. I would be curious to know for instance which way you would like to see it done at No. 2 in your score; would you want the accents to come on the 16th notes, or to have a steady eighth beat running through the whole section with the music making the accents against the pattern?

November 1953. Asked by Ninette de Valois to choreograph something for Britain's Royal Ballet, Robbins proposes *Sacre*. She tells him that Léonide Massine wants to revive his version for her company.

December 1953. Bad terms, letters gone astray and so not answered in time, as well as Robbins's schedule with the New York City Ballet sinks the La Scala *Noces*.

October 1954. Lincoln Kirstein writes Robbins. Balanchine wants to choreograph Stravinsky's *Pulcinella* to star Jerry, and, no, Jerry cannot do *Noces* or *Sacre* for the New York City Ballet.

November 1956. Robbins, busy with *Bells Are Ringing* and coping with the news of Le Clercq's paralysis, mentions in response to a sympathetic letter from his friend Vera Volkova that he'd be interested in doing *Noces* or *Sacre* for the Royal Danish Ballet.

April 1957. Frank Schauffus, now artistic director of the Royal Danish Ballet, writes Jerry: *Sacre*? Great!

October 1957. Robbins hopes Picasso will do the sets for his *Sacre* and writes him a letter: "First allow me to introduce myself . . ."

November 1957. It is discovered that *Sacre* cannot be performed in Copenhagen's Royal Theater because the pit will hold only eighty musicians and there is no score for reduced orchestra. The theater plans to enlarge the pit, but not for two years, and to do so will require permission from Parliament. *Sacre* must be postponed. Everyone is very, very disappointed.

February 1958. Robbins cables the Royal Danish Ballet's executive director, H. A. Brøndsted. How about *Les Noces* this spring? Sorry, not possible for "musical technical reasons." Never mind, he'll do it in Spoleto this coming summer.

March (?) 1958. Doris Humphrey invites him to view her company, Juilliard Dance Theatre; Juilliard School of Music has all the resources to perform *Les Noces.* He travels uptown and takes a look. There aren't enough strong dancers to satisfy him.

June 1958. He doesn't do *Les Noces* in Spoleto.

January 1960. In a long letter to Richard Buckle in London, Jerry lovingly describes an all-star performance of *Les Noces,* for which the pianists were Aaron Copland, Samuel Barber, Lukas Foss, and Roger Sessions.

> Then Stravinsky came on stage, gliding his way past the pianos with wonderful little mincing steps and twisting his body as if fending off blows. The entire house rose and gave him a long and heartfelt standing ovation which was about as exciting a moment as I ever lived through in the theatre. The sweet little man bowed very nicely and turned to conduct his "Noces." The piece was absolutely fantastic. More inspiring than I ever thought it could be and his conducting was so very wonderful because of his lack of an emotional and over-gesticulating quality; instead one saw the tenacious driving economy. No recording that I've ever heard has made the piece sound the way it did when little old Stravinsky was conducting it.

He itches to start choreographing *Noces.* Should he write to Ninette de Valois?

February 1960. The Danes are still trying to do *Sacre.* Stravinsky writes Brøndsted. At Diaghilev's request years ago, he reduced the orchestra for *Petrouchka*'s London performances, but it can't be done for *Sacre:* "I am very sorry not to be able to help you in this, especially as I am a very sincere admirer of Jerome Robbins, and I would be happy to know him staging the *SACRE,* but we must accept the fact that the re-writting [*sic*] this work for a smaller ensemble is already 45 year old headache without result."

February 1962. Plans for Robbins to stage *Les Noces* for the Royal Ballet in London go awry when musical director Colin Davis can't agree to have any of his musicians play on the stage (as Stravinsky always wished). Also, spending two intermissions moving four grand pianos into and out of the pit doesn't seem feasible.

February 1963. Finally asked to choreograph *Les Noces* for the Spoleto Festival, Jerry has to turn the offer down because he can't predict what state he'll be in after *Mother Courage.*

1964. Lucia Chase offers to undertake *Les Noces.* In an article Robbins drafts in 1965 less than two weeks before the ballet's March 30 premiere at the Brooklyn Academy of Music, he thanks her for "the comfort of her company out on a very high limb. I've told her over and over the tree is slippery and the height tremendous, but nothing will avail. 'Forward' she cries. 'Danger!' yell I. 'Onward' she prods me."

———

Stravinsky had begun work on *Les Noces* soon after the premiere of *Le Sacre du Printemps* in 1913. He had been asked by Diaghilev to write another score based on Russian peasant customs, presumably for Nijinsky to choreograph. It took the composer ten years and involved many different ideas about orchestration before he finished the work—barely in time for Bronislava Nijinska to choreograph it in 1923 (she had inherited the project, both her brother Vaslav and Léonide Massine, his successor as Diaghilev's principal choreographer, having by then defected). As text for his scenes from a Russian village wedding, Stravinsky drew on folk songs collected by Peter Vasiliev Kireyevsky and set them to complex, ferociously driving music that underscored the almost cruel rituals of an arranged marriage in which bride and groom are chosen by matchmakers and parents; prepared for the ceremony; and, with much drunken revelry, ushered into bed. Even the parents' grief over losing their children is ritualized. Robbins wrote:

> The music is monolithic and elegant—barbaric, beautiful and frightening. . . . Its form is stubborn, polished, astonishingly block-like and complete unto itself. It is absolutely unyielding. It cannot be disguised or altered by choreography. . . . Once the music starts nothing can stop it. You push a button and this terrifying machine begins to scream, launches into its lamentations, incessant chattering, shocking you with unexpected outbursts and hypnotic murmurings. . . . An overpowering tension is created by the simpleness of the material (the wedding) and by the extraordinary, bizarre and inspired means with which Stravinsky has expressed it.

Robbins hadn't seen Bronislava Nijinska's *Les Noces* when Colonel de Basil's Ballets Russes brought it to Manhattan in 1936. Like many New Yorkers, he was stunned by Nijinska's magnificent 1966 reconstruction of it for Britain's Royal Ballet when the company brought it to New York that fall. Had he seen her *Noces* before he mounted his own version, he would, he later intimated, have been disheartened ("It is a work of majestic inspiration. It curiously combines stiffness & archaic limitations with overt violence & ecstasy. It is as condensed & ritualized as a Japanese Noh drama"). He was, however, familiar with the photographs of Diaghilev's company rehearsing Nijinska's ballet on the roof of Paris's Théâtre de la Gaîté-Lyrique. Patricia Zipprodt's costumes for Robbins are remarkably like Natalia Goncharova's for Nijinska. (He had also, incidentally, seen another vivid dance about an arranged marriage: Sara Levi-Tanai's *Yemenite Wedding* for Inbal.)

Most of the similarities between Robbins's ballet and Nijinska's are due to the fact that both used weighted, down-driving movement and flexed feet (although Nijinska put her women on pointe) and hewed closely to the structure of Stravinsky's scenario. Both choreographers, however, ignored details of the text. No matchmaker tears the Bride's golden tresses; no friends comb the Bridegroom's curls. They make different choices about what to emphasize. Their Brides have artificial braids many feet in length, but in Nijinska's ballet these are taken from her, while in Robbins's, her friends dance on either side of her, braiding six rope strands in a kind of maypole dance, while she, less stoic than Nijinska's Bride, reaches pleadingly to them. In the end, she is carried offstage trussed in the plaits.

Nijinska's ballet is the more austere. Her blocky formations and mountains made of heads laid on top of one another are redolent of the primitivism so captivating to early modernist choreographers like herself and her brother. The force and simplicity of her designs and her use of repetition prefigure modern dance works such as Martha Graham's 1931 *Primitive Mysteries* or Doris Humphrey's 1936 *With My Red Fires*. Nijinska brought out the community's matter-of-fact disregard for the couple's feelings; their bridal dance on a high platform above the stamping, leaping squads of revelers is formal and slightly stiff; the mothers open wide the bedroom doors, close them behind the pair, and sit on a bench in front of it. Robbins has the nuptial pair, willy-nilly, fall in love. On a small platform that suddenly appears, spotlit in darkness, Robbins shows their union in highly condensed form, suffused with their awkwardness and strong emotions. The words Stravinsky gave the chorus emanate, without Nijinska's irony, from their embraces: "Dear heart, little wife, my own dearest treasure. . . . Let us live in happiness that all men may envy us."

Robbins showed the peasant community as driven by ritual—ceremonious and mannerly in their circles and lines. The Bride greets the wedding guests with formal bows; the Groom is steadily driven across the floor by his male friends and relatives as the apex of a wedge. But at times, the behavior is raucous. The guests shove the Bride and Groom together. Several men turn the Groom in midair somersaults. There's some boisterous competing. A matchmaker calls other couples from the throng.

The initial draft of an agreement with ABT, dated February 19, 1965, gave Robbins $1,000 upon signing the contract and another $1,000 five days after the first public performance, as well as royalties (the company proposed $50 per performance; he asked for $75). He required control over the casting, designers, conductors, and program notes and insisted on having the ballet notated. He began choreographing with ABT dancers, but because the company had to go on tour, he assembled a surrogate group that included some former Ballets: U.S.A. dancers. Although all the dancers learned every role, Erin Martin's combination of fragility and strength made her an ideal Bride, and Robbins induced Lucia Chase to take her, as well as James Moore, into the company on a special basis.

A couple of years later, Naomi Isaacson, who was notating the ballet during rehearsals of a revival, took notes on Robbins's directives to the dancers; they reveal how he saw Stravinsky's scenario. Many of Isaacson's paraphrases of Robbins's remarks emphasize his concern with community; these people are not just an ensemble but individuals who know one another. "Pride in making this thing happen is the keynote—each of the people present either has been through the ritual or knows they will be going through it." And (a direct quote): " 'Together we are making this happen.' " He also gave clues to the style he was after: "Girls' movements must be big, bawdy, peasant moves—no fingers—like wood carvings." Chase dropped in to watch the ballet as it progressed and expressed her happiness in a note to the choreographer: "Not since Fokine have I seen such inspiring rehearsals & I enjoyed every moment that I could be there—Thank you for letting me—I attended every one that I could for the joy of seeing a master at work." She hoped Jerry would realign himself with ABT.

Les Noces was a tremendous achievement on Robbins's part—"a triumph," as critic Marcia B. Siegel put it in her *New York* magazine review—although there were some prominent naysayers. Robbins was gratified by the positive responses but thought the ballet flawed. He wrote Robert Graves, whose *White Goddess* he greatly admired and with whom he corresponded about possible projects, that "It's a little athletic, more so than I want it to be, and I think that this is so because of my overzealous attempt to communicate <u>everything</u> about what I heard and saw in the music."

He noted in a letter to Richard Buckle that choreographing a work for the New York City Ballet's rival, American Ballet Theatre, may have endangered his relationship with NYCB, noting that the company was taking only his *Fanfare* to London and presenting only *Interplay* in Manhattan.

In late fall 1965, a slipped disk caused trouble serious enough to land Jerry in the hospital in traction. He sent home for a jigsaw puzzle and, disappointed to find it lacked a piece, queried Le Clercq, whom he remembered having been the last person to work on it at a gathering at his house. Tanny wrote back, only mildly sympathetic, advising him, if he cared that much, to consult Arthur Gold, who had been in the Robbins kitchen with her and had removed for her the tape that kept the box secure. She knew Jerry all too well: "I guess it's just YOU—always a piece missing."

⁓

Involvement in experimental theater was hard to come by in New York, given the demands of the marketplace and Robbins's very large reputation. He made a mistake in developing *The Office,* by Maria Irene Fornés, as a Broadway show with a name star, instead of opening it off-Broadway, as he had Arthur Kopit's *Oh Dad, Poor Dad, Mamma's Hung You in the Closet and I'm Feelin' So Sad. The Office* satirized the kind of behavior that Fornés had observed when she arrived from Cuba as a teenager and took a job as a translator. The play operated on a level of wackiness and fantasy that could give a director and eight actors plenty of room in which to be seriously absurd.

Fornés, an aspiring painter only recently hooked on playwriting, had had her first play, *Tango Palace,* produced in Spoleto. In 1965 she had won an Obie, one of *The Village Voice*'s annual awards to downtown theater, for her *Promenade,* a musical play presented at the avant-garde hotbed Judson Church, with a score by its assistant pastor Al Carmines. When Fornés's agent, Bertha Case, first approached Robbins about *The Office* in August 1965, its first act had already been shown at the Actors Studio, with Gene Wilder in the leading role of Pfancoo, the office manager, and it had been optioned by The Establishment theater.

Robbins aimed higher. Joseph E. Levine, the president of Embassy Pictures, put up the $150,000 necessary to mount the show on Broadway, co-producing it with Ivor David Balding (though not officially listed as a producer, Robbins would receive 25 percent of the profits, in addition to 4 percent of the weekly take and a director's fee of $5,000). Jerry went after known stars. "The author has big talent and I believe in her totally," he wrote to Phil Silvers, whom he envisioned as Pfancoo (Silvers, facing cataract operations, had to decline). The masterly comedian Jack Weston was signed for the role, and Elaine May agreed to return to Broadway, where she hadn't been seen since 1961, and *An Evening with Mike Nichols and Elaine May.*

May was cast as Shirley, the young woman whom Pfancoo sneaks into the office, hoping that Princess (Ruth White), the widow and heir of the office's founder, Hinch, can be persuaded to hire her and fire his nemesis, the sourpuss secretary Miss Punk (Doris Roberts). This is not easy, since, like Fornés herself during her office days, Shirley can type about ten words a minute. Her fingers get tangled in the typewriter keys, and she doesn't know her ABCs well enough to find a file quickly (she has to start with A and work her way through the alphabet each time). Betty Comden remembered as a high point of the play May scrolling a piece of paper into the typewriter, importantly hitting one key, and then crumpling the paper and throwing it away (later, every desk drawer will turn out to be full of nearly blank crumpled paper).

It's never clear what this firm actually does—there is a semidashing Italian salesman named Gucci (Tony Lo Bianco), who occasionally happens by and rouses the usually somnolent Princess to lust—but whatever the business is, it's being conducted with sublime inefficiency. Yet even though nothing about the office works properly, all those connected with it doggedly pursue improbable goals, as if this were their entire world. Pfancoo, in the interests of his own passion for Princess (both as a woman and as a representative of the boss he idolized) and his craving to advance within the firm, attempts to derail her wedding to Gucci, with astonishing results.

Robbins had scene designer Ed Wittstein set up a working model of the set within one of Ballet Theatre's West Fifty-seventh Street studios. The set itself was a replica of a jobber's office, complete with stocked file drawers and stationery engraved with the "Hinch Inc." letterhead. The original plan was to have the entire set gradually tip forward toward the audience, but someone (evidently Jerry) got cold feet. Robert Prince provided incidental music to underline moods, as in a movie score.

The director seems to have had a very good time working out how to give the absurd behavior that Fornés had created a kind of reasonableness. When Pfancoo instructs Shirley in office teamwork, using *The Three Musketeers* as an example, he starts fencing and she duels with him. In the course of a crazy conversation with the Chinese maintenance man (Cliff Arashi), Pfancoo breaks into Hamlet's speech to his mother. In the final, spooky scene, Shirley dances with the portrait of Hinch that Pfancoo has commissioned, in the mad hope of stopping the wedding. The portrait tells Shirley he loves her and they sing "Ah, Sweet Mystery of Life." If Shirley will marry the portrait, Pfancoo thinks, his own position will be assured and the business will thrive. After the "I do" and some business with smoke and mirrors, Shirley appears *in* the portrait (a projection at that point), a tiny figure in bridal regalia perched on Hinch's shoulder, with Pfancoo on his knees before them within a larger frame.

Had *The Office* been performed for an off-Broadway audience, its zaniness might have been relished. At the end of the play's first showing there were boos. And although the house was sold out for every one of the ten previews (with tickets priced at $1) and some people apparently enjoyed themselves, Robbins and the producers decided to close the play before the critics could get their hooks into it. Jerry was not used to receiving angry letters. One began, "Dear Sir, I have never in the 22 years of attending theatre had my intelligence so insulted as I did last Friday nite." The writer added that she was returning the tickets she had bought for her two daughters "for fear of ruining theatre for them."

It's not clear what went wrong. Fornés in 2002 said hesitantly that perhaps Jerry hadn't had enough fun with it. At the time, he apologized to the playwright, shouldering all the blame for the play's failure. He told the actors that if he'd done his job as well as they'd done theirs, *The Office* might have been a hit. Although it was announced that the producers, director, and author were withdrawing the play to revise it for a new production in the fall, it did not reappear.

The Office may have increased Robbins's disenchantment with the pressures of Broadway, but help was on the way. On September 29, 1965, President Lyndon B. Johnson had signed into law the legislation establishing the National Endowment for the Arts, the National Endowment for the Humanities, and councils of experts to go with each, despite a widespread American view of the arts as frivolous. (It was reported that, during the initial debates, two senators were observed prancing down the corridors of power arm in arm, chanting "Yippee, I'm a performing art!") Roger Stevens became the NEA's first chairman and Jerome Robbins one of the first recipients of largesse from its $3 million budget. In August 1966, he received a $300,000 grant to set up an "American Lyric Theater Workshop," in which he planned to experiment with fusions of drama, music, and dance that didn't conform to any commercial model. This was brave thinking on the NEA's part; it affirmed the possibility that experiments—even failed ones—were vital to the health of the arts.

Robbins auditioned performers and, beginning in November, immersed them for almost two years in a rigorous schedule: from 10:00 A.M. to 6:00 P.M. five to five and a half days a week, with a summer break. His American Theatre Laboratory began with eleven people; some dropped out and were replaced, and some joined later. For the first six months or so, sessions were held in the Bohemian National Hall, then at a studio in Ballet Theatre's Fifty-seventh Street building. During the summer of 1967, Robbins was able to rent the entire second floor of the building at 219 West Nineteenth Street, where Dance Theater Workshop was later based. It became a kind of playground for very smart adults, equipped with boxes, flats, and various sorts of basic items, such as dowels and rope, which could stand in for almost anything.

Despite the permission—in effect, the mandate—to simply explore material, Robbins did pursue the idea of public performance. Before he ever met with the lab participants, he was presenting a rough budget to the Spoleto Festival to take the Japanese Noh play *Taniko* and Brecht's *The Measures Taken* there in the summer of 1967, and he presented a much more modest and affordable plan as late as April. For the summer of 1968, he presented another plan for Spoleto, which was accepted but apparently fell through.

The actors, singers, and dancers who participated in ATL* might have been startled to learn that Robbins had been thinking ahead to possible performances. From their perspective, Robbins would involve them all in a promising project and drop it without explanation, since there was no pressure from the NEA to produce and show finished work. Unlike some of the vanguard theater groups of the day, such as the Living Theater, the Open Theater, and the Performance Group, the members of ATL never quite felt like true collaborators. Robbins was protective of this private laboratory. The participants were asked to sign a paper stating that they wouldn't divulge anything that went on in the sessions, although records were kept—in part, perhaps, because he wanted to be able to prove to the NEA that there had been no slacking, in part for his own later perusal. Tom Stone took detailed daily notes, and audiotapes recorded the goings on; during the second year, a video camera was kept running (its mike often too distant to pick up what was said during the long discussions that followed each set of improvisations).

Still, the performers who stuck with ATL found the work days thrilling, if ultimately frustrating. Anna Sokolow, and later others, taught a morning movement class. There were singing lessons. Marion Rich worked on their elocution ("We'd have to do a soliloquy . . . from Shakespeare with a cork in our mouth . . . and really revolting tongue exercises, looking in the mirror, trying not to crack up"). During the second year, Mark Zeller took her place and was more connected to the various projects they worked on. If scripts were involved, Jay Harnick, as Robbins's assistant, or Grover Dale, would do the preliminary labor to prime the actors for Robbins. Other colleagues and invited guests dropped in intermittently: Mary Hunter; Joseph Papp; Leonard Bernstein, who came in to coach the group in the songs for *The Measures Taken*. Young Robert Wilson helped design the ATL space.

The highly formal traditions of Japanese Noh drama were a powerful influence on the ATL projects. Robbins had seen Noh plays in Japan in 1964, when visiting Robert "Robin" Curtis, a dealer in Asian art, and that same year he had sat in on a six-week workshop at the Institute for Advanced Studies in the Theatre Arts (IASTA). Two Noh masters had come

* Performers involved during one or both years were George Bartenieff, Mariclare Costello, Cathryn Damon, James Dybas, Robert Fields, Morgan Freeman, Leonard Frey, Paul Giovanni, Cliff Gorman, Marcia Jean Kurtz, Erin Martin, Julia Migenes, James Mitchell, Barbara Monte, James Moore, James Preston, Barry Primus, Jerome Ragni, and Dorothy Tristan.

to work with American actors on a new English verse translation of *Ikkaku Sennin* by the poet Frank Hoff. Jerry took notes, made sketches, and preserved among his papers sheets with notation for chorus chanting.

Over ATL's two seasons Robbins, who could tell a story so well, seems to have been trying to find strategies for manipulating narrative. He was fascinated by the ways in which, in many Asian theater forms, the performer may shift between narrating his or her story and reenacting it. He was also attracted to ancient Greek theater, which, like Noh, had used masks to objectify and universalize its characters. In the plays of Sophocles and Euripides, as in Noh plays, a chorus supported two or three actors, except that in the Greek dramas, the actors might play several roles each, while Noh's *shite,* or principal actor, presents one or more transformations of his own character (e.g., a simple monk may reveal himself to be the ghost of a warrior seeking closure and redemption).

In April 1967, he wrote to Robert Graves—poet, novelist, exegete of myth—with whom he had earlier bonded during an experience that involved the two ingesting psilocybin, the hallucinogenic mushroom. Robbins mentioned Noh plays as

> rituals in the way that ballets are rituals. But I guess what appeals to me mostly is the austerity and religious atmosphere, the paring away of unessentials, and the final evoking in the temple of some aspect of human relationships which have never been said purer or clearer. There is a relationship between that kind of theatre and things I want to attempt. It might be the intense religious fervor of it and the sense of embarking on a truly holy and perhaps dangerous journey. It has an intensity and a dedication and a solemnization which is enrapturing.

It is easy to understand why Jerry chose *The Measures Taken,* apart from his love of Brecht. In this short 1930 play, intended as a revolutionary proletarian drama, Brecht had resorted to the formality of Noh and some of the devices of classical Greek theater when designing the arguments between a Communist Party tribunal and four agitators who have been sent to propagandize in China, and between the agitators and an idealistic and impetuous Young Comrade working with them. To better infiltrate the workers, the agitators wear masks. In addition to speaking their questions and commands, members of the tribunal, known as the "Control Chorus," take on other roles—for instance, that of the rice barge coolies who sing of their travails. The agitators, explaining to the tribunal why they had to kill the Young Comrade and why he willingly submitted, outline the events of each scene and then enter and reenact it. Because Brecht conceived the play as a *Lehrstück*—intended more as a political lesson for the actors who played it than for an audience—he hoped that each of the four actors would take a turn expressing the Young Comrade's moral dilemmas.

An unlikely and eclectic range of material was also subjected at ATL to the kindred frameworks of classical Greek drama and/or Noh. Barry Primus speaks of simultaneously playing the ghost of Hamlet's father and himself, and of "doing *Hamlet* with two or three Hamlets on my back." A speech from Euripides' *The Bacchae* might be drawn out, Noh style, and take ten minutes to deliver. Lee Harvey Oswald's diaries became fodder for improvising on the text and using the techniques of repetition, choral chanting, and splitting characters that the actors had developed; at one point they all had babushkas over their heads as multiples of Oswald's Russian wife, Olga.

Even some of the very basic movement improvisations at ATL referred back to the austerity of Noh, the weight of each act and word. "He was fascinated," says James Mitchell, "with the impression an actor or dancer left on the stage when he left the stage. What an audience remembered. In other words, how to direct this person so that the image remained on-stage." Videos taken during ATL sessions show exercises in which people enter a space one by one, moving minimally in relation to a previous action by another.

The notion of distancing the performers from their actions took many forms; Erin Martin danced something from *Swan Lake,* while describing what she was doing. In one exercise, two "directors" prescribe actions and spoken lines for another two, who comply moment by moment; e.g., "She walks to the window." "He says, 'What are you doing?' " Afterward, the two are directed to perform the material on their own, assuming full responsibility for the formerly arbitrary actions. Perhaps influenced by Japanese puppet theater or his own early fascination with puppetry, Robbins devised exercises in which one actor manipulated another like a puppet through the "puppeteer's" own fantasy. In the "Black and White" series, these were further jiggered by casting. In one version of a seduction scene, James Preston, a black actor, wore a white mask and scarf and, manipulated by Dorothy Tristan, played a white woman. Leonard Frey, white, wore a black ski mask to play Preston and was manipulated by Barbara Monte.

Among Robbins's papers from July 1966 is a sketch of a play titled *The Mourning Dove,* "a cathartic lamentation and ritualization of grief upon the death of John F. Kennedy." In approaching the assassination with his actors through improvisations based on the testimonies in the Warren Commission Report, he aligned the material with Noh, one of whose central aesthetics is that the principal action is never presented directly but recalled and reenacted. During the second year (perhaps because of Mary Hunter's advice to Jerry to focus on a major project and organize his goals), the group worked extensively on Jacqueline Kennedy's testimony (and were assigned to read the commission's report in full). Judging from the memories of participants and fuzzy video records, the work that developed had stunning possibilities. In one video, the six chorus members take their places ceremoniously, intoning the names of those present. When Jacqueline Kennedy is asked for her account of what happened, Leonard Frey assumes a place on a platform. He takes a mask from a stand when Mrs. Kennedy gives her name; asked if she is the widow of the president, Frey puts a black veil over his (her) head: "Yes." A little later, he pushes the veil back as if it were hair—a wonderful moment. Frey intones her words to striking effect. A stick becomes bouquets. And then he steps down from his platform and improvises a dance that embodies/reawakens the remembered emotions.

The performers were taught the Japanese tea ceremony to intensify and formalize their concentration as judges at the Warren Commission hearings. Robbins had provided all the equipment: green tea, bowls, brushes, hot water. They learned to do it in precise unison. Then they practiced it without the props. Finally, after weeks, they walked in and *thought* it. In unison. "And, of course, we were all so mesmerized," says James Mitchell, "so dizzy from Jerry at that time that we did it." (A few people, apparently, objected to such esoteric demands and disappeared, and the story made for good party gossip among theater people who knew Jerry.)

Many exercises fed into the testimony scene. The workshop members abstracted the moment of the shot that had killed Kennedy and reacted as if they were being blown to pieces. A series of improvisations gave each actor a turn to be, like Jacqueline Kennedy, a public figure or the center of attention in harrowing circumstances (Dorothy Tristan was a patient before a doctor in an institution, Erin Martin a nude model for an art class, etc.). One exercise of January 3, 1968—meant to demonstrate the effect of a chorus or commission against a single person—began with men and women in two parallel lines walking on every other set of four counts, but the ensuing variants became aggressive, with people joining in various ways against others (no touching), until all united against a single person, in this case Jerome Robbins. In view of a possible performance, Tom Stone organized some of the Kennedy assassination material into a workable script.

There was a great deal of group discussion. Robbins gave all the participants subscriptions to what was then known as the *Tulane Drama Review,* the publication edited by Richard Schechner and Michael Kirby that featured articles on radical theater. They discussed Cardinal Spellman's funeral as theater. They discussed Peter Brook's production of *Oedipus* as ritual. They discussed the news about escaped nerve gas killing sheep in Utah. And they analyzed whatever they had just done.

Moments of startling beauty emerged. Primus still thinks of his ATL days as one of the best times in his life. And he was responsible for one of Robbins's own most powerful revelations. Jerry had asked each member to perform a short improvised scene. They were to use masks (very neutral ones)—not wearing them, but holding them and projecting the role into the mask. Primus chose to be an old king entering his throne room for the last time, to say good-bye to it. (Robbins recalled that the scene was to be without words, but Primus remembers that he spoke a kind of narration: "I enter the room," and so on.) A few days later, Robbins asked him to play the scene as a series of animals that corresponded to the thoughts passing through the king's mind and described the result in an enraptured letter to Robert Graves:

> An absolutely astonishing thing happened. The boy disappeared and converted himself (just the way I imagine Dionysus did) into a series of animals, beginning with a mouse, to a young colt, to a wounded lion, to an aged eagle, and back to the mouse as he left. It made me weep because he struck some deep and primitive core within himself and with all those watching. It wasn't at all just an act of imitating animals but he totally disappeared into the animal. His mouse was frightened, timid, anxious; his young colt struggled to get on his feet, snorted and moved and basked in the sun, tossed his mane, galloped about; when he saw his throne he went to it like a dog after a bone, sniffing and smelling away

at it; when he climbed on the throne he was an old wounded lion roaring, licking itself, smelling and keeping an eye out for what was about. His exit, as the plumed eagle, was tremendous. With his back to us he plowed his way through the skies. Without his knowing it the boy had enacted so much of what I have heard you talk about and read in some of your books. It was both frightening and exhilarating to have the New York studio changed into a tribal ceremony for those few minutes. I wish you could have seen it.

Hearing these words years later brought tears to Erin Martin's eyes. If only, she said, Jerry had ever told us all that he felt this moved by anything. They never knew how, or if, what they were doing fit into a larger picture. At one point toward the end of the project, they had a meeting with him and told him of their frustrations. He listened courteously and said that he understood, that he was sorry, but offered no solutions. Instead, he began to show up less, and the American Theatre Laboratory ended in March 1968.

In many ways, ATL's two years were peaceful ones for Robbins. His only commercial venture involved a weekend in Boston in April 1967, when Betty Comden, Adolph Green, Arthur Laurents, and Jule Styne asked for his input on their Broadway-bound show, *Hallelujah, Baby!* He had purchased a town house on East Eighty-first Street that even had room for a small practice studio on the top floor and fretted over its decoration (while he had been sweating over *Fiddler on the Roof,* his loving landlady on Seventy-fourth Street, Muriel Resnick, had decided that due to the success of her play *Any Wednesday,* she and her husband needed her whole house; she spent the next year apologizing and wondering if she couldn't manage to have Jerry back). He had a lover who had nothing to do with the theater and who seems to have spent a lot of time at Ding Dong House in Snedens Landing—working in the garden, painting, and, when Jerry went to Europe to relax in April 1968, attending a Robbins family seder in Jerry's absence and sending flowers on his behalf to Edith Weissman on her birthday.

It was at Snedens that Robbins made some new friends who were to become an important part of his life. The trip from Manhattan took about thirty-five minutes. Daniel Stern, his first wife, and his two young children were living just up the road from Ding Dong House. Jerry met them walking his dog and stopped to watch Stern try to teach his little son to ski.

He found the whole family stimulating. Dr. Stern's work with aspects of infant behavior intrigued dance and theater people—Robbins, Robert Wilson, and Jeff Duncan among them—and continues to interest dance scholars. Stern says he would see Robbins digging in his garden and look over the fence for a chat; "or Jerry would just roam around and come over to our house and knock on the door and say could he do anything for me. So we would take a walk and go somewhere. . . . It was an easy time for him."

However, during this "easy time," other projects both fed into his ATL work and tempted him away from it. For a variety of reasons, including his usual insecurities, none of them materialized, but they reveal where his interests lay. Even before ATL began, Laurence Olivier had been trying to pin him down about directing a play at Britain's National Theatre, and Robbins mentioned *The Bacchae*. After working on the play at ATL, he put forth a heady casting possibility for the fall of 1968: Might John Gielgud be interested? He and Olivier could play any role or roles, "or even triple parts as they were originally done," if masked.

While researching Noh, he had become intrigued by Zeami, the great Japanese playwright of the fourteenth and fifteenth centuries—by his life as a married homosexual, by his plays, by his trenchant advice for actors. He wrote a letter to the noted Japanese writer Yukio Mishima in June 1967, introducing himself, praising Mishima's novels, and inquiring whether Mishima would consider collaborating with him and a composer on a musical-dramatic work about Zeami's life. Mishima, who turned out to be a fan of *West Side Story,* was gracious and very interested, but nothing came of it. The projected work was to be a kind of extended Noh play itself. Robbins's notes to himself suggest that there might be four Zeamis, as well as multiples of other characters and, of course, an onstage chorus. He visualized the characters dancing a ritual in the form of a pavane in which people and events from his life and times would mix and meet to show, if possible, how the playwright had converted the harsh realities of his life into art. (Mishima killed himself in 1970; Jerry saved the newspaper clippings.)

During ATL's second year, Jerry became very interested in directing George Tabori's play *The Cannibals* at the American Place Theatre, in part as an ATL project. Plans seemed to be moving forward, if tentatively, for the play to open in October 1968, after the American Theatre Laboratory experiment was officially ended. The daily notes that Tom Stone took at

ATL record that on the afternoon of December 4, 1967, Robbins dismissed the women and read through the play with the ATL men and other invited actors. Written in memory of Tabori's uncle, who had perished in Auschwitz, and set in a concentration camp in Hitler's Germany in the spring of 1941, the play centered on the death of a pathologically fat inmate and the debate among the starving survivors as to whether they should eat him or not. After the war, the survivors prefer to forget or deny the experience but are forever changed by it. The possibility was raised that the play be acted out by the sons and daughters of the men after the men themselves were dead—remembering and perhaps reenacting events that still troubled them decades later.

Through the summer and fall of 1968, Robbins developed strategies for a film he wanted to direct about Vaslav Nijinsky—his ballets, his amorous relationship with his mentor Serge Diaghilev, his marriage, and his madness—for producer Harry Salzman. The Royal Ballet tentatively agreed to participate, and Rudolf Nureyev was interested in starring. Writers were approached: Harold Pinter, Peter Shaffer, and, in the end, John Bowen. Richard Buckle was at the time writing his biography of Nijinsky; Jerry sent off astute critiques of his friend's chapters-in-progress and learned much from them. The influence of the ATL experimentation is obvious in Robbins's notes. Perhaps, he thought at one point, the principal characters—Nijinsky, Diaghilev, and the dancer's wife, Romola—could introduce themselves to the viewers before triggering the events in flashback form. Even more telling are his notes dated October 15, 1968: "Is it possible to do a ballet-Noh play on N starting him as a sweeper of the stage—attendant at a mad house—gardener at his home in St Moritz—or—England—an attendant on a boat to S.A. [South America—the tour on which Nijinsky married Romola]—& use water waves etc.—& under questioning to relive his past life & madness (become a mad person-woman-man) in struggles between life—loves & dance—ending in calm madness . . ." He envisioned a "really interpretive impressionistic film style" with such effects as this: "Say you film a ballet like Sheherazade from Nijinsky's point of view—his reality—and suddenly have a view from back of house, a grainy little b & w simulated still newsreel camera's view of little figures dancing." Early in 1969, Salzman fired him.

The same complicated juxtaposition of viewpoints figured even more elaborately in a similarly aborted plan to direct Bertolt Brecht's *The Exception and the Rule,* which Jerry worked on at the same time he was thinking about the film and *The Cannibals.* By the time it was abandoned, it involved all the *West Side Story* colleagues but Arthur Laurents (although there is evidence that he was considering being a part of it early on). Like *The Measures Taken,* the play takes place in China, and, like *Measures,* it advances the arguments of communism. The ruling class is represented by an unprincipled merchant out to get to Urga, where oil has been discovered, ahead of other caravans (he expects to be paid off *not* to deal in it). An innocent, abused Coolie stands for exploited labor, and a Guide is the moderately conscientious mediator. The Merchant shoots the Coolie as the latter is advancing on him holding out the last flask of water, because he thinks the flask is a stone and believes that the Coolie must hate him. At the Merchant's trial for murder, the jury believes the Guide's account but rules that because the Merchant had acted in what he thought was self-defense, he owes the Coolie's widow no compensation. No one can believe that the Coolie could have absorbed so much punishment and so many racial slurs and yet not wish to kill the Merchant. This is the skeletal plot. Brecht argues the subtleties of the characters' views and positions in short, emotionally charged scenes.

Robbins enlisted the young playwright John Guare, whose *Muzeeka,* staged at the Eugene O'Neill Theater Center in New London, Connecticut, and then at the Mark Taper Forum in Los Angeles, had received terrific reviews. In 1968, Guare began to reconceive Brecht's play in ways that enthralled Robbins. He set the scene in a television studio, where *The Exception and the Rule* was being rehearsed in front of a gala audience as part of a telethon to raise money and social consciences. With a black actor playing the Coolie (to Zero Mostel's Merchant) and other black actors involved, *The Exception and the Rule*—now a play within a play—was then supposed to tour major cities in a program sponsored by the National Council on Urban Renewal, designed to wake up middle-class whites to their responsibilities toward ending racism. The script mocked white hypocrisy. "There was no dialogue between blacks and whites at this point, and doing something like a telethon, just doing a bleeding-heart thing, was not going to solve anything," Guare says.

The structure was intricate. There were to be fairground booths and comedic acts related to the text before the play began. The performers break out of character to speak as "themselves"; the "star," for instance, stops in the middle of the merchant's "paranoia song" because the tempo is off. He also makes racial slurs and embarrasses his black costar, who plays the Coolie, by inviting the actor's "parents" up from the audience and coaxing them into doing a number from their vaudeville days (it isn't very good).

The project was rocky from the start. Sondheim, disliking Brecht's didacticism, wrote a song and a half and refused to go further. Bernstein worked on a couple of songs with Jerry Lieber but didn't want to pursue the collaboration. Robbins then charged Guare with convincing Sondheim to think again about participating—inviting Guare over, ushering him into a room where Sondheim, whom he had never met, was waiting, and leaving the men alone together. "Well, the irony," Guare says, "is that we got along great. . . . And I said, 'Why haven't you fellas done anything since *West Side Story*?' And he said, 'You'll see, you'll see.' " But he agreed to participate. Guare, being younger and somewhat in awe of his collaborators, did suffer some indignities; one can't imagine Robbins inviting Arthur Laurents to the country for the weekend and then locking him in the guest room until he produced some pages.

Throughout, Robbins was beset by uncertainties. One plan the collaborators discussed was to have Bernstein, Guare, Robbins, Sondheim, and the producer Stuart Ostrow—plus possibly the head of CBS, the head of the National Council for Urban Renewal, the director of the supposed television show, stagehands, costume designers, et al.—appear on video, discussing the show. Jerry wasn't happy about this idea. He also began to worry that the production was mocking Brecht, whom he revered. In addition, Arthur Laurents, styling himself as "Devil's Advocate," wrote a letter that took his erstwhile collaborators aback. Titled "Is the Evening Anti-Semitic?" it noted, among other points, that "Producer, star, director, composer, lyricist are all—consciously or unconsciously—white exploiters of the Negro. They are all Jewish, and their names are Jewish. They are well-known and known to be Jews."

A scene between Robbins and Guare early in the collaboration, as recollected by Guare, illustrates Jerry's chronic insecurity and perhaps something else as well: his feelings of inferiority about his lack of higher education and his admiration/envy of those with a university degree.

One morning I came, and I gave Jerry three pages of a scene. . . . And Jerry said, "Oh, I really like this." "Oh," I said, "thank God." "What do you mean, thank God?" I said, "No, I'm glad you like it." He said, "Well, don't *you* like it?" I said, "Jerry, I just—I've been up all night

working on it and I'm just—and it's so new to me that I don't—I—."
He said, "Well, wait a minute. You mean you don't like these pages?" I
said, "Jerry, I've just finished them and I'm giving them to you and I'm
happy that you like them." He said, "Do you mean—what do you think,
I'm a fool? Are you looking at me like I'm a fool, now? That I like pages
that you know could be better?" I said, "Jerry, it's not like that at all." He
said, "You know what? Take these pages and get out of here. Take these
pages. I don't want them. I hate them."

Bernstein, Robbins, and Guare were sitting in the Shubert Theatre
holding auditions for the show when Jerry excused himself for a moment
and went backstage. The others waited, with a singer and his accompanist
ready, for ten or fifteen minutes. Guare then went in search of him and
queried the doorman. Oh, Mr. Robbins had gotten into a car and headed
for Kennedy Airport. When Bernstein, having anxiously followed Guare,
was told the news, he burst into tears. And that was that.*

Not entirely by accident, Robbins's next accomplishment involved no
script, no speaking, no singing, and no collaborators—just himself, a pianist, and some dancers in a studio. It was called *Dances at a Gathering*.

* In 1987, Robbins brought the collaborators together in a second attempt to stage *The Exception and the Rule*. That production is discussed in Chapter 19.

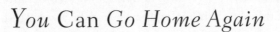

16

You Can Go Home Again

Robbins rehearsing Patricia McBride and Edward Villella
in *Dances at a Gathering.*
Martha Swope/NYPL.

S o the graying prodigal son (he is now fifty) returns to his artistic home, the New York City Ballet, and flourishes there, beginning with the creation of a gorgeous hourlong feast of a ballet
called *Dances at a Gathering* and bestowing upon his "family" the riches of
his accumulated wisdom. So glad is he to be back that he nevermore strays

to Broadway and the demands of the marketplace. Or so the scenario goes. It's a little too neat, though; Jerome Robbins was rarely sure about committing his life to anything on a forever basis.

It is true that he was hungry to make ballets again. The actors and dancers in his American Theatre Laboratory remember afternoons when he would suddenly abandon whatever had been planned and start to choreograph, as if he could no longer hold the urge in check. During the summer of 1968, on one of his impulses, he had considered collaborating with Eliot Feld on the founding of a ballet company. The brash *West Side Story* kid had become a bright new star in the underpopulated firmament of ballet choreographers with his *Harbinger* and *At Midnight* (made for American Ballet Theatre, where he was a soloist). Robbins's lawyer, William Fitelson, almost immediately squelched that plan by alarming Jerry with memos about "financial responsibilities" and inevitable deficits.

Robbins liked to hedge his bets. Through the spring of 1969, when he was rehearsing *Dances at a Gathering,* and for months after its phenomenally successful premiere in May, he was intermittently conferring with Robert Goldman and Glenn Paxton and dashing off script notes to them about their Civil War drama *Hurrah Boys Hurrah,* which he evidently had been planning to coproduce and possibly direct and/or choreograph.

He had never completely severed his connections with the New York City Ballet, occasionally coaching his works, even dropping in to take morning class. The ballerina Patricia McBride recalls how, when she was fifteen years old, Jerry would arrive in the studio where Anatole Oboukhoff was teaching, accompanied by some of his *West Side Story* "guys," such as Tommy Abbott and Jay Norman, and "kind of terrorize the class. They'd come in their sideburns and they'd be gossiping back and forth, and here I was—a little ballet girl." When the Ford Foundation made its first dance grants in 1964 and it was announced that the New York City Ballet and its School of American Ballet would receive almost $6 million over ten years (about 75 percent of the total $7,756,000 in grants), to the outrage of the left-out portion of the American dance community, Robbins contributed a statement to *Dance Magazine* lauding the foundation's good taste and was thanked by Lincoln Kirstein. Therefore, in 1968, when he had become enthralled all over again by Chopin's piano pieces, even trying out some ideas on dancers in Rebekah Harkness's Snedens Landing studio, he considered choreographing a ballet—or maybe just a pas de deux—for NYCB. In November, he received a letter from Kirstein saying that he and Balanchine would love to have Jerry come and do whatever he wanted, adding that George hoped Jerry would use a pianist and not have the pieces orchestrated (apparently Robbins had broached that possibility).

Jerry had earlier coached Edward Villella and the dewy young McBride in *Afternoon of a Faun* in the little top-floor studio in his home and had also worked with McBride on *The Cage*. He asked to start with them, perhaps hoping to feel more secure in what was essentially a new environment; the NYCB was no longer the middle-sized group of peers he had choreographed for in the 1950s. In 1966, the company had moved into its new Lincoln Center home, the New York State Theater, expanding the size of its ensemble and the scale of some of its ballets to fit a stage much bigger than City Center's. Villella, sensing that Robbins might find it difficult "to come back here and try to find his way again after a long time working on Broadway and films," wisely said to McBride, "Why don't we just get really warmed up so that when he gets here we'll be ready for him, and can give him a certain confidence." They were at the barre when he walked into the studio, indeed looking terrified. But the accompanist came, the Chopin Etude, op. 25, no. 5, stormed from the piano, and Robbins began emitting choreography with an ease he hadn't experienced in years.

Consumed by the Chopin music, he wrote passionately in a notebook about his need to get into that world: "to make every chord, every rest, each bar, phrase, confluence of sounds, your skin, your hair, your finger, your sweat, your cock, your toes—the soles of your feet." He played recordings of it over and over. As he narrowed down his musical choices, he selected four more dancers, but he had to face the fact that this was a company with a very large repertory to maintain and enlarge. The dancers he wanted weren't always available. So he assembled a cast of ten,* even though there are never more than six onstage until the very end. He also commandeered a cadre of alternates. Villella, returning from a guest stint on the West Coast, was taken aback when he started to run through a solo variation, and "I look in the mirror and there are about seven people

---

* The original cast members were identified by costume color (costumes by Joe Eula: simple floaty dresses for the women; boots, tights, and loose shirts for the men): in apricot, Allegra Kent; in blue, Sara Leland; in mauve, Kay Mazzo; in pink, Patricia McBride; in green, Violette Verdy; in mustard, Anthony Blum; in blue-green, John Clifford; in plum, Robert Maiorano; in olive, John Prinz; in brown, Edward Villella. Later some of the colors were changed.

[doing it] behind me. One of them is a woman!" Jerry was covering the bases; he later remarked that he also resented Villella's absences.

Whatever frustrations Robbins suffered, he was enthralled to be part of this enterprise, working with Balanchine's dancers and eventually sharing Balanchine's office and dressing room (since there was no extra space, Balanchine had graciously agreed to make room for him). He dashed off a note to Kirstein—who seemed to prefer written correspondence even when both men were in the city—saying how happy he was to be back and commenting on the dancers in his ballet. He's delighted by the two women he's worked with before, Patricia McBride and Kay Mazzo. "Little [John] Clifford is a lovable puppy, eager, willing, bright." Robert Maiorano "is always on the verge of sending me but never makes it." Sara Leland is a "brick."

By March 27, when he sent that letter, he had made about twenty-five minutes of dancing, which he imagined cutting down to eighteen, and wrote Kirstein asking him and George to come look at what he had done, adding, "Don't build up the work to him." They came. And when Jerry worried aloud about length, Balanchine said, "Make more, make it like peanuts." (When Robbins would repeat this to reporters, sometimes the word was "popcorn," but it was usually accompanied by a mime of Balanchine popping tasty nuggets into his mouth as if unable to stop.) Robbins made more. Patricia McBride remembers thirteen weeks of five-hour rehearsals.

When *Dances* entered the repertory on May 22, 1969, the ATL crowd saw it as rooted in the work they had done with Jerry. James Mitchell says that many of them agreed that "after that two-year experience . . . his whole philosophy, his whole look at ballet entirely changed. . . . I thought *Dances at a Gathering* looked like nothing he had ever done before; he had transformed into another artist." It is likely that the ATL experience was partly responsible for the ballet's fluid use of space. The dances spilling onto the stage seemed to refer to a larger society existing beyond the proscenium arch's frame. And ATL had perhaps increased Robbins's taste for simplicity and the illusion of performers communicating with one another rather than playing to an audience. Because of the NYCB dancers' intense schedule—rehearsing during the day, performing at night—they often had to mark the steps in the studio, walking through the material while remembering how it ought to be. Although this sometimes frustrated Robbins, it also inspired him. He admired the fact that these dancers were so beautifully trained that they could still be clear while only indicating the steps, "like someone with a great voice who can whisper and you hear it." Watching Villella mark his opening solo at the last rehearsal before the premiere and loving the thoughtful quality of his performing, Jerry ran backstage and told him, "Now that's what I want."

The ballet contains the residue of his forays into his heritage: the shtetl of *Fiddler on the Roof,* the Russian peasant community of *Les Noces.* In the mid-1970s, trying to understand his Jewishness more fully and take pride in it, he wrote that *"Dances at a Gathering* is also full of the things I loved about dancing & about being Jewish," adding, "But I kept all that deep & under wraps."

The dancers in the ballet are themselves—as Robbins stressed when talking to the press—but they are also members of a community that lives in Chopin's music, especially in the mazurkas of his ancestral Polish homeland, with their lusty downbeats and tautly lilting second beats. However, Robbins's steps suggest Poland only in the way the music does: in a rhythm, a fragment of melody, a folk gesture transformed by creative intellect. There are heel-and-toe steps; feet stamping; heels clicking together; hands placed on hips; men dancing in a line, their arms across one another's shoulders. But these mingle with classical steps that have been eased to look natural and unposed. No man plants himself to spin, and women rise onto pointe as if such an act were the natural consequence of drawing breath. Women fall into men's arms and are spiraled up to sit on a shoulder without visible effort on either dancer's part.

Chopin wrote most of these pieces in Paris, yet all the slow mazurkas are infused with a nostalgia for Polish country life (the composer, like the dance, was born in the province of Mazovia). This quality dovetailed in subtle ways with Robbins's borrowings from Japanese theater during the ATL years, especially the Noh plays' emphasis on remembered action. The people in *Dances at a Gathering* often move as if they were trying to call to mind something they had once known and feel their way back into it. Sara Leland, one of the original cast members and an assistant ballet master at New York City Ballet, said that Robbins told them to imagine that "it's a place you're coming back to years later that you danced in once." One can feel that powerfully in the opening solo made for Villella. With his back to the audience, the man walks into what he makes you imagine as a vast outdoor space. As the quiet mazurka (op. 63, no. 3) catches him up, he breaks tentatively into dance, as if thinking, "Yes, this is how it used to go . . ." until he's rushing in a big circle around the stage, the steps now pouring out of him. During a lighthearted mazurka for three men and two women (the *Fancy Free* dilemma distilled to its essence and stripped of rivalry), the five assume a series of poses as if to fix this happy day for a family photographer. The quality of reverie also appears in a companionable strolling dance for three women (originally McBride, Mazzo, and Leland) out of which tiny solos blossom. Suddenly one of them (Mazzo) sits while the other two, arms entwined, walk to the back and gaze into the distance; a man (Prinz) enters, lifts her into a quiet dance, and backs out, leaving her again on her knees. The other two women retrieve her. You may think they've diplomatically left her alone for a tryst, but you can also imagine that she's daydreaming about a lover.

Leland, who has staged *Dances* for other companies, said that the idea behind Violette Verdy's solo to Etude, op. 25, no. 4, was that this woman—slightly older than the others, gracious, piquant, a bit of a flirt, perhaps "the mistress of the house," is "showing how she used to dance." Her past and her present merge. Verdy has said that when Jerry demonstrated the steps to her, it was as if he were casting a spell on himself. At the end of the hourlong ballet, the cast strolls in to a nocturne (op. 15, no. 1). They pause, gaze into the distance, slowly follow something with their eyes. Robbins told them to watch that cryptic traveling object—whatever they decided it was—without anxiety. It was like a gathering storm cloud that might pass or not; whatever the outcome, they would accept it. Villella kneels and touches the earth firmly and meaningfully. Then they bow to one another and walk away in pairs, arm in arm.

After an interview with Edwin Denby that was published in *Dance Magazine,* Robbins became cautious about promoting specific interpretations of the ballet; he wanted the public to remain open to the simple interplay of music and dancing human beings. And he wanted to erase the image of Jerome Robbins as a man who told stories in movement. Troubled by an interview he and Leland had given to Don McDonagh that had been printed in *Ballet Review,* he sent the following letter to the editor:

For the record, would you please print in large, emphatic and capital letters the following:

THERE ARE NO STORIES TO ANY OF
THE DANCES IN "DAAG"
THERE ARE NO PLOTS AND NO ROLES.
THE DANCERS ARE THEMSELVES DANCING
WITH EACH OTHER TO THAT MUSIC IN
THAT SPACE.

Thank you very much.

Robbins once toyed with the idea of titling the ballet *Dances in Open Air.*
The emotions that transpire in this landscape are, like the music, sunlit or
shadowed, even within individual pieces. In the "B" section of the penultimate brusque scherzo, in which people fly past one another and vanish,
Villella and McBride come together again in an infinitely tender duet. In
the midst of a rapid waltz (op. 42) during which Kent and Clifford chase
playfully about, they turn wistful along with Chopin.

There are other duets beside these and the marvelous pas de deux for
McBride and Villella that Robbins made first. One, to mazurka op. 33,
no. 3, for McBride and Blum, has the feeling of a party dance, with circling
waltz steps, but he carries her off upside down, toes to the ceiling, as if rapture has turned her head over heels, like a woman in a Chagall painting. In
the duet Robbins nicknamed the "wind waltz" (op. 69, no. 2), Prinz and
Kent dance as if being pushed together and apart; on the antecedent
phrases of the "A" section, one follows the other through the movement a
step behind; on the consequent ones they slip into unison.

Despite all the duets, you don't consider any two dancers to be a permanent couple; the suite form and the changing of partners suggest a network of friends and lovers. Villella leads two women through frisky steps,
as if they were fillies. There's a playfully rivalrous mazurka for two men
(Villella and Blum). At the end of the quintet, a third woman arrives just
in time for the man who's been left without a partner, and the six dance.
The Valse Brillante, op. 34, no. 1, yields another exuberant sextet, this time
with the women tossed and spun from man to man. In another section,
Kent rambles along, charming and playful, and one man after another
strolls by daydreaming, sometimes following her path, sometimes even
trying a step with her, yet always leaving. "Oh, well," she seems to say, "I'll
catch them another time."

New York City Ballet dancers unaccustomed to Robbins may have found the rehearsals grueling, but he did not. He wrote to a colleague about his forthcoming ballet: "I've had such a wonderful time working on it—never have I enjoyed work more. The result may surprise people in that it is romantic, lyric, sensuous & delicate—not punchy & sharp & dramatically or theatrically effective as my other works are. But it's theater, & celebrates love & being & togetherness—a rather astonishingly optimistic view in the face of today's fearsome events." While he'd been choreographing *Dances at a Gathering,* the Vietnam War had begun to escalate.

On opening night, May 22, 1969, the ovations, like the reception for *Fancy Free* twenty-five years before, startled everyone. Balanchine came backstage and, without a word, kissed Robbins on both cheeks (a first). Kirstein put his delight into one of his high-style missives to Jerry a couple of weeks later: "In an age when religion has become vestigial, you have provided a ritual about decency, simple consideration, the fruits of the earth and the possibility [of] love which should last as long as virtuosity is a capacity of the human body, and self-discipline a necessity to the human spirit." Edwin Denby noted with pleasure that "You see each dancer dance marvelously and you also see each one as a fascinating individual—complex, alone, and with any of the others, individually most sensitive and generous in their relationships." And—an accolade that must have meant a lot to Robbins—"The music and dance seem to be inventing each other." Almost all the critics wrote in clouds of delight, and Jerry sent them all thank-you notes. He wasn't sure how he had managed to make something everyone loved so much.

Kirstein was anxious to secure Robbins for the company, offering him full participation or freedom to come and go. Robbins chose the latter but accepted the title of ballet master. He was already planning to travel to Stockholm to stage *Les Noces* for the Royal Swedish Ballet and then to Leningrad to sightsee and to Moscow as a guest of honor at the First International Ballet Competition. Christine Conrad, with whom he'd begun an affair in the mid-1960s, was traveling with him, and, despite his continued sexual preference for men, he loved her and relished being able to refer to "my girl." (He later asked himself: "Did DaaG come out of a time with Chris?" And answered, "Possibly. Also Richard, Grover, Bob W., the Sterns et al.")

In June, he expected to visit Saratoga Springs, where the NYCB had begun to offer summer seasons in 1966, before enjoying July and August with Chris in an old farmhouse he'd rented in the Long Island town of Water Mill. Nothing turned out quite as expected. He got sick and couldn't go to Saratoga. The Soviet Cold War bureaucracy thwarted his efforts to watch rehearsals and classes at the Kirov Ballet and speak with members of the Russian dance world until Conrad staged a fit in the Intourist office, telling the officials that they were making a serious diplomatic gaffe giving a major American choreographer the runaround. The Kirov was delighted to see him, but he flew home in a rage anyway, canceling his appearance in Moscow and letting the Russians know why.

By the end of August, his relationship with Conrad was splintering (although they remained close), and he went off to Israel with a male lover to stage *Moves* for the Batsheva Company. Although Sweden's Royal Opera wanted him to direct *Salome* and the Nijinsky film was still simmering intermittently, he returned to the New York City Ballet and in late September began to choreograph *In the Night* to three Chopin nocturnes. He'd been severely depressed. A bad forty-eight-hour drug trip induced by what he had thought was mescaline (but turned out to be "huge amounts of acid and speed") had, he wrote to an intimate, left him "for the next three weeks close to suicide, murder & total anarchy." He rejected his doctor's recommendation of hospitalization and decided instead to start on a new ballet, "hoping to get my head together."

Kirstein, always eager to advise, had suggested that Jerry's next ballet be something different—short, maybe to symphonic music? However, if it was to be Chopin and an onstage piano again, he wasn't going to argue. The company needed Robbins. In 1969, Suzanne Farrell, Balanchine's muse and the object of his intense desire, had left the New York City Ballet and joined Maurice Béjart's Ballet du XXième Siècle in Brussels. Except for *La Source,* Balanchine had made no new works since her departure, assigning choreography for the repertory to Jacques d'Amboise and the ambitious twenty-one-year-old John Clifford, while he went off to Hamburg in the spring of 1969 to direct the opera *Ruslan and Ludmilla* and to Geneva in the fall to stage *Swan Lake.* He told Kirstein (and Kirstein told Jerry) that he was "no longer a cash cow that can be milked for ballets."

In the Night was begun by a not terribly sanguine man. One of the three duets that make it up has moments darker than anything in *Dances at a Gathering.* The dancers show no awareness of being in a place, although Thomas Skelton's lighting design offered them a sky full of stars and a superimposed chandelier for the second duet. Air seems to stir all around the couples, but they themselves are at some still point. A party may be going on somewhere beyond the confines of the stage, but each pair is alone, the man and woman utterly absorbed in each other. At the end, when they come together briefly to exchange courtesies, they look almost dazed, as if their eyes were adjusting to sudden bright light.

If the feeling is less open, less free than in *Dances at a Gathering,* it is perhaps because night breeds a certain elegance and strangeness. Despite their fluidity, Chopin's nocturnes—his night music—are full of shifts and disruptions, and these are reflected in Robbins's phrases. By sometimes traveling hand in hand with the music, sometimes jostling subtly against it, his choreography reflects the changeability of relationships. As Robert Sealy noted, "He never dances *on* the music—he dances in it; he inhabits it."

The first duet (made for Kay Mazzo and Anthony Blum) to op. 27, no. 1, is often airy, yet full of longing, as if these two are discovering a love so wonderful that they can't believe it will last. Over and over he lifts her or twines her through delicate balances; they separate only to rush together. The second man and woman (Violette Verdy and Peter Martins) are more settled, strolling onto the stage arm in arm to Nocturnes, op. 55, nos. 1 and 2, with a hint of a folk-dance step, she always confident that he will be there to support her. Here too, you feel they might be recalling how they used to dance together. Verdy, coaching Elisabeth Platel and Nicolas Le Riche of the Paris Opera Ballet in 2001, said she thought of the duet as a happy marriage, with enough drama (in a good sense) to keep it from "coagulating." It's certainly surprising that, at the end, the man kneels to support his partner's calm arabesque, then picks her up and exits backward, with her kneeling on his shoulder, hovering, neither of them looking where they're going.

Robbins created the third duet to the tumultuous Nocturne, op. 9, no. 2, for Patricia McBride and Francisco Moncion (actually, he had intended it for Moncion and Melissa Hayden, but Hayden withdrew). Moncion, a member of the New York City Ballet since the forming of Ballet Society in 1946, was no longer doing hard-dancing roles, but Robbins made superb use of his gifts and his charismatic presence. This couple is on the verge of a breakup. Their dancing is full of passion and artifice; they're being melodramatic for each other. He touches her; she flings his hand away. They draw close enough to kiss; then she shoves him away and runs past him. One minute they are involved in flashy, tempestuous lifts; the next minute one of them rushes offstage. Just before the end, they both leave, then quietly reenter and gaze at each other across the space. It is she who comes to him, gently touching his face, his arm, his waist, his knee, as she sinks to the floor at his feet, hands optimistically and humbly placed in front of her where he can find them. He pulls her up into a high lift, drops her into his arms, and carries her away.

Balanchine didn't much care for *In the Night*. Revering women as he did, he couldn't bear to see one abasing herself before a man. It's reported that in a private conversation he said (with accompanying gestures), "Can you imagine?! Old man stand, and beautiful woman in beautiful dress goes down on floor. Can you *imagine!!*" Whatever the reason, the ballet, which was enthusiastically received at its premiere in January 1970, was not listed in the repertory for 1971, and Robbins drafted a letter to Kirstein saying how hurt and surprised he was "because no one had informed me that you both felt it was unworthy." Since then, the ballet has never been retired for long and, as a splendid showcase for six stellar dancers, has been performed by a number of companies, including NYCB.

While working on *In the Night,* Robbins took one brief but rewarding holiday from choreographing. In November 1969, Willis Player of Pan American Airlines had invited him on a VIP junket to Cape Kennedy to see the launch of *Apollo 12.* They had watched the ascent from a house-boat, and Robbins thanked Player profusely, noting that the stirring experience had "opened my mind to a whole aspect of man's endeavor and accomplishments from which I'd always signed off."

He took another sort of holiday from the New York City Ballet in September 1970, traveling to London to stage *Dances at a Gathering* for the Royal Ballet. Although he returned the following year to stage *Afternoon of a Faun,* he found the company's style a little restrained for his taste and attributed this to the fact that "The English have been doing Royal ballets too long & in too close proximity of [*sic*] grand opera. Too many crowns, capes, tiaras, swords, trains, necklaces and fake jeweled costumes have been worn." Anthony Dowell's beauty and elegance captivated him (although he found Dowell so schoolboyishly innocent and reticent in *Afternoon of a Faun* that, in order to bring out the sensuality in the role, "I had to change the kiss to a careful cupping of the girl's breast"). Jerry wrote admiringly of Michael Coleman and David Wall ("Wall is interesting indeed. His eyes are there"). Reticence was not, however, the order of the day with the Royal's brilliant Russian member, Rudolf Nureyev, who had planned to wear semitransparent white tights in *Dances at a Gathering*.

"Rudi—is Rudi—an artist—an animal—& a cunt. A child & a smart cookie—much more female & androgynous? than any other stage creature I've seen. He was plenty to handle."

〜

When, in 1970, Balanchine decided to revise his version of Mikhail Fokine's *Firebird,* he tossed Robbins the dance of the monsters to choreograph, which his colleague managed with some wit. However, one can imagine that Jerry—given more or less the run of the New York City Ballet and having come, full of ideas, from a two-year period when he could try out whatever he wished—wanted to see how far he could go and still interest a ballet audience. Like *Dances at a Gathering,* his next two ballets were very long. *The Goldberg Variations* originally clocked in at an hour and twenty dance-packed minutes; *Watermill* ran for fifty-nine minutes in which almost nothing happened.

Bach had written *The Goldberg Variations* for keyboard—theme, thirty variations, and the theme restated in embellished form (most in the key of G major)—for his pupil Johann Gottlieb Goldberg to play in order to sweeten the nights of the insomniac Count Keyserlingk, Goldberg's employer. Perhaps to amuse himself, perhaps to challenge Goldberg, Bach grouped the variations in threes: the first a well-known musical form (sarabande, aria, corrente, gigue, fughetta, etc.), the second a technical study to give the fingers a workout, the third a canon. Harpsichordist and scholar Ralph Kirkpatrick considered the variations to be "like an enormous passacaglia, [reiterating] the harmonic implications of the same bass in thirty different forms."

Robbins, too, might have been setting himself technical challenges, especially in relation to the use of a large ensemble. He said in an interview that after choreographing two ballets to Chopin's music, he wanted to try something different, less romantic. "I wanted to see what would happen if I got hold of something that didn't give me any easy finger ledge to climb." He correctly envisioned Bach's masterwork as something "very big and architectural." In the first few weeks of rehearsal, trying to get a toehold, he kept crashing into its walls. Yet in the end, he succeeded, according to one music critic, in disclosing, through the patterns of the dance, "the inner nature of Bach's own genius."

He also succeeded in creating a feast of classical dancing, a sumptuous array of its forms and its steps. Solos, duets, trios, quartets, quintets, sextets replace one another onstage with skillfully managed transitions. But on some level, Robbins was never able to create "just dancing." When he listened to music, he heard drama and mood—qualities such as "pensive," "playful," "tentative," "intimate." Too, in construing the ballet as being about this company, he found ways to assert the NYCB's identity as a kind of family.

In the ballet, as in daily classes and rehearsals, few perform unwatched. And some of Bach's many canons became studies in conscious imitation, like games of follow-the-leader or anything-you-can-do-I-can-do-too. The third variation is like the center practice of a ballet class, with one man demonstrating elementary steps and the others copying him. However, from a straightforward beginning, in which he watches his "pupils," he begins to thread his steps through theirs, pulling the original lines into clusters and diagonals and ending up drawing out one woman to lead with him. In the first variation, a woman interests two men with her high-flying side leaps on a diagonal. The men then dance canonically and in unison with each other while she watches, before they start swinging her into the air. By the end, they're doing her leaps.

Bach's rigorous, overarching structure does not preclude feeling tones—just not the intimate, private ones that well up in Chopin's music. The musicologist and pianist Charles Rosen has written of the "black despair" of the twenty-fifth variation, and of the "Quodlibet," which incorporates two folk songs of Bach's day, as a "grand and genial finale." Robbins's inventions ranged from passages dense with steps to ones formal but full of air—like the grave pavane he constructed for variation 12, in which six couples do little but walk in various patterns. Some variations are dreamy, others playful. In variation 13, one man partners another in acrobatic moves while two women walk around observing; later one of the women tries supporting her friend in balances on pointe, as if she were standing in for a man in rehearsal.

Robbins divided the ballet into two parts, with two different sets of principal dancers.* Several writers saw the first part as more playful and experimental, the dancers more youthful, and Part II as more formal, classical and mature, with its expanded treatment of an ensemble and its three duets. Elena Bivona, writing in *Ballet Review,* felt also that in the second

* For Part I: Gelsey Kirkland, Sara Leland, John Clifford, Robert Maiorano, Robert Weiss, and Bruce Wells; for Part II: Karin von Aroldingen, Peter Martins, Susan Hendl, Anthony Blum, Patricia McBride, Helgi Tomasson.

half, "the discords shift from experimental outside activities to within the individuals." As a rather contrived and not particularly useful device, Jerry had the pair of dancers who state the theme dressed in suggestions of baroque attire. The rest of the cast starts out wearing designer Joe Eula's leotards in various jewel tones. During the second half of the ballet, they begin altering their attire—shirts for the men, breeches, little skirts for the women, finally tutus and jackets. When the original couple walks in to re-state the theme, they're wearing leotards. The costumes may have been Robbins's way of suggesting a progression from the frisky explorations of classroom steps and compositional strategies to the solidity of classical bal-let, with its pas de deux and its symmetrical formations by the corps de ballet flanking the action by soloists.

Robbins had been full of doubts about *Goldberg* and had worked on it for what seemed to the dancers an eternity. They showed a portion of it in an open rehearsal at Saratoga ten months before it premiered in New York on May 27, 1971. Until very late in the process, he wasn't sure whether he wanted Gordon Boelzner to play the score on a harpsichord or a piano. He himself was not entirely satisfied with the ballet and blamed his least favorite parts on the fact that he'd made them while recovering from a hepatitis attack that had hospitalized him late in 1970. (A torn Achilles tendon and subsequent surgery also hampered him; he did some of the choreographing from a wheelchair.) He wrote in his journal that he found a few sections at the end of the ballet "So uncreative and at shoul-der's length. . . . Ground out rather than created or felt." Three and a half years later—having rehearsed many cast changes due to injury—he had grown fond of it. It had become, he said, the work he was most proud of.

The length of *The Goldberg Variations*—over an hour—taxed the con-centration of its spectators. To Arlene Croce, writing in *Ballet Review,* *Goldberg*'s length was just one more factor in what she saw as pretentious-ness and emptiness. "When Robbins has wrestled every last musical repeat to the mat, we don't come away with a theatrical experience but with an impression of endless ingenious music-visualizations." The ballet was prodigious, alarmingly ambitious, weighted with beauty, almost too much. Critic Nancy Goldner, writing in *The Christian Science Monitor,* thought it was probably the longest storyless ballet ever made:

When the ballet is over, you have witnessed the classical ballet vocabu-lary expanded to its outermost limits and then some. The ballet feels as long as it really is, which also contributes to its monumental effect. It is magnetically fascinating in its variety, lucidity, and ease . . . deliciously exhausting not because it is long but because there is so much to see. And because Robbins has created such clear choreographic lines—they are simultaneously extraordinarily inventive and as naked as classroom exercises—one cannot help but see into the core of technique and choreography.

Balanchine, who had encouraged Robbins to make *Dances at a Gathering* long, thought that *The Goldberg Variations* should be shorter. Why *every* repeat? Jerry deleted a quartet, as well as a dance for Allegra Kent and three women. When the company performed in Russia in 1972, the part of McBride and Tomasson's long pas de deux that fell on a musical repeat was eliminated. (According to dancer Bart Cook, the corps de ballet believed Balanchine had done the pruning, but McBride and Tomasson have no memory of that.) The great Bach pianist Rosalyn Tureck was not disturbed by the ballet's length. In a letter she wrote Jerry years later, she wondered why he had cut the short twenty-seventh variation. She also singled out two of his transitions for their "incredible sensitivity" and offered praise that, coming from her, surely delighted him: "I am more deeply impressed than ever with your extraordinary sensitivity to musical structure and your genius in creating the transfer to the visual and communicative gesture. . . ."

By now the company had acclimated to Robbins—some dancers with pleasure, others by trying to keep out of his way. Those who became known as "Jerry's dancers"—the ones he always requested—quickly learned to remember version A of a given step well after he had gone on to choreograph versions B, C, D, E, and so on, and various combinations thereof. "You had to keep them all in your head," says former corps de ballet member Delia Peters, "because at any given time he'd say, 'Hey, baby, let's try version B3.' And suddenly you think, 'B3?' And you'd blankly look around at all the other dancers and they'd all be trying to figure out what B3 was. And even though he couldn't remember exactly what Version B3 was, he knew it wasn't what you were showing him at that time."

Peters, whose intelligence, good humor, and wit earned Jerry's friendship, remembers (somewhat guiltily) one *Goldberg* rehearsal when she instigated a quiet coup. He had finished the day's rehearsal with the umpteenth version of a particular passage in a trio for Susan Hendl, Betti-jane Sills, and her. None of them liked it: "It was truly verging-on-vulgar ugly." The other two agreed, and the pianist promised cooperation. When Robbins entered the studio the next day and asked to see the last version from the previous rehearsal, they gave him the penultimate one, nodding their heads earnestly when the choreographer asked if they were *sure* this was what they'd finished with the day before and running obligingly through all the previous variants. Luckily this was before videotaping rehearsals became common practice. Robbins never found out.

Generally, however, you didn't mess with Jerry. The guidelines were passed among the dancers by osmosis. You shouldn't challenge him, but if you saw that if you charged out of the wings on a given count, you'd probably bump into five people who hadn't yet left the stage, you could present that possibility calmly and logically. The trouble was that he was so intimidating that most dancers didn't even try this; what Jerry wanted, Jerry got, and what happened happened. You should be aware that he might give you something that he knew wouldn't work, just to test you and see how you'd react. You needed to know that when he said, "Stay with me," he meant you should be focused on what he was doing and saying 100 percent of the time. He appreciated a joke now and then and might erupt in laughter over a dancerly snafu. And it helped to remember that he never met a dog he didn't like.

With dancers he liked but found wanting, Robbins practiced a tough love. Some members of New York City Ballet experienced the stringency exemplified in a letter he wrote to Jane Dudley late in 1969. Dudley was the current artistic director of Israel's Graham-influenced Batsheva Company, for which Robbins had staged *Moves*. She had written wondering why he had left Linda Hodes (like Dudley, a former Martha Graham dancer) stage center in arabesque in the dance with five couples. Hodes's arabesque was "not that presentable . . . and a little shaky besides." She requested permission to switch Hodes with another dancer and make some adjustments. Jerry's response was succinct: "No, don't change Linda. Just force her to keep the arabesque or ask her if she would like to change with someone else who could hold it instead."

Inevitably, the dancers would compare him to Balanchine. Peter Martins, the company's present ballet master in chief, recalls that "rehearsing with Jerry versus rehearsing with Balanchine was very different. Balanchine was—adorable, I was about to say. And he *was* for the most part. Not always—there were times when he sort of cut you down to nothing. But for the most part he was extraordinarily courteous. And Jerry was different. It's not that he wasn't courteous. But he was very matter-of-fact: 'Come on. Come on, boy' [*snaps fingers*], 'let's do it again.' Whereas Balanchine was much more 'Do you think it's okay? Can we go from beginning, dear?' So their personalities reflected very much, I think, how we all felt about them. Maybe there was more fear towards Jerry. Not that there wasn't fear with Balanchine, but it was a different kind of fear. It was more of an aura."

Some NYCB dancers found him more approachable than Balanchine. Balanchine was "Mr. B." Robbins was "Jerry." Balanchine was at ease in his kingdom, if inscrutable. As Martins implies, even remarks that cut to the quick were delivered in a soft voice. Jerry—always pushing, often impatient—had a temper that could take the skin off a dancer's soul (even though his language doesn't seem to have been as coarse or his rants as extreme as they were with Broadway performers—"Mr. B." wouldn't have tolerated that). But Jerry was a guy you could see downing a hamburger and a Coke at O'Neal's Baloon on Columbus Avenue and Sixty-third Street. And, as Christine Redpath (now one of the NYCB's assistant ballet masters responsible for keeping the Robbins repertory in shape) says, "If Jerry liked you, he treated you like gold." Jean-Pierre Frohlich, also an assistant ballet master in charge of the Robbins ballets, was still a student in the School of American Ballet when Robbins asked to use him as the young boy in *Watermill* and only seventeen when he joined the company. It's clear that Robbins glimpsed something of himself as a boy in Frohlich's lean, dark eagerness and New York voice. Jerry, remembers Frohlich, "actually used to give me his clothes at one time: 'Can you use these? 'Cause I don't wear them anymore.' It was very, very sweet." Robbins would perhaps have been surprised to know how quickly the whole company pegged him as being phenomenally insecure.

Watermill was a ballet to try dancers' souls. The piece lasted an hour, and they had to move slowly, for the most part—and move slowly just so. During the piece, which didn't include a single step from the classical lexicon, the seasons turned and a crescent moon waxed, waned, turned dark, and reemerged.

The seventies were a period of intensive self-examination for Robbins.

It was during this decade that he began to keep journals consistently; he also wrote short essays about his childhood and early career—contemplating a sort of nonlinear autobiography—and worked on draft after draft of a play about his father he called *The Poppa Piece*. This preoccupation with the story of a life seems to have surfaced first in *Watermill*. The three men observed by the work's barely mobile protagonist (Edward Villella) could be seen as representing him at various stages of his life, and all relate in some way to Robbins. The title refers to the Long Island village where Jerry rented houses and where many of his friends summered. What appeared to be three shocks of grain standing at the rear of the stage were composed of the tall, feathery-topped phragmites that clog New England marshes. When Grover Dale and the actor Anthony Perkins were visiting Jerry at Water Mill one summer, they shot some 16-millimeter footage of Dale, Robert Wilson, and Robbins dancing on the beach. One film shows Robbins in the dunes, divesting himself of his bathing suit and making slow, intense, self-involved gestures. At one point, he suddenly collapses into a hollow in the sand. At another, he seizes two phragmites and flourishes them somewhat as Villella did in the ballet (Dale remembers that Jerry was on his first acid trip, perhaps the one that proved so alarming). Several friends felt that the ballet was "a big undressing for him." He thought it could have been more so.

However personal the subject matter of *Watermill*, Robbins disguised it with Japanese imagery and postmodern strategies. He could fully indulge his interest in Noh drama, which provided not only the framework of action recollected but elements of a style. The stage is bare except for the shocks of grain and the projected moon—all revealed by Ronald Bates's exquisite lighting. Teiji Ito's spare and haunting score, played in a corner of the stage by six musicians, derived mainly, Robbins wrote in his program note, "from the religious, ceremonial, and theatrical music of Japan," and many of the instruments were traditional: shakuhachi, koto, shō, zither, flutes, and various percussion instruments (the musicians attended rehearsal, and the music developed alongside the dance). Robbins also added a caveat to his note: "However, [the ballet's] world, people, and events are not to be construed as oriental." In keeping with this desired ambiguity, Patricia Zipprodt's costumes suggested practice clothes, beach attire, and Japanese peasant garb all at the same time.

Robbins also displayed his interest in the vanguard theater and dance of the day. The ballet, to the consternation of some and the enchantment of others, was about 10 percent action and 90 percent resonance. Every minimal movement, dwelled on as it is, can set off small associative flickers in the spectator's mind, and there is plenty of time to ruminate. In fact, the primary subject became time—passing, prolonged, remembered, slowing down the watcher's heartbeat.

The windy voice of the shakuhachi is heard. A man enters, turns slightly to survey the scene, lifts his right arm, lowers it, kneels, rises, removes his long cloak (a bell sounds) and his shirt and trousers, carefully laying each on the floor. In his white briefs, he executes a few slow lunges and turns before sitting to contemplate the recollected life of this field, this beach, this inner landscape. His every move is slow and smooth. When the men who arrive with paper lanterns on poles cross one another to exit, their progress seems to tighten and then release a frame around him.

Each element in *Watermill* is as precisely drawn and placed as the shapes in a Japanese painting. The snow falls just so; wind rustles the reeds, and a few leaves, standing for a world of autumns, drift down; a dog barks ominously. Now and then a handful of people passes through or labors quietly at the back of the stage—sowing grain, raking the ground with long gestures, putting potatoes into baskets and walking away. A band of young men carrying sticks runs in right-angled paths, as if intent on some ritual game.

The events that affect the man most directly involve the figures that seem to represent himself at other stages of his life, and he reacts to them. A boy dances, flying high as if to imitate the paper birds on sticks that others hold before him. Villella stretches out a hand as the boy climbs into a "boat" (conveyed, as in Japanese theater, by a man poling himself along). The second visitor engages in a duet whose slow pace intensifies its eroticism. A woman (played by Penelope Dudleston) lingers over her disrobing, hypnotically brushes her long hair, and spreads out her towel to bathe in a remembered sun. When a man (Hermes Condé, to whom Robbins was very much attracted) enters, she serenely offers herself to him, over and over, in different positions. A third visitor (Victor Castelli) is besieged by a nightmare. A masked figure with wild white hair and cuffs and anklets of something like raffia crouches spraddle-legged and leaps around him, shadowed by barely visible lurking figures. A graphic gesture suggests emasculation, and Bart Cook, who played the demon, is sure that's what he was doing to the twitching dreamer. (In his notes, Robbins referred to possible "shamans," one for each season, and may at one point have had a puberty rite in mind.) The last figure to enter is a bent old person in a black robe—perhaps suggesting to the central figure his coming old age, his winter.

In perhaps the most beautiful of the ballet's episodes, women pluck individual stalks from the shocks. One woman stands hers on end and watches it slowly topple. As they exit, carrying some of the stalks, they leave two for Villella, and he wields them like slow, heavy wings or with them forms an X across his shoulders. At the end, the moon is a crescent again, the snow has ceased, and this hourlong ritual has returned almost to the point at which it began, but with the man one step further in self-knowledge.

Robbins fought a battle within himself over *Watermill*—between the savvy man of the theater who could walk into a failing show and shape it into a hit and the man who wanted to be considered as a serious contemporary artist working in ballet. In the month before the premiere, he wrote in his journal, "I am not going to ensure it as I usually can by tightening & hightening [*sic*] & fascinating—I'm going to do it as it is because it is truly my experience & my trip & these are people I have been close with or seen or felt."

Many saw in *Watermill* the obvious influence of the downtown avant-garde choreographers, and especially Robert Wilson's theater works, whose slow parades of images ranged from the fantastic to the mundane. His *King of Spain* had premiered at the Anderson Theatre on Second Avenue in 1969; *The Life and Times of Sigmund Freud* was shown at the Brooklyn Academy of Music in 1970 and *Deafman Glance* in 1971. Robbins saw these; he visited Wilson's Byrd Hoffman School of Byrds at 147 Spring Street; he had even appeared as the seated figure of Freud in a Paris performance and would do so again in New York. Robbins, Wilson, and Wilson's partner, dancer Andy De Groat, had taken a trip through the Yucatán together in 1970. When *Watermill* opened, they sent him a loving poem in an artful homemade book containing postcards, dried flowers, watercolors, and quotes from favorite writers (a year later, Jerry made *them* a book that incorporated images and memories of the Mexican trip). Robbins sometimes slipped away from Lincoln Center to refresh himself in the experimental artistic climate of their downtown world. "Back from Bob's loft," he wrote in his journal, a little over a month after *Watermill*'s premiere. "Danced with Andy—& it felt so beautiful. & we went up in air

& each led & followed at the same time even though we stood in place & touched hands & foreheads. They have true love in life & beauty is shed all over."

It's likely, then, that the two men influenced each other. Several years before Wilson created the aforementioned theater pieces, Robbins had been drawn to his unusual mind and his work with children—some of them brain-damaged—just as he had been fascinated by Daniel Stern's investigations into infant behavior. Wilson remembers Jerry visiting a site in Bedford-Stuyvesant, where Wilson had constructed out of cardboard boxes and fabric a "textured time tunnel" that wound around part of a city block for the children to crawl through—safe, confined, yet adventurous. Jerry tried it too, he recalls. Robbins also traveled out to the Goldwater Memorial Hospital on Welfare Island to see a kind of dance Wilson had created for people in iron lungs; he and his helpers had made and hung constructions, like mobiles with strings, which the patients moved with their teeth. Jerry asked Bob to come to the American Theatre Laboratory as a kind of personal assistant ("To drive him or to get coffee or to buy a toothbrush for him"). In addition to helping design the layout of the raw space of the Nineteenth Street studio, Wilson was also involved with the Kennedy Project, making drawings for an innovative theater with a semi-mobile audience, should that contemporary Noh play ever be developed to the point where it could be publicly performed.

Jerry gave a party for the company and others (one hundred were invited) after *Watermill*'s premiere, undeterred by the fact that a fair number of boos mixed with bravos at the curtain call. Some of the ensuing outrage evoked the days when the Parisian public was affronted by Vaslav Nijinsky's first ballet, *L'Après-midi d'un Faune,* in part because the superb dancer performed only one jump. One NYCB patron wrote, "You are a great choreographer most of the time—but I would like to know why a genius like Edward Villella was wasted in *Watermill.* This was no ballet, and I came to see ballet tonight." Robbins might as well have used her husband, the writer went on; he had an equally magnificent physique and would have cost less money.

Some friends and colleagues did not agree with this disillusioned fan. Virgil Thomson was "ravished by it," music and all. To Sheldon and Margie Harnick, the ballet was "an exquisite theatre poem." Paul Magriel found *Watermill* to be "one of the most moving experiences of my life," ending, "In its humanity and poetry you transformed the theatre into a temple. I am most grateful." Lighting designer Jean Rosenthal wrote Jerry, "I wish you could choreograph my dreams."

The press ran the gamut from John J. O'Connor's "fake deep" in *The New York Times* and Arlene Croce's "rings false at every moment" in *Ballet Review* to Marcia B. Siegel's "very beautiful and evocative" in the *Boston Herald Traveler.*

Lincoln Kirstein, who had encouraged and supported the project, though he had predicted it would cause a ruckus, wrote an emotional note the day before *Watermill*'s premiere on February 3, 1972. It must have pleased Jerry inordinately.

> On the verge of your most lovely catas-trophe, I want to thank you again for the richness of the repertory with which you have endowed us, and in the promise of a succession when George and I are gone. There are those who earnestly pray for such a happy eventuality; I am not among them, but you must know now that you are the heir-apparent, if and when the time comes, if you want it, and if you are then here to take it.

With the note came a Chinese scent bottle, empty because the giver could find no perfume that didn't demean it, and he added, "Scent is the only thing lacking from *Watermill*. So it is apt that this hollow bottle smells of divine nothingness which is the eternal somethingness which you and I adore." Lincoln signed the letter, "With admiration and love."

Watermill was the end, for Jerry, of that kind of experimentation, and, not surprisingly, the ballet didn't become a mainstay of the New York City Ballet's repertory, although it was revived for the company's Robbins Festival of 1990 (the fifty-four-year-old Villella took time off from his own company, Miami City Ballet, and performed magnificently). At one point Jerry hoped to get Baryshnikov to take on the central role, but Baryshnikov, committed to his own White Oak Dance Project, had to refuse.

~

The month after Robbins's Goldberg Variations had premiered in May 1971, Balanchine had produced an expensive and spectacularly bad ballet called *PAMTGG*. Fascinated by certain aspects of American popular culture, he had had the Pan American airlines jingle "Pan Am makes the going great" expanded into a musical score and choreographed an organized hubbub of Lucite luggage, airline personnel, and busy travelers in plastic apparel. The press wondered if Balanchine was losing his touch—or his interest. Clive Barnes published an article in *The New York Times* titled "Balanchine—Has He Become Trivial?" In it, Barnes vaunted Robbins as "clearly the company's future" and wrote some strong words: "[T]he New York City Ballet is becoming increasingly trivial—with the obvious exception of the last three ballets by Jerome Robbins. But take Robbins away and you find a mixture of tinsel and trash." This article and others seemed to imply that it would be a good thing if Robbins took over the company. Barnes qualified his remarks two weeks later: he meant the distant future; Balanchine was, of course, the company's mainstay. It's just that his "serious genius seems to have taken a sabbatical recently."

What few outside the company knew at that point was that just before *PAMTGG* premiered, Balanchine had begun to plan something wonderful, an event that would reassert his status as one of the world's greatest choreographers. Igor Stravinsky had died in April. He was the composer most profoundly connected to Balanchine's career as a choreographer, one of three (Delibes and Tchaikovsky were the other two) Balanchine considered to have written "musique dansante." The company committed itself to a Herculean project—a Stravinsky Festival—as costly as it was exhausting. Staggered rehearsals began in the fall, and at the end of the NYCB's already full 1972 spring season, it presented a weeklong festival beginning on June 18, the day that Stravinsky would have turned ninety. Between then and June 25, thirty-one ballets to Stravinsky's music were staged, twenty-one of which were new. Robbins became part of a team—with Balanchine, John Taras, Todd Bolender, Richard Tanner, John Clifford, and Lorca Massine—of a very different sort from the creative teams of Broadway shows, duking it out as they sleeked a show during its tryouts. Good sportsmanship was mandated. During the planning and the rehearsal period, pieces of music were tossed from one choreographer to another. Robbins, for instance, had plans for the *Octuor;* Tanner ended up with it. When the week was over, Kirstein and Balanchine came in front of the curtain to drink a final vodka to celebrate "Igor Fedorovitch friend of ours Stravinsky." The dancers breathed again, and New York ballet fans—some of whom had attended every performance—resumed their lives. Jerry wrote in his journal:

GB was fantastic—knowing it would work—& to everyone's amazement—it did. If he had said we could all go to the top of the State Theater & fly off & around Lincoln Center, we would have gone & we would have flown, that's how faithful we felt & how awestruck we were by being led into such areas of incredible dangers—& sailing thru them with calm faith & quiet jubilation.

Those who had doubted Balanchine were confounded by three major new ballets, two of which, *Symphony in Three Movements* and *Violin Concerto,* burst on the public the first night. The beautiful duet *Duo Concertant,* for Kay Mazzo and Peter Martins, slipped in on the fourth night.

Robbins, not without difficulty, gave himself over to a new experience: not being able to luxuriate over choreographing one ballet a year. During the rehearsal period for the Stravinsky Festival, while choreographing *Watermill,* he polished up his previous Stravinsky ballet, *The Cage;* created four new short works, *Scherzo Fantastique, Dumbarton Oaks, Circus Polka,* and *Requiem Canticles;* and collaborated with Balanchine on *Pulcinella.*

During the preparations, Robbins voiced a worry to Balanchine:

I said I thought all our work was so derivative because his work was such a model of perfection of the Stravinsky scores. He said look—everything we do will look alike as the company is trained in a very special style & it will all come out like his style. If I were choreographing for Jack Cole dancers, it would come out looking like Jack Cole.

Jerry was under no illusions about *Scherzo Fantastique,* although on the first night of the festival, it pushed into the limelight four young men in the corps de ballet—sending Stephen Caras, Bryan Pitts, and Victor Castelli kiting and skimming about the space and giving Bart Cook the job of partnering the brilliant young principal dancer Gelsey Kirkland. After Jerry showed it to Balanchine, "our eyes turned to each others—and we searched for 3 seconds—me asking & he asking too—his eyes were old and veined & working—then later I could laugh at it—O.K.—did it fast & it looks it—& it's an opener."

Circus Polka, intended as a *pièce d'occasion,* proved to be well worth repeating. Stravinsky had composed the eight-minute piece for Balanchine in 1942 when the latter was making a dance for Barnum and Bailey's elephants and showgirls. Out came Robbins as Ringmaster, wearing a top hat and boots, and flourishing a whip to summon squads of children from the School of American Ballet. Using the theatrical know-how that had produced the "March of the Royal Children" from *The King and I*, he brought on a high-stepping line of little girls, then a group of smaller ones, and, finally, when you thought they couldn't get any smaller, the really tiny ones, tooting imaginary piccolos. They performed their simple steps with aplomb, and Robbins cracked his whip with mock ire and great good humor. He got them going in opposite directions in three concentric circles, their different-colored little tutus creating a pinwheel. There was even the joke of a recalcitrant (or lost) teeny whom he had to glare into her curled-up position as a period in the final formation: the initials I.S. Jerry wrote in his journal: "delightful to audience but 'made' to me."

Robert Craft, an expert on Stravinsky's work, wrote in *World Magazine* that *Dumbarton Oaks (Concerto in E Flat)* belonged among the new festival ballets that should be repeated. It was a skillfully made charmer without a particularly strong idea. A garden set with trellises and lanterns had been borrowed from another ballet and a tennis net strung across the back of the stage, but no obvious games were played by six frisky couples who might have escaped from *The Boy Friend* or an authentic musical of the 1920s. The ballet incorporated some earlier Robbins devices. Three boisterous men in unison evoked *Fancy Free,* a choosing up of partners one by one brought to mind the teams of *Interplay;* there was a hint of a tug-of-war, but all this was embedded in sparky dancing and brightly developed counterpoint. The centerpiece was a "match" for Allegra Kent and Anthony Blum, who entered with rackets but soon engaged in artful pleasantries without them. He obviously found her a marvel, and at the end they picked up their rackets, shook hands, and walked off together. In the final, neatly organized bit of clockwork foolery with teams and couples and line dances, the guys lionized Kent and the women did the same with Blum. For some reason, Robbins wanted a brief passage in tap shoes. Balanchine tried to talk him out of the taps, but Jerry stood firm and felt guilty about it later.

Robbins gave the most thought to *Requiem Canticles (II)*, which began rehearsing in the fall of 1971 and was, appropriately, performed on the last night of the festival. In terms of movement and atmosphere, this spare, tense ballet was more like his sneaker works for Ballets: U.S.A. than anything he'd made subsequently. In darkly dramatic lighting, the black-clad corps of fifteen and the four principal dancers seemed at times to be performing not so much a ritual as an abstraction of one. Their gestures of clenching or trembling occurred in perfectly controlled unison. There wasn't a lot of movement. They raised bent arms, walked, stood. They ran in fits and starts to new positions. They walked on their knees. They cocked a faintly jazzy hip. They sat and watched one another. It was thought by some critics to be self-conscious, its gestures too calculated to ring true, but it had undeniable power. The Royal Ballet immediately asked Jerry to stage it in London.

After a performance of *Requiem Canticles* and his own *Duo Concertant,* Balanchine spoke to Robbins about artists and poets: "We penetrate into that place of silence which everyone is terrified of. . . . It's the place with no words & no names & no objects." Robbins treasured the remark for the rest of his life. What thrilled him was not just the thought and the implied approval; it was the "we" that linked him with Balanchine.

Pulcinella was to have been the extravaganza of the festival, but it bore signs of having been put together in a hurry. Balanchine and Robbins had started planning it well in advance. On November 11, they met to listen to the music together, and someone (probably Tom Abbott, who had been assisting Jerry on all his NYCB ballets so far) took notes. Their idea was a Faustian vision of Pulcinella, who was to die once, sign a pact with the Devil so he could indulge in a little more high living and chicanery, and then try to trick the Devil out of his due. The choreographers had all kinds of farcical ideas for this Commedia dell'Arte romp: chases, men disguised as women, and a spaghetti feast that got out of control.

They worked very much in tandem, judging by Jane Boutwell's account of a rehearsal in *The New Yorker:*

As Miss Verdy [Violette Verdy played Pulcinella's girlfriend] moved diagonally downstage in a series of jumps and turns, Mr. Balanchine stationed himself in the middle of the male chorus and began to improvise complementary movements. "Maybe we do this," he said, playing an imaginary double bass. He broke up the line of dancers into groups of two as Mr. Robbins moved Miss Verdy back across the front of the stage with a sequence of *sautés en arabesque croisé.*

"Don't travel too much," said Mr. Balanchine, looking up.

Miss Verdy nodded and produced an *entrechat-six.*

Mr. Balanchine pushed his male dancers into a semi-circle and invented some elegant steps that took them forward and back. Turning to Mr. Robbins, he said, "It looks like your waltz."

Mr. Robbins grinned and asked Miss Verdy to try three linked turns on *pointe*.

Miss Verdy complied, and Mr. Balanchine nodded, looking pleased. "What do you do next?" he asked her.

"They carry me off!" said Miss Verdy, leaping into the arms of a startled male dancer.

Pulcinella had elegant decor and costumes by Eugene Berman. Edward Villella made a wonderfully roguish Pulcinella. But the ambitious ballet looked unfinished at its premiere, an engaging bawdy mess with some good jokes. A high point was the scene in which spaghetti threatened to flood the stage and baby Pulcinellas cavorted about munching gleefully. Another occurred during the finale, when Robbins and Balanchine came out in masks and ragtag gear, did a ramshackle dance, and pretended to whack each other with big sticks.

The Stravinsky Festival cost close to $350,000 and put the New York City Ballet in debt. However, as Goldner pointed out, "The morale ledger . . . was ensconced in the black."

As soon as the season ended, Robbins took off for a few weeks in Spoleto, where he could slow the pace of his life. He could attend the noon chamber music concert every day, revisit paintings he loved, and ponder beauty, unpressured by the drive to express it onstage. He had invited a young friend, Aidan Mooney—whose energy and enthusiasm for art matched his and whose passionate likes and dislikes he found stimulating—to travel with him.* In museum visits, they might spend an hour and a half in front of one painting. At the Scuola Di San Rocco in Venice, they rented small mirrors to better view the Tintorettos on the ceilings and then turned the mirrors on the pictures on the walls as well, pondering the irregularities that jumped into view. On such vacations, the intensity of Robbins's perceptions and his capacity for sensuous delight shone forth as some of his most endearing qualities:

Aidan shows me a pod, green & young, so big—& squeezes it open—
& out comes a red blood-brilliant orange red—but no—it's a baby

---

* It should be noted that Mooney paid his way on this and other trips (although when Robbins chose a hotel he knew to be above his friend's means, he expected to foot the bill). Robbins loathed being taken advantage of, being taken for granted, or being sucked up to. Paul Sand remembers Jerry once telling him as they walked along a Spoleto street that he enjoyed Sand's company because "You don't think I shit gold."

poppy—but no—he unfurls it further and miracle—compressed into it, rolled up like a Japanese paper water flower is a <u>whole</u> poppy—shiny & damp & crushed—but when unfurled—a whole poppy.

This wondrous moment took place above the tiny town of Pettino, nestled high in mountains. On the slopes above it, Jerry stripped and ran through the grass, writing in his diary, "I'm lying on the swell of a hill in the middle of the magic hills in 'Pettino.' No clothes, being fucked by the sun & washed by the gentleness & quiet."

Sudden mood changes were always a possibility, no matter where he was. But Jerry drinking in what excited him and sharing the experience with those he felt close to was a sweeter man than the Jerry who made dancers tremble or the one who had gotten so furious seven months earlier over the way things were going with his staging of *Afternoon of a Faun* for the Royal Ballet that he had caught an earlier plane out of London, "to show them."

Robbins flew home from Italy on July 16 and a day later performed his bit in *Pulcinella* at Saratoga Springs. At the curtain call, Balanchine picked up a bouquet and hurled it at him. Half in jesting response to this, half sure, for once, of his own mind, Robbins wrote in his journal, "They have me for another eight years."

17

Jerry and George and Lincoln

Mikhail Baryshnikov and Natalia Makarova in *Other Dances.*
Martha Swope.

The *phenomenal undertaking* of the Stravinsky Festival strengthened the relationship between Robbins and the New York City Ballet. When he had flung himself at the company in 1949, he had been too eager to have it all—Broadway musicals, ballets, films, operas, money—to commit himself to Kirstein and Balanchine.

Now in his fifties, he could afford—both literally and figuratively—to settle down with this marvelous assemblage of dancers who were capable of fulfilling all his visions. His relationship with the New York City Ballet's two founders, however, wasn't always harmonious. Kirstein was as touchy and quick to erupt as he was. And Jerry and company manager Betty Cage resumed their cranky interactions as if he had never been away.

Whenever Robbins suspected that he was being taken advantage of, he swung into action. He was not forging a connection with the New York City Ballet to make money—investments and royalties from musicals allowed him to live exceedingly well. But once he had determined that he was addicted to making ballets for this company, he wanted a proper contract with money involved; this was a serious career commitment, not a vanity operation. It took from September 1971 to January 1973 to thrash out an agreement retroactive to September 1968. He needed guarantees of a parking space in the Lincoln Center garage and seats in row A of the New York State Theater's first ring. He wished his name to appear on programs either on the same line as Balanchine's or on a separate line, but never on a line with that of the choreographer–ballet master John Taras. He asked that the company pay part of Edith Weissman's salary, since he didn't have office space of his own in the State Theater. City Center, which controlled the theater, reported a $1.3 million deficit in the fall of 1972, and in January 1973 Robbins agreed to a modest fee of $20,000 per year (to be paid in six installments), plus royalties, rather than a salary that would cost City Center an additional 25 percent in taxes, fringe benefits, and so on. It had taken a great deal of persuasion to bring him to this point, since he was offended by the notion of a "fee." He wanted to be on equal footing with everyone else on the company's staff.

Robbins did not send to City Center's Norman Singer the angry letter he had drafted to express his initial outrage at the idea of a fee. Nor did he, later that year, mail the furious scribble he addressed to Lincoln Kirstein in response to comments by Kirstein that appeared in a newspaper prior to the Stravinsky Festival; he felt they were unfavorable to *Dances at a Gathering* and vaunted the young choreographers Richard Tanner and Lorca Massine over himself. "You really are a shit, Lincoln," he wrote. Kirstein's "consistent message" to him, he felt, was "You are merely serviceable—& whatever you do, even though you work with & for us—you are never to be considered as family."

Throughout Robbins's career, upon reading a colleague's published statement (usually in a newspaper interview) that he felt misrepresented him or learning of a professional decision that affected his own interests adversely, he would fire off a letter to the hapless person, requesting an explanation, an apology, maybe a retraction; he would usually end by noting that a fine friendship had been jeopardized. His files contain drafts of quite a few such letters, as well as the (usually) apologetic replies from the likes of Leonard Bernstein, Oliver Smith, Jule Styne, and quite a few others.

Lincoln Kirstein too was capable of unconsidered explosions; one occurred while the two men were lunching together, and Jerry suggested that the company's programs could be better organized. Yet on some level, the two men got along very well. Jerry was impressed by Lincoln's erudition. They had serious talks. At one, recorded in Robbins's journal on November 17, 1971, "[Lincoln] told me many things about what I was doing & who I was & what my role was. He connected Jew-priest-rabbi, order, discipline & athlete all together. I came out wanting to get to work strongly. Good." They recommended books to each other or offered them as gifts. When Jerry was going to Russia in 1969, Kirstein provided a guide to the street where gay men clandestinely congregated. He sent postcards, some of them with dubious jokes, e.g., "What is 2¾ miles long and Irish? The St. Patrick's Day Parade." And of course, he often and enthusiastically offered suggestions or comments about a choice of music or a ballet he hoped Jerry might pursue. Robbins's relationship with Balanchine continued to be affable, but they never became any closer. Before Balanchine divorced Tanaquil Le Clercq in 1969, the couple was invited to dinner parties chez Robbins, but Balanchine, apparently, didn't enjoy them. After one, in which Robbins, Le Clercq, Fizdale, Gold, Bernard Taper (Balanchine's biographer), and Taper's wife vied enthusiastically in word games, Balanchine told his wife, "It's too fast and American, a language I can't understand." Tanny resolved not to subject him to such an evening again. After the divorce, Robbins and Balanchine rarely socialized outside the theater. Yet Balanchine seems to have bent over backward to make things agreeable for Jerry at work, letting him have his pick of dancers, the larger studio, as much rehearsal time as could be managed. And he evidently admired some of Jerry's ballets very much. When Robbins first returned to work with the company in 1968, Balanchine told Patricia McBride, "You know, dear, you know why Jerry is here? Because he's *good*." Violette Verdy says that Balanchine once confided to her (apparently without irony), "You know, Violette, the real American choreographer at the New York City Ballet is Jerry, not me. He's the one who can capture the fashions, the trends, the relaxed character of American dancers, their lack of a past or a style, but an ability to do all they're asked to do without discussion or preconception." And Robbins's admiration for Balanchine never wavered. "When I watch Balanchine work," he wrote in his journal on December 1, 1971, "it's so extraordinary I want to give up."

When Robbins decided to start seriously keeping a diary in October 1971, he went to Takashimaya, the Japanese department store on Fifth Avenue, and bought some small, slender accordion-pleated books. His journals are little works of art. He created collages on the covers and on some pages. He might glue in a pressed flower, sketch something he'd seen, wind his writing around the space that was left, and then put a watercolor wash over the whole page. Across the top of one set of two pages, he pasted the upper part of a postcard showing a range of the Apennines and then continued it in watercolor. Jerry loved taking his picture, alone or with a companion, in the little booths found in railway stations and other public places, and some of these he affixed also. Reading the journals, one is torn—admiring him, aching for him, and wanting to mutter "Snap out of it!" In them, he wrote a little about his work and a great deal about what he saw, thought, felt, read, and dreamed. The pages vividly reveal his insecurity, his anger, his passions, and his sense of beauty. While preparing for the Stravinsky Festival, he expressed on one elegant yellow-tinted page the fear that never left him: he's internationally famous, "so how come I still think of myself as phoney & my talent is invisible ink?"

The New York City Ballet audience that adored his ballets and eagerly awaited each new one would have been startled to learn of his impostor complex. Watching him take his bows—tanned, immaculate, his graying beard carefully trimmed, his white teeth gleaming, his step youthful— who in the theater would have suspected that he still often thought he had tricked the audience into thinking he was better than he was?

Even his second-best works pleased balletgoers, and the two he created in 1973, *An Evening's Waltzes* and *Four Bagatelles,* while not profoundly satisfying, had passages of great beauty. Robbins's use of music was problematic in both cases. *An Evening's Waltzes* was set to Sergei Prokofiev's 1946 *Suite of Waltzes* (drawn from the composer's *Cinderella, War and Peace,* and *Lermontov*). Discordant in their lyricism, bombastic yet dry, the pieces inspired Robbins to create a ballroom aswirl with waltzing couples in glossy evening clothes, the women crowned with egret feathers. Over the decorous unison of the small corps de ballet, pairs of soloists (Patricia McBride and Jean-Pierre Bonnefous, Christine Redpath and John Clifford, Sara Leland and Bart Cook) enter one at a time to make violent small talk in dance. Small outbursts of movement, sudden changes of heart and direction interrupt the smooth surface of the waltzing. Robbins hinted at dark currents beneath the coquetry and fashionable melodrama without fully exploring them.

He wasn't truly pleased with the ballet; in his journal, he noted that *Waltzes* was "weak in beginning and end. . . . fair—not great & a disappointment." He had intended the third waltz for Gelsey Kirkland and Helgi Tomasson (the latter his "discovery" and very much valued in the company). Tomasson had to withdraw early on, and Kirkland injured herself shortly before the premiere. Redpath and Clifford had done well with the duet, he thought, "but it wasn't made for either of their qualities." To the press, Jerry offered the excuse that the company needed a new ballet and repeated Balanchine's credo that if a choreographer just kept working, some of the ballets were bound to be good, even though others might fall by the wayside: "But it's a hard thing to do—to keep plunging ahead when your instinct is to polish and hone." He was finding his perfectionism a hard thing to keep in check.

Four Bagatelles was first performed at a gala company benefit on May 16, 1973, where it was danced by the company's charming French performers, Violette Verdy and Jean-Pierre Bonnefous, under the title of *A Beethoven Pas de Deux* (when it premiered officially in New York in 1974, Kirkland replaced Verdy). In the duet—structured as a classical pas de deux with an opening adagio emphasizing partner work, a solo for each dancer, and a spirited coda for both—the pair were dressed in ballet-peasant attire, like runaways from *Giselle* or *Napoli:* a full skirt and laced bodice for her, breeches, shirt, and vest for him. Robbins's choreography set Bonnefous dashing around and launching himself into big, rambunctious jumps that suited this bold dancer excellently; and it underlined Verdy's ability to meld vivacity with dreaminess. The mood was as light as her filmy skirt, but the steps were intricate. Some thought the ballet violated the music's flow, but Beethoven's Bagatelles are as playfully perverse and packed with sudden new ideas as Robbins's work. As Nancy Goldner pointed out, the choreographer seemed divided between the wish to present a natural-seeming encounter between two people and a formal pas de deux wherein one person hustles offstage the instant the other shows signs of wanting to do a solo.

If *Four Bagatelles* followed a traditional structure, that may have been because it had been created to figure in Robbins's 1973 project for Spoleto, *Celebration: The Art of the Pas de Deux.* Harvey Lichtenstein, the newly appointed director general of the Spoleto Festival, had hoped to present the New York City Ballet in *Dances at a Gathering,* but that couldn't be arranged. Instead, Robbins proposed that five couples, each representing a different national "school," or style, of ballet, perform two pas de deux of their choice. He would choreograph an opening and a finale. Carla Fracci, prima ballerina of the La Scala Opera Ballet, and Paolo Bortoluzzi of Maurice Béjart's Ballet du XXième Siècle represented the Italian school, Verdy and Bonnefous the French, Antoinette Sibley and Anthony Dowell the British, Patricia McBride and Helgi Tomasson the American, and Malika Sabirova and Muzofar Bourkhanov, from the Tadzhik Theater of Opera and Ballet Aini, the Russian. Robbins's choreography was well represented. In addition to Verdy and Bonnefous performing *Four Bagatelles,* McBride and Tomasson danced *Afternoon of a Faun.*

Robbins had not chosen the Soviet couple. He had seen better Russian dancers earlier in the summer while serving as a judge at the international competition in Moscow, where the hospitality was warm and the company stimulating. The Bolshoi's star ballerina, Maya Plisetskaya, tried to coax a new ballet out of him; he was thrilled to meet Romola Nijinsky, the great dancer's wife; and he had a fine time reminiscing about old days with Alicia and Fernando Alonso. He was impressed by Plisetskaya's performance at the Bolshoi in Roland Petit's new *La Rose Malade* and noted the talent of young Nadezhda Pavlova and others. For Spoleto, however, he was obliged to accept a pair chosen by Gosconcert, the agency of the Soviet Ministry of Culture. Although Sabirova and Bourkhanov hailed from Dushanbe (then Stalinabad), both had trained at Leningrad's prestigious Vaganova Institute. Jerry was a bit taken aback by them but not unimpressed by their power (he counted while Bourkhanov whipped Sabirova through nineteen finger turns). The tiny Malika had arrived toting her costumes in a laundry bag slung over her shoulder. Robbins took note of her street attire: "yellow short sleeve sweater, red mini skirt, large patent leather black belt & huge heavy chunky platform shoes, like those of an old deep sea diver." During rehearsals, while the other dancers marked through their more taxing numbers, the Russians, for whom the steeply raked stage of the Teatro Nuovo held no terrors, charged through their pyrotechnical Russian classics at full steam. In a notebook of Italian impressions he kept that summer, Jerry wrote, "They do *Don Q* 3–4 times and *Corsaire* 2–4 times and entrance walk 4 times. She says to him, 'What are you puffing about, you haven't done anything yet.' " The festival had been warned that a Soviet official or someone in good standing in the Party might be coming. That turned out to be the ballerina.

Robbins didn't often write about dancers in his journals and notebooks, but that summer he did set down some words about those he knew less well than the two NYCB couples. He didn't care for Bortoluzzi's style but found Fracci "lovely—patient—a much better dancer than I thought." He was charmed by Sibley's lyricism, her attentiveness to her partner: "Her use of her small, compact elegant head on top of the neck and her spine is ravishing." He raved even more about Dowell: "a superb partner . . . and a true 'danseur noble.' He has tremendous strength, control, technique & musicality & coupled with all that is an inner sensitivity & vulnerable quality seasoned and guarded by his quiet wit. He is a true artist & a very special one at that." Of the British pair's dancing in Frederick Ashton's *Meditation from Thaïs,* he noted: "So beautiful. Extraordinary!"

Robbins the showman choreographed a knockout opener. Ten male dancers from Rome entered, brandishing pennants as they marched in a series of formations, then used the flags to usher in, one by one and from different directions, each of the five couples (costumed alike but in different colors) for a brief display, in waltz time, of their styles. A quick passage of flying leaps by the men momentarily broke the focus on pairs, and a pleasant meet-and-greet ending established the couples as equals.

Jerry came up with a *coup de théâtre* for the evening's finale. The orchestra, conducted by Christopher Keene, played Tchaikovsky's music for the lyrical pas de deux from *Swan Lake,* Act II, and the couples spelled one another in it, overlapping their entrances and exits. Jennifer Tipton, who did the lighting (commencing a long friendship and professional relationship with Robbins), counts her design for this project among those she's proudest of. Rouben Ter-Arutunian's set consisted of a China silk curtain that could be moved and draped to create different layered effects.

Celebration ultimately showed more about ballet's polymorphous and peripatetic history than it did about national characteristics. The Americans performed a work (*Tchaikovsky Pas de Deux*) by Balanchine, a transplanted Russian, as well as Robbins's *Afternoon of a Faun;* the Italians danced excerpts from the Danish *La Sylphide* and the French *Coppélia;* the French performed *Grand Pas Classique* by the Russian Viktor Gsovsky and the pas de deux by Robbins the American; the English presented, in addition to *Meditation from Thaïs* by "their" Frederick Ashton, Ashton's arrangement of the last-act pas de deux from *The Sleeping Beauty* by Marius Petipa, a Frenchman who had transformed ballet in Russia.

Jerry's summer assistant Rhoda Grauer—very young, new to ballet, and scrambling to fulfill her boss's needs—remembers that time with pleasure. "[Jerry] was so happy, he was just in wonderful shape in Spoleto." Aidan Mooney had joined him again, as well as another friend, Randy Bourscheidt, and, for a while, Tanaquil Le Clercq. But Tanny fell, contracting a long hairline fracture along one immobile leg, and had to fly home in a cast. When Robbins saw the X ray, he almost fainted from "what was it—more than dismay or alarm—but maybe thru the pain of my love for her."

But nothing could quench his delight in being in Italy. He reveled in the view from the loggia on the top floor of 12 Piazza del Duomo, where he had been given lodging. He went to one of the local swimming pools and taught young Spoletini to dive. The *comune* of Spoleto offered him, for the duration of his life, the use of a house known as "Little Falls," high up on the hill above the town, if he would restore it, but he decided against it. He revisited the hill towns of the region and some farther afield, where he could drink in art. His descriptions reveal the acuity and sensuousness of his perception. In Visso, his eye was caught by a curious "Visitation" painted on the curve of the ceiling above the altar: "Elizabeth was in a dark robe & aggressively reaching out to encompass the virgin who was astonishingly thin, like a reed & whose upper body pulled away from Elizabeth at almost right angles. her dress also poured like milk [?] from a pitcher down & at the bottom out." In Messina, he all but memorized the "Entombment of Christ"—its light, its weight, the blurring of the faces when seen close up:

The longer one looks the heavier & like flesh [lifeless?] the Christ becomes. Dead or asleep the angels cannot place him, only aid him, like a somnambulist being helped to bed without completely waking up. . . . The three angels move him carefully, hold him with concern. Little angels—like children angelic and knowing labor—they have the burden of attendant nurse-workers. Their empathy & labor make an enveloping wreath of concern & circle his upper torso & head with attention & wrap him in love—but not pity. They do their jobs. This super-man in ideas and weight—in actuality & in spirit is being attended by children half his size & ¼ his maturity. Like Italian children, they already know that life entails work and death—as a mutual part of life. . . . While the wings of the angels like swallowtail butterflies point upward & flash out—the whole picture is one of sinking.

Drunk on Catholic imagery, he tried to imagine what it might be like to be part of that faith, to "eat the Good God and have him within you to do better." However, unlike Lincoln Kirstein, who had converted to Catholicism, he could not quite take that step away from his heritage, and one of the things he admired about Piero della Francesca was how Jewish his Christs were. He especially loved the muscular and virile risen Jesus in Sansepolcro, one foot on the edge of his open tomb.

Jerry began hatching a plan for a kind of pageant-cum-theater-piece on the Christ story. He imagined the church of St. Eufemia alive with "circus acrobats & tightrope walkers—Angels that swing across the church—or are pulled on tracks—down naves—apostles sit in stacked tiers—flames, clouds & light—float around—candle lit—children play—Christ is lowered from the cross—the dead are healed." His notebook from later that summer contains scattered references to a peripatetic audience, to draping the steps to the Duomo, to a platform stage in the piazza, to something perhaps happening in the cathedral itself and its basement. And at the moment of Christ's death: "A loud noise—huge volume of sound which takes at least 5–10 minutes to decrease—& lessen instruments & voices till finally a single voice of a bell is heard & the simplest thing or action is seen on the stage & light." It might have been a marvelous spectacle.

That summer, wrestling over the insecurities and rages he was trying to stop blaming his mother for, wishing when he was alone that he had company, and, when he had houseguests, wishing for time alone, he wrote a sad and discerning page in his journal:

I straighten my room as if someone I want to love will come into it & find it hospitable to be in. It will welcome them—or is it the kind of neatness I want to find in another. Perfection really rules me v/much—the game I play with, or on me is one always of anticipations—that the face, experience, picture, vista, food—whatever will be extraordinary & have profound & vital meanings. So this is both romantic & discouraging for all I'm with as it projects a dissatisfaction with all around me.

⌒

"Dybbuk Dybbuk Dybbuk," Jerome Robbins had written to Leonard Bernstein in October 1958, in the midst of Ballets: U.S.A.'s successes. "I'm sending over an unseen but continually haunting prodder who will creep into your sleep and into your spare moments and will say the words Dybbuk Dybbuk Dybbuk. With this ghost's effort I know that suddenly something will be on paper that will get us all started." Ben Shahn, he says, tempting the composer further, is excited about designing the production. He continued to prod Bernstein, who, for the next couple of years, continued to try to set aside time within his busy conducting schedule with the New York Philharmonic and elsewhere to write a score.

When Robbins reconnected himself with the New York City Ballet, he began to think again about *The Dybbuk*. And this time Kirstein—who had turned the idea down in 1954 and who didn't care for Bernstein or think highly of him as a composer—approved the project. S. Ansky's play is built on elements Robbins was drawn to: religious mysticism, sense of community, powerful drama, and an Eastern European Jewish ambiance. The story concerns a young man, Chanon, who is cheated of his promised bride, Leah. Their fathers, when young men, had pledged that if ever one had a son and the other a daughter, the two offspring should be wed, but Leah's father breaks the vow when a wealthy suitor appears. A student of theology, Chanon delves feverishly—and dangerously deeply—into the secrets of the Kabbalah, seeking to invoke dark forces that will help him to gain Leah. He dies in the process, and his spirit possesses her body. Exorcised by the community, the demon flees, but the girl dies and joins her true bridegroom. It's small wonder that Robbins asked himself, "Is it an opera? Ballet? Do we need a choir to narrate? What can be danced?" And inevitably, he asked himself, "By now is it a Noh—an abstract interrogation . . . ," toying with the idea of masks and sketching a triangular area with musicians on one side, singers on another, and on the third dancers who'd be able to step into the interior and join actors. At some point, he envisioned an "intense dance" in which Chanon rips from the Torah the magic that will win Leah and "becomes engulfed in the pages (scrolls) of the Torah, like Laocoön" in the grip of the serpent.

In February 1972, taking some time away from Stravinsky Festival preparations, Robbins holed up in Jamaica with Bernstein, and they tried to thrash out a structure. They smoked ganja and shared childhood memories. Lenny was very sensitive, Jerry noted, "like me, but insensitive to the feelings of others. Like me?" One day, the two "had it out—& twenty eight years! (since 1944) of stored up resentments came rushing out—not badly . . . a hard thing to do for both of us—he told me he'd been scared of me for all those years—& all flashed up together—he scared of me & me feeling he's always put me down. Still have strong reactions to him—against him—but I understand some of it now & hope (?) we can be friends. What a load to have been carrying." In October 1973, Robbins dreamed that Bernstein had invited him to a rehearsal of *Dybbuk* (in the dream, Jerry had evidently been off somewhere and Lenny had been working on the ballet in his absence). It started off, then began to look nothing like what he had made, and when he asked, "Where's my ballet?" his collaborator said, "Don't worry, we fixed it—it's now more of a show—you go away & on with your own work & we'll take over this, thanks for your numbers." The horror of it! As the process of agreeing on a structure for the ballet and getting the music written dragged on into 1974, Robbins's sense of the absurd leavened the difficulties. "Lennie & I," he wrote, "well it's a howl. Probably funny if we could see it from the outside . . . RULE: ONLY IF IT'S LENNIE'S IDEA—& HE HAS WRITTEN THE SCORE ALREADY—AND YOU LIKE IT, DO IT. I'm sure we each think the other impossible."

While gearing up for *Dybbuk,* he went to a performance of *The Goldberg Variations* at NYCB and then one of *Fancy Free* at American Ballet Theatre. He hadn't seen the latter for about fifteen years: "What a trip—to see the naiveness of F.F. after the cool clear elegance & craft of G.V." He asked himself how he could put these two pages of his creative life together—the energetic, well-told story, in this case full of references to the culture of its day, and the formal ballet springing from music alone. He tried, in some way, to address this question in *Dybbuk.* Yet the fifty-minute work, which finally premiered on May 16, 1974, turned out to have no blazing identity as either a piece of dance theater or as a ballet. Robbins had begun with brave forays into the plot. He gave the dancers copies of Ansky's play and told them to read it. Bart Cook, who was standing in as Chanon—denatured in the program to the Young Man—for Helgi Tomasson (although Robbins had neglected to tell him that the part wasn't his), recalls that "there was a wedding scene, there was death, there were fires, there were more props than you could count on your fingers. Very interesting props, too. We did the magic circles and talked about the Kabbalah and the fire and the earth and the whole thing." Along the way, scenes were pruned, as were Patricia Zipprodt's costumes. Although Bernstein gave a synopsis of the story in the program, the "argument" that preceded it (possibly by Robbins) told the audience not to expect to see a retelling of the play, which the ballet "uses . . . only as a point of departure for a series of related dances concerning rituals and hallucinations which are present in the dark magico-religious ambience of the play and in the obsessions of its characters."

The eleven-part work emerged as a ritualistic suite of dances pervaded by gloom and imbued with provocative traces of the play's drama. One could imagine it as footage for an eerily pallid film of the play, which some gifted cinematographer had had to abandon. Key scenes were missing; those that remained happened fugitively, in a limbo of time and space. (How was anyone not familiar with the play to know that when Patricia McBride as Leah cast down a veil—or perhaps a *huppa*—she was refusing marriage with a wealthy suitor?) The characters were distanced from the passions that drove them. Yet the powerful dramatic element in the music (which Bernstein himself conducted on opening night) and its residue in the dance made it impossible to think of *Dybbuk* simply as a ballet with a sinister ritualistic atmosphere. Robbins carried his pursuit of abstraction to the point where he originally subtitled the chilling "Possession" scene for the superbly expressive Tomasson and McBride "a) allegro—pas de deux, b) adagio—pas de deux." The movements did not specifically refer to Jewish folk style, despite somber line dances for seven men (Chanon and his fellow students) or eight women, nor were they entirely balletic. Originally, the men wore hats and tallises some of the time, but their costumes—filmy black cassocks over white leotards and tights—invoked the atmosphere of dreams, or of eroticism repressed by austerity. It seems as if, in attempting to reduce the play to its essence, Robbins had pressed some of the juice out of it.

There were superb choreographic and theatrical moments. A bit of sleight of hand made the dead, demonized hero appear as if by sorcery from a group of men. The solos for Bart Cook, Victor Castelli, Tracy Bennett, and Hermes Condé titled "Invocation of the Kabbalah" were fascinating. The dybbuk's spirit seems to flicker through McBride even before the possession duet in which Tomasson, dressed like McBride in a transparent white tunic, clamps himself around her from behind as if to worm his way into her body and soul. Resisting only at first, she wraps herself around him too. At times they seemed to embody Plato's theory of lovers who are only half formed until they meet and merge.

Robbins began cutting the ballet almost immediately. By the end of the year, he had retitled it *The Dybbuk Variations,* rendering it even more at odds with Bernstein's impressive music, whose important, menacing statements suggest cause and effect. Then, in April, he restored some of what he had excised (variations for three "angelic messengers," for instance). In its last incarnation (1980), the ballet was titled *Suite of Dances* and consisted only of the choreography for the men.

In 1986, when Kirstein urged Robbins to revive *Dybbuk* ("it's one of Lennie's best scores and he would love to do it with you. It was a mistake to diminish it into 'Variations'"), Jerry demurred, blaming Bernstein for the ballet's problems: "It was very unsatisfactory as initially it was going to be a small chamber music work about the essences of the spiritual life of the play. Instead Lenny wrote a symphonic work (with two voices yet) without discipline, spreading over the whole story. Thus it was neither an abstract nor a story piece, just an uneasy amalgam of approaches. I did my best to make a whole out of it, but, as you know, I was never satisfied." Bernstein, on the other hand, gave his friend Helen Coates the impression that one of the difficulties plaguing the creative process was that "Jerry can't make up his mind how the ballet should go."

Robbins took the critics' less-than-rapturous reception personally, as he always did. Edwin Denby, whose feedback he always craved and who often tried to avoid giving an opinion for fear of wounding, was no longer reviewing dance, but he wrote a letter that ought to win a prize for ambiguity: "I'm delighted you did such a strange piece. I couldn't tell what you were doing. All along I've always been able to see what you were doing very clearly but this time I didn't know. But I was happy so puzzled it interests me."

⁓

Dybbuk embodies a struggle that shaped Robbins's career choices and the choices he made in his ballets. He was proud of some of his Broadway work, but ballet was a higher form of art. He knew he could tell a story in dance and tell it skillfully, but abstraction was something nobler. He was in awe of Balanchine's ability to suggest or elicit, through the fusion of dancing and music, feelings that couldn't be put into words. Yet he himself had to approach abstraction through conventions that meant a great deal to him: rituals and their lighter sibling, games. The images of community, which sometimes seem to come naturally from his work and sometimes seem contrived, mattered greatly to him. He fought between letting the human feelings that he loved emerge of their own accord and wanting to do what had to be done to *make* them emerge.

His responses to a book he read early in 1975, while he was still tinkering with *Dybbuk*, obliquely shed some light on his attitude toward ballet—and perhaps on his agonizing over that ballet in particular. On January 2, he noticed a review in *The New York Times* of *The Ordeal of Civility: Freud, Marx, Lévi-Strauss, and the Jewish Struggle with Modernity* by John Murray Cuddihy. He later wrote that just from reading the review, "my mind blew open all the shuttered, walled-in, locked away rooms full of rage and hysteria." Early on, Cuddihy announced the "ordeal" as "the ritually unconsummated social courtship of Gentile and Jew that is formative for the labors of the secular Jewish intelligentsia of the nineteenth and twentieth centuries. It is their hidden theme." Moving from the religious gemeinschaft of the Eastern European shtetl to the modernizing society of the West, "The secularizing Jewish intellectual, as the avant-garde of his decolonized people, suffered in his own person the trauma of culture shock." Robbins underlined those last nine words. As he did these: "cultural shame and awkwardness, guilt and 'the guilt of shame,' " in relation to the predicament of the Jew caught between the rough, loving community he had left and the Gentile "host culture" into which he needed to assimilate. (He also underlined sentences in Cuddihy's cultural analysis of Freud's theories.) The book goaded Robbins to probe his ambivalence about his heritage. He constructed a very large and elegant collage of black-and-white photos of religious Jews, with his own portrait—both the little Jerry and the grown one—embedded in the tight clusters, as if this were a game to see how long it took the viewer to spot him. He urged his friend Daniel Stern to read *The Ordeal of Civility,* and he inscribed his own copy, "Jerome Rabinowitz," which, said Stern, "I'd never seen him do in any other book."

Cuddihy's book made Robbins want to learn more about his father and to try to understand him. By January 22, 1975, he was going over his diaries and notebooks of the past few years and musing into a tape recorder about "the rages and discontents deeply deeply rooted inside of me and . . . whirling to get out. . . . It seems to me that anger and anguish [are] caused by this wrenching away from my true cultural background and the constant disciplinary modification—work—to assimilate myself. Pouring myself, filling myself, politely training myself to become an American and by American I mean WASP American." On one hand, his parents had taught him—more through osmosis than intention—"to love the richness the color the quality the roughness the coarseness the faith the despair, the music, the sound the violence and the fears of being a Jew in a shtetl town. But I was born here in America . . . the other part of them was pointing ahead to a land of streets paved with gold and dreams coming true and ships coming in" to which their well-educated children would lead them. Harry and Lena had also indirectly taught their kids that "it was our fate to be persecuted, separated, ridiculed, rejected & always to be an excluded minority lower than all the others (except the schwartzes)."

Robbins had always in his own way honored his heritage (even though the seders he held with friends like the Sterns were hardly by-the-book affairs) and had been gradually letting the things he loved about Jewishness surface in his work. As a youth, he had found Yiddish both magical and ugly, his father's accent a coarse embarrassment, and services at the local New Jersey shul revolting ("Hair shirts and tallises and fringes and beards and drippings and nose runnings and eyes watering, sells [smells?] that I didn't recognize and a language that I couldn't understand. . . . I laid my knife against it").

Robbins had dropped in on Sabbath services when he was working on *Fiddler on the Roof;* now he sampled them for a more personal sort of research, dragging friends with him. He made notes for the autobiographical work he first called "The Jew Piece." As *The Poppa Piece,* it became an ongoing project (he labored on it for many years before finally attempting a workshop production in 1991; his notes and scripts fill many boxes). He began to ask questions about his father's boyhood during periodic dutiful journeys to Florida, where he suffered such trials as being proudly trotted among fifty tables of canasta-playing retirees by Harry and his second wife, Frieda, and being greeted as "Mr. Fiddler." He also asked questions about their father-son relationship and was astonished when Harry said he had loved him and had not, as Jerry had always thought, preferred Sonia.

A number of interesting thoughts related to his work struck him during this probing induced by *The Ordeal of Civility.* None of his frequent dark thoughts surfaced in his ballets, where light and love, laughter, and, at the very least, hope ruled the stage. In Barbados in 1972, he had wondered about that and why he never dealt with "the world of clear unrestrained instinct—the constant and piled up hordes of unconscious hatred, violence, erratic & uncontrolled license. To really let it all hang out." He had fantasized a collage ballet in which *Swan Lake* was spattered by blood from a real dead swan. "An upright man is torn apart, lines of dancers are destroyed, Sylphides raped & all ugliness is allowed." Rereading his thoughts about this *Book of Violences* three years later, he thought the urge might be "a part of those Jew feelings."

One morning in 1975, about to go upstairs to his studio to do a barre and work out, he wondered to his journal whether this ballet business "has something to do with 'civilizationing' of my Jewishness. I affect a discipline over my body & take on another language . . . the language of court & christianity—church & state—a completely artificial convention of movement—one that deforms & reforms the body & imposes a set of artificial conventions of beauty—a language not universal—one foreign to East & 3rd world." And he added, "In what wondrous & monstrous ways would I move if I would dig down to my Jewish self." (He may have known he would never discover the answer, and perhaps wouldn't have dared to jeopardize what he was achieving.)

So while struggling with *The Poppa Piece* and his own autobiography, Robbins continued to dedicate himself to ballet's world of beauty. In the New York City Ballet's Ravel Festival in May 1975, it was George Balanchine who choreographed a strange and nightmarish piece, *Gaspard de la Nuit,* along with six other new works, the most memorable of which were *Le Tombeau de Couperin,* a jewel of a contredanse that starred the corps de ballet, and *Tzigane,* the first work he choreographed for Suzanne Farrell after she returned to the company in January after a six-year absence.

Unlike the Stravinsky Festival, presented in a thrilling, tightly packed week, the three programs dedicated to Ravel were scattered amid the repertory during three weeks in May, each performed three times in a row. Why Ravel? "Why not Ravel?" countered Balanchine. Ravel was not a musician whom Balanchine had associated himself with overmuch (he had choreographed *L'Enfant et les Sortilèges* for Diaghilev's Ballets Russes in 1925 and his great *La Valse* for NYCB in 1951). However, it was Ravel's centennial; festivals caused excitement and might yield usable new ballets.

The French connection might enhance publicity, but, says Barbara Horgan, then Balanchine's assistant, "his heart wasn't really in it."

Robbins choreographed five new ballets. One, *Concerto in G* (subsequently retitled *In G Major*), became an enduring favorite; another, *Ma Mère l'Oye,* is one of his most delicious works. The other three were less memorable: the pretty *Introduction and Allegro for Harp* for McBride and Tomasson, plus three couples; *Une Barque sur l'Océan* for five male corps de ballet members—a light dance that tilted and sailed and rocked, with the men sometimes like sailors, sometimes like billows; and *Chansons Madécasses,* a quartet that featured two black dancers wearing black and two white ones dressed in white (Debra Austin and Hermes Condé, McBride and Tomasson).

Barque, like the earlier *Scherzo Fantastique* and *Dybbuk,* pointed up one of Robbins's important contributions to the company: his interest in showing off its young male dancers. Balanchine, despite having made some superb roles for men, had once remarked to a Cooper Union audience, "You can put sixteen girls on a stage and fill it—it's everybody, the world. But put sixteen boys . . . and it's always nobody." Whether he actually felt that way or not, it's certain that featuring male ensembles wasn't a priority. For Robbins it was.

Patricia McBride feels that *Madécasses* was a ballet that meant a lot to Jerry, and he wanted to get it right. He was charmed by the music—Ravel's setting of three poems by Évariste Parny. But the ballet, despite lovely moments, was opaque, especially in relation to the songs. Robbins brought out the languor and delicate heat of the music; the dancers moved slowly through angular positions into watchful stillness. The choreography didn't refer much to Parny's words—some of which are extremely erotic and others that, like "Place not your trust in the white man . . . ," bring up racial tensions. For Robbins, all four dancers simply dwelt together in wary companionship. He himself found black men very beautiful, and had once confided impetuously to his diary, "And why do I feel better with blacks than whites. This has become stronger & stronger—so that I almost don't dig whites."

When *In G Major* was first performed in Paris in 1976 as part of a mini–Ravel Festival, it acquired a stylized backdrop by Rouben Ter-Arutunian suggesting the sea. The NYCB adopted that decor, which gives it more the air of a beach romp, and the ballet is often performed as if the dancers think of it that way, with men and women kicking up their heels as they run. It has something of the sporty feel of *Dumbarton Oaks,* but, in keeping with Ravel's music, its jazzy overtones are cooler, though still perky.

In 1975, the queen and king of the moment were Suzanne Farrell and Peter Martins, both tall, fair, and handsome. Kneeling, the men watch this woman, rising up two by two to assist her in looking even more lovely. Later the women form a chain with her partner at the middle (an effect reminiscent of Balanchine's *Piano Concerto No. 2*). The long, rich second-movement duet is one of Robbins's finest. It begins with a simple walking passage on a diagonal. The woman walks toward the man, then backs up; when she repeats this, he walks toward her as she retreats; then the walk brings them together and apart and past each other. Variations of this serene motif recur as the two move into complex but fluid lifts and other forms of partnering. A stroll on the shore, a conversation full of questions becomes something more than a beach-blanket romance. Curiously, Robbins, while choreographing the ballet, saw it as "another dance pure ballet—not my cup of tea." Was he viewing it momentarily in the light of *The Ordeal of Civility,* as irrelevant to his Jewish identity?

Robbins subtitled *Ma Mère l'Oye* "Fairy Tales for Dancers." The beginning was more than a trifle unbelievable (dancers lounging around on a stage studded with remnants of sets, trunks, a barre, and so on—apparently listening to a story, which was read at the premiere by the company wardrobe mistress, Sophie Pourmel, standing in for Mother Goose). But the ballet is a charmingly conceived escapade. Robbins surrendered to telling stories—actually, fairy tales within a story (*The Sleeping Beauty*) within his own favorite story: lovely young people working at the rituals of theater with all their precocious professional skill and all their youthful, unmannered freshness. The silent storytelling done, the dancers find things they can use—a plumed hat here, a paper lantern there. And Robbins followed Ravel's scenarios for "Sleeping Beauty," "Beauty and the Beast," "The Empress of the Pagodas," and "Hop o' My Thumb" in a wispy, almost improvisatory way. As in Ravel's plan, the *Sleeping Beauty* tale is the frame. The princess (Muriel Aasen) enters skipping rope and does some fancy tricks when two of her friends start turning the rope for her. In place of the fairy-tale dances in Marius Petipa's ballet, celebrating her awakening and marriage, she dreams the stories; the performers acknowledge her where she sleeps on her bed, and the Good Fairy (Delia Peters) gives a stern "Shh!" to any who might disturb her.

The ballet offers no choreographic feats on Robbins's part, but many bright theatrical ideas. The Beast, touched sympathetically by Beauty, rises, and as he does so, his lumbering crookedness gradually slips from him like a discarded cloak. The clueless brothers in "Hop o' My Thumb" are grown-up dancers, while a child plays the smart youngest one. The dancers look like children who on a rainy day have ransacked the attic to find props for a game of charades, and they perform with the naïveté of children. Only these children are dancers, and their attic is the NYCB prop and wardrobe department. Aficionados could recognize the bed from *The Nutcracker,* the window from *Liebeslieder Walzer,* and the lanterns from *Watermill. Watermill*'s phragmites become a handheld hedge for Prince Charming to push his way through. Transparent fabric panels are held horizontally to make an ocean for Laideronette, the Empress of the Pagodas, and her snaky lover. There are also allusions to other ballets: a bit of mime from Petipa's *Sleeping Beauty,* the pseudo-Chinese movements that recall the "Tea" dance from Lev Ivanov's *Nutcracker,* the stately wedding procession like the one that ends *The Firebird.*

Some people found the ballet contrived or too comedic or underchoreographed, or—worse from Robbins's point of view—mocking in its attitude toward ballet. "In truth," he said, "I have felt only love and tenderness for all the pieces represented." Arlene Croce, so often critical of Robbins, wrote warmly about this work:

> In the poetic style of *Ma Mère l'Oye* Robbins returns to those qualities that first defined him as a unique theater artist. . . . [It] is bound to be underestimated because it looks so easy and hasn't a lot of dancing, but it's a New York artifact of wide significance. It catches up the beloved Robbins myth about dancers as children and relocates it in our current world of young dancers' workshops, professional children's schools, and incubators of the performing arts. The point of overlap is the ancillary myth, so real to the stagestruck kids of Robbins' generation, of puttin' on a show.

Responding to a letter from one who followed his career, the choreographer wrote: "Best of all, Mr. B. likes it immensely, and you know what that means to me."

He was nonetheless disheartened by the festival. In 1978, he recorded in his journal that his "deep depression" over the Ravel Festival had started him "signing off on work." Kirstein tried to cheer him up and engage his interest. "It seems incontestable that *Chansons Madécasses, Ma Mere l'Oye* and the *Concerto* are repertory pieces; what more can one ask? Ravel wasn't Stravinsky but we did the best Spring season money wise than ever; 10% better than last year, and we only lost $50,000 on a $400,000 outlay; so don't fret." He was planning a Copland gala for next spring "in which you ought to do three 'serious' i.e. non-folkloristic works from his early, middle and late periods, with the possibility of a new commission which we would find money for and which he would conduct, or Lennie, if he were of such a mind. . . . It would be YOUR evening as Balanchine has no real sympathy for Aaron." As for the critics: "What do you expect; Love? . . . We work as we can and must for ourselves."

~

The years 1974 and 1975 had been trying for Robbins for a number of reasons. A relationship with one young lover had come apart while another was beginning; then that one had soured. Jerry felt that *Dybbuk* had been a failure, and it took him a long time to get over that. He found much to criticize in the day-to-day running of the New York City Ballet. Although he enjoyed Balanchine's 1974 production of *Coppélia,* he thought the company should be above pandering to audiences by feeding them another old story ballet (sensitive to matters of money, he was, nevertheless, inexperienced in the business of what a company had to do to survive). Lincoln Kirstein had a mild heart attack at the end of 1975, and Balanchine began to show signs of ill health. Joseph Mazo, dance critic of *Women's Wear Daily,* spent the 1973 season observing the life of the New York City Ballet and in 1974 produced a lively and uncomfortably revealing book, *Dance Is a Contact Sport,* with a chapter devoted to Robbins as the resident monster (the company was upset by the way Mazo had interpreted events and repeated off-guard remarks).

Even so, in this period of intense and painful self-scrutiny, Robbins had many happy times—and busy ones. He served on the National Council of the Arts and the New York State Council on the Arts. As ever, he took in plays, movies, and art exhibitions and spent evenings and weekends with friends (he felt lost without weekend plans). He traveled abroad. He gave dinner parties, often drawing the seating plan in his journal. In the summer of 1974, he visited Ahmet and Mica Ertegun in Bodrum, Turkey. The Erteguns were neighbors on Eighty-first Street; Mica—who heads Mac II, the design firm she founded with the late Chessy Rayner—made highly effective alterations to his living room (he loved the result and loved her too). Yachting around the Mediterranean with the Erteguns and friends, having the ruins at Cnidos explained by archaeologist Iris Love, buying a dress for Tanny, he could relax and enjoy himself. He wrote in his journal—and later polished his remarks for his possible autobiography—an account of a hot afternoon in a deserted gallery of the Topkapi Palace and a fleeting, wordless sexual adventure with a young museum guard (both of them fully clothed) that remained in his mind as an enigmatic, sensuously poetic encounter.

In 1973, Jerry bought an 8-millimeter movie camera. He also purchased a video camera and tested it by filming the office and dressing room he shared with Balanchine. In this tape, the photographer, first checking focus and zoom, pans silently around the desks, the two easy chairs, the shelves of ancient Russian books, the piano, the pictures of Balanchine's cat, Mourka, and so on. Then, as the camera more confidently reexamines the room, Robbins starts to talk quietly: "This is George's desk. . . . This is my desk. . . . The books on George's desk have been there for a month or more, some of them for a year." One could make too much of this, but the impression the clumsy videotape gives is that the person who is holding the camera still thinks of himself as an interloper who can't quite believe this is his office too but likes reminding himself that it is.

In the summer of 1975, Robbins slid into a severe depression, perhaps a breakdown. Daniel Stern thinks it could well be true that the issues raised in *The Ordeal of Civility* and Jerry's probing of his past were tearing him apart more than he let on, but Stern also raises other possible causes, such as the various drugs that Robbins had experimented with during some summers at the beach and that had perhaps had too strong an impact on his somewhat delicate constitution and imaginative sensibility. Also, at the end of June, Jerry had moved out of the Snedens Landing house. In recent years, he had been spending more summers in rented houses in the Hamptons, subletting the riverside place where he had been happy for so long. It wasn't moving out per se that upset him, but the packing and all the decisions. In his calendar, he crossed out a meeting he was evidently scheduled to attend on July 3 and across his calendar from that day to July 24, he scrawled in red "FREAK OUT," letting the cross of the T tumble down the page. To his journal, he was uncomfortably playful:

Dear Diary. Guess where I'm writing from?—Oh you'll never guess!
I'll give you three little hints. It's near Boston—it has lots of trees &
grounds & facilities (except a pool)—& the service is so good that you're
almost never out of sight of one of the staff!!!
Well?
No—Not Nantucket or the Cape
no—not the Ritz Carlton in Boston
I'm at McLeans—Wheeeeeeeeee

McLean Hospital, housed on a former estate in Belmont, Massachusetts, is the main psychiatric teaching hospital of the Harvard Medical
School. Dr. Shervert Frazier, at this time Robbins's psychiatrist for almost
eight years, had moved from Columbia Presbyterian in New York City to
become chairman of McLean's Department of Psychiatry. The point of
Jerry's stay, as he stated it in his journal, was to build up his tolerance to the
antidepressant Elavil until he could handle 150 milligrams. He worried
about possible publicity—"a Jewish ex commie fag who had to go into a
mental hospital"—but even many close friends knew nothing about his
sojourn at McLean. His current boyfriend, Ronald Ifft, came up often to
visit, bringing Nick, the beloved mongrel terrier that Aidan Mooney, Slim
Keith, and her stepson had picked out at Bide-A-Wee and presented to
Jerry for his fifty-sixth birthday. And Robbins went home after three
weeks to houseguests who knew how to make a guy laugh: Nora Kaye and
his former boyfriend Howard Jeffrey, on their way to London.

After weathering a grievous event—John Kriza drowned off the coast
of Naples, Florida, on August 18, 1975—Jerry recovered his balance and
flew to Paris in October to arrange extra time for Tom Abbott to stage *In
G Major* for its December premiere with the Paris Opera Ballet. He also
rehearsed *Fanfare* with the NYCB and celebrated Thanksgiving with a
cookout in Bear Mountain State Park for eight men friends who included
Buzz Miller and his partner, Allen Groh; Aidan Mooney and William
Earle; and Ronald Ifft (two former lovers of Jerry's were present to shiver
in the November chill). He then traveled to London to mount *The Concert*
on the Royal Ballet, to Paris to fine-tune *In G Major* and reap the acclaim,
and to Marrakech, where he hoped to see some dancing.

Even as the Ravel Festival was being prepared, he had begun to test his
commitment to his work at New York City Ballet (which included
mounting ballets created there on other companies). In February 1975, he

had sounded out the great Swedish director Ingmar Bergman about the not-quite-dead-in-the-water Nijinsky film: "Would you consider working together with me collaboratively on the film?" Bergman was busy until spring 1978, and *Nijinsky,* the final disappointing 1980 product, was directed by Herbert Ross. Robbins considered making a piece for American Ballet Theatre's thirty-fifth anniversary season (nothing came of it). David Merrick flew him out to the coast to give advice about his production of *The Baker's Wife,* and Leonard Bernstein needed him in Philadelphia, where his latest foray into musical comedy, *1600 Pennsylvania Avenue,* was ailing. Jerry went to Philadelphia and gave advice but declined to doctor the show. The visit boosted his self-confidence and confirmed his decision to avoid Broadway: "The Philly experience was fruitful because I discovered how very good I am at theater, how easily my ideas & clarity flow again, that doing a show as far as my muscles are concerned, would not be difficult; that I'm not out of practice, & that most of all how happy I am <u>not</u> to be doing them when I see the shoddiness of 1600. . . . But I am still undecided what to do next." The trip to Philadelphia also incited a revealing entry in his journal:

> Lennie never learns; he fucks around with Christ, God & his country in each work, forgetting his best work came out of looking warmly at his life around him—On the Town, Wonderful Town—: He sees himself a Sage, Prophet, Einstein—& all gets stuffed into symbols, fake statues, LARGE & IMPORTANT pieces. They come out hollow, sentimental.

It seems not to have struck him that his assessment of Bernstein was similar to the opinions about his own work expressed by critics who preferred *Fancy Free* and *Ma Mère l'Oye* to *The Goldberg Variations* and *Watermill.*

Robbins's style was becoming more and more securely grounded in neoclassical ballet, despite his self-questioning and the fact that he was often moved by dancing that had nothing to do with the ballet aesthetic. He went twice to see the Moroccan company that came to the Brooklyn Academy of Music in 1971. He wrote joyously about the calypso dancing at a New York outdoor festival he attended with a boyfriend: "3 boys— strong, sure, show me what the 3 drunks in Petrushka should be like . . .

wild, joyous with each other & not afraid of the improvisation going wrong or astray, they sprawl—careen, flaunt spill around & their contagion is terrific." He continued to drop by Bob Wilson's studio and join in the dancing and to attend downtown dance performances, often with Edwin Denby as a guide. He didn't like everything he saw, but "God, the guts of these kids! . . . how relieving!" he exclaimed in one interview. He was particularly drawn to Twyla Tharp's work (and to her as a person). "She is elegant & crafted & there is a continuous delight & everydayness in the light floating drunken & heady improvisational quality of her work; eccentric & perversely independent, she noodles her way into her own descriptive vocabulary." (He could not understand, though, why she did not push more for variety and contrast.) Her vision of women excited him:

> Martha's women are pious, dedicated, religious, noble seers and monuments. George's are elegant glamorous "stars"—Garbo elevated, mysterious, provocative, extremely refined—a product of richness of taste & elegance. But Twyla gives you the body of women, their strength, ability, work, sex, work, co-partners to men & adds to the body of dance & presents a full-bodied down-to-earth woman, capable of sharing and abetting man's world as an equal, uncompetitive, feminine, equally capable. That's tremendous.

But just as *Watermill* was Robbins's only defiantly antitraditional work for NYCB, his presentation of strong women in ballet began and ended with *The Cage,* where power was expressed as violence toward men. Most of his works, especially beginning in 1969, view women with tenderness. They are unmannered, dreamy, and slightly flirtatious in their movements, but never do they court the audience. Their bodies are not just supple in the sense of dancerly flexibility; they arch and curl their way into windblown movement.

One can certainly see this in *Other Dances,* a small, lapidary work created in 1976 for a May 9 gala held at the Metropolitan Opera House to benefit the Library for the Performing Arts at Lincoln Center. Set to Chopin waltzes and mazurkas, it featured New York's cherished defectors from the Kirov Ballet, Natalia Makarova and Mikhail Baryshnikov. Although the duet might have been snipped out of *Dances at a Gathering,* found in a dark corner, and polished up for the occasion, it was also adroitly tailored to those two superb performers.

Robbins loved Makarova's dancing and often went to see her perform with American Ballet Theatre. He also found her extremely alluring. Baryshnikov had thrilled him from the dancer's first appearances with ABT in 1974, when it seemed as if he were redefining ballet steps, making them look invented on the spot. In an interview, Robbins marveled over the modesty of Baryshnikov's bows and the way he filled a role or a gesture completely, without mannerism and without what he elsewhere called— in reference to that other admired star Russian, Rudolf Nureyev, with whom he had worked in London— "[doing] a number on the audience."

Other Dances begins with a bit of a tease. Here were two virtuosos, yet in the opening adagio to a slow mazurka (op. 17, no. 4), Robbins gave them hardly a step that was beyond the capabilities of any technically accomplished dancer. Instead, he offered them as immensely subtle artists and fellow Russians (and, fortunately, allowed their performances to be captured on video for *Dance in America*). During the first few seconds of music, standing side by side in one corner, all they do is take hands and begin to stroll along a diagonal toward the onstage pianist. It makes one instantly want to cheer. As the adagio developed, Robbins mingles more than a few Slavic folk steps and gestures with the classical lexicon and focuses, in the moments where Baryshnikov lifts or turns his partner, on making the whole exchange into a fond conversation. In one lovely repeated passage Makarova, bourréeing, attempts to lead her companion somewhere; although she's holding his hand, he keeps pulling back to execute a huge cabriole, smacking his legs together in the air as if in delight at embarking on a journey with this woman.

Although the pianist is onstage for this ballet, suggesting the gemütlich atmosphere of Balanchine's *Duo Concertant,* an orchestra is also playing. The dancers exit during each other's solos rather than watching and listening. They also bow to the audience after each section: a duet, two solos each, and a final duet. Robbins either felt the audience would need to applaud for this stellar pair or knew the dancers would prefer not to hang around panting. Makarova does approach the piano once and gazes at the player, and, in a jokey moment, Baryshnikov pretends to get dizzy during a sequence of turns and he staggers, recovering before he runs into the instrument. Baryshnikov remembers that Robbins wanted his second solo to be "very, very muted and quiet and bravura, the first one very strong and explosive." In the first, the choreographer let Baryshnikov unleash all his startling jumps; in one sequence, with his legs bent into a diamond in the air, he uncannily shivers them. The second solo has that quality of gradually intensifying memory and rediscovery that infuses the opening solo of *Dances at a Gathering*. A small, delicately built woman, Makarova had the gift of making all her movements lavish, extending far into space, without overstressing their extravagance. "She goes and goes and goes and he just loved that in her," Baryshnikov said. Robbins makes her look as fleet as a butterfly in one solo, twisting this way and that as she dances, and in the other lets her flow into the long, improbable, breath-caught balances at which she excelled. Another slow mazurka (op. 63, no. 2) serves for both of the dreamier solos; and that, in some way, seems to bring them closer to-gether—two people commenting on the same landscape—before they embark on the last, more spirited mazurka (op. 33, no. 2).

In his obligatory roundup for *The New York Times* of the most impor-tant dance events of 1976, Clive Barnes counted *Other Dances* as among the best ballets of 1976. American Ballet Theatre immediately snapped it up—an obvious decision, since Makarova and Baryshnikov topped its ros-ter of stars. When ABT performed in London in the fall of 1977, Peter Williams rhapsodized in *Dance and Dancers* that this was the most gor-geous dancing he had seen since the war, and he would be very happy to "see both these dancers in this piece every night of my life."

When *Other Dances* entered the New York City Ballet's repertory on November 26, 1976, Peter Martins and Suzanne Farrell were inevitably compared to the Russians, but their slightly more distanced performing was also praised. Slightly later, Helgi Tomasson and Patricia McBride made debuts in the ballet, and at American Ballet Theatre, Baryshnikov also performed the duet with Gelsey Kirkland to stunning effect (Kirk-land had defected from NYCB to ABT primarily to be his partner).

The satisfaction derived from *Other Dances,* and picking up the Capezio Dance Award in April 1976 and New York City's Handel Medal-lion less than a month later, must have reassured Robbins that his career in ballet was well worth concentrating on. When the New York City Ballet performed in Paris in September and October, all his ballets went beauti-fully and were adored, especially *Dances at a Gathering.* When he stepped forward to take a bow with the company at the Théâtre des Champs-Élysées on October 10, the audience roared.

Although at home he continued to work on what he intended as a three-part, full-evening project, *The Arts of the Gentleman,* for a number of reasons he did not mount a new ballet for NYCB until 1978. A musicians' strike wiped out all but the last few weeks of the 1976 fall season. In March

1977, he was hospitalized with diverticulitis; the problem recurred with complications, and at the end of November he underwent surgery. In a letter to Peter Martins, scolding Martins and Farrell for performing the pas de deux from *In G Major* in a guest appearance outside the company without explicit permission, he noted about his impending operation, "All should go well, and I'll be around and scowling again in the Spring."

He was indeed around and scowling in rare form, but a new love was making him happy. While phasing out an affair with independent filmmaker Warren Sonbert, he began another, more lasting one with the gifted young photographer Jesse Gerstein, whose black curls and olive skin gave him the look of a faun. Gerstein, nineteen to Jerry's fifty-seven when they met in 1976, would be the love of his life for a number of years. However, 1977–1978 was a time marked by illness—and not only Robbins's gastrointestinal crisis—and by loss. Dan Stern and Jerry's father were hospitalized close to the same time. Stern recovered from his heart attack, but Harry Rabinowitz died on December 16, 1977, and in March 1978, Jerry traveled to Jersey City for the burial of his lively, witty Aunt Mary, the fourth Rips sister to die. (One salutary outcome: he and his sister finally made peace with each other after a long period of animosity.) Late in 1976, he had gone to Boston to rehearse the revival of *Fiddler on the Roof*. Less than six months later, Zero Mostel was dead, and only then did Jerry realize that Zero would have been ideal to play Harry Rabinowitz in *The Poppa Piece*. In the spring of 1978, George Balanchine had his first heart attack.

18

When the King Dies

Jerry and George, ca. 1972.
Martha Swope.

*B*alanchine, at seventy-four, was working at a remarkable pace. Robbins marveled that by the closing night of the 1978 winter season, he had choreographed three ballets in seven months: *Vienna Waltzes* (Johann Strauss the younger, Richard Strauss, and Franz Lehar),

Ballo della Regina (Giuseppe Verdi), and *Kammermusik No. 2* (Paul Hindemith).

For the spring season, having saluted Great Britain in 1976 with *Union Jack,* Balanchine planned to choreograph a tribute to another country he loved and had worked in as a young man. *Tricolore,* his salute to France, would form part of an "Entente Cordiale" program that would include *Union Jack* as well as the 1958 *Stars and Stripes.* Like *Union Jack, Tricolore* had the ambitions—and the budget—to be what Lincoln Kirstein called an "applause machine." It might have been, had Balanchine's cardiovascular system not rebelled. Instead, he parceled out *Tricolore* to three choreographers: Peter Martins, whose first ballet, the duet *Calcium Light Night* (1977), had shown unmistakable evidence of choreographic flair; the resident Frenchman Jean-Pierre Bonnefous, who was currently making a piece for the annual School of American Ballet recital; and Jerome Robbins. They rallied to execute the master's ideas, burdened with a disappointing score commissioned from Georges Auric (no longer as adventurous as he had been in 1920s Paris as a member of the group of young composers known as "Les Six").

Robbins had been considering a little moonlighting: engineering a revised version for Broadway of *Heartaches of a Pussycat,* which was playing in Paris that spring. This adaptation of a droll, tart Balzac tale, in the form of a genteel, upwardly mobile young feline's memoir, was performed in animal masks and appealed to his love of fantasy. He may have had some input into the show that opened in New York two years later, but in April he wrote to the producer of the French version, Kim d'Estainville, that he wouldn't be coming to Paris: "Mr. Balanchine isn't well and I have had to take up some of the slack. This means doing some extra choreography that I wasn't prepared for."

From his hospital bed, Balanchine instructed *Tricolore*'s three choreographers in some detail as to what he envisioned. Martins drew the ballet-peasant opener, "Pas de Basque"; in "Pas Degas," Bonnefous choreographed for the ballet girls and jockeys who populated Edgar Degas's paintings. Robbins was assigned the "Marche de la Garde Républicaine," deploying an elegantly uniformed and helmeted coed platoon plus four "officers" in fancy drill formations—hands reining in horses, feet representing the prancing steeds. These were followed by Majorettes led by Karin von Aroldingen—it was Balanchine's idea to present these as saluting cancan girls. In the apotheosis, Nina Fedorova as the Spirit of Liberty was hoisted aloft while behind her red, white, and blue curtains assembled into a French flag. A behemoth like this goes down spectacularly, thrashing in a tangle of dancers, music, and fancy costumes (in this case, distractingly beautiful ones by Rouben Ter-Arutunian). Audience and critics greeted the ballet, when it first appeared on May 18, 1978, as second only to *PAMTGG* in the annals of New York City Ballet flops. By the time the complete "Entente Cordiale" program closed the company's season on July 2, 1978, the ballet had been improved, according to Lincoln Kirstein, but only somewhat.

Work on this extravaganza had delayed Robbins's own ballet, *The Arts of the Gentleman.* Loving to choreograph for young male dancers, he was inspired in part by an eighteenth-century manual *L'École des armes,* and its wonderful plates; by Pierre Rameau's 1725 manual, *The Dancing Master;* and by the work of Baroque dance scholar Wendy Hilton. He drew up lists of music to listen to and plotted a full-length entertainment, presided over by a king and court, with a small group of musicians in an onstage box. A display of fencing, with a possible staged war, was to be followed by court dances, including a solo for the king. He also envisioned an equestrian display and mock hunt (with dancers both horse and rider as in *Tricolore*). After a ceremonious finale, lackeys would clean up. Along the way, he dropped plans for a second half to be set at the king's supper, with a parade of allegorical figures, entertainment by popular acrobatic dancers, a royal ballet, toasts, salutes, and fireworks.

As early as October 1976, Robbins's calendar had noted "Fencing rehearsal NYCB." By the late spring of 1978, he had choreographed only the first section of this grandiose spectacle, *Fencing Dances and Exercises.* He was also at work on *Four Seasons,* set primarily to ballet music from Verdi's opera *I Vespri Siciliani.* Three weeks after the premiere of *Tricolore,* on June 8, the finished portions of these, along with a solo for Daniel Duell and a pas de deux by Peter Martins, were presented under the title *A Sketch Book: Works in Progress*—a first for the NYCB, although everything that was shown was, in itself, "finished."

To excerpts from Handel's *Water Music,* the sixteen young "gentlemen" in *Fencing Dances* strode in, doffed their cocked hats, donned gloves, took up foils handed them by servants, and struck the basic poses—manual illustrations come to life. Under the watchful eye of a Master (Bonnefous), they began to lunge and thrust, parry, and recover their stances. Robbins placed each swift, strong move with precision, sometimes on a musical accent, sometimes not; you could believe the nobles to be piercing the music with their rapiers as it flowed on. Gradually, Robbins eased the men into dancing: skirmishes in pairs, a trio, a sextet. The high point was a duet for the two gifted Duell brothers, Daniel and Joseph. For their bellicose flourishes—slashing the air while leaping and turning—Robbins interrupted Handel's elegant geniality with an eccentric piece by Heinrich von Biber, whose curious violin timbres sound as if they are being produced by bows equipped with sandpaper, and punctuated the music's frequent silences with the swish of foils. Lincoln Kirstein wondered whether the imagination, vigor, and confidence of this and Robbins's other contributions to *Sketch Book* owed more to Jerry's "enforced rest" from choreographing for the company because of his ailments or to his "enthusiasm for a thrilling new wave of strong young dancers."

Daniel Duell also performed, to Georg Philipp Telemann's Fantasy for Unaccompanied Violin, a solo that Robbins intended as part of a suite of three, each to music for a different single instrument. It was the kind of solo Robbins loved most and did best. Although it involved difficult steps, Duell attacked them as if he were trying them out—trying to discover how they felt rather than how they looked. Critic Jack Anderson said it was as though Duell were "daydreaming about performing court dances." And John Howlett, writing perspicaciously of both *Fencing Dances* and *Solo,* noted that "Robbins' genius lies in his ability to make ballet seem like the natural means of expression of a thinking person."

Robbins never continued his ambitious scheme for *The Arts of the Gentleman.* His planned solo suite eventually emerged in 1994, in a different form: *A Suite of Dances,* set to Johann Sebastian Bach's unaccompanied cello pieces, for Mikhail Baryshnikov. *Verdi Variations,* his third contribution to *Sketch Book,* had a longer life, taking its place as the "Spring" section of *Four Seasons* the following January.

⁓

NYCB dancers sometimes asked permission to perform a Robbins ballet—usually *Afternoon of a Faun*—when making guest appearances elsewhere, and he chided them if they assumed that his permission was good for more than the specific date requested. In 1978, he transferred to Edith Weissman the revenues from concert performances of *Faun* and the right to authorize them. He then proceeded to give her lessons in how to be

Jerry. In the margin of a letter to Edith from Betty Cage's assistant, Edward Bigelow, noting that Suzanne Farrell and Peter Martins were planning to perform *Faun* in West Palm Beach, he wrote "Please tell Peter that he <u>must ask in writing</u> for every permission to dance Faun. This is a <u>legal</u> stipulation . . . & that you are very shocked he went ahead without permission from you as it is your property [arrow pointing up]: all this from you not from me."

That the New York City Ballet would go to some length to accommodate Robbins and keep him as happy as possible was never less in doubt than during the crisis that developed a week after *Sketch Book*'s premiere. His dog, Nick, was abducted while tied up outside a store. While Jerry and his friends leafleted Manhattan and phoned the shelters, the NYCB press office went into high gear; announcements of Nick's disappearance and offers of a reward for his safe return aired on radio and television and appeared in newspapers and on an insert in the New York City Ballet program. When a patron phoned in a tip that a dog answering Nick's description had been seen in the Times Square area, Rosemary Dunleavy, one of the company's assistant ballet masters, hastened down there (Robbins being out of town) and interviewed doormen, shopkeepers, and hotel desk clerks. Thanks to the persistence that yielded a description of the dognapper, Jerry patrolled the Times Square area until he spotted man and dog a week after the abduction. The man, who had a police record, accepted $20, released Nick, and ran.

When Robbins worked, he worked demonically hard, but he was an exceptionally skilled loafer. On August 21, reading and sunbathing at a rented beach house, he planned an elaborate dinner menu for an all-male party the next evening. The meal was to begin with carrot soup and end with plums, peaches, and bucheron cheese, to be followed by pot and poppers. He also decided to chart this particular day:

> Awake
> walk dog
> meditation
> breakfast
> read Tolstoy
> clean house
> wash clothes
> play Bach

go to bank
real estate agent
shop King Kullen
home
feed dog
antiques show . . .

Another, similar list includes "stalling." And he filled a double-page spread of his journal by watercoloring a vast deserted Long Island beach and pasting a tiny photograph of Tolstoy reading in the middle of it.

After accompanying NYCB to its Copenhagen engagement in August ("It was George's week, but I had to fill in a lot for him"), he began work again on *Four Seasons.* That fall he had a new company member to add to his cast. In April 1978, Mikhail Baryshnikov left American Ballet Theatre and joined the New York City Ballet, willing to be listed alphabetically among its principal dancers and forgo a superstar salary for the pleasure of working with George Balanchine. And with Jerome Robbins, who had urged Balanchine and Kirstein to accept him, when the former had worried about the impact of such a star on company morale.

Four Seasons was the first new ballet Baryshnikov appeared in at NYCB.

"I'm working on Verdi—& just am trying to spit it out," Robbins joked to his journal a week after his sixtieth birthday. "Is this going to be my super wasp ballet before I do my super Jew opus?" (He was still, intermittently, laboring over *The Poppa Piece.*) *Les Vêpres Siciliennes,* Giuseppe Verdi's five-act opera of 1855, with a libretto by Eugène Scribe, had been written for the Paris Opera. Translating the title and libretto into Italian didn't alter its somewhat ponderous French elegance, its five-act length, or its de rigueur ballet in the third act. Robbins followed the Scribe-Verdi scenario for the divertissement (interpolating short excerpts from the composer's *I Lombardi* and *Il Trovatore*), and the music's easy charm inspired him to create a breezy, accomplished work that was destined to become a repertory choice. The creation of the ballet, however, was no breeze for him or anyone concerned. Jean-Pierre Frohlich, who played the antic, high-springing faun in the "Fall" ballet, remembers Robbins at one point inviting Balanchine to come take a look and advise him on how best to manipulate the large ensemble. He tried his leading dancers in various parts before settling on which they'd dance. "STUCK," he wrote exasperatedly during the early stages of rehearsal. "Everything frozen. Sounds familiar? Encased in ice & anxiety & completely out of contact with people, self etc." He almost melted in delight when Balanchine sat in on a November rehearsal and told him, "What you're doing is very hard to do—it looks easy—but only a few can do it—Petipas, Noverre—me—you" (Robbins added three exclamation points to his journal entry).

As in the opera, the god Janus introduces four figures representing Winter, Spring, Summer, and Autumn. Each then reenters to introduce his or her season, bowing graciously to the waning one. Yet, for all the formality, Robbins exercised his predilection for creating little communities with their own laws and relationships.

He could call on his expertise with comedy to depict Verdi's nine shivering winter girls, huddling together against the icy blasts of two boyish winds. It takes a brave later arrival (Heather Watts), whom they won't allow into their clusters, to teach them that snappy échappés and passés can warm a girl and bring the men to heel for a pas de trois. "Winter" ends with a well-ordered storm of leaps and turns and ice-skating steps for all. Despite its wit, the section showed Robbins's increasingly relaxed handling of classicism. The lovely Spring section featured the two dancers Robbins had used in the last third of *Tricolore,* Kyra Nichols and Daniel Duell (both now soloists), in a delicately frisky engagement with each other. While Robbins was still trying to make up his mind about casting and was working on "Spring" with Stephanie Saland, he told her "he wanted it to be very Plisetskaya-Violette." And you can see in the pas de deux a trace of Maya Plisetskaya's Russian abandon, and more than a little of Violette Verdy's capricious charm in the challenging solo. Although the pas de deux and solos are only gently frisky, as are the admiring games the four men play with the ballerina, the four left alone onstage indulge in swaggering politesse, bowing to one another before popping up into jumps (first one, then another, then two, then all). "Summer" was led by Bart Cook and Saland, whose sumptuous personal style and gift for conveying a mood appealed to Robbins and struck him as suiting this season better than it did "Spring." For the disappointingly brief and underdeveloped section, Jennifer Tipton's lighting creates a blazing sun on the cyclorama, and the six women attendants sway and sink into languorous, seductive steps in tune with the "oriental" hints in the music.

Autumn is the gaudy jewel of the ballet, and, for Verdi's bacchanale, Robbins pulled out all the stops and introduced the company's new principal dancer in a role that displayed his Russian heritage and training. The ballet is like a highly educated spoof on Leonid Lavrovsky's *Walpurgis Night,* a staple of Soviet ballet and an opera tradition long before that. The corps interrupt the flexed-footed jumps and scamperings of Pan (Jean-Pierre Frohlich), as they rush on and leap into a crouch, the women's hair flying. Those invited to this orgy lounge about, egging on the faun in his antics. Baryshnikov played a delightedly lecherous satyr in what Arlene Croce referred to as a "headlong debauch," with Patricia McBride (in a wig of curly black hair) as a willing nymph. For Robbins, Baryshnikov turned himself into scissors, daggers, tops, gliders, knitting machines, and more. Whipping off a series of turns à la seconde, he occasionally doubled up his supporting leg and landed still spinning. "Images of sensual abandon," wrote Croce, "arise purely from fertility of technique."

Robbins gave fans a bonus by offering an alternate cast for "Autumn" and choreographing for Peter Martins a completely different solo that showed off the Dane's skill at the beats that stud Auguste Bournonville's ballets. Suzanne Farrell's solo differed only in certain details from McBride's, but it appeared very different on Farrell's taller body and more willful style. "Good piece," Balanchine said to writer-editor Robert Gottlieb (then a member of the New York City Ballet board) while they were watching a rehearsal in London, but he wished Jerry would get rid of those costumes.

That spring, Robbins again had to fill in for Balanchine, whose condition necessitated a bypass operation in May. This time, his task was to finish the choreography for the New York City Opera's production of a score by Richard Strauss, originally written as incidental music for a production of Molière's play *Le Bourgeois Gentilhomme.* It was to be part of a double bill with Purcell's *Dido and Aeneas,* which Balanchine was also slated to choreograph. Balanchine had tackled the Strauss music before in 1932 and 1944, without notable success. Jean-Pierre Bonnefous, padded and monstrously bewigged, played the credulous and snobbish parvenu, Monsieur Jourdain, whom the not-quite-penniless Cléonte, craving his daughter's hand, has no trouble outwitting and making a fool of. Patricia McBride played Lucile with her usual beautiful conviction.

In the blend of mime and dancing, Rudolf Nureyev as Cléonte performed a tour de force of costume changes and impersonations (during which he inevitably remained Nureyev). In this scenario, the enterprising suitor not only disguised himself as the Son of the Grand Turk, he was also

Monsieur Jourdain's tailor, his fencing master, and his dancing master. It was difficult to figure out which dances or parts of dances—some performed by students from the School of American Ballet—had been set by Balanchine and which by Robbins, but aficionados had fun trying. As well as contributing one dance to *Le Bourgeois Gentilhomme,* Peter Martins choreographed *Dido and Aeneas* (with Balanchine's help on the mime scenes) using primarily the Opera's dancers.

It was unfortunate that the advent of Baryshnikov into the company coincided with Balanchine's health problems. Balanchine created no new ballets for Baryshnikov, more or less inviting him to look over the repertory and choose what he wanted to learn and, memorably, coaching him in *Prodigal Son* (a performance fortunately captured by *Dance in America*). Many of the roles Baryshnikov took on were those created on another dynamic performer of relatively short stature, Edward Villella, who, plagued by injuries, had stopped dancing them.

Robbins clearly wanted to explore Baryshnikov's chameleonlike aptitude for unfamiliar styles and his ability to suggest emotional depths, as well as his formidable technique. *Opus 19/The Dreamer,* shows a man searching for something in a shifting world. The music, Prokofiev's Violin Concerto no. 1 in D Major, Baryshnikov is fairly certain, was suggested to Jerry by Robert Fizdale and Arthur Gold. The concerto is classical in form, romantic in its passion, and twentieth-century in its harmonies. Robbins responded to all these facets. Its dissonances underscore the impression the hero gives of an archetypal "modern man"—brooding, self-doubting, fragmented in his energy, suspicious of flow. The woman (Patricia McBride) who invades his world—for all her mysterious appearances and disappearances—is no wispy ideal. The dreamer's introspective opening solo, performed at first almost in place, has the weight and pressure of modern dance. A small corps of six men and six women, shadowy at first, echoes his steps. He can banish them or (in the last movement) draw them in. Throughout the ballet, they're never away for long; whether benign or eerily distorted in their movements, they often act as living curtains—framing the stage, gliding across it, parting and drawing together.

The woman makes her entrance dancing in the women's ensemble. It takes a while for the watching man (and the audience) to realize that she is more important than the others; it's almost a shock when she throws herself against him. The dancing of the two is slightly dissonant, although she echoes his gestures—amplifying them as she bourrées around his station-

Jerome Robbins 444

ary reaching figure. Robbins devised a magical effect to make the dream woman recede. The pair stand at the head of a line of people that stretches from the front of the stage toward the rear, and he begins gently pushing her to the rear. Helped by the others, she braids her way backward through the line until, when the group re-forms, she's again anonymous.

Later, we seem to be at an odd party at which the men sit while the women dance for them, the women sit as the men perform, and couples pursue a folk dance. At the end, in accord with a musical repeat, the long line of the first movement reverses itself, redelivering the mysterious woman to the front where the dreamer is waiting, and her arms wind around his. There's more than a residue of *Dybbuk* in the ballet, but without fangs and claws.

Opus 19—compelling to some, opaque to others—has had a long life and some subtly diverse interpretations. The hero can look as if he's controlling his dream or being drawn into it. Helgi Tomasson replaced Baryshnikov when the latter was offered the post of artistic director of American Ballet Theatre and left New York City Ballet a year after joining it. Bart Cook and Heather Watts and, more recently, Peter Boal and Wendy Whelan have given memorable performances in the ballet.

⌐⌐

Robbins's dithering over casting often drove dancers mad. Bart Cook thought he would be playing Chanon in *Dybbuk* until Helgi Tomasson appeared one day in rehearsal and watched him closely as he danced his heart out. Jerry would even ask company members to audition for him. The upside of this demoralizing shuffling was that he watched dancers closely and helped make them look wonderful. And most of them knew that. Sometimes his use of certain performers would bring them to Balanchine's attention. Balanchine, however, trusted dancers with his marvelous steps once he had choreographed them. As Barbara Horgan puts it, "He gave them the largesse of their art. And Jerry really didn't. He didn't really trust the performer." There were, of course, those he came to trust, whose choices delighted him. But in general, he monitored performances closely and came backstage afterward to give notes. If Balanchine offered his ballets in black and white and allowed the dancers to color them in, as Suzanne Farrell once said, then Robbins, thinks assistant ballet master Victor Castelli, offered a more limited, paint-by-numbers freedom: "He wants blue here but he doesn't say what color blue. He lets the dancer [decide]. . . . And this has to be red. It doesn't matter what tone of red it is, but it's gotta be red." Some dancers flourished in this freedom within limits, happy to strive for the perfect interpretation. Patricia McBride loved the fact that he was still coaching her in *The Cage* when she was forty-six and on the brink of retirement. "I always felt like he was my fan," she said in 2002. "All I really wanted . . . was to dance for myself and just to know that he was happy with me." He always was.

One of the reasons his ballets need so much polishing is that much depends on *how* they are performed. Atmosphere is crucial to his work, and, as Horgan says, "atmosphere is very hard to rehearse." How many times in a single session did Edward Villella have to practice touching the floor at the end of *Dances at a Gathering?* Fifteen? Twenty? If Robbins was crabby when he thought dancers were slacking off, it was because he was afraid that what he was seeing in the studio would be what the audience saw onstage. Stephanie Saland, who was one of his favorites (and who also says "I cried for Jerry on a dime") understood that "without that musicality and without that specificity, it's like a soufflé; it goes, it's lost." This can be true of any dance, but it's particularly true of Robbins's. The aura of intimacy his ballets often project is very fragile. At their best, they draw spectators into a private world of thoughts and relationships, in which steps are rarely displayed for their own sake. Choreographing for George Balanchine's company, Robbins still showed the influence of an early guru, Antony Tudor.

The idiosyncrasies of Robbins's choreography during these years—his variant of the company's neoclassical style—were more than a matter of the cartwheels or somersaults that dancers joke figured at least once in every ballet of his—along with claps, slaps, or finger snaps. He often had performers lying or sitting on the floor. When he returned to the New York City Ballet and began work on *Dances at a Gathering,* he must have felt his lack of a strong classical background. Sometimes, says Violette Verdy, he would ask the female dancers if it was possible to do such-and-such a step on pointe; when he very occasionally taught class, it was to understand better how the ballet vocabulary worked. Even as he became increasingly fluent in his use of pointe work, he gave the women quite a lot of steps that weren't on pointe. Balanchine took pleasure in emphasizing the women's footwork. In a Robbins ballet, the dancer's focus is fixed so intently on some other aspect of the movement or on a partner that we simply don't see how she rises onto pointe; she breathes, and there she is. In

Peter Martins's words, Balanchine "always wanted more—more energy, faster, more emphasis, more commitment, move bigger. . . . It was always give everything you've got and a little bit more. . . . And Jerry would often say to you, 'Take it easy, baby, take it easy. Calm down, calm down, calm down.'"

Robbins's choreography almost always acknowledged the earth. And as much as he loved the classical lexicon, he didn't have Balanchine's penchant for affirming the beauty of fifth position or a centered preparation for a turn. He didn't want to break the flow, unless for dramatic or comedic purposes. He didn't want the mechanics to show, no matter how difficult, whereas Balanchine often wanted to reveal what could be done, and how, without compromising his profound musicality. In some ways, dancers found Robbins's ballets less technically challenging than Balanchine's, but there were certainly extremely difficult movements to master and exhausting passages to get through—"puffy," as dancers term work that gets them panting. Some rehearsal footage from the 1990s shows Jerry rehearsing Philip Neal and Lauren Hauser over and over in a lift in *Interplay*—once the woman has rushed at her partner, done a half turn in the air and landed in his arms, he has to help her swing one leg backward around him as he dips her toward the ground. Done the way Robbins wants it, it looks like a spiral that unwinds. Even with Robert La Fosse and Melinda Roy—the ballet's first cast—moving in to help and kibitz, Neal's back rebels before the dancers quite get it.

Robbins used more lifts than Balanchine, and he wanted these, too, to look effortless, born of a feeling. Castelli, who has taught *In the Night* to other companies and rehearsed new casts, explains a typical snafu: "There are lifts in which you've got every single thing working against you. You're lifting the girl here. You've got her by the leg and you've got her by the armpit here, and she's doing a jeté and you have to land her on this leg and lower it, but where?—there's nothing to hold on to. Her armpit is here, but not only that; he's got the port de bras going the opposite way, so she's lifting this arm as you're trying to lift her. Somehow it works. It's a pain in the butt to do. And the effect is—it's glorious. It's like she's floating."

In trying to present dancers as thinking human beings, Robbins needed them to avoid the heroic stance that often figures in nineteenth-century ballets, with the leading performers stalking onto the stage, chests puffed up. His dancers should be aware of one another and strive to create an illusion that they're making up the dance as they go along, or, in the case of unison, sharing a new experience of something they already know. Robbins himself, of course, never let actual improvisation be part of a performance. Instead, as Lincoln Kirstein once cannily put it, he excelled at "the artificed use of the apparently accidental." When a moment in a Robbins ballet looks contrived, it can be because one is not simply moved by it but aware of how the choreographer calculated its effect.

However rough he was on the NYCB dancers, he knew that in them he had a treasure chest to explore. Late in 1978, he had noted in his journal that young Kyra Nichols and Stephanie Saland had "an authority that other principals lack."* Two years later, he created *Rondo,* to Mozart's Rondo in A Minor for Piano, a modest duet for the two of them about trying out some dancing for and with each other, with the help of Gordon Boelzner at an onstage piano. Robbins saw clearly their individual qualities as dancers and made use of these, but—and this is generally true in his mature works—he also saw the women through ballet's rose-colored glasses and classical forms as idealized and gracious creatures. Saland, by her own admission, lacked the technical "grit" of some Balanchine dancers, but she was a marvel at shading movement, at giving it richness. Nichols was lighter and tauter, her steps crystalline. It was Saland who showed the theme, Nichols who later, and spiritedly, complicated it. When the two began to dance side by side, they weren't in perfect unison; Nichols inserted tiny embellishments that Saland then picked up. Much of the choreography had the feeling of a friendly, challenging dialogue, with now one woman leading, now the other. They held hands to support each other in balances. Although a few critics saw *Rondo* as yet another example of Robbins's self-conscious attempts to make a work appear simple and unpretentious, it was a ballet that induced other writers to use words such as "sweet," "charming," and "a gem."

Robbins's various journals and private writings reveal how little it took to make him question his talent or his status in the New York City Ballet. A bad review could devastate him. When Balanchine blew up at him in December 1978 for requesting a reordering of an opening-night program, he cooled down for a few days and then, assuring Balanchine of his devotion, offered to leave the company. (Balanchine ended up being the one to

---

* Nichols was a newly minted soloist when he wrote that, but Saland was still in the corps de ballet.

apologize for losing his temper.) Such set-tos were unusual. Balanchine, relaxed about his own ballets and a pragmatist, knew Robbins's worth to the company, regardless of his own like or dislike of any given Robbins ballet. The impression in the company was that Balanchine gave Jerry what he wanted.

This wasn't always possible, of course. Robbins didn't care to understand the complicated formulas that the company management used to decide which ballets would be programmed in a given season: the need to show the subscription audience some works it hadn't seen the previous season, the amount of rehearsal time required for a given ballet, and myriad other issues. The ballet master, the technical director, the music department all had to look over a schedule for feasibility. If Robbins wanted to present a large number of his works, that could be a problem, because, as Barbara Horgan says, "You didn't just rehearse his ballets for two days, you rehearsed his ballets for days and days and you had to have an orchestra dress rehearsal *and* a dress rehearsal [something Balanchine himself rarely demanded]. Those were the fights when Balanchine and Jerry were together."

Robbins also tended to mistrust the skills of backstage personnel and of costume designers. He had his own strong vision of costumes for his ballets and gave designers little leeway to be creative. Trying to please him was so frustrating that some gave up working with him. He didn't have such a detailed picture in his head when it came to the more elusive business of lighting, and "trust" is a word he used when it came to lighting designer Jennifer Tipton. He once wrote that after she had watched a run-through of one of his ballets, he "showed her the drop and left her alone. One can do that with Jenny. I think I called her attention to only five things or less, but she is such a supreme empathic artist that one is completely trustful of her perceptions."

⌒

In October 1979, Robbins bought an unpretentious gray shingled cottage in Bridgehampton. It was small but right on the beach, and he enlarged its two decks to accommodate summer gatherings. He acquired another dog, Annie, who'd been found wandering in the subway; Annie was more of a tyrant than her size and winsome, ragamuffin looks would have led anyone to believe. He and Jesse Gerstein went to Italy; they visited Egypt and voyaged down the Nile. He took a group of NYCB dancers to China and traveled to Israel with the entire company. He was fairly pleased with *A Suite of Dances,* his final assault on *Dybbuk.* In 1979, he enjoyed setting *Interplay* for the School of American Ballet's annual recital and then for the company. Having finally wrested *Fancy Free* from the contract he had signed with Ballet Theatre in 1944, he restaged it, to acclaim, for NYCB—casting Jean-Pierre Frohlich, Bart Cook, and Peter Martins as the three sailors and working the pants off them (although he claimed he didn't get enough rehearsals). In 1982, he finished his analysis with Dr. Robert Michels, the successor to Shervert Frazier, and wrote less frequently in his journals.

Up to now, Robbins had been reluctant to have his ballets filmed—ironically, since it was he who had helped fund the New York Public Library's film archive. He feared that an inevitably imperfect performance would come to stand for the work, and he also feared plagiarism. But, collaborating with a sensitive director, Emile Ardolino, he was relatively pleased with *Dance in America*'s presentation of *Other Dances* in 1980 on a program, "Two Dances," shared with Peter Martins's first and highly praised ballet, *Calcium Light Night.*

An unpleasant experience the same year was NBC's taping of *Afternoon of a Faun, The Cage,* and excerpts from *Fancy Free, The Concert,* and *Dances at a Gathering* for its new and much-touted cultural venture *Live from Studio 8H.* Jerry had expected to be in control; instead he was presented with several different sorts of directors and some ultimatums. He wanted to break the contract, but Balanchine wouldn't hear of it, since the company's repertory and dancers were involved. Robbins loathed the resulting program but couldn't prevent it from being shown. According to Rhoda Grauer, who worked with him on it, the experience was "horrendous"; she couldn't imagine how he'd ever agreed to do it. Perhaps it was the high fee that had persuaded him, although he had to sue NBC to get some of what he felt he was owed. "Major network shit," he called the whole process, and had one word for it: "Ychacht!!!"

He was not looking forward to the New York City Ballet's Tchaikovsky Festival in June 1981. He was neither stirred at the prospect of choreographing to Tchaikovsky's music nor interested in turning out his share of festival fodder. Tchaikovsky, however, mattered a great deal to Balanchine, as he had to Stravinsky. As a child student in Saint Petersburg, Balanchine had performed in the Petipa-Tchaikovsky ballets and in Tchaikovsky's operas. He had made his stage debut as a page in Petipa's

The Sleeping Beauty, and, perhaps in memory of that, he restaged for the festival its lovely "Garland Dance" for company members and children from the School of American Ballet. Many of the works he had composed over the years to the composer's music honored and commented on the grand-scale order and clarity, the theatrical zest and sparkle of that era in ballet.

Architect Philip Johnson, who had designed the New York State Theater, created a controversial set that was used for all the programs—a glittering ice palace of clear plastic tubes that altered its shape from ballet to ballet. But by the time the glorious array of Balanchine ballets and premieres by Robbins, John Taras, Peter Martins, and Jacques d'Amboise came to a close, it was possible to conjecture that the master foresaw his own death, just as he had perhaps prefigured his deterioration from Creutzfeldt-Jakob disease in his 1980 *Robert Schumann's "Davidsbündlertänze,"* with its references to the composer's madness.

The festival began with a prayer (Balanchine's beautiful new version of his 1933 *Mozartiana*) and closed with a funeral. This strange choreographic setting of Tchaikovsky's Sixth Symphony in B Minor, the "Pathétique," omitted the first movement. Robbins choreographed the second one, the Allegro con Grazia, with its oddly lilting waltz in 5/4 time, deploying ten women in handsome patterns for his favorite dance couple, Patricia McBride and Helgi Tomasson, to thread their way through. Robert Irving conducted the orchestra in the martial Allegro. Then, in the final Adagio Lamentoso, Balanchine layered veils of dancers, making the simplest of gestures, around an imaginary bier; like guardians or attendant muses, three women in blue dresses wove their way through others who came and went. There were more women in peach-colored dresses— all with their hair loose—two squads of angels with enormous wings, a horde of purple-cloaked figures, and others in black who lay down at the end to form a huge, seething cross, while a little boy entered with a lighted candle and a voice cried out. To Robbins, the Adagio was "heartbreaking in intent—& nearly corny in execution—& finally crushing." When the curtain came down on the Tchaikovsky Festival, one felt not just Balanchine's homage to a composer whose music he loved but a statement about his past, the past of the New York City Ballet, and its future without him.

For a man who wasn't wild about Tchaikovsky, Robbins did wonderfully well by him. A pas de deux (later called *Andantino*) to the second movement of the composer's First Piano Concerto featured the young newcomer Darci Kistler and Ib Andersen, recently arrived from the Royal Danish Ballet, as a most adventurous and glistening pair of lovers. And *Piano Pieces* turned out to be one of his most relaxed, accomplished, and effortlessly charming works. This was simply a suite of dances to various short piano works, but Robbins gave it the look of a village festival in balletland, in which happy peasants and members of the gentry pass one another on their way to dancing and mingle in a final celebration. It's perhaps fortunate that he abandoned a more ambitious structure, along the lines of *Ma Mère l'Oye* but more contrived, in which the dancers, in practice clothes, would be warming up and rehearsing their way into a fictitious Tchaikovsky ballet.

In *Piano Pieces,* it's the patterns and choreographic ideas that create a sense of a village, not just the device of people watching others dance. A nimble, larky fellow (Andersen) acts as revels leader, vaulting through a couple of solos and a trio with two village maidens. When all assemble for the finale, he sets steps for them to copy. The six couples in festive but uncomplicated peasant attire—with their heel-and-toe steps, their polkas, their maiden chains—at one point dance in a circle (a familiar dance symbol of community); at another, they form a clump and sink into plié to reach toward the sky and earth. Most magical is the brief contredanse in which lines of men and women facing each other open out and become more complex, until, as one pair after another moves down the center, there are no lines left.

Threaded through the ballet are three lovely, lyrical duets for a more aristocratic group, danced at the premiere by Kyra Nichols and Daniel Duell, Heather Watts and Bart Cook, Joseph Duell and Maria Calegari. The pas de deux for Calegari and J. Duell is particularly enthralling, calling to mind *Dances at a Gathering.* The man scarcely dances. He wanders close to his dreamy partner, almost always holding her hand, enabling her intrepid steps or stepping in to grasp her waist for more daring ventures. There are also solos: the lovely "Natha Waltz" for Nichols, the easygoing "Mazurka" for Cook, and the mercurial "June-Barcarolle" for Watts. This was the first role Robbins had made for Calegari, and she bloomed in it. Perhaps the happy aura of *Piano Pieces* proceeds from the relative ease with which Robbins choreographed all his contributions to the Tchaikovsky Festival. Although the dancers remember endless rehearsing, he wrote with amazement of his unexpected "work streak . . . a high like I can't recall since Dances and Goldberg." *Piano Pieces* turned out to be the hit of the June festival, but Robbins's pleasure in his success was offset by guilt (and by problems in his relationship with Gerstein). Why did he need approval to verify his worth? he wondered. "If I can have it," he wrote, "it isn't good enough. If I can do it it isn't worthwhile. If someone loves me, they are not with taste or are lacking in strength of character. . . . All this ain't good!"

He was irritated that Balanchine had no interest in contributing to the September tour to China and hadn't wanted Jerry to undertake the venture. Robbins persisted; this was a prestigious undertaking, the first American group to go to China under the new cultural agreement between that country and the United States. Between September 7 and September 29, 1981, fourteen NYCB dancers traveling as the Jerome Robbins Chamber Dance Company performed in Beijing, Shanghai, and Canton—giving workshops in the last two; allowing Chinese dancers to take company class in Beijing; being treated to receptions, banquets, and tours. The critic of *The China Daily* praised the dancers and the program.* She only wished there had been more than one sample of Balanchine's choreography.

It's hard to tell whether it was dissatisfaction with the way things were going at NYCB, Jerry's appetite for variety, or a vestigial hankering to direct offbeat plays that led him in the spring of 1981 to get involved with a Broadway-bound project called *C. C. Pyle and the Bunion Derby* by Michael Cristofer. The historical Pyle had been a sports manager (Red Grange was a major client). In 1928, he organized a marathon that began in Los Angeles and ended in New York City. A lot went wrong: runners dropped out starting on the first day; they griped about the poor quality of the food and accommodations along the way; towns were not as eager to chip in as Pyle had thought, wooing them with prophecies of the tourism the race would bring.

In this scenario, Robbins saw possibilities for all the sorts of things that interested him in terms of unconventional theater, and he was drawn to Pyle's character: the hustler who sees beauty in athletic prowess. In one script, the play begins in a cell (Pyle was arrested in 1937 for refusing to pay

* Kyra Nichols, Heather Watts, Lourdes Lopez, Judith Fugate, Alexia Hess, Melinda Roy, Bonita Borne, Daniel Duell, Joseph Duell, Bart Cook, Sean Lavery, Christopher d'Amboise, Kipling Houston, and Peter Frame performed *Afternoon of a Faun, Interplay,* an excerpt from *Fancy Free,* "Spring" from *Four Seasons,* the duet from *In G Major,* excerpts from *Dances at a Gathering,* and Balanchine's *Tchaikovsky Pas de Deux.*

a parking ticket) with a surreal chorus of runners, "frozen in shadows but talking." Jerry had montages in mind: "On the backdrop flash the head-lines and some texts of the race. On the middle stage, a stylized running dance. The towns passed, states, weather and number of racers left an-nounced as radio reports. Way downstage C.C. is talking to reporters, i.e. 'the human foot is going to come into its own,' etc. There is a wealth of fun and color in the hoopla surrounding the race which is so culturally typical of the late 20's."

On and off for about a year, Robbins made notes and conferred with the author about the script but delayed and delayed signing the contract that producer Alexander Cohen had offered. Finally, on May 4, 1982, with Cohen still trying to get a commitment and set a schedule, Cristofer telegraphed Jerry:

> IT'S BEEN A LOVELY, LONG TIME WORKING ON C. C. PYLE BUT WE REALLY CAN NOT GO ON WITHOUT A DECISION. I KNOW YOU ARE WORRIED ABOUT TIME, SCHEDULES, REWRITES, PRODUCERS, ENERGY, REPUTATION, ART, LOVE, LIFE AND HEMORRHOIDS BUT ALL YOU REALLY NEED TO DIRECT THIS PLAY IS A COMMITMENT TO THE MATERIAL. I CAN NOT GIVE YOU THAT AND IT IS HUMILIATING FOR ME TO BEG FOR IT. I SEE THE PLAY CLEARLY IN YOUR HANDS LIKE A MIRROR HELD UP TO THE AMERICAN VISION AND I THINK YOU'RE A FOOL NOT TO DIRECT IT. CALL ALEX, MAKE A DECISION. LIFE IS TOO SHORT. LOVE

Robbins answered, bowing out with his familiar justification. He loved the idea and the flexible structure of the script but couldn't make *Pyle* as a whole cohere in his mind.

When he made his decision, he was still embedded in NYCB. Being honored by the Kennedy Center in December 1981 (along with Count Basie, Cary Grant, Helen Hayes, and Rudolf Serkin) must have reaffirmed to him the value of what he was accomplishing in the realm of ballet. He flew to Washington, D.C., with Mica and Ahmet Ertegun in their private plane to celebrate the occasion with his sister and brother-in-law and a cluster of friends. In a video of the gala, Robbins—having been entertained at a State Department dinner the night before, a brunch given by the Erte-guns in their hotel, and a White House reception where he received his sash and medal from President Reagan—looks flushed and happy. Mikhail Baryshnikov not only spoke eloquently about him but, to his delight, danced the role of the second sailor in an excerpt from *Fancy Free*.

When Robbins pulled out of *C. C. Pyle,* his *Gershwin Concerto* had pre-miered, and he was polishing his *Four Chamber Works* for the company's second Stravinsky Festival in June. It's possible that no one in the company knew of his outside foray.

Gershwin was not an easy piece for Robbins. Bart Cook, who'd been as-signed by Balanchine to be Robbins's ballet master, remembers that Jerry had a lot of trouble with the large corps and wanted to cancel the ballet. George Gershwin's Piano Concerto in F (1925) is rife with New York en-ergy and variegated drama. Like Gershwin, Robbins was attempting to braid vernacular motifs into a symphonic structure. He saddled himself with a corps de ballet of twenty-four, as if he were re-creating the am-biance of a 1920s Broadway show with its characters abstracted and move-ments like a jazzy strut and a Charleston step so groomed for a date with ballet that they lose in spontaneity what they gain in clarity of design. Robbins's inventions are happiest when he doesn't deal with the whole corps at once or sets them whirling briefly in ballroom style. He elegantly deploys eight men in attentive lines while a sinuous siren (Maria Calegari) dances through them, cool but aware of their interest. Four women and four men back a sassy duet, made for Darci Kistler and the second-generation NYCB dancer Christopher d'Amboise. Six women strike the familiar Balanchine pinup-girl pose.

There's a very faint trace of a story. When Mel Tomlinson, the company's sole and underused black male dancer, enters, he bows to the ladies like the new guy on the block; watching Kistler dance, he's moved to take on a pas de deux with her. Then Calegari steps in from the sidelines, and Kistler literally bows out. But after Calegari's duet with the new-comer, she's left alone.

The public loved *Gershwin*. After the premiere, Kirstein and Balan-chine said not a word. Robbins wrote in his journal, "It's O.K.ish. . . . I'm glad to have good reviews, yet feel—I got away with it." The critics did, for the most part, approve, although Arlene Croce, who wrote brilliantly about Balanchine, published a lengthy essay in *The New Yorker.* She criti-cized not only the choreography but the way it presented the dancers:

> The two ballerinas, who are sharply differentiated at the outset, soon become interchangeable. To be sure, Kistler and Calegari are sisters under the N.Y.C.B. skin, but, having stated Kistlerian and Cale-gariesque themes in the choreography and related them to different

themes in the music (red-hot and blue), Robbins apparently feels free not only to intermingle his themes in the second movement but to lose them completely in the third. . . . Right at the end, Robbins has the two women change partners; The effect is all but unnoticeable.

Jerry, who was proud of his insights into particular dancers' qualities, thought the review undermined him with the company.

He redeemed himself in his own eyes with *Four Chamber Works.* Balanchine wanted to present one more homage to Igor Stravinsky that summer, this time on the occasion of the composer's centennial. The company choreographers—Balanchine, Robbins, Martins, Taras, and Jacques d'Amboise—pitched in, but for this festival, the ailing Balanchine didn't produce any new works that could compare with his creations of ten years before.

Like *Piano Pieces,* Robbins's bright new four-part ballet was danced to unrelated musical selections, but he made no effort to link them. If the earlier ballet, buoyed by Tchaikovsky's lilting melodies, played with the heritage of nineteenth-century ballet, the new one, digging into Stravinsky's more acerbic pieces, invoked the jazz that had influenced both the composer and the Balanchine vocabulary. The finest and most imaginative of the miniballets were a trio set to Stravinsky's Concertino for Twelve Instruments and Three Pieces for Clarinet Solo, and a quintet to his Septet. The first showed off three tall dancers—Merrill Ashley, Sean Lavery, and Mel Tomlinson—their relationship as subtle and wry as the composer's musical ones. They dance together as equals; each has a smart solo; and the men partner the women. The central trio might almost be a very contemporary take on the original Act II pas de deux in *Swan Lake,* in which the Prince's friend Benno assists with the job of partnering.

In Robbins's ballet, one man turns the woman in arabesque while the other walks quietly behind her extended leg, hands just above it, as if it were a turnstile into a new part of the music. In *Septet,* too, there is an air of equality between the sexes; the three men and two women dance alike in the opening section, and in the "Passacaglia," they step in to replace one another or take over in a duet. The ballet has something of the feeling of *Interplay,* only this group of friends is more sophisticated and both more individualized and more abstract.

The other two sections are lighter in weight and more theatrical in tone: *Ragtime,* a slick little 1920s duet for Heather Watts and Bart Cook, with four brightly costumed women doing the Charleston behind them; and, to the sour-sweet *Octet for Wind Instruments,* a romp for four nimble men. They make jokes about timing and being on the same foot; they do stunts; they dress up in sketchy homemade outfits and do quick skits (warriors and maidens, etc.); they hide under cloaks and make their hands into the heads of big querulous birds. The men (Christopher d'Amboise, Jean-Pierre Frohlich, Christopher Fleming, and Douglas Hay) got so imaginative in rehearsal that they had the choreographer dissolving in laughter. The comedy was perhaps a bit overextended, but in its good-mannered way, it had something of the air of inspired improvisation with which the Proteans had raced through "Comedy Tonight" in *A Funny Thing Happened on the Way to the Forum.*

Jerry's summer involved both pleasure and pain. He had wanted to reconstruct *New York Export: Opus Jazz* and other pieces from the Ballets: U.S.A. repertory for the Spoleto Festival with a handpicked group of dancers. Since the festival couldn't deal with the large budget involved, Rhoda Grauer, then working at American Ballet Theatre, and Mikhail Baryshnikov, its artistic director, brokered a compromise. ABT, hoping to acquire more Robbins ballets, would assume some of the cost. Jerry was grumpy at first, coaching unfamiliar dancers in *Fancy Free, Afternoon of a Faun, Other Dances,* and *Opus Jazz.* But Baryshnikov remembers the venture as successful (probably due in part to the salubrious artistic climate of Spoleto): "It was a great program with the orchestra and everything. And Jerry was so happy. We were eating in little piazzas, spaghetti with truffles and him drinking red wine. And he was in heaven—in heaven."

The painful part began with a drop-by visit to Balanchine in August. Mr. B., caught off guard, was playing the piano, wearing only Jockey shorts and an unbuttoned shirt. Jerry put the flowers he'd brought in a vase and made motions of leaving. Balanchine beckoned him to stay, his "hair astray, one eye black & very old & fragile looking—his Don Quixote come off the stage to visit him." Robbins tried to recapture Balanchine's words for his journal: "They tell me to be patient with my eye—I said all right I have lots of patience now. I don't want to do anything more—I did enough—now, eat, travel—& I will go to Europe—I'd like to go to Monaco—I want to be buried there—There is where I started—There I want to end." He griped a little about the NYCB board's pressure to add new works to the repertory, adding, "It doesn't matter—do something new and small. I can't anymore—my legs won't hold me up—no muscle—some performers can work from a chair—not me—I must <u>show</u> them." He didn't get to Europe. In a few months, his trip would be to the hospital and what Robbins called "a slow elevator down."

Then, on December 2, Edith Weissman died, with Jerry holding her hand. In his journal, he wrote simply, "It's left a hole in the galaxies." Not until that summer, weakened by heart trouble, had Weissman begun to train an assistant to take over. She had been a vital part of Jerry's professional life; his friends and business associates were indebted to her efficiency, her tact, and her sound, tart advice. They liked her, even if few were as extravagant in their affection as Richard Buckle, who years before had closed a letter to his friend Jerry with "best love, also to Edith Princess of Xeroxia, whom I adore most constantly and kiss on both ears." Lucia Chase, Arthur Laurents, Oliver Smith, and many others sent letters of sympathy and regret. Leonard Bernstein, down with the flu, wrote, "I wanted so much to be with you today, especially at your house where I most frequently saw and got to know the good and devoted Edith. . . . I do know the pain you must be feeling at this loss, and I send you a warm hug and whatever consolation that can bring."

Robbins was in the throes of choreographing two contrasting ballets for the spring season when George Balanchine died on April 30, 1983, and the hearts of ballet lovers all over the world fell to half-mast.

19

Pressing Onward, Looking Back

Jerry's "nymphs": left to right: Stephanie Saland, Simone Schumacher, Heléne Alexopoulos, Jeri Kummery, Kyra Nichols, Maria Calegari, Victoria Hall, and Florence Fitzgerald in *Antique Epigraphs*. *Paul Kolnik*.

*T*he issue of "the succession" had been pondered long before Balanchine's Requiem Mass in the Russian Orthodox Cathedral of Our Lady of the Sign at Ninety-third Street and Park Avenue, where wet-faced dancers, choreographers, friends, and dance lovers— more than twelve hundred mourners—stood for the three hours or more it took to send his invaluable soul on its way. No one could replace Balanchine, but someone had to run the company. Peter Martins got the job.

He was, in several ways, an obvious choice to succeed Balanchine. Like Balanchine, he had grown up in the ambiance of a large, state-run institution—trained since childhood at the Royal Danish Ballet in the Bournonville tradition that Balanchine very much admired. Already listed among the company's ballet masters, he had been running the company as Balanchine's illness advanced. He was young and capable and had many years ahead of him. And he was a talented choreographer. According to Barbara Horgan, Balanchine's personal assistant, and Martins himself, a few years before his death Balanchine had invited Peter to meet him for breakfast and asked, in effect, How would you like to run this company? (He had hoped to have five years to groom his successor for the job; he got three.)

Robert Gottlieb confirms the choice of Martins, saying that Balanchine had mentioned it twice; on one occasion, "we were standing in the wings together. . . . Peter was partnering—I guess it was Suzanne—and [George] said to me, 'It has to be Peter. He understands what ballerinas need.'" A telling, if ambiguous, remark. In the fall of 1982, Balanchine, apparently concerned that Lincoln Kirstein might wish to add the function of artistic director to his duties as general director and president of the School of American Ballet, asked Horgan to bring Orville Schell, chairman of the NYCB Board, and Gillian Attfield, its president, to his bedside at Roosevelt Hospital. Horgan remembers: "Balanchine said, and I quote, 'I want Peter to be director. Don't give it to Lincoln. He'll destroy it.' No one will believe me because no one wants to believe me. They want to think it was a cabal and there was all this sinister stuff going on. Balanchine was very clear." And he wanted the appointment announced before he died.

One who clearly thought a cabal was at work was the company's general administrator, Betty Cage. Speaking not long after Robbins's death, she told biographer Greg Lawrence, "[Balanchine] had no idea of appointing Peter. I think all of us who were there knew that Balanchine had never chosen anybody." She fulminated to Lawrence against Schell (deceased at the time of the interview), enraged that he and unidentified board members had "leaked" to the press that Martins was being handed the company before the master had expired.

Where did that leave Robbins? An article by Ken Sandler that appeared in the *Reporter Dispatch* of White Plains, New York, on January 23, 1983, had quoted Schell on the issue of the succession:

> "To speak of succession now is not appropriate," Schell added, but he confirmed co-founder Lincoln Kirstein's suggestion that Martins will be named ballet-master-in-chief—the company's artistic director—should Balanchine not return. Robbins . . . would most likely not wish to assume full-time artistic control of the company, City Ballet has concluded, Schell said, and therefore the board hopes Robbins will act as senior advisor and counsel to Martins.

Robbins did see this article (it was found among his files and in his scrapbook), though probably not right away. Clipping services weren't speedy, and after the season ended in mid-February, he had taken a vacation in the Caribbean. Then another more prominently placed article appeared. After months of arguments and back-and-forth at New York City Ballet, *The New York Times* came out on March 12 with an article by Fred Ferretti, this time stating that Robbins had "turned down an offer to be the company's artistic director." Lincoln Kirstein immediately drafted a press release:

> There has been some loose talk about a successor to George Balanchine. There is no successor to be thought of, now or in the future. Mr. Balanchine took great pains in nominating himself as ballet-master, which is what he was and is, a master of ballets. As for the function of artistic-director, a title never claimed by Mr. Balanchine, this will be undertaken by Lincoln Kirstein whose title for some thirty years has been and will remain General Director. The ballet-masters of the New York City Ballet are, in alphabetical order: Peter Martins, Jerome Robbins and John Taras.

It's hard to say whether the article(s) or the press release made Robbins angriest. Perhaps he *would* have refused an invitation to lead the company, but the board hadn't shown him the courtesy of asking him. And judging by later correspondence, the notion of being in the middle of an alphabetical listing of ballet masters could not be countenanced. He drafted a resignation from his position with the company. The board managed to mollify him, and a few days later, it was settled that Martins and Robbins would—

on paper, at any rate—run the company together. Everyone took a deep breath.

Oliver Smith expressed the sentiments of many New York City Ballet admirers in telling his old friend how glad he was to learn that Jerry had decided to share the codirection: "You are America's greatest choreographer, and your presence is essential to [the company's] future." On March 27, back from two weeks in St. Bart's, Jerry reviewed the fracas in his journal: "All angers flare up—Got thru it all—some story to be told re: <u>Lincoln, Betty, Barbara, Bob Gottlieb, Orville—etc. Whew!!!</u>" noting that "long swallowed resentments & public & private injuries surfaced in the Schell affair. I guess I was not going to remain in the company as a side kick supplier of 'other' works, no matter how it was foreordained by G.B. . . . The company, to keep me, would have to want my oar in its running."

Robbins's reaction to Martins's appointment was complicated. He wouldn't have wanted to run the company on a day-in-day-out basis for the rest of his life, and he didn't have the temperament or the diplomatic skills for the job. But Balanchine had been a father figure to him, and he was not the heir apparent—the thought that Kirstein had so frequently flattered him with many years ago. Now he would have to make his requests and demands to a much younger man.

In the months following Balanchine's death, the hassles over titles continued. In one of many drafts of a response he never sent, Robbins debated the options offered him by Kirstein, who found the wrangling distasteful: He, Jerry, will *not* be designated principal choreographer: "George never called himself that, although he <u>was</u> and still <u>is</u> it." He will not be named as a ballet master on an alphabetical list, sandwiched between Martins and John Taras. He doesn't fancy being associate artistic director to Martins's director (a title Balanchine had dispensed with). "In no way can I consider Peter an equal as choreographer (if Ballet Master refers to that) or <u>artistic</u> director. He may prove able as a 'director' to run the company and handle its problems, and I sincerely do wish him success at that." In the end, he accepted the title of ballet master in chief, as did Martins—their names on the same line in the programs—and got on with the business of making ballets people loved and making Peter's life difficult. Martins says that his first priority was to ensure that the company would survive without Balanchine and next "to make sure that we didn't also lose Jerry. . . . I could never let Jerry feel that he had a boss. . . . It wasn't so difficult, because I admired and respected him. I had to find the way not to defer to him, because we were equal, and yet also not make him feel that he had to defer to me. It was very, very tricky."

As for Jerry, he operated according to a personal credo he imparted to Penelope Dudleston a few years later, when she needed advice in handling a difficult business deal (Dudleston, the long-legged beauty who had combed her hair so persuasively in *Watermill,* had been one of his favorites, and they'd corresponded ever since she had left the company in the 1970s). "I have to think hard," he wrote, "that what I want is important—and let them adjust to me. If I worry about how they may not like it, or me, I never get my just rights and am full of depression and anger about being taken advantage of." Especially in the early years after Balanchine's death, he seemed, as Robert Gottlieb put it, to be "always looking to be offended or marginalized," which meant he was hell on wheels in business meetings.

During the last weeks of Balanchine's illness and after his death, the company had rallied in the master's honor and danced superbly. And now Robbins was the senior figure, the link with company traditions. Some of those who had considered it a soul-threatening experience to work with him thought again.

⌒

In choosing to choreograph a ballet to the music of Philip Glass, Robbins was again trying to align himself with avant-garde artists in theater and dance, as he had in *Watermill*—wanting perhaps to bring something from that world into ballet, but this time without entirely bypassing the language of the academy. Glass and Robbins had met in Paris in 1976, when Robbins saw the composer's collaboration with Robert Wilson, *Einstein on the Beach.* So enraptured was he that he called Jane Hermann at the Metropolitan Opera and told her she had to send someone to see the work, that it belonged at the Met. It was, therefore, partly due to him that *Einstein* came to the opera house for two special performances. He had also seen and admired a work by *Einstein*'s choreographer, Lucinda Childs: her evening-long *Dance,* a collaboration with Glass and artist Sol LeWitt, which premiered at the Brooklyn Academy of Music in 1979 (that same year, he wrote a highly enthusiastic recommendation for Childs, who was applying for a Guggenheim Fellowship). Shortly thereafter, Glass approached Robbins about directing his opera *Satyagraha,* but Jerry wasn't able to take it on.

When *Glass Pieces* premiered on May 12, 1983, the final section turned out to be a musical premiere as well. Philip Glass's *Rubric* and *Facades* were followed by music from the composer's yet-to-be-seen opera *Akhnaten,* which was set to premiere in Stuttgart and later play at the Houston Grand Opera and at the Brooklyn Academy of Music. Fascinated by Egyptian history and art and knowing that Glass developed his librettos with the input of his collaborators, Jerry had wanted to be in on the process of shaping this opera. He ordered additional books on the subject of the monotheistic pharaoh, roamed the Egyptian galleries at the Metropolitan Museum, and planned a summer trip to Egypt.

Between February 1982 and February 1983, he met with Glass on eleven occasions—sometimes alone, sometimes in sessions that also involved Egyptologist Shalom Goldman, set designer Robert Israel, and lighting designer Robert Riddell. When there was some doubt about the number of rays in Akhnaten's sun, he put Goldman in touch with Robert Graves. Glass found Robbins's input invaluable as he worked his way through several drafts of the opera, spurred on by his colleagues' reactions. To Glass, Jerry's queries "were like critiques. . . . His questions were the mother of the answer in a way. By asking the right question, you could find your way through a work." The printed libretto was to have Robbins's name on it, and he was to receive a 4 percent royalty along with the other authors. While he was serving as a kind of dramaturge, it became obvious to all concerned that he should direct the opera.

But in early February, because of Balanchine's rapidly declining health and the NYCB's need of him, Robbins decided he couldn't take on that job. Glass very much regretted the decision, although Christopher Keene, who was to conduct the opera and knew Jerry from Spoleto, allowed that "a certain inartistic sigh of relief went up when Jerry withdrew, because we all knew that having him on the project meant it was going to be even more of a nightmare than new work generally is simply because of his totally uncompromising nature." Keene also noted that the refusal to compromise on the part of an artist of Robbins's stature "reminds us of why we're here in the first place, which is to create something beautiful and as close to perfect as we can come."

When Robbins had thought he would be directing *Akhnaten,* he had asked Glass if he could use some of the composer's music for a ballet, "to get my feet wet" in terms of dealing with Glass's style and musical structures. In late 1982, Glass sent Robbins his *Rubric* and *Facades* for the first two sections of the ballet, and, early in 1983, the funeral march that opened *Akhnaten,* which Jerry had already advised the composer to pare down for maximum effect.

The Glass ballet was in itself an adventurous project, born not only of Robbins's involvement with the opera but of his interest in the postmodern choreographers whose careers he followed and the contemporary music they used. The score certainly sounded unlike what usually came out of the NYCB's orchestra pit. His task was to wed the ballet vocabulary with structures and other movements that suited Glass's minimalist compositions. Instead of long, melodic lines, he was more often faced with brief motifs built of neighboring notes that repeat over and over, plus rhythmic patterns that shift subtly across a vibrating pulse and harmonic chords. In the three pieces Robbins used, Glass's emphasis is on the ensemble, and what often appears circular is actually spiral, accumulating and gathering momentum until it seems about to lift off. The resultant ballet, wrote Nancy Goldner in *The Christian Science Monitor,* was "an absolute victory of complex simplicity."

Notable in the first two sections is the way the choreography pits soloists against the group. In *Rubric,* twenty-four dancers variously dressed in bright practice clothes and looking like a horde walk briskly across the white stage the way pedestrians navigate a plaza, giving the impression of being on private errands, yet sharing a common beat. Each time this scene recurs, a little something is added: a few people turn, a little dodgy step occurs, they all stop and bend their knees briefly. And each time, as the crowd is beginning to thin, soloists jump into their midst. First one pair of athletes in gleaming unitards dances ("I want you to be a steel angel from outer space," he told dancer Heléne Alexopoulos); the next time, it's two pairs, then three, until the throng reappears for a final time and the music suddenly stops and freezes them in their tracks.

In *Facades,* a silhouetted stream of women moves steadily across the back of the stage, embellishing a chugging walk with small variations; circling one another to change places, sidestepping, pausing, raising an arm, they're the train bearing Glass's beat. In front of them, to a sweetly singing solo clarinet, a man and woman dance a romantic pas de deux. Robbins prefigures the Egyptian ambiance of *Akhnaten* by having them occasionally pause in hieratic two-dimensional poses that recall the pharaoh and his Nefertiti. The scene requires a dual focus on the part of the viewer; the women at the back are almost more compelling than the soloists. But both the couple and the women stop from time to time, as if to allow one's shifting gaze to alight.

The ensemble section to the march from *Akhnaten* gave Robbins some headaches. It begins vividly with three men in crisp, space-covering patterns. Three become six become twelve; unison splits into counterpoint and reforms. Twelve women introduce a circle. Up to this point, the impeccable formations have a ritualistic drive. But as Glass's texture gets denser and all twenty-four dancers are moving in groups, Robbins—gradually working his way back to the image of a mob—makes the movements more elaborate. The ear can absorb a complexity that baffles the eye. By mid-February, he had finished the ballet and wrote, "Glass looks like a so what so so work"; later it was "Glass goes nowhere. Finishes poorly." He was, as usual, much harder on himself than the audience was. *Glass Pieces* was a tremendous success, and he came to value it ("What do I know?"). The composer liked it too. The influence of Childs and another postmodern minimalist, Laura Dean (for whom Robbins had also written a Guggenheim recommendation), was noted by certain critics but not disparaged. This was hardly copycat work.

Maria Calegari and Bart Cook danced the pas de deux marvelously. You'd never have guessed that practically every time she'd start a phrase in rehearsal, Robbins would stop her with a whistle and a clap. The two dancers made their own small contributions to the ballet. "At first," says Calegari, "[Jerry] wasn't quite sure what to do with those poses. They were a little bit more Etruscan, and then all of a sudden Bart and I Egyptianed them, and they stayed that way." Because the women in that second-movement line had a terrible time remembering the minute changes in their ongoing pattern, Cook, as ballet master, pasted sheets of graph paper together, wrote in the steps, and laid the chart out on the floor for them. Although Robbins had hoped that the painter Cy Twombly might be persuaded to design the ballet, the backdrop ended up being simply graph paper blown up; the stoic women, in effect, danced the patterns against it.

Something Violette Verdy once said about Robbins's approach to music could be applied to his ideas for ballets as well. "I think," she told an interviewer, "the musicality is extreme but I think that his own personal, intellectual complexity does not allow him to content himself with a simple solution. And I think that he looks for something more inventive, more original, more intricate, and [un]expected." He needed the challenge of making work that might tell him something different about the world and about himself.

Although *I'm Old Fashioned (The Astaire Variations)* premiered on June 16, 1983, only a month after *Glass Pieces,* Robbins had been hatching it for several years. For the theme on which to build his variations, he didn't, surprisingly, choose one of the many great duets Astaire had danced with Ginger Rogers. Instead, while watching the 1980 PBS Astaire special *Change Partners and Dance* (for which he had been interviewed), he became fired up over a number from the film *You Were Never Lovelier,* which paired Astaire with Rita Hayworth: "What a simple, clear and miraculous dance. How lovely, how easy and most of all how choreographically delightful. . . . It struck such a deep response in me and more than anything I wanted to use it, study it, become a part of it and in my way dance it." He procured a clip; he wrote to Astaire, and Astaire responded, "I'm honored that you want to do what you suggest."

Making the ballet was anything but simple, clear, and easy. It was also complicated by the fact that a documentary on the process was planned, and camera crews attended several rehearsals and shot Robbins and Morton Gould conferring, before someone (probably Robbins) put a stop to the project. Bart Cook, Sara Leland, pianist Richard Moredock, and Jerry worked for hours to decode the steps under and behind Hayworth's long, swirling black dress. According to Edward Bigelow, then company manager, Hershy Kay declined the task of composing a set of variations on Jerome Kern's tune; lovely as the melody was, he couldn't see manipulating it over twenty minutes. Nor could Morton Gould, but Jerry talked him into it and sent off a list of points for the composer to keep in mind, recapitulating the qualities of Astaire that he hoped to hear in the score: "debonair, delightful, jaunty, elegant, a sophistication of musical and rhythmic expertise. An ease—dexterity, lightness, concentrated but playful."

By the time rehearsals began in September, Robbins was already dissatisfied with some of Gould's variations, although he loved the man, who came helpfully to the studio: "[H]e's so wonderfully laid back, incredible humor—ironic & self-mocking." Gould complained that he found it hard to satisfy the choreographer when Jerry couldn't explain what he wanted. Jerry had a hard time clarifying even to himself what was wrong with the music. He wrote in a log he was keeping that Gould, in his variations, "uses the whole construction of the song instead of seizing on the bars or section that applied to specific steps & making use of that particular material to develop." Ten days later, however, he wrote that, although the composer has "done some good variations, they seem not to reflect enough of the original dance itself." He choreographed some variations to the original tune as it appeared in the film and then wondered why Gould had trouble pinning new music on finished choreography. " 'Nice' is not good enough for an Astaire Variations Ballet." Gould joked about committing suicide but arrived with new material two days after Jerry wrote this comment in his log.

At one point, Robbins had created eighteen variations. He ended up with fourteen. At one point Judith Fugate had a lot to do; in the final version she was left with just one duet and the finale. Robbins lured Victor Castelli into giving up two of his vacation weeks to come into the studio. Who wouldn't oblige if Jerome Robbins called and said, "I have a ballet for you"? "We had the best time. He had a whole number called 'Honi Coles'; we tapped together. Jerry was dancing around me. I was dancing around him. We got into the season, and all of a sudden I realized I was starting to teach all of this stuff he did for me to everybody else." Castelli went to Robbins's office and told him he wouldn't work with him again. The breach lasted two years.

Robbins and those who assisted him—notably his lawyer, Floria Lasky—went through difficult and expensive processes to get the rights to show the film sequence as a statement of the ballet's theme and to project the ballet's program credits in a 1940s typeface as a lead-in to the film, while the singer who had dubbed the song for Rita Hayworth spooled it out. At the premiere—as at every performance thereafter—spectators clapped when the words "Dedicated to Fred Astaire" appeared on the screen. The ending—when the entire cast, clad in black costumes somewhat like Astaire and Hayworth's, danced the original steps by Astaire and Val Raset beneath the projected film sequence—brought the audience to its feet and earned the dancers eight curtain calls.

Robbins never thought his ballet was worthy of Fred Astaire, and many critics felt the same way, although most of them also praised his ingenuity and the beauty and charm of some of his inventions. He had set himself an enormous challenge, an almost quixotic one: to make variations that would show off the ballet company he loved doing the kinds of things they did best, while not violating the qualities of the original duet. Watching the ballet—it is a repertory favorite, regularly revived—one can see how he went at it. After the film, one couple (originally Judith Fugate and

Joseph Duell) slightly "classicizes" Astaire's and Hayworth's number—the first, gentle part of it—and hints at variations to come. They enlarge the initial rocking step by adding an arabesque; a fan kick becomes a développé, a slight raising of Astaire's leg becomes an attitude, an embrace lifts the woman off the floor, the many swirling ballroom turns can encompass pirouettes.

In a subsequent variation for two couples, Astaire's springier steps broaden into a leap, and Robbins introduces the film dance's ending, in which Astaire and Hayworth, attempting simultaneously to exit onto a balcony, bump shoulders, back up and bow to each other, and then succeed in walking through the door side by side. Six couples vary the film pair's jaunty, quick-stepping passage. Of the ballet's other duets—two choreographed for Kyra Nichols and Sean Lavery, two for Heather Watts and Bart Cook—three are lyrical and lovely, riffing in various ways off the romantic aspect of the original duet; in the fourth Nichols and Lavery play competitive little games with the "after you" bow and the bump (this comes to seem overused in the ballet, primarily because it's instantly identifiable and isn't subject to much manipulation on Robbins's part). The sound of Astaire's taps is picked up in Gould's percussion section and in the dance by one man (Cook) slapping his hands on his body and sending quizzical looks toward the pit that turn the drummer into his partner. In the second Watts-Cook duet, when another man briefly takes her away, Robbins refers to a device in other Astaire films. The dejected dancing by the man left alone is echoed by an ensemble of eight men.

A year later, Martha Graham, grateful to Robbins for speaking at the ceremony where she had received the first National Medal of Arts, wrote him, "I know the ancestral footsteps dog you as they do me and I know so deeply how, as every artist experiences, you justify a line from [the] Edda, 'I hung nine nights and nine days upon the tree.' That's what you do in your work and I love you for it." He did, indeed, hang on the tree while creating *I'm Old Fashioned,* which may be one of the reasons Astaire's ease often eluded him.

⁓

Having pursued in *The Arts of the Gentleman* a vision of the New York City Ballet's men as both elegant and vigorous, Robbins turned his attention to making a ballet for only women, albeit on a much less ambitious scale. His motive was also pragmatic. On a typical New York City Ballet program, his *Afternoon of a Faun,* being brief and involving only two dancers, was usually paired with another "small" ballet from the repertory rather than being framed by intermissions. Following it with a galloping bit of virtuosity, such as Balanchine's dazzling *Tarantella,* didn't allow its spell to sink in. On February 2, 1984, Robbins premiered another short ballet, *Antique Epigraphs,* and made it clear that the two ballets were to be programmed together.

For the new work, he returned to Debussy and the same pieces he had used for *Ballade* in 1952: the composer's flute melody *Syrinx* (as both overture and finale) and *Six Épigraphes Antiques* (the orchestral version). The latter were musical impressions of selections from *The Songs of Bilitis,* erotic prose poems evoking an island community of women resembling Sappho's on Lesbos. The real writer was a fin-de-siècle Frenchman, Pierre Louÿs; perhaps for that reason, the poems have a slightly voyeuristic, occasionally decadent cast. A blind old man speaks to Bilitis of nymphs:

Their necks were inclined beneath their long hair.
Their nails were as thin as the wings of grasshoppers. Their
nipples were hollowed like the cups of hyacinths.

. . .

They trailed their fingers upon the water and drew up,
from an invisible vase, the long-stemmed water-lilies. Around
their parted thighs, the ripples slowly widened.

Having choreographed an *Afternoon of a Faun* without the attendant nymphs who had created agitated border designs and rhythmic punctuation for Vaslav Nijinsky's 1912 version, Robbins now considered "nymphs." His suite of dances for eight New York City Ballet women isn't as suffused with eroticism as Louÿs's poems. Like Debussy's music, it is mysterious, nostalgic, voluptuous only in the most refined and formal ways. What Robbins has taken from Louÿs is a certain ambiance: a sunlit isle where desirable women exchange confidences and meditate on love. At the end, lined up as if pressed into a frieze, they strike various archaic poses borrowed from four life-sized sculptures of women with enamel eyes that had fascinated Robbins in the National Museum in Naples in 1963. It is the statue-come-to-life scenario, seen retrospectively and promoting a nostalgic vision: how lovely they were just seconds ago, how alive! The artful conclusion, a few earlier postures, and Florence Klotz's subtly Grecian gowns are the only concessions to Louÿs's embrace of fabled antiquity.

Robbins's approach to his subject is echoed in an essay about the music filed among his papers; it links "classical clarity and the supple finesse of the modal melodies, Greek or oriental" in an illusion of timelessness. In the beginning, the women of this island community stand at one side of the stage, staring toward the other side and gradually moving in that direction; they might be pondering some distant shore or wished-for ship, or simply taking in air. The solo created for Stephanie Saland to the music titled "The Nameless Tomb" is tinged with darkness; the dancer echoes Debussy's arpeggios with incantatory gestures to the ground. She could be a priestess, or just a woman allying her own physical and emotional tides with the earth. Kyra Nichols's solo is more rapturous, more yielding, lighter and quicker. The choreography as a whole creates an illusion of simple, fluent utterance typical of Robbins's lyricism. The dancers make an attitude turn on pointe look as if they were sailing on invisible wind. Three women holding hands, entwining, have the chasteness of young girls frolicking on a beach; two lift another in a leap.

Robbins's vision of this sisterhood of women*—or, rather, of these women dancers he cherished—is idealized. Young, lithe, gracious, and gentle, they inhabit the *danse d'école* as if it were a convent with all its windows open to the sun and salt air. There's a startling moment close to the end in which they move into their frieze, looking like Nijinsky's nymphs: Their curved arms cross and form ovals, their fingertips not quite touching. But these women's heads and feet are not twisted into profile. They face us, enigmatic yet forthright. Their gazes breach the separation. It's almost like a warning. No faun would dare to thread his way among them.

On July 3, 1984, a month after the premiere of *Brahms/Handel,* a ballet he had cochoreographed with Twyla Tharp, Robbins was on a boat anchored in a bay off Turkey. He was always welcome at Mica and Ahmet Ertegun's house in Bodrum, and this summer he, Aidan Mooney, and Brian Meehan (with whom Jerry was having a very romantic affair that would last into the 1990s) spent time cruising along the coast on the Erteguns' yacht, *Miss Leyla,* attended by a crew of four. When not swimming, sunbathing, or eating well, they went ashore to explore ruins,

---

* Kyra Nichols, Stephanie Saland, Maria Calegari, Simone Schumacher, Heléne Alexopoulos, Jerri Kumery, Victoria Hall, and Florence Fitzgerald.

tombs, and Byzantine churches. One evening, as he watched the sea turn from blue to dark green and listened to a Handel concerto he'd been wanting to choreograph, images from Balanchine's ballets kept coming to mind, along with his venture with Tharp. He started to think about that:

> We all try to speak "Balanchine." We, Peter—Helgi [Tomasson had begun to choreograph]—Taras—even Jacques [d'Amboise]—have a working understanding of his language & even how he constructs, etc. Peter has the best grasp on the technical aspects of the language—but no matter—we all speak with the heavy accents of our natures—& only George can spin out the seamless flow of a natural native tongue. Even when we get fluid, even when it's grammatically correct (as it is most in Peter's constructions), it still doesn't have the deep ease, knowledge, poetry & certainty of what it means to say; or the profoundly absolute understanding of the music. We'll never pass in his language. . . . [I] know that trying to "do" a Balanchine-like work is a futile effort—like trying to paint a Leonardo-like painting. I've learned a lot from Twyla. Her daring, her outrageousness, her insistence, her invention . . . the belief that all is possible is a deep & inspiring lesson—& awakes in me again earlier & younger dares—when every second was to be invented and filled. At NYCB I've fallen backward & [been] put asleep by trying to trust more the GB vocabulary—it's lazy. She made me feel that way. Go ahead, try, anything is possible—turn it upside down, inside out, on its head—

Inviting Tharp to join him at New York City Ballet had been in itself adventurous, although she, with works like *Push Comes to Shove* (1976) to her credit, had proved long before that she could triumph with large ballet companies as well as with her own small one, that a maverick could function within the establishment, and that her own slippery idiosyncratic vocabulary with its bone-deep jazz influence could mate happily with ballet.

The very last entry in Robbins's journal says only of *Brahms/Handel,* "that story is a chapter." He had wanted for several years to collaborate on a ballet with Tharp. She had finally agreed, hoping to learn how he developed a narrative, while he wanted to understand how she approached structure. He opted out of narrative, though, and the choice of music, Brahms's *Variations and Fugue on a Theme by Handel,* mandated a field day of structural games. Balanchine had asked that they use the orchestrated version of the music rather than the single piano original Tharp preferred; that decision more or less paved the way for a "big" ballet.

They chose their casts—a principal couple for each, two demisoloist pairs, and a small corps de ballet—and color-coded them: blue for him, green for her. Presumably they divided up the music, although the dancers involved say that Robbins often changed his mind about who had what. Tharp, thrilled to be working with Balanchine's dancers, remained diplomatic. "I think," says Bart Cook, her principal male dancer, "that she almost cracked some of her teeth biting her tongue." The idea was not just that Jerry would choreograph one variation and she another (they did do that), but that in a given variation, his dancers might be doing his choreography in the foreground while she set hers to creating counterpoint in an upstage corner, or vice versa. They could build not just on the theme but on each other's variations. They might lend each other dancers. In a "dialogue" between Cook and Ib Andersen, Robbins's male principal, Tharp devised the steps for her man and Robbins for his, the two choreographers working together in the same space. They hoped to cover their tracks and create a unified work. Tharp says they made a pact not to advertise who had done what.

Their working methods were very different. Tharp, for instance, sometimes choreographed movement in silence and then tailored it to the music. She worked swiftly. Robbins exercised his usual need to revise and rethink. "He basically made me crazy," recalls Tharp good-humoredly, "because it would be like, you know, I plan what I'm going to do, I do it, I'm ready to go on; he plans what he's going to do, he does it, he's ready to go *back*." In one of the cochoreographed sections, she might create a pause or some pared-down movement in order to allow an important step of his to emerge, only to find that, at the next rehearsal, he had eliminated that step.

They worked in adjoining studios most of the time. Her ease must have driven *him* crazy. Delia Peters, by then no longer dancing in the company and assigned to videotape Tharp's work sessions, remembers a day near the beginning of rehearsals. "He walked through at one point, saw what she was doing, said, 'Hmm,' and went into his rehearsal; came back at the end of the three hours and we were doing the same thing. He looked and said, 'Didn't get too far today, huh, baby? Ha-ha.' She said, 'Oh, no, this is the first movement. I've done the next two already.' And he said, 'Oh.' "

According to Tharp, neither of them thought *Brahms/Handel* was great. Since the ballet had, of necessity, been constructed piecemeal, it couldn't be run through until the last stages of rehearsal. But Jerry liked it enough to have it included in the Robbins retrospective that the NYCB staged in 1990. The public loved it, and so did the critics, including some, such as Dale Harris of *The Wall Street Journal,* who didn't like most of Robbins's work for the NYCB. What was exhilarating about *Brahms/Handel* when it premiered on June 7, 1984, was the fact that it looked at home in the New York State Theater, danced by these dancers yet did not look like anything else in the company's repertory. Watching the 1990 revival on videotape confirms that impression. Although Robbins's austere theme, with its orderly tendus and turns, alludes to the grand manner that Balanchine established at the opening of his *Theme and Variations,* the variations almost never confirm the hierarchies derived from Petipa. Instead of discreetly framing and echoing the principal dancers, the demisoloists and/or corps often have intense, off-center activities of their own. And when Tharp is involved, these activities may involve scorchingly fast petit allegro. The effect is visually complex and, in spirit, democratic. In Variation VI, for instance, Robbins sets two units, Andersen and Merrill Ashley and three demisoloists, dancing in counterpoint to one another, while in the upstage left corner, Tharp swings three couples into their own close canon.

The two costume colors are not always a reliable guide to authorship, but those familiar with the two choreographers' styles can pretty much tell who did what. When the men run, kicking up their heels, that would be Robbins, or when a lift reminds you of *Dances at a Gathering.* Tharp's touch is unmistakable in a fluid, slightly funky solo for Andersen or in a sequence for Ashley and a horde of racing men that looks death-defying. While putting the piece together, the choreographers riffed off each other. Robbins starts Variation IX with flying lifts for his entire group. Tharp brings Maria Calegari onstage standing on the shoulders of a group of men, alluding not only to Jerry's aerial statement but to the last moment of Balanchine's *Serenade.* After some intricate dual activities, the teams rush out on opposite sides, each bearing its ballerina like a battering ram. For the audience, deciding what to look at in this ballet is part of the pleasure, with well-timed passages of unison to rest the eyes.

⁓

In the year George Balanchine died, Robbins turned sixty-five. He minded. "It's pushing me up into the A-K [*alte kocker*] category." Yet at sixty-five, he was in love with the twenty-three-year-old Meehan, who found him immensely attractive, and his creative energy blazed undiminished. He didn't need to worry about money. The contract he signed with the New York City Ballet in 1983 gave him $100,000 a year, plus royalties of between $150 and $350 per ballet (depending on length) per performance. A list of his fees and royalties dated June 7, 1986, is typical of what he earned licensing his ballets to other companies. In a given period, seven American companies and nine foreign ones paid him fees ranging from $1,500 to $25,000 to set—or send someone else to set—a ballet, plus royalties. Then there were the royalties from his musicals; in 1986, from *Fiddler on the Roof* alone, he made $115,186. His net worth at the end of that year was more than $5 million.

He had trouble thinking of himself as rich. "It was hard for him to spend money," says his financial adviser Allen Greenberg, "especially on himself." A true child of the Depression, he liked to have more of his earnings invested in bonds than in stocks. Once, when his father was visiting Manhattan, Jerry had tried to get him to take a taxi to the Port Authority bus station. "You don't understand," said Harry. "When I get into a cab, with each click of the meter, my heart gives a powerful jump. It's like a little knife stick in the heart." Writing this down as research material for *The Poppa Piece,* Robbins added, "With those words, he put the same curse on me."

He gave interesting Christmas presents but not ostentatious ones. One year, many of his friends got subscriptions to art magazines; another time it was twenty-five-pound bags of Vidalia onions. Lighting designer Jennifer Tipton always received a potted amaryllis. The two men who assisted him while he was assembling *Jerome Robbins' Broadway* were vastly amused when he bought a new camera and inquired every day as to whether his modest rebate had arrived. His house had many beautiful things in it, but he was not, for example, a collector of expensive contemporary art. He had a cook, a housekeeper, a secretary, a handyman, and a classic Mercedes, but he seems to have flown first class for the first time in 1982 (and loved it). He formed the habit of stashing money away among his books; after his death bills amounting to about $600 were found in record jackets. And he was suspicious of those who might want to pry some money out of him, while still helping family members through gifts and loans, paying out money to artists through his foundation, and continuing to support the Jerome Robbins Archive of the Recorded Moving Image at the New York Public Library's Dance Collection.

Like many people in the performing arts, he lost friends, lovers, and colleagues to AIDS. As the disease mushroomed, more and more of his foundation's money began to go to organizations for AIDS research and care, and he donated his services to coordinate *Dancing for Life,* a benefit performance at the New York State Theater on October 5, 1987 (as Leonard Bernstein did in the *Music for Life* benefit at Carnegie Hall that same year). Robert Rauschenberg designed the posters. Thirteen companies participated.* Jerry gave the program a great deal of agonized thought. At one point, Ellen Sorrin, who was assisting him, says he called her and "used more 'de' and 'dis' words . . . than I probably ever heard in my life," including "disappointed" and "disgruntled" (the envisioned audience) and "discouraged" and "depressed" (himself). However, he knew just where to place the poignant male duet from Lar Lubovitch's *Concerto Six Twenty-Two* (Mozart) to make its images of tenderness and support the symbol of the evening. And the programming in moving ways affirmed the solidarity of the dance community in the face of AIDS. In the second half of the evening, a three-part Bach piece was formed from the first movement of Mark Morris's *Marble Halls;* the second movement of Balanchine's *Concerto Barocco,* performed by Dance Theatre of Harlem; and the last movement of Paul Taylor's *Esplanade.* As a finale, each movement of Balanchine's *Symphony in C* was danced by leading couples from four different companies—NYCB, ABT, DTH, and the Joffrey Ballet—backed by the NYCB corps. In his opening speech, Mikhail Baryshnikov announced that the benefit had raised $1.4 million for the American Foundation for AIDS Research, the National AIDS Network, and GMHC.

~

If age had no impact on the scope of Robbins's activities or his financial status or his energy, it did influence his creative life. In 1989, he wrote in one of the notebook-diaries he sometimes started (unable to completely kick the journal habit), "Anyone should be able to see that 'In Memory Of . . . ,' 'Ives,' and 'JR Bway' are farewell pieces, personal closing up shop pieces." Of the five ballets he made between 1985 and 1988, three—

* Alvin Ailey American Dance Theater, American Ballet Theatre, Merce Cunningham Dance Company, Dance Theatre of Harlem, Laura Dean Dancers and Musicians, Feld Ballet, Martha Graham Dance Company, The Joffrey Ballet, Lar Lubovitch Dance Company, Mark Morris Dance Group, New York City Ballet, The Paul Taylor Dance Company, and Twyla Tharp Dance.

In Memory of . . . , Quiet City, and *Ives, Songs*—commemorated the past and contemplated death. His 1989 show *Jerome Robbins' Broadway* was a retrospective of his best musical comedy numbers. You could consider the production of Bertolt Brecht's *The Exception and the Rule,* which he had dropped in 1968 and took up again in 1986, as unfinished business that still interested him and that he wanted to resolve, and two minor ballets, *Eight Lines* and *Piccolo Balletto,* as a return to something he had done before and was trying to do differently.

His slight dissatisfaction with *Glass Pieces,* as well his interest in new music in the minimalist vein, may have prompted Robbins, in 1985, to tackle Steve Reich's *Octet,* in an orchestral version (played on tape with the addition of two live pianists). As he had reconsidered the Debussy music he had used in *Ballade* for *Antique Epigraphs,* he set *Piccolo Balletto* (1986) to the same Stravinsky music he had used for *Dumbarton Oaks* in 1972; the cast was the same size: a principal couple and six supporting pairs.

With Reich's music, as with Glass's, Robbins had to deal with a hypnotically steady pulse overlaid with gradually changing rhythmic patterns, and he was able to capture some of the spatial aspects of Reich's music—its spirals and helixes and asymmetries—in the patterns dancers traced on a white floor. As in *Glass Pieces,* he created a recurring background motif— spaced-out flights by three men in blue—and a canon for Maria Calegari and five women came close to being a visual equivalent of Reich's technique of "phasing," one part gradually slipping out of unison with another. The ballet was lean and smart, boasting an intriguing legato duet for Kyra Nichols and Sean Lavery, although to anyone familiar with the works Laura Dean had set to Reich's music, the New York City Ballet dancers in sleek, bright-colored unitards seemed light—skating on the pulse rather than digging into it.

For his second go-round with the Stravinsky concerto, he dropped the 1920s tennis party for a festival in a small Italian town (a handsome backdrop of umber and sienna buildings by Santo Loquasto), the classical steps seasoned with dashes of circus and Commedia dell'Arte. This time, he involved the ensemble more in the antics of the stars, Darci Kistler and Robert La Fosse, both charmers. Mildly rambunctious and a bit cute, *Piccolo Balletto,* like *Eight Lines,* pleased audiences without leaving much of an impression. Robbins himself liked *Eight Lines* enough to include it on a wish list for the company's 1990 Robbins Festival. At the time, however, he had finished it early and turned his attention to a ballet that he felt more deeply.

In an interview with Rosamond Bernier that punctuated *Dance in America*'s live broadcast of *In Memory of* . . . , Robbins spoke of its music, Alban Berg's Violin Concerto, as a cryptogram. As he had learned from composer George Perle's two volumes on Berg's operas, Berg had written the piece in 1935, the year of his death, and dedicated it to Manon Gropius, the daughter of Alma Mahler and Walter Gropius, who had just died of infantile paralysis at the age of eighteen. The music interweaves a portrait of the girl and the Vienna society in which she moved with memories of women Berg had loved, his intimations of death, and his awareness of the rise of fascism. As a Jew, he had already felt some pressures, and Germany invaded Austria twenty-seven months after his death. Robbins's intimations of his own mortality and his grief over the loss of George Balanchine, Edith Weissman, and others merged with Berg's musical sorrow. While he denied that the ballet was an elegy for Balanchine, by molding it around Suzanne Farrell, one of the most exquisite of Balanchine's ballerinas, he ended up creating a memorial to the choreographer that is infinitely more poignant than an overt homage.

He began to work out his ideas with Victor Castelli and Cathy Ryan, a talented corps dancer. Farrell was having serious problems with her hip, and he didn't want to call her in until he had something set. He also didn't want to flounder in front of her. While working with her on *In G Major,* he had often felt as if she were evaluating him, comparing him unfavorably to Balanchine. He was choreographing two pas de deux—an innocent and loving one and a darker one in which the man represents Death. (In the very early stages, he seems to have been considering having Farrell dance both duets with the same partner, Alexandre Proia, whose poetic quality he admired.) The music, with its dissonant twelve-tone texture and quiveringly sweet violin, created a complex interior landscape. At some point, he got stuck, but after deciding to abandon the ballet, he returned from a week in California to give it another try. Not completely satisfied with the way Proia was working, he had invited Adam Lüders to the rehearsal: "[I]f the male lead was to represent death, Adam might well do." On an impulse, he got Lüders on his feet and started working on a new pas de deux with him and a surrogate partner.

The first session with Farrell was, he noted in a log written in Turkey the summer after the premiere, "the most extraordinary rehearsal I've ever had . . . It was as near to automatic writing as I've experienced. Suzanne was incredible. . . . We were all possessed; high; amazed, spent, inspired.

At <u>that</u> point the ballet fused; Suzanne and I fused; Suzanne and the ballet fused." It took only two weeks to finish the work, including retooling the first group dance. Because of Farrell's hip, he couldn't work her too long at a time. That didn't matter. He was thrilled not only by her dancing, but to find her an example to all: "Her concentration, attentiveness and efforts were complete & she gave them with extreme quietness, calm and a concentration of energy. She would never slack off repeating a section over and over. To boot, (& it was miraculously relieving) she had a light, free, quiet, sense of humor which . . . [made] everyone relaxed, happy, & delighted to be with each other." After the first full run-through, the cast applauded—something that had never happened to Robbins.

As the ballet was developing, he brought in Joseph Duell—whose gifts he had first made use of in *Fencing Dances and Exercises*—to partner Farrell in the first pas de deux. In that trusting duet, the woman is often off the ground, led and turned by her partner, gently kept from the dark corners of the stage that seem to beckon her. Certain moments prefigure the second duet: her young lover rocks her gently, as the Death figure does later; falling backward into his arms, she goes fleetingly limp. In delineating his heroine's milieu, Robbins goes more deeply into the image of community than simply having people watch one another. Farrell all but disappears into a women's dance. When couples skein a country waltz over the floor, the men lift their partners in leaps, one after another; it's as if they're inciting their companions to try this joyful step.

The first exit of the group puzzled many viewers. They stalk stiffly out on tiptoe, revealing Lüders, who has entered behind Farrell, now seated warily on the floor. One note Robbins wrote to himself sheds some light on this scene: he wondered if the corps could be "her country folk slowly giving in to Nazism. <u>But</u> must be used, if used, subtly, delicately, also hidden & ambiguous."

Fortunately, *Dance in America* taped a performance of the ballet in December 1986 (a year and a half after its premiere on June 13, 1985). Farrell's extraordinary performance with her exemplary partner in the second duet is hair-raising even on tape. With Lüders as his surrogate, Robbins forces her to extend her range, to undertake movements you can believe have never been tried before, movements that are both beautiful and strange, like words in an unfamiliar language. Twice her partner leaves her exhausted on the floor, then reclaims her. Although he entraps her and she struggles, he is also the gentle puppet master and the tender lover. In the end, after she has taken her place in an angelic society very like the one she has left, where the moves are familiar to her, both men, like her now garbed in white, return to carry her further. Robbins wanted us to see that "she is now accepting Life and Death, transported to a place to be able to WALK ON AIR, which is what she is doing."

In the taped performance, Proia has replaced Duell, and by then the ballet could memorialize one more person. On February 15, 1986, Joseph Duell, severely depressed, jumped from the fifth-floor window of his apartment.

Lincoln Kirstein was especially heartbroken over Duell's death. He had loved him and believed in his talent as a choreographer. (Ironically, the backdrop for *In Memory of . . .* was the one David Mitchell had designed for Duell's ballet *La Création du Monde;* for Robbins, Mitchell hung a black scrim in front of the drop and added to it a few subtle lines and shadings.) Two years earlier Kirstein had commissioned from Michael Leonard a portrait of Duell "as the Chevalier Noverre," as if foreseeing his elevation into the pantheon that included that eighteenth-century theorist and choreographer. Jerry, too, grieved, worried that his having replaced Duell with Proia in *In Memory of . . .* might have contributed to Joe's depression. In an undated letter to Jerry, the dancer had written, "I wish I was a more worthy person to be close to" and "I love you very much but I know that I will always disappoint you." Robbins, in Europe at the time of the suicide and unable to get an immediate flight back, sent the company a message: "Know that I join you in grief, and wish we were together, I put my arms around you & miss feeling yours around me." Once home, he did what he could to comfort the dancers and Duell's family. He was not only sorrowful but furious that Duell's circle of friends had been unable to see his suicide coming and forestall it.

Robbins dedicated *Quiet City,* to the music of the same name by Aaron Copland, to Duell's memory. Robert La Fosse, the former ABT principal dancer whom Robbins had just invited to join NYCB, recalls that the short ballet took shape "in no time flat"—maybe in a week. Perhaps that's why it had the force of an undifferentiated flood of emotion, sleeked into theatrical shape—beautiful yet impersonal, like one of those formal eulogies that make all the dead sound virtuously alike. Not surprisingly, it also evokes *Requiem Canticles* and might almost be a simpler, miniature version of the last section of *In Memory of . . .* People in dark street clothes stand around as if waiting for something, making small, consoling gestures to one another. Three men in white, like the first "angels" to enter in the last section of *In Memory of* . . . (two of them played by the same young corps members, Peter Boal and Damian Woetzel), dance along a golden path of light. As they launch themselves into flights, La Fosse clearly stands for Duell—sometimes falling into the arms of his companions, sensing something frightening or alluring in the distance.

By the time *Ives, Songs* premiered in 1988, Jerry had lost others who were important to him. Nora Kaye died of cancer on February 2, 1987. He had flown out to Hollywood to say good-bye to her. Antony Tudor died in April. Tom Abbott died too young, undone by alcohol. Bob Fosse died, leaving a sum of $25,000 to be divided equally among about sixty-five people, "so that when my friends receive this bequest, they will all go out and have dinner on me." A few days after Kaye's death, Jerry's beloved dog Nick died, despite all the veterinary help that had been lavished on him. His master wrote a heartbroken page in a notebook; here was one fellow creature who had needed him and loved him unquestioningly.

⁓

During the early stages of planning his Ives ballet, Robbins resurrected a ghost from 1968: *The Exception and the Rule.* The Lincoln Center Theater's two houses, the Vivian Beaumont and the Mitzi Newhouse, had had checkered careers.* When Gregory Mosher took over as artistic director in 1985, with Bernard Gersten as executive director, he was advised to get Jerome Robbins to come and do something—whatever Jerry wanted. What he wanted was to work on a production of the Brecht play in a workshop situation, with no guarantee that it would ever be presented in front of a paying audience. John Guare's *The House of Blue Leaves* had had a successful run at Lincoln Center in the spring of 1986, which, says Mosher, "meant we had some cash to play with." Of the original collaborators, Leonard Bernstein was initially enthusiastic. Guare, although remembering the traumas of the earlier production, agreed to return to the project. Stephen Sondheim had no desire to become involved but con-

---

* Robert Whitehead and Elia Kazan, codirectors of what was to be its first constituent, the Repertory Theater Association, resigned in 1964 before the theater was completed. Julius Irving ran what was called the Repertory Theater Association of Lincoln Center, from 1965 to 1973, with Herbert Blau codirecting for the first year. Joseph Papp's New York Shakespeare Festival took over the theater from 1973 to 1977. While Richmond Crinkley was in charge from 1980 to 1984, the theater was dark for some of those years, due to reconstruction.

sented to let his lyrics be used. It was agreed that any plans to present the work publicly would involve more negotiation.

One issue the collaborators had to thrash out was whether to proceed with the version of *The Exception and the Rule* that they had developed in 1968 with all the elements—the play-within-a-telecast structure, the tensions between black and white actors, the speeches to the audience, and the possible involvement of the authors as characters—that they had added to Brecht's tale of greed and suspicion against a background of class warfare and racism.

On November 6, 1986, in response to a meeting several days earlier and a subsequent early morning call from Robbins, Bernstein articulated the problems facing them:

> [I]t is wonderful to try to organize our discussions, arguments, alternatives, choices, auditions, multiple castings and heterogeneous approaches into a new and great and unprecedented theatre-piece. But it is also, at this moment, dealing with pure and beautiful chaos, with the problem of freedom riding the waters. You can't choose A without <u>un</u>choosing B; that's a law. Of course, <u>you can,</u> and present <u>part</u> of A and part of B, in opposition or in tandem, but then you ultimately have neither. . . .
>
> It would be great fun, and deeply interesting, for the audience to hear the Big Minds bickering and building and bulldozing their way through Brecht's China, for maybe a half hour. Then what? We get the point, OK, basta, get on with it, tell the story. . . . A MAN HAS BEEN KILLED. What man? Does it matter who, or what his importance, or if he's a grain of salt in a vast population? Are men created equal, and if so why is it so fucking hard to live our lives as if that were really true?
>
> Do we really want to hear and see a writer and a director argue this cosmic subject onstage for two hours? OK, one hour. OK, three hours. Nine Acts. As I say, Finnegans Wake.

For months, says Mosher, Robbins, Guare, and Bernstein

argued about what this show should be. What relevance did it have, both small and large 'R?' What was the theatrical point, what was the social point, should it have a narrator, shouldn't it have a narrator . . . should it be about a racial conflict, was it inevitable? John would pipe up every now and then, but mostly Lenny and Jerry would just go at it.

And there it was, the legendary Bernstein-Robbins relationship. And then one of them would leave and the other person would say, "Can you believe how insane he is? He is insane!" He'd come back and they'd argue about it some more, and the other one would leave and the one that remained would burst into tears and say "I can't stand it, I can't stand it. I hate this!"

Yet for Mosher, watching the two of them work together "was one of the greatest experiences of my life." When Bernstein and Robbins were in sync, they made shimmeringly clear the intimate connections between movement and music.

Gradually, most of the additions were stripped away from Guare's translation of Brecht's play, now called *The Race to Urga*. Josh Mostel played the Merchant, the part intended for his father back in 1968; Thomas Ikeda was the Coolie and the Judge; and Joe Grifasi the Guide. There was a chorus of four and a small ensemble of male actors, all of whom played several parts. The bulk of the musical numbers had lyrics by Sondheim; the rest were by Guare, with one (possibly two) by Bernstein and one by Jerry Lieber—the pidgin English "The Coolie's Dilemma." Most of the lyrics are terse, and Bernstein's music is forthright and driving, sometimes rollicking. One of the songs, says Sondheim, had already found a very different life in Bernstein's *Mass*.

As of February 1987, according to notes on the contract negotiations, Bernstein wanted no further part of the venture. They could use his music only for these invitational performances. However, something Robbins wrote in a diary on March 13 en route to his favorite island, St. Bart's, before rehearsals makes it sound as if Bernstein was still considering a run for the production: "Meanwhile L'Affaire Lenny goes in & out, up & down. He's up & down & as of today I said no to a 7-wk. run after a workshop. The material is not ready nor would be unless LB was there to solve problems." Guare stuck it out through rehearsals. In contact sheets of photos taken during the process, you can see him and Robbins, heads together in the audience or onstage perusing a script, although Robbins is more often demonstrating with gusto.

There was no danger of this production being faulted for being too clean, neat, and spare, like Robbins's *Mother Courage*. Not only did Jerry seem to be aiming for something rougher and more like street theater, but there was almost no budget. He improvised brilliantly, drawing also on his actors' imaginations. Nine men manage all the roles, including the Coolie's widow. They don hats to become Chinese, run in and out carrying signs and small objects. The ongoing race across the desert is engineered in two supermarket shopping carts, with the merchant and his rival whizzed around by their servants—careering off track, nearly colliding, trying to cut each other off. According to ensemble actor Magnus Ragnarsson, who was doing odd jobs for Robbins (organizing his video library, checking his scrapbooks, etc.) while studying at the Neighborhood Playhouse, "We played whatever—rivers and deserts and suns . . ." In a video made at one of the showings, two low "walls" of fabric stand for the raging river that the Merchant forces the simple, good-hearted Coolie to enter. Tiny boats and bridges are carried on and then sink. Men-as-river ripple the cloth and then roil it wildly around the travelers.

In the opening song, the actors set up the plot and, true to Brecht, adjure the spectators to consider the possibility that they can change society for the better, but they do it in a raucous song by Bernstein and Guare, marching in like ragtag circus performers, one of them banging on cymbals. And in addition to the songs, musical director Michael Scott Barrett and a small group of musicians provide links between scenes and punctuate the action with drumbeats or whistles. Under Robbins's direction, the Merchant becomes comical as well as terrible—a big self-centered baby, Josh Mostel isn't as venal as one imagines his father would have been, but he has the same elephantine grace and surprising flexibility. Guare's script provides laughs for him ("I *love* ethnic," enthuses the Merchant to the audience as he squats beside the Coolie, feigning solidarity). Casting the small, wiry Ikeda as both Coolie and Judge gives an ironic twist to the play's social inequities.

As the actors are taking their bows, a tenor unexpectedly sings out from the audience. He's a Lincoln Center subscriber; he doesn't want any fingers pointing at *him* as an exploiter. Three other do-gooders (all with fine legit voices) also sing out—their rather lame justifications of their greatheartedness cleverly written to take the edge off Brecht's sober didacticism. An argument with the actors ensues before the last song is reprised, ending with those pointing fingers and "What do *you* think?"

Many of those who saw *The Race to Urga* at its several invitational performances in May were enthusiastic about it. Brecht wasn't one of Oliver Smith's favorite authors; however, he wrote Jerry, "Your delightful production brought me a totally new aspect of the playwright's world. Trenchant and tough and remorseless it was, but with your direction so deft, so totally unselfconscious, humorous and affecting, I was totally involved. . . . Even though the play is a terrible condemnation of Greed, it is also about interdependence which you so deftly expressed in your work."

John Guare says that Bernstein, after seeing the workshop production, said, in effect, "I know how to do it. I love it. I have to start work tomorrow." Guare remembers saying, "I have other things that I have to do." Jerry, who in May, close to the opening date, had said he was "exhausted & happy & frustrated," wrote back to Oliver Smith, "URGA took six weeks out of my life, and after it was over I wished I'd done a ballet instead." Instead, he did a ballet too: *Ives, Songs.*

In the summer after the Brecht adventure, Robbins had a waking dream. He was having breakfast in the little Piazza del Mercato in Spoleto, noticing with a choreographer's eye the many different ways in which streets entered the square: from lower down the hill, through an arch, via a narrow Roman street, along the straight road for automobiles. All these created "an easy constant flow of people of all ages: strollers, shoppers, visitors, and equally, thru the single swimming uncrowded current, were meetings, conferences, decisions, dawdlings, all flowing in an unhurried way like being borne on a gentle tide, passing thru, passing thru." He glimpsed a woman who seemed to be coming toward him.

> At first, as I craned my head around, it flashed upon me, without a moment's rationale, that it could be Edith [Weissman], who could be there, very simply, alive again, in this town at this moment, passing thru. And that there was, on consideration, not a thing odd, wrong, or unreal about it. I could easily be visited by all who had passed on, and there wouldn't be anything extraordinary about it—As I thought that, I could see Nora [Kaye] coming down that hill street, all glowing with humor & delight at bumping into me; I could see Tommy [Abbott] walk by & say Hi—& talk a little & nothing would be forced or portentous. David Heaton, Tudor, Ronnie Bates, Michael Bennett, Joe Duell. . . . But it was all with a safe security, without fuss or dream or psychic phenomenon that this easy visitation to heaven came about.

Ives, Songs was a current of remembered scenes and people who had passed on. In *In Memory of . . .* and *Quiet City,* Robbins had thought of angels—although he would never publicly identify the dancers as such for fear of pinning down what was best left to the individual spectator to interpret. In *Ives, Songs,* he equates other winged creatures with resurrection. His dance to "The White Gulls" follows scenes that conjure up World War I; young men proudly don helmets, level imaginary bayonets, and, like the soldiers in Kurt Jooss's great ballet *The Green Table,* advance into the darkness that lurks offstage. They're already falling as they go. And as the next song ends, a son leaves his loving family and follows them. It was not hard, in February 1988, to link the loss of these golden young men to the scourge of AIDS; although there is no evidence that Robbins himself consciously intended this, the *Dancing for Life* benefit that he had coordinated while creating the ballet must have affected him, as it did all who saw it.

If in *Watermill* he had obliquely revealed his intimations of age and mortality in a Japanese landscape, in *Ives, Songs,* he transferred his feelings about the passage of time and the nearness of death into a dark, yet nostalgic vision of the America in which Charles Ives (1874–1954) had grown up—a white, Anglo-Saxon, Protestant society very different from that of Robbins's parents. The songs of Ives were not his only source. In the spring of 1987, while wrestling with *The Race to Urga,* he'd seen a show of monotypes by Maurice Prendergast and become fascinated anew by the work of this artist, born sixteen years before Ives. Many of the monotypes, like Prendergast's watercolor-and-pencil paintings and his oils, vividly evoke the American past: little girls hitching up their ruffled skirts to wade in the sea, women in long dresses carrying parasols as they pick their way across rocky beaches. His works teem with people—enjoying May Day in Manhattan's Central Park, congregating on Rome's Pincian Hill.

With Neel Keller, recommended to him as a research assistant by John Guare, Robbins traveled to Williamstown, Massachusetts, to take in an extensive Prendergast exhibition. He wondered how he could make the pictures dance. Then he listened to a record of Dietrich Fischer-Dieskau singing some of Ives's songs, "& it was as if I hadn't heard these songs ever before. What a revelation. They seemed perfect, made for Prendergast!" The next day, he listened to recording after recording in a state of agitation he likened to the first stages of love. On the next he wondered, "Is there a possible sequence which follows from childhood thru adolescence, young manhood, love, marriage, the war, etc.—till old age?" Keller remembers comparing Ives catalogues in order to list every song the composer had written and to obtain recordings of all of them. For months, Robbins played with ideas about how to juxtapose Ives, Prendergast, and ballet. Gradually the composer crowded out the painter.

Ives's songs are a wonder: they can be pastel, yet pungent; wry and spare, then suddenly effulgent. Inconclusive harmonies subvert romantic outpourings. The America Ives celebrated was the small-town country of Thornton Wilder's *Our Town,* yet under his ministrations, sentimental poems such as Henry Wadsworth Longfellow's "The Children's Hour," with its "patter of little feet," or soothing hymn tunes such as "Shall We Gather at the River?" acquire unexpected shadows. After Robbins had finished the ballet, he worried that it was "somewhat sentimental." It *is* sentimental, but Ives's sweet astringency works against this, as does Robbins's insistence on unmannered performing. The three clamorous little girls popping around on a bench to "We're Going to the Opera" are more zealous than cute, despite their hair bows; and even the Norman Rockwellian cliché of the same eager girls facing two shy boys at a dance manages to avoid coyness.

This ballet doesn't give the impression of being about steps or even of having much "choreography." Most of the songs are short, and Robbins uses a limited vocabulary and relatively simple steps for each, with the exception of a young boy's boisterous solo (made for Michael Byars). The father (Robert Lyon) who prowls back and forth in "The Caged Leopard," with his smaller "son" (Tom Gold) copying him, does almost nothing but that. People stroll their way into dancing. Women are lifted tenderly. "Children" sit to watch the grown-ups (Heléne Alexopoulos and Alexandre Proia) in a summer-evening love duet but follow the couple offstage and don't stay to watch the darker, more haunted dancing of Stephanie Saland and Jeppe Mydtskov. There's a hint of continuity in "Songs My Mother Taught Me"; two of the dancers playing children (Stacy Caddell and Margaret Tracey) join the four women in longer dresses and learn their steps. There are images of death, or leave-taking, in a solo for Alexopoulos, and three men dance to Ives's eerily discordant sliding phrases in "Like a Sick Eagle."

A man (originally Laurence Matthews) links the episodes together. Since the singer and pianist are in full view, off on the side extension of the stage's apron, one can imagine him as the composer reliving scenes from his own music. Robert La Fosse, who also played the part, says that in 1988, "they had pictures of Ives for the makeup and hair and they tried to make Larry Matthews look like Ives." The man is standing onstage when the curtain rises, and he is left alone there when it falls. Occasionally he enters to watch events as if wandering through a museum gallery, and at the end, he seems to summon up all the figures from his remembered life, until the adults stand gazing, while two children continue to race around them as if they were trees in a forest. As Susan Reiter has pointed out, this one-who-remembers has a link to the lady in the green gown who seems to invoke the lovers in Antony Tudor's *The Leaves Are Fading.* But Robbins's onlooker, like the protagonists of Noh dramas or the heroines of Martha Graham's dances, seems to be looking back at his life in order to make sense of it before he enters a new state—even though he stands apart from the pretty, bittersweet pictures he has created. Robbins had intended the role for the fine actor-dancer Adam Lüders, who was unavailable but who in 1994, according to Reiter, gave an apparently "mesmerizing" performance in the ballet. A few days after *Ives, Songs* premiered on February 4, 1988, and still not entirely pleased with what he had created, Jerry asked himself, "Did I show my own fears & loves more than I knew I had?" And "If someone asked me what was it about, I could easily say it's about me and my dancers. I see them & my life as children, as enthusiasts, as worshippers or believers, as lovers, as losers—at the last collected, loved, & outside me—left alone."

20

The Final Chapter

Jerry, Annie, and Tess.
Jesse Gerstein. Courtesy of the Jerome Robbins Foundation.

I keep going," Robbins wrote as he was finishing *Ives, Songs,* "but oh my mortality raises its invisible barriers in constant signs every day. My eyes, my ears, my cock, my fatigues, my desires & most of all how others react <u>to</u> me. The loneliness within my bones. I work not to recognize it." He still took pleasure in juggling several projects at the same time—rehearsing one ballet or show, planning or negotiating for another, and beginning to think about a third. Switching mental gears was one way he refreshed himself, just as he enjoyed spending time with friends who had nothing to do with the theater or dance. *Ives, Songs* and *The Race to Urga* scurried about in his mind together, along with the retrospective of his most sterling musical comedy numbers, which would open in 1989 as *Jerome Robbins' Broadway*. And he was seriously listening to Johann Sebastian Bach's Two and Three Part Inventions, which he would not choreograph until 1994.

It had once been hoped on separate fronts that the Robbins Festival at the New York City Ballet and *Jerome Robbins' Broadway* might fall in 1988, the year he turned seventy, putting before the public the best of his work in the two worlds he straddled. Conflicts postponed both. In the spring of 1988, the NYCB staged its American Music Festival, for which he provided advice and criticism but no new ballet; he was already deep in his musical comedy retrospective.

In one of his notebooks, on August 15, 1988, Robbins wrote, "WE BEGIN! First day of rehearsals for 22 wks. Final press opening—<u>FEB. 26th.</u>" Then, in slightly smaller writing: "Here comes a trip." He demanded, and won, an unprecedentedly long rehearsal period for what was originally referred to as *Hit Dances,* which the Shubert Organization was producing at the Plymouth Theatre. There weren't many big dance shows on Broadway at the time, and almost every gypsy in New York wanted to get into this one. Robbins held auditions for months before rehearsals started, occasionally warranting intervention by Actors' Equity. The performers he liked were called back many times over the next few months for workshops in which they would learn some of the choreography, or for two-hour private auditions if they were being considered for an important role, such as Anita in *West Side Story.* A few, Robert La Fosse and Alexia Hess of the New York City Ballet, for instance, didn't have to wade through the whole process. Robbins probably knew early on that he wanted Charlotte d'Amboise (daughter of Jacques and his wife, Carolyn George; sister of Christopher) and Scott Wise, a seasoned Broadway performer. Meanwhile, Neel Keller was tracking down old scraps of films, videos, photographs—anything that would help in reconstructing some of the long-gone numbers.

When rehearsals finally began, the company took almost two floors—four or five studios—at 890 Broadway (the Lawrence A. Wien Center for

Dance and Theatre, owned by ABT and the Feld Ballet). Several rehearsals went on simultaneously, and Robbins had enough helpers to staff them: Grover Dale as assistant director and Victor Castelli, Cynthia Onrubia, and George Russell as assistants to the choreographer. He, of course, supervised them all. The schedule was grueling: an abbreviated ballet class or a warmup for the nondancers, a 10:30 rehearsal with an hour lunch break, followed by afternoon rehearsals that might last until 6:45. A ten-minute break could become five if Robbins grabbed a dancer by the arm and said, "Let me try something . . ." The cast worked a five-day week for the first months, with an occasional week off; later a week meant six days.

Despite frustrations, Robbins had a wonderful time recovering the best of his musical comedy past and tweaking it into shape. For one thing, the process reunited him with some colleagues he hadn't worked with in years. Young dancers who called him "Mr. Robbins" watched dumbfounded when Yuriko, coaching "The Small House of Uncle Thomas" from *The King and I,* would shoo him away with commands such as, "No, Jerry, that's not the way you do that. Wrong! You not dance. I dance lead part. Go, go!" Sondheim came. Bernstein came and wept when his music played. Jule Styne came. So did Betty Comden and Adolph Green, Oliver Smith, Nancy Walker and Cris Alexander from the cast of *On the Town,* Sondra Lee from *High Button Shoes* and *Peter Pan,* James Mitchell from *Billion Dollar Baby,* and many others. Kevin Joe Jonson, a dancer in *High Button,* turned out to have made detailed notes on the Mack Sennett chase scene. Neel Keller sensed that "to put these numbers back on, [Jerry] had to—in his mind in some way—be back at the moment in which the original idea for the number was born."

So when Betty and Adolph and Cris Alexander and Nancy Walker would come to work on *On the Town,* they would sit in the room and they would talk about the number but then the conversation would become about "When did we put this number in the show?" "Oh, right, it was when we were in Boston." And "Why did we need this number?" "Oh, because we felt we weren't following this character enough. And then there was the night when we were all having dinner at that deli, do you remember?" And they would all remember the name of the deli. . . . "And then someone said 'What if we sang this number over and over again—but it was different nightclubs?' " They would literally go back to the moment they had the idea. And then Jerry could restage the numbers because then it would all come to him again. Sort of from memory but more as though he was actively solving the same storytelling problem again. These weren't just numbers in this revue. They were suddenly numbers in *On the Town* and it was 1945.

Robbins had a fine time demonstrating various roles. At one rehearsal of the Mack Sennett ballet from *High Button Shoes,* when the cast was engaged in the tug-of-war for the missing handbag, it was Jerry, sneaking in from his directorial place at the front of the studio, who tiptoed gleefully away with it. Said one dancer, "He was the best Bathing Beauty. When he did it with us he was so good that we would just drop character and watch him in amazement. It was incredible, he was a hysterical Bathing Beauty, a great Cop, the most frightening Crook. He became every character."

Over the months, standout numbers from other shows came to life— from *Look Ma, I'm Dancin'!, A Funny Thing Happened on the Way to the Forum, Gypsy, Fiddler on the Roof.* Sometimes music had to be edited and new transitions concocted. The jinxed "Mr. Monotony," dropped from both *Miss Liberty* and *Call Me Madam,* was choreographed anew. So was the heroine's dream of herself as a movie queen from *Billion Dollar Baby* and the sleepwalking scene from *Look Ma* (neither of these made the final cut; during previews the show turned out to be three hours long). It was ironic that this celebration of Robbins's work in the theater concealed an important part of his achievement; his genius for contextualizing a show's musical numbers couldn't come into play here. Jason Alexander functioned as a "setter," telling the audience a little about the shows the numbers were drawn from, setting the scene, and introducing the characters. (Alexander, who collaborated with Robbins on the narration, also entered the action, taking on major roles like Tevye.)

Inevitably, performers who'd been in the original shows faulted the new versions. Steps had been changed, they complained; details had been lost; the dancers of 1989 could toss their legs higher but didn't have the individuality of those in the heyday of big musicals. Watching a preview at SUNY Purchase done in practice clothes with no set, Grover Dale thought the whole show would have been stunning performed just that way and told Robbins so. But Jerry wasn't just contractually committed to a full production; he wanted to bring to life a time when musicals had drawn people to the theater and sent them out into the street light in their hearts and on their feet, wishing they could sing and dance, or teary over Maria's loss or the vanished Anatevka.

This anthology covering his twenty years on Broadway accomplished that, even though there were no famous stars in it. John Simon missed "that pristine glow that musical comedy performers used to have." But most of the critics praised the young cast Robbins had assembled. And of course, Robbins: "No one has ever used dancing in the musical theater like this" (Clive Barnes). The prevailing tone of the reviews was that of delight—and more than a trace of nostalgia for the good old days. There were digs at current hyperproduced musicals, such as *Cats* and *Phantom of the Opera*. Frank Rich wrote in *The New York Times,* "Audiences inured to the hydraulic scenic gizmos, formless acrobatics, deafening amplification and emotional vacuity of this decade's Broadway spectaculars will find Mr. Robbins' musical theater a revelation."

The year 1990 was not the most salubrious for Robbins. While cycling through Central Park that spring with a young companion, he fell off his bike, hit his head on a curb, and lost consciousness. His friends think that the concussion gradually affected his equilibrium and general health more than anyone realized at the time. In April, he lost one of the people he loved most: Lady Nancy Keith (Slim, sometimes Pearl to him, or Old Smokey)—Slim, who had written in her posthumously published autobiography that he was one of the few people she would trust "to the ends of the earth." In October, Leonard Bernstein died, and Robbins wrote to the composer's children that "I felt as if a big piece of my life's construction had dropped away." Jerry's seven-year love affair with Brian Meehan was showing signs of strain, and in April 1989, Jesse Gerstein—no longer a lover but still a friend—had told Robbins that he had AIDS. A couple of weeks later, Jerry wrote that Jesse was "handling it well—so far—but ever so often he'll say a sentence that will break my heart."

Robbins had insisted that the gloriously ambitious Balanchine Celebration in the spring of 1989 include the master's *Danses Concertantes* and offered to supervise the revival but bowed out because of a change in the schedule. In April, pleading exhaustion, he took a leave of absence. During the summer Lincoln Kirstein announced his intention to resign, and Jerry sent him an urgent telegram: DEAREST LINCOLN, PLEASE DO NOT LEAVE. WE NEED YOU, AND IT IS IMPERATIVE YOU STAY WITH THE COMPANY FOR THE SAKE OF ALL YOU MADE AND BUILT AND ACHIEVED. PLEASE DON'T GO AWAY. THIS IS A PERSONAL MESSAGE SENT WITH ALL MY LOVE.

One wonders whether the passing of this last and vital connection to the company's history unnerved him more than he might have expected, because in the fall he, too, relinquished his position at the New York City Ballet, leaving Peter Martins the sole ballet master in chief. Kirstein's emeritus status kept him in contact with the company, however. His name now appeared after Balanchine's as a "founder," and Robbins was listed after Balanchine as a "founding choreographer." Never mind that the billing was convoluted; it satisfied Jerry, and after the Robbins festival, the following year, he was in love with the company all over again.

It had taken some persuading to get him to agree to a banquet of his ballets—to believe that a retrospective of his work could sustain a three-week season. But Martins, resigned to the fact that festivals were integral to the company's survival, was wily, and he knew Jerry. He burned considerable midnight oil making out a schedule that displayed all the major Robbins ballets in the repertory, taking into consideration that many of them were piano ballets and that the orchestra needed to play on every program. Also, there had to be a musical shape to the evening. He thought about potential conflicts in casting, by now pretty well able to predict whom Jerry would want to dance his ballets. Naturally, Robbins viewed the schedule he was handed with suspicion, sure that something wasn't going to work. But Martins knew his plan was foolproof: "If he moved one piece, the whole thing would fall apart, basically. . . . The bottom line is that he accepted the whole thing: the programs, the order, and the casting were exactly as I had predicted." In the years since Balanchine's death, Martins had worked his way to a black belt in Robbins management, although he and Jerry tussled over dancers that spring. ("You promised me to do a small work," wrote JR to PM, "employing only three I wasn't using. So far, you have called some 22 dancers, some of whom dance in 14 or more of my ballets. There is no way for this to work out.") They worked it out.

"A Festival of Jerome Robbins Ballets," which began on June 5, 1990, was costly and required special fund-raising; the theater had to be darkened for a week in order to rehearse all twenty-eight ballets onstage. American Ballet Theatre dancers performed an excerpt from *Les Noces,* and, for the final performance, six dancers from the Paris Opera Ballet* flew over to perform *In the Night.* That last evening, all the dancers—

* Isabelle Guérin, Jean Guizerix, Fanny Gaida, Manuel Legris, Elisabeth Platel, and Laurent Hilaire.

including Edward Villella, who (after much persuasion on Robbins's part) had returned to re-create his role in *Watermill*—plus Kirstein and Martins, paraded onstage with roses for the choreographer. He was thrilled. He told *The New Yorker* in July that he realized he couldn't quit this company "cold turkey."

⌒

In the fall, Jerry must have sent an uneasy and despondent letter to Mary Hunter, and she responded encouragingly: "Your own creativity and ability to start new projects from scratch is really only shifting gears. The fact that your concussion occurred about the same time could be expected to sharpen and deepen feelings of anxiety about everything from what next to will I really recover, to today I'm better but is it going to last? You will, and you are, emerging into a new phase not less, just different."

Perhaps she was referring to Slim Keith's death. She also perhaps imagined that finally staging *The Poppa Piece* would propel Robbins toward the music-theater-dance form that he had been struggling intermittently to define since the 1960s. If nothing else, getting out of his system and onto a stage material that had been fermenting for almost thirty years could only be salutary. He'd been through at least ten drafts of the autobiographical material, conferring over the years with friends such as Dan Stern and Slim Keith about his hang-ups with it. Now Gregory Mosher and the Lincoln Center Theater offered him an opportunity to rehearse and present the piece in a workshop situation, as he had with *The Race to Urga*. Jerry waded in.

While his mother had dominated his early life and continued to haunt him, his father had become the central figure in his autobiographical writings. That he had most of the time perceived his father as a cipher during his childhood had increased Lena's power over him yet made Harry the one he needed to understand. He had spent many hours researching his father's background and paternal feelings, and he had written about his childhood view of his parents. But *The Poppa Piece* was not really about Harry Rabinowitz; it was about Jerome Robbins/Gershin Rabinowitz and the monkey on his back he called Pop—the immigrant Jew with the accent, whose love he had craved and whom he had so passionately wanted not to be like.

All through the spring of 1991, he conferred with writer John Weidman, who was assisting him to shape his script, with Doug Wieselman,

495   *The Final Chapter*

who was writing music, and with Gerald Freedman—now a respected director himself—whom he had persuaded to serve as his assistant. The actors and dancers Robbins eventually assembled in the basement rehearsal room at Lincoln Center never understood what the shape of the piece would be, but they knew—or divined—that it wasn't about a fictitious character called Jacob Vitkowitz, aka Jay Whitby—played both by a little boy and a young man (Jace Alexander); it was about the man up there directing them. Two well-known actors, Ron Rifkin and Alan King, worked on the role of Poppa. Robbins conceived some of the scenes simply and fairly literally, just as he remembered them. In one bleak episode, the boy lies on the floor doing his homework; the father enters with his newspaper, turns on the radio, and sits down to read; the mother talks quietly on the telephone; the sister dances while the "Anniversary Waltz" plays softly; no one speaks. The mother hugs her daughter, and they exit together, while the boy sits up and watches them go. The grandmother walks in, the father leaves. Seated on a couch, the grandmother bends sideways and half lies down, keeping her feet planted, and the boy lying on the floor echoes her almost fetal position.

Judging from the many drafts of the script, from the memories of those involved, and from bits of poor-quality rehearsal video, other scenes are staged more fancifully. In the beginning, having spoken to the audience about how "all my life I've been dragging a dead body around," the grown-up "Jake" lugs a sheet-covered corpse off a table and tries to make it dance with him. Eventually this spectral Poppa gets into gear, spurred on by klezmer music, and unveils to reveal a big-nosed clown mask; now he's the one luring his son into dancing, he's the puppeteer. In the end, he claps the mask on his son and punctuates the last musical note with a spirited "Hey!"

Robbins found some magical ways to dig beneath his memories and, in the workshop, to transform them in a rudimentary setting, with lengths of fabric, accessories such as hats and yarmulkes, and smaller pieces of white cloth to stand for towels, prayer shawls, angel wings. He contrasted a scene in the Turkish baths his father frequented, and to which he had once dragged his reluctant son, with a WASP locker room scene full of jock revelry and subliminal homoeroticism (one could also posit a relationship to the gay bathhouses that had flourished in New York before AIDS). In the first jocular scene, a group of chatty old men joke with the cringing "boychik" that Poppa proudly introduces, pinching his cheeks, checking the size of his penis, singing and dancing around him. The steam emerges from a vat of soup with huge matzoh balls that the men fling about. In the complementary locker room scene, young athletes indulge in postgame horseplay—slapping one another with towels and raucously celebrating their victory. The boy Jake is carried into this scene in triumph. Small for his age (as Jerry was in high school), he's the team's mascot. He leads them in a cheer and doesn't seem to mind when they lay him on a bench and, spraddling it, jump along, their crotches inches above his face. A third very brief scene—a tableau almost—brings these two boyhood memories together. The old men in the bathhouse cry out and crumple to the floor, while, framed in a doorway, looking like golden gods, the athletes gaze past the bodies in what's now a gas chamber toward the boy, like a vision of a promised land both Gentile and gay. "[T]here is the faintest hint of something more than curiosity in their fascinated stares," Robbins wrote in his ninth revision (1985).

The image of non-Jewish faces looking into a Jewish world repeats itself in that scene from Robbins's childhood that he never forgot. The little boy is bicycling with his Gentile friends, the four of them (the others are played by adult dancers) trying to outdo one another—look, no hands; look, feet in the air—when Poppa calls the reluctant Jake in to study for his bar mitzvah. Here's the venerable Tzaddik correcting his weak and imperfect chanting; here are the other more accomplished kids who turn the lesson into an occasion for song and then into a rowdy game before running off. The bicycling boys crowd around to look in the window, mock the imperturbable teacher, even climb into the room, until Jake shouts at them to go and runs to get his mother.

The script contrasts the hero's humiliating bar mitzvah with the loving memory of all that his paternal grandfather taught him about Judaism. The narrator re-creates in words the shtetl of Rejanke and all that happened there that wonderful summer when the boy was six. With his head in his grandfather's lap, listening to the old man softly singing, Jake gets a Bible lesson. The grandfather silently conjures up scenes, and the Old Testament rolls by at a lickety-split pace, masterminded by three male angels who also serve as living scenery. Eve offers Adam the apple, a furious Moses holds up the tablets, Delilah shears Samson, the Red Sea (two pieces of fabric) parts for the faithful and swallows Pharaoh's army, and so on. Little Jake runs around looking at everything and gets a chance to be David and fell Goliath.

Jerry's paternal grandfather died before his bar mitzvah, and he's the one the boy cries for when his voice breaks on the chanting. Robbins directed and choreographed the bar mitzvah as a festive ordeal. While in the background, people in prayer shawls whirl and stamp, four men lift Jake, carry him to a table, manipulate him, and dress him. When he can't continue the chanting and yells out in rage, the others roll away like a receding tide, and he's left with his mother, who comforts him gently and asks if he wants to continue. He manages a dignified speech—"Dear Parents . . ."—but after all have shouted "mazel tov" and left, he tears off his ceremonial garb and kicks it.

As if to show that a choreographer does best starting with what he knows, Robbins reintroduces elements of previous events as his hero moves from dancing to dancemaking. The young adult Jake, rather clumsily doing his pliés in a ballet class, drifts away from the barre and begins to conduct a bicycle ballet. He lifts one leg in an arabesque; the four riders copy him as they wheel lazily around in circles and figure eights. He does a port de bras; they too lift a graceful arm. They manipulate their bikes. Gerald Freedman and dancer Elaine Wright both remember this sequence as "exquisite." By the end of the scene, Jake has orchestrated three jocks flicking their towels, three people holding prayer shawls, two cyclists, and four revelers moving with and on huge beach balls (this refers back to a planned scene about family weekends in Bradley Beach).

Robbins wrote scenes that he didn't attempt to stage: the time he looked through a keyhole, saw his parents having sex, and thought his father was killing his mother, or the time Santa Claus/Harry threatened to take away the toy train he'd just brought, or his parents' dream about their children's gilded future, or a polite mealtime scene backed by a video of the family flinging food and stabbing one another with cutlery. But to get to the end of the story, to reconcile himself to his father and to the Jewish heritage that he both loved and resented, to understand his career, he strongly felt he had to present his appearance before the House Committee on Un-American Activities and its aftermath.

He had struggled with these scenes in draft after draft. He had been able finally to peruse a transcript of the session and disliked his performance before HUAC intensely. But how to show that his capitulation had been prompted by the terror that "they" would take it all away from him—all that he had achieved—and that if they did so, he would somehow become like his father? In rationalizing his actions, would he inevitably be seeming to justify himself? Gerald Freedman says that although Robbins tried the trial scene in many different ways—several of them quite effective—he was never satisfied with it. "My own feeling was that he felt something about it wasn't the real truth. . . . Maybe he kept on trying to get into a different layer but he never did. So that section was always vague or it was skipped over or he tried different ways of doing it, and I thought, God, that this event should still be torturing him."

In 1992, when Jerry was wondering about tackling *The Poppa Piece* again, he wrote in a notebook about the hearing:

One of the keenest feelings is that I betrayed the Poppa—the Jewish Poppas to keep me from going down, & back to my being—no one, like <u>him</u>—that all I had gained, gotten, achieved, changed—would be wiped out: thus my work, which gave me my public identity was at stake. To sacrifice for it I had to betray the Poppas. . . . This rupture of all respect for myself & my denial of my father stuck with me—haunted me.

Poppa—Herschel Vitkowitz in the play—figures in all the versions of the trial scene. In some drafts, the questions and remarks by members of the committee and some of Jake's answers are very close to what had actually been said: he had joined the Communist Party as a way of protesting anti-Semitism, and so on. In another draft, the committee speaks as a threatening chorus. In one of the late drafts, Poppa is standing off to the side, as a kind of spokesman for both Jewish traditional views and Jake's conscience, urging his son not to name names and venting his own negative feelings about Jake in counterpoint to Jake's answers to the committee's questions. He wears a clown suit that he removes in the middle of the proceedings. Agonized, Jake cries, "You want to drag me back to where you are. They're gonna take it all away." And with his back to the wall, he points to his father and says to the committee, "Take him!" It's not hard to understand why he worried that this could come across as simple scapegoating, an easy out—whether the Poppa figure represented Robbins's father, the aspects of Jewishness he was rejecting, every creative hang-up that had plagued him, or simply his own terror.

So Jerry never staged the rest of his story—never got to the part where Jake and his father dance together and the dead body Jake's been dragging around is laid to rest once and for all. In his 1992 notes he wrote, "Maybe I can't—will never find a satisfying release from the guilt of it all."

When he wrote that, he had just finished living out another story: the long dying of Jesse Gerstein. With the help of Jesse's friends and, later, of three nurses, Jerry had taken charge of his former lover. Jesse moved back into the Eighty-first Street house, and while he was still fairly strong, they rented an apartment in Paris at 58 Boulevard Raspail; they both loved the city, and Robbins was staging *In the Night* for the Paris Opera Ballet. They went together to Japan, but Jesse got sick and had to return. In the spring of 1991, they still sometimes went to the theater together, and Robbins's appointment calendar for March 29 notes that they are to dine at the home of his good friends Louis and Anka Begley and attend their seder the next day. Part of the summer of 1991 was spent in Bridgehampton. Among Robbins's papers are instructions he wrote for whoever was looking after Jesse at the beach house when he had to go into the city. Pillows and throws, portable telephone, water or juice, medicines, his books, etc., must always be within arm's reach. "The sun moves fast outside & when he is on the lounge (in the R corner facing the ocean) the umbrella must be moved and tilted. . . . He should be checked periodically for what he wants and needs—& these change from hour to hour, sometimes from moment to moment."

As always, they celebrated Jesse's birthday (his thirty-fourth) with a lobster fest on the deck: Jerry; the Erteguns; another close friend, the architect D. D. Allen (who had designed an addition to the beach house); and Jesse's devoted friend Lisa Stevens, who commemorated the event in a little book she made for Jesse's mother, Cassandra, after his death. By the fall, Jesse needed around-the-clock care. The nurses' reports make almost unbearable reading. He died on October 14. In accordance with his wishes, his ashes were scattered on the beach. They had to pay a rabbi extra to say kaddish for one who'd been cremated.

The notice that Robbins sent to the *Times* included the names of his housekeeper and cook, who had endured the long months with him: "Jesse Gerstein, 34, photographer, died October 14, 1991. He brought happiness, delight, sensitivity, intelligence, gentleness, and most of all love into the hearts of all of us who lived with him. His life and his work were infused with an unerring sense of beauty and taste. We mourn him deeply. Jerry, Pam, Alicia, and all his friends and family."

⌒

Because Robbins's thoughts were often of death and debility, and because he had been working in a retrospective mode during the late 1980s and early 1990s, does not mean he slowed down or stopped pursuing a variety of projects. His calendars for the first half of the 1990s are filled. He dined at friends' houses, he attended parties and gave them. He took in numerous plays, films, concerts, dance events, galleries, and museums. He did not think of himself as too old to pick up a new language, and, frustrating as he found it, he tried to learn a little Russian when the Kirov Ballet was to mount *In the Night* in 1992. He took the time to praise Massachusetts Congressman Barney Frank for revealing his homosexuality ("What a fine brave and noble thing you have done. . . . You have cleared the air not just for yourself; your response will go deeply into the consciousness of all concerned and will be deeply honored") and joined his name to those of Gloria Steinem and Mathilde Krim on the invitations to a New York fund-raising salute to Frank. He chastised New York's mayor, Ed Koch, in 1988 for his proposal to cut the city's budget for culture and the arts. He joined the scrimmage when a conservative uproar over Andrés Serrano's *Piss Christ* and Robert Mapplethorpe's homoerotic photographs threatened the National Endowment for the Arts' budget and prompted Senator Jesse Helms to propose an amendment to an Interior Department bill that would ban arts subsidies that "promote, disseminate, or produce obscene or indecent materials." In 1989 and 1990, he sent a blitz of letters to senators and congressmen and telegraphed President George H. W. Bush.

In the spring of 1990, Gregory Mosher got Robbins fired up again about *The Bacchae* as a possible Lincoln Center Theater production.* Jerry dug into Euripides and got as far as inviting selected actors for a reading and wondering about Diamanda Galas as composer-singer. He now perceived a connection between the Greek tragedy and *The Poppa Piece:* "In Bacchae it's rage & power—In Poppa it's rage & need to understand—come to some peace & digestion of what happened. I think that's one of the main pulls to Bacchae—the unappreciated son, (the son of a God!) gets revenge." Robbins renewed his interest in Richard Strauss's opera *Salome,* which had been floating around in his mind and his notebooks since the 1970s—a version that would double-cast each role with a singer and a dancer—and approached several opera houses (the Théâtre du Châtelet in Paris was a possibility for 1992).

---

* Oddly, Robbins never told Mosher he had been thinking about how to do *The Bacchae* back in the 1960s, acting as if it were all new to him—and maybe, in a sense, it was. Mosher gave him a copy, and Jerry told him he hadn't been able to sleep—had been up all night reading it. How had he liked it? Oh, he'd only gotten through the first act. Mosher was amazed and impressed.

He labored fairly intensively with John Guare between 1992 and 1994 on the "Berlin Project," a music-theater work linking Irving Berlin's songs with a scenario (one possibility focused on the composer and his immigrant beginnings). He vigorously, and sometimes vituperatively (according to producer Craig Zadan), pursued the idea of codirecting, with Emile Ardolino, the television movie of *Gypsy* starring Bette Midler that aired on CBS in 1993. It was clear to Zadan that Robbins was still brooding over having been fired from the *West Side Story* film: "It was not that he had a passion to direct the movie of *Gypsy;* it was all about showing Hollywood that he could do it."

He monitored his shows, traveling to Japan in 1991, when *Jerome Robbins' Broadway* played Tokyo (where he could seize the opportunity to see more Noh and Kabuki plays). He wrote to Theodore Bikel, who was playing Tevye in the current touring production of *Fiddler on the Roof.* Sheldon Harnick and Joseph Stein had caught the show in Boston and been delighted by the production. However, the sung portions of Tevye's monologues that had been cut in Las Vegas (where, evidently, short audience attention span mandated a maximum length for shows) had not been restored. Robbins's complimentary letter to Bikel included a firm request to reinstate the material: "It means a lot to those of us who did the work originally."

In 1993, the Alvin Ailey American Dance Theater learned *New York Export: Opus Jazz*—a frustrating experience on all sides. (The dancers, unused to a finger snap, a point, and a "You!" to get their attention, interpreted his behavior as disrespect—with perhaps a hint of racism—and gave him little respect in turn.) And of course, even after leaving his position as NYCB's co–ballet master in chief, Robbins continued to rehearse his works, once his ballet masters had them in decent shape. An in-house video of his coaching captured a nice moment in an *Interplay* rehearsal. The man leading one section of the ballet goes up to some of the other dancers, using a demi-plié as a perky greeting; they respond by imitating him. Jerry doesn't like the way one of the women does this; she's too used to the plié to make it look like a discovery. Taking the guy's place, Robbins tells her to do what he does. Instead of bending his knees, he shrugs his shoulders; caught off guard, she giggles but manages to copy him. Aha, that's the timing and quality he wants! (And don't forget it.)

He also responded generously to "his" dancers when they were troubled. When Maria Calegari was sufficiently upset with the way things were going for her in the company to think about leaving and taking up teaching, he wrote a concerned and furiously loving letter that told her to "do your work. You owe it to yourself—and to your public[—]& to let anyone get in your way is a mistake. . . . To hell with them. Dance. They are small. You are great." Stephanie Saland had very much wanted to dance Suzanne Farrell's part in *In Memory of* . . . ever since Farrell had retired. The summer before the 1990 Robbins Festival, Kyra Nichols was given the role. Saland wrote Robbins of her great disappointment and got a hand-delivered letter that she was afraid to open. Instead of a scolding, she got these words: "You are an extremely fine and rare dancer. And you have a striking & deeply authoritative presence. At times it is also coupled with dark and dramatic undercurrents. All of this makes you fascinating to watch. It is very womanly and voluptuous. But it's exactly all those qualities which I saw get in the way of the direct and simple fragility of the girl in 'In Memory of.' " He hadn't called her to rehearsals because, at this point, he wouldn't be around to guide her. He ended with "You are special, and I love you and your dancing—if you want to go after that role again—wonderful."

He traveled frequently to Paris, where his ballets had always been loved. When the NYCB had performed there in the 1970s, bringing with it a repertory that included Balanchine's masterworks from the Stravinsky Festival, it was *Dances at a Gathering* that had received the most rapturous response. Barbara Horgan remembers being at dinner with Balanchine and Paris Opera bigwigs; they told him, " 'Oh, you've had such a successful season,' and he said, 'I didn't; Jerry did.' " By 1986, when Robbins, with the help of Victor Castelli, was staging *In Memory of* . . . for the Paris Opera Ballet (by which time Rudolf Nureyev was its artistic director), the company had already presented *Circus Polka, Scherzo Fantastique, Afternoon of a Faun,* and *In G Major* (titled *En Sol*). Jerry was taken with the Palais Garnier's opulence and the aroma of history that clung to it, with the dancers' elegance, sophistication, and sense of drama. Sylvie Guillem in Suzanne Farrell's role in *In Memory of* . . . was "a dream"; he loved her dancing and was astonished to find himself "emotionally grabbed" by her.

But he chafed at the strict hierarchies. The POB was not like the NYCB, where a member of the corps de ballet might step into a leading role at one performance and a principal dance it the next, or a gifted young soloist partner an established ballerina. Nor were the dancers at first accustomed to the intense rehearsals that Robbins and his assistants took for granted. In this hallowed, state-run bureaucracy, yelling and screaming were sometimes necessary to get what the choreographer wanted in terms of casting, lighting, costumes, and rehearsal time onstage. After one lighting rehearsal that Robbins termed "hair-raising," he noted, "But I do my fuse explode act—," which was, apparently, all it took. Nevertheless, he and his ballets were cherished, the company gave him carte blanche, and the Paris Opera became a second home for his works. *In the Night* entered the repertory in 1989; *Dances at a Gathering* and *Glass Pieces* came in 1991. The company had expected to get *Dances at a Gathering* in 1989, but after auditioning (unheard of!) and rehearsing for several weeks, Robbins felt the dancers weren't ready for it (Castelli, charged with informing the management of the switch to *In the Night,* says he was glad he didn't understand French). Over the decade, the company, under Patrick Dupond's direction, also acquired *Moves, Four Seasons,* and *A Suite of Dances* and revived *The Concert* and *En Sol.* When the New York City Ballet gave a two-week season at the Théâtre du Châtelet in 1995, including two different all-Robbins programs, the Opera's Jean Guizerix took on Villella's role in *Watermill* and felt that the experience had deeply affected his life.

⌒

Three of Robbins's last four ballets are set to the music of Johann Sebastian Bach. *A Suite of Dances* used the composer's Suite for Solo Cello; *2 & 3 Part Inventions,* his piano studies; and *Brandenburg* was danced to Brandenburg Concerto no. 3 plus excerpts from nos. 2, 1, and 6. The return to Bach's sunny clarity so many years after *The Goldberg Variations* may have inspired him to travel further along that pleasant path, just as *Dances at a Gathering* had led him deeper into Chopin's world.

A Suite of Dances, a solo choreographed for Mikhail Baryshnikov, premiered in 1994. Baryshnikov, by then directing his own White Oak Dance Project, remembers that he'd said to Robbins, " 'Listen, at some point, if you need a body to work with just give me a call.' And he called me and said 'I have an idea for a little dance.' " The two of them worked on and off for more than a year. At some point, Robbins seems to have thought about a duet for Baryshnikov and another man; there is some 1992 footage of him working out movements with Peter Boal and Victor Castelli; he was stiff but still spry enough to indicate steps and flourish his arms. However, in the finished ballet, Baryshnikov's only partner is the musician seated onstage to play Bach's Suite for Solo Cello. That the latter is a woman

(Wendy Sutter) gives their transactions a slightly flirtatious edge. When the lights come up, he's sitting at her feet. As Baryshnikov says, the atmosphere is "a bit of a casual setup . . . friends are playing around; it's sort of 'Okay; what've you been practicing?' . . . 'How about this one?' 'Let's start.' That kind of approach."

Baryshnikov was in his forties when the ballet was made and had undergone several knee operations. Although some of the choreography is very difficult, it was constructed to highlight his artistry in terms more of nuanced performing than of bravura skills. As in the opening solo of *Dances at a Gathering,* the man begins almost tentatively, marking the steps, remembering them. His manner is easy whether he's skimming the stage with small jumps and beats, looking as if he's lost his feet for a moment, or recalling his way into a folk-dance step. In the last of four sections, he repeatedly strides toward and away from the audience, adding different steps as if this were a game—now cocky, now bewildered, now matter-of-fact. And, intermittently, he and the cellist acknowledge each other. You can imagine them dining together afterward. Two months after White Oak premiered *A Suite of Dances* on March 3, 1994, it entered the New York City Ballet's repertory, where it has been performed by Damian Woetzel and Nikolaj Hübbe. And three months later Robbins had another Bach ballet to show.

Choreographers face a problem that no composer, painter, or sculptor has to cope with. As they age, their materials get younger, bred in a different cultural climate. The Jerry who could collapse in a laughing heap with Todd Bolender, Frank Moncion, and Tanny Le Clercq after a hard rehearsal was now working with dancers who could be his grandchildren. This was particularly true when he began making his *2 & 3 Part Inventions* on the graduating class of students at the School of American Ballet, rather than on the company. He had elected to do this because in the spring of 1994 it was the only way he could get the rehearsal time he needed. If all went well, the ballet would be performed at the SAB's annual workshop in June.

After watching many classes, he taught some young dancers excerpts from the "Spring" section of *Four Seasons* before settling on a cast: Kristina Fernandez, Benjamin Millepied, Eliane Munier, Amaury Lebrun, Riolama Lorenzo, Alex Ketley, Jennifer Chipman, and Seth Belliston, most of them sixteen or seventeen years old. Quite a few of these kids didn't even know who Robbins was, much less his reputation as a Tartar. Fernandez, who'd noticed him smiling in the front row of some previous school show-ing, felt it a natural thing to go up to this nice-looking old guy before re-hearsals and chat. (Robbins loved that almost as much as he loved the uncomplicated freshness of her dancing—what critic Rick Whitaker called her "early-in-the-morning sense of herself.") He was fairly patient with his cast, although hardly easy on them. After he made Munier cry over her solo, someone from the school must have reminded him that these weren't hardened professionals. Thereafter, says Fernandez, when frustrated, he'd lower his gaze, stamp his feet a little, maybe go watch a next-door class for five minutes, and return ready to work. (Also, after the ballet had been staged, he sent Munier a note thanking her "for being so patient with me.")

Like *Interplay, 2 & 3 Part Inventions* features four men and four women, and its tone is similarly fresh and clear—that of the "American outdoor party" to which Edwin Denby had likened the 1945 ballet. But Bach's in-tricacy made limpid prompted a style and atmosphere very different from those engendered by the pushy vigor of Morton Gould's music for *Inter-play.* The games are not so obvious. The dancers are not brash young ath-letes challenging one another; they emerge like fine racehorses in training, their bloodlines showing in an elegance that's beguilingly undercut by a trace of coltishness. The women wear pointe shoes, but while the work ac-knowledges ballet's traditional gender roles, it doesn't emphasize them; the females are as adventurous within the musical patterns as the males. *Interplay* asks adult ballet dancers to behave like kids; the new piece shows these kids as the professionals they are.

The training pieces Bach wrote for one of his young sons are rich in their simplicity. Robbins's choreography of *2 & 3 Part Inventions* is also a primer in counterpoint. Two couples dance two different pas de deux si-multaneously. Two men partner one woman with an "After you, Alphonse" courtesy, rather the way Prince Siegfried and his friend Benno took turns handling Odette in Ivanov's original *Swan Lake* choreography. The many different kinds of canons emphasize the group's solidarity with their inevitable follow-the-leader effect. Four men indulge in a familiar Robbins you-go-up-I-go-down pastime. The ballet seems full of air; its steps may become strenuous, but the texture never feels dense or the atmo-sphere anything but unstrained, sweet-natured, playful. Two women pick their way across the stage on pointe, as if the spaces between Bach's notes were stepping-stones.

Robbins asked the dancers to make the movements they'd struggled over the years to master look simple and easy, and to dance with, to, and for one another. Millepied came into the studio bursting with sixteen-year-old energy, "and Jerry was trying to teach us how to dance—that it wasn't always about giving it everything you had, but like maybe giving only seventy percent of it and showing the audience that you had another thirty percent." Says Fernandez, "One of the things I really loved about the experience of *2 & 3 Part Inventions* was that I felt I could just *dance*. I don't remember him ever giving me a technical correction; he just allowed me to dance and enjoy myself . . . and that was so much fun."

2 & 3 Part Inventions entered the repertory of the New York City Ballet six months later, where—with Ethan Stiefel, Christopher Wheeldon, and Wendy Whelan in the cast—it looked no less charming but bolder in space and a little less fresh—a summer garden party rather than a spring outing.

Lincoln Kirstein, who even in "retirement" was alert to ways to add the right sort of contrast to the repertory, wrote Robbins one of his flattering letters in April 1994, hoping that the choreographer was "giving earnest consideration to the marvelous idea of doing *WSS* as a choral ballet. Not only would it be a terrific boost for the company which needs a new *Sleeping Beauty,* but it would put us in a more stable condition, for continuity. There are no older classics that make sense. The Royals have *Romeo and Juliet.* If we had *WSS,* I would not feel so desperately worried about our repertory and the ageing of our audience."

It's not clear what Kirstein meant by "a choral ballet." What he (and Martins, who shared his enthusiasm) got in *West Side Story Suite* was a reworking of the *Reader's Digest* version of the musical that had closed the first act of *Jerome Robbins' Broadway,* with a spoken introduction and bows between numbers to emphasize the suite form. A singer provided a voice for Tony (Robert La Fosse), and Nancy Ticotin (of Broadway and Ballet Hispánico) and Natalie Toro were imported to play Anita and Rosalia in "America." Jock Soto was a splendidly moody Bernardo and, to everyone's delight, the Danish Nikolaj Hübbe as Riff could sing "Cool" himself. Later, Heléne Alexopoulos and Jenifer Ringer, too, turned out to have voices and could take on Anita.

Robbins put the dancers through the expected rigors of inventing characters and family histories for themselves. Some, predictably, embraced this; others resisted it. But he got the necessary toughness, the street smarts, and the pent-up hostility out of them. Years before, he had told Balanchine he was thinking of doing a condensed version of *West Side Story* for American Ballet Theatre, "and without a moment's pause, Balanchine said, 'Oh, that's okay, <u>our</u> boys can't fight.' " For Jerry, they fought. Kirstein felt the finale was "irresolute" but wrote Robbins that "Nevertheless [*West Side Story Suite*] was a magnificent spectacle for which I am grateful."

It is especially hard for dancers to accept infirmities. Robbins, like Balanchine in his last years, was feeling more and more like an alien in his body. There were the hearing aids (plural because he kept losing them), the cataract operations. His equilibrium was iffy, and he had an especially bad fall in 1996 (the dogs, Annie and Tess,* tended to take him for a walk rather than vice versa). He had an elevator installed in his town house. Starting in 1994, he was seeing two or three doctors almost every week: the cardiologist, the neurologist, and others, plus a physical therapist. After a series of minor strokes, he had a heart valve replaced in December 1995 and was put on the blood thinner Coumadin, which necessitated having a blood test every week. He thanked a friend who'd written him a note in the hospital: "The operation wasn't so hot but what can you expect when they stop your heart?"

It was time for Jerry to say a few good-byes and make sure his affairs were in order. He flew down to Palm Beach, Florida, to spend Thanksgiving Day 1994 with Viola Balash, the second cousin he'd been so close to as a boy. In the tradition of the Rips and Rabinowitz clans, he had always helped out family members with gifts and loans, guaranteed other loans for them, and had his financial advisers assist them with their affairs. He had supported his father and mother since the 1940s; later he took responsibility for Harry's second wife, Frieda, too. He assisted Sonia and George Cullinen when, for example, in 1987, Les Clochettes, the progressive nursery school they had opened in Bayside, New York, in 1949, ran into financial difficulties. He helped their son, his nephew Robbin Cullinen, with restaurant ventures, and, for the last four years of his life, paid his great-nephew Matthew's tuition at Ethical Culture. Often, in making gifts of money, he would say to the family beneficiary something to the effect of "You may as well have this now" or "Better you have this now than later," as if he intended to deduct the sum from what he planned to leave them, but there's no evidence he did that.

He had, of course, drafted a will—or wills—years earlier. He must

---

* Tess, a sweet mutt, had been found on the steps of the Metropolitan Museum.

have had fun planning the last one he drew up in 1995. It forgave all debts to him and doled out carefully chosen personal bequests that may have come as a surprise to some: quite a few close friends, ex-lovers, and colleagues whom he felt to be in need, such as Anna Sokolow and Mary Hunter, received sums of $50,000 and up. Robert Fizdale stood to inherit $100,000. Robbins's ballet masters and household and office staff were also generously honored. He left money to the children of certain friends and articles he valued to people who had meant the most to him. To Mica Ertegun, he willed the ravishing Korean screens that hung on the wall above the banquette sofas she had designed to run the length of one side and around a corner of his living room. Kitty Hawks (the daughter of Slim Keith and her first husband, Howard Hawks, whom Jerry had loved since she was a little girl) got the naïf nineteenth-century painting by Martinet of a little boy holding a marionette and a rosebud that had hung on the wall of his ground-floor office. Those on a long list of friends were invited to visit his home after his death and choose one of the many tchotchkes he had collected on his travels. And there were more complicated bequests related to the income from his estate, the setting up of his trust and an advisory board to handle the licensing of his ballets, and the allocation of funds and the distribution of his papers to the New York Public Library.

Robbins worked on and off for two years choreographing his last ballet, *Brandenburg,* becoming increasingly tottery during the process. On November 10, he sent a fax to Andy De Groat, Robert Wilson's former partner, who had been running a company in France for some years:

> I can't show them what I want them to do so they all move around with stiff-legged movements imitating me and not my intentions. The pas de deux is fine. It is Wendy Whelan and Peter Boal and they work beautifully. I don't know how much longer I'll be going on. I've got another pas de deux already done, and I'm going to work on a dance for four couples and see if I can do that. It's such very hard work for me now. If I stay on my feet, my hips do not lock; it's when I sit down that I get stiff all over. The kids realize I'm not my old self and are trying to be helpful. They are a lovely bunch. I don't know how they remember all the changes I make all the time.

The dancers noticed that after his operation, he seemed to have slid downhill a little; his memory began to be shaky. Cast member Emily

Coates says that "in those rehearsals it was amazing. When he was watching dance, he'd be completely focused, he'd see everything. It's like his world, his reality had reduced around him, but what was real was the dance. And so all his perceptions, all his mental capacities were still going strong for that. . . . But then as soon as the rehearsal ended he would totter off." Everyone in the building knew when he'd left the floor because, rather than negotiate a flight of stairs, he'd go out the fire door, setting off the alarm.

It never failed to surprise Robbins that some of his finest inventions were those that came to him quickly and easily, and he might have been even more startled to learn that dancers who sweated through many versions of a swatch of choreography often felt that the first version was the best. Given his usual worries over how to deploy large ensembles without losing a vision of community, *Brandenburg* was a comparative breeze. Jean-Pierre Frohlich thinks that the movement for the ensemble was the best Jerry ever made. "He moved the corps de ballet like I've never seen him move a group of dancers. And he did that very quickly. It could have been because he wasn't demonstrating as much at the time and he was just telling people 'Go here, go here, go here, and do this here. And, okay, for eight counts do this and you guys go over here and would you—' It was amazing that it went so fast."

Unlike *The Goldberg Variations,* which had taken its tone from the fiendish intricacy and rigorous structure of the piano music, *Brandenburg* creates the ambiance of a long afternoon game that winds among the hedges, flower beds, and shadowed arbors of a grand park. During the first section, set to the third concerto, dancers rush with dazzling rapidity through crisscrossing patterns, circles, zigzags, London Bridges; the whole stage seems to fold and unfold like images in a kaleidoscope held by a playful hand. Peter Boal and Wendy Whelan led this first section and came together in their pas de deux. Probably the most memorable of the other duets—some very brief—was the mysterious one made for Nikolaj Hübbe and Lourdes Lopez, in which for much of the time their hands hover six inches apart, the space between them as charged as a grip or an embrace.

Brandenburg is not a flawless ballet, but it's full of beauties. Robbins may, consciously or unconsciously, have been casting his eyes back. Barbara Newman wrote in London's *Dancing Times* that Robbins, "weaving his cast through Bach's delicate intricacies with unerring skill . . . slips echoes of other dances into this one like reminders. I spotted *Dances at a Gathering, The Goldberg Variations, Glass Pieces, Fanfare, Interplay,* and *Dumbarton Oaks* as they flashed by." The following praise, coming as it did from Louis Begley, who was not only a friend but a writer Jerry very much admired, must have pleased him greatly: "You are an extraordinary being. When I look at your work, I really think that there isn't a single element of human behavior—motion—that you have not observed, analyzed and re-membered."

Jerry was mellower. Costume designer Holly Hynes had talked to other designers who swore they'd never work for him again, but although he gave her many directives, such as "green with a little bit of yellow and not too close to blue" and caused seemingly endless re-dyeing jobs, she earned his respect. Although there were still dancers who asked not to be cast in his ballets, many understood that if they could just try to let his intensity and occasional harsh words roll over them, they could learn a great deal (it takes a brave sense of humor if you're one of the skinniest young women in the company and he tells you to "get your fat ass off the stage"). "The way he pushed us to think in his ballets," says Peter Hanson, "to take note of where's your emphasis or what's the point of these steps or where are you taking that, you come off as a better dancer. You look like a better dancer. But it's not just like paying attention to details like how turned out you are or showing off how far you can stretch; it's about making sense of all these steps, [taking] the vocabulary you have to speak and making it interest-ing." Learning what Robbins had to offer meant being involved in every moment of the choreography even if you were in the ensemble. He did not appreciate people who telegraphed the attitude that Emily Coates de-scribes as "I want to wear my tiara tonight and that's it or else I'm not in-terested. . . . You have to imagine a world around you. And that's what I remember so much about doing his ballets, is that it left room for that imagined world, it required that imagined world."

Hanson and some of his friends—half in fun, half realizing that this somehow lovable old curmudgeon who was also a genius would soon no longer be with them—hid a little tape recorder near him during stage re-hearsals. They didn't capture anything immortal, just typical Robbins carping into a mike: "All the girls, please give into this a lot more, just give into it a lot more. Dance it happily. It's a little happy song. That's all it is." Or "Hey, boys, watch your lines, please, otherwise we're going to be here all day." Once, addressing the rehearsal pianist playing the *Brandenburg,* he says, "If you could take it a little sniveling bit faster, it would help a lot. Okay?" and you can hear faint, amused little dancer voices repeating to one another, "*Sniveling?*" "Sniveling *bit?*" Hanson mixed Jerry's comments into the disco at a party the dancers threw for themselves. Robbins came, which impressed everyone, and looked happy all evening. Given his hearing, he probably didn't pick up his own voice issuing orders through the music; the dancers loved the whole idea.

Lincoln Kirstein died on January 5, 1996. That year Robbins began to husband his energy, cutting down on his activities, maybe not descending on his office staff until noon. He often fell asleep in the middle of things or had lapses of memory. But he marshaled himself to restage *Les Noces* for NYCB, celebrating his fiftieth year with the company. It was lucky George Balanchine wasn't around, given that he had considered *Noces* and *Sacre* to be two Stravinsky scores that no one should choreograph. "Mr. B said that Jerry's hell would be having to sit there watching *Les Noces* over and over and over and over," remembers Bart Cook. Rehearsals began in March 1998. James Moore, who had restaged the ballet for American Ballet Theatre, the Royal Swedish Ballet, and the Finnish National Ballet, taught the piece to the company. Moore says that Jerry did more than just coach: he excised some movement from the finale and brought separate contrapuntal groups together into unison. He was going to get it right. The ballet premiered on May 20, with Alexandra Ansanelli as the Bride and Robert Wersinger as the Groom.

Various of the company dancers came to see Jerry before they left for the company's summer season in Saratoga, realizing that he mightn't live out the summer. Fernandez, Coates, and Millepied went to his house with Deborah Koolish (ex–company dancer, now Peter Martins's assistant). He had invited them but didn't recognize them at first. Then he wanted to know how they had gotten there. He seemed to think he lived on Eighth Street. "But he was very sweet and endearing." They ordered Chinese food and sat with him afterward in his living room talking quietly, while he leaned back on the long couch and fell asleep with Koolish stroking his forehead. They kissed him good-bye without waking him, alerted the nurse, and left.

In July, he had a massive stroke. At the New York City Ballet Memorial in November, Daniel Stern movingly described his family's long friendship with Robbins and told the audience in the New York State Theater about Jerry's last hours—how Stern's wife, Nadia, who had the responsibility for carrying out Robbins's living will, had persuaded the hospital to release him (that both Sterns were doctors made it easy). Jerry had wanted to die at home. He was in a coma, but there was a second when his eyes opened. Maybe he heard the Bach music they had put on, maybe he saw the circle of friends holding hands, holding his hands, and Tess on the bed. It was July 29, 1998.

Family and friends scattered his ashes on the beach behind his Bridgehampton house on Dune Road. There were several memorial tributes. Broadway paid its respects with warm reminiscences, jokes, film clips, and montages of photographs in a show organized by his old friend Donald Saddler. The Paris Opera honored its cherished guest with a gala program of four of his ballets: *In the Night, Other Dances, A Suite of Dances,* and *The Concert,* and the thrilling spectacle of a *grand défilé,* with the school's students leading on the entire immense company in order of rank. The New York City Ballet's ceremony was more modest, with heartfelt speeches and film clips of Robbins talking about his career. It closed with *Dances at a Gathering,* and at the end, the performers were joined by what seemed like legions of company dancers—all appropriately costumed—strolling alone or in small groups, arm in arm, hand in hand. It was Jerome Robbins's favorite sight in all the world: dancers gathering together, walking in beauty across a stage—his ideal kingdom.

Afterword

Martha Swope.

Five years before his death, Jerry received a letter from Gerald Freedman, saying how much his "respect and continued collaboration" had meant to Freedman over the years: "And you've been such a wonderful mentor in demonstrating your commitment to the work, your resistance to compromise, your ruthless examination of your own work and your continuous and restless search for the truth. The right gesture—the absolute essence."

It was that search that defined Robbins's career and his work. In the process of searching, he remade the American musical, going beyond what George Balanchine and Agnes de Mille had already achieved. In such shows as *West Side Story, Gypsy,* and *Fiddler on the Roof,* he not only integrated dancing into the plot, he made it subservient to a larger choreographic picture of humanity. The kiddie vaudeville acts he concocted for *Gypsy* had to be dreadful, because the real choreographer for them was Mama Rose. In *Fiddler on the Roof,* everybody in the cast danced when celebration was in order, "dancers" or not, and they all had names; but he knew better than to contrive, for example, a sad dance of farewell to Anatevka.

In the course of trying to find his way in classical ballet, Robbins enlarged and invigorated the art form, not just by popularizing it or making it enjoyable but by training on it a completely American imagination and, in so doing, contributing to its survival. He considered his talent inferior to Balanchine's, as do many others. In the end, that doesn't really matter. At the time of his death, Robbins was considered the greatest American-born choreographer working in ballet. And no one had achieved an equal degree of success and artistry in both ballet and American musical theater.

Some artists—whether their field is music, theater, dance, or the visual arts—focus almost unhesitatingly on what art means for them, and out of that create a style, modifying it according to changing times or their own changing views. Martha Graham was such an artist in dance. So are some of later generations: Merce Cunningham, Trisha Brown, and Twyla Tharp, for instance. This is not to deny that Robbins had a style; he did. But he approached each project as if to discover a new world that he could be part of, one that had the potential to educate and transform him.

If "community" became an icon for him and a defining feature of his work, it may be because he never felt unequivocally part of one. From an early age, he was faced with a dichotomy that dogged many of the offspring of immigrant Jews. His parents, admonishing him not to be a "greenhorn," to "fit in" in order to succeed in a culture dominated by Gentiles, deprived him of Jewish tradition in its full richness. But neither could he, as a young man, feel fully a part of that other culture. American ideology might champion cultural diversity, but American society didn't always embrace it. Too, even in America, a Jew coming of age during

World War II and the years immediately preceding it had reason to feel vulnerable.

Some people believe with the *New Yorker* critic Joan Acocella that "as good as [Robbins's ballets] got, they were never as good as his Broadway work, the thing he walked away from." She posited a conflict within Robbins: "Had he left his real home only to spend the rest of his life banging on the gates of someone else's property?" I think a conflict existed, but a different one. Robbins very much enjoyed working on Broadway and continued to consider offers to do so even after he returned to work with the New York City Ballet, although he saw ballet as something finer. What he struggled with was controlling the degree to which his theatrical know-how could influence his ballet choreography. *Fancy Free,* made when he was young and as cocksure as he'd ever be, is a perfect blend of dance invention and the subtle use of showbiz savvy, but the more he knew and the more he wanted to embrace the delicious ambiguity that dance permits, the harder the task he set himself. You often see in a ballet of his a moment when his talent for creating an "effect" took over (usually to the delight of his audience), but there was always the Jerry who would storm backstage and, say, tear Peter Martins to shreds because he'd done a double pirouette instead of a single in *In G Major.* He worked hard to make each project into a perfect whole; sometimes in his ballets that labor shows—for better or for worse—and may even have something to do with the humanity they exude.

Out of that struggle to find himself, he created art that made an enormous contribution to theater and dance almost worldwide. In the course of it, sadly, he left many associates angry and wounded, cursing him even as they called him a genius. But he was also a remarkable friend and a stimulating one. What Brian Meehan says about traveling with Robbins could also be applied to his work: "It was wonderful to see the world with him. The world was a more exciting place with Jerry in it."

Notes

JR = Jerome Robbins; JRP = The Jerome Robbins Papers. I have used JRP to designate the archive of papers Robbins bequeathed to the New York Public Library. This includes private correspondence, journals, and similar papers, in addition to materials pertaining to Robbins's professional life. The archive is housed in the Jerome Robbins Dance Division, at the New York Public Library for the Performing Arts Dorothy and Lewis B. Cullman Center in Lincoln Center, New York (NYPL), where additional material about Robbins's career, including videotapes and his scrapbooks of press clippings, may also be found. Publication details for books cited can be found in the bibliography.

1. A Boy of Many Talents

Note: Information about the Rabinowitz family in New York was obtained from the Department of Commerce, Bureau of the Census (Fourteenth Census: 1920—Population). Information on JR's family history and genealogy comes primarily from informal lists compiled for JR by his cousin Jean Handy (JRP), and almost all the material on Robbins's father, Harry Rabinowitz, and on Robbins's childhood comes from JR's research for a possible autobiography and for his unproduced music-theater work *The Poppa Piece*.

PAGE

1 "I stand before a mirror": JR, "My Selves," essay in hand-decorated folder, 1935, JRC.

2 "By saying Art": Ibid.

2 "I do think he'd stop": JR, Journal No. 4, December 11, 1972, JRC.

2 "They didn't really know": Sonia Robbins, interview with the author, May 23, 1999.

3 there were Passover riots: Iwo Cyprian Pogonowski, *Jews in Poland: A Documentary History,* 304.

3 Information about the Comfort Corset Company is scanty and confusing. Ben Goldenberg is listed at the business in R. H. Polk & Co.'s 1922–1923 Directory for Jersey City, but his position is not stated. The Certificate of Incorporation dated May

22, 1931, lists the principals as Edward Herrmann, Mary E. O'Brien, and Elsie J. Huck (Division of Revenue, Department of the Treasury, State of New Jersey). The 1934 New Jersey State Industrial Directory lists Harry Rabinowitz as Comfort Corset's president, purchasing agent, and plant manager and Lena Rabinowitz as its secretary. The directories are located in the New Jersey Room of the Jersey City Public Library.

3   farther north in Weehawken: The addresses Sonia sent to her brother on September 30, 1984, were: 108 Boerum Avenue, Jersey City, and, in Weehawken, Carroll Place, 60 Highwood Terrace, 157 Edgar Place, 63 Hudson Place, and in two different apartments at 17 Fifty-first Street. After leaving Manhattan, the family first stayed with Lena's mother, Ida Rips, who had a small grocery store on Franklin Avenue. JRP.

3   "stylish stouts": Comfort Corset sign that once hung in Robbins's office, now owned by Sonia Robbins Cullinen.

4   According to the program: Schlussfeier des Kindergartens der Hudson City Academy von Jersey City (last-day-of-school program), June 23, 1923, JR, "Family Research," material assembled for an autobiography, JRP.

4   he later recalled: JR, "Early Home Life," August 6, 1976, notes toward an autobiography/*The Poppa Piece,* JRP.

4   "A special feature": "Students Display Musical Ability," unidentified newspaper clipping, "Jerry Rabinowitz Poetry & Music Compositions, 1924–35" (a small homemade scrapbook), JRP.

4   "they listened as": JR, "Sister continued B," September 1, 1976, notes toward an autobiography/*The Poppa Piece,* JRP.

5   "reception for Brother Edward C. Havens": program for Reception to Brother Edward C. Havens by the Masonic Club of the City of New York, June 1, 1919, JRP.

5   "Little Sonia": Ibid.

5   danced a "Spring Song": An undated clipping promoting the Christmas celebration of the *Evening World*'s Kiddie Klub at the Metropolitan Opera House and a repeat performance at the Stage Children's Christmas Festival at the Hudson Theater. Sonia's offering was categorized as "Rhythmic Dance." A review (also undated) states that the child dancers were pupils of Florence Fleming Noyes and that Sonia Rabinowitz danced "A Poem." "Memorabilia," JRP.

5   "A tiny fleck": Harold G. Broland, untitled poem about Sonia Rabinowitz (typed), "Memorabilia," JRP.

5   Sonia was chosen: Julia Levien and Hortense Kooluris, interviews with the author, March 16, 1999.

5   "various aspects of rhythmics": Alys Bentley's obituary in *The New York Times,* January 9, 1951.

5   Bentley's ideas: Mary Alice Brennan, "Interview with Margaret H'Doubler," October 8, 1972. Courtesy of Janice Ross. (An almost identical transcript exists at the NYPL.) Dance educator Margaret H'Doubler, visiting New York as a young woman, commented on the innovative floorwork in Bentley's classes.

5   "We did things like 'folding' ": JR, "How I Almost Did Not Become a Dancer," August 25, 1976, notes toward an autobiography, JRP.

5   his sister, Sonia: Sonia Robbins Cullinen, interview with the author, February 13, 1999.

6   "World Renowned Acrobats": Scrapbook of the Davenport Brothers' appearances in the possession of Jackye Lee Madura, daughter of JR's cousin Jack Davenport.

6   Lena encouraged: JR, "Reading Chekhov's Biography—on the beach," August 6, 1976, notes toward an autobiography, JRP.

7   "like a bird": Viola Zousmer Balash, interview with the author, October 30, 1999.

7   "He did all kinds of performances": Ibid.

7   thrilled that when he performed: JR, "Reading Chekhov's Biography—on the beach," August 6, 1976, notes toward an autobiography, JRP.

8   "I guess my family": Ibid.

8   "They were funny ladies": Donald Saddler, interview with the author, June 1, 1999.

8   "doing splits off the piano": Sonia Robbins Cullinen, interview with the author, August 19, 2000.

8   Harry, Jerry later wrote: JR, "Family Life," July 24, 1976, notes toward an autobiography/*The Poppa Piece,* JRP.

9   "double betrayal": JR, "Grudges," ca. 1976, notes toward an autobiography/*The Poppa Piece,* JRP.

9   "It'd start in the kitchen": JR, "Sister-Family," September 1, 1976, notes toward an autobiography/*The Poppa Piece,* JRP.

9   "brilliant. . . . She could speak": Viola Zousmer Balash, interview with the author, October 30, 1999.

9   " 'Mother Knows Best' ": JR, "Yiddish Art, etc. continued," July 23, 1976, notes toward an autobiography, JRP.

9   "[She] set me up": JR, Journal No. 2, February 28, 1972, JRP.

10 "Hello, is this the orphanage?" (part quote, part paraphrase): JR, "Yiddish Art, etc. continued," July 23, 1976, notes toward an autobiography, JRP.

10 "Dear Mommy": "Jerry Rabinowitz, Poetry & Music Compositions, 1924–35" (scrapbook), JRP.

11 "All the sun long": Dylan Thomas, "Fern Hill," in *The Collected Poems of Dylan Thomas* (augmented edition) (New York: New Directions, 1953), 178–179.

11 "They told me I spoke": JR, notes toward an autobiography/*The Poppa Piece;* also in various drafts of *The Poppa Piece* itself, JRP.

11 Reminiscing: JR, audiotape, *"Poppa Piece,"* January 25, 1975, JRP.

11 "making faces and jeering": Ibid.

11 "mother-cuddled": Ibid.

11 "My being a Jew": JR, "The Times of the 35 40s continued into being a Jew," September 8, 1976, notes toward an autobiography/*The Poppa Piece,* JRP.

12 "Sometimes I dream": "Jerry Rabinowitz, Poetry & Music Compositions, 1924–35" (scrapbook), JRP.

12 "Youth is a thing": Ibid.

12 he and his cousin: Jack Davenport, interview with the author, May 19, 2000.

13 "Come on girls": Harry Rabinowitz, quoted in JR, "Sister Family continued C," September 1, 1976, JR, notes toward an autobiography/*The Poppa Piece,* JRP.

13 "most terrifying": Ibid., JRP.

13 his highest grades: Transcript, New York University, Office of the Registrar, 1935–1936.

2. First Steps

15 "America's Only Ballet Company": Program for a concert by Dance Center at the Barbizon-Plaza Concert Hall, December 10, 1932, JRP.

15 "I think he must": JR, "A Story of Hands," July 14, 1976, notes toward an autobiography, JRP. For an additional source on Robbins's days with Gluck Sandor, see JR's interview with Ellen Sorrin about Sandor for the NYPL's Oral History Project, November 28, 1995, NYPL.

16 "He took good dancers": José Limón, *An Unfinished Memoir,* 47.

16 "a beauty quite out of keeping": Robert Benchley, *The New Yorker,* September [?], 1931, from a typed chronology, "Critical Reviews of Ballets, Dances, Performances, Revues, Productions, Direction and Painting by Gluck Sandor and Felicia Sorel," probably prepared by Philip Lanza, Sandor's adopted son, JRP.

16 " 'Madame Butterfly' conceived and directed": *Billboard,* March 1926, included in the above list.

16 "The surprise of the season": John Martin, "The Dance: One Year of an Adventure," *The New York Times,* June 19, 1932.

17 "German Technique and Dance": advertisement for Dance Center in *The Dance Magazine,* October 1931.

17 His idea of having: JR, "How I Almost Did Not Become a Dancer," August 16, 1976, notes toward an autobiography, JRP.

17 José Limón: Programs of Dance Center concerts can be found in Senia Gluck-Sandor, programs, NYPL.

18 "Her lids never seemed": JR, "Training," September 7, 1976, notes toward an autobiography, JRP.

18 "[using] space": Ibid.

19 "look into the hearts": Charles D. Isaacson, "Dance Events Reviewed," *The Dance Magazine,* November 1931, 31.

19 "Everything was a source": JR, "How I Almost Did Not Become a Dancer," August 16, 1976, notes toward an autobiography, JRP.

19 "there was always a prop": Martin Green, interview with the author, March 15, 1999.

19 "The men and women of Herod's": unidentified typed review of *Salome* at the Barbizon-Plaza Concert Hall, April 19, 1933, in Senia Gluck-Sandor, clippings, NYPL.

19 "an infinitely subtle blend": José Limón, *An Unfinished Memoir,* 47.

19 "as if to plead": Ibid.

20 "evil genius": Program notes for *The Eternal Prodigal* in the program for the Dance Center performances at the Ritz Theatre under the auspices of the WPA's Federal Dance Project, Senia Gluck-Sandor, programs, NYPL.

20 "subway stampede": The production was supposed to open on November 29, 1936, and run through December 5 but did not actually open until December 2, according to John Martin, "The Dance: WPA in Action," *The New York Times,* December 6, 1936, Senia Gluck-Sandor, clippings, NYPL.

20 "ideals shattered": Possibly from advance press information quoted in John Martin, "The Dance: WPA Debut," *The New York Times,* November 22, 1936. Senia Gluck-Sandor, clippings, NYPL.

20 "always searching, fighting": Ibid.

20 "few stage artists": Sulamith Ish-Kishor, *The Jewish Times,* February 1, 1929, Senia Gluck-Sandor, clippings, NYPL.

20 Robbins later said: JR, "The Times of the 35 40s continued into being a Jew," September 8, 1976, notes toward an autobiography/*The Poppa Piece,* JRP.

20 "I didn't want to be a Jew": Ibid.

20 "high jinks": undated, unsigned review in Senia Gluck-Sandor, clippings, NYPL.

21 and was overcome: JR, draft of a projected speech about Danilova marked "D.C."

and "Dec–Jan?" (scribbled on a birthday card sent him by his sister), October 12, 1989, JRP.

22   the YMHA concert was twice postponed: see *The New York Times,* October 17, 1937, *New York Sun,* November 20, 1937, and additional clippings in Lisa Parnova, clippings, NYPL.

22   "and Gerald Robbins' partnering": Anatole Chujoy, *The Dance Magazine,* January 1938. JR quotes this in "Flopping," September 9, 1976, notes toward an autobiography, JRP.

22   "I never could get her": JR, "Flopping": Ibid.

23   "skinny me": Ibid.

23   "announce the fall opening": pamphlet announcing classes by "Sonya and Jerry Robyns," JRP.

23   "It started with 'bending' movement": JR, "Training," August 17, 1976, notes toward an autobiography, JRP.

23   Schönberg claimed to remember: Tribute to Bessie Schönberg, held at what was then known as the NYPL's Dance Collection, January 31, 1995.

24   It was on that couch: JR, "The Story of Hands," July 14, 1976, notes toward an autobiography, JRP.

24   "Yes, Papa": JR, "Training 2, Yiddish Art Theater and Classes," August 20, 1976, notes toward an autobiography, JRP.

24   earned him a mention: *Daily Mirror,* September 22, 1937; *The Brothers Ashkenazi,* clippings, programs, etc., NYPL (Billy Rose Theater Collection).

24   Writing on Yiddish theater: David S. Lifson, *Yiddish Theatre in America,* 28.

25   "men, women, Germans": program, Maurice Schwartz's production of *The Brothers Ashkenazi,* September 20, 1937; *The Brothers Ashkenazi,* clippings, programs, etc., NYPL (Billy Rose Theater Collection).

25   "dance of shame": Ibid.

25   holding on to the washbasin: JR, "Training 2, Yiddish Art Theater and Classes," August 20, 1976, notes toward an autobiography, JRP.

26   John Martin had often: "The Dance: A Reopening," *The New York Times,* September 20, 1936.

26   "Gluck Sandor said": Robert Lewis to JR, May 6, 1989, JRP.

26   it was announced: *The New York Times,* November 13, 1938, Senia Gluck-Sandor, clippings, NYPL.

26   "Gluck-Sandor now feels": Ibid.

27   "and the guys were looking": Ruthanna Boris, interviews with the author, August 9 and August 10, 2000.

27   ten lectures by visiting scholars: A large cache of material on Tamiment is to be found in the Rand Institute Archives in New York University's Bobst Library.

27   "wield a wicked": Max Liebman, quoted in Martha Schmoyer Lo Monaco, "Broadway in the Poconos: The Tamiment Playhouse 1921–1967," 165.

27   "If Sandyville liked": Boris, interviews with the author, August 9 and August 10, 2000.

28   "You came in": JR, "Training 2, Yiddish Art Theater and Classes," August 20, 1976, notes toward an autobiography, JRP.

28   "Wear a coat": Boris, interviews with the author, August 9 and August 10, 2000.

28   "feel her lips": JR, 1939 diary, October 23, 1939. JRP.

28   "seduced . . . It felt funny": JR, "Tamiment," September 12, 1976, notes toward an autobiography, JRP. He also mentions that he was "a whit drunk" at the time.

29   Boris remembers: Boris, interviews with the author, August 9 and August 10, 2000.

29 "schloch night" and "a porridge": JR, "Tamiment," September 12, 1976, notes toward an autobiography, JRP.

29 "Danny," said Boris: Boris, interview with the author, August 9 and August 10, 2000.

29 "In the cabaret environment": Dorothy Bird and Joyce Greenberg, *Bird's Eye View,* 154–155.

30 "jumping joint": Anita Alvarez, interview with the author, December 7, 1999.

31 "a ferocious": JR, "Anita Alvarez," in "Training," August 17, 1976, notes toward an autobiography, JRP.

31 "was the degenerate": Alvarez, interview with the author, December 7, 1999.

31 "revealed them as superlative": "Possibilities" column, *Billboard,* September 1939.

31 "a party of white slummers": JR, interviewed in *NY PM,* April 30, 1944, JR scrapbooks, NYPL.

32 "a typical French farce": Ibid.

32 "as attentive a fan": JR, "Tamiment," September 12, 1976, notes toward an autobiography, JRP.

33 According to Dorothy Bird and Joyce Greenberg: Bird and Greenberg, *Bird's Eye View,* 158. Bird also claims that the dancers had pretty much choreographed the original version themselves and that Robbins was responsible for the ending. Bird's memory may be inaccurate. When "Piano and Lute" was premiered at Tamiment on August 5, 1939, Robbins did not dance in it, nor did his name appear on the program for that week's show, *What Goes On.*

33 "attacked the problem": John Martin, "The Dance: Ballet et al," *The New York Times,* September 30, 1939.

33 "brought in a touch of": Burns Mantle, *The Best Plays of 1939–1940,* 4.

33 "21 gone": JR, 1939 diary, October 10, 1939, JRP.

34 "My rising eating loving": JR, 1939 diary, October 28, 1939, JRP.

3. From Broadway to Ballet

PAGE

36 "natural process of American": George Amberg, *Ballet in America,* 36.

36 "Everything was done": JR, "Training," August 17, 1976, notes toward an autobiography, JRP.

36 "Where's the dagger?": JR, "Appearance in—Two Fokine Ballets," September 1, 1976, notes toward an autobiography, JRP.

37 "Yakeflopf": Ibid.

37 "celebrating their wild": Ibid.

37 "whip-like turning": Ibid.

37 "it was good": Ibid.

37 "Bobbsey Twins": Ibid.

37 "Will you be asked": JR, "Auditions," draft of an article, June 24, 1986, intended for inclusion in Ken Marsolais, Rodger McFarlane, and Tom Viola, *Broadway: Day & Night* (1992) (it does not appear in the book), JRP.

38 "Oh my God": Ibid.

39 "it missed": Burns Mantle, *The Best Plays of 1939–1940,* 4.

39 "for contractual reasons": *Choreography by George Balanchine: A Catalogue of Works,* 141.

39 "wore themselves out": Brooks Atkinson, "The Play: 'Great Lady' . . . ," *The New York Times,* December 2, 1938.

40 "swooning waltz music": John Anderson, "Great Lady Curtsies into Majestic Theatre," *Journal American,* December 2, 1938.

40 Director Joshua Logan: Stanley Green, *The World of Musical Comedy,* 169.

41 "the gustiest performances": Brooks Atkinson, "The Play: Ethel Merman and Jimmy Durante . . . ," *The New York Times,* February 10, 1939.

41 "there is always something": Richard Lockridge, " 'Keep Off the Grass,' with Jimmie Durante, Opens at the Broadhurst," *New York Sun,* May 24, 1940.

41 "Age cannot wither": Burns Mantle, " 'Keep Off the Grass,' A Lively Burlesk with Jimmie Durante," *Daily News,* May 24, 1940.

42 "You go in center": José Limón, *An Unfinished Memoir,* 93.

42 "Dances and Choreography by Jerry Robbins": Program for *Melodies and Moods* ("in honor of the Shop Chairladies of Local 62"), JRP.

42 a "choreographic poem": program for Ballet Theatre's performance at Robin Hood Dell, Philadelphia, June 25, 1940, JRP.

42 "comedy of flirtations": Ibid.

43 "the best that is traditional": Selma Jeanne Cohen and A. J. Pischl, "The American Ballet Theatre: 1940–1960," *Dance Perspectives* 6 (1960), 6.

43 "Negro Unit": Ibid., 8.

43 "Spanish Unit": Ibid.

43 "A Balletplay": Ibid., 9.

43 "the ballet stepping out": from a press release cited in Walter Terry, "The Ballet Theatre," *New York Herald Tribune,* December 31, 1939.

44 "I am not a classical dancer": JR to Harry and Lena Rabinowitz, from Mexico, July 23, 1942, continued "Saturday eve" (July 25, 1942), JRP.

44 "because there was real": Sono Osato, interview with the author, April 22, 1999.

44 shot in performance: Barzel's films are housed in the Jerome Robbins Archive of the Recorded Moving Image, NYPL.

44 However, a home movie: "Fire & Shadow" ("Family Photos including Cydney's flashbacks of her early years as she experiences Robbins' early years"), shot by JR's brother-in-law, George Cullinen, 1940s, Jerome Robbins Archive of the Recorded Moving Image, NYPL.

45 "I remember the first": JR, draft of an article, typed with corrections in his hand. Penned at top: "Frenchman's Leave, Bahamas?—date?," JRP.

46 "a gypsy recital divertissement": Robert Pollack, undated clipping, Chicago, JR scrapbooks, page dated November 1940, NYPL.

46 "Jerome Robbins, whose style": Alexis Dolinoff, "Chicago," *The American Dancer,* January 1941, JR Scrapbooks, NYPL.

46 "essentially the best": John Martin, "Hightower Wins Ovation in Ballet," *The New York Times,* October 28, 1943.

46 "We must have been": JR, "Appearance in—Two Fokine Ballets," September 1, 1976, notes toward an autobiography, JRP.

47 "running set": George Freedley, review in [. . . *graph*—first part illegible], May 21, 1941, American Actors Company, clippings, NYPL (Billy Rose Theater Collection).

47 Laing recommended Jerry: JR, "February 1994, Agnes" ("Misc. Writings"), notes toward an autobiography, JRP.

47 "He came sort of tripping": Osato, interview with the author, April 22, 1999.

47 "Jerome Robbins": John Martin, "The Dance: Query Please," *The New York Times,* March 9, 1941.

48 "One night you might": Donald Saddler, interview with the author, May 24, 2000.

48 "Why, even the ballerinas": Walter Terry, "An Opportunity for All," *New York Herald Tribune;* included in Terry, *I Was There,* 108–109.

48 "Russian Ballet": Robert Lawrence, "Dance Returns to the Metropolitan Opera House," *New York Herald Tribune,* March 28, 1943, JR scrapbooks, NYPL.

48 "the Russian invasion": Saddler, interview with the author, June 1, 1999, and Miriam Golden, interview with the author, February 17, 2000.

48 Robbins later said: JR mentioned his "Russian" getup in many later interviews, including in an interview with Rosamond Bernier in *In Memory of . . . ,* a presentation by *Great Performances/Dance in America,* January 25, 1986, produced for WNET/13 by Judy Kinberg and directed by Emile Ardolino, and a videotaped interview with the author for the Kennedy Center Honors Oral History Program, July 11, 1995.

49 "five minutes after": Miriam Golden, interview with the author, February 17, 2000. Shirley Eckl, interview with the author, July 14, 1999, also mentions unscrewing the seat backs.

49 "returned to train": JR, Dailyaide ("The Silent Secretary"), January 4, 1944, JRP.

49 "The hormones were racing": Miriam Golden, interview with the author, February 17, 2000.

49 "Army game": Ibid.

49 "Have you ever had": This is not an actual quote; the information came from Brian Meehan, interview with the author, March 4, 1999.

49 "Last night": Ibid.

49 "Report of Induction": The draft board's report was prepared by Louis Schneider, first lieutenant, Medical Corps, Assistant Medical Officer, April 18, 1941. The draft card is dated April 23, 1941, JRP.

49 "Please save me": JR, 1942 yearbook, January 13, 1942, JRP.

50 "Be wary": Ibid., front of book.

50 He records: Ibid., January 1 and 2, 1942.

50 "Sang songs": Ibid., January 16, 1942.

50 In Quebec: Ibid., January 30, 1942.

50 In Montreal: Ibid., February 6, 1942.

50 "Kids thought I'd do it well": Ibid., January 17, 1942.

50 "fantastically agile": "Audience Thrilled," *Daily Province* (Vancouver), January 21, 1943, JR scrapbooks, NYPL.

51 "cringing inwardly": JR notebook, ca. 1941–1942, JRP.

51 "When the boys decided": Ibid.

51 "[T]here were things he knew": Ibid.

51 "I've got to take care": JR, "Lullabye" (short story), 1942 (returned years later, with a note to JR by Charles Payne, who couldn't remember why JR had sent it to him), JRP.

52 One curious unfinished tale: JR, sketch for a short story, "December 3, 1943, Personal Writing, Jerry Robbins," JRP.

52 "lived in large sure brushstrokes": Ibid., February 5, 1942, JRP.

52 Annabelle Lyon had urged: JR, 1942 yearbook, January 31, 1942, JRP.

4. Learning from the Masters

53 Robbins later said: JR, speech at a tribute to Antony Tudor, "Toasting Tudor: The Capezio Awards," *Ballet Review* 14, no. 3 (Fall 1986).

54 "One could see him": JR, draft of speech at Antony Tudor Memorial, June 9, 1987, JRP.

54 "*Peter* went better": JR, 1942 yearbook, January 16, 1942, JRP.

54 "the time of day": Sono Osato, *Distant Dances,* 193.

54 "the color of the wallpaper": Ibid., 194.

54 "get right to the inner you": Miriam Golden, interview with the author, February 17, 2000.

54 "When you choreograph": Antony Tudor, interviewed by John Gruen for *The Private World of Ballet,* 262.

55 He used to speak: Ibid., 263.

55 "oozing": Donald Saddler, interview with the author, June 1, 1999.

55 "a vital characterization": Kathleen Grealish Perper to JR, April 11, 1945, JRP.

55 "I was always trying out": JR, draft of speech at Tudor Memorial, June 9, 1987, JRP. Also quoted in Jennifer Dunning, "The Complex Antony Tudor Is Remembered," *The New York Times,* June 10, 1987.

55 "a little one-minute": JR, draft of speech at Tudor Memorial, June 9, 1987, JRP.

56 "got in his own way": Ibid.

56 "ham-and-eggs" program: There are many references to this in Ballet Theatre lore. JR uses the term in a long newsy letter to Donald Saddler (in the Army and stationed at Fort Richardson, Alaska), written from Joplin (n.d., but Saddler replied on April 5, 1944).

56 "delightful": Walter Terry, "The Ballet Theatre," *New York Herald Tribune,* November 13, 1941, JR scrapbooks, NYPL.

56 Margaret Lloyd, reviewing *Bluebeard:* "[torn off] . . . ws—Ballet Season Closes," *The Christian Science Monitor,* January 26, 1942.

57 he accidentally threw: JR, 1942 yearbook, January 13, 1942, JRP.

57 "one of the high spots": uncredited, untitled review of Ballet Theatre at Forty-fourth Street Theatre, New York, *American Dancer,* November 12, 1941, JR scrapbooks, NYPL.

57 "Whenever [Jerry] did it": Annabelle Lyon, interview with the author, October 29, 1999.

57 "pièce d'occasion and not": Margaret Lloyd, *The Christian Science Monitor,* January 30, 1942, quoted in Selma Jeanne Cohen and A. J. Pischl, "American Ballet Theatre: 1940–1960," *Dance Perspectives* 6 (1960), 25.

57 "Who is against": Mikhail Fokine, quoted by Sono Osato, interview with the author, April 22, 1999.

57 "We quickly found out": JR, "Further on Fokine," July 22, 1976, notes toward an autobiography, JRP.

58 "that awful 'Kije' ": JR, 1942 yearbook, January 22, 1942, JRP.

58 "making mad changes": Ibid., January 23, 1942. Fokine rehearsed the cast from 1:30 to 5:00 P.M.

58 "a hard variation": Ibid., January 23, 1942.

58 "I did very well": Ibid.

58 Robbins felt that: JR, "Training," August 17, 1976, notes toward an autobiography, JRP.

58 "Good, good . . .": JR, "Further on Fokine," July 22, 1976, notes toward an auto-biography, JRP.

58 "It was never a put down": Ibid.

59 "$11 a week": JR, 1942 yearbook, May 8, 1942.

59 "I have control": Ibid., August 8, 1942.

59 "And there is an Indian": JR, "essay" on Mexico, in letter addressed to "Hello fel-low" [last page missing], Monday night [summer 1942], JRP.

60 "I have class at nine": JR, letter to Jean Handy (undated, but he mentions having written to Jean in a letter to his parents, July 23, 1942). Courtesy of Jean Handy.

60 Donald Saddler remembers (footnote): Donald Saddler, interview with the author, June 1, 1999.

61 "my film": JR, 1942 yearbook, August 28, 1942.

61 "now that things": JR to Harry and Lena Rabinowitz, July 23, 1942, JRP.

61 "I only wish": JR to Harry and Lena Rabinowitz, undated letter sent from the Hunter Hotel in Mexico City (where he resided that summer), JRP.

61 although he later said: JR, videotaped interview with the author for the Kennedy Center Honors Oral History Program, July 11, 1995.

61 "Started work with Massine": JR, 1942 yearbook, July 7, 1942, JRP.

61 "He was the kind": Saddler, interview with the author, June 1, 1999.

61 "especially wonderful": JR, 1942 yearbook, September 8, 1942, JRP.

61 "It does have a kind": Ibid.

62 "had an overly rich": quoted in Selma Jeanne Cohen and A. J. Pischl, "American Ballet Theatre: 1940–1960," *Dance Perspectives* 6 (1960), 30.

62 Charles Payne had to: Charles Payne, *American Ballet Theatre,* 20.

62 a wig he compared to: JR, "Further on Fokine," July 22, 1976, notes toward an auto-biography, JRP.

62 "I had to do": Ibid.

62 "after working on": JR, letter to Harry and Lena Rabinowitz from Mexico, July 23, 1942, continued "Saturday eve" (July 25, 1942), JRP.

62 "force [himself] to know": JR, "Further on Fokine," July 22, 1976, notes toward an autobiography, JRP.

62 He'd had a dream: JR, "Training," August 19, 1976, notes toward an autobiography, JRP.

64 "to understudy the understudy": Ibid.

64 "badly painted": JR, transcript of an interview with Clive Barnes, 1973, JRP.

64 "wonderful analogy": JR, 1942 yearbook, September 8, 1942, JRP.

64 Tudor told him: JR, 1942 yearbook, September 14, 1942, JRP.

64 Sevastianov pronounced him: Ibid.

64 "Oh god": JR, 1942 yearbook, September 15, 1942, JRP.

64 "a short slap": JR, 1942 yearbook, October 26, 1942, JRP.

64 "His approach": Robert Lawrence, "Elegant and Tough," *New York Herald Tribune,* October 26, 1942, JR scrapbooks, NYPL.

64 "for dramatic power": Lawrence, *New York Herald Tribune,* November [?], 1942, JR scrapbooks, NYPL.

65 "that it was the first": JR, 1942 yearbook, October 16, 1942, JRP.

65 "Arrived home": JR, 1942 yearbook, September 25, 1942, JRP.

65 "an uncle!": JR, 1942 yearbook, October 13, 1942, JRP.

65 "captured precisely": Claudia Cassidy, "Ballet Theatre Brings Stay to Brilliant Close," *Chicago Tribune* [no date listed on clipping; March 1943 noted on scrapbook page], JR scrapbooks, NYPL.

65   "The indefatigable Jerome": Ibid.

66   "Did *I* give you that?": JR, transcript of an interview with Clive Barnes, 1973, JRP.

66   "perhaps the single": John Martin, "The Dance: Honor Roll," *The New York Times,* August 29, 1943.

66   "He chewed gum": Keith M. Thompson, " 'Helen of Troy' Crowns First Week of Ballet," *Musical America,* March 10, 1943.

66   "Robbins sometimes seems": Edwin Denby, "Rosella Hightower; Jerome Robbins," *New York Herald Tribune,* November 8, 1943, collected in Denby, *Dance Writings,* eds. Robert Cornfield and William MacKay, 171.

66   "Jerome Robbins, as Mercury": Edwin Denby, "Tudor's 'Lilac Garden'; Lichine's 'Helen of Troy,' " *New York Herald Tribune,* October 18, 1943, collected in Denby, *Dance Writings,* eds. Robert Cornfield and William MacKay, 156–157.

5. *I'm* the Choreographer

PAGE

68   Ruthanna Boris remembers: Ruthanna Boris, interview with the author, August 9 and 10, 2000.

69   "Mary said, 'Well' ": Horton Foote, interview with the author, January 11, 2001.

70   Robbins envisioned: "New York Ballet," 1938–1940, JRP.

70   "like a stirring": Ibid.

70   "born during the": Hyde Parnow, "War Babies," *Direction,* May 1941. Clipping filed with "War Babies Ballet," 1941–1942, JRP.

70   "use for ballet": JR, notes for "War Babies Ballet," 1941–1942, JRP.

70   "Lennie is tough": Ibid.

70   "until it's completely": "The Wild West," scenario for a ballet, pre-1943 (?), JRP.

70   Foote remembers: Foote, interview with the author, January 11, 2001.

71   "get anything done": JR, 1942 yearbook, January 15, 1942.

71   It was probably (footnote): JR, "Flopping," September 9, 1976, notes toward an autobiography, JRP. He guessed the number to have been choreographed in 1940 or 1941. However, in a diary entry dated August 28, 1942, he mentions "material for Coca," which may refer to his plans for this number.

71   "Dorati [Antal Dorati]": JR, 1942 yearbook, January 21, 1942, JRP.

71   The script for *Stack:* JR, "Stack O'Lee"—ballet, 1941–1942. A later note at the top of the scenario says, "Ballet submitted to Ballet Theatre 1942." It was to have had narration by Horton Foote, although Foote has no memory of this.

72   "wonderful": JR, 1942 yearbook, February 5, 1942, JRP.

72   "the first breaking away": JR, "Early '40s Ballet Stories" (notes apparently for *Clan Ritual*), JRP.

72   Charles Payne remembered: Charles Payne, *American Ballet Theatre,* 119.

72   "And then out of": "Cain," draft of a narrative for a ballet, JRP.

73   Robbins mentioned: JR, interviewed by Tobi Tobias, "Bringing Back Robbins' 'Fancy,' " *Dance Magazine,* January 1980, 69.

73   "This ballet is so essential": JR, "Early '40s Ballet Stories" (notes apparently for *Clan Ritual*), JRP.

73   some wise person: JR, interviewed by Tobias, "Bringing Back Robbins' 'Fancy,' " *Dance Magazine,* January 1980, 69.

73   a letter: Charles Payne to JR, January 28, 1943, JRP.

73   "an American Beau Danube": Payne to JR, January 18, 1942, JRP.

73   "to be different": Payne to JR, January 28, 1942, JRP.

73   "An opening ballet": Ibid.

73   "Can you make Aunt Polly": Payne to JR, June 6, 1943, JRP.

74   Mary Hunter fed Robbins: JR, interviewed by Tobias, "Bringing Back Robbins' 'Fancy,' " *Dance Magazine,* January 1980, 69.

74   "a most disgraceful": Secretary of the Navy Swanson, *Time,* April 30, 1934. Cited in Lincoln Kirstein, *Paul Cadmus,* 25.

74   almost 30 percent: Thomas Schatz, *Boom and Bust: The American Cinema in the 1940s,* 240.

74   Betsy Blair (footnote): Beth Genné, "Freedom Incarnate": The Dancing Sailor as American Icon in World War II," paper presented at the Society of Dance History Scholars Conference, July 2000. Courtesy of Beth Genné.

75   he noticed that they often: JR, interview with Rosamond Bernier in *In Memory of . . .* , a presentation by *Great Performances/Dance in America,* January 25, 1986, produced for WNET/13 by Judy Kinberg and directed by Emile Ardolino.

75   Robbins recalled later: JR, interview with Clive Barnes, 1973 (draft), JRP.

75   "distinctly American": Charles Payne to JR, January 28, 1942, JRP.

75   "jockey crotch down": Paul Magriel, *Chronicles of the American Dance from the Shakers to Martha Graham,* 21.

75   As Gene Kelly: Genné, "Freedom Incarnate: Jerome Robbins, Gene Kelly, and the Dancing Sailor as an Icon of American Values in World War II," *Dance Chronicle* 24, vol. 1 (2001).

75   *Les Matelots:* Cyril Beaumont, *Complete Book of Ballets,* 742–743.

76   "ideal sel[ves]": program for American Concert Ballet at the Ninety-second Street Y, November 14, 1943, at 3:30. American Concert Ballet clippings, NYPL.

76   "touching and exciting": S. L. M. Barlow, "Dancing on Broadway," *Modern Music,* January–February 1944.

76   Todd Bolender remembers: Todd Bolender, telephone conversation with the author, subsequent to April 7, 2000, interview.

76   "spruce themselves up": *Fancy Free* scenario, in George Amberg, *Ballet in America,* 132–139.

77   Gould, Robbins later said: JR, interview with Nancy Reynolds, June 8, 1974, in preparation for her book *Repertory in Review.* Courtesy of Nancy Reynolds.

77   Gould himself remembered: Joan Peyser, *Bernstein: A Biography,* 136.

77   "Dear Mr. Persichetti": JR to Vincent Persichetti, August 3, 1943, Vincent Persichetti Collection, Music Division, NYPL.

78   "Jerry went through": Humphrey Burton, *Leonard Bernstein,* 126–127.

78   later described by Bernstein: "Dramatists Guild Landmark Symposium: *West Side Story,*" *Dramatists Guild Quarterly,* Autumn 1985, 20.

78   Humphrey Burton reports: Humphrey Burton, *Bernstein: A Biography,* 117.

78   "Tomorrow start on my": JR, 1942 yearbook, January 11, 1943, JRP. Note: In November 1942, this diary jumps a year (JR himself notes that), JRP.

78   "Very very exciting": JR, 1942 yearbook, January 12, 1943, JRP.

79   "A lot of counting": Shirley Eckl, interview with the author, July 14, 1999.

79   "[W]e were in Bloomington": Janet Reed, interviewed by Tobias, "Bringing Back Robbins' 'Fancy,' " *Dance Magazine,* January 1980, 69.

79   "If we were on": Janet Reed, taped message read at the memorial "Broadway Salutes Jerome Robbins," April 8, 1999.

79 "I guess he saw me": Harold Lang, interviewed by Tobias, "Bringing Back Robbins' 'Fancy,' " *Dance Magazine,* January 1980, 71.

79 "Jerry really caught": Muriel Bentley in ibid., 71.

79 "That role is me": Ibid.

79 "like patent leather": Jennifer Dunning, "Muriel Bentley, 82, Dancer in Jerome Robbins's Ballets," *The New York Times,* March 15, 1999, quote attributed to a *Time* interview "last year."

79 "never really thought": Reed, interviewed by Tobias, "Bringing Back Robbins' 'Fancy,' " *Dance Magazine,* January 1980, 71.

80 "small, dark and": Agnes de Mille, cited in typed publicity material on JR sent out by Bill Watters in Los Angeles and Bill Doll in New York, JRP. I have been unable to locate the original source.

80 Reed had only: Janet Reed, interview with the author, October 9 and October 17, 1999.

80 Bentley did not: Bentley, interviewed by Tobias, "Bringing Back Robbins' 'Fancy,' " *Dance Magazine,* January 1980, 72.

80 "his first fuck": Bentley, quoted by Tony Mordente, in Greg Lawrence, *Dance with Demons,* 260.

80 "I don't remember": JR, interviewed by Tobias, "Bringing Back Robbins' 'Fancy,' " *Dance Magazine,* January 1980, 74.

80 "Must save now": JR, 1944 Dailyaide, January 22, 1944, JRP.

80 "1/20, Kansas City": Ibid., January 20, 1944, JRP.

82 Jerry felt let down: JR to Oliver Smith, undated, in response to a March 10, 1944, wire from Smith, JRP.

82 arguing with the union: Smith to JR, March 16, 1944, JRP.

82 they didn't actually rehearse: Reed, interview with the author, October 17, 1999.

82 "Dear Jerry": Leonard Bernstein, speaking on one of the 78-rpm records of sections of *Fancy Free,* played by Bernstein and Aaron Copland on two pianos, Photo & Sound Studios, February 2, 1944. Courtesy of Douglas Lackey.

83 the dancers remember: Reed, interview with the author, October 17, 1999.

83 "About the two extra": Leonard Bernstein to JR, undated (prior to a trip to Montreal), *Fancy Free* Correspondence, JRP.

83 "There's a phrase": Ibid.

83 "For God's sake": Bernstein to JR, undated (after return from Montreal), *Fancy Free* Correspondence, JRP.

83 "Got music settled": JR, 1944 Dailyaide, March 30, 1944, JRP.

83 "and raved": Ibid., April 4, 1944, JRP.

83 "Leonard said he": Ibid., April 15, 1944, JRP.

84 The radio was (footnote): "Dramatists Guild Landmark Symposium: *On the Town,*" Leonard Bernstein, Betty Comden, Adolph Green, Jerome Robbins, Oliver Smith (Arthur Laurents, moderator), *Dramatists Guild Quarterly* 18, no. 2 (Summer 1981), 11–24. Comden and Green have told this story elsewhere.

85 A newspaper item asserted: Leonard Lyons, "Lyons Den," *Palm Beach Times,* West Palm Beach, Florida (syndicated), August 26, 1953, JR scrapbooks, NYPL.

86 The composer Ned Rorem: Ned Rorem, interview with the author, April 3, 2000.

86 "I have a nervous": Antony Tudor to JR (handwritten note to JR on a small card), April 18, 1944, JRP.

86 "The whole production": Arthur V. Berger, "Ballet Theater in 'Fancy Free,' " *New York Sun,* April 19, 1944, JR scrapbooks, NYPL.

86 "aggressive self-intrusiveness": B. H. Haggin, "Dance," *The Nation,* May 6, 1944, JR scrapbooks, NYPL.

86 John Martin praised: John Martin, "Ballet by Robbins Called Smash Hit," *The New York Times,* April 19, 1944, JR scrapbooks, NYPL.

86 "smash hit": Edwin Denby, "Fancy Free," *New York Herald Tribune,* April 19, 1944, collected in Denby, *Dance Writings,* eds. Robert Cornfield and William MacKay, 218.

87 "I showed them!": Betty Comden and Adolph Green, interview with the author, March 15, 2000.

87 "This is young Robbins's": Martin, "Ballet by Robbins Called Smash Hit," *The New York Times,* April 19, 1944, JR scrapbooks, NYPL.

6. Choreographer on the Town

PAGE

89 "Yesterday I was": Robert Silverman, interview with the author, May 21, 2001.

89 "I've got a dozen": JR, interviewed in *NY PM,* April 30, 1944.

89 "ballet dance play": JR, draft of *Bye-Bye Jackie,* May 1, 1944, JRP.

89 "[T]he whole scene": Ibid.

90 Both men: Oliver Smith, quoted in Didier C. Deutsch, liner notes for the 1998 CD of *On the Town* by Sony Music Entertainment, a reissue of the Columbia Broadway Masterworks recording (1961).

90 "the desperate remains": Betty Comden and Adolph Green, *The New York Musicals of Comden and Green,* 2.

91 "My Coney Island": Oliver Smith to JR, August 8, 1944, JRP.

91 "I think we were all": Adolph Green, "Dramatists Guild Landmark Symposium: *On the Town,*" with Leonard Bernstein, Betty Comden, Adolph Green, Jerome Robbins, and Oliver Smith (Arthur Laurents, moderator), *Dramatists Guild Quarterly* 18, no. 2 (Summer 1981), 11–24.

91 "the subject matter was light": Leonard Bernstein, quoted in Terry Teachout, "It's Still a Helluva Town," *Civilization,* December 1997–January 1998.

91 "I like the kids": George Abbott, quoted in *New York Times* news item, October 4, 1944.

92 "a marvelously limber girl": Wolcott Gibbs, in *The New Yorker,* quoted in Sono Osato, *Distant Dances,* 221.

92 both McNichols and: Interviews with the author: Dorothy McNichols, January 14, 2000, and Jean Handy, January 10, 2000.

93 "a valentine": Oliver Smith, "Dramatists Guild Landmark Symposium: *On the Town,*" *Dramatists Guild Quarterly* 18, no. 2 (Summer 1981), 11–24.

93 "I feel like I'm": Comden and Green, *The New York Musicals of Comden and Green,* 8.

93 "New York, New York": Ibid.

94 "that Prokofieff stuff": George Abbott, quoted by Leonard Bernstein, "Dramatists Guild Landmark Symposium: *On the Town,*" *Dramatists Guild Quarterly* 18, no. 2 (Summer 1981), 11–24.

94 "[Jerry] would say": Bernstein, ibid.

94 "this little polka-like": Ibid.

95 "She's a home-loving type": Comden and Green, *The New York Musicals of Comden and Green,* 12.

95 "the monkeyshines of the principals": Edwin Denby, "On the Town, Sing Out Sweet Land, Song of Norway," *New York Herald Tribune,* January 21, 1945, collected in Denby, *Dance Writings,* eds: Robert Cornfield and William MacKay, 282.

95 "You got my whole": Comden and Green, "You Got Me," *The New York Musicals of Comden and Green,* 69.

95 "very well how to": JR, notes with one copy of *On the Town* script, JRP.

95 "What am I doing": Richard D'Arcy, interview with the author, December 12, 2000.

96 "she thinks": Ibid.

96 "Then from the end": JR, notes on *On the Town,* inside a copy of the script (black snap-back binder), JRP.

96 "wonderful, suspended": Ibid.

96 "It was a long, hard": Allyn McLerie, interview with the author, October 18, 2001.

97 "Next, with a slight": Sono Osato, *Distant Dances,* 235.

97 "[H]c had done a dismal": Sono Osato, interview with the author, April 22, 1999.

97 remarking years later: JR, "Dramatists Guild Landmark Symposium: *On the Town,*" *Dramatists Guild Quarterly* 18, no. 2 (Summer 1981), 11–24.

97 "You know, most people": Osato, interview with the author, April 22, 1999.

98 "dullish": John Chapman, *Daily News,* December 29, 1944, quoted by Didier C. Deutsch, liner notes for the 1998 CD of *On the Town* by Sony Music Entertainment, a reissue of the Columbia Broadway Masterworks recording (1961).

98 "opportunity to heave": Jack O'Brien, Associated Press, December 29, 1944, JR scrapbooks, NYPL.

98 "Just now, his ideas": Edwin Denby, "On the Town, Sing Out Sweet Land, Song of Norway," *New York Herald Tribune,* January 21, 1945, collected in Denby, *Dance Writings,* eds. Robert Cornfield and William MacKay, 282.

98 "We're used to actors": Louis Biancolli, "On the Town Ballet Dusts Off Tradition," *New York World-Telegram,* February 3, 1945, JR scrapbooks, NYPL.

98 Robbins and Nancy Walker: 78 rpm Voice-O-Graph recording, 1945. Courtesy of Douglas Lackey.

98 "The bonds that you purchase": *Playbill* for *On the Town* at the Adelphi Theatre, week beginning February 25, 1945.

99 "based on an idea by": Ibid.

99 he mentioned that: "From New York's *On the Town* to Hollywood's *Milky Way,*" *Cue,* March 17, 1945, JR scrapbooks, NYPL.

99 told John Kriza: Kirsten Valbor, interview with the author, June 22, 2001.

99 "Jerry! I can't *lie!*": Rhoda Grauer, interview with the author, October 29, 2000.

99 Comfort Corset as a corporation: Department of State, New Jersey, Certificate of Dissolution for Comfort Corset Corporation, June 5, 1943. Filed with the Division of Revenue, Department of the Treasury, Trenton, New Jersey.

100 "they complained": Sonia Robbins Cullinen, interview with the author, August 19, 2000.

100 one writer has Robbins: Marie Torre, "Robbins Going into Films," *World-Telegram,* February 20, 1945, JR scrapbooks, NYPL.

100 Leonard Lyons reported: Leonard Lyons, "The Lyons Den," *New York Post,* April 2, 1945.

100 "OK, you can tear up": Ibid.

100 "a Sardi romance": Dorothy Kilgallen, "Notebook of a Broadway Cinderella," *Toledo Blade,* March 16, 1945. Kilgallen's syndicated column appeared under a number of different titles.

100 in 1999 Wheeler told: Lois Wheeler, quoted in Greg Lawrence, *Dance with Demons,* 80.

100 talking about the new: JR, "Ballet Puts on Dungarees," *New York Times Magazine,* March 11, 1945.

100–01 signed a new principal's: contract between Ballet Theatre and Jerome Robbins, March 24, 1945, JRP.

101 Sol Hurok presented Robbins: R.B., "3 Dances at the Met," *New York World-Telegram,* April 20, 1945.

101 "the veteran vaudevillian": Leonard Lyons, "The Lyons Den," *New York Post,* April 11, 1945.

101 he drew up a list: JR, list of ballets planned ca. 1945, "Early 1940s Ballet Stories," JRP.

101 He also outlined: JR, plan for *Cook Book Ballet,* 1940, JRP.

102 "By the way, I'm": Ibid.

102 Robbins approached Bernstein: Humphrey Burton, *Leonard Bernstein,* 140.

102 "He worked in": Paul Bowles, *Without Stopping,* 273.

102 "This would be": JR, list of ballets planned ca. 1945, "Early 1940s Ballet Stories," JRP.

102 "*Fancy Free* . . . was so": JR, interview with Nancy Reynolds, June 8, 1974, in preparation for her book *Repertory in Review.* Courtesy of Nancy Reynolds.

103 "halfway between": Louis Kronenberger, "Culture Larded with Comedy," *NY PM,* June 3, 1945.

103 "a wonderful show": JR, interview with Reynolds, June 8, 1974.

103 "If you are going": George Jean Nathan, "When Deems and Dems Is Followed by Doze," *The New York Times,* June 11, 1945.

103 she loathed it: Janet Reed, interview with the author, October 9, 1999.

104 "There is interplay": *Playbill, Billy Rose's Concert Varieties,* 1945, JRP.

104 "musical architecture": Edwin Denby, "Robbins' 'Interplay'," *New York Herald Tribune,* November 4, 1945, collected in Denby, *Dance Writings,* eds. Cornfield and MacKay, 337.

105 "romantic out of all proportion": Marcia B. Siegel, *Shapes of Change,* 250.

106 "the landlord may remove": One-year lease for apartment at 24 W. Tenth Street, dated August 17, 1945, JRP.

107 "We didn't know who": Story reported by Brian Meehan, March 4, 1999.

107 "Somehow we'd all be lying": JR, "Interim Years," September 3, 1976, notes toward an autobiography, JRP.

107 "Oliver, producing it": Ibid.

107 Jerry's cousin Robert Silverman: Robert Silverman, interview with the author, May 21, 2001.

107 "Both seemed to be": JR, "Interim Years," September 3, 1976, notes toward an autobiography, JRP.

108 He explained: Harriett Johnson, "The First Step in a Robbins Dance," *New York Post,* January 4, 1946.

108 "His attitude": Humphrey Burton, *Leonard Bernstein,* 116.

109 Helen Gallagher: Helen Gallagher, interview with the author, June 8, 2000.

109 "We tackled the end": Betty Comden and Adolph Green, interview with the author, March 15, 2000.

109 John Chapman: John Chapman, " 'Billion Dollar Baby' An Engaging Musical About Speakeasy Days," *Daily News,* December 22, 1945.

109 a "honey": Howard Barnes, "The Theaters," *New York Herald Tribune,* December 22, 1945.

109   "considerable life": Ward Morehouse, "The New Play," *New York Sun,* December 22, 1945.

109   "For one thing": Louis Kronenberger, "A Fine Try Just Misses," *NY PM,* December 22, 1945.

109   "She had fat legs": George Abbott, interview with Kenneth Geist, September 15, 1983.

110   Adolph Green thought: Adolph Green (with Betty Comden), interview with the author, March 15, 2000.

110   "A bit later": Ann Hutchinson Guest, interview with the author, July 14, 2000.

111   "ballet plays": JR, quoted in Harriett Johnson, "The First Step in a Robbins Dance," *New York Post,* January 4, 1946.

111   "I don't think" (footnote): Agnes de Mille to JR, October 24, 1945, JRP.

112   "He choreographed": James Mitchell, interview with the author, June 9, 2000.

112   Dancers remember: Arthur Partington, interview with the author, July 9, 2001.

112   "Dapper's girls": Ibid.

112   "They [Robbins, Abbott . . .]": Danny Daniels, interview with the author, January 12, 2002.

112   "generally accepted": Lewis Nichols, "Billion Dollar Baby," *The New York Times,* December 30, 1945.

112–13   "screen version": JR, penciled note in a film script for *Billion Dollar Baby* (brown, striped), JRP.

113   "jazzy distortion": JR, single-spaced typed notes for *Billion Dollar Baby* "movie script," JRP.

113   Robbins was paid: JR, income book for 1946, JRP.

7. The Broadway-Ballet Seesaw

116   "Nobody moved": James Mitchell, interview with the author, June 29, 2000.

116   "That's not exactly": Brian Meehan, interview with the author, March 4, 1999.

116   "He was": Mitchell, interview with the author, June 29, 2000.

116   William Weslow: William Weslow, interview with the author, January 18, 2000.

117   "I think Jerome": JR, diary, October 9, 1939, JRP.

117   "He had the temper": JR, "Knockout Numbers," *Vanity Fair,* December 1984, 114–118.

117   "What *are* you doing?": Ann Hutchinson Guest, interview with the author, July 14, 2000.

117   "The way I remember": Helen Gallagher, interview with the author, June 8, 2000.

118   "I want this lively": Virginia Gibson, interview with the author, May 5, 2000.

118   "He would turn black": Sondra Lee, interview with the author, March 30, 1999.

118   "If he got blocked": Gallagher, interview with the author, June 8, 2000.

118   "You had to scrape": Beverly Emmons, conversation with the author, ca. 2001.

119   "If it had been anyone": Suzanne Johnston, interview with the author, January 23, 2000.

119   when his young assistant: Rhoda Grauer, interview with the author, October 29, 2000.

119   "He said, 'I don't know' ": Allyn McLerie, interview with Francis Mason, July 28, 1998; for *Ballet Review.* The interview appeared in edited form in the journal *Ballet Review* 28, vol. 1 (Spring 2000). Courtesy of Francis Mason.

119 "When Jerry could smell": Lee, interview with the author, March 30, 1999.

120 "full out, all the screams": Weslow, interview with the author, January 18, 2000.

120 Rall doesn't recall: Tommy Rall, interview with the author, September 11, 2002.

120 "He was *it*": Arthur Partington, interview with the author, July 9, 2001.

120 "That little squab": Monte Proser, quoted in Lee Rogow, "Hottest Thing in Show Business," *Esquire,* November 1948.

121 His $10 per-performance royalties: JR, income book for 1946, JRP.

121 "due to the pressure": Arthur Laurents to JR, February 15, 1946, JRP.

121 "This man made me crazier": Arthur Laurents, interview with the author, June 12, 2000.

122 but he had planned: Charles Payne, *American Ballet Theatre,* 52.

123 "Its characteristics are": *The Times* (London), July 5, 1946, quoted in Selma Jeanne Cohen and A. J. Pischl, "The American Ballet Theatre: 1940–1960," *Dance Perspectives* 6 (1960), 51.

123 "Ballet Theatre Wins": Edwin Denby, *Dance Magazine,* November 1946.

123 he upped his sessions: JR, 1946 calendar, JRP.

124 "*Facsimile* was intended": Charles Payne, *American Ballet Theatre,* 145.

124 "Small inward treasure": Santiago Ramón y Cajál, program note for *Facsimile,* quoted in Cohen and Pischl, "The American Ballet Theatre: 1940–1960," *Dance Perspectives* 6 (1960), 53.

124 silent film: "Interplay and Facsimile" (Ballet Theatre, 1945–1946), Jerome Robbins Archive of the Recorded Moving Image, NYPL.

125 "a choreographic observation": Ballet Theatre program, City Center Theater, December 5, 1947, JRP.

125 "Scene: A lonely place": "Facsimile Is the Smartest of the Ballet Novelties," clipping, no author, date, or paper, JR's files on *Facsimile,* JRP.

125 "beach robe": Robert Lawrence, *The Victor Book of Ballets and Ballet Music,* 171.

125–26 "Without inner resources": John Martin, "Robbins Ballet Has Premiere Here," *The New York Times,* October 25, 1946.

126 "a big step forward": Edwin Denby, "Ballet Theatre vs. Hurok; A War of Attrition," *Dance Magazine,* December 1946, included in Denby, *Dance Writings,* eds. Robert Cornfield and William MacKay, 357.

126 "In comes John Kriza": Robert Sylvester, " 'Facsimile' Is Just Too Much," *New York World-Telegram,* October 25, 1946.

126 *Life* magazine devoted: *Life,* January 27, 1947.

126 "Do a pirouette": Mitchell, interview with the author, June 29, 2000.

127 "an irreverent and diverting": Lillian Moore, "American Notes," *The Dancing Times* (London), May 1947.

127 John Martin cited with relish: John Martin, "Robbins' Ballet Satire on Dance," *The New York Times,* March 28, 1947.

127 "[T]hey sneak glances": Ibid.

127–28 "Children while playing": Ballet Theatre program for City Center Theater, December 2, 1947, JRP.

128 "I think he wore tights": Annabelle Lyon, interview with the author, October 29, 1999.

128 "Quite naturally": Walter Terry, *New York Herald Tribune,* December 7, 1947, quoted in Cohen and Pischl, "The American Ballet Theatre: 1940–1960," *Dance Perspectives* 6 (1960), 56.

128 "Dear Boys": JR to Jerome Lawrence and Robert E. Lee, June 22, 1946, filed with *Look Ma, I'm Dancin'!* material in JRP.

129　roller-skating with Nancy Walker: JR, 1946 calendar, December 30, 1946.

129　Mary Hunter was slated (footnote): Paul Moor, "Lady on Her Way," *Theatre Arts Monthly,* January 1949.

130　"First I had to": JR, quoted in *NY PM,* December 1947, JR scrapbooks, NYPL.

130　He read up on: Robbins's material on *High Button Shoes* includes newspaper clippings from 1914 on the "denatured tango," JRP.

131　"Is that number finished, Jerry?": Gallagher, interview with the author, June 8, 2000.

131　"In would walk": Ibid.

131　"At six o'clock": Ibid.

132　"The little kid": Lee, interview with the author, June 28, 1999.

132　"And then": Partington, interview with the author, July 9, 2001.

132　"the little girl": Lee, interview with the author, June 28, 1999.

132　"I think": Ibid.

133　"a masterpiece": *Time,* cited in Theodore Taylor, *Jule: The Story of Composer Jule Styne,* 122.

133　"That kind of stuff": Laurents, interview with the author, June 12, 2000.

134　"My group": Robert Lewis, *Slings and Arrows: Theater in My Life,* 183.

134　"his physical movement": Ibid., 185–186.

135　$6,000 fee: Contract dated September 22, 1947, JRP.

136　"I think the essence": JR to Jerome Lawrence and Robert E. Lee, June 22, 1946, filed with *Look Ma, I'm Dancin'!* material in JRP.

137　"Lucia had aspirations": Laurents, interview with the author, June 12, 2000.

137　"I'm the first girl": Hugh Martin, *Look Ma, I'm Dancin'!,* script, JRP.

138　Richard D'Arcy remembers: Richard D'Arcy, interview with the author, December 12, 2000.

138　However, it seemed to Ross: Herbert Ross, interview with the author, November 8, 2000.

138　"husband—lech theme": JR, notes for *Look Ma, I'm Dancin'!,* JRP.

139　"full of Jerryisms": Ross, interview with the author, November 8, 2000.

139　"I wound up": Ibid.

139　"We figured": Lawrence and Lee, *Look Ma, I'm Dancin'!,* JRP. Eddie's line, last act.

140　"One thing we've learned": Frank Rasky, "Authors of Abbott Musical Learn Theater Isn't Radio," *New York Herald Tribune,* February 1, 1948—feature written during tryouts at the Forrest Theater in Philadelphia, JR scrapbooks, NYPL.

140　"top-drawer Broadway show": Brooks Atkinson, "At the Theatre," *The New York Times,* January 30, 1948.

140　"another hit": Robert Coleman, *Daily Mirror,* February 1, 1948.

140　"one of the brightest": Louis Kronenberger, "A Joke About Ballet Falls Somewhat Flat," *NY PM,* February 1, 1948.

140　"A good idea": Ward Morehouse, "The New Play," *New York Sun,* January 30, 1948.

140　"[F]or whatever reason": Walter Terry, "Look Ma, I'm Dancin'!, New Musical Comedy on Broadway Is About Ballet by Ballet Star," *New York Herald Tribune,* January 30, 1948.

140　"She dives into": unsigned, *New York Herald Tribune,* February 18, 1948, JR scrapbooks, NYPL.

141　Richard D'Arcy thinks: D'Arcy, interview with the author, December 12, 2000.

141　*The New York Times* reported: *The New York Times,* December 20, 1949, JR scrapbooks, NYPL.

141 Robbins's notes: JR, notes for film script (hardcover binder), pages dated April 13 to April 21, 1950, JRP.

141 "As she waltzes": Ibid., page dated April 14, 1950, JRP.

142 According to Sturges's biographer: Donald Spoto, *Madcap: The Life of Preston Sturges,* 235.

8. Balanchine's Right-hand Man

PAGE

143 An article in *Esquire:* Lee Rogow, "Hottest Thing in Show Business," *Esquire,* November 1948.

144 "rapturously": JR, interview with the author for the Kennedy Center Honors Oral History Program, July 1, 1995.

144 "So I wrote": JR, interview with Nancy Reynolds, June 8, 1974, in preparation for her *Repertory in Review: 40 Years of the New York City Ballet.* Courtesy of Nancy Reynolds.

144 "From the very beginning": Isabel Brown (Mirrow), interview with the author, September 19, 2001.

144 Robbins asked to observe: JR, "Notes on Meeting Balanchine," March 12, 1984, JR, notes toward an autobiography, JRP.

144 he also referred: JR mentioned the Nantucket meeting in several interviews, including one with Ellen Sorrin, "A Conversation with Jerome Robbins: Working with Balanchine," New York City Ballet Guild Seminar, March 8, 1993, and in his "Notes on Meeting Balanchine," March 12, 1984, JRP.

144 "And in those days": JR, interview with Ellen Sorrin, "A Conversation with Jerome Robbins: Working with Balanchine," New York City Ballet Guild Seminar, March 8, 1993.

144 "It was just like": JR, transcript of interview with Clive Barnes, 1973, JRP.

145 Balanchine managed: Charles Payne, *American Ballet Theatre,* 154.

145 "[Joe] tore up": JR, "Flopping," September 9, 1976, notes toward an autobiography, JRP.

146 "One of the reasons": Allyn McLerie, interview with the author, October 18, 2001.

146 "I made mistakes": JR, "Flopping," September 9, 1976, notes toward an autobiography, JRP.

146 "hamstrung by the script": Isabel Brown (Mirrow), interview with the author, September 19, 2001.

147 "one of the most unusual": *Variety,* cited in Patricia Bosworth, *Montgomery Clift: A Biography,* 153.

147 "make up her mind" (footnote): JR to Robert Fizdale, ca. 1950, JRP.

148 he suggested: Lincoln Kirstein to Lucia Chase, quoted in Charles Payne, *American Ballet Theatre,* 162.

149 "Mr. Balanchine has once again": John Martin, "2 New Works Given by Ballet Society," *New York Times,* March 23, 1948.

149 Kirstein wrote to Robbins: Kirstein's letters to Robbins are preserved in JR, correspondence, JRP.

150 "[Y]ou never could tell": Maria Tallchief with Larry Kaplan, *Maria Tallchief: America's Prima Ballerina,* 86.

150 "Well, what's he coming for?": Todd Bolender, interview with the author, April 7, 2000.

150 "He could be absolutely": Ibid.

150 he denied that: JR, draft of letter to Doris Hering in response to an article about him she contributed to *Dance Magazine,* April 1989, JRP.

150 "Leftist attachments": Lincoln Kirstein, *Thirty Years: Lincoln Kirstein's the New York City Ballet,* 125.

151 "*The Guests* portrayed": JR, "Thoughts on Choreography (as told to Selma Jeanne Cohen)," 1954, typed, with handwritten corrections and queries by JR, "Articles by JR," JRP.

151 as Walter Terry pointed out: Terry, "Dance Me a Dance with Social Significance," *New York Herald Tribune,* October 2, 1966, 499–500.

151 "drama of space": Terry, "New York City Ballet," *New York Herald Tribune,* January 21, 1949, reprinted in Terry, *I Was There,* 227.

151 "A ballet in one scene": program, New York City Ballet, City Center Theater, March 17–18, 1950.

151 "the included": JR, notes marked "Ballet of Distinction" (ca. 1949). JR later told Nancy Reynolds (June 8, 1974) that it was Balanchine who had first dubbed the two groups by these names.

152 The Host subtly: There is a useful account of the ballet in George Balanchine and Francis Mason's *Balanchine's Complete Stories of the Great Ballets,* 1954 edition, reprinted in "Four Lost Robbins Ballets," *Ballet Review,* vol. 26, no. 3 (Fall 1998), 33–38.

152 "[The masks] are": JR, notes for *The Guests,* December 17, 1948, JRP.

152 "chipper, assured": JR, notes for *The Guests,* undated, JRP.

152 "with lyrical arm movements": Ibid.

152 "This work shouldn't be": JR, typed sheet, notes for *The Guests,* undated, JRP.

152 "a supportive gesture": quoted in Bernard Taper, *Balanchine: A Biography,* 228.

153 "Here I was": Ibid.

153 "newborn child": Doris Hering, "Reviewers' Stand," *Dance Magazine,* March 1949.

153 "floored": JR to Robert Fizdale, March 3, 1949, JRP.

153 "what emerges now": Martin, "Robbins Does Lead in His Own Ballet," *The New York Times,* November 26, 1949.

153 "[Robbins] has done": James Monahan, *The Manchester Guardian,* August 2, 1950, quoted in Reynolds, *Repertory in Review: 40 Years of the New York City Ballet,* 95.

153 "Jerry R. called": Leonard Bernstein, "Excerpts from a West Side Story Log," *Playbill,* September 1957, quoted in Humphrey Burton, *Leonard Bernstein,* 187.

154 "The bird-girl drapes": Balanchine and Mason, *Balanchine's Complete Stories of the Great Ballets,* 1954 ed., 239.

154 "Dancing in Todd's ballet": JR to Robert Fizdale, March 3, 1949, JRP.

154 he was able to tell Fizdale: Ibid.

155 "Zing like an arrow": JR, draft of speech for Irving Berlin Memorial, 1990, JRP.

155–56 had a "ball": Ibid.

156 "We spent the first": JR to Mary Martin and Richard Halliday, April 13, 1955, JRP.

156 putting up, it was said: Greg Lawrence, *Dance with Demons,* 175.

156 "They were always": McLerie, interview with the author, October 18, 2001.

157 "These songs will be": Philip Furia, *Irving Berlin: A Life in Song,* 239.

157 opening-night review: Robert Coleman, "Miss Liberty is Saluted as New B'way Hit," *Daily Mirror,* July 16, 1949.

157 "Irving was always": McLerie, interview with the author, October 18, 2001.

157 "*I* like it": Ibid.

157 "a pallid part": Brooks Atkinson, "At the Theatre," *The New York Times,* July 16, 1949.

158 "Probably the authors": Ibid.

158 "[she] ought to be": Robert Sylvester, *"Miss Liberty* and Miss Griffies," *Daily News,* July 16, 1949.

158 "It is Robbins": Howard Barnes, "The Big Three Miss," *New York Herald Tribune,* July 16, 1949.

158 "Of Robbins' five": John Martin, "The Dance: Broadway," *The New York Times,* July 17, 1949.

158 a "tumultuous": Brooks Atkinson, "At the Theatre," *The New York Times,* July 16, 1949.

159 "Dear Jerry—": Moss Hart, undated note to JR, tucked in with *Miss Liberty* script in black bend-back cover, JRP.

159 Rall remembers: Tommy Rall, interview with the author, January 28, 2002.

159 "Go Away!!": JR, 1949 datebook, JRP.

160 "French Christmas tree": Doris Hering, "Balanchine Makes New Ballet Dazzle," *Compass,* December 4, 1949.

160 "takes a fleeting jab": Terry, "The Ballet: A Sheer Delight," *New York Herald Tribune,* December 2, 1949, included in Terry, *I Was There,* 229–232.

160 "Jerry always said": Tanaquil Le Clercq, interview with Rick Whittaker, *Ballet Review,* vol. 26, no. 2 (Summer 1998), 13.

160 "agile as a leprechaun": Terry, "The Ballet: A Sheer Delight," *New York Herald Tribune,* December 2, 1949, included in Terry, *I Was There,* 229–230.

162 he told Nancy Reynolds: JR, interview with Reynolds, June 8, 1974, in connection with her *Repertory in Review: 40 Years of the New York City Ballet.* Courtesy of Nancy Reynolds.

162 The difficult part: JR in Reynolds, *Repertory in Review: 40 Years of the New York City Ballet,* 105.

162 "like the best kind": Robert Sealy, typed article, annotated by JR, intended to be included in the program for a Robbins Retrospective at New York City Ballet, n.d., JRP.

162 "Discretion is not": J. C. Vignes to JR, undated [ca. 1950], JRP.

163 Invited to dinner: Maria Tallchief with Larry Kaplan. *Maria Tallchief: America's Prima Ballerina,* 109.

163 Humphrey Burton: Humphrey Burton, *Leonard Bernstein,* 189.

163 "an almost autobiographical protagonist": Leonard Bernstein, *The Age of Anxiety, Symphony for Piano and Orchestra (after W. H. Auden),* two-piano version (New York: G. Schirmer, Inc., 1950), 2, JRP.

163 "the four faculties": John Fuller, *W. H. Auden: A Commentary,* 371. Fuller has also mentioned the allegorical use of these faculties in connection with Auden's *The Ascent of F6* (1936) and persuasively posits Auden's familiarity with Jung's *Modern Man in Search of a Soul* (1933); see 193–201, especially 197.

163 "dream odyssey": Bernstein, *The Age of Anxiety,* 2, JRP.

164 "For the world": W. H. Auden, *The Age of Anxiety: A Baroque Eclogue* (London: Faber & Faber, 1948), 90.

164 "What is left": Ibid.

164 "[Robbins] makes no": Hering, "Reviewers' Stand," *Dance Magazine,* April 1950.

165 "watching, observing": W. H. Auden, *The Age of Anxiety,* JR's annotated copy (New York: Random House, 1947), title page between 28 and 29, NYPL.

165 "his inner life": Ibid., 30.

165 "however violent / Their": Ibid., 37.

165 "To be young": Ibid., 42.

165 "Unattached as tumbleweed": Ibid., 44.

165 "become obstructions": Francisco Moncion, quoted in Reynolds, *Repertory in Review: 40 Years of the New York City Ballet,* 110.

165 "where they were like": Moncion, quoted in ibid., 110.

165 In black-and-white fragments: The *Age of Anxiety* footage by Ann Barzel appears in a film titled "Nora Kaye," Jerome Robbins Archive of the Recorded Moving Image, NYPL.

165 "And then we reached": Todd Bolender, interview with the author, April 7, 2000.

166 "[Jerry] seemed to focus": Bolender, quoted in Reynolds, *Repertory in Review: 40 Years of the New York City Ballet,* 110.

166 Auden's reputed dislike: Kirstein, *Thirty Years: Lincoln Kirstein's the New York City Ballet,* 76.

166 "high wedgies" on which: Edward Bigelow, interview with the author, June 12, 2001.

167 "Jerry would call us": Bolender, interview with the author, April 7, 2000.

167 "quite as obscure as": Martin, "City Troupe Gives Ballet by Robbins," *The New York Times,* February 27, 1950.

9. Walking a Tightrope

PAGE

170 "I hate mosquitoes": George Balanchine, quoted in Nancy Reynolds, *Repertory in Review: 40 Years of the New York City Ballet,* 114.

170 "I was rehearsing": JR, interview with Ellen Sorrin, "A Conversation with Jerome Robbins: Working with Balanchine," New York City Ballet Guild Seminar, March 8, 1993.

170 "seven pretty little": Doris Hering, " 'Jones Beach' Takes Ballet to the Sea," *Compass,* March 12, 1950.

171 "They came tearing": Tanaquil Le Clercq, interview with Rick Whittaker, *Ballet Review,* vol. 26, no. 2 (Summer 1998), 13.

171 "a piece of vivacious nonsense": John Martin, "City Troupe Gives Ballet Premiere," *The New York Times,* March 10, 1950.

171 "artistic maturity": Martin, "The Dance: Robbins," *The New York Times,* March 12, 1950.

171 it was also reported: Claudia Cassidy, *Chicago Tribune,* April 13, 1950, among others, JR scrapbooks, NYPL.

171 the contract he signed: Contract between the New York City Ballet and Jerome Robbins, signed on June 11, 1950, stipulates five weeks—four of rehearsals, one of performance—at a salary of $84 (not less than $72) for the performance week and $35 for the rehearsal weeks, with one rehearsal week in London at $42, JRP.

171 "nice fee and percentage": JR to Robert Fizdale, n.d., JRP.

172 "There is, in the best examples": Lincoln Kirstein, *Ballet* 9, no. 6, (June 1950), 18.

172 "passionate admiration": Mary Clarke, "Lend Lease in Ballet," *Dance Magazine,* September 1950.

172 "psycho-sexo-dramas": Richard Buckle, "Critics' Sabbath," *Ballet* 10, no. 2 (October 1950), 4–10 (9).

172 *The Guests* and *Age of Anxiety*: J. H. Bradley, in ibid. (Fourteen prominent London

critics were invited to review different parts of the NYCB repertory in this issue of *Ballet*.)

172 "firm favorites in London": Clarke, "Ballet Theatre Welcomed Back to Covent Garden," *Dance Magazine,* October 1950.
173 "opportunities": JR, draft of speech for Irving Berlin Memorial, 1990, JRP.
173 "great turmoil and anxiety": JR to Robert Fizdale, August 22, 1950, JRP.
173 "Neither the character": *Call Me Madam, Playbill* for the Imperial Theatre, April 1951.
173 "for Uncle Sam": Irving Berlin, "Washington Square Dance," *Call Me Madam,* Act I.
174 "Wild Man from the Mountain": William Weslow, interview with the author, January 18, 2000.
174 "They talked about": Kirsten Valbor, interview with the author, June 22, 2001.
174 "k-ta-k-ta-k-ta-k-ta": Ibid.
174 "those beautiful reds": Weslow, interview with the author, January 18, 2000.
174 "looked like an out-of-work": Slim Keith with Annette Tapert, *Slim,* 171.
175 "It went like gangbusters": Donald Saddler, interview with the author, May 24, 2000.
175 " 'Look, just give me' ": JR, draft of speech for Irving Berlin Memorial, 1990, JRP.
175 Valbor remembers: Valbor, interview with the author, June 22, 2001 (Karinska screaming in horror); Saddler, interview with the author, May 24, 2000; and Weslow, interview with the author, January 18, 2000.
176 "Let's not pretend": Brooks Atkinson, "Ethel Merman Is an American Envoy in 'Call Me Madam,' with Berlin's Music," *The New York Times,* October 12, 1950.
176 "smart, bright": John Chapman, "Call Me Madam Comes to Town with Its Plot as Its Big Handicap," *Daily News,* October 13, 1950.
176 "gay": Howard Barnes, "Her Excellent Excellency," *New York Herald Tribune,* October 13, 1950.
176 "fresh, young dances": William Hawkins, "Call Me Madam Is a Winner . . . and It's Here to Stay," *New York World-Telegram,* October 13, 1950.
176 "(sound of a falling body)": JR to Slim Hayward ("Dearest Pearl"), April 1956, JRP.
176 "horrified (yet amused . . .)": JR to Robert Fizdale, August 22, 1950.
176 the show's sponsor, Ford Motors: Disclosed by JR's agent, Howard Hoyt, at a meeting with FBI agents at the Bureau's New York office on April 25, 1950, with Robbins, Hoyt, and Hoyt's lawyer, Paul Williams. FBI report ("Confidential letter to the Director" dated April 27, 1950, recorded May 11, 1950).
176 "or some such excuse": Ibid. (JR requested the FBI files on him when he was working toward a possible autobiography and *The Poppa Piece.* They were surrendered, heavily censored, on May 8, 1981.)
177 "The Committee's inquisitorial zeal": Arthur Schlesinger, "Liberals, Stalinists, and HUAC," a review of Victor Navasky's *Naming Names, The New Leader,* December 15, 1980, 6–8.
177 "that it was to his": FBI report, April 27, 1950 (see above).
177 he said he'd attended: Ibid.
177 "squeeze play": Ibid.
177 "unable" to remember: Ibid.
178 "it" . . . "Will it still come out": JR, informal journal on blue onionskin, Monday, November 13, "1951–52 Personal Writings, Jerry Robbins," JRP. (JR has penciled "Paris? 51–52 notes"; however, per his calendar the correct year is 1950.)
178 "Not as an aged man": Ibid.
178 "Nora [Kaye] is staying": Ibid., November 15, 1950.

179   "I have gotten to be closer": JR to Robert Fizdale, undated (at some point JR asked if Fizdale would return letters written to him by JR—presumably in connection with his autobiographical research. Fizdale dated this letter 1950), JRP.

179   "war news looking": JR to Robert Fizdale, December 6, 1950, JRP.

180   a newspaper article dated: Claudia Cassidy, "On the Aisle," *Chicago Tribune,* April 19, 1951.

180   useful material: JR's files for *The King and I,* JRP.

181   "No!!!": Mara, handwritten comments on typed pages of *The King and I.* Courtesy of Mara.

181   she taught Robbins: Mara, January 1951 log of dealings with JR. Courtesy of Mara.

181   "Consultant on Oriental Dancing": Billing on program of *The King and I.*

182   "Dancers never made any noise": Gemze de Lappe, interview with the author, May 2, 2000.

182   Robbins asked Yuriko: Yuriko, interview with the author, February 21, 2002.

182   his penciled notations: JR notations on a script of *The King and I,* JRP.

182   "He would say": Yuriko, interview with the author, February 21, 2002.

184   "BEST WISHES FOR A": Telegram to JR from George Balanchine and Lincoln Kirstein prior to New York opening of *The King and I,* March 29, 1951. Folder of telegrams dated March 26, 1951, filed with JR's materials on *The King and I,* JRP.

184   "Strictly on its own": Brooks Atkinson, "At the Theatre," *The New York Times,* March 30, 1951.

185   "After Bar 55": JR, three-page memo to Alfred Newman, November 19, 1955, JRP.

185   "Needless to say": JR to Arthur Laurents, November 7, 1955, JRP.

185   "the scars and bullet holes": JR to Laurents, November 15, 1955, JRP.

185   "the reviews and the clink": Charles Brackett to JR, July 9, 1956, on Twentieth Century–Fox Film Corporation stationery, JRP.

186   "at the top of": John Martin, "City Ballet Group Opens in Top Form," *New York Times,* November 22, 1950.

186   "And what a company": Ibid.

186   "It is a waste to": Lincoln Kirstein to Betty Cage from London, August 25, 1950, JRP.

187   "after all": Claudia Cassidy, "On the Aisle," *Chicago Tribune,* April 19, 1951.

187   It was also noted: *Long Island City Star Journal,* December 2, 1950. The wedding was announced for April 16, 1951. JR scrapbooks, NYPL.

187   "She was going to marry us all" (footnote): Arthur Laurents, interview with the author, June 12, 2000.

188   Not since Doris Humphrey's: Walter Terry, *New York Herald Tribune,* June 24, 1951.

188   "I did not have to": Robert Sabin, draft annotated by JR of "The Genesis of 'The Cage,' " which appeared as "The Creative Evolution of 'The Cage': Jerome Robbins Reflects on His Most Controversial Ballet" in *Dance Magazine,* August 1955, JRP.

188   Kirstein noted: Kirstein, *Thirty Years: Lincoln Kirstein's the New York City Ballet,* 198.

188   Robbins had been struck: JR, draft of an article on *The Cage,* "Articles by JR," JRP.

188   The highly effective (footnote): JR interview with Charles Gleaves, rough transcript with corrections, prior to February 25, 1971, in connection with a book Rosenthal was working on with Lael Wertenbaker at the time of her death (*The Magic of Light: The Craft and Career of Jean Rosenthal, Pioneer in Lighting for the Modern Stage* [Boston: Little Brown and Company, 1972]).

189 "love and tenderness": JR, draft of an article on *The Cage,* "Articles by JR," JRP.

189 "almost went into": John Martin, "Ballet by Robbins in Local Premiere," *The New York Times,* June 15, 1951.

189 "to 'project' what": Robert Sabin, "The Genesis of 'The Cage' " (see above).

189 According to Arthur Laurents: Laurents, interview with the author, June 12, 2000.

189 "decadent in its concern": Martin, "Ballet by Robbins in Local Premiere," *The New York Times,* June 15, 1951.

189 "remorseless beauty": Terry, "Dance World," *New York Herald Tribune,* June 24, 1951.

190 "I loved you for": Leonard Bernstein to Nora Kaye, June 18, 1951, passed on to JR, JRP.

190 "frighteningly inhuman": Terry, "The Ballet," *New York Herald Tribune,* June 15, 1951.

190 "She didn't ever play": JR, draft of an essay about Nora Kaye, possibly for inclusion in his projected autobiography, JRP.

190 "you don't like women": Karen Kissin to JR, November 22, 1951. Kissin was the daughter of Robbins's parents' (and his own) doctor.

190 "I don't see *love*": Tanaquil Le Clercq to JR, penciled P.S. at bottom of undated note written on Queens College stationery (Le Clercq's father, Jacques Le Clercq, was on the faculty), JRP.

190 "clattering around the studio": Jack Anderson, *Stagebill* for New York City Ballet, copyrighted 1978, reprinted from *The New York Times.*

190 Interestingly, Robbins: JR, interview with Clive Barnes, 1973, annotated draft, JRP.

191 "TIP TO RED": Ed Sullivan, *The Philadelphia Inquirer,* March 24, 1951, quoted in Greg Lawrence, *Dance with Demons,* 167.

191 "figured importantly in Hollywood": Ibid.

191 "preeminent attorney": Victor Navasky, *Naming Names,* 342.

191 "stated that the subject": FBI report: "Letter to Director," April 20, 1951.

192 "if not perfect": Buzz Miller, speaking alone into a tape recorder at the behest of Brian Meehan, 1998, after JR's death. Courtesy of Brian Meehan.

192 "wonderful . . . so many": JR to Fizdale, July 15, 1951, JRP.

192 "The initial, impossibly": Ibid.

193 "We would like to explore": JR, remarks at a press conference arranged by the American Fund for Israel Institutions, July 20, 1951, after his arrival in Israel. Report filed in "Trip to Israel," JRP.

193 "Can't you just imagine": JR to Fizdale, July 15, 1951, JRP.

193 "Dearest Sweetest Jerry": Lena Robbins to JR, n.d. [1951], JR correspondence, JRP.

193 "found in Israel": JR to Judith Gottlieb, July 1951. Quoted in Ruth Eshel, *Li-reḳod `im HaHalom (Dancing with the Dream: The Development of Artistic Dance in Israel, 1920–1964)* (Tel Aviv: Sifriyat po`alim and the Dance Library of Israel, 1991), 45. I am grateful to Judith Brin Ingber for bringing this book to my attention and translating the relevant pages.

194 "They would like to": Hoyt to JR, July 12, 1951, JR correspondence, JRP.

194 a letter from Siegel: Robert Lawrence Siegel to JR, August 1, 1951, JRP.

194 "If anything did happen": Hoyt to JR, August 21, 1951, JRP.

195 Robbins sought to determine: On January 8, 1991, Clifford Forster of Fitelson, Lasky, Aslan, and Couture (Floria Lasky was and, as of 2004, still is Robbins's lawyer) received a letter from Allan Robert Adler of Cohen and Marks, Washington, D.C., January 28, 1991. The letter explained that the FBI had withheld ninety full pages from its file on Siegel—almost one half of its total information on him—pro-

viding only material that had no connection with either Robbins's HUAC testimony or Siegel's possible onetime FBI connections. That might lead one to suppose that the FBI had something it considered worth concealing.

195 "not dark but bright": Siegel to JR, August 1, 1951, JRP.
195 He comforted Robbins: Ibid., JRP.
195 "[Oliver] Smith has threatened to": Siegel to JR, September 6, 1951, JRP. Siegel claimed that Howard Hoyt had told him this over the telephone.
195 "What's this all": JR to Oliver Smith, August 1, 1990, Post-it in JR's writing attached to copy of Siegel's September 6, 1951 letter [sent?], JRP.
195 "looking for you": Hoyt to JR, August 30, 1951, JRP.
196 "Melissa [Hayden] is": Lincoln Kirstein to JR, September 1, 1951, JRP.
196 "terrible series of hysterical": Kirstein to JR, September 8, 1951, JRP.
196 "Hugh [Laing] tore off ": Ibid.
196 "On two occasions now": Francisco Moncion to JR, September 21, 1951, JRP.
196 "The company is growing": Ibid.
197 "much against his will": Kirstein to JR, September 6, 1951, JRP.
197 "forcing us more": Ibid.
197 "Here is a plot": Tanaquil Le Clercq to JR, n.d. [1951], JRP.
197 "I just love": Le Clercq to JR, n.d. [summer 1951], JRP.
197 decor for *Tyl:* Kirstein to JR, September 6, 1951, JRP.
197 "he's a cuties-pie": Ibid.
197 he stresses the value: Kirstein to Betty Cage, April 1, 1950, signed "Nastypants," Lincoln Kirstein Collection, NYPL.
198 "I would give ANYTHING": Ibid.
198 "If Robbins has to": Kirstein to Betty Cage, September 1, 1950, signed "Nostropanins," Lincoln Kirstein Collection, NYPL.
198 *Age of Anxiety* badly needs: Kirstein to JR, September 10, 1951, JRP.
198 "an important American score": Kirstein to JR, September 6, 1951, JRP.
198 "fit in films, shows": Ibid.
198 "we will be able to pay": Ibid.
198 "Balanchine wants to give": Ibid.
198 "I believe you are": Ibid.
198 "being stranded in Paris": Le Clercq to JR, undated (summer 1951), JRP.
198–99 He wrote Kirstein that: JR to Kirstein, unfinished draft, n.d., JRP.
199 "Hy—": Le Clercq to JR, envelope postmarked October 19, 1951.
199 "Can't you think": Ibid. (?). The two pieces of paper seem to belong together, although the first sheet has both salutation and signature and the other has neither.
200 Siegel wrote Robbins (footnote): Siegel to JR, October 31, 1951, JRP.
200 Rorem gave (footnote): Ned Rorem, introduction to " 'Ballet for Jerry': Three Letters from Jerome Robbins to Ned Rorem," *Dance Chronicle: Studies in Dance and the Related Arts* 23, no. 3, 20.

10. Ballet Haven

201 "Top B'way Choreographer": *Variety,* November 7, 1951.
202 "rain stained ceilings": JR to Ned Rorem, October 31, 1951, reprinted as " 'Ballet for Jerry': Three Letters from Jerome Robbins to Ned Rorem," *Dance Chronicle: Studies in Dance and the Related Arts* 23, no. 3 (2000), 256–273.

202 "I feel absolutely": JR to Rorem, November 1951, in ibid.

202 "From ten in the morning": Ibid.

202 "American ballet": Edwin Denby, "A Letter on New York's City Ballet," *Ballet,* August 1952, included in Denby, *Dance Writings,* eds. Robert Cornfield and William MacKay, 415–430.

202 "dance ballets": Ibid., 418.

202 "long ago learned": Ibid., 425–426.

203 Robbins later recalled: JR, quoted in Nancy Reynolds, *Repertory in Review: 40 Years of the New York City Ballet,* 127.

203 "sense of conspiracy": Todd Bolender, interview with the author, February 28, 2000.

204 "Tyl just did not": Anatole Chujoy, *The New York City Ballet,* 305.

204 A set of contact prints: Walter Owen's photos of *Tyl Eulenspiegel,* NYPL.

204 ". . . the backdrop suddenly": Lincoln Kirstein, quoted in M.S. [associate editor Marilyn Silverstone?], "Stage and Artist in the Television Era," *Art News,* February 1952.

204 critic Doris Hering's account: Doris Hering, "Season in Review," *Dance Magazine,* January 1952.

204 "In a fright wig": Robert Sealy, typed article, annotated by JR, intended to be included in the program for a Robbins Retrospective at New York City Ballet, n.d. [late 1970s, not used], JRP.

205 "a detailed, complicated": Chujoy, *The New York City Ballet,* 305.

205 "grunting and groaning": F.O. (Ethel Schwartz Tyne) to JR, "Friday the 16th" (November 16, 1951), JRP.

205 "because [Tyl's] antagonists": Walter Terry, "A World Premiere," *New York Herald Tribune,* November 15, 1951.

205 "storyless": George Balanchine, "Balanchine Celebration," part 1, a video presentation by *Great Performances/Dance in America,* produced for WNET/13 by Judy Kinberg and directed by Matthew Diamond.

205 "two moonbeams who play": JR, unfinished scenario written on the back of a letter drafted to Lincoln Kirstein, JRP. In the 1980s, Robbins returned to the unfinished idea and amused himself by developing it on paper into a wistful romantic tale (even casting it on current New York City Ballet dancers, such as Stephanie Saland, Hélène Alexopoulos, Gen Horiuchi, etc.), but he never choreographed it.

205 "Lincoln had the marvelous": JR to Rorem, October 31, 1951, reprinted as " 'Ballet for Jerry': Three Letters from Jerome Robbins to Ned Rorem," *Dance Chronicle: Studies in Dance and the Related Arts* 23, no. 3 (2000), 256–273.

206 "they couldn't afford": JR to Rorem, November 1951 (see preceding note).

206 "[T]hey lie on the floor": Terry, "The Dance World: The Pied Piper in New Guise, Works His Enchantment Once More," *New York Herald Tribune,* December 9, 1951.

207 the scraps of film: [Dance films by Ann Barzel], *MGZHB 12-2537, Jerome Robbins Archive of the Recorded Moving Image, NYPL.

207 "It was more like": Tanaquil Le Clercq, interview with Rick Whittaker, May 1, 1998, intended for publication in *Ballet Review,* vol. 26, no. 2 (Summer 1998). The version that appeared in the journal was considerably revised by Le Clercq. Transcript courtesy of Francis Mason.

207 "It seemed to me": Janet Reed, interview with the author, October 19, 1999.

207 "American": Various critics quoted in Reynolds, *Repertory in Review: 40 Years of the New York City Ballet,* 135.

207 "You are a bright boy": Frederick Ashton to JR, n.d. [late 1951 or early 1952], JRP.

207 Fizdale and Gold: Ned Rorem, interview with the author, April 3, 2000.
208 "cute, cloying": John Martin, "Robbins Ballet Has World Debut," *The New York Times,* February 15, 1952.
208 "enchanting": Terry, "Dance: New York City Ballet," *New York Herald Tribune,* February 15, 1952.
208 "didn't get started": Denby, "A Letter on New York's City Ballet," *Ballet,* August 1952, included in Denby, *Dance Writings,* eds. Cornfield and MacKay, 427.
208 "Robbins's dramatic line": Ibid., 428.
208 1954 interview: JR, "Thoughts on Choreography (as told to Selma Jeanne Cohen)," 1954, typed, with handwritten corrections and queries by JR, JRP.
209 "There's that Petrouchka": JR, interview with Reynolds, June 8, 1974, quoted in Reynolds, *Repertory in Review: 40 Years of the New York City Ballet,* 136.
209 "rushing, circusy number": George Balanchine and Francis Mason, *Balanchine's Complete Stories of the Great Ballets,* 1954 ed. Reprinted in "Four Lost Robbins Ballets," *Ballet Review,* vol. 26, no. 3 (Fall 1998), 33–38.
209 "No sets—just": JR to Robert Fizdale, 1952, JRP.
210 "heavenly": Denby, "A Letter on 'Caracole,'" *Ballet,* September 1952, included in Denby, *Dance Writings,* eds. Cornfield and MacKay, 430–431.
210 "new ballet": JR to Tanaquil Le Clercq, January 22, 1957, JRP.
210 "sugarhead": Maria Tallchief, interview with the author, February 23, 2002.
210 "Jerry woke up": Brian Meehan, interview with the author, March 4, 1999.
210 "He even would forbid": Ibid. Whether he feared "they" would use evidence of a homosexual liaison to blackmail him or was simply terrified that the government was keeping a frighteningly close eye on him isn't entirely clear.
211 Robbins was dumbfounded: Ibid.
211 they reminisced: JR to Buzz Miller, n.d. [summer 1952], JRP.
211 He wrote Buzz the next day: JR to Miller, May 9, 1952.
212 Photos show him: Photocopies courtesy of Judith Brin Ingber.
212 A six-page letter: JR to Judith Gottlieb, July 1952, JRP.
213 "shock": JR to Fizdale, n.d. [summer 1952], JRP.
213 "his name plastered": Ibid. Fizdale, also a friend of Balanchine, was glad to hear of Robbins's success but wrote (undated letter to JR), "It seems insane that it's causing difficulty between you and G.B. Write us the details." JRP.
214 "I'm coming home": JR to Miller, July 6, 1952, JRP.
214 "As Tanny said": JR to Fizdale, n.d. [summer 1952], JRP.
214 "The rage of the first": Ibid.
214 "I think George": Le Clercq to JR, n.d. (European tour of 1956), JRP.
214 "right under George's": JR to Fizdale, n.d. [summer 1952], JRP.
214 *The Cage* received: Lincoln Kirstein, *Thirty Years: Lincoln Kirstein's the New York City Ballet,* 128. The entry, dated June 1952, The Hague, notes, "Our embassy wants thirty tickets; none to be had."
214 "Igor now calls": JR to Fizdale, n.d. [summer 1952], JRP.
215 "Can't you see": Ibid.
215 "Scattered around": JR to Miller, "Sunday morning" [probably June 14, 1952, because Robbins mentions that *The Cage* had its first birthday "last night"], JRP.
215 "O Christ I feel": JR to Fizdale, "Sunday in Paris" [summer 1952, probably June, since it contains news similar to that in the letter to Miller cited directly above], JRP.
215 "and Robbins injected": E. J. Kahn, Jr., "The Tough Guy and the Soft Guy—II," *The New Yorker,* April 11, 1953, JR scrapbooks, NYPL.
216 "blew his stack": Nancy Franklin, interview with the author, June 23, 2001.

216 In his lengthy July letter: JR to Judith Gottlieb, July 1952, JRP.
216 "not the world's greatest": Russell McLauchlin, *Detroit News,* October 20, 1952, quoted in Whitney Stine (with a running commentary by Bette Davis), *Mother God-dam: The Story of the Career of Bette Davis,* 264.
216 "like a bear": Arthur Laurents, interview with the author, June 12, 2000.
216 Robbins told Miller: Meehan, interview with the author, March 4, 1999.
216 "moderately painful scene": *The New Yorker,* December 27, 1952, quoted in Stine with Davis, *Mother Goddam,* 265.
217 She told the newspapers: Stine with Davis, *Mother Goddam,* 263.
217 The dancers told Arthur Laurents: Laurents, interview with the author, June 12, 2000.
217 "You can't say I didn't": Stine with Davis, *Mother Goddam,* 263.
217 "My feeling was": Laurents, interview with the author, June 12, 2000.
217 "I strongly suggest": Laurents to JR, "Tuesday" [possibly post-Detroit], JRP.
217 "sex loving": Frances Herridge, *New York Post,* January 20, 1953, JR scrapbooks, JRP.
217 "a Fanny Brice routine": Laurents, interview with the author, June 12, 2000.
218 "[O]ver the course": JR, notes on "Haunted Hot Spot," filed with *Two's Company* material, JRP.
218 "putting their heads together": Brooks Atkinson, "The Case of Bette Davis," *The New York Times,* December 21, 1952, JR scrapbooks, NYPL.
218 "Jesus, Baby": Nancy Walker to JR, November 1, 1953, JRP.
218 "The producers were going": Laurents, interview with the author, June 12, 2000.
218 Davis refused (footnote): James Spada, *More Than a Woman: An Intimate Biography of Bette Davis,* 300–301.
219 "You like her": McLauchlin, *Detroit News,* October 20, 1952, quoted in Stine with Davis, *Mother Goddam,* 264.
219 "Indeed, Miss Davis": Walter Kerr, *New York Herald Tribune,* December 16, 2002.
219 "Dear Jerome Robbins": Bette Davis to JR, December 15, 1987, in response to his letter congratulating her on receiving a Kennedy Center Honors award, JRP.
220 For one thing, Saddler says: Donald Saddler, interview with the author, May 24, 2000.
220 " 'Don, why don't you' ": Ibid.
220 "Everything was very": Betty Comden, interview with the author, March 15, 2000.
220 "When they got": Ibid.
220 "Don, don't spare me": Saddler, interview with the author, May 24, 2000.
221 "Oh, George, please": William Weslow, interview with the author, January 18, 2000.
221 "In days to come": Olin Downes, "Wonderful Time," *The New York Times,* May 10, 1953.
221 "It is understood": Contract between JR and Robert Fryer and Thomas Whyte, general partners, January 26, 1953, JRP.
221 "That whole period": JR, interview with Reynolds, June 8, 1974, in preparation for her *Repertory in Review: 40 Years of the New York City Ballet.* Courtesy of Nancy Reynolds.
222 "That is me": Meehan, interview with the author, March 4, 1999.
222 "I walked into": JR, interview with Reynolds, June 8, 1974, quoted in Reynolds, *Repertory in Review: 40 Years of the New York City Ballet,* 147.
222 Johnson had one: Louis Johnson, interview with the author, June 8, 2002.

222   Jerry wrote to Buzz: JR to Miller, April 22, 1952, JRP.
223   Romola Nijinsky said: Romola Nijinsky with Lincoln Kirstein, *Nijinsky,* 239.
224   "suddenly began to stretch": JR, quoted in Reynolds, *Repertory in Review: 40 Years of the New York City Ballet,* 147.
225   "pushing through": Francisco Moncion, quoted in ibid., 148.
225   they might be seeing: I am indebted to Yaping Chen for alerting me to the reflection imagery in this lift in her unpublished paper "Jerome Robbins's *Afternoon of a Faun:* From Male Mythological Narcissism to the Sublimation of Female Beauty," New York University–Tisch School of the Arts, 1991.
226   "Reflect . . . whether": Stéphane Mallarmé, *L'Après-midi d'un faune,* author's translation.
226   "What you have understood": Jacques Le Clercq to JR, n.d., JRP.
227   "I fixed it": JR, interview with Ellen Sorrin, "A Conversation with Jerome Robbins: Working with Balanchine," New York City Ballet Guild Seminar, March 8, 1993.
228   "plan has provided": Terry, "Coronation Ballet," *New York Herald Tribune,* June 3, 1953.
229   "there have always been": Arnaud d'Usseau's testimony, "Investigation of Communist Activities in the New York Area—Part 2," Hearing Before the Committee on Un-American Activities, House of Representatives, Eighty-third Congress, First Session, May 5, 1953, 1315.
229   "getting into the field": Harold H. Velde in ibid.
229   "theatrical transient group": JR's testimony, in ibid., 1317.
229   "fascistic, bourgeois": Ibid., 1319.
229   He related that: Ibid., 1317.
229   he spilled them out: Ibid., 1322–1323.
230   she had clued him in: Madeleine Lee, quoted in Greg Lawrence, *Dance with Demons,* 58.
230   Representative Bernard Kearney thanked: Bernard W. Kearney of New York, in ibid., 1323.
230   Representative Gordon Scherer revealed: Gordon H. Scherer of Ohio, in ibid., 1324.
230   "yes, sir": JR testimony, in ibid., 1324.
230   "In other words, you feel": Clyde Doyle of California, in ibid., 1324.
230   "Now, let me say": Ibid.
230   "American quality": JR's testimony, in ibid., 1324.
230   "even put more": Doyle, in ibid., 1325.
230   Others . . . expressed sympathy: Mary Hunter to JR, May 6, 1953; George Abbott to JR, May 6, 1953.
230–31   he sought . . . to find: "References to Lionel Berman, Edward Chodorov, Jerome Chodorov, Lloyd Gough, Madeleine Lee, Edna Ocko, Lettie Stever, and Elliot Sullivan in House Committee on Un-American Activities Testimony by Jerome Robbins on May 5, 1954," submitted to Clifford Forster by Anthony Henley, January 23, 1989.
231   Many years later: Michael Koessel, interview with the author, March 26, 1999.
231   "It was my homosexuality": JR, "The Times of the 35 40s continued into being a Jew," September 8, 1976, JR, notes toward an autobiography/*The Poppa Piece,* JRP.

11. Taking Charge

PAGE

232 Arthur Laurents believes: Arthur Laurents, interview with the author, June 12, 2000.

233 *Daily Variety* noted: *Daily Variety,* June 30, 1953, JR scrapbooks, NYPL.

233 In July he was said: "Broadway Beat," *Salt Lake City Tribune,* July 12, 1953, JR Scrapbooks, NYPL.

233 *Dance News* was presenting: *Dance News,* September 1953, JR scrapbooks, NYPL.

233 "You must explain": Tanaquil Le Clercq to JR, November 27, 1956.

233 "Try if possible": JR to Buzz Miller, "Tuesday, May 27" [May 27, 1952], JRP.

234 "who we are": Mary Hunter to Leland Hayward, July 27, 1953, filed with material on "The Ford 50th Anniversary Show," JRP.

234 "Concurrent with each": JR, penciled note to Hayward, re "The Ford 50th Anniversary Show": "Robbins notes—Sunday night," JRP.

235 "thrust upon us": Oscar Hammerstein II, on "The Ford 50th Anniversary Show" ("The American Road"), June 15, 1953, broadcast simultaneously over NBC and CBS television. A kinescope of the program is archived at the Museum of Television and Radio in New York City.

235 "[if] we confuse": Edward R. Murrow, on "The Ford 50th Anniversary Show" ("The American Road"), June 15, 1953 (see above).

235 "destroy itself": Ibid.

235 "Sad Spots Flaw": Dorothy Kilgallen, "The Voice of Broadway," *New York Journal American,* June 17, 1953.

235 seated on stools: Myron Stitt, interview with the author, February 28, 2002.

236 "In view of the fact": agreement between Mary Martin and Jerome Robbins, July 29, 1953, JRP.

236 *Newsweek* reported: *Newsweek,* June 29, 1953, JR scrapbooks, NYPL.

237 "outstanding individual": Clipping in JR scrapbooks, NYPL.

237 *Musical Americana:* Flyer with inked date, February 15, 1954, *Musical Americana,* clippings, NYPL (Billy Rose Theater Collection).

237 Although the New York News Service: *Salt Lake City Tribune,* July 12, 1953, JR scrapbooks, NYPL.

238 "He didn't think the sun": Anna Sokolow, interview with the author, March 9, 1999.

239 "fantasia on Israeli folk themes": John Martin, "Robbins' 'Quartet' Danced at Center," *The New York Times,* February 20, 1954.

239 "the lyric oriental flavor": Rosalind Krokover, "The Dance," *Musical Courier,* March 15, 1954.

239 "Once he put that": JR, interview with Nancy Reynolds, June 8, 1974. Quoted in Reynolds, *Repertory in Review: 40 Years of the New York City Ballet,* 161.

239 "charmingly composed": John Martin, "Robbins' 'Quartet' Danced at Center," *The New York Times,* February 20, 1954.

240 "inept book": [Author's name not included in clipping], "Music to My Ears," *Saturday Review,* April 17, 1954, JR scrapbooks, NYPL.

241 "mannered": Douglas Watt, "Copland Work in World Premiere," *Daily News,* April 15, 1954, JR scrapbooks, NYPL.

241 "quota of plastic posturing": Robert Bagar, " 'Tender Land' in Rustic Setting," *World-Telegram and Sun,* April 2, 1954, JR scrapbooks, NYPL.

241 "The most deeply emotional": Olin Downes, "Music: One-Act Opera Has Premiere," *The New York Times,* April 2, 1954, JR scrapbooks, NYPL.

241 "one of the worst": JR to Laurents, March 29, 1954, JRP.

241 "a good experience": JR to Lincoln Kirstein, April 5, 1954, JRP.

241 he still fired off notes: JR, notes to Jean Rosenthal and Robert Pageant, filed with *Tender Land* material, JRP.

241 Buzz Miller urged: Miller, quoted in Kevin Boyd Grubb, *Razzle Dazzle: The Life and Work of Bob Fosse,* 41. Martin Gottfried, *All His Jazz,* 76, credits Joan McCracken, then Fosse's wife, with trying to get everyone involved with *Pajama Game* to see *Kiss Me, Kate.*

242 "I, while agreeing": Harold Prince to Greg Lawrence, June 11, 1999, quoted in Lawrence, *Dance with Demons,* 220.

242 "1. Helped re-stage": JR to David Hocker of the Music Corporation of America, December 6, 1955, JRP.

242 he offered opinions: JR to George Abbott, March 26, 1954, JRP.

243 "was the best stager": Stephen Sondheim, interview with the author, August 3, 2000.

243 "I think I learned": Bob Fosse, interview with Kenneth Geist, May 16, 1983. Courtesy of Kenneth Geist.

243 "I think Balanchine": Ibid. Fosse also notes in the interview that he made the same remark in a recent interview for *Rolling Stone.*

244 "It was destined that Jerry": Mary Martin, "All About *Peter Pan,*" a symposium held at Marymount Manhattan Theater, February 23, 1982. Published in *The Journal for Stage Directors and Choreographers,* June 1982, no. 7. Martin could not be present but contributed an Afterword.

244 "Still dreams of youth": "Jerry Rabinowitz, Poetry & Music Compositions, 1924–35" (scrapbook), JRP.

244 "find a way of doing it": JR, in "All About *Peter Pan,*" a symposium held at Marymount Manhattan Theater, February 23, 1982.

245 "The only possible problem": JR to Edwin Lester, March 18, 1953, JRP.

245 "small, young boys" . . . "practically midget girls": JR to Eugene Loring, May 27, 1954, JRP.

245 In January, it was announced: Bert McCord, "Theater News: Mary Martin as Peter Pan, Her Daughter as Wendy," *New York Herald Tribune,* January 29, 1954.

245 "prim, proper and": JR, typed notes on *Peter Pan,* "Main Points to Consider in Planning Changes," with handwritten bits not in JR's hand, JRP.

246 Sondra Lee remembers: Sondra Lee, interview with the author, June 28, 1999.

246 The collaborators: Betty Comden and Adolph Green, interview with the author, March 15, 2000.

246 "Occasionally someone": JR to Miller, September 1954, JRP.

246 "It ended with Jule": JR, draft of speech to be given at a 1990 tribute to Jule Styne, JRP.

247 "It wasn't a musical": Betty Comden, interview with the author, March 15, 2000.

247 "We wrote songs": Adolph Green, ibid. (Comden and Green were interviewed together).

247 "We felt it needed": Comden, ibid.

247 The San Francisco critics: quoted in Bruce K. Hanson, *The Peter Pan Chronicles: The Nearly 100 Year History of "The Boy Who Wouldn't Grow Up,"* 195–196.

247 "It's the way": Walter Kerr, "Theater: 'Peter Pan' Something to Crow About," *New York Herald Tribune,* October 21, 1954.

248 "His right hand": JR, set of pages with cues giving details of the shadow play, filed with *Peter Pan* material, JRP.

248 The choreographer has said (footnote): Paul Taylor, *Private Domain,* 57.

248 Sondra Lee corroborates this (footnote): Lee, telephone conversation with the author, ca. 2000.

249 "thinks he has to do": Kirstein to JR, October 1, 1954, JRP.

249 He had listed *Dybbuk:* JR, list of ballets planned ca. 1945, "Early 1940s Ballet Stories," JRP. *New York News,* May 28, 1948, mentions JR's "long-projected ballet version" of *The Dybbuk.*

249 Neither of the two: Kirstein to JR, October 31, 1954, JRP.

249 "[George's] suggestion that I do": JR to Kirstein, November 11, 1954, JRP.

250 "convert the material": Ibid.

250 "long, turbulent": Edward Sothern Hipp, " 'Silk Stockings' Slick," *Newark Sunday News,* March 6, 1955, JR scrapbooks, NYPL.

250 it had been announced: Hedda Hopper, "The Talk of Hollywood" (syndicated column), *Baltimore Evening Sun,* April 12, 1954, JR scrapbooks, NYPL.

250 "This is the story": Guy Bolton and Eddie Davis, script of *Ankles Aweigh,* JRP.

251 "something I never would": JR to Mary Martin and Richard Halliday, April 13, 1955, JRP.

251 "Dearest Crow": Laurents to JR, dated only "Friday eve" [1955].

252 "A Half Riot": John Martin, "A Half Riot," *The New York Times,* March 7, 1956.

252 Robbins once said: JR, interviewed by Reynolds, June 8, 1974. Quoted in Reynolds, *Repertory in Review: 40 Years of the New York City Ballet,* 172.

252 "Nineteen Days to Go": Draft of an idea for a show or ballet, dated October 8, 1953, JRP.

254 "quite a job": Sam Lurie to JR, March 9, 1956, JRP.

255 Robbins told Maria Tallchief: Maria Tallchief with Larry Kaplan, *Maria Tallchief: America's Prima Ballerina,* 210–211.

255 a number of urgent cables: the correspondence is filed with Royal Danish Ballet materials, JRP.

255 Volkova and her husband: Vera Volkova to JR inviting him, March 11, 1956, JRP.

255 Svend Kragh-Jacobsen invited: Svend Kragh-Jacobsen to JR, April 3, 1956, JRP.

255 The Ballet Club persuaded him to: Ballet Club to JR, April 10, 1956, JRP. Robbins did so on April 20, 1956.

255 "beautiful, wonderful atmosphere": JR to Slim Hayward ("Dearest Pearl") from Copenhagen, "April, 54" penciled in later, but this is actually 1956, JRP. Robbins also drafted an article, "Working with the Royal Danish Ballet," intended for *Theatre Arts.*

255 "The children themselves": Ibid.

256 "fart" and "prik": JR to Slim Hayward ("Dearest Pearl"), Copenhagen, "April 1950" penciled in later, but this letter too is 1956, after the Royal Danish Ballet's performance of *Fanfare,* JRP.

256 "Dear Verushka": JR to Volkova, June 26, 1956, JRP.

256 "his marvelous cooperation": H. O. Brøndsted to JR, December 12, 1956, JRP.

256 "I know I should": JR to Slim Hayward ("Dearest Pearl"), from Copenhagen, "April, 54" penciled in later (this is the first of the two 1956 letters mentioned above), JRP.

256 "getting into a snit": Ibid.

258 Debates over whether Peter Larkin: Betty Comden, Adolph Green, and Jule Styne, cable to JR, April 12, 1956, JRP.

258 "So finish with the": Comden and Green to JR, April 19, 1956, JRP.

258 "[Jerry] didn't tell": Gerald Freedman, interview with the author, May 12, 2000.

258 "You can use imagery": Ibid.

259 "a corny little": Comden and Green, *The New York Musicals of Comden & Green*, 256.

259 "He was so extraordinary": Freedman, interview with the author, May 12, 2000.

259–60 in 1959 she persuaded Jerry: Correspondence February 1959 among JR, Judy Holliday, and Morris M. Schrier, filed with *Bells Are Ringing* material, JRP.

260 "One terrible part": JR to Tanaquil Le Clercq, December 3, 1956, JRP.

260 "You would have been": JR to Le Clercq, October 8, 1956, JRP.

260 "I don't care for it": JR to Volkova, October 29, 1956, JRP.

260 Robbins was, he regretted: JR to Volkova, November 9, 1956, JRP.

260 "an inspired masterwork": Volkova to JR, October 29, 1956, JRP.

260 According to Barbara Horgan: Barbara Horgan, interview with the author, March 11, 2002.

261 "She is so brave": Edith Le Clercq to JR, November 14, 1956, JRP.

261 "all the time": Tanaquil Le Clercq to JR, undated [late November 1956], JRP.

261 she never . . . let Balanchine: Edith Le Clercq to JR, November 14, 1956, JRP.

261 "like a filet of sole": Tanaquil Le Clercq to JR, December 31, 1956, JRP.

261 remarking that "someone": Tanaquil Le Clercq to JR, n.d. [late January or early February 1957; JR refers to it in his letter to Le Clercq of February 6, 1957], JRP.

261 "I would like an animal": Tanaquil Le Clercq to JR, November 25, 1956, JRP.

261 "Morgan": Tanaquil Le Clercq (including note from Edith Le Clercq) to JR, December 21, 1956, JRP.

262 a helpful overseas friend: [Illegible] to JR, reporting the purchase on a German greeting card, filed in envelope with letter from Tanaquil Le Clercq to JR, December 4, 1956, JRP.

262 Betty Cage . . . has said: Betty Cage, quoted in Greg Lawrence, *Dance with Demons*, 239.

262 "the new show": JR to Tanaquil Le Clercq, December 3, 1956, JRP.

262 "all those new little": JR to Tanaquil Le Clercq, December 12, 1956, JRP.

262 "All the new kids": JR to Tanaquil Le Clercq, January 27, 1957, JRP.

262 "Don't laugh": JR to Tanaquil Le Clercq, January 25, 1957, JRP.

263 "Then they began": JR to Tanaquil Le Clercq, January 28, 1957, JRP.

263 Tanny had heard: Tanaquil Le Clercq to JR, January 27, 1957, JRP.

263 Jerry obliged: JR to Tanaquil Le Clercq, February 6, 1957, JRP. Lee Becker was shortly to be cast as "Anybodys" in *West Side Story* and to become a girlfriend of Robbins's. *The Unicorn, the Gorgon, and the Manticore* (referred to by NYCB dancers—not affectionately—as "Kukla, Fran, and Ollie") premiered on January 15, 1957.

263 "The long table": JR to Tanaquil Le Clercq, February 20, 1957, JRP.

264 She wondered if she might: Tanaquil Le Clercq to JR, November 25, 1956, JRP.

264 "in a long romantic cape": JR to Tanaquil Le Clercq, February 20, 1957, JRP.

12. Tony Loves Maria

PAGE

266 "That's who he was": Peter Martins, interview with the author, May 14, 2002.

266 "You *are* Anita": Rita Moreno, speaking at the reunion connected with the fortieth anniversary of the *West Side Story* film at Radio City Music Hall, October 2001. The

speeches by Moreno and others aired with showings of *West Side Story* on Turner Classic Movies around the same time.

266 "I wanted to find out": JR, speaking at "Dramatists Guild Landmark Symposium: *West Side Story," Dramatists Guild Quarterly,* Autumn 1985.

267 As Laurents had foreseen: Arthur Laurents, speaking at "Dramatists Guild Landmark Symposium: *West Side Story," Dramatists Guild Quarterly,* Autumn 1985.

267 Robbins has said: JR, speaking at "Dramatists Guild Landmark Symposium: *West Side Story," Dramatists Guild Quarterly,* Autumn 1985.

267 "agonizingly brilliant" (footnote): Kevin McCarthy, quoted in Patricia Bosworth, *Montgomery Clift: A Biography,* 157.

267 One early version: A number of early drafts of *West Side Story* material are archived in JRP.

267 they gradually drifted: Laurents, *Original Story,* 337. See also Robert Emmet Long, *Broadway, The Golden Years: Jerome Robbins and the Great Choreographer-Directors: 1940 to the Present,* 96.

267 Nora Kaye counseled: Arthur Laurents to JR, n.d., in response to JR to Laurents, October 16, 1955, JRP.

268 Judging by a letter: Laurents to Leonard Bernstein, July 19, 1955, JRP.

268 as producer Harold Prince confirms: Harold Prince, *Contradictions: Notes on Twenty-six Years in the Theatre,* 33.

268 sent him a Franklin stove: Brian Meehan, interview with the author, March 4, 1999.

268 Edith Weissman's daily memos: 1956 memos, JRP.

268 Oliver Smith ends: Oliver Smith to JR, April 5, 1956, JRP.

268 Miller told a friend: Meehan, interview with the author, March 4, 1999.

269 "that contained a lot": Keith Garebian, *The Making of West Side Story,* 35. See also "Early Story Plan for Romeo," typescript using Shakespeare's names for the characters, JRP.

269 "as fresh as theirs": Laurents to JR on yellow paper, "Monday," JRP.

270 "Tante": "A. Laurents, Rough Outline," in *West Side Story* materials, JRP.

270 Gerald Freedman: Gerald Freedman, interview with the author, May 12, 2000.

270 "You are away": JR to Laurents, October 18, 1955, JRP.

270 "to tread the fine line": Leonard Bernstein, "Excerpts from a *West Side Story* Log" (entry for March 17, 1956), *Playbill* for *West Side Story,* September 26, 1957.

270 "relaxes into a legitimate": JR to Laurents, November 16, 1955, JRP.

271 "True, I have found": Laurents, "Friday," in response to the above letter from JR, JRP.

271 "brilliant and exciting": Ibid.

271 "prettier, more melodic": Ibid.

271 "[w]e might tend": Laurents to JR from Paris, "Friday," JRP.

271 "Clam it!": Laurents, *West Side Story,* fairly early script (carbon on yellow paper), JRP.

272 "Lenny was very nervous": Laurents to JR, "Wednesday" [November 24, 1955] (addressed to "Dear Almost Home," it crossed Jerry on his return trip to New York and had to be forwarded from Beverly Hills), JRP.

272 "could be a wonderful": Ibid.

272 "on again": Bernstein, "Excerpts from a *West Side Story* Log" (entry for March 17, 1956), *Playbill* for *West Side Story,* September 26, 1957.

272 "Your idea": Smith to JR, April 5, 1956, JRP.

273 Gene Gavin remembers (footnote): Gene Gavin, "B.C. to Broadway: The Memoir of a Broadway Gypsy," manuscript, NYPL.

273 "both feel that exciting": Cheryl Crawford to JR, June 15, 1956, JRP.

273 "sketchy": Crawford to JR, January 3, 1957, JRP.

273 on April 2, 1957: Humphrey Burton, *Leonard Bernstein,* 268.

274 "I hereby engage you" (footnote): Contract between JR and Peter Gennaro, June 14, 1957, JRP.

274 He jotted down possibilities: There are many notes on casting in the *West Side Story* material, JRP.

274 Robbins told her to hide: Carol Lawrence, interview with the author, May 10, 2000.

274 she screamed: JR to Tanaquil Le Clercq, February 15, 1957, JRP.

275 "both crazy and wonderful": JR to Le Clercq, February 20, 1957, JRP.

275 "They do dances": JR to Le Clercq, February 25, 1957, JRP.

275 Chita Rivera remembers: Chita Rivera, interview with the author, May 25, 2000. Rivera remembers the picture showing sixteen-year-old Salvador Agron ("The Capeman") of the Vampires standing over the bodies of two teenagers he'd stabbed in a rumble. If she is correct, Robbins must have posted it much later, for the London company. The killing occurred on August 30, 1959, several years after the Broadway *West Side Story.*

275 "Tony is really *in*": Chita Rivera to JR in St. Thomas, November 24, 1957, JRP.

275 "an explosive little ferret": Laurents, *West Side Story,* stage directions that open Act I, scene 1.

275 "catlike ball of fury": Ibid.

276 "the gentle one": Lawrence, interview with the author, May 10, 2000.

276 "Big Daddy": various cast members mention this or address their letters to him this way, e.g., Rivera to JR, November 24, 1957, JRP.

276 Robbins told her: Garebian, *The Making of West Side Story,* 110.

276 "magnificent. . . . But I do not": Laurents to JR, undated letter written during rehearsals for *West Side Story,* JRP.

276 "make him better or not": Ibid.

276 Carol Lawrence tells: Lawrence, monologue in Tina Croll and James Cunningham's dance-theater piece, *From the Horse's Mouth,* performances. Lawrence's was one of those printed in *Ballet Review,* vol. 29, no. 4 (Winter 2001), 53–66. Jay Norman, interview with the author, September 11, 2002, remembers that although the "Maria Catchers" were not in place, the stage was deceptively full of people; the "Maria Lifters," he said, would never have tossed her had they not thought the "Catchers" were on hand.

276 "I just loved him": Rivera, interview with the author, May 25, 2000.

276 "You can't manipulate": Lawrence, interview with the author, May 10, 2000.

277 both Lawrence and Kert: Ibid.

277 "We were young": Rivera, interview with the author, May 25, 2000.

277 "It's really going to save": Leonard Bernstein to Felicia Montealegre Bernstein, August 8, 1957. Quoted in Burton, *Leonard Bernstein,* 272.

277 According to Sondheim: Sondheim, speaking at "Dramatists Guild Landmark Symposium: *West Side Story,*" *Dramatists Guild Quarterly,* Autumn 1985.

277 "It's alarming how charming": Stephen Sondheim, "I Feel Pretty," *West Side Story.*

278 Nora Kaye had predicted: Nora Kaye, quoted in Garebian, *The Making of West Side Story,* 31. JR to Laurents, November 16, 1955, notes that Betty Bogart (Lauren Bacall) feels the same way: "You three characters will never get on together." JRP.

278 Sondheim told: Meryle Secrest, *Leonard Bernstein: A Life,* 218.

278 "I would pick up": JR to Charles Harmon, December 27, 1994, JRP.

278 "unequivocally one of the most": Stephen Sondheim, interview with the author, August 3, 2000.

278 Laurents tried and failed: Laurents, *Original Story,* 363; Burton, *Leonard Bernstein,* 275.

279 "Despite everything": Laurents, interview with the author, June 12, 2000.

279 shrug their way: Beth Genné has pointed out in a note to the author (Spring 2003) that the device of making everyday behavior gradually expand into dancing did not originate with Robbins. She mentions the melding of ordinary movement, dancing, and song in, for instance, Rouben Mamoulian's 1932 film *Love Me Tonight,* but Robbins's pulling back from a climax at the end of musical numbers isn't typical of earlier films.

280 "More than subject matter": Sondheim, speaking at "Dramatists Guild Landmark Symposium: *West Side Story,*" *Dramatists Guild Quarterly,* Autumn 1985.

280 "The floating fire escapes": Garebian, *The Making of West Side Story,* 52.

280 Justice Felix Frankfurter: Burton, *Leonard Bernstein,* 273.

280 John Chapman ... loved it: John Chapman, " 'West Side Story' a Splendid and Super-Modern Musical Drama," *Daily News,* September 28, 1957.

280 Robert Coleman declared it: Robert Coleman, "Robert Coleman's Theatre: 'West Side Story' a Sensational Hit," *Daily Mirror,* September 28, 1957.

281 "I admired it": Ward Morehouse, "Shakespeare Goes Modern in Teen Gang Musical," *Staten Island Advance,* September 27, 1957, JR scrapbooks, NYPL.

281 "rushingly acted": Walter Kerr, "West Side Story," *New York Herald Tribune,* September 28, 1957.

281 "probably over-stylized": Kenneth Tynan, 1958. Reprinted without attribution in Kenneth Tynan, *Tynan on Theatre,* 170–171.

281 "The score": Ibid., 170.

282 the four creators agreed: Carl Fisher, general manager of the *West Side Story* company, to JR, July 13, 1960. This letter thanks JR and says that all four have agreed to royalty cuts in New York. JRP.

282 firing off notes: JR to Kenneth Le Roy, March 31, 1961 (also January 24, 1961 and January 30, 1961), JRP.

282 laying down the law: JR to Hugh Beaumont, December 27, 1960, JRP.

283 Lee Becker told Gavin: Gavin, "B.C. to Broadway: The Memoir of a Broadway Gypsy," manuscript, NYPL.

283 "When I see him": JR to Robert Fizdale, November 15, 1957, JRP.

284 "Our approach to": JR to Robert Wise, April 4, 1960, JRP.

284 "We have to find a": Wise to JR, April 8, 1960, JRP.

284 "Its absolutely true": JR to Wise, n.d. (a reply to the above), JRP.

285 She addressed him (footnote): Natalie Wood to JR, February 6 [?], January 10, 1968, and January 1973, JRP.

285 "My garage idea is": JR to Bernstein, June 3, 1960, JRP.

285 "The musical material": JR to Bernstein, interoffice memo, July 18, 1960.

286 "the camera WHIPS": Ibid.

286 "My father is a": Sondheim, "Officer Krupke," *West Side Story,* Act II, scene 2.

286 Wise, who was: Robert Wise, interview with the author, March 17, 2000.

286 "That's the way": Ibid.

287 "We'd write on little": David Bean, interview with the author, July 27, 1999.

287 And the records show: One script of the film of *West Side Story* (red cover) lists scenes according to the daily log that records number of takes, etc., JRP.

287 Margaret Banks, says: Margaret Banks, interview with the author, October 2, 2000.
287 "I would say": Ibid.
287 it is George Chakiris's: Chakiris, interview with the author, January 10, 2000.
288 Harold Mirisch's note: Mirisch to Robert Wise and JR, September 12, 1960.
288 "9–9:52 rehearse": Memo from Mirisch to "Messrs. Robert Wise and Jerome Robbins," September 15, 1960.
288 Wise has since: Wise, interview with the author, March 17, 2000.
288 According to Gina Trikonis: Trikonis, interview with the author, April 28, 1999.
288 Howard Jeffrey . . . reported: Jeffrey in Beverly Hills to JR in London, December 4, 1960 and December 16, 1960, JRP.
288 "the atmosphere absolutely": Chakiris, interview with the author, January 10, 2000.
289 Robbins estimated: JR to William Fitelson, June 2, 1961, JRP.
289 "There is possibly": JR, "Cutting Notes," December 1960, JRP. A later letter (April 1, 1961) indicates that these notes were primarily for Thomas Stanford, but copies were sent to Harold Mirisch and Wise.
289 "Would like to see how": Ibid.
289 "the cutting away from": Ibid.
290 "The most important aspect": JR, "Notes on *West Side Story* Film," April 12, 1961, JRP. The content and an initial note indicates they were primarily intended for Wise, but JR also says he was sending a copy to Mirisch.
290 "marvelously done" . . . "an absolutely": Ibid.
290 Wise reported: Robert Wise to JR, April 24, 1961, JRP.
291 Ray Kurtzman: Kurtzman to Jay Kanter, May 8, 1961, JRP.
291 more than $250,000: Some financial information is contained in a memorandum from Floria Lasky to JR, February 7, 1964. The Jerome Robbins Papers contain information on all JR's financial transactions, earnings, tax statements, accounts, etc.
291 "the late Bobby Griffith": JR, Academy Awards acceptance speeches, April 11, 1962, film clips in the Jerome Robbins Archive of the Recorded Moving Image, NYPL.
291 Bosley Crowther . . . and Stanley Kauffmann: Crowther, "Screen: 'West Side Story' Arrives," *New York Times,* October 19, 1961; Kauffmann, "West Side Story," *The New Republic,* October 23, 1961; reprinted in Kauffmann, *A World on Film,* 134–137.
291 "the best film musical": Ibid.
291 "How can so many critics": Pauline Kael, KPFA broadcast, 1961; *Film Quarterly,* Summer 1962; included in Kael, *For Keeps: 30 Years at the Movies,* 34–38 (36).
292 "Saw film of *West Side Story*": JR to Richard Buckle, October 16, 1961, JRP.
292 "no faces, no fingers": JR to Buckle, May 30, 1962, JRP.

13. Exporting America

PAGE
294 writing a testimonial: JR statement about Inbal, April 30, 1957, to be sent out with letters, apparently to be signed by him and Anna Sokolow, requesting funding to facilitate the company's U.S. tour, JRP. The "list" was in good part Roger Stevens's.
294 He and Anna Sokolow: guest list and draft of invitational telegram from JR to various friends (Carol Lawrence, Nora Kaye, Lena Horne, et al.), JRP.
294 the American Israel Cultural Foundation: American Israel Cultural Foundation to JR, January 12, 1960, JRP.

294 He wrote a letter: JR to the Rockefeller Foundation, October 31, 1957, JRP.

294 he signed over his royalty: Jean Rosborough, executive director, the Greater New York Chapter of the National Foundation for Infantile Paralysis, to JR, December 4, 1957, thanking him for his contribution, JRP.

294 He was glad: Bernard Taper to JR, March 13, 1958, thanking him for agreeing to be interviewed, JRP.

294 "The Relaxation Guidance Center": Marthann Doolittle, Ed.D., to JR, April 27, 1958, JRP.

294 David I. Zeitlin: Zeitlin to JR on *Life* magazine stationery, January 24, 1958, JRP.

295 "The negative is somewhat": JR to Zeitlin, January 30, 1958, JRP. For some reason, Zeitlin's book, *Shooting Stars,* was not published until 1998, after Zeitlin's death ("Restored and revised" by Harriet Zeitlin), and perhaps after Robbins's as well. The comments JR sent to Zeitlin are more detailed than those that appear in the book.

295 "falling apart": JR to Richard Buckle [early January 1960], JRP. Buckle had been visiting New York but had returned to London before Christmas.

295 "She walked into the kitchen": Ibid.

295 "could be a hell": JR to Leland Hayward, October 25, 1957, JRP.

295 he also wrote to Rudolf Bing: JR to Bing, November 27, 1957, JRP.

296 Leo Kerz: Leo Kerz to JR [early 1958], JRP.

296 excited him by proposing: Kerz to JR, February 12, 1960, telling JR he needs a decision by Monday. JR to LK, February 18, 1960, can't commit himself at this point. JRP.

296 "found myself settling": JR to Robert Fizdale, November 15, 1957, from St. John, JRP.

296 "a horrifying children's fairy tale": JR to Lincoln Kirstein, September 25, 1958, JRP.

296 In 1957, the composer: Gian Carlo Menotti to JR, August 1957, JRP.

297 "The Arts in Spoleto": Alberto Moravia in the 1958 souvenir program for the Festival of Two Worlds, NYPL.

298 "wiser heads have": John Martin, "Dance: Spoleto," advance piece on Ballets: U.S.A., *The New York Times,* June 1, 1958.

298 "financial endorsement": JR, cable to Spoleto Festival, April 18, 1958, JRP.

299 Carolyn Brown: Carolyn Brown, in-process book about her years in the Merce Cunningham Dance Company. Courtesy of Carolyn Brown.

299 she was overheard: Ibid.

299 "I think we": Sondra Lee, interview with the author, June 28, 1999.

299 "a shipload of immigrants": Ibid.

299 Lida Gialoretti: Lida Gialoretti, interview with the author, July 9, 2002.

300 "[draping] like a swag": JR, 1973 notebook, August 2, 1973, JRP.

300 they were served: Gialoretti, interview with the author, July 9, 2002.

300 "a hurricane . . . sweeping over": Alexander Bland (nom de plume of Nigel Gosling and Maud Lloyd), "The Balletic Missile," *The Observer,* August 19, 1961, Ballets: U.S.A. clippings, NYPL.

301 Humphrey had been trying: Author was a member of Juilliard Dance Theater, 1957–1959.

302 "like she was a": James Moore interview with the author, May 29, 1999.

302 "Ballet: Rousing Success": Howard Taubman, "Ballet: Rousing Success," *The New York Times,* June 9, 1958, Ballets: U.S.A. clippings, NYPL.

303 Robbins heard from Leland Hayward: Hayward, cable to JR, June 12, 1958, JRP.

303 "delightful improvisation": Review signed "Geor.," *Variety,* September 10, 1958, Ballets: U.S.A. clippings, NYPL.

303 a film prepared by: "Ballets: U.S.A," USIA program, "Americana Cultural Series," United States Information Agency, 1958, Jerome Robbins Archive of the Recorded Moving Image, NYPL.

303 Robert Sabin: Robert Sabin, "Jerome Robbins Company in Broadway Engagement," *Musical America,* October 1958, Ballets: U.S.A. clippings, NYPL.

303 John Martin disliked: John Martin, "Ballets U.S.A. Opens," *The New York Times,* September 5, 1958.

303 Robbins wasn't satisfied: JR to Robert Ponsonby at the Edinburgh Festival, December 16, 1958, mentions that for the company's 1959 appearances there, he may substitute a new ballet for *3 X 3,* "as I was not too happy with it." JRP.

303 Martin also found fault: Martin, "Ballets U.S.A. Opens."

303 "You are hereby": Paul Godkin, telegram to JR, September 4, 1958, JRP.

303 "Now don't be nervous": telegram to JR signed Tony, Lisa, and Chita on behalf of the whole *West Side Story* company, September 4, 1958, JRP.

304 "YOU MURDERED THEM": Jule Styne, telegram to JR, September 4, 1958, JRP.

304 "[N]o one but you": Lincoln Kirstein to JR, May 20, 1958, JRP.

304 "BEST WISHES": Kirstein and George Balanchine, telegram to JR, September 4, 1958, JRP.

304 Barbara Horgan: Barbara Horgan to JR, December 30, 1958, JRP.

305 ANTA's Dance Panel: This and other information about the International Cultural Program comes from Naima Prevots, *Dance for Export: Cultural Diplomacy and the Cold War.*

305 "[H]e established": David Denby, "The Gift to Be Simple," *The New Yorker,* December 13, 1999, 102–111.

306 "pure dance terms": JR to Aaron Copland, January 9, 1959, JRP.

306 "a declarative statement": Ibid.

306 "These are only ideas": JR, note handwritten at top of above letter to Copland, JRP.

306 "Copland's highly stylized" (footnote): Howard Pollack, *Aaron Copland: The Life and Work of an Uncommon Man,* 487.

306 Robbins wrote that Copland: JR, one of many drafts of an article or program note on the genesis of *Moves,* JRP.

306 "a beautiful score": Ibid.

307 James Moore has a memory: Moore, interview with the author, May 29, 1999.

307 "Let's try something": Erin Martin, interview with the author, March 19, 1999.

307 Schnitzer predicted: Robert Schnitzer to JR, June 8, 1959, JRP.

307 "[H]e said he felt": JR to Schnitzer, June 18, 1959, JRP.

307 suggested that *Interplay*: Schnitzer to JR, June 23, 1959, JRP.

307 Robbins had suggested: JR to Schnitzer, June 9, 1959, JRP.

307 the attaché in Dubrovnik: JR to Schnitzer, August 22, 1959, JRP.

307 "It is absolutely": JR to Schnitzer from Salzburg, August 15, 1959, unsent, JRP.

308 "places the dancer's body": JR, one of many drafts of an article or program note on the genesis of *Moves,* JRP.

309 Jets and Sharks gone "arty": John Martin, "Robbins' Dancers Open at the ANTA," *The New York Times,* October 9, 1961, Ballets: U.S.A. clippings, NYPL.

309 "It's like having lost": *Politiken,* included with extracts of reviews sent JR by USIS, April 8, 1960, JRP. Note: Many of the items below pertaining to Ballets: U.S.A.'s 1959 European tour sent on by USIS, April 8, 1960, JRP.

309 "The Greatest Thing in Ballet": Julian Holland, "The Greatest Thing in Ballet," September 14, 1959, extracts of reviews sent to JR by Robert Schnitzer, JRP.

310 *Le Figaro* also mentioned: François de Santerre, *Le Figaro,* among the Paris reviews sent to JR by the American Embassy in Paris, JRP.

310 "None of the illustrious": "Young America Dancing," *Der Tagesspiegel,* October 4, 1959, press comments on Ballets: U.S.A. translated and sent from Germany, JRP.

310 "There have been brilliant": 1959 "Tour Analysis" (July 3–November 4, 1959), no authorship attributed, presumably prepared by ANTA for the State Department, JRP.

310 "[I]t's like rolling": JR, draft of statement on his process, with corrections; begun June 3, 1959, revised June 15, 1959, JRP.

310 "We in America dress": JR, program essay, quoted in Alexander Bland, "The Robbins Affair," *The Observer,* September 20, 1959.

310 He delighted: Heath Bowman to JR, October 25, 1960, JRP.

310 "You know": JR, quoted by Moore, interview with the author, May 29, 1999.

311 Alte Kocker: Ibid.

311 "a treasure": JR to Leland Hayward, August 14, 1959, JRP.

311 "The kissing bandit": JR to Robert Fizdale, August 2, 1959, JRP.

311 "Fabulous day": JR, entry in small diary, "1959 BUSA," July 23, 1959, JRP.

311 official in the latter city: 1959 "Tour Analysis," JRP. See note above.

311 "invite adverse propaganda": Ibid.

312 Robbins . . . made: Edinburgh reviews of September 7, 1959, opening mention lost scenery and costumes, etc., and JR's speech, JRP.

312 "The dancers themselves": JR to Schnitzer, July 12, 1959, JRP.

312 Jenny Nicholson Cross: JR to Jenny Nicholson Cross, October 1, 1959, thanking her for all her help, JRP.

312 Tony Mordente . . . flew over: Tony Mordente, cable to JR, September 24, 1959, announcing his arrival in Copenhagen, JRP.

312 "Jerome Robbins' Ballets: U.S.A.": Edinburgh review, no author or date, among those press extracts sent to JR by Schnitzer, JRP.

312 Sullivan presented: "The Concert" *(Ed Sullivan Show),* Jerome Robbins Archive of the Recorded Moving Image, NYPL, *MGZHB 6-46.

313 "the Arthur G. [Gold] thing": JR to Fizdale, July 20, 1958, JRP.

313 "the consequences or actualities": JR, note added to the above the next day. It's reasonable to believe the letter was never sent, even though Fizdale years later returned to JR the letters he'd received from him—presumably in connection with JR's projected autobiography.

313 "practically my foster parents": JR, transcript of interview for "The American Showmen," BBC-TV, 1975. As of September 17, 1975, JR notes that he can't approve the transcript he's been sent, but will either correct this version or a final one.

314 "I have to work": JR to Slim Hayward [Keith], quoted in Slim Keith with Annette Tapert, *Slim: Memories of a Rich and Imperfect Life,* 259.

314 "That was just": Ibid., 259.

314 "He's so cool": JR, notes, green notebook labeled "Italian Notes. Celebrations & large mysteries for church" [1973], JRP.

314 a letter from Robbins: JR, draft of letter to Richard Buckle, n.d. [January 1960], JRP.

314 "balance the program": Schnitzer to JR, July 12, 1960, JRP.

314 "American Ballet Company of Monaco": Correspondence between Albert Sarfati and JR in Hollywood, October 2 and October 7, 1960, and cable to JR from Audrey Wood, JRP.

315 "just the end": JR to Nora Kaye, March 6, 1961, JRP.

315 "The fall out": JR, "Events—notes," JRP.

316 In a silent: *Events,* filmed in 1961, silent, Jerome Robbins Archive of the Recorded Moving Image, NYPL, *MGZHB 8-90 or *MGZIA 4-3712.

316 Erin Martin also learned: Erin Martin, interview with the author, March 19, 1999.

317 "pleased and profoundly moved": Ben Shahn to JR, August 3, 1961, JRP.

317 "a quest to find": Walter Terry, "Dance: Ballets: U.S.A.," *New York Herald Tribune,* October 18, 1961.

317 "The bomb": Richard Buckle, "Robbins Takes His Time," *The Sunday Times* (London), August 6, 1961.

317 "many marvelous": Terry, "Dance: Ballets: U.S.A.," *New York Herald Tribune,* October 18, 1961.

318 "The choreography": Buckle, "Robbins Takes His Time."

14. Everything's Coming Up Roses?

319 "The best damn musical": Walter Kerr, "First Night Report: 'Gypsy,' " *New York Herald Tribune,* May 22, 1959.

320 "the Queen Mary coming": Gerald Freedman, interview with the author, May 12, 2000.

320 "*Gypsy* had two producers": Arthur Laurents, *Original Story: A Memoir of Broadway and Hollywood,* 375.

320 "seething with volcano-force": Keith Garebian, *The Making of Gypsy,* 9.

321 "ETHEL MERRICK": Leland Hayward, cable to JR, June 17, 1958, JRP.

321 Sondheim's mentor, Oscar Hammerstein II: Meryle Secrest, *Stephen Sondheim: A Life,* 134.

322 Jack Haskell: On February 5, 1959, plaintiff's lawyer, David Neuwirth, sent JR a list of nine numbers in *Gypsy* that Haskell claimed had originated in ideas he had given to Robbins. JR penciled "no" beside six of them. Vis-à-vis "Pony Trot," "Heads," and "Aerial Number," he wrote, "Don't know what these are." Haskell apparently sued Jule Styne as well. JR's papers imply that there was a transcript of JR's examination before a trial, which was scheduled for May 27, 1959. The transcript is not among the papers, and the case must have been settled out of court. Floria Lasky, Robbins's lawyer, has no memory of the case.

323 "I didn't just do" (footnote): Danny Daniels, interview with the author, January 12, 2002.

323 "Well, someone tell me": Stephen Sondheim, *Gypsy,* Act II, scene 6.

324 "It was. . . . one": Secrest, *Stephen Sondheim: A Life,* 138.

324 "Ethel's imagination and brain": Sondheim, interview with the author, August 3, 2000.

324 "commitment": Gerald Freedman to JR, December 27, 1993.

325 in a Dramatists Guild symposium: "Dramatists Guild Landmark Symposium: *Gypsy,*" *Dramatists Guild Quarterly,* vol. 18, no. 3 (Autumn 1981), 1–30.

325 he later refuted: JR, "Footnote to *Gypsy* symposium" (typed notes), May 18, 1985, JRP.

325 he was not pleased: JR to David Merrick, Leland Hayward, Arthur Laurents, Stephen Sondheim, and Jule Styne, December 8, 1959, confirms this ("Lane Bradbury . . . with whom none of us was too pleased"), JRP.

325 "DEAR JERRY, THANK YOU": David Merrick, telegram to JR, May 21, 1959, JRP.

325 "obscenity, lewdness": Memorandum prepared by a lawyer, found among Robbins's material pertaining to *Gypsy,* JRP.

325 "We are all absolutely": Arthur Laurents to JR, undated note on Hotel Warwick stationery, JRP.

326 "I know you're so rich": Leland Hayward to JR, August 25, 1959, JRP.

326 Robbins advised a new costume: Hayward to JR, September 23, 1959, indicates that JR has wired saying that a new costume was needed for Church. Hayward countered: "Raoul DuBois is in Europe, so I can't get him to do a new costume." The debate continued: JR to Hayward, Merrick, Laurents, Styne, and Sondheim, December 8, 1959, and JR to Hayward and Merrick, January 11, 1960, JRP.

326 Hayward wondered slyly: Hayward, cable to JR, September 16, 1959, JRP.

326 "No other choreographer": JR to Hayward, October 3, 1959.

327 "as a cross between": Secrest, *Stephen Sondheim: A Life,* 140

329 By August 18: JR, cable to Roger Stevens, August 18, 1961, JRP.

329 "The feeding": Arthur Kopit, interview with the author, September 15, 2002.

329 "It just bubbles along": Ibid.

329 "for all its horror": JR, notes in a spiral binder pertaining to *Oh Dad . . . ,* JRP.

329 "cunts with teeth": Muriel Resnick to JR, March 7, 1962, JRP.

329 "a romantic sort": Kopit, interview with the author, September 15, 2002.

330 "it seemed as if ": Ibid.

330 "a world waiting to": Kopit, *Oh Dad, Poor Dad, Mamma's Hung You in the Closet and I'm Feelin' So Sad,* scene 3.

330 "You just followed": Nancy Franklin, interview with the author, June 23, 2001.

330 As one critic: Harry Altshuler, " 'O Dad' Hilarious Novelty," *New York Mirror,* August 28, 1963.

330 "As a mother": Kopit, *Oh Dad, Poor Dad, Mamma's Hung You in the Closet and I'm Feelin' So Sad,* last scene.

330 "They [mother and son]": JR, notes in a spiral binder pertaining to *Oh Dad . . . ,* JRP.

331 Kopit wrote Jerry notes: These are preserved in JRP, along with materials pertaining to *Oh Dad . . .* One set of typed comments is dated February 17, 1962.

331 "visual brilliance and sense": Kopit, interview with the author, September 15, 2002.

331 At the end: Kopit, *Sing to Me Through Open Windows,* in *The Day the Whores Came Out to Play Tennis and Other Plays,* 77.

331 It has been suggested: Bill Daniels, quoted in Greg Lawrence, *Dance with Demons,* 502.

331 Kopit has said: Kopit, interview with the author, September 15, 2002.

331 Kopit, Austin Pendleton, Barry Primus, and Gerald Hiken: Kopit, interview with the author, September 15, 2002; Pendleton, interview with Kenneth Geist, September 9, 1983; Primus, interview with the author, January 12, 2001. Hiken, quoted in Greg Lawrence, *Dance with Demons,* 301.

332 "a series of still images": Kopit, interview with the author, September 15, 2002.

332 "on the second or third day": Primus, interview with the author, January 12, 2001.

332 Primus found out later: Ibid.

332 "In rehearsal": Pendleton, interview with Geist, September 9, 1983.

333 Robbins . . . asked Pendleton: Ibid.

333 "Arthur Kopit's little rasher": John McClain, "Bit Funnier Second Time Around," *Journal American,* August 28, 1963.

333   "remains original": Paul Gardner, "Theater: 'Dad' Returns," *The New York Times,* August 28, 1963.

334   "Jerry dear": Cheryl Crawford to JR, July 12, 1961, JRP.

334   "Everyone has been": Ibid.

334   "Ethel Merman!": Crawford to JR, July 26, 1961, JRP.

334   "but I must be honest": Ethel Merman to JR, March 26, 1962.

334   Robbins admitted: JR, interview with the author for the Kennedy Center Honors Oral History Program, July 11, 1995.

334   He attacked it optimistically: JR's files of research for *Mother Courage* contain all the items mentioned, JRP.

335   "It's been too influential": JR to Estelle Parsons, n.d. [1962?], JRP.

335   "It goes very much": Ibid.

335   "isn't really an anti-war": JR, "Day to Day Notes—Telling the Story of Mother Courage," November 26, 1962, JRP.

335   "Let all of you": Bertolt Brecht, *Mother Courage and Her Children: A Chronicle of the Thirty Years' War,* trans. Eric Bentley, 111.

335   At one point: JR, "Day to Day Notes—Telling the Story of Mother Courage," November 26, 1962, JRP.

336   that she was too young: Ibid.

336   he took her: Ibid., entry dated December 5, [1962].

336   Eric Bentley thinks: Bentley, conversation with the author, November 24, 2003.

336   "It may be": Eric Bentley to JR, January 19, 1963, JRP.

336   Robbins asked for cuts: Bentley, in notes to JR during rehearsals, refers to the request for cuts, JRP.

336   and warned Jerry: Bentley to JR, March 13, 1963, JRP.

336   "The Epic character": Mordecai Gorelik, "An Epic Theatre Catechism." JR got a copy of the essay from the Maria Ley Piscator Institute. JRP.

337   "ability to button": Stephen Sondheim, interview with the author, August 3, 2000.

337   "I didn't know shit": Conrad Bromberg, interview with the author, June 23, 2001.

337   Several critics noted: Walter Kerr, "Brecht on Broadway At Last—and Alas," *New York Herald Tribune,* April 14, 1963; Michael Smith, "Courage, Brothers" ("Theatre Uptown" column), *The Village Voice,* April 4, 1963.

337   "Annie often stops": Crawford to JR, "Notes. C.C.," undated [1963], JRP.

337   "Isn't the emotion": Bentley to JR, undated [1963] notes, JRP.

338   "Mother Courage is a queen": Crawford to JR, undated [1963] notes, JRP. The critical comment came from "a friend of Dick Chandler."

338   "lights 10 up": JR, marginal comment on Bentley's undated 1963 notes referred to above.

338   "Our text, too": Bentley to JR, "A Note," March 15, 1963, JRP.

338   "I would like <u>more</u>": JR, marginal comment on the March 15, 1963 note directly above.

338   Stuart W. Little: Stuart W. Little, " 'Mother Courage': High in Previews," *New York Herald Tribune,* April 2, 1963.

338   with the exception: Martin Gottfried, "Brecht's 'Mother Courage' Murdered on Broadway," *Women's Wear Daily,* March 29, 1963. Gottfried thought that JR had tried to make the play into popular entertainment.

338   "visually stunning": John Chapman, "Anne Bancroft Shines Again in Brecht Play," *Daily News,* April 14, 1963.

338 "has been staged": Howard Taubman, "Theater: 'Mother Courage' by Brecht," *The New York Times,* April 14, 1963.

339 "power of the theater": Walter Kerr, *New York Herald Tribune,* April 14, 1963.

339 Both Melvin Maddocks . . . and Richard Watts: Melvin Maddocks, "Brecht's 'Mother Courage,' " *The Christian Science Monitor,* March 30, 1963; Richard Watts, "Berthold Brecht's 'Mother Courage' " (Watts's "Two on the Aisle" column), *New York Post,* April 14, 1963.

339 "This is the season": Michael Smith, "Courage, Brothers" ("Theatre Uptown" column), *The Village Voice,* April 4, 1963.

339 "[I]t seems to me": JR, "Day to Day Notes—Telling the Story of Mother Courage," November 26, 1962, JRP.

340 "I found it interesting": Crawford to JR, May 21, 1963, JRP.

340 The bad news: Leland Hayward, cable to JR, July 17, 1958, JRP.

340 "WHAT CAN BE DONE": JR, draft cable to Hayward from Brussels in response to the above.

341 "Yesterday Paddy Chayevsky": William Fitelson to JR, June 3, 1963.

341 a Rockland County enclave: Isabelle K. Savell, *The Tonetti Years at Snedens Landing.*

342 By June: Harold Prince to JR, June 6, 1961, JRP.

342 Sondheim says: Sondheim, quoted in Secrest, *Stephen Sondheim: A Life,* 149.

342 "pretty teed off": JR to Prince, August 2, 1961, JRP.

342 In the remarkably courteous: Prince to JR, July 27 and August 9, 1961, JRP.

343 "a disaster": Stephen Sondheim, interview with the author, August 3, 2000.

343 "couldn't finish the thing": George Abbott, interview with Kenneth Geist, September 15, 1983.

343 "sort of guru": JR, transcript of interview with Craig Zadan for Zadan's book *Sondheim & Co.* (1974). On November 28, 1973, Zadan sent JR the transcript, which JR edited heavily. His contribution did not appear in the published book.

343 "[Jerry] could work": Abbott, interview with Geist, September 15, 1983.

343 "I just didn't think": Sondheim, quoted in Secrest, *Stephen Sondheim: A Life,* 150.

343 According to Stone: Tom Stone, interview with the author, September 17, 2002.

343 "Hiya, loose lips!": Tony Walton, quoted in Greg Lawrence, *Dance with Demons,* 311.

344 "hummable": Secrest, *Stephen Sondheim: A Life,* 152.

344 "[T]he opening song": JR, transcript of interview with Craig Zadan for Zadan's book *Sondheim & Co.* (1974). See above.

344 "A proud Roman": Sondheim, "Comedy Tonight," *A Funny Thing Happened on the Way to the Forum,* Act I, scene 1.

344 "funniest bit": Sondheim, interview with the author, August 3, 2000.

344 Robbins wrote: JR, itemized list of his contributions in regard to doctoring the production of *A Funny Thing Happened on the Way to the Forum.* This must have been intended for his lawyer; it ends with a note: "The above are the things I can remember right off the bat and hastily, but there may be more. J.R." JRP.

344 Abbott recalled: Abbott, interview with Geist, September 15, 1983.

344 "magic little finger": JR to Richard Buckle, May 30, 1962, JRP.

344 "beef up trill in orchestra": JR, one of the notes written on a little pad, "Don't Forget," JRP.

344 "He said, 'You're being' ": Sondheim, interview with the author, August 3, 2000.

345 "its composer was grateful": Sondheim to JR, n.d., postmarked May 16, 1962, JRP.

345 He also negotiated: In the heated correspondence at this time among Ray Stark, his

lawyer, Albert da Silva, Robbins, and *his* lawyer, William Fitelson, these facts are revealed in a letter from Stark to da Silva, August 31, 1962, that was passed on to JR (and occasioned a vitriolic response). JRP.

345 letting her know: JR to Isobel Lennart, August 9, 1962, JRP.

346 "ghastly": Lennart to JR, n.d., postmarked September 20, 1962, JRP.

346 he had persuaded: JR to Ray Stark, n.d. [the contents suggest fall 1962], JRP.

346 "most active participant": JR, draft of contributions to the script of *Funny Girl* in response to a request from Fitelson in a memo dated September 20, 1962, JRP.

346 "I've told you": Lennart to JR, n.d., JRP.

346 "Ladies and gentlemen": Larry Fuller, interview with the author, October 1, 2002.

347 "I want you to know": JR to Garson Kanin from the Hotel Barclay in Philadelphia, February 16, 1964, JRP.

347 Stone and Karen Kristin: Stone, interview with the author, September 17, 2002; Kristin, interview with the author, September 15, 2002.

347 "It's wrong": Kristin, interview with the author, September 15, 2002.

347 "chicken scramble": Fuller, interview with the author, October 1, 2002.

347 "We came marching": Ibid.

347 "Look, you're her neighbors": Kristin, interview with the author, September 15, 2002.

348 "his biggest contribution": Fuller, interview with the author, October 1, 2002.

348 "During the rehearsal": JR, "Barbra: Some Notes," December 22, 1965, JRP. Robbins occasionally wrote short essays about performers, perhaps intended for his projected autobiography.

348 "I HAD TO GO": Stark (and the cast), telegram to JR [February 1964], JRP.

348 He also proposed: Stark to JR, February 8, 1964, JRP.

349 "Much luck and": Buzz Miller, telegram to JR, March 26, 1964, JRP.

15. The Sixties—A Fiddler on His Roof

351 Bauer thinks: Jamie Bauer, conversation with the author, December 8, 2002.

351 According to one: Renzo Tian, "I Tre Balletti," *Il Messaggero,* July 11, 1963. Translation courtesy of Karen Wilkin.

351 "delicious dessert": Giorgio Prosperi, *Il Tempo,* July 11, 1963.

351 Luis, a young: Paul Sand, interview with the author, November 25, 2002.

351 Allen Midgette: Allen Midgette, interviews with the author, January 25 and February 6, 2002.

351 "*Fiddler on the Roof*": John Chapman, " 'Fiddler on the Roof' Great Musical; Zero Mostel Heads Superb Cast," *Daily News,* September 23, 1964.

352 Robbins goaded his cast: Maurice Edwards, conversation with the author, September 13, 2000.

352 "For Joe, this show": Richard Altman and Mervyn Kaufman, *The Making of a Musical:* Fiddler on the Roof, 44.

352 "*Fiddler* was a glory": JR, "The Times of the 35 40s continued into being a Jew," notes toward an autobiography/*The Poppa Piece,* JRP.

352 "Dear Ruthie—": JR, cable to Ruth Mitchell in London, August 29, 1963, JRP.

353 Harold Prince: Altman and Kaufman, *The Making of a Musical:* Fiddler on the Roof, 21.

353 Robbins nagged: JR to Jerry Bock and Sheldon Harnick ("Dear Boys"). Letter ac-

companies "Notes on Score," April 4, 1964, sent to Bock and Harnick in London, JRP.

353 delved into the culture: One source was Dvora Lapson, "Jewish Dances of Eastern and Central Europe," the published digest in the *International Folk Music Journal* of a paper given at a 1962 Conference of the IFMC in Gottwaldov, Czechoslovakia, JRP. Among the dances Lapson described was a "Flaschen-tanz," in which a man dances with a bottle on his head to prove himself sober; Robbins may have stored this information away for his rousing bottle dance in *Fiddler's* wedding scene. Lapson also inveigled the Broadway Central Hotel Caterers into letting her attend one or more *simchas,* bringing "a relative" (Robbins) as her escort; Lapson to Mr. Tennenbaum of Broadway Central Hotel Caterers, October 21, 1963, and Lapson to JR, November 18, 1963. According to Betty Comden and Adolph Green, Harry Robbins had told his son that he'd do better to ask caterers than scholars for details of ceremonies: Comden and Green, interview with the author, March 15, 2000.

353 "the virile ferocity": JR, draft of a letter replying to Harold Clurman, who had apparently written him admiring the show but missing a "cozy" quality in the dancing, JRP.

353 Chagall had politely: Marc Chagall, cable to JR, September 7, 1963: "Merci votre attention regrette trop occupé pour accepter faire décors," JRP.

353 "was like the world's greatest": Harnick, quoted in Altman and Kaufman, *The Making of a Musical:* Fiddler on the Roof, 30–31.

353 "the most *powerful*": Pauline Kael, "A Bagel with a Bite out of It," *The New Yorker,* October 13, 1971. Included in Kael, *For Keeps: 30 Years at the Movies,* 395.

354 "would say again and again": Harnick, quoted in Altman and Kaufman, *The Making of a Musical:* Fiddler on the Roof, 31–32.

354 "The drama of the play": JR, handwritten notes on yellow paper, January 1, 1964, JRP.

354 He accompanied her: Joanna Merlin, interview with the author, February 6, 2001.

355 "Dear Zee": JR to Zero Mostel, draft of a telegram, with "sent the 25th" penciled across the top, JRP.

355 Actors, singers, and dancers: The Jerome Robbins Papers relevant to *Fiddler on the Roof* include many letters from performers asking for parts, following up on auditions ("I can do better"), and letters and notes indicate that some did reaudition.

355 "They are tough": JR, "Jerry Robbin's [*sic*] Note—1963," typed; title and "Written during the pre-Rehearsal period—" handwritten (not JR's hand), JRP.

355 "Again I feel": JR, "Notes on Tevye", addressed to "Dear Boys," March 18, 1964, JRP.

355 having said: JR, "Notes on Score," April 4, 1964, JRP.

355 "one-dimensional": Ibid.

355 "No arguments on this": JR, "Book Changes to Be Completed by Author in April," intended for Joseph Stein, April 3, 1964, JRP.

355 "which was well written": JR to Joseph Stein, April 3, 1964, letter accompanying the above "Notes," JRP.

356 "How about cutting out": Stein to JR, n.d. [1964], JRP.

356 "lacklustre" . . . "serviceable" . . . "pedestrian": "Tew," *Variety,* quoted in Altman and Kaufman, *The Making of a Musical:* Fiddler on the Roof, 9.

356 "What Jerome Robbins has done": Martin Gottfried, "Fiddler on the Roof," *Women's Wear Daily,* September 23, 1964, included in Gottfried's *Opening Nights,* 113.

357 music would sound better: Norman Nadel, " 'Fiddler on the Roof' Is Humorous, Tender Musical," *New York World-Telegram and The Sun,* September 23, 1964.

357 "something of the compelling": Richard Watts, Jr., "Two on the Aisle: The Brilliance of Zero Mostel," *New York Post,* September 24, 1964.

357 "criticism of a work": Howard Taubman, "Theater: Mostel as Tevye in 'Fiddler on the Roof,' " *The New York Times,* September 23, 1964.

357 "the shifting of a tub": JR, quoted in Altman and Kaufman, *The Making of a Musical:* Fiddler on the Roof, 73.

357 "To see him dance": Gottfried, "Fiddler on the Roof," *Women's Wear Daily,* September 23, 1964, included in Gottfried's *Opening Nights,* 114.

357 "I think it might": Walter Kerr, "Fiddler on the Roof," *New York Herald Tribune,* September 23, 1964.

357 Jerry drafted a long: JR, draft of letter to Kerr, written in response to Kerr's piece in the *New York Herald Tribune,* October 11, 1964, JRP.

357 "to lift a dozen": Kerr, "Broadway in Anatevka," *New York Herald Tribune Sunday Magazine,* October 11, 1964.

359 "It faithfully reflects": Rabbi Judah Nadich to JR, November 5, 1964, JRP.

359 "he didn't seem able": Walter Mirisch, quoted in Altman and Kaufman, *The Making of a Musical:* Fiddler on the Roof, 182.

359 New York Public Library: The details of Robbins's arrangements with the New York Public Library in relation to the Jerome Robbins Archive of the Recorded Moving Image are among the Jerome Robbins Papers.

359 "purpose of producing": Drafts of agreement among Leonard Bernstein, Betty Comden, Adolph Green, and Jerome Robbins, December 27, 1962, JRP.

360 "The four plan": Leland Hayward, memo to Frank Goodman, January 4, 1965, JRP.

360 "No—we did not": JR, comment in margin of a list of questions sent to him by Humphrey Burton in the fall of 1993, in connection with Burton's in-progress biography of Leonard Bernstein, JRP.

360 La Scala invited him: JR to Igor Stravinsky, October 27, 1953: "Last month I had the honor of having La Scala ask me to stage *Les Noces* for them," JRP.

360 he writes to Stravinsky: Ibid.

361 Stravinsky is encouraging but: Stravinsky to JR, October 29, 1953, JRP.

361 "I notice that sometimes": JR to Stravinsky, November 11, 1953, JRP.

361 She tells him: Ninette de Valois to JR, November 10, 1953, JRP.

361 Bad terms: The final demise of the La Scala *Les Noces* is explained in a letter from JR to La Scala's director, Dr. Ghiringhelli, December 23, 1953, JRP.

361 Lincoln Kirstein writes: Kirstein to JR, January 1, 1954, JRP.

361 Robbins . . . mentions: JR to Vera Volkova, November 9, 1956, JRP. (The correspondence among Volkova, Robbins, and H. A. Brøndsted, dating from 1956 through 1960, is sizable and gives interesting insights into the workings of the Royal Danish Ballet.)

361 Frank Schauffus . . . writes: Frank Schauffus to JR, April 8, 1957, JRP.

361 "First allow me": JR to Pablo Picasso, October 31, 1957, JRP.

361 It is discovered: Vera Volkova to JR, November 22, 1957, in response to one from JR expressing his disappointment. He must have previously received news of the cancellation by cable. JRP.

361 Robbins cables: JR, cable to H. A. Brøndsted, February 11, 1958, JRP.

361 "musical technical reasons": Brøndsted, cable to JR, February 15, 1958, JRP.

361 he'll do it in Spoleto: JR to Brøndsted, February 17, 1958, JRP.

362 Doris Humphrey invites: The author was present when Humphrey announced this and when Robbins came to audition the company.

362 "Then Stravinsky came on stage": JR, draft of letter to Richard Buckle, n.d. [possibly late October 1959]. (Buckle writes November 17, 1959, enclosing a letter from Ninette de Valois to Buckle, November 3, 1959, about Robbins's earlier attempt to interest her in *Sacre*. This suggests that Buckle had possibly approached her on Robbins's behalf.)

362 "I am very sorry": Stravinsky to Brøndsted, February 8, 1960, JRP (sent by Brøndsted to JR). In his letter, Stravinsky advised that the revised 1947 version, which he's been using himself (Boosey & Hawkes), is scored for fifty-nine instead of sixty-six instruments and has better balance; but that still evidently involved more musicians than the pit of Copenhagen's Royal Opera House could hold.

362 Colin Davis can't agree: de Valois to JR, March 18, 1962, JRP.

362 Finally asked to choreograph: JR to Gian Carlo Menotti, February 8, 1963, JRP.

363 "the comfort of her company": JR, "Robbins on Les Noces," *The New York Times,* March 28, 1965 (Sunday). A final draft, dated March 19, 1965, is among the Jerome Robbins Papers.

363 "The music is monolithic": Ibid.

364 "It is a work of majestic": JR, "Nijinska's Les Noces," n.d., JRP.

365 "Dear heart": Igor Stravinsky, *Les Noces,* printed libretto in English translation, JRP.

365 the company proposed $50: The initial draft of the agreement and related correspondence are in the Jerome Robbins Papers.

365 "Pride in making": This and subsequent quotes are from notes Naomi Isaacson took on JR's comments during rehearsals of *Les Noces,* probably in 1966–1967. Courtesy of Naomi Isaacson.

365 "Not since Fokine": Lucia Chase, note to JR, n.d., JRP.

365–66 a "triumph": Marcia B. Siegel, "Troubles, Trifles, and the Return of a Prodigal Son," *New York* magazine, July 14, 1969. Reprinted in Siegel's *At the Vanishing Point: A Critic Looks at Dance,* 14.

366 prominent naysayers: See Arlene Croce, "The Relevance of Robbins," *Ballet Review,* Spring 1972. Reprinted in Croce, *Afterimages,* 395–406.

366 "It's a little athletic": JR to Robert Graves, April 25, 1967, JRP.

366 He noted in a letter: JR to Richard Buckle, September 27, 1965, JRP.

366 "I guess it's just YOU": Tanaquil Le Clercq to JR, n.d. [November 1965], JRP.

367 Bertha Case: Bertha Case to JR, August 4, 1965, JRP.

367 "The author has": JR to Phil Silvers, December 2, 1965, JRP.

367 Betty Comden remembered: Betty Comden, interview with the author, March 15, 2000.

368 The set itself: Stuart W. Little, " 'The Office' in Rehearsal," *New York Herald Tribune,* March 30, 1966, JR scrapbooks, NYPL.

368 someone (evidently Jerry): Maria Irene Fornés, interview with the author, October 28, 2002.

368 there were boos: Tony Lo Bianco, quoted in Greg Lawrence, *Dance with Demons,* 357.

368 "Dear Sir, I have never": Mrs. Joseph Randall of Highland Park, New Jersey, to JR, envelope postmarked April 22, 1966, JRP.

368 he apologized: Fornés, interview with the author, October 28, 2002.

368 He told the actors: Lo Bianco, quoted in Lawrence, *Dance with Demons,* 359.

369　"Yippee, I'm a performing art!" (or maybe it was "Whoopee!"): For years, I have cherished and retold this episode, recounted in one of *The New Yorker*'s "Wind on Capitol Hill" squibs, but I cannot locate the date.

369　presenting a rough budget: Bob Weiner to Bill Crawford, October 28, 1966, JRP.

369　much more modest: a proposed budget for $19,560 dated April 27, 1967, JRP.

369　For the summer of 1968: Frank Rizzo to David Payne, manager, ATL, February 19, 1968, accepting a proposal for a company of eighteen to be the first dance attraction of the Spoleto Festival, budgeted at $25,000, JRP.

370　participants were asked: Eric Martin, interview with the author, March 19, 1999.

370　Tom Stone took detailed: Stone's notes are among the Jerome Robbins Papers. Audiotapes and videotapes of sessions (the last from the second year only) are also in the NYPL.

370　"We'd have to do": Martin, interview with the author, March 19, 1999.

371　"rituals in the way": JR to Robert Graves, April 25, 1967, JRP.

372　Barry Primus speaks: Barry Primus, interview with the author, January 12, 2001.

372　A speech from Euripides': I am especially indebted to Erin Martin, Barry Primus, and Tom Stone for their insights into the processes of the work at ATL.

372　"He was fascinated": James Mitchell, interview with the author, June 29, 2000.

372　Martin danced: Information about the exercises described in these pages comes from the ATL Daily Notes, JRP. Some are also shown in the daily videotapes, Jerome Robbins Archive of the Recorded Moving Image, NYPL.

373　"a cathartic lamentation": JR, "The Mourning Dove," JRP.

373　Mary Hunter's advice: Mary Hunter to JR, June 6, 1967, written from Stratford, Connecticut (Hunter was associated with the Shakespeare Festival), JRP.

373　"And, of course, we": Mitchell, interview with the author, June 29, 2000.

374　Tom Stone organized: Stone, interview with the author, September 17, 2002, and scripts among the Jerome Robbins Papers.

374　Primus still thinks: Primus, interview with the author, January 12, 2001.

374　"An absolutely astonishing": JR to Graves, April 25, 1967, JRP.

375　If only, she said: Martin, telephone conversation with the author [exact date unrecorded: prior to 2001, probably 2000].

375　she spent the next year apologizing: There is a sizable file of letters and notes passing between JR and Muriel Resnick in the Jerome Robbins Papers.

376　"or Jerry would just": Daniel Stern, interview with the author, April 5, 1999.

376　Laurence Olivier: Olivier to JR, February 4, 1966, JRP. Olivier had heard from John Dexter that JR might be interested in directing a play at the National Theatre.

376　he put forth a heady: JR to Olivier, March 23, 1967, JRP.

376　He wrote a letter: JR to Yukio Mishima, June 16, 1967, JRP.

376　Mishima, who turned: Mishima to JR, June 26, 1967, JRP.

376　Robbins's notes: JR, notes on Nijinsky film dated October 15, 1968, JRP.

377　The possibility was raised: "General thoughts about a treatment," note from [name illegible] to JR on yellow lined paper, July 23, 1968, JRP. In 1978, JR penciled "Buckle's?".

377　Writers were approached: Harold Pinter turned the job down (Pinter to Harry Salzman, June 10, 1968; letter sent on to JR), saying he was not interested in this fictionalization of history, but showed some interest in July (JR to Salzman, July 3, 1968; Peter Shaffer to JR, October 29, 1968). Bowen did work on the project.

377　Perhaps, he thought: JR [?], "General thoughts about a treatment." JR penciled "Buckle's? (found 1978)." JRP.

377　"Is it possible to do": JR, notes to himself on Nijinsky film, October 15, 1968, JRP.

378 although there is evidence: Stuart Ostrow, cable to JR in London, September 24, 1968: "Laurents ready to begin work. Come home and get headstart of Bernstein and Sondheim Love Stu," JRP.

378 Guare began to reconceive: John Guare's scripts for *The Exception and the Rule* are among the Jerome Robbins Papers.

378 "There was no dialogue": John Guare, interview with the author, August 16, 2000.

379 "Well, the irony": Ibid.

379 One plan: Ambiguous notes found in folders with plans for *The Exception and the Rule,* JRP.

379 "Producer, star": Arthur Laurents, "Is the Evening Anti-Semitic?" note addressed to Bernstein, Sondheim, and Robbins, JRP.

379 "One morning—I came": John Guare, interview with the author, August 16, 2000.

380 Guare then went: Ibid.

16. You *Can* Go Home Again

382 he had considered: Eliot Feld, interview with the author, June 28, 1999.

382 Robbins's lawyer, William Fitelson: Fitelson, memo to JR, June 3, 1968, JRP.

382 he was intermittently conferring: The earliest correspondence in JR's files is dated January 6, 1969. By the end of July 1970, the authors submitted one last rewritten draft, hoping it might meet with the producers' approval. Evidently it did not, and in October, Goldman and Paxton took *Hurrah Boys Hurrah* to another production company. In the spring of 1971, Robbins finally surrendered his rights, title, interest, and copyright, etc.—but not his author's share—in the project. The letter from JR to Paxton and Bolton, c/o their lawyers, is dated March 15, 1971, JRP.

382 Patricia McBride recalls: McBride, interview with the author, May 6, 2002.

382 it was announced: *Dancing Times* (London), February 1964, 246.

382 Robbins contributed: "Ford Foundation Controversy Pros and Cons," *Dance Magazine,* February 1964, 34–37, 82.

382 was thanked by: Lincoln Kirstein to JR, March 15, 1964, JRP.

382 even trying out: Among JR's papers pertaining to *Dances at a Gathering* is a note in his hand that he "worked a bit in Mrs. H's Snedens studio with five or six dancers from her school and her dancers," JRP.

382 In November: Kirstein to JR, November 29, 1968, JRP.

383 Villella, sensing: Edward Villella, interview with the author, January 12, 2003.

383 "Why don't we": Ibid.

383 "to make every chord": JR, " '69 JR/Personal" (black notebook), June 24, 1969.

383 "I look in the mirror": Villella, interview with the author, January 12, 2003.

384 He dashed off a note: JR to Kirstein, March 27, 1969, JRP.

384 "*Don't* build up": Ibid.

384 "Make more": JR, interview with the author, summer 1974.

384 McBride remembers: McBride, interview with the author, May 6, 2002.

384 "after that two-year experience": James Mitchell, interview with the author, June 29, 2000.

385 "Like someone with": JR, interview with Edwin Denby, "Robbins on Robbins," *Dance Magazine,* July 1969. Reprinted in Nancy Reynolds, *Repertory in Review: 40 Years of the New York City Ballet,* 259–261 (260).

385 "Now that's what": Ibid., 261.

385 *Dances at a Gathering* is": JR, "The Times of the 35 40s <u>continued into being a Jew</u>," September 8, 1971, notes toward an autobiography/*The Poppa Piece*, JRP.

385 "it's a place": Sara Leland, quoted in Reynolds, *Repertory in Review: 40 Years of the New York City Ballet*, 264.

386 "the mistress of the house": Ibid.

386 Robbins told them: JR, interview with Edwin Denby, "Robbins on Robbins," *Dance Magazine*, July 1969. Reprinted in Reynolds, *Repertory in Review: 40 Years of the New York City Ballet*, 261.

386 After an interview: Ibid.

386 "For the record": JR to *Ballet Review*, May 10, 1971, JRP. Printed in *Ballet Review*, vol. 4, no. 2, 1972.

387 Robbins once toyed: A sheet with various possible titles is filed with material on *Dances at a Gathering*, JRP.

388 "I've had such": JR to John Bolton, May 5, 1969, JRP. Bolton is the writer he worked with on plans for the aborted Nijinsky film.

388 "In an age": Lincoln Kirstein to JR, May 23, 1969, JRP.

388 "You see each dancer": Denby, "Robbins on Robbins." *Dance Magazine*, July 1969. Reprinted in Reynolds, *Repertory in Review: 40 Years of the New York City Ballet*, 261.

388 "The music and dance": Ibid.

388 Jerry sent them all: The author received one, and other critics said the same in conversation at the time.

388 "my girl": JR to A. Z. Propes, January 10, 1969, JRP. The correspondence is filed with material on Batsheva Dance Company.

388 "Did DaaG come out of": JR, "My Father Harry Rabinowitz," January 23, 1976 [JR notes the day as "Thursday," but July 23 fell on a Friday that year]. The portion in which JR asks the questions quoted is dated July 19, 1976. JR, notes toward an autobiography/*The Poppa Piece*, JRP.

389 Conrad staged a fit: Christine Conrad, interview with the author, April 8, 1999.

389 letting the Russians know why: JR to Intourist bureau in Leningrad, June 19, 1969, JRP.

389 "huge amounts of acid": JR to Allen Midgette, November 10, 1969, JRP.

389 "for the next three weeks": Ibid.

389 Kirstein . . . had suggested: Kirstein to JR, May 23, 1969, JRP.

389 "no longer a cash cow": Kirstein to JR, March 27, 1969, JRP.

390 "He never dances": Robert Sealy, "Mr. Robbins, Mr. Balanchine, Mr. Boelzner," *Ballet Review*, vol. 3, no. 3, 1970, 16–22 (17).

390 Verdy . . . said: *Violette et Mr. B.*, videotape by Dominique Delouche (2001).

390 "coagulating": Ibid.

391 It's reported that: Robert Greskovic was present when Peter Martins described Balanchine's response to the last duet in *In the Night* and recounted the story to the author.

391 "because no one had": JR, draft of letter to Lincoln Kirstein, February 12, 1971, JRP.

391 "opened my mind": JR to Willis Player, November 17, 1969, JRP. He wanted to come again and see the whole process. Player invited him to a rollout and launch on November 9, 1970, and January 31, 1971. Robbins accepted but had to cancel both times.

391 "The English have been": JR, "Trip to London (rehearsals *Faun*)," in Pen-Tab spiral notebook, "London 71," JRP.

391 "I had to change": Ibid.

391   "Wall is interesting": Ibid.

392   "Rudi—is Rudi": JR, "London Sept–Oct 70 NY Nov Dec 1971" (beige spiral Pen-Tab notebook), JRP.

392   "like an enormous passacaglia": Johann Sebastian Bach, *The "Goldberg" Variations,* edited for the harpsichord, or piano by Ralph Kirkpatrick (New York: G. Schirmer, Inc., 1938), vii.

392   "I wanted to see": JR, interview with Nancy Reynolds, June 8, 1974, in Reynolds, *Repertory in Review: 40 Years of the New York City Ballet,* 275.

392   "very big": Ibid.

392   "the inner nature": Alan Rich, "Going through the Motions," *New York* magazine, July 5, 1971.

393   "pensive," "playful": JR, notes for *The Goldberg Variations,* May 14, [1970], JRP.

393   "black despair": Charles Rosen, liner notes for his Columbia Odyssey recording of Johann Sebastian Bach's *The Goldberg Variations* (prior to 1970). Copy found among JR's notes for the ballet, JRP.

393   "grand and genial finale": Ibid.

393   "the discords shift": Elena Bivona, "The World of 'Goldberg Variations,' " *Ballet Review,* vol. 3, no. 6 (1971).

394   wasn't sure: Delia Peters, interview with the author, October 7, 1999, and McBride, interview with the author, May 6, 2002.

394   "So uncreative": JR, journal no. 1, November 2, 1971, JRP.

394   "When Robbins has wrestled": Arlene Croce, "Waterloo," *Ballet Review,* vol. 4, no. 2 (1972). Reprinted as "The Relevance of Robbins" in Croce, *Afterimages,* 395–406 (405).

394   It had become: JR, journal no. 10, May 12, 1974, JRP.

394   "When the ballet is": Nancy Goldner, "Robbins' 'Goldberg Variations': a great ballet," *Christian Science Monitor,* June 7, 1971.

395   the corps de ballet believed: Bart Cook, interview with the author, February 6, 2000.

395   McBride: Patricia McBride and Helgi Tomasson, conversation with the author, April 6, 2004.

395   "incredible sensitivity": Rosalyn Tureck to JR, May 3, 1989, JRP.

395   "You had to keep": Peters, interview with the author, October 7, 1999.

395   Peters . . . remembers: Ibid.

396   "It was truly": Ibid.

396   "not that presentable": Jane Dudley to JR, September 8, 1969, JRP.

396   "No, don't change Linda": JR to Dudley, October 1, 1969, JRP.

396   "rehearsing with Jerry": Peter Martins, interview with the author, May 14, 2002.

397   "If Jerry liked you": Christine Redpath, interview with the author, July 18, 2000.

397   "actually used to give me": Jean-Pierre Frohlich, interview with the author, April 6, 1999.

398   One film shows: "Personal Beach Sequences," September 1971, 16 millimeter, color, silent, Jerome Robbins Archive of the Recorded Moving Image, R850, NYPL.

398   Dale remembers: Grover Dale, interview with the author, April 15, 2000.

398   "a big undressing": JR, journal no. 1, January 9, 1972, JRP.

398   "from the religious": JR, program note in *Stagebill* for New York City Ballet, February 1972.

399   Bart Cook: Cook, interview with the author, February 6, 2000.

399   "shamans": JR, "Watermill II" (pink notebook with red spine), December 8, 1971, JRP.

400   "I am not going to": JR, journal no. 1, January 4, 1972, JRP.

400 they sent him: Robert Wilson and Andy De Groat, "To Jerry for opening Watermill," February 3, 1972, JRP.

400 Jerry made *them:* "Artist's Book," dated February 28, 1973, is in the possession of Robert Wilson; a photocopy exists in the Jerome Robbins Papers.

400 "Back from Bob's loft": JR, journal no. 2, March 12, 1972, JRP.

401 "textured time tunnel": Robert Wilson, interview with the author, February 14, 2001.

401 "To drive him": Ibid.

401 "You are a great choreographer": Mrs. Julie Fine to JR, May 28, 1972, JRP.

401 "ravished by it": Virgil Thomson to JR, February 12, 1972, JRP.

401 "an exquisite theatre poem": Sheldon and Margie Harnick to JR, June 1, 1972, JRP.

401 "one of the most moving": Paul Magriel to JR, February 20, 1972, JRP.

402 "I wish you could": Jean Rosenthal to JR, n.d., JRP.

402 "fake deep": John J. O'Connor, "Television: Don't Look Now, Busby, but Some of Those Dancers Are Nude," *The New York Times,* February 20, 1972.

402 "rings false": Arlene Croce, "Waterloo," *Ballet Review,* vol. 4, no. 2 (1972). Reprinted as "The Relevance of Robbins" in Croce, *Afterimages,* 395–406 (395).

402 "very beautiful": Marcia B. Siegel, " 'Watermill' Ballet by Jerome Robbins," *Boston Herald Traveler,* February 22, 1972.

402 "On the verge": Kirstein to JR, February 2, 1972, JRP.

402 Baryshnikov . . . had to refuse: Mikhail Baryshnikov, interview with the author, April 4, 2002.

403 Clive Barnes published: "Balanchine—Has He Become Trivial?" *The New York Times,* June 27, 1971.

403 "clearly the company's": Ibid.

403 Barnes qualified: Barnes, "Ballets About People, Not Princes," *The New York Times,* July 12, 1971.

403 "serious genius": Ibid.

403 "musique dansante": George Balanchine, speaking at a press conference, March 6, 1972. Quoted in Nancy Goldner, *The Stravinsky Festival of the New York City Ballet,* 13–14.

403 "Igor Fedorovitch": Kirstein and Balanchine, toasting Stravinsky on the final evening of the Stravinsky Festival, June 25, 1972. Quoted in Goldner, *The Stravinsky Festival of the New York City Ballet,* 38.

404 "GB was fantastic": JR, journal no. 2, June 29, 1972 (written en route to Spoleto), JRP.

404 "I said I thought": JR, "Stravinsky Journal 1972," April 29, 1972, JRP.

404 "our eyes turned": Ibid.

405 "delightful to audience": JR, journal no. 2, June 29, 1972.

405 Robert Craft: Craft, "Celestial Motions: The City Ballet," *World Magazine,* 1972, quoted in Goldner, *The Stravinsky Festival of the New York City Ballet,* 239–240.

406 thought by some critics: Anna Kisselgoff, *The New York Times,* January 12, 1974; Nancy Goldner, *The Nation,* July 10, 1972, quoted in Reynolds, *Repertory in Review: 40 Years of the New York City Ballet,* 305.

406 Balanchine spoke to Robbins: JR, journal no. 2, June 29, 1972 (written en route to Spoleto), JRP.

406 "We penetrate into": George Balanchine, quoted by JR, "1971—Some Theater & Dance Reports" (large red spiral binder), June 22, 1972, JRP. Robbins worded this quote differently and said it pertained to *Watermill* in "A Conversation with Jerome

Robbins: Working with Balanchine," interview with Ellen Sorrin, New York State Theater, March 8, 1993.

406 "As Miss Verdy": Jane Boutwell, "Festival," *The New Yorker,* 1972, quoted in Goldner, *The Stravinsky Festival of the New York City Ballet,* 240.

407 The morale ledger: Goldner, *The Stravinsky Festival of the New York City Ballet,* 244.

407 It should be noted (footnote): Aidan Mooney, interview with the author, February 3, 2003.

407 "You don't think" (footnote): Paul Sand, interview with the author, November 25, 2002.

407 "Aidan shows me": JR, journal no. 2, July 7, 1972, JRP.

408 "I'm lying on": Ibid.

408 "to show them": JR, journal no. 1, December 13, 1971, JRP.

408 "They have me": JR, journal no. 3, July 19, 1972, JRP.

17. Jerry and George and Lincoln

PAGE

410 It took from September 1971: The contract negotiations involving Kirstein, Robbins, and Cage, representing New York City Ballet, and Norman Singer, representing New York City Center, are filed with the Jerome Robbins Papers.

410 He needed: JR, memo on meetings with Betty Cage, January 11, 1973, JRP.

410 City Center . . . reported: *The New York Times,* November 4, 1972, and *Variety,* October 11, 1972, reported the deficit and noted that City Center needed to raise $5.3 million to close its first budget gap in twenty-nine years.

410 Robbins agreed: $20,000 is the fee Cage proposed to JR on March 2, 1972. Singer had informed him that accepting a fee would benefit City Center; see above memo, January 11, 1973, JRP.

410 notion of a "fee": JR, draft of a letter to Norman Singer, November 27, 1972, not sent, JRP.

410 "You really are a shit": JR, draft of a letter to Kirstein, n.d. [1972?], JRP.

411 the (usually) apologetic replies: Oliver Smith to JR, January 9, 1971, JRP. Jule Styne to JR, June 2 and June 10, 1980.

411 Jerry suggested: JR, journal no. 4, February 12, 1972, JRP.

411 "[Lincoln] told me": JR, journal no. 1, November 17, 1971, JRP.

411 Kirstein provided: Lincoln Kirstein to JR, May 23, 1969, JRP.

411 "What is 2¾ miles": Kirstein, postcard to JR, n.d., postmark illegible, JRP.

411 "It's too fast": Tanaquil Le Clercq to JR, June 23, 1966, JRP.

411 Balanchine seems: Barbara Horgan, interview with the author, March 11, 2003.

411 "You know, dear": Patricia McBride, interview with the author, May 6, 2002.

412 "You know, Violette": Violette Verdy, *Violette et Mr. B.,* videotape by Dominique Delouche (2001).

412 "When I watch Balanchine": JR, journal no. 1, December 1, 1971, JRP.

412 "so how come": JR, journal no. 1, January 9, 1972, JRP.

413 "weak in beginning": JR, journal no. 6, June 7 and May 29, 1973, JRP.

413 "but it wasn't": Ibid.

413 "But it's a hard thing": JR, interview with Nancy Reynolds, June 8, 1974, in Reynolds, *Repertory in Review: 40 Years of the New York City Ballet,* 308.

413 Some thought the ballet: Reynolds, *Repertory in Review: 40 Years of the New York City Ballet,* 308.

413   As Nancy Goldner: Goldner, "Dance/Nancy Goldner," *The Nation,* March 2, 1974.

414   Harvey Lichtenstein: Rhoda Grauer, interview with the author, October 29, 2000.

414   was thrilled to meet Romola: JR, journal no. 7, June 10, 1973, JRP.

414   counted while Bourkhanov: JR, notebook: "Spoleto, 1973," June 21, 1973, JRP.

414   "yellow short sleeve": Ibid., June 25, 1973.

415   "They do *Don Q*": Ibid.

415   "lovely—patient": Ibid.

415   "Her use of her small": Ibid., June 21, 1973.

415   "a superb partner": Ibid. The word transcribed as "seasoned" is not fully legible but is the most likely choice.

415   "So beautiful": Ibid., June 25, 1973.

415   Jerry came up with: Films of the three parts of *Celebration* (not labeled in the correct order) can be found in the Jerome Robbins Archive of the Recorded Moving Image, NYPL. One lacks sound, and the finale could not be filmed because the lights were too dim.

415   Jennifer Tipton, who did: Tipton, interview with the author, March 18, 2003.

416   "[Jerry] was so": Grauer, interview with the author, October 29, 2000.

416   "what was it": JR, journal no. 7, July 3, 1973, JRP.

416   He reveled in the view: JR, notebook: "Spoleto, 1973," n.d. [July 1973], JRP.

416   Spoleto offered: JR, draft on an agreement between him and the commune, JRP.

416   "Elizabeth was in": JR, notebook: "Spoleto, 1973," n.d. [July 1973], JRP.

416   "The longer one looks": Ibid.

417   "eat the Good God": JR, journal no. 8, August 15, 1973, JRP.

417   "circus acrobats": JR, journal no. 7, June 23, 1973, JRP.

417   "A loud noise": JR, notebook: "Spoleto, 1973," August 2, 1973, JRP.

417   "I straighten my room": JR, journal no. 8, August 19, 1973, JRP.

418   "Dybbuk Dybbuk": JR to Leonard Bernstein, October 13, 1958, JRP.

418   "Is it an opera?": JR, black softcover notebook with Japanese paper on cover, entry for December 27, 1971, JRP.

418   "By now": Ibid., February 14, 1972.

418   "intense dance": Ibid., February 9, 1972 (a line separates this entry from the date above it, but no new date is given).

419   "like me": JR, journal no. 2, February 16, 1972, JRP.

419   "had it out": Ibid., February 26, 1972.

419   Robbins dreamed: JR, journal no. 9, October 17, 1973, JRP.

419   "Lennie & I": Ibid., February 28, 1974, JRP.

419   "What a trip": Ibid., March 11, 1974.

420   "there was a wedding": Bart Cook, interview with the author, February 6, 2000.

420   "uses . . . only as": Program note for *Dybbuk,* quoted in Reynolds, *Repertory in Review: 40 Years of the New York City Ballet,* 311.

420   "a) allegro": JR, notes for *Dybbuk,* JRP.

421   "it's one of Lennie's": Kirstein to JR, November 12, 1986, JRP.

421   "It was very unsatisfactory": JR to Kirstein, November 17, 1986, JRP.

421   "Jerry can't make": Helen Coates for Alan Fluck, February 24, 1974, quoted in Humphrey Burton, *Leonard Bernstein,* 422.

421   "I'm delighted": Edwin Denby to JR, n.d., JRP.

422   he noticed a review: JR, "The Times of the 35 40s continued into being a Jew," September 8, 1976, JRP. ("What blew the lid off all of this was reading a review of *The Ordeal of Civility*.")

422 "my mind blew": JR, "Notes—Poppa—<u>Histories, Changing It</u>," October 6, 8, 9, 1976, JR, notes toward an autobiography/*The Poppa Piece,* JRP.

422 "the ritually unconsummated": John Murray Cuddihy, *The Ordeal of Civility: Freud, Marx, Levi-Strauss, and the Jewish Struggle with Modernity,* 3–4.

422 "The secularizing Jewish": Ibid., 4.

422 "cultural shame": Ibid.

422 "host culture": Ibid.

422 He urged his friend Daniel Stern: Stern, interview with the author, April 5, 1999.

423 "the rages and discontents": JR, "The Times of the 35 40s <u>continued into being a Jew,</u>" September 8, 1976, JR, notes toward an autobiography/*The Poppa Piece,* JRP.

423 "to love the richness": Ibid.

423 "it was our fate": Ibid.

423 "Hair shirts and tallises": JR, "Poppa Bar Mitzvah Jan '75," January 25, 1975, audio-tape (this part dated January 22, 1975), JRP.

423 canasta-playing retirees: JR, journal, Miami, March 1970, JRP.

424 "the world of clear": JR, journal no. 2, March 6, 1972, JRP.

424 "An upright man": Ibid., March 9, 1972.

424 "a part of those": JR, "My Father Harry Rabinowitz," January 23, 1975 [?], notes toward an autobiography/*The Poppa Piece,* JRP. [JR has dated it Thursday, January 23, 1976, but he is wrong about either the day or the year.]

424 "has something to do with": Ibid.

424 "Why not Ravel?": George Balanchine, quoted in Reynolds, *Repertory in Review: 40 Years of the New York City Ballet,* 319.

425 "his heart": Horgan, interview with the author, March 11, 2003.

425 "You can put": George Balanchine, speaking to an audience at Cooper Union. Quoted in Arlene Croce, "Risky Business," *The New Yorker,* June 8, 1987.

425 Patricia McBride feels: McBride, interview with the author, May 6, 2002.

425 "Place not your trust": Évariste Parny, quoted in the program for *Chansons Madécasses,* New York City Ballet, May 1975.

425 "And why do I feel": JR, journal no. 1, November 1, 1971.

426 "another dance": JR, journal no. 12, January 29–30, 1975, JRP.

427 "In truth": JR to the author, June 25, 1975 (not sent), JRP.

427 "In the poetic": Arlene Croce, "It's a Wise Child," *The New Yorker,* June 9, 1975. Included in Croce, *Afterimages,* 155.

427 "Best of all": JR to the author, June 25, 1975 (not sent), JRP.

427 "deep depression": JR, journal no. 19, January 9, 1978, JRP.

428 "It seems incontestable": Lincoln Kirstein to JR, July 2, 1975, JRP.

428 Jerry felt that: JR, journal no. 11, September 25, 1974, JRP.

428 he found much to criticize: JR, journal no. 10, July 3, 1974, JRP.

429 an account: JR, journal no. 11 [exact date unclear: after September 13, 1974, and before September 18, 1974], JRP.

429 "This is George's desk": JR, "George Balanchine/Jerome Robbins, Room & Office, '73," videotape, R28, Jerome Robbins Archive of the Recorded Moving Image, NYPL.

429 Daniel Stern thinks: Stern, interview with the author, April 5, 1999.

429 he crossed out . . . he scrawled: JR, 1975 appointment calendar, July 3–24, 1975, JRP.

430 "Dear Diary": JR, journal no. 13, July 9, 1975, JRP.

430 as he stated it: Ibid.

430 "a Jewish ex": Ibid., September 7, 1975, JRP.

430 Nora Kaye and: JR, 1975 appointment calendar, JRP. Robbins left McLean on July

24, 1975. Kaye and Jeffrey arrived either the same day or the next (not entirely clear in the calendar) and left July 31, 1975.

431 "Would you consider": JR to Ingmar Bergman, February 15, 1975, JRP.

431 Bergman was busy: Bergman, cable to JR, March 12, 1975 ("Dear Friend"), JRP.

431 "The Philly experience": JR, journal no. 15, March 8, 1976, JRP.

431 "Lennie never learns": Ibid., March 4, 1976, JRP.

431 "3 boys": JR, journal no. 12, March 31, 1975, JRP.

432 "God, the guts": JR, interview with the author, summer 1974. Quoted in Jowitt, "Back Again to Ballet," *The New York Times Magazine,* December 8, 1974.

432 "She is elegant": JR, journal no. 15, March 28, 1976, JRP.

432 "Martha's women": Ibid.

433 Robbins marveled over: JR, interview with the author, summer 1974, in preparation for *The New York Times Magazine* article mentioned above.

433 "[doing] a number": JR, journal no. 10, August 7, 1974, JRP.

433 captured on video: "Two Duets," a video presentation by *Dance in America,* February 20, 1980, produced for WNET/13 by Emile Ardolino and Judy Kinberg and directed by Emile Ardolino (the other duet, Peter Martins's *Calcium Light Night,* was directed by Ralph Holmes).

433 "very, very muted": Mikhail Baryshnikov, interview with the author, April 4, 2002.

434 "She goes": Ibid.

434 Clive Barnes counted: Barnes, "Dance View: Who Pirouetted out of the '76 Cake?" *The New York Times,* December 26, 1976.

434 Peter Williams rhapsodized: Williams, "Less American Activities," *Dance and Dancers* (London), September 24, 1977, 20–24.

435 he was hospitalized: JR, journal no. 18, March 10, 1977; October 5, 1977; and November 29, 1977, JRP.

435 "All should go well": JR to Peter Martins, November 2, 1977, JRP.

18. When the King Dies

436 Robbins marveled: JR, journal no. 19, January 16, 1978, JRP.

437 Robbins had been considering: Correspondence and other materials pertaining to JR's involvement with *Heartaches of a Pussycat* are filed with the Jerome Robbins Papers.

437 "Mr. Balanchine isn't": JR to Kim d'Estainville, April 10, 1978, JRP.

438 according to Lincoln Kirstein: Kirstein, *Thirty Years: Lincoln Kirstein's the New York City Ballet,* 321.

438 He drew up lists: JR, Notes on *Arts of the Gentleman,* July 21, 1976, JRP.

438 plotted a full-length: Ibid.

438 "Fencing rehearsal NYCB": Entry in JR's 1976 "bedroom calendar," JRP. During the 1970s and beyond, JR's staff maintained an office calendar for his activities, in addition to his "bedroom calendar."

439 Kirstein wondered whether: Kirstein, *Thirty Years: Lincoln Kirstein's the New York City Ballet,* 327.

439 "daydreaming": Jack Anderson, "New York Newsletter," *Dancing Times,* August 1978, 648.

439 "Robbins' genius": John Howlett, "New York City Ballet in 4 Premieres," *Albany Times Union,* June 10, 1978.

439 he transferred: Legal assignment dated February 21, 1978, JRP.

440 "Please tell Peter": JR, marginal note on letter from Edward Bigelow to Edith Weissman, February 17, 1979, JRP.

440 Nick's disappearance: Maitland McDonagh, draft of the story for American Kennel Club Newsletter, JRP. This recounts the tale of the abduction, search for, and retrieval of Nick, JRP. *The New York Times,* July 2, 1978, announced Nick's return. JRP.

440 he planned an elaborate: JR, journal no. 19, August 21, 1978, JRP.

440 "Awake": Ibid.

441 "stalling": Ibid. [possibly August 22, 1978; the layout of the journals sometimes makes dating entries difficult].

441 "It was George's": Ibid., August 21, 1978.

441 "I'm working on Verdi": JR, journal no. 20, October 18, 1978 [possibly October 17, 1978], JRP.

441 Jean-Pierre Frohlich . . . remembers: Frohlich, interview with the author, April 6, 1999.

441 "STUCK": Ibid., October 18, 1978.

442 "What you're doing": George Balanchine, quoted in JR, journal no. 20, November 9, 1978, JRP.

442 he told her he wanted: Stephanie Saland, interview with the author, November 8, 1999.

443 "headlong debauch": Arlene Croce, "Other Verdi Variations," *The New Yorker,* February 5, 1979. Included in Croce's *Going to the Dance,* 152.

443 "Images of": Ibid.

443 "Good piece": Robert Gottlieb, interview with the author, June 25, 2003.

444 fortunately captured by: *Choreography by Balanchine,* a video presentation by *Dance in America,* produced by Emile Ardolino and Judy Kinberg for WNET/13 and directed by Merrill Brockway, 1978.

444 Baryshnikov is fairly certain: Mikhail Baryshnikov, interview with the author, April 4, 2002.

445 Bart Cook thought: Bart Cook, interview with the author, February 6, 2000.

445 "He gave them": Barbara Horgan, interview with the author, March 11, 2003.

445 "He wants blue": Victor Castelli, interview with the author, July 18, 2000.

446 "I always felt": Patricia McBride, interview with the author, May 6, 2002.

446 "atmosphere is very hard": Horgan, interview with the author, March 11, 2003.

446 "I cried for Jerry": Saland, interview with the author, November 8, 1999.

446 "without that musicality": Ibid.

446 cartwheels or somersaults: Robert La Fosse, interview with the author, May 29, 1999, and Castelli, interview with the author, July 18, 2000.

446 Sometimes, says Violette Verdy: Verdy, interview with the author, March 27, 2002.

447 "always wanted more": Peter Martins, interview with the author, May 14, 2002.

447 Some rehearsal footage: The New York City Ballet sometimes videotaped rehearsals for later use within the company. Occasionally Robbins had a copy made for his own use, this one labeled "Interplay working rehearsal," R7, Jerome Robbins Archive of the Recorded Moving Image, NYPL.

447 "There are lifts": Castelli, interview with the author, July 18, 2000.

448 "the artificed": Kirstein, *Thirty Years: Lincoln Kirstein's the New York City Ballet,* 107.

448 "an authority": JR, journal no. 20, November 11, 1978, JRP.

448 Saland, by her own admission: Saland, interview with the author, November 8, 1999.
448 "sweet," "charming" . . . "a gem": "sweet," Clive Barnes, "First Views of 'Lille Suite' & 'Rondo,' " *New York Post,* November 12, 1980; "charming" and "a gem," Bob Micklin, "City Ballet in Martins' 'Lille Suite,' " *Newsday,* November 30, 1980.
448 When Balanchine blew up: JR, journal no. 22, December 24–28, 1978, JRP.
449 The impression in the company: Martins, interview with the author, May 14, 2002.
449 "You didn't just": Horgan, interview with the author, March 11, 2003.
449 "showed her the drop": JR, "In Memory of," Ostürk notebook bought in Turkey, July 1, [1985]. JRP.
450 although he claimed: JR, journal no. 21, January 28, 1980, JRP.
450 he was relatively: Rhoda Grauer, interview with the author, October 29, 2000.
450 He wanted to break: Ibid.
450 "horrendous": Ibid.
450 "Major network shit": JR, journal no. 21, December 10, 1980, JRP.
451 "heartbreaking in intent": JR, journal no. 22a, July 1, 1981, JRP.
452 he abandoned: JR, journal no. 22, April 5, 1981, JRP.
452 "work streak": Ibid., April 12, 1981.
453 "If I can have it": Ibid., June 4, 1981.
453 He was irritated: Ibid., March 16, 1981, JRP.
453 The critic of *The China Daily* praised: Ma Xia, "A Taste of American Ballet," *The China Daily,* September 16, 1981. Review found among JR's material for "China Tour 1981," JRP.
454 "frozen in shadows": Michael Cristofer, *C. C. Pyle and the Bunion Derby,* script b, JRP.
454 "On the backdrop": JR, notes for *C. C. Pyle* . . . January 12, 1981, JRP.
454 "IT'S BEEN": Michael Cristofer, telegram to JR, May 4, 1982, JRP. Alexander Cohen had written to JR on April 26, 1982, informing him of the production schedule and warning that all plans would become academic if JR didn't instruct his lawyer, Floria Lasky, to release the signed contracts to him.
454 Robbins answered: JR to Michael Cristofer, draft of a letter dated May 5, 1982, JRP.
454 Being honored by: Invitations, travel plans, schedule, guests, etc., can be found in the Jerome Robbins Papers. They cover the December 5, 1981 award presentation by George Stevens during cocktails at the National Academy of Science; the State Department dinner afterward, given by Alexander and Mrs. Haig; and the White House reception and ensuing gala at the Kennedy Center, December 6, 1981. Scheduled to sit at Robbins's table at the postgala dinner: Slim Keith, Jesse Gerstein, Rhoda Grauer, Sonia & George Cullinen, Chessy Raynor "& husband," Mikhail Baryshnikov, Dicran Berberian, Aidan Mooney, Oliver Smith, and Bart Cook "(Fancy Free Dancer)." Edith Weissman seems to have attended the proceedings too.
454 In a video of the gala: "Kennedy Center Honors" [videorecording], CBS-TV 1978–1991, Jerome Robbins Archive of the Recorded Moving Image, NYPL.
455 Bart Cook . . . remembers: Cook, interview with the author, February 6, 2000.
455 The public loved: JR, journal no. 22a, February 5, 1982, JRP.
455 "It's O.K.ish": Ibid., February 6, 1982, JRP.
455 "The two ballerinas": Arlene Croce, "This Space and That Jazz and These Dancers," *The New Yorker,* February 22, 1982; included in Croce, *Sightlines,* 37.
456 Jerry . . . thought: JR, journal no. 22a, February 25, 1982, JRP.
457 dissolving in laughter: Jean-Pierre Frohlich, special presentation for donors, New York City Ballet, held at the School of American Ballet, April 14, 2003. Joan Qua-

trano moderated a panel consisting of Frohlich, Nikolaj Hübbe, Wendy Whelan, and Holly Hynes.

457   Baryshnikov . . . brokered a compromise: Grauer, interview with the author, October 29, 2000.

457   "It was a great program": Baryshnikov, interview with the author, April 4, 2002.

457   "hair astray": JR, journal no. 23, August 25, 1982, JRP.

458   "a slow elevator down": Ibid., March 27, 1983.

458   "It's left a hole": Ibid., December 2, 1982.

458   Not until that summer: Barbara Whipple, who worked with Weissman that summer, says that Weissman gradually began to come to the office less in the fall but kept her hand in. Whipple, conversation with the author, September 26, 2003.

458   "best love . . . to Edith": Richard Buckle to JR, November 24, 1968, JRP.

458   Lucia Chase . . . and many others: Most of the sympathy letters arrived within a few days of Weissman's death on December 2, 1982.

458   "I wanted so much": Leonard Bernstein to JR, n.d. [circa December 5, 1982], JRP.

19. Pressing Onward, Looking Back

PAGE

460   Balanchine had invited: Barbara Horgan, interview with the author, March 11, 2003; Peter Martins, speaking on "Balanchine Celebration, Part 1," a video presentation by *Great Performances/Dance in America,* January 25, 1986, produced for WNET/13 by Judy Kinberg and directed by Matthew Diamond.

460   He had hoped to have: Horgan, interview with the author, March 11, 2003.

460   Robert Gottlieb confirms: Gottlieb, interview with the author, June 25, 2003.

460   asked Horgan to bring Orville Schell: Horgan, interview with the author, March 11, 2003.

460   "Balanchine said": Ibid.

460   "[Balanchine] had no idea": Betty Cage, quoted in Greg Lawrence, *Dance with Demons,* 450–451.

461   "To speak of succession": Ken Sandler, "Ballet in Master's Absence," *Reporter Dispatch* (White Plains, N.Y.), January 23, 1983.

461   "turned down an offer": Fred Ferretti, "Martins Seen Succeeding Balanchine," *The New York Times,* March 12, 1983.

461   "There has been some": Lincoln Kirstein [?], typed carbon on onionskin. At top JR wrote, "from L.K. on Tues. March 12 or Wed ditto 13"; at bottom he wrote, "announcement made on Wed. March 14" [? March 14 was a Monday], JRP.

461   He drafted a resignation: JR, draft of a resignation, [March 1983], citing the board members' recent release to the press as the cause. He regrets having had to make this decision and notes that he has no quarrel with the company.

461   The board managed: A letter from Gillian Attfield to JR (March 17, 1983, JRP) attests to much conferring and to the board's desire not to lose Robbins. After thanking JR for his help and telling him of his value, she writes, "I know that the last week was a very unhappy time for a lot of people, you in particular."

462   "You are America's": Oliver Smith to JR, March 25, 1983, JRP.

462   "All angers flare up": JR, journal no. 23, March 27, 1983, JRP.

462   Robbins debated: JR to Lincoln Kirstein, July 21, 1983, JRP.

462   who found the wrangling: Kirstein to JR, June 23, 1983, JRP. In addition to using

the words "unseemly" and "embarrassing," Kirstein found the idea of two "in chiefs" anomalous and reminded JR of the example of modesty set by Balanchine.

462   "George never called himself": JR to Kirstein, July 21, 1983, JRP.

462   "In no way": Ibid. This letter may be in response to a list of possible titles for JR sent by Betty Cage to Floria Lasky, June 23, 1983.

462   "to make sure": Peter Martins, interview with the author, May 14, 2002.

463   "I have to think hard": JR to Penelope Dudleston, April 15, 1987, JRP.

463   "always looking": Gottlieb, interview with the author, June 25, 2003.

463   he called Jane Herman: Philip Glass, interview with Kenneth Geist, May 15, 1984. Courtesy of Kenneth Geist.

463   he wrote a highly enthusiastic: JR, strong endorsement for a Guggenheim for Childs, 1979–1980. Childs got the fellowship and wrote to thank him. JRP.

463   Glass approached Robbins: Glass, interview with Geist, May 15, 1984.

464   he met with Glass: JR, "Akhnaten—Misc. Notes, Schedules, Corr," JRP. A bundle of small sheets of lined paper with holes, clipped together, contains a list of meetings, etc.

464   he put Goldman in touch: JR to Shalom Goldman, February 26, 1983, JRP.

464   Glass found Robbins's input: Glass, interview with Geist, May 15, 1984.

464   "were like critiques": Ibid.

464   The printed libretto: A 1984 draft of a contract has the credit line "Libretto by Philip Glass in association with Shalom Goldman, Robert Israel, Richard Ridell [sic] and Jerome Robbins" and gives the royalties. A letter from lawyer David Gunn to Freddie Reppond of the New York City Opera, October 23, 1984, JRP, explains that JR wishes his name removed because since he had ended his involvement with the opera more than a year before, numerous changes in the libretto had occurred and he felt that his work on it was "no longer represented in the opera's present form."

464   Robbins decided he couldn't: After the final meeting on February 21, 1983, listed in JR, "Akhnaten—Misc. Notes, Schedules, Corr," is the notation "(JR has decided to become less involved w/ the project, only in consulting capacity. Meetings of others will continue tomorrow & Weds. at City Center.)." JRP.

464   "a certain inartistic sigh": Christopher Keene, interview with Geist, May 8, 1984.

464   "to get my feet wet": JR, quoted by Glass, interview with Geist, May 15, 1984.

465   "an absolute victory": Nancy Goldner, "Music by Glass Meets Dance Steps by Robbins—and It's a Draw," *The Christian Science Monitor,* June 10, 1983.

465   "I want you to be": JR, quoted by Heléne Alexopoulos, New-York Historical Society Symposium, May 24, 1999—Alexopoulos and Jean-Pierre Frohlich in conversation with the author.

466   "Glass looks like": JR, journal no. 23, March 27, 1983, JRP.

466   "Glass goes nowhere": Ibid., April 3, 1983.

466   "What do I know?": Ibid., June 25, 1983.

466   Robbins would stop her: Maria Calegari, interview with the author, February 6, 2000.

466   "At first": Ibid.

466   Because the women: Bart Cook, interview with the author, February 6, 2000 (Cook and Calegari were interviewed together).

466   Robbins had hoped: JR, "New Ballet—Philip Glass Music Project," in "Akhnaten—Misc. Notes, Schedules, Corr," JRP, records a February 14, 1983, phone call from Steven Mazo of Mazo Gallery. He's going to Key West to speak with Twombly about decor for the Glass ballet. In a previous phone conversation

Twombly was uninterested, but Mazo thinks he might have more luck in a face-to-face meeting.

466 "I think": Violette Verdy, interview with Charles France, October 12, 1974, in connection with Nancy Reynolds, *Repertory in Review: 40 Years of the New York City Ballet.* Courtesy of Nancy Reynolds.

467 "What a simple": JR, "Astaire Variations," a log of the process of *Making I'm Old-Fashioned,* June 19, 1982, JRP.

467 "I'm honored": Fred Astaire to JR, April 12, 1981, JRP.

467 and shot Robbins and Gould: JR's "Astaire Variations" documents, on August 23, 1982, a meeting with Morton Gould in Great Neck being videotaped "for a possible tv show" and taping being done at a rehearsal, September 25, 1982. "Two hours with lights, cameras and a crew of seven!!" In October, Joel Gold replaced Dewitt Sage as director (JR hadn't been satisfied with the rehearsal footage). JR recorded that Gold had taped another conversation, on October 12, 1982 ("terrific"), and a rehearsal on October 27, 1982. Then the log ceases.

467 Hershy Kay declined: Edward Bigelow, interview with the author, June 12, 2001.

467 "debonair, delightful": JR to Morton Gould, June 30, 1982, JRP.

467 "[H]e's so wonderfully": JR, "Astaire Variations," September 29, 1982, JRP.

467 Gould complained: Barbara Horgan, interview with the author, March 11, 2003.

467 "uses the whole construction": JR, "Astaire Variations," October 12, 1982, JRP.

468 "done some good variations": Ibid., October 22, 1982.

468 " 'Nice' is not": Ibid., November 9, 1982.

468 Gould joked: Ibid.

468 Robbins lured Victor Castelli: Castelli, interview with the author, July 18, 2000.

468 "I have a ballet": Ibid.

469 "I know the ancestral": Martha Graham to JR, October 4, 1985, JRP.

470 and made it clear: Noted among suggestions sent by JR to Peter Martins concerning the repertory for the New York City Ballet's spring season, 1989, JRP.

470 "Their necks were inclined": Pierre Louÿs, "The Old Man and the Nymphs," *The Songs of Bilitis,* trans. by M.S.B.

470 that had fascinated Robbins: Pictures of these statues are included in Robbins's notes for *Antique Epigraphs.* William Crawford, in a conversation with the author, ca. March 2003, mentioned that he knew that Robbins had seen the statues during the summer of 1963.

471 "classical clarity": Harry Halbreich, photocopied essay found among JR's notes on *Antique Epigraphs.* JRP. Its format suggests that it may have come from a record jacket.

472 "We all try to speak": JR, entry in red spiral binder marked "Bodrum, July–August—84," July 3, 1984, JRP.

472 "that story is a chapter": JR, journal no. 23, December 9, 1984, JRP.

472 hoping to learn: Twyla Tharp, interview with the author, April 28, 2003.

473 piano original Tharp preferred: Ibid.

473 "I think": Cook, interview with the author, February 6, 2000.

473 Tharp says: Twyla Tharp, interview with the author, April 28, 2003.

473 "He basically made me crazy": Ibid.

473 "He walked through": Delia Peters, interview with the author, October 7, 1999.

473 neither of them thought: Tharp, interview with the author, April 28, 2003.

474 some, such as Dale Harris: Dale Harris, interview with Kenneth Geist, June 5, 1984. Courtesy of Kenneth Geist.

474 Watching the 1990 revival: All of JR's ballets shown during the 1990 Robbins Retro-

spective at the New York City Ballet were shot in both wide-screen and tight-screen formats for the Jerome Robbins Archive of the Recorded Moving Image, NYPL.

474 "It's pushing me up": JR, journal no. 23, April 4, 1983, JRP.

475 who found him: Brian Meehan, interview with the author, March 4, 1999.

475 The contract he signed: Draft of a contract between the New York City Ballet and JR, August 1, 1983, JRP.

475 A list of his fees: The Robbins Rights Trust office maintains a list of Robbins ballets licensed to other companies. Detailed data on his earnings are included among the Jerome Robbins Papers.

475 He had trouble: Allen Greenberg, interview with the author, June 5, 2003.

475 "You don't understand": Harry Robbins, quoted in JR, "Grudges," December 12, 1980, notes toward an autobiography/*The Poppa Piece,* JRP.

475 "With those words": Ibid.

475 subscriptions to art magazines: JR [office staff?], Christmas lists 1961–1963, JRP.

475 Jennifer Tipton: Tipton, interview with the author, March 18, 2003.

475 The two men: Magnus Ragnarsson, interview with the author, April 24, 2000.

475 he seems to have flown first class: JR, journal no. 23, July 24, 1982, JRP. Companies, festivals, competitions, etc., usually gave him business-class tickets. On this occasion, he wrote that he "loved it & it gave me a big push (needed!) into spending more."

475 bills amounting to $600: Aidan Mooney, interview with the author, February 8, 1999.

476 "used more 'de' and": Ellen Sorrin, interview with the author, May 15, 2000.

476 Baryshnikov announced: "Dancing for Life (Benefit)," clippings, NYPL.

476 "Anyone should be able": JR, "Notes, etc. 89–91 etc." (black leather-bound notebook), April 13, 1989, JRP.

478 Robbins spoke of its music: JR, interview with Rosamond Bernier in *In Memory of . . . ,* a presentation by *Great Performances/Dance in America,* January 25, 1986, produced for WNET/13 by Judy Kinberg and directed by Emile Ardolino.

478 he didn't want: JR, "In Memory of . . . ," Ostürk notebook bought in Turkey, JRP. The retrospective account was begun on July 1, 1985, in Bodrum.

478 he had often felt: Ibid.

478 "[I]f the male lead": Ibid.

478 "the most extraordinary": Ibid.

479 "Her concentration": Ibid.

479 something that had never: Ibid.

479 "her country folk": Ibid.

479 Fortunately, *Dance in America: In Memory of . . . ,* a presentation by *Great Performances/Dance in America,* January 25, 1986, produced for WNET/13 by Judy Kinberg and directed by Emile Ardolino.

480 "she is now accepting": Ibid.

480 "as the Chevalier": Kirstein sent a copy of this picture to the author.

480 "I wish I was": Joseph Duell to JR, undated [1986], JRP.

480 "Know that I join": JR, draft of message from Paris to New York City Ballet, February 26, 1986, JRP.

480 He was not only sorrowful: Aidan Mooney, interview with the author, February 8, 1999.

480 "in no time flat": Robert La Fosse, interview with the author, May 29, 1999.

481 "so that when": JR filed the invitation with the quote from Fosse's will and his own response, dated October 27, 1987, in a file labeled "Fosse," JRP.

481 His master wrote: JR, " 'Ives Etc.' (notebook bound in brown marbled paper). The choreographer writes of the development of *Ives, Songs* from March 13, 1987 until February 10, 1988 (six days after the ballet's premiere) etc.," February 5, 1988, JRP.

481 "he was advised to": Gregory Mosher, interview with the author, May 5, 2003.

481 "meant we had": Ibid.

481 Guare, although remembering: John Guare, interview with the author, August 16, 2000.

481 Sondheim had no desire . . . but consented: Sondheim, interview with the author, August 3, 2000.

482 "[I]t is wonderful": Leonard Bernstein to Jerome Robbins and John Guare, November 6, 1986, JRP.

482 "argued about what": Mosher, interview with the author, May 5, 2003.

483 "was one of the greatest": Ibid.

483 Bernstein's music is forthright: As of this writing, an uncatalogued videotape of an informal workshop performance of *The Race to Urga* (aka *The Exception and the Rule*) was found in the New York Public Library's "Theater on Film and Tape" Collection. Also, an audiotape dated November 3, 1986, in the Jerome Robbins Collection has Bernstein providing a cursory narrative and singing the songs, along with—possibly—Guare (the tape label mentions Bernstein, Robbins, and Guare). Stephen Sondheim recalls singing on a tape with Bernstein, but this may have been during the 1968 sessions.

483 One of the songs: Sondheim, "Q & A Stephen Sondheim, Part II," The *Dramatists Guild Quarterly,* vol. 2, no. 2 (Summer 1991), 10–17.

483 "Meanwhile L'Affaire Lenny": JR, "Ives Etc." (notebook bound in brown marbled paper), March 13, 1987. This log of the creation of *Ives, Songs* was begun en route to Bodrum on March 13, 1987, and continues until February 10, 1988 (six days after the ballet's premiere). JRP.

483 In contact sheets: The photos of *The Race to Urga* rehearsals (no photographer credited) are in the Jerome Robbins Collection.

484 "We played whatever": Ragnarsson, interview with the author, April 24, 2000.

484 "Your delightful production": Oliver Smith to JR, May 12, 1987, JRP.

485 "I know how": Guare, interview with the author, August 16, 2000.

485 "exhausted & happy": JR, "Ives Etc.," May 5, 1987, JRP.

485 "URGA took six": JR to Oliver Smith, June 10, 1987, JRP.

485 "an easy constant flow": JR, "Ives Etc.," July 5, 1987, JRP. Later, JR added to this entry that he recounted this vision at the memorial for Nora Kaye, January 5, 1988, and tears flowed down his face.

485 Robbins had thought: JR, "In Memory of . . . ," Ostürk notebook bought in Turkey, JRP. The retrospective account was begun on July 1, 1985, in Bodrum.

486 With Neel Keller: Neel Keller, interview with the author, February 2, 2000.

486 "& it was as if ": JR, "Ives Etc.," March 13, 1987, JRP.

486 "Is there a possible": Ibid., March 15, 1987.

486 Keller remembers: Keller, interview with the author, February 2, 2000.

486–87 Robbins played: JR, "Ives Etc.," JRP.

487 "somewhat sentimental": Ibid., February 5, 1988.

487 "they had pictures": La Fosse, interview with the author, May 29, 1999.

488 As Susan Reiter: Susan Reiter, "A Robbins Celebration," *Danceview,* Autumn 1994, 11.

488 Robbins had intended: JR, "Ives Etc.," August 9, 1987, JRP.

488 "mesmerizing": Reiter, "A Robbins Celebration," *Danceview,* Autumn 1994, 11.
488 "Did I show": JR, "Ives Etc.," February 10, 1988, JRP.
488 "If someone asked": Ibid.

20. The Final Chapter

489 "I keep going": JR, "Ives Etc." (notebook bound in brown marbled paper), January 15, 1988, JRP.
490 "WE BEGIN": Ibid., August 15, 1988.
490 occasionally warranting intervention: Elaine Wright, interview with the author, July 29, 1999.
490 Robert La Fosse and Alexia Hess: La Fosse, interview with the author, May 29, 1999.
491 "No, Jerry": Wright, interview with the author, July 29, 1999.
491 Bernstein came: Ibid.
491 "to put these numbers": Neel Keller, interview with the author, February 2, 2000.
491 "So when Betty": Ibid.
492 "He was the best": Unidentified dancer quoted by Neel Keller in a draft about the process of creating *Jerome Robbins' Broadway* ("Swope-Keller Project"), JRP. Keller and photographer Martha Swope planned to collaborate on a book. It was never published.
492 Inevitably, performers: Ann Hutchinson Guest to JR, June 26, 1989; Greg Lawrence, *Dance with Demons,* 483–484.
492 Grover Dale thought: Dale, interview with the author, April 15, 2000.
493 "the pristine glow": John Simon, "Whose Broadway Is It, Anyway?" *New York* magazine, March 15, 1989.
493 "No one has ever": Clive Barnes, "Old Gold, New Again," *New York Post,* February 27, 1989.
493 "Audiences inured to": Frank Rich, "From Jerome Robbins, 20 Years of Broadway the Way It Was," *The New York Times,* February 27, 1989.
493 His friends think: Daniel Stern, telephone conversation with the author, spring 2003.
493 "to the ends of the earth": Slim Keith, *Slim,* 173.
493 "I felt as if": JR, draft of a letter to Bernstein's three children, October 18, 1990, JRP.
493 "handling it well": JR, "Ives Etc." (notebook bound in brown marbled paper), April 16, 1989, JRP.
493 "Dearest Lincoln": JR, telegram to Lincoln Kirstein, August 22, 1989, JRP.
494 "If he moved": Peter Martins, interview with the author, May 14, 2002.
494 "You promised me": JR to Martins, March 19, 1990, JRP.
495 "cold turkey": JR, quoted in "Talk of the Town," *The New Yorker,* July 9, 1990.
495 "Your own creativity": Mary Hunter to JR, November 21, 1990, JRP.
495 Gershin: JR spelled this name in various ways in his *The Poppa Piece* notes and drafts: "Gershin," "Gershen," and, less often, "Gershon."
495 he conferred with: Entries in JR's 1991 appointment calendar, JRP.
496 poor-quality rehearsal video: The taping was done for JR's own private use in reviewing certain scenes, and restricted to that use. R16, Jerome Robbins Archive of the Recorded Moving Image, NYPL.
496 "all my life": JR, *The Poppa Piece* script, February 8, 1991, JRP.

497 "[T]here is the faintest": JR, *The Poppa Piece,* draft, ninth revision, April 25, 1985, JRP.

498 as "exquisite": Gerald Freedman, interview with the author, May 12, 2000; Wright, interview with the author, July 29, 1999.

498 Robbins wrote scenes: All the scenes mentioned occur in JR's many drafts—over a period of about sixteen years—of scenes in *The Poppa Piece* and in his notes toward an autobiography. These fill a number of boxes in the Jerome Robbins Papers.

499 "My own feeling": Freedman, interview with the author, May 12, 2000.

499 "One of the keenest": JR, "Plans 92" (brown steno pad, yellow lined paper), JRP.

499 "You want to drag me": JR, *The Poppa Piece* script, JRP.

499 "Maybe I can't": JR, "Plans 92" (brown steno pad, yellow lined paper), JRP.

500 and Robbins's appointment calendar: JR, calendar, March 29, 1991, JRP.

500 "The sun moves": JR, instructions about the care of Gerstein, handwritten, n.d., JRP.

500 commemorated the event: Lisa Stevens, "Dear Cassandra," JRP.

500 The nurses' reports: The reports are included in the Jerome Robbins Papers.

500 "Jesse Gerstein, 34": JR, draft of a notice sent to *The New York Times,* JRP.

501 His calendars: JR's appointment calendars, usually marked "office" and "bedroom" for the same year, are included along the Jerome Robbins Papers.

501 he tried to learn: JR's calendar for 1992 records these. See also the account by Faye Greenbaum (then working for Robbins), who tutored him, in Lawrence, *Dance with Demons,* 510.

501 "What a fine": JR to Barney Frank, June 4, 1987, JRP.

501 He chastised New York's mayor: JR to Ed Koch, April 28, 1988, JRP.

501 He joined the scrimmage: JR to Senator Strom Thurmond, August 1, 1989, JRP.

501 "promote, disseminate, or": Helms's amendment, quoted in a letter from Senator John Heinz to JR, thanking JR for his letter, JRP.

501 he sent a blitz: The bulk of JR's letters were mailed in May 1990 (Senator Al Gore responded to his concern on November 20, 1990, and so did several others). In response to a postcard from Strom Thurmond concerning the punitive measures the senator wished might be taken against organizations that presented art he found offensive, JR drafted a letter to Thurmond, August 1, 1989, saying, "I find your reaction out of line, as I am sure you would if the credibility and honesty of the entire Senate body were to be criticized and changed on the basis of a history of corruption amongst politicians in Washington in recent years." JRP.

501 Robbins never told Mosher (footnote): Gregory Mosher, interview with the author, May 5, 2003.

501 wondering about Diamanda Galas: JR's files on *The Bacchae,* 1990, contain the liner notes for a Galas CD and a note about where she'll be performing next. JRP.

501 "In Bacchae": JR, "Personal Notes," *The Poppa Piece,* August 6, 1990, JRP.

502 according to producer Craig Zadan: Zadan, quoted in Lawrence, *Dance with Demons,* 513.

502 "It was not that": Ibid.

502 and been delighted: Sheldon Harnick to JR, October 21, 1994, JRP.

502 "It means a lot": JR to Theodore Bikel, October 28, 1994, JRP.

502 The dancers . . . interpreted: Sarita Allen and Edward Verso in Greg Lawrence, *Dance with Demons,* 514–515.

502 Robbins tells her to do: "*Interplay*—Working Rehearsal," New York City Ballet, videotape R7, Jerome Robbins Archive of the Recorded Moving Image, NYPL.

503 "do your work:" JR to Maria Calegari, photocopy of undated response to her letter

of April 19, 1984, JRP. The letter meant a lot to Calegari; she can quote its last lines from memory (Calegari, interview with the author, February 6, 2000).

503 Saland wrote Robbins of her: Stephanie Saland, interview with the author, November 8, 1999.

503 "You are an extremely": JR, draft of letter to Stephanie Saland, May 26, 1989, JRP.

503 " 'Oh, you've had such' ": Barbara Horgan, interview with the author, March 11, 2003.

503 "a dream": JR, "Paris, December '86" (small red marbleized notebook), entry for December 2, 1986, JRP.

503 "emotionally grabbed": JR, unlabeled red-checked notebook, October 21, 1986, JRP.

504 "hair-raising": Ibid., December 13, 1986.

504 Castelli . . . was glad: Victor Castelli, interview with the author, July 18, 2000.

504 felt that: Jean Guizerix, "Le Moulin de Jerry ou Watermill aux sources de mon imaginaire," an essay for JR, written between July 1996 and March 1997.

504 "Listen, at some point": Mikhail Baryshnikov, interview with the author, April 4, 2002.

504 some 1992 footage: "Work in Progress, Spring '92," New York City Ballet, video-tape R5, Jerome Robbins Archive of the Recorded Moving Image, NYPL.

505–7 Fernandez . . . felt: Kristina Fernandez, interview with the author, August 23, 2000.

506 Robbins loved that: Benjamin Millepied, interview with the author, July 11, 2002.

506 "early-in-the-morning": "Jerome Robbins," Kristina Fernandez, interview with Rick Whitaker, *Ballet Review,* vol. 26, no. 2 (Summer 1998).

506 he made Munier cry: Dena Abergel, "Jerome Robbins Choreographs at SAB," School of American Ballet Newsletter 34 (Winter 1999).

506 Thereafter, says Fernandez: Fernandez, interview with the author, August 23, 2000.

506 "for being so patient": Abergel, "Jerome Robbins Choreographs at SAB."

506 "American outdoor party": Edwin Denby, "Robbins' 'Interplay,' " *New York Herald Tribune,* November 4, 1945. Included in Denby, *Dance Writings,* eds. Robert Corn-field and William MacKay, 337.

507 "and Jerry was": Millepied, interview with the author, July 11, 2002.

507 "giving earnest consideration": Lincoln Kirstein to JR, April 29, 1994, JRP.

507 Martins, who shared: Aidan Mooney, informal conversation with the author, winter 2003.

508 "and without a moment's pause": JR to Kirstein, November 17, 1986, JRP.

508 "irresolute": Kirstein to JR, May 22, 1995, JRP.

508 "Nevertheless [*West Side Story Suite*] was": Ibid.

508 Annie and Tess: Daniel Stern, interview with the author, April 5, 1999, says that when Dr. Stern was walking around Robbins's neighborhood after JR's death, a doorman reported having sometimes seen JR pulled off his feet by his dogs. Other friends corroborate the dogs' eagerness.

508 he was seeing two or three: JR's appointment calendars for 1994 and after note the many visits to doctors. JRP.

508 "The operation wasn't so": JR to Carol Arbo, December 2, 1995, JRP.

508 He assisted Sonia: JR's correspondence with family members is included in JRP.

509 forgave all debts: "Last Will and Testament of Jerome Robbins," December 1, 1995.

509 "I can't show them": JR to Andy De Groat, November 10, 1995, JRP.

510 "in those rehearsals": Emily Coates, interview with the author, September 20, 2000.

510 Everyone in the building knew: Ibid.

510 "He moved the corps": Jean-Pierre Frohlich, New-York Historical Society Symposium, May 24, 1999, conversation among Frohlich, Heléne Alexopoulos, and the author.

510 "Weaving his cast": Barbara Newman, "January in New York," *The Dancing Times,* April 1997, 619.

511 "You are an extraordinary": Louis Begley to JR, January 27, 1997, JRP.

511 "green with a little bit": Holly Hynes, New York City Ballet Guild Seminar with Joan Quatrano (moderator), Jean-Pierre Frohlich, Nikolaj Hübbe, Wendy Whelan, and Hynes, April 14, 2003.

511 "get your fat ass": Peter Hanson, interview with the author, August 23, 2000.

511 "The way he pushed us": Ibid.

511 "I want to wear": Coates, interview with the author, September 20, 2000.

511 "All the girls": JR, captured on audiotape during stage rehearsals, 1995. Courtesy of Peter Hanson.

512 maybe not descending: Christopher Pennington, conversation with the author, spring 2003.

512 "Mr. B said": Bart Cook, interview with the author, February 6, 2000.

512 He had invited them: Coates, interview with the author, September 20, 2000.

512 "But he was very sweet": Ibid.

512 They ordered Chinese food: Ibid. Millepied, interview with the author, July 11, 2002, corroborates Coates's account of the evening.

512 Daniel Stern movingly described: Daniel Stern, speech delivered at the New York City Ballet's memorial for Robbins, November 16, 1998, New York State Theater. Courtesy of Daniel Stern.

513 Broadway paid its respects: "Broadway Celebrates Jerome Robbins," April 8, 1999.

513 The Paris Opera: "The Arts: Ballet Master Must Be Smiling from Heaven," *Financial Times* (London), March 17, 1999; Alan Riding, "In Paris, Paying Tribute to Jerome Robbins with Pomp and Humor," *The New York Times,* March 12, 1999. The memorial took place on March 11, 1999.

Afterword

PAGE

514 "respect and continued": Gerald Freedman to JR, September 1, 1993, JRP.

516 "as good as": Joan Acocella, "American Dancer," *The New Yorker,* May 28, 2001.

516 "It was wonderful": Brian Meehan, interview with the author, March 4, 1999.

Selected Bibliography

Abbott, George. *"Mister Abbott."* New York: Random House, 1963.

Altman, Richard, and Mervyn Kaufman. *The Making of a Musical:* Fiddler on the Roof. New York: Crown Publishers, 1971.

Amberg, George. *Ballet in America: The Emergence of an American Art.* New York: Duell, Sloan and Pearce, 1949.

Auden, W. H. *The Age of Anxiety: A Baroque Eclogue.* New York: Random House, ca. 1947, fourth printing. Jerome Robbins's annotated copy, NYPL.

Balanchine, George [no author listed]. *Choreography of George Balanchine: A Catalogue of Works.* New York: Viking, 1984.

Balanchine, George and Francis Mason. *Balanchine's Complete Stories of the Great Ballets.* Garden City, N.Y.: Doubleday and Company, 1954.

Beaumont, Cyril W. *Complete Book of Ballets.* New York: G.P. Putnam's Sons, 1938.

Bergreen, Laurence. *As Thousands Cheer: The Life of Irving Berlin.* New York: Viking Press, 1990.

Bird, Dorothy, and Joyce Greenberg. *Bird's Eye View: Dancing with Martha Graham and on Broadway.* Pittsburgh, Pa.: University of Pittsburgh Press, 1997.

Bordman, Gerald. *American Musical Theatre.* New York: Oxford University Press, 1986.

Bosworth, Patricia, *Montgomery Clift: A Biography.* New York: Harcourt Brace Jovanovich, 1978.

Bowles, Paul. *Without Stopping.* New York: Ecco Press, 1972.

Brecht, Bertolt. *The Measures Taken.* Trans. Eric Bentley. *The Modern Theatre,* vol. 6. Garden City, N.Y.: Doubleday, 1960.

—————. *Mother Courage and Her Children.* Trans. Eric Bentley. New York: Grove Press, 1966.

Buckle, Richard. *In the Wake of Diaghilev.* New York: Holt, Rinehart and Winston, 1983.

Burton, Humphrey. *Leonard Bernstein.* New York: Doubleday, 1994.

Burton, William Westbrook, ed. *Conversations About Leonard Bernstein.* New York: Oxford University Press, 1995.

Chujoy, Anatole. *The New York City Ballet: The First Twenty Years.* New York: Alfred A. Knopf, 1953.

Cohen, Selma Jeanne, and A. J. Pischl. "The American Ballet Theatre: 1940–1960." *Dance Perspectives* 6 (1960).

Comden, Betty, and Adolph Green. *The New York Musicals of Comden & Green.* New York: Applause Books, 1997.

Conrad, Christine. *Jerome Robbins: That Broadway Man, That Ballet Man.* London: Booth-Clibborn Editions, 2000.

Croce, Arlene. *Afterimages*. New York: Alfred A. Knopf, 1977.

———. *Going to the Dance*. New York: Alfred A. Knopf, 1982.

———. *Sight Lines*. New York: Alfred A. Knopf, 1987.

Cuddihy, John Murray. *The Ordeal of Civility: Freud, Marx, Levi-Strauss, and the Jewish Struggle with Modernity*. New York: Basic Books, 1974.

De Meyer, Adolphe. *L'Après-midi d'un Faune, Vaslav Nijinsky, 1912: Thirty-three Photographs*. New York: Dance Horizons, 1983.

de Mille, Agnes. *And Promenade Home*. Boston: Little, Brown and Company, 1956.

Denby, Edwin. *Dance Writings,* eds. Robert Cornfield and William MacKay. New York: Alfred A. Knopf, 1986.

Dubnow, Simon. *History of the Jews in Russia and Poland from the Earliest Times Until the Present Day,* vol. 3 [ca. 1916–1920], trans. I. Friedlaender. New York: Ktav Publishing House, 1975.

Easton, Carol. *No Intermissions: The Life of Agnes de Mille*. Boston: Little, Brown & Company, 1996.

Fuller, John. *W. H. Auden: A Commentary*. Princeton, N.J.: Princeton University Press, 1998.

Furia, Philip. *Irving Berlin: A Life in Song*. New York: Schirmer Books, 1998.

Garebian, Keith. *The Making of* Gypsy. Oakville, Ontario: Mosaic Press, 1998.

———. *The Making of* West Side Story. Oakville, Ontario: Mosaic Press, 1998.

Gavin, Gene. "B.C. to Broadway: The Memoir of a Broadway Gypsy,*"* manuscript, NYPL.

Goldner, Nancy. *The Stravinsky Festival of the New York City Ballet*. New York: Eakins Press, 1973.

Goodman, Walter. *The Committee: The Extraordinary Career of the House Committee on Un-American Activities*. New York: Farrar, Straus and Giroux, 1968.

Gordon, Joanne. *Art Isn't Easy: The Theater of Stephen Sondheim*. New York: Da Capo Press, 1992.

Gottfried, Martin. *All His Jazz: The Life and Death of Bob Fosse*. New York: Da Capo Press, 1998.

———. *Opening Nights: Theater Criticism of the Sixties*. New York: G. P. Putnam, 1969.

———. *A Theater Divided: The Postwar American Stage*. Boston: Little, Brown and Company, 1967.

Green, Stanley. *The World of Musical Comedy: The Story of the American Musical Stage as Told Through the Careers of Its Foremost Composers and Lyricists,* 4th ed. New York: Da Capo Press, 1980.

Grubb, Kevin Boyd. *Razzle Dazzle: The Life and Work of Bob Fosse*. New York: St. Martin's Press, 1989.

Gruen, John. *The Party's Over Now: Reminiscences of the Fifties—New York's Artists, Writers, Musicians, and their Friends*. New York: Viking Press, 1972.

———. *The Private World of Ballet*. New York: Viking Press, 1975.

Hanson, Bruce K. *The Peter Pan Chronicles: The Nearly 100 Year History of "The Boy Who Wouldn't Grow Up."* Secaucus, N.J.: Carol Publishing Group, 1993.

Kael, Pauline. *For Keeps: 30 Years at the Movies*. New York: Plume/Penguin, 1994.

Kanfer, Stefan. *A Journal of the Plague Years*. New York: Atheneum, 1973.

Kauffmann, Stanley. *A World on Film: Criticism and Comment*. New York: Dell Publishing, 1967.

Keith, Slim, with Annette Tapert. *Slim: Memories of a Rich and Imperfect Life*. New York: Simon & Schuster, 1990.

Kirstein, Lincoln. *Paul Cadmus*. New York: Horizon Press, 1984.

———. *Thirty Years: Lincoln Kirstein's the New York City Ballet*. New York: Alfred A. Knopf, 1978.

Kislan, Richard. *The Musical: A Look at the American Musical Theater,* rev. expanded ed. New York: Applause Books, 1995.

Kopit, Arthur L. *The Day the Whores Came Out to Play Tennis and Other Plays.* New York: Hill and Wang, 1965.

———. *Oh Dad, Poor Dad, Mamma's Hung You in the Closet and I'm Feelin' So Sad.* New York: Hill and Wang, 1960.

Laurents, Arthur. *A Clearing in the Woods.* New York: Random House, 1957.

———. *Original Story: A Memoir of Broadway and Hollywood.* New York: Alfred A. Knopf, 2000.

Laurents, Arthur and Stephen Sondheim. *Gypsy.* New York: Theatre Communications Group, 1989.

———. *West Side Story.* London: Heinemann, 1959.

Lawrence, Greg. *Dance with Demons: The Life of Jerome Robbins.* New York: G. P. Putnam's Sons, 2001.

Lawrence, Robert. *The Victor Book of Ballets and Ballet Music.* New York: Simon and Schuster, 1950.

Leonard, Maurice. *Montgomery Clift.* London: Hodder and Stoughton, 1997.

Lewis, Robert. *Slings and Arrows: Theater in My Life.* New York: Stein and Day, 1984.

Lido, Serge. *Ballet Panorama,* photographies de Serge Lido, préface par Jerome Robbins (commentaires et textes par Irène Lidova, avec la collaboration de George Skibine—Maître de Ballet du Théâtre National de l'Opéra de Paris, Maurice Béjart—Maître de Ballet du Théâtre Royal de la Monnaie de Bruxelles). London: A. C. Black, 1961.

Lifson, David S. *The Yiddish Theatre in America.* New York: Thomas Yoseloff, 1965.

Limón, José. *An Unfinished Memoir.* Hanover, N.H.: University Press of New England (Wesleyan University Press), 1999.

Lo Monaco, Martha Schmoyer. "Broadway in the Poconos: The Tamiment Playhouse, 1921–1967." Dissertation, New York University, 1988.

Long, Robert Emmet. *Broadway, The Golden Years: Jerome Robbins and the Great Choreographer-Directors: 1940 to the Present.* New York: Continuum, 2001.

Louÿs, Pierre. *The Songs of Bilitis,* trans. M.S.B. Privately printed, 1919.

Magriel, Paul, ed. *Chronicles of the American Dance from the Shakers to Martha Graham.* New York: Da Capo Press, 1978.

Manor, Giora. *The Life and Dance of Gertrud Krans.* Tel-Aviv: Hakibbutz Hameuchad Publishing House, n.d.

Mantle, Burns. *The Best Plays of 1926–1927.* New York: Dodd, Mead and Company, 1927.

———. *The Best Plays of 1938–1939.* New York: Dodd, Mead and Company, 1939.

———. *The Best Plays of 1939–1940.* New York: Dodd, Mead and Company, 1940.

Massine, Léonide. *My Life in Ballet.* London: Macmillan and Co., 1968.

McClure, Arthur F., ed., *The Movies: An American Idiom—Readings in the Social History of the American Motion Picture.* Rutherford, N.J.: Fairleigh Dickinson University Press, 1971.

Merman, Ethel, with George Eells. *Merman.* New York: Simon & Schuster, 1978.

Navasky, Victor. *Naming Names.* New York: Viking Press, 1980.

Nijinsky, Romola, with Lincoln Kirstein. *Nijinsky.* New York: Simon & Schuster, 1934.

Osato, Sono. *Distant Dances.* New York: Alfred A. Knopf, 1980.

Payne, Charles. *American Ballet Theatre.* New York: Alfred A. Knopf, 1977.

Peyser, Joan. *Bernstein: A Biography* (rev. and updated). New York: Billiard Books, 1998.

Pogonowski, Iwo Cyprian. *Jews in Poland: A Documentary History: The Rise of Jews as a Nation from Congressus Judaicus in Poland to the Knesset in Israel.* New York: Hippocrene Books, 1993.

Pollack, Howard. *Aaron Copland: The Life and Work of an Uncommon Man.* New York: Henry Holt and Company, 1999.

Prevots, Naima. *Dance for Export: Cultural Diplomacy and the Cold War.* Hanover, N.H.: University Press of New England (Wesleyan University Press), 1998.

Prince, Harold. *Contradictions: Notes on Twenty-six Years in the Theatre.* New York: Dodd, Mead and Company, 1974.

Reynolds, Nancy. *Repertory in Review: 40 Years of the New York City Ballet.* New York: Dial Press, 1977.

Savell, Isabelle K. *The Tonetti Years at Snedens Landing.* New City, N.Y.: Historical Society of Rockland County, 1977.

Schatz, Thomas. *Boom and Bust: The American Cinema in the 1940s.* New York: Scribner's, 1997.

Secrest, Meryle. *Leonard Bernstein: A Life.* New York: Vintage Books, 1995.

————. *Stephen Sondheim: A Life.* New York: Delta, 1998.

Siegel, Marcia B. *At the Vanishing Point: A Critic Looks at Dance.* New York: Saturday Review Press, 1972.

————. *The Shapes of Change: Images of American Dance.* Boston: Houghton Mifflin Company, 1979.

————. *Watching the Dance Go By.* Boston: Houghton Mifflin Company, 1977.

Smith, Wendy. *Real Life Drama: The Group Theatre and America, 1931–1940.* New York: Alfred A. Knopf, 1990.

Spada, James. *More Than a Woman: An Intimate Biography of Bette Davis.* New York: Bantam Books, 1993.

Spoto, Donald. *Madcap: The Life of Preston Sturges.* Boston: Little, Brown and Company, 1990.

Stein, Joseph, Jerry Bock, and Sheldon Harnick. *Fiddler on the Roof.* In Stanley Richards, ed., *Best Plays of the Sixties.* Garden City, N.Y.: Doubleday and Company, 1970.

Stine, Whitney, with Bette Davis. *Mother Goddam: The Story of the Career of Bette Davis.* New York: Berkley Books, 1984.

Tallchief, Maria, with Larry Kaplan. *Maria Tallchief: America's Prima Ballerina.* New York: Henry Holt and Company, 1997.

Taper, Bernard. *Balanchine: A Biography.* New York: Times Books, 1984.

Taylor, Paul. *Private Domain: An Autobiography.* New York: Alfred A. Knopf, 1987.

Taylor, Theodore. *Jule: The Story of Composer Jule Styne.* New York: Random House, 1979.

Terry, Walter. *I Was There: Selected Dance Reviews and Articles—1936–1976,* compiled and edited by Mark Andrew Wentink. New York: Marcel Dekker, 1978.

Tynan, Kenneth. *Tynan on Theatre.* Bungay, Suffolk: Richard Clay and Company, 1964.

Walker, Kathrine Sorley. *De Basil's Ballets Russes.* New York: Atheneum, 1983.

Zadan, Craig. *Sondheim & Co.* New York: Macmillan Publishing Co., 1974.

Zborowski, Mark, and Elizabeth Herzog. *Life Is with the People: The Jewish Little-Town of Eastern Europe.* New York: International Universities Press, 1952.

Zeitlin, David I., and Harriet Zeitlin, *Shooting Stars: Favorite Photos Taken by Classic Celebrities.* Los Angeles: General Publishing Group, 1998.

Index

American Ballet of, 22; Stravinsky and, 360, 403–7, 456, 503, 512 *(see also titles of specific ballets below)*; Tallchief and, 152; Taper's biography of, 153, 294, 411; Tchaikovsky and, 450–51 *(see also titles of specific ballets below)*; women revered by, 391, 432; Zorina and, 66

works: *Agon,* 308; *Allegro Brillante,* 255; *Apollo,* 188, 190, 197, 249; *Ballet Imperial,* 172; *Ballo della Regina,* 437; *Bourrée Fantasque,* 160, 171, 180, 187, 209, 211, 213; *Caracole,* 202, 209, 214; *Concerto Barocco,* 172, 202, 476; *Danses Concertantes,* 493; *Divertimento No. 15,* 209, 210; *Duo Concertant,* 404, 406, 433; *L'Enfant et les Sortilèges,* 424; *Errante,* 144; *Firebird,* 168, 172, 392, 427; *Four Temperaments,* 202; *Gaspard de la Nuit,* 424; *Jones Beach* (with Robbins), 170–71; *Kammermusik No. 2,* 437; *Mozartiana,* 451; *Opus 34,* 239; *Orpheus,* 172, 188; *PAMTGG,* 402–3, 438; *Pas de Trois,* 179; *Piano Concerto No. 2,* 426; *The Prodigal Son,* 18, 19, 160–63, 168, 171, 172, 203, 444; *Pulcinella* (with Robbins), 404, 406–8; *Robert Schumann's "Davidsbündlertänze",* 451; *Serenade,* 172, 239, 474; *La Source,* 389; *Stars and Stripes,* 437; *Swan Lake,* 197, 389; *Symphonie Concertante,* 172; *Symphony in C,* 144, 149, 202, 476; *Symphony in Three Movements,* 404; *Tarantella,* 470; *Tchaikovsky Pas de Deux,* 415, 453n; *Theme and Variations,* 144, 145, 474; *Le Tombeau de Couperin,* 424; *Tricolore,* 437, 438, 442; *Tyl Ulenspiegel,* 195–99, 203, 210, 213, 249; *Tzigane,* 424; *Union Jack,* 437; *La Valse,* 179, 209, 424; *Vienna Waltzes,* 436; *Violin Concerto,* 404; *Waltz Academy,* 144; *The Wanderer,* 144

Balash, Viola Zousmer, 6, 7, 9, 508
Balding, Ivor David, 367
Bales, William, 27, 33
Ball, Lucille, 74

Ballard, Kaye, 146
Ballet Caravan, 36, 39, 43, 69, 149
Ballet Hispánico, 507
Ballet Intime, 16
Ballet Russe de Monte Carlo, 32, 36, 39, 46, 56, 61, 127, 138, 203
Ballet Society, 108, 122, 144, 148, 149, 196, 390
Ballets Russes: of de Basil, 19, 21, 32, 36, 75–76, 123, 127, 138, 203, 363; of Diaghilev, 15, 18, 62, 75, 160, 223, 360, 424
Ballet Theatre, 8, 41–48, 53–66, 69, 71–73, 75–77, 99, 127, 195, 197, 213, 221, 250, 287, 303, 368, 369; Artistic Advisory Committee, 122; Balanchine and, 144; ballets choreographed by JR for, 75–80, 82–86, 88, 103, 105, 123–6, 128, 199–200, 450; Broadway appearances by members of, 92, 131, 137, 158, 354; financial difficulties of, 120–21, 147–48; JR joins, 31, 32, 42–44; JR's income from, 101, 121, 147; in London, 122–23, 128–29, 172; in Mexico, 59–62; in Paris, 178, 179; Russian style of, 48, 203, 254; U.S. tours of, 24, 46, 49–50, 80–81, 90; and World War II, 48–49 *(see also* American Ballet Theatre)
Ballets: U.S.A. (BUSA), 252, 296–318, 320, 326, 329, 340–43, 347, 365, 405, 418, 457
Ballet du XXième Siècle, 389, 414
Balzac, Honoré de, 437
Bancroft, Anne, 334–36, 339
Band Wagon, The (revue), 32
Banks, Margaret, 44, 138, 287, 288
Barber, Samuel, 198, 214, 300, 362
Barnes, Clive, 64, 75, 172, 434, 493
Barnes, Howard, 109, 158, 176
Barnett, Robert, 263
Baronova, Irina, 44, 48, 56, 60
Barrett, Michael Scott, 484
Barrie, James M., 237, 244, 247
Barry, Philip, *The Philadelphia Story,* 39
Bartenieff, George, 370n
Bartholdi, Frédéric, 157
Barto, Leon, 69

Eglevsky, André, 39, 40, 123, 127, 210
Eisenhower, Dwight D., 173, 298
Elizabeth II, Queen, 222
Ellis, Anita, 270
Ellis, Michael, 218n
Embassy Pictures, 367
Emmons, Beverly, 118
Enters, Angna, 22
Epstein, Julius J. and Philip G., 145, 146
Erickson, Leif, 145
Ertegun, Ahmet and Mica, 428–29, 454, 471, 500, 509
Establishment, The, 367
Estainville, Kim d', 437
Eula, Joe, 383n, 394
Euripides, 371; *The Bacchae,* 372, 376, 501; *The Trojan Women,* 69
Evans, Maurice, 39
Evans, Richard, 347
Evans, Walker, 240
Everett, Horace, 240
Everett, Tanya, 356

Fabray, Nanette, 130, 131
Fadiman, Clifton, 41
Fain, Sammy, 250
Faine, Hyman, 305n
Fairbanks, Douglas, 7
Falla, Manuel de, 17,
Fallis, Barbara, 44
Fancy Free (Robbins), 31, 68, 74–90, 99, 102, 104, 105, 139, 167, 229, 300, 386, 405, 419, 431, 453n, 516; Americanness of, 66, 86; Ballet Theatre performances of, 75, 86, 88, 101, 123, 172, 179, 199, 388; Bernstein's score for, 70, 77–78, 80, 82–86; danced by Baryshnikov at Kennedy Center Gala, 454; musical comedy based on, *see On the Town;* rehearsals for, 76, 80; reviews of, 86–87; royalties for, 88; 121, 147; scenario for, 76–78; sets for, 81–82; at Spoleto Festival, 457; television production of, 450; variants of social dancing in, 95, 230
Farrar, Geraldine, 5
Farrell, Suzanne, 389, 424, 426, 434, 435, 440, 443, 445, 460, 478–79
Faye, Joey, 129

Federal Bureau of Investigation (FBI), 177, 191, 195, 210, 230
Federal Dance Project, 19
Fedorova, Nina, 438
Feigay, Paul, 90
Feld, Eliot, 285, *At Midnight,* 382; *Harbinger,* 382
Feld Ballet, 476n, 491
Fernandez, José, *Goyescas,* 43, 46, 55
Fernandez, Kristina, 505–7, 512
Ferretti, Fred, 461
Feuer, Cy, 250
Fiddler on the Roof (musical), 17, 351–60, 385, 423, 475, 492, 502, 515; film of, 359
Fields, Dorothy, 40
Fields, Joseph, 219, 230
Fields, Robert, 370n
Fille Mal Gardée, La (ballet), 43, 60
Fine, Sylvia, 27, 30, 32, 33
Finnish National Ballet, 512
Fiorello! (musical), 353
Fischer-Dieskau, Dietrich, 486
Fisher, Eddie, 235
Fisher, Nelle, 95, 132
Fiske, Cora E., 12
Fitelson, William, 129n, 288–89, 341, 346, 382
Fitzgerald, Florence, 459, 471n
Fizdale, Robert, 108, 206, 207, 294, 341, 411, 444, 509; correspondence of JR and, 147n, 153, 154, 171, 173, 176, 179, 192, 193, 213–15, 283, 311, 313
Fleming, Christopher, 457
Flippen, Colonel Jay C., 101
Fluxus, 328
Fokine, Mikhail, 16, 62–66, 75, 225, 365; *Bluebeard,* 35, 48, 50, 56, 81; *Carnival,* 58; *Cléopâtre,* 161; *Firebird,* 172, 392; *Helen of Troy,* 62, 64, 66, 81, 101, 122, 160; *Narcisse,* 225; *Petrouchka,* 15, 18, 19, 59, 62–65, 101, 122, 362; *Russian Soldier,* 48, 57–58; *Schéhérazade,* 36, 56; *Spectre de la Rose,* 48; *Les Sylphides,* 43, 56, 81, 254; *Thamar,* 161; *The Thunderbird,* 16
Fokine, Vitale, 36
Fokine Ballet, 36
Follow the Fleet (film), 75

Lost Angel (film), 345
Lost in the Stars (musical), 159
Lost Weekend (film), 185
Louÿs, Pierre, 470, 471
Love, Iris, 429
Love, Kermit, 81
Love Me or Leave Me (film), 345
Lubovitch, Lar, 476
Lüders, Adam, 478, 479, 488
Lukas, Paul, 173
Lumet, Sidney, 134
Lunt, Alfred, 66
Lurie, Sam, 254
Lyne, George Platt, 170, 171, 211
Lyon, Annabelle, 39, 40, 43, 44, 47, 52, 54, 56, 127
Lyon, Robert, 487
Lyons, Leonard, 100, 101

Macero, Teo, 301
Mackintosh, Bob, 311
Maddocks, Melvin, 339
Magallanes, Nicholas, 152, 160, 169, 170, 189, 206, 210
Magdalena (musical), 192
Maggio Festival, 303
Magnani, Anna, 334
Magriel, Paul, 401–2
Mahler, Alma, 478
Mahler, Gustav, Kindertotenlieder, 53
Maiorano, Robert, 383n, 384, 393n
Makarova, Natalia, 432–34
Malden, Karl, 327
Malina, Judith, 328
Mallarmé, Stéphane, 223, 225–26
Mandia, John, 263, 299n
Mann, Thomas, 197
Mantle, Burns, 33, 39, 42
Mapplethorpe, Robert, 501
Marais, Jean, 206n
Margaret, Princess, 343
Markova, Alicia, 44, 48, 50, 56, 61, 123, 127
Marsh, Reginald, 19
Martin, Dean, 260
Martin, Erin, 299n, 304n, 307, 311, 315, 316, 365, 370n, 372, 374, 375
Martin, Ethel, 233
Martin, George, 233
Martin, Hugh, 129, 137

Martin, John, 33, 64, 171, 186, 262, 298; Balanchine's ballets reviewed by, 149; on Dance Center, 16–17; JR's ballets reviewed by, 86, 87, 103, 125–27, 153, 167, 189, 208, 239–40, 252, 303, 309; on JR's Broadway shows, 158; JR's dancing praised by, 21, 47, 66
Martin, Mary, 92, 156, 232, 235–37, 243–47, 249, 251, 295
Martins, Peter, 266, 396–97, 404, 435, 447, 456, 472, 507, 512; ballets choreographed by, see works below; in ballets by JR, 390, 393n, 426, 434, 440, 443, 495, 516; in Stravinsky festival, 456; as successor to Balanchine, 460–63, 494; in Tchaikovsky festival, 451
  works: Calcium Light Night, 437, 450; Dido and Aeneas, 444; Pas de Deux, 438
Mason, Francis, 209
Mason, Jane, 304n, 307
Massine, Léonide, 120, 361, 363; Aleko, 60n, 61, 62, 74; Capriccio Espagnol, 53, 65, 81; Don Domingo de Don Blas, 61–62, 73; The Fantastic Toyshop, 65; Gaîté Parisienne, 45; Mademoiselle Angot, 138; Les Matelots, 75–76; Saratoga, 136; The Three-Cornered Hat, 65; Union Pacific, 136
Massine, Lorca, 403, 410
Mata and Hari dance team, 28
Matthews, Laurence, 487–88
Mature, Victor, 74
Maule, Michael, 196, 304n
May, Elaine, 332, 367
Mayehoff, Eddie, 103
Mayer, Christine, 304n
Mayer, Louis B., 91
Mazo, Joseph, 428
Mazzo, Kay, 315, 317, 383n, 384, 386, 390, 404
McBride, Patricia, 381–84, 386, 387, 390, 393n, 395, 411, 413, 414, 420–21, 425, 434, 443, 444, 446, 451
McCarran, Patrick, 195
McCarthy, Joseph, 177, 305
McCarthy, Kevin, 267n

Musser, Tharon, 338
My Fair Lady (musical), 40
Mydtskov, Jeppe, 487

Nadel, Norman, 357
Nadich, Judah, 358
Nash, Ogden, 217, 218
Nathan, George Jean, 103
National Broadcasting Company (NBC), 450
National Council of the Arts, 428
National Council on Urban Renewal, 378, 379
National Endowment for the Arts (NEA), 298, 369, 370, 501
National Endowment for the Humanities, 369
National Foundation for Infantile Paralysis, 294
National Theatre, British, 376
Navasky, Victor, 177, 191
Neal, Philip, 447
Neff, Hildegard, 250
Neighborhood Playhouse, 484
New Dance Group, 21
Newman, Alfred, 185
Newman, Barbara, 510–11
New York City Ballet (NYCB), 179, 186–87, 221–22, 238–39, 248–49, 261–63, 268, 297, 306n, 308, 409–12, 415, 428, 448–49, 505, 507; American Ballet Theatre and, 366; American Music Festival of, 490; Balanchine Celebration of, 160, 493; and Balanchine's decline and death, 436–37, 444, 457–61, 464, 474; Ballets: U.S.A. and, 299, 304, 312, 315; ballets choreographed by JR for, 150–54, 163–67, 169–70, 180, 187–90, 222–28, 239–40, 252, 303, 381–95, 397–402, 412–14, 419–21, 432, 434–35, 438–48, 463–74, 477–81; classes for dancers of, 154; in *Dancing for Life* AIDS benefit, 476; European tours of, 211, 213–14, 238, 260, 305; flops of, 402–3, 437–38; in Israel, 449–50; JR joins, 144, 146, 148–50; JR's absences from, 179, 186, 191, 195–200, 202; JR's income from, 475; JR's

retirement from, 493, 502; in London, 153, 171–72, 186, 214, 443; Martins appointed to head, 460–63; Memorial for JR at, 512–13; in Paris, 503, 504; performances of JR with, 143, 159–62, 180, 219, 361, 407, 408; Ravel Festival at, 424–28, 430, 494–95; rehearsals of, 106, 159, 395–97; return of JR to, 266, 381–83, 388–89, 418, 516; Robbins Festival of, 477, 490, 494, 503; Stravinsky Festivals of, 403–7, 409, 410, 412, 419, 424, 455–57, 503; Tchaikovsky Festival of, 450–53; withdrawal of JR from, 155, 264, 296
New York City Opera, 148, 149, 155, 197, 240, 283, 443–44
New York Philharmonic, 418
New York Public Library for the Performing Arts, 432, 509; Dance Collection, 359, 450; Archive of the Recorded Moving Image, 359, 475
New York Shakespeare Festival, 481n
New York State Council on the Arts, 428
New York World's Fair (1939), 37, 38
Nichols, Kyra, 442, 448, 452, 453n, 459, 469, 471, 477, 503
Nichols, Lewis, 112
Nichols, Mike, 332
Nijinska, Bronislava, 43, 360, 363–64; *The Beloved,* 48
Nijinsky, Romola, 223, 377, 414
Nijinsky, Vaslav, 36, 62, 198, 233, 360, 363, 377, 389, 431, *Après Midi d'un Faune,* 48, 222–25, 401, 470, 471; *Jeux,* 198
Nijinsky (film), 431
Nillo, David, 28, 31
Nimura, Yeichi, 21
Ninotchka (film), 250
Nixon, Marni, 284
Nixon, Richard, 315n
Norman, Jay, 285, 289, 299, 303, 304n, 311, 382
Nureyev, Rudolf, 377, 391–92, 433, 443, 503

Obie Awards, 366
Oboukhoff, Anatole, 382

President's Emergency Fund for
International Affairs, 298, 304
Preston, James, 370*n,* 372–73
Primus, Barry, 331, 332, 370*n,* 372, 374–75
Prince, Harold, 242, 268, 273, 274, 282,
291, 342–43, 353, 359
Prince, Robert, 298, 301, 302, 315, 318,
329, 368
Prinz, John, 383*n,* 387
Producers' Showcase, 247
Proia, Alexandre, 478, 480, 487
Prokofiev, Sergei, 94; *Children's Suite,*
127; *Cinderella,* 412; *Lermontov,* 412;
Lieutenant Kije Suite, 57; *Prodigal
Son,* 161; String Quartet no. 2, 239;
Violin Concerto no. 1, 444; *War and
Peace,* 412
Proser, Monty, 120
Psota, Vania, *Slavonika,* 48
Public Broadcasting System (PBS),
467
Puccini, Giacomo, *Turandot,* 26
Pulitzer, Joseph, 157
Purcell, Henry: *Abdelazar, or the Moor's
Revenge,* 226; *Dido and Aeneas,* 443,
444

Quintero, José, 297

Rabinowitz, Harry (father), *see* Robbins,
Harry
Rabinowitz, Julius (uncle), 2, 3
Rabinowitz, Lena Rips (mother), *see*
Robbins, Lena
Rabinowitz, Ruth (aunt), 3
Rabinowitz, Samuel (uncle), 3
Rabinowitz, Sonia (sister), *see* Cullinen,
Sonia Robbins
Rabinowitz, Theodore (uncle), 2
Ragnarsson, Magnus, 484
Ragni, Jerome, 370*n*
Raitt, John, 241, 242
Rall, Tommy, 104, 119–20, 137–39, 158,
159, 174, 175
Rambert, Marie, 54
Rameau, Pierre, 438
Ramin, Sid, 320
Ramirez, Tina, 298
Ramon y Cajál, Santiago, 124
Rand Institute, 27

Randall, Carl, 40, 41*n*
Raset, Val, 468
Rauschenberg, Robert, 476
Ravel, Maurice, 424–28; *Une Barque sur
l'Océan,* 425; *Chansons Madécasses,*
425, 428; *L'Enfant et les Sortilèges,*
424; *Gaspard de la Nuit,* 424;
Introduction et Allegro, 425; *Ma Mère
l'Oye,* 154, 425–27; Piano Concerto
in G, 425; *Le Tombeau de Couperin,*
424; *La Valse,* 424
Rayner, Chessy, 429
Reagan, Ronald, 454
Rebel Without a Cause (film), 275
Red Pony, The (film), 306*n*
Red River (film), 146
Redpath, Christine, 396, 413
Reed, Janet, 43–44, 77, 79–82, 85, 103–6,
137, 160, 207, 209
Reed, Richard, 33, 44, 50
Reich, Steve, 477
Reik, Theodore, 121
Reilly, Bill, 304*n*
Reilly, Flash, 92
Reiter, Susan, 488
Resnick, Muriel, 268, 329; *Any
Wednesday,* 375
Respectful Prostitute, The (play), 129*n*
Revueltas, Silvestre, 61
Reynolds, Nancy, 162, 221
Rice, Elmer, *Street Scene,* 89
Rich, Frank, 493
Rich, Marion, 370
Richardson, Ralph, 122
Richman, Harry, 26
Riddell, Robert, 464
Riesman, David, 301
Rifkin, Ron, 496
Rimbaud, Arthur, 172
Rimsky-Korsakov, Nikolai, *Le Coq d'Or,*
16
Ringer, Jenifer, 507
Rips, Aaron, 3, 8
Rips, Anna, 3
Rips, Frances, 3
Rips, Ida, 3, 8
Rips, Jacob, 3
Ritchard, Cyril, 245, 247–49
Rittman, Trude, 138
Rivera, Chita, 273–77, 303

About the Author

Deborah Jowitt has been the principal dance critic for *The Village Voice* since 1967. Her articles on dance have appeared in numerous publications, among them *The New York Times* and *Dance* magazine. She was chair of the Dance Critics Association and a founding member of Dance Theater Workshop. She was recipient of a Bessie, the New York Dance and Performance Award, and of the prestigious dance book award, the de la Torre Bueno Prize. She has lectured and conducted workshops in the United States and abroad and is currently on the faculty of the Dance Department of New York University's Tisch School of the Arts, where she has taught since 1975. Jowitt was awarded a Guggenheim Fellowship in 2002 to write the critical biography *Jerome Robbins: His Life, His Theater, His Dance.*